The John F. Sonnett Memorial Lectures
at Fordham University School of Law

The John F. Sonnett Memorial Lectures at Fordham University School of Law

A Half-Century of Advocacy and Judicial Perspectives

Dennis J. Kenny and Joel E. Davidson, Editors

FORDHAM UNIVERSITY PRESS

NEW YORK 2018

Fordham University Press also publishes its books in a variety of electronic formats. Some content that appears in print may not be available in electronic books.

Visit us online at www.fordhampress.com.

Library of Congress Control Number: 2017960015

Printed in the United States of America

20 19 18 5 4 3 2 1

First edition

CONTENTS

FOREWORD

Encouraged by a former member of the Supreme Court of Ireland, the idea for this book took shape more than twelve years ago. The Justice's concern was that priceless lectures on the law in Fordham University School of Law's almost forty-five-year-old John F. Sonnett Memorial Lecture series, including three given by former chief justices of his country, were worthy of perpetuation and deliverance to the broader world. The Sonnett lecture series has featured many of the finest jurists in the United States, including Supreme Court Chief Justice Warren E. Burger, Supreme Court Justice Tom Clark, and Federal Circuit Court judges, including Judges Wilfred Feinberg, John J. Gibbons, Dennis Jacobs, Irving G. Kaufman, William Hughes Mulligan, and Lawrence W. Pierce, as well as former New York Court of Appeals Chief Judge Judith Kaye. Jurists from Great Britain, Ireland, South Africa, and Israel also delivered Sonnett lectures. Many of the lectures have been published in the *Fordham Law Review*. In fact, as of September 2014, "Special Skills Advocacy" by Chief Justice Warren E. Burger was the single most cited article in *Fordham Law Review* history. As dean of the law school at the time, I began to seek out ways to best distribute the broad knowledge and insight contained in these lectures.

Time flew by and the project remained incomplete until 2013, when two senior Fordham Law School alumni heard of this unfinished work and volunteered to bring it to conclusion: Dennis J. Kenny, who enjoyed a wonderful career as a corporate general counsel and a contributor to innumerable causes and good works, including churches and institutions of higher education; and Joel E. Davidson, who served as a corporate litigation counsel and then founded his own law firm. Like Kenny, Davidson is a contributor to many worthy causes, especially those involving children, family, and the poor. This book is a tribute to their efforts and the efforts of the editors and staff of the *Fordham Law Review* who wrote the Introductions that precede each lecture and helped in many other ways to bring this book to fruition.

John F. Sonnett, a Fordham graduate, enjoyed a life of excellence as a lawyer. He served as head of the Antitrust Division of the Department of Justice and was a senior partner at Cahill Gordon & Reindel, formerly Cahill Gordon Sonnett Reindel & Ohl, until his untimely death. Another Fordham graduate and former partner of Sonnett, Denis J. McInerney, together with Boris Kostenlantez, who served with Sonnett in the Justice Department, conceptualized and instituted the Sonnett lectures. For many years, they collaborated in identifying possible Sonnett lecturers, suggesting them to the deans of Fordham's Law School and then extending invitations to those chosen. There seemed to be no one they did not know or from whom an invitation as a prospective lecturer would be declined.

In their lifetimes, Denis and Boris expressed the fervent hope that this undertaking would one day receive additional recognition. It is hoped that this work—which includes the actual Sonnett lectures and brief Introductions about the lecturers and the long-term impact of their lectures—will prove to be of value to legal scholars, law professors, law students, and those who are interested in the perspectives of some of the leading scholars on legal issues and principles that remain significant to the present day.

I am privileged to contribute this background note to this remarkable work.

John D. Feerick[1]

1. Professor John D. Feerick served as dean of Fordham University School of Law from 1982 to 2002. He is the recipient of the American Bar Association Robert Kutack and D'Alemberte Raven awards and the founder of the Feerick Center for Social Justice at Fordham University School of Law. Professor Feerick is a leading expert on presidential succession and author of *From Failing Hands: The Story of Presidential Succession* (1965) and *The Twenty-Fifth Amendment: Its Complete History and Application, Third Edition* (2013). He also has served as president of the New York City Bar Association, chairman of the Board of Directors of the American Arbitration Association, chairman of the New York State Commission on Government Integrity (a Moreland Act Commission) from 1987 to 1990, and the New York State Public Integrity Commission from 2007 to 2009, and has made substantial contributions to numerous social causes. Dean Feerick is currently the Sidney Norris Professor of Law at Fordham University School of Law and teaches courses in Alternative Dispute Resolution, Constitutional Law, and Legal Ethics. He is a former partner of Skadden Arps.

EDITORS' NOTE

Putting together the collection of the Sonnett lectures and accompanying Introductions brought us great joy. We wish to acknowledge the leadership of Professor John D. Feerick and the generous assistance of the *Fordham Law Review* editors and staff, with special thanks to Editor Alexander McCabe, whose extra efforts contributed greatly to this collection. We also thank Dean Robert Reilly of the Feerick Center for Social Justice for his help both in locating archives and because he has played a key behind-the-scenes role with respect to many of the Sonnett lectures. We are also grateful to the University of Texas School of Law for assisting us in locating the text of the first lecture, given by Supreme Court Justice Tom Clark. We pay tribute to Denis McInerney and Boris Kostenlantez for their herculean efforts over many years to bring many of the leaders of the world bar and judiciary to participate in the Sonnett lecture series. Of course, their personal efforts were accompanied by Cahill Gordon & Reindel's ongoing financial support of the lectures given in the name of their former partner, John Sonnett. The edits of the Introductions to the lectures were handled by Ann Marie Denning. Finally, we express our gratitude to those who took the time to prepare and deliver these remarkable addresses.

The Sonnett lectures remain as relevant today as when they were given and provide keen insights and observations regarding many of the issues we continue to grapple with as we seek to improve the legal profession and the administration of justice. We were amazed at the number of recommendations made in the course of the lectures which later became part of the everyday life of the profession and the continued legal debate involving legal ethics, prisoner rights, legal training, the role of the executive in our judicial system, and many other current issues. We hope those that have an interest in the lecturers will find this volume to be a valuable source on the thinking of the deliverers of the lectures and that those who have an interest in the study of the evolution of legal ethics, legal training, prisoner rights, and other jurisprudential issues will find this book to be a valuable tool.

Unless otherwise noted, the text of the lectures remains substantially as it was delivered or transcribed. Edits were limited to ensure consistency in punctuation and spelling, as well as clarity.

Dennis J. Kenny, Editor[1]
Joel E. Davidson, Editor[2]

1. Dennis J. Kenny graduated from Fordham University School of Law in 1961 where he served as an editor at the *Fordham Law Review*. He was associated with the firm of Cleary Gottlieb and later was senior vice president and general counsel of Transamerica Leasing, Inc. He has been a generous supporter of Fordham University School of Law and the Feerick Center for Social Justice and was significantly involved in the latter's program to bring Alternative Dispute Resolution training to the legal profession in Ghana.

2. Joel E. Davidson graduated from Fordham University School of Law in 1975 and was Editor-in-Chief of the *Fordham Law Review*. He worked at Cahill Gordon & Reindel and, after serving as in-house counsel at several brokerage firms, started the firm of Davidson & Grannum in 1999. He has served as an adjunct professor at Fordham University School of Law and has done pro bono work for several of the Feerick Center projects.

The John F. Sonnett Memorial Lectures at Fordham University School of Law

The Art of Advocacy

Hon. Thomas C. Clark

Former United States Supreme Court Justice Tom C. Clark delivered the inaugural Sonnett lecture on December 15, 1970. Tom C. Clark devoted most of his career to public service.[1] He served as U.S. Attorney General in Harry S. Truman's administration from 1945 to 1949, and later served as a Supreme Court justice from 1949 to 1967.[2] Born in Dallas, Texas, in 1899, Clark attended the University of Texas, where he earned both his B.A. and J.D. degrees.[3] Clark began his public service career as a Civil District Attorney of Dallas County, Texas, in 1927.[4] In 1937, Clark joined the U.S. Department of Justice where he served, among other roles, as special assistant to the Attorney General and as coordinator of a program for the evacuation and internment of Japanese Americans during World War II.[5] Later, as Attorney General, Clark initiated a case against leaders of the American Communist Party for conspiring to overthrow the government.[6]

In 1949, President Truman appointed Clark to the Supreme Court of the United States.[7] While serving as an Associate Justice, Clark was known as generally conservative when it came to upholding government powers.[8] Yet, Justice Clark may be best remembered for at least two landmark opinions expanding individual rights in major civil liberties cases.[9] In 1961, Justice Clark wrote the opinion in *Mapp v. Ohio*,[10] in which the Court restricted police from using the fruits of illegal searches and seizures as evidence in state trials.[11] Writing for the majority, Justice Clark maintained that the Due Process Clause of the Fourteenth Amendment prohibited the use of illegally obtained evidence in both state and federal courts.[12]

1. *See* James A. Gazell, *Justice Tom C. Clark as Judicial Reformer*, 15 Hous. L. Rev. 307, 307 (1977).
2. *Tom C. Clark, Former Justice, Dies; On the Supreme Court for 18 Years*, N.Y. Times, June 14, 1977, at 1; *Biographical Directory of Federal Judges: Clark, Tom C.*, Fed. Judicial Ctr., http://www.fjc.gov/servlet/nGetInfo?jid=444&cid=999&ctype=na&instate=na (last visited Feb. 21, 2017).
3. *Tom C. Clark, Former Justice, Dies*, *supra* note 2, at 38.
4. *Id.*
5. *Id.*
6. *Id.*
7. *Id.*
8. Martin Well, *Former Supreme Court Justice Clark Dies at 77*, Wash. Post, June 14, 1977, at C6.
9. *Id.*
10. 367 U.S. 643 (1961).
11. Well, *supra* note 8, at C6.
12. 367 U.S. at 655.

Justice Clark often wrote the decision in significant controversial cases, including the First Amendment decision in *School District of Abington Township, Pennsylvania v. Schempp*,[13] a case in which the Court ruled that Bible-reading exercises in public schools violated the Constitution.[14] Furthermore, Justice Clark demonstrated his political independence on the Court when he concurred in the Court's decision that President Truman's seizure of the steel mill industry was unconstitutional in *Youngstown Sheet Tube Co. v. Sawyer.*[15]

When Justice Clark's son, Ramsey Clark, was appointed Attorney General in 1967, Justice Clark stepped down from the Court to avoid any conflicts of interest.[16] After leaving the Supreme Court, Justice Clark remained active, accepting assignments on various circuits of the U.S. Courts of Appeals. Indeed, at the time of his death, Justice Clark was sitting on the Second Circuit.[17] After Justice Clark's death, Chief Justice Warren E. Burger remarked that "[n]o one in the past 30 years has contributed more to the improvement of justice than Tom Clark."[18]

Justice Clark's Sonnett lecture reflected his passion for advocacy. Noting that lawyers are "essential to a fair administration of justice," Justice Clark proposed significant changes to the third year of law school that would prepare students to be better advocates and improve the problems he saw in trial court practice.[19] Justice Clark suggested third-year studies should be changed to include clinical programs and more time spent observing court proceedings.[20] Justice Clark also encouraged trial lawyers to be more prepared and then explained discovery in criminal cases. He also opposed the philosophy that a lawyer's sole duty is his client and that he has no duty to the fair administration of justice. Although delivered in 1970, Justice Clark's lecture remains relevant and insightful as practitioners, educators, and regulators recommend and vigorously debate changes in legal education today.[21] The text reprinted here was provided by the University of Texas Law School, which houses Justice Clark's papers.

---

13. 374 U.S. 203 (1963).

14. *Id.* The scope of the religious freedom afforded by the first amendment continues to evolve, and the recent Supreme Court decision in *Burwell v. Hobby Lobby Stores*, 573 U.S 221 (2014), construing the Religious Freedom Restoration Act and employer payment for contraceptives and abortion services reflects a significant shift in the law.

15. 343 U.S. 579 (1952); *see also* Gazell, *supra* note 1, at 308.

16. Well, *supra* note 8, at C6.

17. *Id.*; *Tom C. Clark, Former Justice, Dies*, *supra* note 2, at 1.

18. *Tom C. Clark, Former Justice, Dies*, *supra* note 2, at 1.

19. *See* Transcripts of the Proceedings of the Lecture Inaugurating the John Sonnett Memorial Lecture Series at 36–40 (1970).

20. *Id.* at 37–38.

21. *See, e.g*, Brody v. Maryland, 373 U.S. 83 (1963); Ethan Bronner, *Lawyers Call for Drastic Change in Educating New Lawyers*, N.Y. Times, Feb. 11, 2013, at A11; *Report and Recommendations: American Bar Association Task Force on the Future of Legal Education* (Jan. 2014), http://www.americanbar.org/content/dam/aba/administrative/professional_responsibility/report_and_recommendations_of_aba_task_force.authcheckdam.pdf.

Inaugural Sonnett Lecture

Mr. Kostelawitz, Dean Mulligan, my brothers of the bench and the bar, ladies and gentlemen—all friends of John Sonnett.

Mr. Chairman, you were most generous with your introduction and I thank you for its warmth, which is reciprocated. I am proud of your accomplishment in and devotion to the law, and to think that I may have had a small part in it gives me great satisfaction.

Dean Mulligan, you honor me greatly by your invitation to participate in the initial John Sonnett Memorial Lecture series of the Fordham University School of Law. It is always pleasing to visit the law school, but even more so in the company of so many old friends of John Sonnett. The law school and you have my hearty congratulations upon the initiation of this memorial to a distinguished graduate.

To have known John Sonnett was to love him. He was one of God's noble men. It is most fitting that we gather here in his honor tonight and re-dedicate ourselves to the great principles to which he devoted his life. John is not dead. He lives in the hearts of all of us. Through us he continues to perform the good works that were the hallmark of his life.

When Dean Mulligan first asked me to deliver the opening lecture I immediately selected the topic about which I wanted to speak: the art of advocacy. It was selected because I believe it would please John to know that the act for which he had such proficiency was chosen as the initial subject. John was a consummate advocate.

Boris, you were generous in your introduction, much better than I got last Friday down at Salado, Texas. That's a very sore spot in Texas. I was introduced as the "late" Mr. Justice Clark. I had just flown from San Francisco to Salado. I had been sitting in San Francisco off and on for three or four months in the trial court.

One of the judges met me at the airport in Boston and the first thing he said to me was, "Tom, it's too bad you didn't sit on the trial court before you sat on the Supreme Court. You would have learned both ways."

Then, after some time, through my experiences on the trial court, I came to rather agree with him that it might be well if all of us, before we get into the appellate courts, would take a little sojourn in the trial courts.

Dean, it's a high honor for me to come here tonight at the first series in the John Sonnett lectures and particularly to visit you in this historic spot that has nurtured so many minds in the legal profession, and that continues to render such great service to it, to this community, and to our nation.

I take it as a high privilege to speak at a lecture that is named for one so eminent as John Sonnett. I worked with him for many years. I, indeed, argued one case with him in the Supreme Court. He did all the work and I claimed all the credit. That was the John Lewis case. Most of you are too young to remember that case, but it had to do with the seizure of coal mines by Mr. Lewis through the United Mine Workers soon after the war.

I suppose the largest fine that was ever paid, to my knowledge, in the history of the United States, was paid by Mr. Lewis about a year later because of the good work of John Sonnett.

I will never forget—his office was on the third floor and I was on the fifth. I would go by and see him about eight or nine o'clock at night, he and I being the only ones in the building—we would have been killed if the building had fallen in because everybody else had gone home. He was still there working on the John Lewis case then.

I remember he had a problem of having a little pinkeye. I don't know whether you remember it or not, but after he had been working nights, and he always stayed there—well, sometimes he would stay all night, I found out later—and his eye would get a little bloodshot. I would try to get him to take off a day or two, but not John Sonnett.

He believed in being prepared and he was prepared. He not only prepared himself, but he also had prepared me, and I thought when the dean was so gracious to ask me to open this series, that it would be well if we devoted a few minutes to a discussion of advocacy, because having been with and heard John in two or three different courts, all the way from the District Court to the Supreme Court, I held him in high esteem as an advocate.

I think that it would be well if we talked some about him in the spirit that he might talk if he were here tonight.

For that reason, I thought I might say a few words tonight about advocacy through permissiveness—that is, well I guess you would call it a Stanford University word. I am going to speak somewhat extemporaneously tonight with the understanding that the young man who is so studiously there with his stenotype machine, and the other who is making a recording of this, I understand—when I was in the Cabinet, we used to look under the table to see if there was a machine under it—will give me a copy I will be able to follow because of an old and very honored custom that is in almost all of our deliberative bodies, that of extending your remarks in the record, extending and revising, they call it.

So, Dean, with your indulgence, I will do that.

I need not tell you that the art of advocacy is one of the oldest arts in history because many of you here tonight are what we would call old advocates yourselves. You have been in the courtrooms and you know what goes on there, but if you took the art of advocacy back even to the days of Demosthenes, Cicero, or through the English hierarchy of efficacious, you would find that there was a theme that was in them that continues to be in the minds of advocates today; that is, those that ever taught how an advocate goes about presenting a case.

Now, it was, I believe, Jeff Lawrence, who is a distinguished barrister over in London—I'm sure I see Whitney Seymour here and I'm sure he knows him. He is a member of one of the Inns of the Court there, possibly the same Inn Jeff belongs to.

He said that the study of advocacy was entirely different from the study of law. I agree with that. I rather think that the law schools agree, to some extent. They don't teach advocacy.

However, as I will develop a little bit further along, I have come to the conclusion that perhaps we should have a little bit of a closer relationship, perhaps a marriage, between the study of law and advocacy, so that we might improve and make more effective the advocacy that we have today.

I think that Sir Jeffrey was right when he said that. He said that the qualities of an advocate were, as he put it, high-spirited. I take it that this means one who is effervescent, not in the word of spirit as we think of it nowadays, you know, of spirits.

Also, he has a good humor. He has an optimistic outlook on life, which is part of being in high spirits. He also has common sense.

An advocate, according to Sir Jeffries, has vitality, and I must say it takes vitality for a good advocate—a good trial lawyer—because he has great stresses upon his physical condition and his physical ability to carry through some of the things that were assigned to him.

He has to have—Sir Jeffrey says—a penchant for hard work. He really has to love it; as a result, he devotes himself to whatever task he has.

In addition, he says that it might be helpful if the advocate had thrown in with these qualities a little bit of law—that is the way he puts it, a little bit of law. That does help, I found out, since I have been sitting on the trial court.

Of course, it is pretty easy, as you well know, you trial lawyers at the trial level, to get up in the Supreme Court and read a statement and talk from a brief, but it is quite different when you are trying a case in the trial court.

Of my now recent experience, I found that true, particularly in the area of judgeships. First, the Rules of Evidence had changed some since I was last in trial court, back in 1944, and I found out that I had forgotten much about the Rules of Evidence. So I took down some of the recent works on it, the recent provisions that the very generous committee had prepared, and tried to learn, but I found out that the way it is written is so much different from the way it occurs in the courtroom.

Just all of a sudden, someone jumps up and suddenly says he objects—and, of course, he never tells you why. So when you ask him, like I always do, hoping that perhaps I can get a little light, then he has four or five words, that it only is hearsay, but it is a compound question, irrelevant and immaterial with three or four other adjectives thrown in, none of which helps me.

So I turn to his opponent and I say, "What do you say about that?"

So, he says about the same thing. Then I have to just grasp around and decide.

So far, the Lord has had his arm around me. Either the jury has decided for the one who has raised these questions to rulings I have made in my error, or the case has been settled, or something of the kind.

So out of all the cases I have tried, an enormous number, I'm on my fifteenth now, in my four weeks out in San Francisco—we have lawyers from New York, Philadelphia, San Francisco, Los Angeles. I don't know whether they will be appealed or not, possibly they will be, but I think there is one I'm sure that will be appealed where the jury gave the plaintiff $591,000 which I trebled and then gave him $275,000 attorneys' fees.

I told him that if I were in New York they would have to double that.

I sat on the Court of Appeals here not long ago and we were talking in conference over what a fee would be worth in a certain case. I was amazed when one of the judges said $350,000—I was going to say $50,000. I don't know how much he got. We left that up to the trial court.

Fees come higher over here then they do in San Francisco. There is no appeal, no exception to the $250-an-hour when entered in judgment. There wasn't any exception to the setting of $275,000 fee for the plaintiff in this action. So I found that it is good if the advocate has added in a little law, particularly for the judge.

I have set up a new set of rules that they never heard of before on the West Coast—that is, if you want to introduce a study or to raise an objection to a study, you have to let me know before we go to trial.

Now when they bring in all these long studies, they hire an economist to make a study of how much damages has been made to this party or that party, then they will get, well, they will have a survey, a very beautiful survey all made up with figures blown up on a board. They have to address the jury, and when I toss it out, you never saw so much confusion in your life. All this work gone.

Quite often, I am unable to get the lawyers to abide by my ruling, to tell me about these studies before we go to trial.

One of the things that Sir Jeffrey says is that an advocate needs zeal. I think that's true. Of course you can have perhaps too much zeal.

In jury cases I have been trying I have noticed that the advocate that is sort of overzealous seems to go out on the shorter end of the stick as far as the jury is concerned. So I think there is a line there that you have to rather meet pretty carefully before you go over on the wrong side, because if you are not careful, why, the jury or if you have just a judge, well, the fact-finder may think that perhaps you are overzealous.

I remember it was said way back in early English history that the defense counsel would always tell his lordships that he was reminding them, not that they needed reminding, that he owed his sole allegiance and his entire feeling and everything he had to his client, and that he was obligated to do anything he could to bring about justice for his client, which he found, of course, to be an acquittal in the criminal case or victory in the civil case.

Of course, that's a little bit too much zeal and we don't agree with that.

However, there has been a growing tendency, I think, in some circles for lawyers to think that they do owe everything in this world to their client and that for some reason, they hold no obligation at all to the court or to the public.

Now, that's contrary to the commonest trends. I don't go for them either, but you remember when Mr. Kostov was prosecuted in 1949 in Bulgaria. He was charged with being guilty of treason. The prosecutor, in addressing the court, in a hearing of Mr. Kostov, said that he, the defense counsel, and the judge had the same duty and the same responsibility, and that while Mr. Kostov claimed that he could not have been friends with Tito because earlier, in earlier years when Tito was in a little bit better relationship with the Soviets, he had proposed a motion to throw Tito out of the Communist Party.

Counsel said, well, that's very well phrased, but, of course, you are only acting for the Central Committee, so you can't claim that at all.

I can't imagine an American lawyer or an English lawyer saying that, but they did. Then, also, his second defense was that Tito himself had accused Mr. Kostov of being a spy of a foreign country back in earlier days when things were happier and that, therefore, there was evidence that they were not too friendly.

His lawyer said, well, Tito was trying to build up an answer for any charges that might be filed against him later.

So it seems that the idea in that jurisprudence is that the defense lawyer must try to tell the court everything that seems to be against the defendant, rather than trying to help him out.

Now, of course, we don't go that far here, nor do we go all the way the other way as did the early English, that is that we owe all our fealty to the client himself. We take a more common ground, you might say, in our adversary system. Why, we think that we should do everything that is legitimate in the defense of our client.

That's not to say that if we thought him guilty, if we insisted on pleading not guilty, that we would withdraw from the case and not put on evidence and things of that kind, but it is to say that we would not use any means, such as has been indicated in some countries, that would mislead the court. In some areas, counsels have been found in contempt when that happened.

So we have developed what we call our adversary system. It is a fair bit different from the English adversary system, although it is copied very closely.

Today, we are drifting a bit closer to the English system. We have an elite practicing bar that is somewhat like its barristers and we have a large core, as it does, of non-court lawyers, you might say those who are not in the actual trial practice and who might be termed as solicitors.

Some states have gone so far as to suggest that perhaps they might prefer to adopt such a system.

I think that perhaps Sir Jeffrey would say that there really are three Ps to the adversary system, particularly where you have a criminal case and you represent a defendant. The first one would be your *pleading*, the next one would be your *proof*, and the final one would be your *persuasion*.

Perhaps in some areas a lot of persuasion is more important than the other two. In one case I tried in California, I thought the plaintiff was going to prevail with a verdict. The jury was out in about a half hour. They came back with a verdict for the defendant, only on four or five different questions that I thought had been asked.

I tried to get the parties to agree on the formal parts of the verdict, so we wouldn't have any trouble with that. So they reviewed this verdict for themselves, the yeses and nos.

This plaintiff, I think, was rather shocked when they came back "no" on every one of the counts. I think, rather, that it was because of the third P that Sir Jeffrey puts into the adversary system—persuasion—because the defense lawyer seemed to have more sincerity.

He was the one who left the greater weight with the type of argument that he made and, although I used to reprimand him in our luncheon and sometimes at coffee break, because he had an unfortunate habit of sitting on the rail, the jury rail, of all places. The jury would be sitting back here and he would come up and start off leaning on the rail at first and the first thing you know, he was getting on his toes and sort of leaning up on the rail.

So I would ask him not to do that, that's why we had the lectern, but evidently it had some effect on the jury because they decided with him. Of course, he paid no attention to what I said. I didn't dare reprimand him in the presence of the jury because I was afraid that I might prejudice him, or the other side, or myself, or somebody, and I knew that all of them would jump up and object the minute I did that. So I had enough problems already without going into that.

I think that Justice Cardozo pointed out a very important aspect of the adversary system that we overlook quite often nowadays. I notice that there are some very distinguished lawyers here tonight. I have had some experience since I have been trying cases that cause me to be a little critical.

Indeed, some of my folks told me that I ought to pipe down, but it is somewhat like the nun that died. She devoted herself to the Lord and she found herself in hell and she was very much disappointed and surprised. She had led a life for the Lord and then he let her go to hell.

So she called up St. Peter and she said, "Hello, St. Peter? This is Sister Agnes. I am down here in hell—"

St. Peter interrupted her and said, "Yes, I know. We are crowded up here, but if you will be patient, I will send down for you in a few days."

So she waited a few days and didn't hear a thing. Then she called him up again and said, "Hello, St. Peter? This is Sister Agnes. I am still down here."

He said, "Yes, I know that."

She interrupted and said, "Well, they got drinking and smoking down here and you better hurry and help me get out of here."

He said, "Now I told you to be patient and I will come there in about ten days with a chariot and I will bring you up here."

So she hung up and waited ten days. When she didn't hear anything, she called him a third time. She called up and she said, "Hello Pete? This is Agie. Just forget about the whole thing."

So, if I stepped on any toes, we can forget about the whole thing and we will still be friends and maybe I will have learned my lesson someday, but as Mr. Justice Cardozo so well pointed out, we—we lawyers—have more than just a license. Some lawyers seem to think that their license got a little bit further than the wording of it and they try to not only have a license for practicing law, but also a license for doing almost anything—particularly of late in disrupting court and things of the kind.

I remember reading, not long ago, a report by Mr. Seymour, a very distinguished committee member of the College of Trial Lawyers in this area. I concurred with his findings and told him I congratulated him on his report. Soon after that, *Allen*[1] came out of Illinois which gave the trial courts a little more leverage in this area where they might be able to control the situation.

1. Illinois v. Allen, 397 U.S. 337 (1970).

Now, the English passed that bridge long ago. One day when one of the prisoners jumped out of the box and onto the counsel table and commenced to holler and jump and then try to undress, the judge ordered him out of the courtroom. After they got him calmed down, they brought him in a little bit later and the judge told him, "If you behave yourself, then you can stay."

He continued to disrupt the proceedings, so the judge expelled him again. Later, the judge gave him a ten-year sentence in abstentia, holding him in the next room and offering him not only counsel, but to let him stay in the courtroom if he behaved.

We didn't come down that far. Indeed, we had gone so far the other way, because we had an idea of confrontation. It is more than that. Indeed, it is part of the Constitution. We thought that that included the right to be present at one's trial, which it does, so long as one does not disrupt the trial to such an extent that he, by his own actions, deprives himself of this right of being present.

So, the *Allen* case has held to that effect.

We still have disruptions. About forty miles from where I was sitting in San Francisco, a judge was killed, as you remember. Not too long ago, another one was shot. Indeed, when I was trying a case there, as a novice, I did not have a bailiff. All I had was a clerk.

While I was trying this case, a relative was testifying about some back taxes—this was a refund tax action—and all of a sudden someone jumped up in the back of the courtroom—there might have been two or three people, that was all—and he hollered, "How much did he pay you?"

You could hear him all over the courtroom. All of a sudden, he went scooting out of the door of the courtroom. I didn't have any bailiff or anybody to go after him, so I pushed a button that lighted the lamp where the clerk sat and he looked up at me and I motioned to him and said, "Go out and see if you can catch that fellow."

In the meanwhile, I said something to counsel and we went on trying the case and I didn't see anything.

Well, the clerk came back in about ten minutes and said that the man had run down the stairwell and out onto the seventeenth floor. So I forgot about it.

I asked Judge Harris, the chief judge, at lunch, what he would do. He said, "What did you do?"

I said, "Nothing."

He said, "That's what you did right."

I don't know what else I could have done. Even if I could have caught him, what would I have done about it? But those are the things that occur. I don't think there was any connection between lawyers there and this gentleman, but at the same time, it gives you an idea of the atmosphere and the climate in which even courts operate today.

It seems to be more prevalent in the West than it does in the East. In four or five different jurisdictions in one or two states, there have been these disturbances again and again—some of them violent disturbances. We will have to find an answer or else the court system is going to be so disrupted that it will not be able to function.

Well, after Cardozo's remark, I thought Felix Frankfurter, who was a great justice—he had an office next-door to me. I loved him and I revere his memory.

I shall never forget the three or four times a day he would come into my chambers, walking along, bouncing along, rather, and he would have some remark to make about a case then under consideration. Most of the time it was a pretty good remark.

I remember he said in one of his dissents that—I believe one of his last cases—the relationship of the lawyer was really a most intimate relationship and that it was just more than even an officer of the court. That it was a relationship in which trust was essential. He indicated also that this might not be true of all officers of the court.

I suppose that since I have been out in California I found that to be true also. But he said that he thought that the lawyer was essential to the judicial process. Certainly, that is true.

After sitting on the trial court, I have seen that the trial court can be practically shackled by the activities of the lawyer. After all, it is not the court that goes out and says I will look into this lead and investigate this suggestion. It is the lawyers who do that.

So whatever is brought in before the judge, is brought there by the lawyers. The judge had no part in deciding what he will even leave out.

Many, many times, when I was practicing law, I would say "Let's don't put that in. It might have a bad effect on the jury and the judge might not understand it" and we would just cast all that aside, although we may have spent considerable time investigating that phase of our case.

I remember when I argued my first case before the Supreme Court. I bought a book by Frankfurter and Green and I practically memorized it.

Frankfurter was on the bench, and I used practically all of the Frankfurter and Green that I could. Just as Frankfurter said himself, I overargued my case. I suppose he thought that perhaps the book was influencing me or I was trying to use the book to influence the Court. When it came down, Justice Murphy wrote the opinion and Justice Frankfurter didn't sit in it at all.

So if I had excised all of that from my argument, I probably would have had him sitting on the case and I would have saved all that time. I didn't realize that. It was a message that I got pretty quickly after I got the result of the case, which was favorable. So those are the things the lawyer must judge, and not the court.

Presently, I am trying a case that has over four thousand exhibits in it. I know that there are quite a number of those exhibits that don't have any relevancy, that they could just be cast aside. I told them one day that they don't need over four hundred. Perhaps even that remark was too much.

I told them I thought they ought to try to cut some of them and we recessed so that they might be able to do that. They told me that they would like to have another day. I noticed that they told me that at three days over two weeks, it would take three months to try this case.

When all the documents came in and the only testimony that's left is about five or six witnesses that they are going to put on on January 4 when I got back there.

So I think that perhaps this little nudging that I have them on the four thousand exhibits made a little difference. I asked the clerk how many documents had been introduced and he said six hundred.

I brought home a stack of them. I have a Stetson box that some kind soul gave me when I was Attorney General. You use this box to send your Stetson back to the Stetson Company to get it refurbished. So it was just the right size for these records. It is about a foot high, just about the size of a Texas Stetson.

So I brought that back to the West Coast and I went through those exhibits and out of the stack that I had, which was about a hundred, I'd say about twenty-five of them had no place there at all. So I imagine that the balance of the six hundred will be in the same place.

However, the lawyers, in their determination that they should get everything in, to be certain about it, they have placed them in. So I am going through all of them to make certain that I get everything that is there.

Now, there is another theory of justice and that is the idea that justice is a game. It is a parting theory of justice, Chief Justice Warren used to call it in which he described in one of his calls when he dedicated the University of Cincinnati College of Law. The theory is that the lawsuit belongs to the lawyers and that anything that you could conceal and bring on as a surprise to your opponent is really the highest of the art. That's the test of whether or not you really are a great advocate.

He said that he didn't believe that truth in a trial of case sprang from ignorance and, therefore, he was opposed to that theory. I completely agree with him. I don't think that justice should be a sport or a game of chance; I believe that we should have, as the rules indicate, and particularly the new rules, discovery even, in the area of criminal law, which I know is walking on thin ice.

I was happy to see that the Supreme Court decided that a state had the power within constitutional restrictions to require the defendant to file sixty days before trial, any notice of alibi that he might have.

Now, some would say that that would violate all of our principles, particularly the Fifth Amendment, prohibition of incrimination, that it would violate our ideals of a fair trial in criminal cases, but I rather think that it is helpful to the defendant for us to have discovery.

If we require the U.S. Attorney, for example, to give the defendant the theory of the case, any confessions that he has made with reference to the matter, very often they don't do this and any names of witnesses, indeed, almost giving the files to counsel so he might go through it, we have found in many of the jurisdictions, six to be exact, that where we use this technique, which we call the omnibus hearing, that the defendant's lawyers like it and the District Attorneys eventually like it. He doesn't like it at first.

We also find that the pleas of guilty jump up to eighty-five to ninety percent, while a district, like the Southern District, would have about fifty percent and some say that's bad. But I say that when that file shows a picture of the defendant robbing a bank, why waste the time of the court and the expense of the lawyers and the defendant too.

Why don't we get along with this business? That would be fair to the defendant and certainly fair to the public. We would then be able to try the rest of the criminal cases within reasonable dispatch.

But you must remember that every time that we have to try the criminal case, it takes more time than before, now about three or four days at trial. It used to be a day.

Whenever pleas of guilty are fifty percent, if you get them up to sixty percent, you see you are reducing them twenty percent right there. If you get them up to ninety percent, you have reduced them down to ten percent of trial.

So, you can see that the courts would be able to reach cases much more quickly. I am not advocating anyone to plead guilty when they are not guilty, but I am advocating that there ought to be a change of philosophy, a change of climate in this area.

I don't often mention the districts, but take Brooklyn, for example, which is close by. They have a philosophy there and climate where everybody pleads not guilty, practically everybody. As a result, they have a hundred and some odd cases pending over there. Of course, their number did increase in the filings since last year, but I believe if they had the philosophy that when a defendant is guilty, he should plead guilty and get the case out of the way, we would be able to dispose of more cases.

Indeed, the four judges in the Southern District of New York, who are now, and for the past year have been trying criminal cases individually, as well as civil [cases], have their four dockets down an average of thirty cases, give cases less than the average throughout the whole United States.

When they started, just a year ago, they had almost a hundred cases apiece. So, you can see that when the judge indicates that he thinks that the defendant is guilty, he should plead guilty.

When there are more guilty pleas—those are not cases that are more easily disposed of that are not tried. So I think it would be helpful in that area.

Now, I have just one more thing and I will be done. We need better preparation. I would change the three Ps Sir Jeffrey mentioned to preparation, preparation, preparation.

I find that lawyers are not prepared. As I mentioned earlier, in one case in California, I had to recess two days while they got their documents straightened out. Time after time after time, one of the lawyers walked to the witness stand with the wrong document in his hand.

He looks at it and I can hear him muttering. Then he walks all the way back to the lectern to a stack of papers this high and he has to look and, when he finally finds the document, he walks back to the witness stand and has it identified and wastes two or three minutes. By the time he does that ten or twelve times a day, it is thirty minutes lost. He is not prepared.

When it comes to arguing motions, for example, a motion like we had the other day to exclude some evidence, the lawyer was not prepared. He didn't know this case.

Now, I find, Dean, that the young men that come out of law schools, they really don't know anything about advocacy at all. Of course, you haven't taught them anything, but that's not your business.

Of course, I really think we will have to change that and I am going to propose at this first Sonnett lecture that we change the third year of law school altogether. I don't know whether John would object to this or not, I rather think not from my experience with law schools—and I haven't had much.

I went to a few these past two weeks. A few in California, one in Texas, and one here, and I talked to some students. All of them, they don't seem to get much out of the third year. I was up at Yale, by the way, a week ago last Saturday and you should have heard what the kids said there about the third year.

I don't say that we should abolish it. I say that we ought to devote our time to critical studies during that time and we ought to start at eight o'clock and have regular formal classes, like you do now, from eight to nine o'clock and then take off from nine to eleven o'clock, take off to the court house.

If you want to, say, go into labor law, why, go into that. Study that. Or if you want to go into some other specialty, study that. Then at noon, why, you would have lunch and at one o'clock you would come back to your formal study.

Then after that, until five o'clock, you stay in that specialty. If you want to be a trial lawyer, then you have some lawyers assigned to you or your cases assigned to you and you participate in those trials.

I know that some states have to have their rules changed, but I found out since, indeed, Connecticut doesn't have any rules at all, permitting the students there to practice.

I think, for misdemeanor cases, the student can appear without counsel or assistance. He has to have a certain certificate from the dean though. In other cases, he has to have assistance, which I think he should have in all cases, but I think you should find a different student, a graduate. After doing that for a year, they would come out.

I believe that then we would be able to start indoctrinating this student with some of the problems that we have in the courts. We have so many problems that we don't have much help to solve them.

Most of the lawyers are too busy, they don't have the time to help us. It is hard to get them to change.

I found some of the judges don't want to change because they're just not used to it. I can understand that. If I were practicing law, I wouldn't want all the rules to change over night either. But you have to make some changes if we are going to make progress.

I suggested that to the College of Lawyers about ten years ago. Perhaps they ought to establish some schools in the metropolitan area for young lawyers just starting their careers. Of course, they have never been established, but they do have a school for prosecutors in Houston that I think would have been helpful.

I am going to go a step further now in saying that I think the law students in the third year should have clinical programs, as the University of Miami does. They are getting ready to build a new law school near the courthouse and they are going to require the law students to stay in that building so that they will be able to either observe or take part in court proceedings, as the court system permits.

That way, when a graduate begins to practice, he wouldn't have to use the public as a guinea pig. That will be helpful to the lawyer because he will get new ideas from these youngsters and it will also build up our trial bar. I have told this to the trial lawyers some ten years ago.

Trial lawyers are a diminishing race and we are going to have to build it up. I grant you that since that time it has been built up some because of the 1965 Justice Act.

Even now we have had to try various gadgets to educate lawyers on how to try criminal cases. We have a list about six or seven pages long that outlines every possible defense that one could raise and we require lawyers to go over that with their clients in order that they won't miss anything because there are so many. Indeed, there are so many claims that lawyers are often ineffective and we have to reverse cases on that account and for that reason, why, we give him this list so he will know what available defenses there are and he can run down them and see what he wants to raise. Then he can go over it with the U.S. Attorney and try to get the U.S. Attorney to agree to tell him just what his case is all about. We have found this to be very helpful.

So, these are some of the ideas that I have and that we should have interest in so a new advocacy training will begin in law school. There we have young minds, not already in the groove. They are not yet steeled to a committed practice or a specific procedure. They are inquisitive. They want to know what they can improve and why. And I say to you, Dean, frankly, the young students that come out now are so far, so far ahead of the ones that came out when I first went on the court, it is just like darkness and light.

You have done a tremendous job in the area that has been assigned to you, but I believe that you ought to embrace a little more and, with the help of the bar, with the help of the courts, which I am sure you will get—I haven't found a judge yet who is not anxious to try to get more experienced lawyers before him—because that, as I said in the beginning, is the part of the judicial process that is essential, essential to be a fair administration of justice.

So, in closing, let me say that many of you may think, well, why should I get into it. After all, I have been practicing some time or, I am not a lawyer, so I couldn't be of any influence.

I tell you that you could be of some influence whether you are a lawyer or not. You could influence people in your neighborhood. You could get them interested in court matters and you, who are lawyers, could take a definite interest in it.

Many years ago, Daniel Webster said that the greatest interest of man on earth was justice, and I think that's true. That is not only men and women in our country, but men and women in countries that do not have the great protections that we have. We don't realize what great protection we have until we look around the world and find that more people in the word are without it than with it.

We are fortunate to have them, but we may lose them. We are going to lose them unless we try to protect them, unless we try to give the courts more opportunity to protect them, more opportunity to bring efficient justice, more opportunity to develop new procedures and new techniques that can bring to the courts the present techniques of business management that have been so helpful and that will work to strengthen these foundations of justice.

Daniel Webster went on to say, you who worked to strengthen these foundations and to build its abutment higher and higher and higher are going to be blessed not only by the judge who looks down and guides all of us, but you are also going to be blessed by your fellow man.

So I hope you may take a part in this new advocacy that I hope we may be inaugurating in the name of John Sonnett.

The Role of the Judge

Hon. Cearbhall Ó Dálaigh

Former President and Chief Justice of Ireland Cearbhall Ó Dálaigh delivered the second Sonnett lecture, entitled "The Role of the Judge." Although he served as president of Ireland from 1974 to 1976, his greatest legacy is as a jurist.

Born on February 12, 1911, in Bray, County Wicklow, Ó Dálaigh graduated from University College Dublin in 1931 with a degree in Celtic Studies.[1] He studied law at King's Inns in Dublin and was called to the bar in 1934.[2] Ó Dálaigh served as Attorney General of Ireland from 1946 to 1948 and 1951 to 1953 during two Fianna Fáil administrations.[3]

In 1953, Ó Dálaigh became a judge of the Supreme Court of Ireland, and later was appointed Chief Justice by Taoiseach Séan Lemass in 1961.[4] One scholar observed that "it was the appointment of Cearbhall Ó Dálaigh as Chief Justice in 1961 which signaled the beginning of the new era" of judicial activism.[5] During his tenure as Chief Justice, the Supreme Court asserted itself as a "guardian of the rights of citizens enshrined in the Constitution,"[6] which at that time was a relatively young document having only come into force in 1937.[7]

The new approach of the Court under Ó Dálaigh was evident in the landmark case *Ryan v. Attorney General*,[8] where the Supreme Court ruled that the rights guaranteed under the Constitution were not limited to those expressly enumerated; rather, it also guaranteed a range of unenumerated rights, such as a right to bodily integrity.[9] This era of reform was due, in part, to Ó Dálaigh's willingness to look to the U.S. Supreme Court for

Introduction written by Emer Stack, J.D., Class of 2014, Fordham University School of Law.

1. *Ó Dálaigh, Cearbhall*, University College Dublin, http://www.ucd.ie/archives/html/collections/odalaigh-cearbhall.htm (last visited March 7, 2014).

2. *The Hon. Mr. Justice Cearbhall Ó Dálaigh (1961–1972)*, Supreme Court of Ireland, http://www.supremecourt.ie/supremecourt/sclibrary3.nsf/pagecurrent/B8E6388E466B6FB680257315005A41D3?opendocument&l=en (last visited March 7, 2014).

3. *Ó Dálaigh, Cearbhall*, *supra* note 1.

4. *The Hon. Mr. Justice Cearbhall Ó Dálaigh*, *supra* note 2.

5. Ronan Keane, *Judges as Lawmakers: The Irish Experience*, 4 Jud. Stud. Inst. J. 1, 9 (2008).

6. *The Hon. Mr. Justice Cearbhall Ó Dálaigh*, *supra* note 2.

7. *See* Constitution of Ireland 1937, http://www.taoiseach.gov.ie/eng/Historical_Information/The_Constitution/December_2013_-_Bhunreacht_na_hEireann_Constitution_Text.pdf.

8. [1965] IR 294 (Ir.).

9. *Id.*

guidance in interpreting the Irish Constitution.[10] According to one scholar, because the Ó Dálaigh Court welcomed that practice, "[n]owadays a barrister arguing a point of constitutional law in the High or Supreme Courts will, as a matter of course, refer to decisions of the American Federal Supreme Court as persuasive authority."[11]

Ó Dálaigh's Sonnett lecture reflects the influence of U.S. courts, and focuses on an enduring debate over judicial activism. Ó Dálaigh's lecture focused on the debate over whether the role of the judge is lawmaker or a mere interpreter of the law. Quoting Justice Brandeis's notable dissent in *Olmstead v. United States*,[12] Ó Dálaigh argued that the proper role of the judge is to interpret the law in a way that adapts to a changing world and meets modern conditions. In other words, Ó Dálaigh posited "the rigid rule of stare decisis must in a court of ultimate resort give place to a more elastic formula." Ó Dálaigh's lecture remains relevant as this debate over whether the courts should take an activist or restrained approach to deciding cases is enduring and animates constitutional interpretation today.

1971 Sonnett Lecture

What can I say, Mr. Chairman, after your words? Like a good judge, I am perplexed. Not sorely; that wouldn't be true; pleasantly perplexed.

I wonder if the autobiography of Henry Adams, the work entitled *The Education of Henry Adams*, makes as much an impact on an American as it does on an outsider? Somewhere in *The Education of Henry Adams* the author says that judges are the only class in society who are specially adapted to defend themselves. He means, of course, against attack. Faced with barefaced praise, a judge is caught off his guard—as I said perplexed, pleasantly perplexed. Then his professional reflex mechanism comes into play immediately. First, he says: "This is a preposterous statement." Next, he says: "Well, look here it's plausible; it could, after all, be true." Finally (he runs for cover), he says: "Thank you, gentlemen, I'd better look into this." *Curia advisari vult*. The court will reserve judgment.

This, Mr. Chairman, must be my course. In face of your statement—your very plausible statement—I would belie the office of judge if, at this stage, I were to say more than "Thank you very much. I will take the matter under advisement." *Dia annso isteach*. So, let God guide us.

10. *See* Donal Barrington, *The Constitution in the Courts*, *in* The Constitution of Ireland 1937–1987 110, 115 (Frank Litton ed., 1988), ftp://78.153.208.68/bkp/ipa/PDF/B4_constitutioninthecourts.pdf.

11. *Id.*

12. 277 U.S. 438 (1928).

I

The late Mr. John F. Sonnett, to whose memory we pay pious tribute to-night, I never met; and I cannot therefore speak directly of the man or the lawyer. But the overwhelming evidence of the warm esteem in which he was held by his colleagues, for his personal merits no less than for his professional ability, leave me in no doubt that it is a high honor, for a brother lawyer from Ireland, to be invited to join in this tribute.

This honor, I appreciate, is not for me personally but for my country—green as always, and still distressful—and the invitation of the trustees is enhanced by the fact that it comes immediately after the inaugural lecture by Justice Tom Clark.

John F. Sonnett died in the fullness of his powers. Life still held much promise for him. His achievements were in three fields, private practice, the Navy, the Attorney General's office, and in each of these he reached the heights.

In private practice, his name is associated with the largest verdict that has yet been handed down in the U.S. courts in the case *TWA v. Hughes*.[1]

In the Navy, he rose to the rank of Lieutenant Commander; and he filled the offices of Judge Advocate and Special Assistant Secretary.

In the Attorney General's office, he was twice Assistant Attorney General, first in charge of war claims and then, in charge of antitrust problems.

If, in terms of ethnic origins, it is permissible to speak of the alley of American life, then three strains went into the making of J.F.S. He was Irish, he was French, he was Dutch. And the testimony of his closest and dearest friends is that he was chiefly Irish; characteristically Irish.

No other strains could be more appropriate to the molding of a New Yorker and Fordham alumnus. New York was once New Amsterdam. Fordham was once a French Jesuit foundation. But, of course, it was fatally infiltrated by the Irish. It is, therefore, for me a very special privilege to come from Ireland, where J.F.S.'s forebears, on his mother's side, the McLaughlins, were kings whose descent can be traced to St. Patrick's deacon *St. Secondinus* and to say as we say, in the Irish saga stories: let this lecture be my stone on the cairn of the memory of John F. Sonnett here at Fordham, of which he was so distinguished an alumnus.

Peace to his spirit.

II

A few months ago, when I received your letter of invitation and was asked to say what title I would give my lecture, I had just been reading those words of Judge Jerome Frank which you, here in New York have heard so often—that the theory of a trial can be expressed algebraically, in the formula $R \times F = D$ (Rules times Facts equals Decisions).

It had occurred to me that the formula was, perhaps, a trifle stark; and that however it is done, a third factor should be introduced to account for *The Role of the Judge*, to be symbolized

1. TWA v. Hughes, 332 F.2d 602 (2d Cir. 1964). (Ed. note, but see 409 U.S. 343 [1973], decided after the Ó Dálaigh lecture.)

by the letter *J*. It would be too much to think of *J* as an additional multiplier, but I felt that here perhaps was my subject, too inaccurate to be called *The Third Factor* but legitimate enough in the unweighted words *The Role of the Judge*.

Over and above this, it is now almost twenty years since I last tried a case—that is, in the American usage of the verb *try*—and whatever I was to say should perhaps be said from the slightly elevated, though not necessarily better-vantaged position of the bench.

It was Mr. Dooley (who has so much of value to observe about life and law) who said: "If I had a job to pick out, I'd be a judge. I've looked over all th'others, an' that's th' on'y wan that suits. I have the judicial temperament: I hate work."

I would not wish to reverse my choice of almost twenty years ago, though I think I should say I have failed to find the leisure that Mr. Dooley prophesied.

III

As a preliminary, I propose to sketch in, very rapidly, the Irish jurisdictional background.

Ireland, once an island, is now two peninsulas. I speak of the larger peninsula, still constitutionally named "Ireland." Ireland is, in a sense, a common law country. It has, however, a written Constitution, with the equivalent of a Bill of Rights under the chapter heading *Fundamental Rights*, with five subdivisions for personal rights, the family, education, private property, and religion respectively (Articles 40–44); I should add as a sixth subdivision, trial of offences (Articles 38–39).

The Constitution, one might say, is drawn on the American model, except that we have a parliamentary executive, and the President is a formal head of state. We are a unitary republic—not unitary enough, as you may gather. Without the necessity which arises, in a federal system, for judicial review, Ireland has expressly written judicial review into its Constitution, in a straightforward formula in Article 15(4):

> 1°. The Oireachtas [both Houses of Parliament] shall not enact any law which is in any respect repugnant to this Constitution or any provision thereof.
> 2°. Every law enacted by the Oireachtas which is in any respect repugnant to this Constitution, or to any provision thereof, shall, but only to the extent of such repugnancy, be invalid.

Moreover, the pre-existing law, statute law, and common law was carried over or continued in force, but only to the extent to which it was not inconsistent with the Constitution. But the legislature has not engaged in the exercise of revising the statute roll and amending the common law to ensure that they accord with the Constitution; and one might therefore say that the preexisting law is, constitutionally speaking, an unexplored minefield.

Mr. de Valera, now President and in his ninetieth year (a citizen of Manhattan, not of Brooklyn, as he insisted, when I called to see him on Tuesday last) who played a major role in drafting the Constitution, considered, but rejected, the concept of a special Constitutional

Court, which would consist of representatives of parliament in addition to judges, a scheme by the way which has since been embodied in the Italian Constitution.

The Constitution of Ireland came into force on December 29, 1937. In a review of the work of the Supreme Court, covering the first dozen years of the Constitution, Professor Edward McWhinney, then of Yale University, says:

> In spite of the Irish judges' insistence on the distinction between "law" and "policy," involving the notion that judges in exercising judicial review of the Constitution have no concern with "questions of ethics, morals, economics, and sociology," empirical, case-by-case examination of the Irish Supreme Court's work shows that the judges' function, in practice, has been much more than any simple law-finding role that might reduce, ultimately, to a merely mechanical "squaring" of statutes with the Constitution. It still seems true to say, however, that the approach to judicial policy-making on the part of the Irish judges has been much less sustained, and it is suggested also, much less conscious or informed than is the case, for example, with the United States Supreme Court. As a result, no doubt, of Ireland's long historical association with the United Kingdom, the influence of English judicial techniques and English methods of legal training, and the strictly professional nature of the criteria for selection for appointment to the Supreme Court Bench, the Irish judges have moved rather cautiously in translating the policy norms set out in the guarantees and directives of the Constitution of 1937 into law-in-action. The positive law of the Constitution of 1937, from the opening remarks of the Preamble onwards through the Fundamental Rights and the Directive Principles of Social Policy, purports to represent a society whose "living law" is Roman Catholic and social democratic. But the actual approach of the Irish judges to the cases . . . has been but rarely innovatory, and in general, fairly conventional throughout. To this extent, it is clear that the impact of modern Catholic political, social and economic ideas on legal development in present-day Ireland has been rather less significant or substantial than the adoption of the radically new Constitution of 1937 might have seemed at the time to foreshadow.[2]

Since those early years—and most of them were war years—a new race of *rights-conscious* citizens has grown up; and secondly, I would think there has also been a new race of rights-conscious young lawyers; and, thirdly, though the crop has been slower, there has been a new breed of judges.

It is only fair that I should acknowledge that this change has come about largely, if not entirely, under the influence of the study of the American Constitution and the decisions of the United States Supreme Court.

In parenthesis, let me urge that this is a field of study in which Irish law schools require to extend and deepen their activities; and I, for one, would do all I could to encourage American constitutional lawyers to find their way to Ireland for sabbatical leave, or, preferably, longer sojourns.

2. 29 Tul. L. Rev. 69, 85 (1954).

IV

Let me begin by resort to the casebook method.

A.B. sues C.D. for breach of promise of marriage. C.D. sets up, as a defense, that his promise to marry A.B. was made after he had obtained a decree nisi in divorce proceedings but before decree absolute, and that the contract was therefore void as being against public policy.

This was the problem presented to the Court of Appeal in England in 1938 in the case of *Fender v. St. John Mildmay* Sleeser and Roche, L.JJ. upheld the defense, Greer, L.J. dissenting.[3] The House of Lords, by a 3-2 vote, reversed the Court of Appeal, and held that the lady's action was maintainable. Lord Wright in delivering the leading speech said:

> The question in the present case is whether after decree nisi there is any public interest in seeking to preserve, at the expense of the solid detriment of sanctioning a breach of contract, the transitory and unsubstantial form of a marriage which by the decree of the Court is practically doomed to extinction in a brief period of months. In the language of the Divorce Court there are innocent and guilty parties. It is said that public policy imposes on both equally a contractual disability of a particular kind after decree that the marriage is to be dissolved until it is finally dissolved. The reasons adduced for this proposition seem to me to be vague and problematical, and not sufficient to weigh against the solid fact that the parties may legitimately be anxious to stabilize their position against the time when the decree absolute takes effect. The assumed promise is to marry when and if it becomes legally possible to marry, that is, after the decree absolute. The guilty party in such cases may properly be anxious to regularize, as the law permits him to do, his union with his partner in adultery. The innocent party may properly desire, now that the Court has declared the practically certain dissolution of the marriage, to lay the foundation of another and happier union. The decree nisi has put an end to the common home, to the consortium vitae, to what are crudely called the conjugal rights. These new relationships are not in their nature bad on the ground of immorality or likely to lead to immorality any more than the engagement of affectionate couples who have not suffered the miseries of an illassorted union. On the footing that the marriage of divorced persons is legal in this country, it is true that such a promise may possibly place at least in theory a new obstacle to the parties being reconciled and coming together again. But it is agreed that in the vast number of divorces there is no reconciliation. A mere possibility of that kind cannot to my mind counterbalance the solid and certain considerations which I have indicated.[4]

In conclusion, Lord Wright runs up to the mast-top the flag "*Pacta sunt servanda.*"

By contrast, the speech of Lord Russell of Killowen is illuminating. Lord Russell of Killowen was a son of Charles Russell, counsel for Parnell at the Parnell Commission and a great-nephew of Rev. Charles Wm. Russell, President of Maynooth College. Lord Russell launches forth with great vigor:

3. [1936] 1 KB 111 (Ir.).
4. [1938] A.C. 1.

> My Lords, when England was a Catholic country matrimony was a sacrament, conferred upon themselves by the spouses. This sacramental nature of marriage, the holy state of matrimony, was the basis of the civil law of Europe with regard to it. When in the reign of Elizabeth England abandoned the old faith, and became a Protestant country, matrimony ceased, according to the new dispensation, to be ranked among the sacraments of the Gospel. The 25th of the 39 Articles so provided. The status of marriage became the product or result of a contract between the parties. But the obligations resulting from the status, the solemnity of the status, the importance to a civilized community of its maintenance, remained almost unimpaired. Until the first Divorce Act in 1857 the marriage tie was indissoluble except by legislation. The question now arises whether as a result of that Act and subsequent divorce legislation, there has come about such an alteration in the public view of the status of marriage, its obligations, and the importance of its maintenance, that without any offence to public policy or public opinion, a spouse may validly contract to marry another, provided only that the jurisdiction of the Divorce Court has been invoked in relation to his or her existing marriage.
>
> My Lords, I use those words advisedly, because as it seems to me, every argument for the Appellant which depends upon the existence of a decree nisi, is applicable to a case where the suit has not yet proceeded beyond the presentation of the petition. The decree nisi as I understand it effects nothing. It does not dissolve the marriage. The parties are just as much man and wife as they were before. It is true that the right to consortium could not be enforced; that duty and obligation between spouses is no doubt in suspense. So it is, once a petition for divorce has been presented. Other duties or obligations, however, remain. The duty and obligation to refrain from sexual intercourse with others, surely continues. To break it would be to commit adultery, just as much as to marry another would be to commit bigamy. I confess that I do not understand how the existence of a decree nisi is really relevant or essential to this case. The parties at the time of the contract are either married or not. If they are married, can either of them, while still married, enter into an enforceable contract to marry someone else?[5]

As was well said by Beasley, C.J., in the American case of *Noice v. Brown*: "The institution of marriage is the first act of civilization, and the protection of the married state against all molestation or disturbance is a part of the policy of every people possessed of morals and laws."[6] In my opinion, any contract, the effect or tendency of which would be to create an obstacle or bar to the reconciliation of husband and wife, must necessarily be a contract against public policy. In divorce proceedings nothing is final until decree absolute. Up to that time there is always the possibility, I put it no higher than that, of a reconciliation, and of that being maintained which it is in the interest of the State to maintain—namely, the marriage tie: "My Lords, as I see this case, there is here no question of inventing a new rule of public policy. It is only an illustration of an old rule applied to new facts."

The case of *Fender v. St. John Mildmay* shows better than many words, how the law is shaped by men and history as much as by judicial precedent.

5. *Id.*
6. 38 NJL 228 (1876).

V

But in our jurisdiction, in Ireland, the doctrine of judicial precedent, stare decisis, has now been formally dethroned.

Speaking for a unanimous Court, Kingsmill Moore J. in 1964 in *A.G. v. Minister for Defence and Ryan's Car Hire Ltd.*[7] said:

> This Court is a new court (established in 1961) and it is free to consider whether it should adopt the rule which prevails in the House of Lords. . . . However desirable certainty, stability and predictability of law may be, they cannot in my view justify a court of ultimate resort in giving a judgment which they are convinced, for compelling reasons, is erroneous. In my opinion the rigid rule of stare decisis must in a court of ultimate resort give place to a more elastic formula. Where such a court is clearly of opinion that an earlier decision was erroneous, it should be at liberty to refuse to follow it, at all events in exceptional cases.

That decision was handed down on December 11, 1964. Eighteen months later, on July 26, 1966, in the House of Lords the Lord Chancellor, Lord Gardiner, made the following statement:[8]

> Their Lordships regard the use of precedent as an indispensable foundation upon which to decide what is the law and its application to individual cases. It provides at least some degree of certainty upon which individuals can rely in the conduct of their affairs, as well as a basis for orderly development of legal rules.
>
> Their Lordships nevertheless recognise that too rigid adherence to precedent may lead to injustice in a particular case and also unduly restrict the proper development of the law. They propose, therefore, to modify their present practice and, while treating former decisions of this House as normally binding, to depart from a previous decision when it appears right to do so.
>
> In this connection they will bear in mind the danger of disturbing retrospectively the basis on which contracts, settlements of property and fiscal arrangements have been entered into and also the especial need for certainty as to the criminal law.
>
> This announcement is not intended to affect the use of precedent elsewhere than in this House.

In the law reports the Lord Chancellor's statement is blandly published under the caption "Practice Statement (Judicial Precedent)." In fact, the statement is a revolutionary pronouncement, and it is even more surprising that it should have been made, not in deciding a specific case but, so to speak, in vacuo. The House of Lords may, however, have felt driven to this course by the inconveniences of the doctrine of prospective invalidity, developed

7. [1965] ILR 642 (Ir.).

8. [1966] 1 WLR 1234. (Lord Gardiner L.C., Viscount Dilhome, Lord Reid, Lord Denning, Lord Parker of Waddington, Lord Morris of Borth-Y-Gest, Lord Hodson, Lord Pearce, Lord Upjohn and Lord Wilberforce were present. Lords Donovan, Guest, and Pearson were absent.).

by the United States Supreme Court in constitutional cases. All in all, it was perhaps fairer to give notice that in the future the rules of the game would be altered.

The Chancellor's declaration had an unusual sequel in the Court of Appeal three years later, in the case of *Gallie v. Lee*.[9] The Court, on this occasion, consisted of Denning, M.R. and Salmon and Russell, L.JJ. Denning, M.R. had been a party to the Lord Chancellor's declaration. You will, however, remember that the last sentence of the declaration had said that the announcement was not intended to affect the use of precedent elsewhere than in the House of Lords.

Gallie v. Lee found only one authority which was inconsistent with the course that he considered should be taken in the case, but this case was inconsistent with many others and could therefore be disregarded.

He then continues:

> But even if there were authorities against it, they are only to be found in this Court, and are not in the House of Lords. We are, of course, bound by the decisions of the House, but I do not think we are bound by prior decisions of our own, or at any rate, not absolutely bound. We are not fettered as it was once thought. It was self-imposed limitation: and we who imposed it can also remove it. The House of Lords have done it. So why should not we do likewise? We should be just as free, no more and no less, to depart from a prior precedent of our own, as in like case is the House of Lords or a judge of first instance. It is very, very rarely that we will go against a previous decision of our own, but if it is clearly shown to be erroneous, we should be able to put it right. I propose, therefore, to apply the principle which I have stated.

Salmon, L.J. approaches with more caution. He begins by pointing out that the dicta to the effect that the Court of Appeal is bound by its own decisions rests on the concept of judicial comity. Then he continues:

> Surely today judicial comity would be amply satisfied if we were to adopt the same principle in relation to our decisions as the House of Lords has recently laid down for itself by a pronouncement of the whole House. It may be that one day we shall make a similar pronouncement. I can see no valid reasons why we should not do so and many why we should. But that day is not yet. It is, I think, only by a pronouncement of the whole court that we could effectively alter a practice which is so deeply rooted. In the meantime I find myself reluctantly obliged to accept the old authorities, however much I disagree with them. My only consolation is that in spite of the present unsatisfactory state of this branch of the law, it enables us, on the facts of this case, to reach a decision which accords with reason a justice.

The third member of the Court, Russell, L.J., takes a firmly conservative line. His words are:

> I add that I do not support the suggestion that this Court is free to override its own decisions, now that the House of Lords has given itself ability to override its own

9. [1969] 2 Ch. 17; *affirmed sub nom.* Saunders v. Anglia Building Society [1971] AC 1004.

> decisions. I am a firm believer in a system by which citizens and their advisers can have as much certainty as possible in the ordering of their affairs. Litigation is an activity that does not markedly contribute to the happiness of mankind, though it is sometimes unavoidable. An abandonment of the principle that this Court follows its own decisions on the law would I think lead to greater uncertainty and tend to produce more litigation. In the case of decisions of the House of Lords error, or what is later considered to be error, could only previously be corrected by statute; and the other demands on parliamentary time made this possibility so remote that the decision was justifiable at the expense of some loss of certainty. But the availability of the House of Lords to correct error in the Court of Appeal makes it in my view unnecessary for this Court to depart from its existing discipline.

Here you have an example of whole spectrum of judicial temperament: green, amber, red; or go, caution, stop.

I have been discussing the fate of stare decisis; but I think I should not pass over a case in which the existing law was changed not by the Court, but, in a manner of speaking, by the litigants themselves.

We are in the delicate field of testamentary dispositions.

One Chancery judge (Eve, J.) is reported to have said: "I shudder to think that, in the hereafter, I shall have to meet those testators whose wishes on earth have been frustrated by my judgments." But it was an Irish judge, who was also a philosopher, who had the good sense to adjust the law, this side of Paradise, to accord with the testator's wishes.

The specific case raised the important question of the meaning of the term "money."[10] Meredith J. observed that the judiciary had waged a long fight to teach testators that "money" means "cash;" but, as the ordinary testator does not study the law reports, he persists in constantly using the word in a wider sense. Meredith J. continued:

> The Court must do its best. For two centuries, the Courts have been endeavoring to force testators to use the word "money" in the sense of "cash." They have signally failed, notwithstanding a number of decisions in which they regretfully held that as a matter of law the testator said what they were convinced he did not mean. It is time to hoist the white flag. Testators evidently prefer to say 'cash' when they mean "cash."

The Court's capitulation in this case is refreshing.

The House of Lords, after an interval of thirteen years, apparently thought so too. In 1943, they followed Meredith J. in *Perrin v. Morgan*.[11]

By the way, I don't wish you to think that the House of Lords spends all its time following Irish decisions.

10. Meredith, J. was a noted Kantian scholar. The case was *In re* Jennings, dec. (Caldbeck v. Stafford and Lindemere [1930] IR 196 (Ir.)).

11. [1943] AC 399.

VII

In modern times, what I have been illustrating, the clash of temperament in interpreting and administering the law, has been, by the academics, conveniently contrasted as mechanical jurisprudence and realist jurisprudence or (in a European context) the jurisprudence of free legal decision.

The history of law, as Sir Maurice Sheldon Amos has well said, reveals a perpetual oscillation between the introvert ideal of stability and static perfection, with the primary emphasis on the abstract rule, and the extrovert ideal, which commands that the law be remolded in conformity with the new interests and the new moral standards of the outside world. Mechanical jurists have tended to place uppermost the first of these ideals, and the school of free legal decision has been inclined to give emphasis to the second ideal. Each group of jurists has profoundly influenced American constitutional interpretation.

If you come to visit the Supreme Court in Dublin, in the Court Conference room you will see, as the dominant element in the carpet design, a gold collar, shaped like the new moon. These lunular neck ornaments were worn by judges in Ireland in pagan times. One of the most famous of the Irish judges in pre-Christian times, Morann, had a collar that had the useful property that it began to tighten around his neck—in protest—if he were about to deliver an unjust judgment. Is this an early example of mechanical jurisprudence?

The Greeks of prehistoric times had perhaps what might be considered a superior method. Do you remember your Homer? And, more particularly, the scenes depicted on the shield of Achilles, one of which depicts a trial:

> The men had flocked to the meeting-place, where a case had come up between two litigants, about the payment of compensation for a man who had been killed. The defendant claimed the right to pay in full and was announcing his intention to the people; but the other contested his claim and refused all compensation. Both parties insisted that the issue should be settled by a referee; and both were cheered by their supporters in the crowd, whom the heralds were attempting to silence. The Elders sat on the sacred bench, a semicircle of polished stone; and each, as he received the speaker's rod from the clear-voiced heralds, came forward in his turn to give his judgment, staff in hand. Two talents of gold were displayed in the centre; they were the fee for the Elder whose exposition of the law should prove the best.[12]

Does anyone doubt that the Greek method *if it could be acceptable* (I emphasize these words) would have two unusual results: (i) a marked drop in judicial employment, and (ii) a marked rise in the quality of judgments.

A good deal of this debate about mechanical and realist jurisprudence begins with the words of a post-reformational English Lord Chancellor; the only Lord Chancellor who, so far as I know, was deprived of the Great Seal. He was charged with bribery, and he confessed that he was guilty of "corruption and neglect." I refer to Francis Bacon.

12. The Iliad 350 (E.V. Rieu trans., Penguin).

Bacon plunges into his dissertation on Judicature with these words:

> Judges ought to remember that their office is *jus dicere*, and not just dare; to interpret the law and not to make law, or give law. Else it will be like the authority claimed, by the Church of Rome, which, under pretext of exposition of scripture, did not stick to add and alter; and to pronounce that which they do not find; and by show of antiquity to introduce novelty. . . . Cursed (said the Law) be he who removeth the landmark.[13]

It was a Jesuit (Lewis Watt, S.J.) who, having read this passage, said that "no doubt Bacon thought that the possibility of resembling the Church of Rome would be a sufficient deterrent to judge-made law," and then added "but the difficulty of drawing a line between interpreting the law and making a new law is admittedly greater than he (Bacon) realised."

Medieval lawyers, under the influence of canon law, upheld the *ratio acquitatis* in preference to the *ratio stricti juris* (the fourteenth-century Luca de Penna might be quoted); and Ullmann, no mean medievalist, has himself said that mechanical, literal interpretation of law frequently results in the paradox "*summa jus, summa injuria.*" In Irish we say (I think, with more force,) *ní haincheart go lomcheart* (there is no injustice to compare to literal justice).

But the opposing school has never been silent. I might refer to the work of another Italian, Ludovico Antonio Muratori, born exactly three hundred years ago. His work *Dei diffetti della giurisprudensa* (Of the Defects of Jurisprudence) was dedicated to Pope Benedict XIV, and appeared in 1742, the year after Blackstone entered the Middle Temple.

Let me quote a single sentence from him. (I will offer no apology in this great Italo-Irish city, or should I *not* say, Hiberno-Italian, for quoting him in Italian, but I will apologize for my accent.) Let's listen carefully: "Tornerò bensì ad inculcare, che l'equita *cervellstica* dei giudici non è da tollerare, equando Ie leggi e gli statuti son chiari, ancorché rigorosi, equando Ie volontà dei contraenti sono manifeste e sevisa frode, la giustizia e non l'equitâ ha da decidere Ie liti." I should, I think, offer a prize for the best translation of the phrase: "*l'equita cervellstica dei giudici.*"[14]

I have searched through the textbooks and the judgments for what I consider some acceptable statement of what I personally would regard as defining a judge's task in interpreting the law, and I think I may say that I have found no better exposition than the words Justice Brandeis, used in *Olmstead v. United States* 227 US 472 (1927): "[T]his Court," he says, "has repeatedly sustained the exercise of power by Congress under various clauses of that instrument"—he is here speaking specifically of the Constitution, but he broadens his grounds as he proceeds—"*over* objects of which the Fathers could not have dreamed."[15] He continues:

> We have likewise held that general limitations on powers of Government, like those embodied in the due process clauses of the Fifth and Fourteenth Amendments, do not forbid the United States or the States from meeting modern conditions by regulations

13. Francis Bacon, *Of Judicature*, *in* Essays, civil and moral (Charles W. Eliot, ed. 2001).
14. My own rendering is the "hair-brained equity of the judges"; I received no other entries.
15. Olmstead v. United States, 277 U.S. 438, 472 (1927) (Brandeis, J., dissenting).

> which, "a century ago, or even half a century ago, would have been rejected as arbitrary and oppressive."[16]

Then he balances this by observing: "Clauses guaranteeing to the individual protection against specific abuses of power must have a similar capacity of adaptation to a changing world."[17] Then he quotes from *Weems's* case:

> It was with reference to such a clause that this Court said in *Weems v. United States*: "Legislation both statutory and constitutional [—here broader ground is being taken—] is enacted, it is true, from an experience of evils, but its general language should not therefore, be necessarily confined to the form that evil had theretofore taken."[18]

I emphasize the words "necessarily confined" and the words "the form that evil had theretofore taken." He continues: "Time works changes, brings into existence new conditions and purposes. Therefore the principle must be capable of a wider application than the mischief which gave it birth."[19] The quotation from *Weems* ends by returning to the problem of constitutional interpretation as follows:

> In the application of a constitution . . . our contemplation cannot be only what has been but of what may be. Under any other rule a constitution would indeed be as easy of application as it would be deficient in efficacy and power. Its general principles would have little value and be converted by precedent into impotent and lifeless formulas. Rights, declared *in words* might be lost *in reality*.[20]

Brandeis and Holmes were colleagues in the Court for many years. Am I right in thinking that, to some extent, Holmes J. (O.W.H.) is on the other side?

Do I detect a contradiction in Holmes's position? He was eminently an admirer of the common law which he described as "a far more developed, more rational and mightier body of law than the Roman." As an admirer of the common law, which is an organic thing, one would expect that he would not react as he did to Judge Learned Hand's tease, as they parted one morning at the steps of the Supreme Court. Hand said: "Well, good-bye, sir, Do justice." Holmes turned sharply: "That's not my job. My job is to play the game according to the rules."[21] A common lawyer is instinct (I would suggest) with the desire to do justice. Is it too much to say that Holmes's hostility to the absolutes of natural law drove him to opposite extreme—to the point where, in words at least, he reduced his role to playing the game according to the rules?

It is therefore with reluctance that I call attention to what I consider a wholly admirable feature of the Swiss Civil Code. (I say with reluctance, because the Swiss are only now

16. *Id.*
17. *Id.*
18. *Id.* at 472–73 (internal citations omitted).
19. *Id.* (quoting *Weems v. United States*, 217 U.S. 349, 363 (1910)).
20. *Id.* at 473 (emphasis added).
21. Quoted by Biddle.

about to get around to a referendum to alter the constitutional ban on Jesuits.) The Code, in its first article, defines the judge's function in these words:

> The Civil Code applies to all cases for which it contains provisions, either according to its letter or its spirit. If the Code contains no provision applicable to the question at issue, the judge should decide according to customary law; and, where that is also absent, according to recognised legal doctrine and science: In the absence of all these sources, he shall render judgment in accordance with such rules as he would enact if he were legislator.

Here we have express authority for what has been called by Holmes "intersticial legislation."

The formula of the Swiss Code would end the debate—or would it? In any event, it is, in my opinion, a very practical approach, and I suggest the so-called common law countries might consider adopting it.

Coming down to a less exalted level, I don't think anyone has better formulated, or more succinctly set forth, the rules for trial courts than the unfortunate Francis Bacon. Let me quote: "Judges ought to be more learned than witty, more reverend than plausible, and more advised than confident. Above all things, integrity is their portion, and proper virtue."[22]

The "Essays" were first published in 1597; Bacon's tragic downfall was in 1621:

> A judge ought to prepare his way to a just sentence, as God useth to prepare his way, by raising valleys and taking down hills: So, when there appeareth on either side, an high hand, violent persecution, cunning advantages taken, combination, power, great counsel, then is the virtue of a judge seen, to make inequality equal; that he may plant his judgment, as upon even ground. . . . Judges must beware of hard constructions and strained inferences; for there is no worse torturer, than the torture of laws. Specially in the case of laws penal, they ought to have care, that that which was meant for terror be not turned into rigour.[23]

He is perhaps, after all, less an adherent of the mechanical school than he first holds himself out to be.

> In causes of life and death judges ought (as far as the law permitteth) in justice to remember mercy and to cast a severe eye upon the example, but a merciful eye upon the person.
>
> . . . . For the advocates and counsel that plead, patience and gravity of hearing is an essential part of justice.
>
> . . . . an overspeaking judge is no well-tuned cymbal. It is no grace in a judge first to find that which he might have heard, in due time, from the bar; or to show quickness of conceit in cutting off evidence or counsel too short.
>
> The parts of a judge on hearing are four: to direct the evidence; to moderate length, repetition or impertinency of speech; to recapitulate, select, and collate the material

22. Bacon, *supra* note 16. "Plausible" in the sixteenth and seventeenth centuries meant deserving of applause.

23. *Id.*

> points of that which hath been said. And to give the rule, or sentence. Whatsoever is above these is too much; and proceedeth either of glory and willingness to speak; or of impatience to hear; or of shortness of memory; or of a want of staid and equal attention.
>
> There is due from the judge, to the advocate some commendation and gracing where causes are well handled and fair pleaded, especially towards the side which obtaineth not; for that upholds, in the client, the reputation of his counsel.

Bacon had only taken silk the year before, 1596.

> There is likewise due to the public a civil reprehension of advocates where there appeareth cunning counsel, gross neglect, slight information, indiscreet pressing and an over-bold defence. And let not the counsel at the Bar chop with the judge or wind himself into the handling of the cause anew after the judge hath declared his sentence; but on the other side, let not the judge meet the cause half way; nor give occasion to the party to say his counsel or proofs were not heard.[24]

The American Bar Association could not have better formulated the rules.

I don't overlook that the members of the bar have their own remedies, by courage and otherwise, in dealing with judges. Might I take an illustration, not from a court case but from a tribunal of inquiry presided over by an English judge.

The scene in Ireland; the occasion the sitting of the tribunal to inquire into wholesale evictions of tenants in Ireland; the year, 1892. Edward Carson appeared for Lord Clanricarde. When Carson rose to cross-examine the first witness, the English High Court judge, who was President of the tribunal and who should have known his man, refused to allow him to do so. The following dialogue ensued:

PRESIDENT: I decline to hear you.

CARSON: I must press this matter. I will ask for a vote to be taken to see if every Commissioner takes your view.[25]

PRESIDENT: I will not hear you further, and I will order you to withdraw.

CARSON: I insist upon my right till every Commissioner orders me to withdraw. I will stand up here and now for justice to be done to Lord Clanricarde as well as to everyone else.

PRESIDENT: The Commissioners have consulted and we have come to the unanimous conclusion that we will not hear you . . .

CARSON: My Lord, if I am not allowed to cross-examine I say the whole thing is a farce and a sham. I willingly withdraw from it. I will not prostitute my position by remaining longer as an advocate before an English judge.

PRESIDENT: I am not sitting as a judge.

CARSON (in a loud whisper): Any fool could see that.

And having remained on his feet throughout this exchange, Carson threw down his papers and walked out of the room.

24. *Id.*

25. It was a multimember tribunal.

One point in favor of the presiding judge: he had the good sense not to pretend he heard what Carson said.

When a judge is in the wrong the only answer is silence; or, better, an apology.

You will remember that Bacon commended gravity in a judge as against plausibility (that is to say, desire for applause). There are, however, some cases where the latter is permissible and, perhaps, a useful example is a case that came before Sir Peter O'Brien (in his days as Attorney General he was better known as "Peter the Packer," for his capacity to pack juries).[26]

A Local Government Board Auditor had disallowed certain payments by the Dublin Corporation, one item being the cost of a luncheon by members of the Corporation on the occasion of the "Annual Inspection" of the Vartry Waterworks. The validity of this disallowance came before the Irish Queen's Bench Division on an application for mandamus. when the Attorney-General (The MacDermot, Q.C.) appeared for the Auditor, and the Solicitor-General (C.M. Hemphill Q.C.) for the Local Government Board. The leading judgment was delivered by Sir Peter O'Brien C.J.:

> Now I think it is relevant to refer to the character of this luncheon. I have before me the items in the bill. Amongst the list of wines are two dozen champagne, Ayala, 1885—a very good brand—at 84s. a dozen; one dozen Marcobrunn hock—a very nice hock; one dozen Château Margaux—an excellent claret; one dozen fine old Dublin whiskey—the best whiskey that can be got; one case of Ayala; six bottles of Amontillado sherry—a stimulating sherry; and the ninth item is some more fine Dublin whiskey! Then Mr. Lovell supplied the "*dinner*" (this was a dinner, not a mere luncheon!) including all attendance, at 10s. per head. There is an allowance for brakes; one box of cigars, 100; coachmen's dinner; beer, stout, minerals in syphons, and ice for wine. There is dessert, and there are sandwiches, and an allowance for four glasses broken—a very small number broken under the circumstances.
>
> In sober earnestness, what was this luncheon and outing? It seems to me to have been a pic-nic on an expensive scale. What authority is there for it? No statutable authority exists. By what principle of our common law is it sustainable? By none that I can see. In *McEvoy's* case, to which I have already referred, there was a question of maintaining the Mansion House, being the property of the Corporation. But this is a question of providing a sumptuous repast for the members of the Corporation on the Wicklow hills. It is not certainly for the benefit of the property of the Corporation, or of the rate-paying citizens of Dublin, that the members of the Corporation should lunch sumptuously.
> I asked for statute or for case, but neither was cited. The Solicitor-General in his most able argument—I have always to guard myself against his plausibility—appealed pathetically to common sense; he asked, really with tears in his voice, whether the members of the Corporation should starve; he drew a most gruesome picture; he represented that the members of the Corporation would really traverse the Wicklow hills in a spectral condition, unless they were sustained by lunch. I do not know, whether he went so far as Ayala, Marcobrunn, Château Margaux, old Dublin whiskey, and cigars. In answer to the pathetic appeal of the Solicitor-General, we do not say that the members of the

26. R. (Bridgeman) v. Drury [1894] 2 IR 489 (Ir.).

> Corporation are not to lunch. But we do say that they are not to do so at the expense of the citizens of Dublin.[27]

Finally, in American context, let me remind you of the lawyer whose witnesses were constantly being taken out of his hands by an impatient judge.

Counsel grew alarmed at the judge's line of questioning. "Your Honor," he said, "I have no objection to your trying my case for me; but, for God's sake, don't lose it."

I must end.

Judge Jerome Frank to whom I referred earlier, wrote an article in the *University of Pennsylvania Law Review* in 1931: He entitled it *"Are Judges Human?"*[28] My answer is "yes"; and like the bar, where judges have had their formation, judges believe profoundly in justice and the use of law to achieve it.

27. *Id.* at 496–97.
28. *See generally* Jerome Frank, *Are Judges Human?*, 80 U. of Pa. L. Rev. 17 (1931).

Prison: The Judge's Dilemma

Hon. Irving R. Kaufman

Judge Irving Kaufman delivered the third Sonnett lecture, entitled *Prison: The Judge's Dilemma*, on November 20, 1972.[1] Arguably most well-known for his decision to sentence the convicted spies Julius and Ethel Rosenberg to death, Judge Kaufman also wrote a number of prominent opinions regarding the First Amendment, civil rights, and antitrust law throughout his nearly forty-three-year service on the federal bench.[2] Born in New York City in 1910, Judge Kaufman attended Fordham University and graduated from Fordham University School of Law in 1931, at the age of twenty.[3] Between 1932 and 1950, Judge Kaufman alternated between private practice and public service, working for several years as an assistant U.S. attorney in the Southern District of New York, and later as a special assistant to the Attorney General of the United States.

In 1950, President Harry S. Truman nominated Judge Kaufman to sit on the United States District Court for the Southern District of New York.[4] He was confirmed that same year and served as a district court judge until his appointment to the United States Court of Appeals for the Second Circuit in 1961 by President John F. Kennedy.[5] In 1951, he gained national attention by sentencing the Rosenbergs to death after a jury convicted them of conspiring to deliver secrets pertaining to the atomic bomb to the Soviet Union.[6] Although the Court of Appeals, Supreme Court, and the President let the sentences stand, Judge Kaufman's decision was controversial to many.[7] In another noteworthy decision, Judge Kaufman, in *Taylor v. Board of Education*,[8] ordered an

Introduction written by Daniel Marcus-Toll, J.D., Class of 2015, Fordham University School of Law.

1. Irving R. Kaufman, *Prison: The Judge's Dilemma*, 41 Fordham L. Rev. 495 (1973).

2. Marilyn Berger, *Judge Irving Kaufman, of Rosenberg Spy Trial and Free-Press Rulings, Dies at 81*, N.Y. Times (Feb. 3. 1992), http://www.nytimes.com/1992/02/03/nyregion/judge-irving-kaufman-of-rosenberg-spy-trial-and-free-press-rulings-dies-at-81.html.

3. *Id.*

4. *Biographical Directory of Federal Judges: Kaufman, Irving Robert*, Fed. Judicial Ctr., http://www.fjc.gov/servlet/nGetInfo?jid=1231cid=999ctype=nainstate=na.

5. *Id.*

6. Berger, *supra* note 2.

7. *Id.* Current commentators and the Rosenberg's sons now acknowledge that Julius Rosenberg was a spy and that there is evidence that his wife Ethyl was an accomplice. *See* Radosh Milton, The Rosenberg File (2d ed. 1997).

8. 191 F.Supp. 181 (S.D.N.Y. 1961).

elementary school to desegregate, a first in the North[9] following *Brown v. Board of Education*.[10]

Judge Kaufman served as Chief Judge from 1973 to 1980.[11] His ruling in *Berkey Photo, Inc. v. Eastman Kodak Company*[12] is considered a landmark in antitrust law.[13] Moreover, in cases such as *Edwards v. National Audubon Society, Inc.*[14] and *Reeves v. American Broadcasting Companies, Inc.*,[15] Judge Kaufman established his reputation as a staunch defender of the First Amendment. Perhaps most notably, Judge Kaufman dissented in *United States v. New York Times Company*,[16] which concerned the issue of whether publication of the Pentagon Papers would pose a sufficient threat to national security to justify prior restraint. Ultimately, the Supreme Court agreed with his position and reversed the decision.[17]

In 1983, he was named chairman of the President's Commission on Organized Crime, which urged action to combat organized crime.[18] In 1987, President Ronald Reagan presented Judge Kaufman with the Presidential Medal of Freedom, the country's highest civilian honor.[19] At the ceremony, President Reagan praised Judge Kaufman's "willingness to go even beyond [his] achievements on the bench"—specifically his efforts on behalf of jury reform and against organized crime—and also lauded Judge Kaufman's "noble and heroic work" in "protecting the courts from political pressures."[20] In 1987, Judge Kaufman assumed senior status on the Second Circuit.

Judge Kaufman's Sonnett lecture, *Prison: The Judge's Dilemma*, focused on the nature of prisoner rights, the appropriate response by the judiciary to convicted individuals, and complaints about the prison system in general.[21] Focusing on the increasing frequency of prisoner applications to the courts for assistance,[22] Judge Kaufman noted that this development had the significant effect of familiarizing judges with prisons and prisoners.[23] Judge Kaufman remarked that the essential role of the courts was to function as "guardians of basic rights,"[24] and justified judicial intervention in the prison system where the purpose was not to assert "superior penological wisdom," but rather, to protect prisoners' constitutional rights.[25] The significance of the judiciary's role in this area—and the

9. Berger, *supra* note 2.
10. 347 U.S. 483 (1955).
11. *Id.*
12. 603 F.2d 263 (2d Cir. 1979).
13. Berger, *supra* note 2.
14. 556 F.2d 113 (2d Cir. 1977).
15. 719 F.2d 602 (2d Cir. 1983).
16. 444 F.2d 544 (2d Cir.), *rev'd*, 403 U.S 713 (1971).
17. Berger, *supra* note 2.
18. *Id.*
19. Times Staff, *Irving R. Kaufman; Judge in Rosenbergs' Spy Trial*, L.A. Times (Feb. 4, 1992), http://articles.latimes.com/1992-02-04/news/mn-1246_1_judge-irving-r-kaufman.
20. President Ronald Reagan, Remarks on Presenting the Presidential Medal of Freedom to Irving R. Kaufman (Oct. 7, 1987), http://www.reagan.utexas.edu/archives/speeches/1987/100787c.htm.
21. *See generally* Kaufman, *supra* note 1.
22. *Id.* at 504–5.
23. *Id.* at 507.
24. *Id.* at 510.
25. *Id.* at 515.

challenge of adequately structuring the way the judicial system operates with respect to prisoners and the prison system—remains timely today, as evidenced by the Supreme Court's recent decision in *Brown v. Plata*,[26] which authorized a court-mandated population limit to remedy constitutional violations in California's prisons.[27]

1972 Sonnett Lecture

In choosing the subject matter and then in preparing the lecture, it became apparent to me how appropriate to this occasion were Learned Hand's introductory comments to his Holmes Lectures on the Bill of Rights. He said: "My subject is well-worn; it is not likely that I shall have new light to throw on it; but it is always fresh, and particularly at the present time it is important enough to excuse renewed examination."[1] No one, I am sure, will take issue with my view that the subject of prisons and prisoners has occupied so many people for so long that it can withstand just one more reexamination.[2] The temptation to speak of prisons as rotten, fetid cages of inhumanity, which breed more crime than they prevent, and to use similar language to describe our modern system of corrections, is ever-present.[3] But I shall resist the temptation,[4] and I shall attempt to speak instead with a more

26. 563 U.S. 493 (2011).
27. *Id.* at 502.

1. L. Hand, The Bill of Rights, 1 (1958).
2. For some recent views *see, e.g.*, R. Clark, Crime in America (1970); D. Clemmer, The Prison Community (1958); K. Menninger, The Crime of Punishment (1966); D. Rothman, The Discovery of the Asylum (1971); G. Sykes, The Society of Captives (1958). A particularly interesting volume, written by four inmates of the Indiana State Prison, is L. Griswold, M. Misenheimer, A. Powers & E. Tromanhauser, An Eye for an Eye (1970). *See also* New York State Special Comm'n on Attica, Attica: The Official Report (1972) [hereinafter cited as Attica Report]; The President's Comm'n on Law Enforcement and Administration of Justice, Task Force Report: Corrections (1967). Several older accounts of prison life continue to make fruitful reading today. *See, e.g.*, A. Berlman, Prison Memoirs of an Anarchist (1970, originally published in 1912). Few people realize that Alexis de Tocqueville, the eighteenth-century Frenchman, whose *Democracy in America* continues to be required reading for students in every field relating to American political or social science, came to this country originally to study the prison system. His work in this regard remains highly instructive. *See* G. de Beaumont & A. de Tocqueville, On the Penitentiary System in the United States and Its Application in France (1964).
3. One federal district court judge, in response to the flood of prisoner rights cases brought in the courts, has stated: "I am persuaded that the institution of prison probably must end. In many respects, it is as intolerable within the United States as was the institution of slavery, equally brutalizing to all involved, equally toxic to the social system, equally subversive of the brotherhood of man, even more costly by some standards, and probably less rational." Morales v. Schmidt, 340 F. Supp. 544, 548–49 (W.D. Wis. 1972).
4. "The only thing I can't resist," Oscar Wilde is known to have said, "is temptation."

muted, but hopefully analytic voice. While I do not wish to imply that I blindly endorse the present penological system, I wish also to avoid a fashionable despair that serves to excuse inaction.

As I have indicated, the fact that prisons and courts are the subject of my talk is neither accidental nor of minor significance. Five years ago, this lecture more likely would have dealt with *procedures* in criminal courts. I might have explored the implications of the then brand new *Miranda* rule[5] and stressed the overall significance of increased supervision by federal courts of state criminal procedure. However, my concern is not with criminal suspects, or criminal defendants, but with criminals, and with society's response to the convicted lawbreaker. That difference is symbolic of how thought and emotions about the criminal law have developed in a half-decade. During that period of time a large segment of the public, and the inner sanctum of professionals who deal with crime and criminals on a daily basis, have focused their attention on the same issues. This was not always the case. Five years ago, criminal and constitutional lawyers were occupied primarily with fairness and equity in the ways people were processed through the criminal courts. Today, however, the focus seems significantly different. Attention has shifted from how people are processed through the criminal justice system to an intensive examination of the system itself. I will describe at greater length throughout this talk how our concern at present has shifted from what I shall loosely call procedure to substance. Stated in broader terms the core of the dilemma that is the subject of my lecture is shaped by a certain confusion, or at least ambiguity, concerning the purpose of the criminal law and the most appropriate method of responding to those who violate the law. This ambiguity prompts a number of important questions, some examples of which are: What function is served by sending drunks, drug addicts, prostitutes, and gamblers to prison? What can prisons, or police, or the criminal law generally do to prevent violent street crime like mugging? Although these questions and others like them are being asked by people of different interests and disciplines, they in essence raise two issues: What is the aim of the criminal law, and what role do prisons play in giving effect to that aim?

Clearly, the impulse behind this kind of questioning is an increasing professional and societal concern over what happens to a convicted criminal after he is sent to prison.[6] Despite the fact that even the Supreme Court has spoken of the "substitution of deterrence and reformation in place of retaliation and vengeance as the motivation for public prosecution,"[7] the hard truth is that punishment and retribution are the primary, if not the only, functions currently served by most correctional institutions.[8] In the foreground of

5. Miranda v. Arizona, 384 U.S. 436 (1966).

6. Chief Justice Burger recently stated: "It must be ironic to a prisoner to recall that society spared no expense to afford him three, four or five trials and appeals, at enormous costs, but then proceeds to forget his plight." N.Y. Times, Nov. 18, 1972, at 39, col. 8.

7. Morissette v. United States, 342 U.S. 246, 251 (1952).

8. The view that prisoners are sent to prison not as punishment, but for punishment, is held by at least four prisoners, see Griswold et al., *supra* note 2, at 32. *See generally* Mead, *The Psychology of Punitive Justice*, 23 Am. J. Soc. 577 (1918).

the public's mind, it seems to me, are two thoughts. One is the horror of Attica and all it symbolizes about the daily life of prisoners and about society's attitudes toward them. The second involves the inmate recently discharged from a prison who shortly thereafter is arrested for another mugging, or for armed robbery, or for rape. This is the familiar problem of inmate recidivism that plagues our system of corrections. The magnitude of this problem is largely responsible for an increasing public awareness that "rehabilitation," the great battle cry of prison reform, is one of the great myths of twentieth-century penology.[9] In New York State prisons, for example, in 1970, eighty-two percent of those committed to a correctional center had prior adult criminal records.[10] Federal statistics are equally depressing: sixty-three percent of federal parolees—the "golden boys of the prison system"—and seventy-six percent of those inmates released at the end of their regular terms of confinement were rearrested within six years.[11] In the face of these shocking statistics, the public rightfully demands to know exactly what is happening to prisoners inside those walls, and why the inevitable result of confinement does little good for the prisoner and even less good for society. Lawyers also ask this question, but in their own legalistic and obscure language. When translated, their queries become questions about what the courts will do, if anything, if the institutions in which we put criminals fail to properly perform the job they are required to perform.

On this question, I shall attempt to shed some light.

It is appropriate at this point to take a necessary detour in order to reach my destination.[12] The disillusionment with our correctional system and the search for alternatives to prison has opened a wide area of investigation. The public, lawyers, and thus inevitably the courts are increasingly concerned with a fuzzy and largely uncharted area outside the criminal law—"the borderland of criminal justice"—in which people who have not been convicted of any crime are placed in large institutions and forced to remain there for long periods of time. I am referring to compulsory confinement of persons who are thought to be inappropriate subjects for a strictly criminal sanction. Among these are alcoholics, drug addicts, social misfits, the mentally ill, and even troublesome children whom many, if not all, states control by the operation of special noncriminal statutes.[13] Exactly what happens

9. For a contrary view, see *In re* Timbers, 226 F.2d 501 (6th Cir. 1955), and note the remarkable "rehabilitation" of that distinguished gentleman.

10. N.Y. Dep't of Correction, Characteristics of Inmates Under Custody 1970, Table IIIc, at 9.

11. Committee for Economic Dev., Reducing Crime and Assuring Justice 44 (1972).

12. T. S. Eliot, in *Four Quartets: Little Gidding V* (1943), made the point in this fashion: "We shall not cease from exploration/And the end of all our exploring/Will be to arrive where we started/And know the place for the first time."

13. It has been estimated that ninety percent of all patients in American mental hospitals are placed there by some form of involuntary commitment. *See generally* Hearings Before the Subcomm. on Constitutional Rights of the Senate Comm. on the Judiciary, 87th Cong., 1st Sess. 11 (1961). New York's "treatment" laws are not atypical. For example, N.Y. Mental Hygiene Law § 31.27 (McKinney Supp. 1972), provides: "Involuntary admission on medical certification (a) The director of a hospital may receive and retain therein as a patient any person alleged to be mentally ill and in need of involuntary care and treatment upon the certificates of two examining physi-

to people who are committed under their authority is a most fascinating subject in its own right but one which I will only touch on, lest it swallow up my main subject. I simply urge you to keep in mind, in the interstices, as it were, the thought that the conditions of civil commitment are often difficult to distinguish from the conditions of imprisonment.[14] For that reason, prison problems are not unique to penal institutions but apply as well to a host of restraining and detention facilities.

To make my subject more manageable, I will commit myself to speak primarily as a federal judge who has dealt with some of these questions, and who fears that what we have heard so far of these issues in the federal courts are only faint rumblings of an impending tremor. Whether, when it subsides, that tremor will have left confusion and disrepair in its wake or whether instead it will have given those in positions of responsibility the motivation to rebuild and reshape our institutions on much firmer foundations, is a question that will be decided by the thoughtfulness and perseverance of the men and women who lead us.

For judges, these crucial issues will be posed in the form of lawsuits that unfortunately require enormous expenditures of time, and further congest our courts. This, however, is not the only dilemma facing courts in attempting to resolve the prison mess, for it is an essential theme of this lecture that one attribute shared by all lawsuits that challenge the constitutionality of conditions of confinement is a demand upon courts to reform a system dominated by coercion by applying more coercion. We know that prisoners cannot be forced into rehabilitation. The question remains how far can courts go in compelling prison officials to undertake the task of reform.

I propose, then, to try, haltingly and with some trepidation, to sketch the contours of the problems I have just noted. Having done so I will recommend some ways of analyzing these problems—although I do this with still a greater sense of setting out, without a guide,

---

cians, accompanied by an application for the admission of such person." Identical language appears in N.Y. Mental Hygiene Law § 35.23 (McKinney Supp. 1972), treating involuntary admission of alcoholics to alcoholism facilities. For New York's treatment of narcotic addicts see N.Y. Mental Hygiene Law §§ 81.01–36 (McKinney Supp. 1972), particularly § 81.03, which defines a narcotic addict as "a person who is at the time of examination dependent upon opium, heroin, morphine, or any derivative or synthetic drug of that group or who by reason of the repeated use of any such drug is in imminent danger of becoming dependent," and § 81.13(e) (1), which provides that "[t]he period of commitment to the [narcotics addiction control] commission shall be a period of unspecified duration."

As to treatment of juveniles, see N.Y. Family Ct. Act §§ 711–84 (McKinney 1963). Section 712(b) defines a "[p]erson in need of supervision" as a "male less than sixteen years of age and a female less than eighteen years of age who is an habitual truant or who is incorrigible, ungovernable or habitually disobedient and beyond the lawful control of parent or other lawful authority." Sections 754 and 756 authorize the Family Court to place a person adjudged to be a "person in need of supervision" in a "youth opportunity center" for an initial period of eighteen months, "and the court in its discretion may, at the expiration of such period, make successive extensions for additional periods of one year each," not to extend beyond the child's eighteenth birthday, if male, and twentieth birthday, if female.

14. *See, e.g.*, Wyatt v. Stickney, 325 F. Supp. 781 (M.D. Ala. 1971).

into territory about which little is known except that the terrain is exceedingly dangerous. In this task, I take comfort in the words of Mr. Justice Holmes, who said: "[C]ertainty generally is illusion, and repose is not the destiny of man."[15] We shall have to be satisfied not with conclusive answers but with the probings of a restless mind.

PUNISHMENT OR TREATMENT?

The question I would initially like to explore with you is fundamental to any investigation of the problem of prisons: To what extent and under what kinds of laws is imprisonment justifiable as punishment for crimes, and to what extent and under what kinds of laws is coercive restraint justified as treatment for a socially dangerous "illness"? This is a basic issue society must face in its approach to harmful conduct and in its search for solutions to the prison dilemma.

That this problem is, as I have asserted, fundamental to the problem of prisons is well-illustrated by a recent publication of the American Friends Service Committee, entitled *Struggle for Justice*.[16] Although my reference to the publication is not to be considered an endorsement of its conclusions, I believe it is very important for people who think about the criminal justice system, and for judges in particular, to understand the thrust of the attack on prisons discussed in that book. The argument made there underscores the fundamental challenge to the prison system currently confronting the courts and legislatures. It represents the most widely discussed alternative to the traditional role of prisons currently espoused by some responsible reformers. Were it a fully effective alternative, I would not need to speak about problems in our prisons. But a brief analysis demonstrates the limits of this proposed alternative, and points us in the proper direction for our discussion of the central problems courts will continue to face in attempting to aid in resolving the prison crisis.

The debate has deep roots in history. Prisons were introduced in this country as part of a major reform effort in the early nineteenth century, an effort aimed at relieving the criminal justice system of being compelled to choose between freedom or death as the only available responses to criminal conduct.[17] Prisons evolved, largely under the influ-

15. Holmes, *The Path of the Law*, 10 Harv. L. Rev. 457, 465 (1897).

16. American Friends Serv. Comm., Struggle for Justice: A Report on Crime and Punishment in America (1971).

17. Prisons have not always existed. There was a time when society's response to the commission of crime was swift and decisive. Through the eighteenth century, execution was generally the only available "sentence" for a wide range of offenses, while less serious offenders faced public punishment, including whipping and maiming. *See* Attica Report, *supra* note 2, at 6. Thomas Eddy, a Quaker philanthropist living during the colonial period, commented: "The tears of the sympathetic, and the voice of the benevolent, had made but slow progress against the apathy of the great mass of mankind, and the vindictive spirit of a few, who believe, or profess to believe, that the world should be governed by a rod of iron. The hearts of the people were made callous by the sight of the stocks, whipping posts, pillories in every shire town or considerable village. Flagellation with cat-o'-nine tails burning in the hand or forehead with a hot iron, cropping the ears of prison-

ence of the Pennsylvania Quakers,[18] into institutions that established, for those convicted of crimes, a regimen of hard work, discipline, training in practical skills, moral education, and solitary confinement—an agenda of life that was conducive to meditation and silent penitence. The aim of this enterprise was not merely to punish wrongdoing, but to reform the wrongdoer as well.

Gradually, toward the end of the second half of the nineteenth century, a second reform impulse led to the formation of what is considered to be the standard liberal approach to prisons. Ever since, despite its failures, it has been touted as the "new" penology,[19] a penology that is presently about a century "new."[20] It is based on the idea that prisoners should be *treated* rather than *punished.*

I wish to stress that the "new penology" is not simply an academic game conjured up one sleepless night by an insomnious professor. This theory, unlike most, seeks to translate its philosophical musings into actual statutory language. It urges a response to criminal conduct that focuses on the individual, and the causes of his unlawful behavior, in the hopes of "curing" him of a social "illness."[21]

---

ers in the pillory, were all common sights to the youngest as well as the oldest portion of the community." Quoted in 2 M. Haft & M. Hermann, Prisoner's Rights 332–33 n.9 (1972) [hereinafter cited by volume as Prisoner's Rights]. Imprisonment during the early 1800's was the reform movement's response to the horror of public capital and corporal punishment. *See* O. Lewis, The Development of American Prisons and Prison Customs, 1776–1845, at 7–24 (1967).

18. The Walnut Street Jail, a pretrial detention facility in Philadelphia, was remodeled into a new prison around 1790, after prompting by the Society of Friends. This prison is generally believed to be the first of its kind in the United States. *See* 2 Prisoner's Rights, *supra* note 17, at 334.

19. *See, e.g.*, Knuckles v. Prasse, 302 F. Supp. 1036, 1047–48 (E.D. Pa. 1969), *aff'd*, 435 F.2d 1255 (3d Cir. 1970), *cert. denied*, 403 U.S. 936 (1971).

20. The new penology, perhaps, may be even older than that. *See, e.g.*, Jeremy Bentham's model prison plans sketched in his *Panopticon*, 4 The Works of Jeremy Bentham 37 (J. Bowring ed. 1843).

21. The so-called beneficiaries of a regimen of involuntary treatment number in the tens of thousands. This group of prisoners includes drug addicts and other perpetrators of what is commonly referred to as the victimless crime. It embraces men and women convicted of crimes without victims, whose prison term depends upon someone's decision that they are in need of special treatment and assistance. It counts among its members that class of people who have been found too unsound mentally to be capable of standing trial for an offense for which they are charged, and those persons found to have committed crimes at a time when they were insane. And, finally, it includes those who fall within the jurisdiction of juvenile and family courts—in New York, they are called "persons in need of supervision," and in other states, they are called incorrigible or morally depraved children—who find themselves arrested, forcibly detained, and incarcerated not necessarily because they have committed criminal acts but because they have not acted in the way responsible children are required to act. *See supra* note 13. What all these persons have in common is that pursuant to statute they are involuntarily confined in many instances without the benefit of the full range of procedural protections that our system of justice normally affords a criminal defendant. As the Supreme Court has noted, it is one virtue of the criminal justice system that the duration of incarceration is limited by statute. Therapeutic commitment, however, lacks this feature because a "patient" is generally committed indefinitely, or until he is cured. Powell v. Texas, 392 U.S. 514,

This leads me to mention a line of relevant case law, represented by the important decision of *Robinson v. California*,[22] decided by the Supreme Court in 1962. In *Robinson*, the Court ruled that the criminal law could not be used against a person merely because he suffered from the condition or status of being addicted to a narcotic drug. In sum, the Court said legislatures cannot make it a crime to be a drug addict. I hasten to add that acts associated with addiction remain crimes: a person may not purchase drugs, or possess them, or sell them, free of criminal liability. But the Court laid down the doctrine that drug addiction itself is an illness and therefore no more open to criminal punishment

529 (1968). For a discussion of the problem of indeterminate sentences see Frankel, *Lawlessness in Sentencing*, 41 U. CIN. L. REV. 1, 29–40 (1972).

Presumably, there must be some feature characterizing treatment of this kind that permits the imposition of concededly coercive sanctions in such cases without the benefit of due process afforded the criminally accused. The fundamental questions posed by this class of prisoners are: What rule of law justifies their incarceration, and how long may their confinement continue?

One approach to these questions is to look at the rationale of those cases that prohibit criminal laws from being overly vague. The cases teach that criminal laws must define crimes with sufficient specificity to give adequate notice as to exactly what conduct is outlawed and what conduct permitted. A law that says "You must not be bad" and then goes on to punish persons who are "bad" hardly gives a law-abiding citizen much in the way of guidance as to how he may hope to avoid being punished. The vagueness doctrine compels legislatures, in drafting criminal codes, to spell out exactly what they mean by "bad." If they cannot accomplish that relatively simple task, the constitution would seem to be a barrier to permitting them to punish others for their legislative failures. The vagueness doctrine, as applied in the criminal law, has the salutary effect of controlling the discretionary authority of persons empowered to enforce the law, including police, prosecutors, and judges. It prevents law-enforcement authorities from administering the criminal law as they would like to see it written, and compels the legislature, the only body with any rightful power to enact laws, to make those hard judgments. For an interesting discussion of the problem of discretion in the criminal law see Goldstein, *Police Discretion Not to Invoke the Criminal Process: Low-Visibility Decisions in the Administration of Justice*, 69 YALE L.J. 543 (1960).

The vagueness doctrine has particular relevancy to the problem of "treatment" statutes. One cannot seriously urge that a law that triggers involuntary restraint for persons found to be "morally depraved," for example, measures up to the rigorous standards defined by that doctrine. The hard question to be answered is: Under what conditions will a non-criminal state sanction be appropriate for persons who are indeed morally depraved to the extent that they pose a substantial threat to the safety of society?

If there is to be confinement that is not "punishment," so as to justify less than full due process safeguards, it would seem that there would have to be a trade-off at some point. A jurisprudence that undertakes to analyze these treatment statutes might conclude that incarceration on the basis of a condition or a status may be legitimate and justifiable only when the regulatory statute is narrowly drawn so as to reasonably define, within the scope of current knowledge and expertise, the status or condition regulated. And, of course, the law must authorize a treatment regimen that is appropriate to the malady.

The use of the vagueness doctrine, which I have suggested, would permit courts to deal with all coercive laws—penal and treatment—with a single tool and along a single line of analysis. The generally applicable principle would be that all coercive laws may not give those who enforce them unreasonable discretion to use the laws for purposes not authorized or justified by the legislature.

22. 370 U.S. 660 (1962).

than other kinds of illnesses. In the Supreme Court's view, punishing a man for being a drug addict was like punishing a man for having a cold. There was, however, a caveat to that decision. Although the Court said that punishment for addiction was unconstitutional, other forms of state response to the problem of addiction were not prohibited. Specifically "treatment," and here I mean *involuntary* so-called civil treatment of drug addicts, was approved by the Court.[23] *Robinson* implies that a similar response is appropriate for other persons such as the mentally ill and troublesome children whose "status" raises serious social problems.[24]

The *Robinson* case leaves us wrestling with the problem of how to distinguish treatment from punishment. This is becoming an acute problem for courts because there is an increasing awareness that many putative treatment institutions have the attributes of prisons. The problem, as Mr. Justice Marshall saw it in 1968 in *Powell v. Texas*,[25] is to avoid sacrificing procedural rights for the sake of treatment when all that is accomplished is the hanging of a new sign reading "hospital" over one wing of the jailhouse. As Mr. Justice Cardozo once said: "Metaphors in law are to be narrowly watched, for starting as devices to liberate thought, they end often by enslaving it."[26] We must beware, therefore, that treatment does not simply become a euphemism for punishment.

Recently, a three-judge court on which I sat struck down a statute that permitted the incarceration of adolescents in prisons that housed adult criminal offenders[27]—and the Supreme Court affirmed the ruling without hearing argument.[28] The law in question was a treatment statute,[29] which triggered imprisonment based on a finding that an offender was "morally depraved" or in danger of becoming so. We decided that the statute was clearly criminal in character and that it not only was overly vague but punished a status as well.[30]

If, as some say, one way of solving the prison problem is to *treat* offenders rather than to punish them, we cannot escape facing up to the problem this alternative will pose. Because of the too often blurry distinction between treatment and punishment, many have argued that institutions charged with the responsibility of treating individuals committed to their control must provide *some* special therapy that is suited to the disease. It will not do, as I have said, simply to recast the nasty problem with a more palatable label, and hope in that way that the agonizing dilemmas posed by the Atticas in our land will gracefully disappear. The treatment of criminal offenders is obviously not the panacea for the

23. *Id.* at 666.
24. *But see* Powell v. Texas, 392 U.S. 514 (1968).
25. 392 U.S. 514, 529 (1968).
26. Berkey v. Third Ave. Ry., 244 N.Y. 84, 94, 155 N.E. 58, 61 (1926).
27. Gesicki v. Oswald, 336 F. Supp. 371 (S.D.N.Y. 1971), *aff'd*, 406 U.S. 913 (1972).
28. 406 U.S. 913 (1972).
29. N.Y. Code Crim. Pro. § 913-a(5)–(6) (McKinney 1958) (repealed 1971).
30. The children in Gesicki were confined in an adult prison, a feature which earmarked the statute as at least ancillary to the state's criminal code and which seriously undermined the state's argument that treatment, not punishment, was the aim of the law.

problems of rehabilitation that we might have hoped it to be.[31] While there may be more humane and more constructive alternatives to punishment or prisons, I have tried to show that we cannot get far by skirting the issue. To that issue, I would now like to turn.

JUDICIAL INVOLVEMENT IN PRISON PROBLEMS

I have tried to suggest thus far that the problem of prisons goes much deeper than the issues normally presented in so-called prisoner rights litigation. Mr. Justice Holmes, in his treatise *The Common Law*, insisted:

> The first requirement of a sound body of law is, that it should correspond with the actual feelings and demands of the community, whether right or wrong. If people would gratify the passion of revenge outside of the law, if the law did not help them, the law has no choice but to satisfy the craving itself, and thus avoid the greater evil of private retribution. At the same time, this passion is not one which we encourage, either as private individuals or as law-makers.[32]

Justice Holmes's view may be called the "fall-back theory of collective vengeance." It says that when all else fails, at the very least punishment has the virtue of preventing private vengeance. This is hardly a roseate picture of our corrections system, but a closer look reveals that on the whole Justice Holmes's view is one that accurately describes prison life. For no matter what function apart from vengeance we may assign prisons to serve—be it deterrence, rehabilitation, or even isolation—the clear consensus is that performance of those functions by the prison system is at best sub-optimal. No doubt this failure of performance is inherent in a system based upon conflicting premises and competing goals. If so, it is time we recognized that fact.

But prisons will be with us for a long time to come, and they will not cease to be a focus of the most bitter controversy. As long as this problem persists, courts will be confronted with the perplexing dilemma of applying the Constitution to the complex relationship that exists between a prisoner and the state.

The Constitution, however, is not the private preserve of courts alone, and certainly judges make no claims to superior political wisdom. Other branches of government, and private citizens as well, have an obligation under our system to remedy social ills.[33] Only when there has been a failure of alternative solutions will the machinery of judicial intervention be activated. There has been just such a failure with respect to the prison problem.

In this light, it is a remarkable tribute to the capacity for growth inherent in our legal institutions that courts have found ways of securing at least minimal compliance with the Constitution in our nation's prisons. The development of this area of the law has been

31. The leading cases developing the "right to treatment" doctrine are Holt v. Sarver, 442 F.2d 304 (8th Cir. 1971); Rouse v. Cameron, 373 F.2d 451 (D.C. Cir. 1966); and Wyatt v. Stickney, 325 F. Supp. 781 (M.D. Ala. 1971). *See also* Note, *The Nascent Right to Treatment*, 53 VA. L. REV. 1134 (1967).

32. O. W. HOLMES, THE COMMON LAW 41–42 (1881).

33. *Cf.* Beal v. Lindsay, 468 F.2d 287 (1972).

startling. To speak only of the federal courts, with which I am most familiar, I can say that the frequency with which prisoners turn to the courts for assistance has taken on amazing proportions. In 1930, the number of post-conviction motions and petitions filed by state prisoners was less than 100. In fiscal year 1972, their number increased to 12,088. An additional 4,179 motions and petitions for relief were filed by federal prisoners, for a total of 16,267 so-called prisoners' rights suits reaching federal judges.[34] Among these suits there are, without question, many frivolous claims. For example, one inmate has brought suit against a prison warden for denying him the right to read *Playboy* magazine. And not long ago, a group of prisoners insisted that they had a constitutional right to be served chateaubriand in their dining room—and with wine too![35] Perhaps this indicates that we are getting a better class of prisoners. But undeniably, the rush of litigation has resulted in a substantial enlargement of prisoner rights. The legal debate no longer seriously questions the existence of those rights, or the competence of courts generally to enforce them although some still argue that federal courts should not become involved in state prisoner cases, or that at the very least access to federal courts should be barred until after state courts have ruled.[36] I shall not address myself to that issue for to do so could consume the balance of the lecture. Suffice it to say, that in the main, the debate now focuses on the precise nature of prisoner rights and the role courts ought to play in the prison process, as compared to other agents of reform such as legislatures, executive branch officials, administrators, and private citizens. These two heated issues—the content of prisoner rights and the role of the courts in prison administration—will occupy center stage for the remainder of the lecture.

Turning first to the content of these rights, I cannot hope to go through the encyclopedia of inmate rights that have received judicial protection over the years.[37] It will be enough if I recount something of the history of that struggle, and summarize some of the more important decisions in the field. Of primary significance is the fact that the legal wall that courts formerly erected to shield themselves from prisoner litigation is crumbling. This shield—known as the "hands-off doctrine"—found its fullest expression over one hundred years ago in the Supreme Court of Virginia's disdainful and paternalistic

34. Annual Report of the Director of the Administrative Office of the United States Courts, Table 17, at 11–29 (1972).

35. Wall St. J., Oct. 10, 1972, at 1, col 1.

36. In Rodriguez v. McGinnis, 451 F.2d 730 (2d Cir. 1971), a panel of the Second Circuit, with one judge dissenting, held that prisoners must first exhaust state judicial remedies before bringing suits challenging the conditions of their confinement under 42 U.S.C. § 1983 (1970). The court, en banc, disagreed, 456 F.2d 79 (2d Cir. 1972), and the Supreme Court granted certiorari, sub nom. Oswald v. Rodriguez, 407 U.S. 919 (1972).

37. An in-depth consideration of all aspects of the prisoner rights problem is the two-volume edition of M. Raft & M. Hermann, Prisoner's Rights (1972). Also valuable is *The Prison Law Reporter*, published by the Administration of Criminal Justice and Prison Reform Comm. of the Young Lawyers Section of the American Bar Ass'n. For a proposed code of prisoner's rights, see Comm. on the Model Act, Nat'l Council on Crime and Delinquency, *A Model Act for the Protection of Rights of Prisoners* (1972).

portrayal of prisoners as "slave[s] of the State," with only those rights "which the law in its humanity accords to him."[38] More often than not this meant no rights at all. The hands-off doctrine has now taken its place in the dustbin of legal history. The effect of the hands-off rule was to isolate prisoners from society to an even greater extent than the physical segregation resulting from their imprisonment. It is clear that neither society nor the prison population reaped any discernible benefits from judicial adherence to the hands-off approach.

The total isolation of prisons from society was the most destructive aspect of our penal system. It is fitting, therefore, that the earliest decision to cast doubt on the hands-off rule, *Ex parte Hull*,[39] a 1941 Supreme Court case, guaranteed prisoners access to at least one responsive forum by forbidding officials from screening prisoner petitions to courts for habeas corpus relief. Because full and free access to the courts is absolutely indispensable to the full development and effective enforcement of even the most minimal of other safeguards, currently the law in this area is the most expansive and well developed of any in the field of prisoner rights. Marked ancestral features are recognizable in *Hull*'s most recent progeny. Thus, in 1969 the Supreme Court assured prisoners help in preparing court petitions when they can find a willing colleague ready to play the part of jailhouse lawyer.[40] The Court ruled that unless prisons provide inmates with legal assistance, officials may not prevent inmates from helping each other in the preparation of legal documents. And only last term, the Supreme Court reiterated and strengthened the well-established rule that prisoner petitions must be viewed with unusual generosity, and may not be dismissed by a trial judge when a federal claim can possibly be extracted from documents submitted to the court.[41] Finally, other courts have sought to protect communications between prisoners and courts, lawyers, and public officials against unnecessary official censorship.[42]

Armed with books, technical assistants, unlimited supplies of paper and pencils, guarantees of anonymity, and open channels of communication, prisoners cannot be expected to become suddenly shy or reticent in the coming years. It is a prospect no conscientious and hence overworked judge will entirely welcome, yet it is also not the unexpected end result of the cases I have described. The important effect of these decisions is to provide prisoners with a forum in which to air legitimate grievances. An important by-product of these cases is that it brings judges into closer contact and familiarity with prisons and prisoners. Both of these developments—prisoner access to courts and court access to prisoners—are responsible for the rapid development of prisoner rights in other major areas. I refer to prisoners' first amendment rights, rights to procedural due process in

38. Ruffin v. Commonwealth, 62 Va. 790, 796 (1871).

39. 312 U.S. 546 (1941).

40. Johnson v. Avery, 393 U.S. 483 (1969).

41. Haines v. Kerner, 404 U.S. 519 (1972) (per curiam).

42. *See, e.g.*, Moore v. Ciccone, 459 F.2d 574 (8th Cir. 1972); Smith v. Robbins, 454 F.2d 696 (1st Cir. 1972); Sostre v. McGinnis, 442 F.2d 178 (2d Cir. 1971), *cert. denied*, 404 U.S. 1049 (1972); Guajardo v. McAdams, 12 Crim. L. Rep. 2086 (S.D. Tex., Sept. 29, 1972). *See generally* Note, *Prison Mail Censorship and the First Amendment*, 81 Yale L.J. 87 (1971).

serious prison disciplinary proceedings, and the constellation of substantive rights secured to inmates that is associated with the eighth amendment's ban on cruel and unusual punishment.

Apart from access to courts, attorneys and public officials, probably the most often litigated and well-established area of prison law involves freedom of religion, a phenomenon largely attributable to litigation initiated by Black Muslims. Federal courts seem to be in substantial agreement that prisoners may gather for religious services, consult ministers of their faith, subscribe to and possess religious books, and correspond with their spiritual leaders, subject only to reasonable regulation of time, place, and manner.[43]

Where freedom of religion is not an issue, the law is more nebulous and ill-defined. In general, courts have approached questions of a prisoner's right to possess literature and his right to correspond with people outside prison who have no specially protected legal or religious status with a measure of caution. Judicial restraint in these areas is a result of the absence of any reasonably defined limiting standards once courts begin to overturn the discretion of prison administrators. Courts are simply not equipped with the tools or experience to decide whether, for example, a prisoner's correspondence list should be limited to three people or thirty people, or whether it should be restricted at all.[44] Moreover, courts are naive in their understanding of the operation of clearly volatile prison subcultures. The end results that might accompany unrestricted recognition of first amendment rights in prison are largely unpredictable. Speech otherwise innocuous may have a direct, immediate, and serious impact upon the community of inmates. Without knowledge of the reasonable consequences of intervention, courts must proceed with caution. Thus, although judges realize that institutions that rely on a veil of silence to protect themselves from criticism may become calcified, prison officials still must retain substantial discretion in day-to-day decision-making. I would suggest, however, that the presence of restraining influences on aggressive court action makes this area especially appealing for nonjudicial solutions.

The courts also seem to have exercised judicial caution in dealing with prison disciplinary proceedings that impose administrative sanctions on inmates. The strategy of litigators in this area has been to try to import into prison disciplinary proceedings the full range of procedural safeguards guaranteed to a defendant in a criminal case. Judicial response has been patterned on the developing law of procedural due process as it relates to other important governmental actions, such as parole revocation[45] and termination of welfare benefits,[46] in which the seriousness of a threatened loss is balanced against the state's

43. *E.g.*, Walker v. Blackwell, 411 F.2d 23 (5th Cir. 1969); Long v. Parker, 390 F.2d 816 (3d Cir. 1968); Cooper v. Pate, 382 F.2d 518 (7th Cir. 1967); Sostre v. McGinnis, 334 F.2d 906 (2d Cir.), *cert. denied*, 379 U.S. 892 (1964).

44. *See, e.g.*, Lee v. Tahash, 352 F.2d 970 (8th Cir. 1965); Palmigiano v. Travisono, 317 F. Supp. 776 (D.R.I. 1970).

45. *See* Morrissey v. Brewer, 408 U.S. 471 (1972); United States ex rel. Bey v. Board of Parole, 443 F.2d 1079 (2d Cir.), vacated as moot, 404 U.S. 879 (1971).

46. *See* Goldberg v. Kelly, 397 U.S. 254 (1970).

interest in speedy and efficient administration. Case-by-case adjudication must be the rule in this area.

In the closed prison world where none is free to escape the company of unknown enemies, the apparent or actual erosion of official authority may have serious consequences unforeseeable not only to the courts but to prison officials as well. The risks involved in hedging disciplinary authority with trial-type formalities must therefore be justified by something more than a remote and speculative gain in the accuracy of the fact-finding process. Without considering in detail how these general considerations might be applied to each asserted procedural right, I suggest that there are strong reasons for enforcing the requirements of notice, of a neutral decision-maker, and of an opportunity for the prisoner to present a case in opposition to that brought against him.[47] These guarantees may be viewed as minimally necessary to safeguard the integrity of the fact-finding process. Beyond these requirements, however, there may be sound reasons for not imposing procedures appropriate to criminal trials upon prison disciplinary proceedings.[48] Indeed, greater accuracy in fact-finding may better be assured by other measures, such as a guarantee that prison authorities affirmatively conduct a thorough and impartial investigation of the questioned conduct before charging the prisoner. In the prison context, it may be well to stress the virtues of a fair investigative rather than a strictly adversarial process. Otherwise, inmates will find themselves challenging their accusers, a rather awkward posture for a prisoner who knows he will be subject to the control of those authorities he presumes to challenge for a substantial time to come.

I have been portraying the judge's dilemma faced with prisoners' claims as turning on a conflict between values protected by the Constitution on the one hand, and the unpredictable effects of court intervention in prison affairs on the other. This dilemma seems most acute in the area I have left for last: the application of the Eighth Amendment's ban on cruel and unusual punishment to conditions of confinement.

I believe courts are moving toward a satisfactory resolution of the problems in this area by requiring prisons to conform to commonly accepted minimum conditions of a decent and healthy life. Such patent barbarisms as those disclosed in *Wright v. McMann*,[49] a case decided several years ago by a panel on which I sat, no longer will be tolerated. The allegations in the complaint, which for purposes of the appeal we were bound to take as true, since the complaint was dismissed without a hearing by the district judge, told Wrights story of conditions in Dannemora prison [today: Clinton Correctional Facility] in most eloquent language. It said:

47. *Cf.* Sostre v. McGinnis, 442 F.2d 178, 194–99 (2d Cir. 1971), *cert. denied*, 404 U.S. 1049 (1972).

48. *But see* Krause v. Schmidt, 341 F. Supp. 1001 (W.D. Wis. 1972); Landman v. Royster, 333 F. Supp. 621 (E.D. Va. 1971); Clutchette v. Procunier, 328 F. Supp. 767 (N.D. Cal. 1971). These cases have extended due process protection to include the right to call witnesses, the right to cross-examine witnesses against the prisoner, and the right to representation at a hearing, if such assistance is required.

49. 387 F.2d 519 (2d Cir. 1967).

> [T]he . . . solitary confinement cell wherein plaintiff was placed was dirty, filthy and unsanitary, without adequate heat and virtually barren; the toilet and sink were encrusted with slime, dirt and human excremental residue superimposed thereon; plaintiff was without clothing and entirely nude for several days . . . until he was given a thin pair of underwear to put on; plaintiff was unable to keep himself clean or perform normal hygienic functions as he was denied the use of soap, towel, toilet paper, tooth brush, comb, and other hygienic implements and utensils therefore; plaintiff was compelled under threat of violence, assault or other increased punishments to remain standing at military attention in front of his cell door each time an officer appeared from 7:30 A.M. to 10:00 P.M. every day, and he was not permitted to sleep during the said hours under the pain and threat of being beaten or otherwise disciplined therefore; the windows in front of his confinement cell were opened wide throughout the evening and night hours of each day during subfreezing temperatures causing plaintiff to be exposed to the cold air and winter weather without clothing or other means of protecting himself or to escape the detrimental affects thereof; and the said solitary confinement cell was used as a means of subjecting plaintiff to oppression, excessively harsh, cruel and inhuman treatment specifically forbidden by the Eighth Amendment to the United States Constitution.[50]

It was not too difficult for a court to find the conditions described by the prisoner in his complaint to be "subhuman." Accordingly, we reversed the dismissal and directed the district court to proceed to trial.[51] The recent litigation history of that case is worth mentioning. Upon remand, a trial was held and Wright successfully proved that the charges he had asserted were true.[52] Judgment was entered on his behalf and compensatory damages were awarded to him. Our court affirmed that decision,[53] and the Supreme Court recently denied certiorari.[54]

Courts are now confident enough of their role as guardians of basic rights to recognize that human dignity demands more than mere freedom from a bestial, subhuman existence. Courts are increasingly willing, for example, to require prisons to provide a diet meeting minimum nutritional standards recommended for the general population,[55] to furnish prisoners with sufficient opportunity for physical exercise to maintain their bodies in reasonably good condition,[56] and to refrain from imposing conditions that will impair the prisoner's mental health.[57] No longer will courts approve the absolute denial of reading

50. *Id.* at 521.

51. *Id.* at 527.

52. Wright v. McMann, 321 F. Supp. 127 (N.D.N.Y. 1970), *aff'd*, 460 F.2d 126 (2d Cir.), *cert. denied*, 409 U.S. 885 (1972).

53. 460 F.2d 126 (2d Cir. 1972).

54. 409 U.S. 885 (1972).

55. *See* Landman v. Royster, 333 F. Supp. 621, 647 (E.D. Va. 1971).

56. *See, e.g.*, Jones v. Wittenberg, 323 F. Supp. 93, 99 (N.D. Ohio 1971), *aff'd sub nom.* Jones v. Metzger, 456 F.2d 854 (6th Cir. 1972); Krist v. Smith, 309 F. Supp. 497, 501 (S.D. Ga. 1970), *aff'd*, 439 F.2d 146 (5th Cir. 1971).

57. *Cf.* Sostre v. McGinnis, 442 F.2d 178, 190, 193–94 (2d Cir. 1971), *cert. denied*, 404 US. 1049 (1972).

matter, and the insistence upon total prisoner silence as routine punishment for prisoner misconduct.[58]

Thus, it is apparent that this area of the law is in a state of flux. Courts have been responding on a case-by-case basis, as if tiptoeing in a garden of delicate flowers. But try as they do, courts, in the end, are simply not up to the task of policing and administering, much less devising, new rehabilitative programs for our nation's prisons. A judge is far removed from the atmosphere of the maximum security prison and his sole personal contact with the hard tensions of the prison comes in the form of arid, though able, adversarial debate within the secure walls of a courthouse. He simply does not have the precise sense for the nuances or even the sweat of prison life.

There are encouraging signs, however, that courts will not be left to go it alone in trying to reform prisons. I will briefly indicate what I believe are the most interesting remaining alternatives and complements to judicial intervention. I shall then conclude with some reflections, and perhaps even some predictions, for the future.

One very hopeful sign of legislative and administrative willingness to assume some of the burden of ameliorating conditions in prison is reflected in regulations recently promulgated by the New York Department of Corrections that govern prisoner correspondence. I will not go into a detailed analysis of the new provisions, but one development is of particular interest because it illustrates the kind of healthy interplay between courts and other branches of government that may be the hope for the future of prison reform. The Court of Appeals for the Second Circuit, sitting en banc, held in *Sostre v. McGinnis*,[59] a case of importance in this branch of the law, that censorship of inmate letters to courts, lawyers and public officials violated First Amendment rights of prisoners.[60] But the court did not prohibit prison officials from reading mail—incoming and outgoing—to or from courts, attorneys, and others, to ascertain whether these letters contained contraband, or included possible escape plans.[61] Three weeks after *Sostre* was decided, the New York Department of Corrections adopted a policy of permitting inmates to send sealed letters to legal and public officials, and to receive letters from such persons without any censorship.[62] The department adopted the sensible rule of requiring only that letters be opened in the presence of guards so as to permit a spot check for contraband.

This example of judicial restraint and administrative initiative illustrates a point I stressed earlier that courts need not be the sole guarantor of individual liberties, although they must always be available to serve that purpose. Courts generally will be unable to compel adoption of what they believe to be the best prison policy. For despite what

58. *Id.* at 193–94. Courts have even been willing to hold an entire prison system unconstitutional in violation of the Eighth Amendment. *See* Holt v. Sarver, 442 F.2d 304 (8th Cir. 1971); Jackson v. Hendrick, 40 U.S.L.W. 2710 (Phila. C. P., Apr. 7, 1972).

59. 442 F.2d 178 (2d Cir. 1971), *cert. denied*, 404 U.S. 1049 (1972).

60. *Id.* at 200.

61. *Id.*

62. *See* N.Y. Dep't of Correction Administrative Bull. No. 20, Jan. 31, 1972.

conservative critics of the courts have said, there *are* many policies judges favor that they cannot find written into the Constitution.

Enlightened rule-making is most certainly a necessary element in any program of prison reform. But just as courts have learned the difficulty of securing prison compliance with their orders, progressive administrators have also experienced the frustration of attempting to move an intractable bureaucracy of prison guards, whose ideas about maintenance of prison discipline may conflict with attempted efforts at reform. Thus, it may be important to bring an independent but nonjudicial agency into the prison system—a concept represented by the ombudsman, now in practice in Minnesota,[63] and suggested as a device for general adoption by a Committee of the Bar Association of the State of New York[64]—to give prisoners a forum in which the merits of their complaints may be rationally considered. The mediation function served by the ombudsman is potentially very significant for the courts for it provides a screening device which may effectively limit the number of less important prisoner cases now finding their way into the federal courts. Any progress in that direction is, of course, a welcome sign.

These suggestions for reform by no means exhaust the possibilities available to diligent and nimble minds, but hopefully they illustrate the different directions that are open to us. And the extent to which courts will continue to intervene in prison problems will depend, to a large extent, upon how effective other methods prove to be in the long run. Litigation, as we know, generally represents a failure of other ways to solve problems. If that failure persists, courts will continue to intervene.

CONCLUSION

I have spoken on several important topics that currently share the spotlight in the debate over prison reform. My principal concern has been with the function of institutions of confinement in our system of criminal justice and the appropriate attitude courts should take in responding to complaints about the prison system. It is the general drift of the lecture that in both areas, performance has been sub-optimal.

But there is a unity between these two themes that transcends this mere shared lack of success. It is at least arguable that intervention by prison administrators in the lives of prisoners and intervention by judges in the lives of prison administrators are unsuccessful for the same basic structural reasons.

The first is the most obvious: if we assume that the central aim of any criminal justice system is to effect a decrease in the incidence of future crime, and we then agree that decriminalizing persons who are now criminal would contribute substantially to that end,

63. Minneapolis Star, Apr. 19, 1972, at 16B, col. 1. A prisoner ombudsman has also been established in Oregon. Ore. Statesman, Mar. 13, 1971, § 1, at 1, col. 6. A state ombudsman, with jurisdiction over prisoner complaints, has been established in Hawaii. Hawaii Rev. Stat. tit. 8, ch. 96 (1968). Legislation has recently been introduced into the New York State Assembly to set up prison ombudsmen in state correctional facilities. N.Y. Times, Mar. 1, 1973, at 55, col. 2.

64. Comm. on Civil Rights, New York State Bar Ass'n, *Report on Prison Reform* (June 30, 1972).

we come up shorthanded at the end of the proposed syllogism for the sad reason that no one has any real idea how to go about doing the job with any degree of consistent success. Few would suggest that prison administrators are trying to achieve high recidivism rates. They obviously think, however, that alternatives to their present techniques will be no better, and will likely be worse on that score. Though they know that they do not have the answers, and that present trends will not be allowed to continue indefinitely, still they do not know what else to do.

What they do know is that judges do not know how to cut down on recidivism either, especially when they sit outside the system and peek in, only to launch through the peephole an occasional thunderbolt. They also know that judges' traditional concerns are, by and large, not really with rehabilitative success. Judges are bound to maximize due process, but there is absolutely no demonstrable relationship between greater due process for prisoners and greater rates of rehabilitation.

This, I think, points up a second unity in the themes I have presented, and one that I find more interesting, more significant than the unity of shared ignorance. It is that the relationship between courts and jailors, and the relationship between jailors and prisoners, are ones in which there is an attempt to coerce virtue as defined by the coercer. Even if we were of one mind about the function of prisons, it is hard to imagine a more inefficient system of administration than the coercion of unwilling people over whom one has authority.

Let me expand on this point through the use of a metaphor. Picture the correctional system for a moment as a division of a large corporation. Imagine that there is a corporate desire to expand foreign sales, and that to that end selected personnel have been designated to learn foreign languages prior to becoming salesmen. A staff of teachers has been hired to effect this acquisition of language skills.

Now assume that the salesmen candidates are selected after tests have been administered to them, designed to uncover (a) their linguistic skills and (b) their desire to learn foreign languages. But remarkably, only those who have scored the lowest on both tests have been selected. The teachers are then chosen from the rather shallow pool of those willing to take on the job of teaching something hard to a group of students preselected on the basis of deficiencies in motivation and talent. Before beginning their assignment, the teachers are informed by corporate officers that they must force the salesmen to learn foreign languages or their jobs are on the line.

It soon becomes obvious that no one knows very much about language teaching. The teachers are closest to the online problems but they haven't been doing very well. Deep down they believe they are doing about as well as they can, given the material and the nature of the students. The corporate heads have a great many other things to do. They worry not only about teaching languages, but also about corporate public relations, costs, shareholder desires, and so on. But from time to time, a vice president in charge of language improvement may descend, deus ex machina, and punish the teachers, not only for failing to teach languages to more than two-thirds of the students, but also for other things too, for instance getting stories about nasty teaching techniques into the newspapers or for failing to hold long, individual conferences with each student. That is, the teachers are generally punished for things that, if done the way the bosses want them done, would in the opinion of the teachers cut down on teaching success.

And so it goes, with this division running about as inefficiently as any division can run. For it has been set up so that the bosses must try to *force* the teachers to *force* the students to learn, and most of the expense of the system goes into trying to make people do things that they do not want to do. This is the antithesis of sound managerial organization. The whole idea in a sound system is to bring about cooperation in a common endeavor among top management, line personnel, and employees. You cannot run a good business by concentric levels of threat and punishment any more than you can efficiently so run a family, a baseball team, or a corrections system.

That has been a pretty extended metaphor but, I believe, a sound one. The corrections system will never run with any real efficiency until (a) prisoners want to be "reformed," (b) prison administrators want to help them to reform, (c) courts want to help toward a system of reform, and (d) they all define reform in the same way. That is going to take a lot of social change. I like to think for instance, that most prisoners do not want to be "crooks" but I also doubt that all of them want to be what we generally conceive of as "productive members of society" either. Pending those millennial changes it would seem that our corporation ought to shoot for the following direction or transition:

1. Top management—courts, legislatures and the executive—ought to determine the cost of not being efficient in deterring crime, no matter how effective it may be. That is, even if flogging, or year-long solitary confinement under subhuman conditions could be shown to decrease recidivism, that would be irrelevant because at a certain point there are criteria other than efficiency that must guide our system of corrections. But the most important point here is that courts—and others—in setting out these definitions, should make clear that they do not pretend to know penology better than the jailors but only to know the moral and legal principles that override penological efficiencies. No one should pretend that due process decreases crime, but rather that it increases due process, an independent goal.
2. Line administrators—wardens, guards, and others—should be chosen for their congruence with the socially determined aim—deterrence, rehabilitation, punishment, or whatever mix—and then once chosen, should be allowed some play in attempting to reach it, so long as they willingly share the overriding goals like due process. If they do not, they must be coerced or replaced.
3. Prisoners should be convinced that they are part of the process of their own change, an irreplaceable part, and if they refuse to cooperate they can seriously interfere with, if not destroy, the process of rehabilitation for all others incarcerated.

For a long time to come, then, if not forever, the criminal justice system will continue to operate on the model of concentric layers of coercion, a grossly inefficient model, but its tendency ought to be in the direction of replacing that model with one of communication and cooperation. Courts cannot keep hands-off prison problems, and the dilemmas of which I have spoken tonight will continue to be bothersome. But courts, to be effective, must justify their interventions as the product of trying to preserve nonpenological values, such as protecting constitutional rights, not as the product of superior penological wisdom.

I have spoken of the new penology and the problems involved in a program of treatment of prisoners. I have reviewed some of the more significant developments in the law of prisoner rights, especially concerning the application of the First, Eighth, and Fourteenth Amendments in the prison setting. My intention has been to indicate that willing as they are, courts simply cannot solve the dilemmas of the prison mess by themselves. Prisoners and their lawyers who look only to the courts for relief are, in effect, trying to replace one system of coercion with another, a result that will have some momentary advantage but will be of little social benefit in the long run. Mutual commitment—and I do mean commitment—to change and improvement on the part of courts, prisoners, administrators, legislatures, and community groups is, I have suggested, a far better approach to achieving lasting prison reform.

Even this, however, is not the final answer. The impetus for change, as we all know, stems from mounting public criticism of the manner in which prisoners are treated under our present system of corrections. The public, I believe, has finally come to realize that its past attitude of not-so-benign neglect toward prisoners and the schools of crime in which they are confined has largely been responsible for many of the problems of which I have spoken. Society is beginning to see the direct link between crime in the streets and the shame of our prison system, and it is this understanding that holds out the greatest promise of significant change for the future.

Of one thing, at least, I can be certain. It is the fact that only when the public is willing to pay the price of reform, and to commit adequate funds—I mean tax dollars—to improve the conditions of confinement in prison, will we be able to move on from the stage of diagnosing an illness to prescribing a cure for it. And I leave you with the hopeful thought that, at least, from where I sit, there are encouraging signs that the dream of prison reform may yet become a reality.

The Special Skills of Advocacy: Are Specialized Training and Certification of Advocates Essential to Our System of Justice?

Chief Justice Warren E. Burger

Chief Justice Warren E. Burger is the only person to have delivered two of the Sonnett lectures at Fordham University School of Law: On November 26, 1973, while he was Chief Justice of the Supreme Court of the United States,[1] he delivered the fourth annual Sonnett lecture, and on January 23, 1995,[2] six months before his death, he delivered the twenty-fourth Sonnett lecture.[3] His first speech, entitled *The Special Skills of Advocacy: Are Specialized Training and Certification of Advocates Essential to Our System of Justice?*, emphasized the need for specialized training for litigators and a system reflecting some of the training and specialization provided for English barristers.[4] In that lecture, Chief Justice Burger stressed the needs for greater professionalism, ethics, and decorum in the courtroom and the need for specialized litigation training analogous to specialization in the medical profession.[5] The second lecture, entitled *The Decline of Professionalism*, discussed the evolution of the legal profession, lamenting a growing trend of lawyers eschewing bedrock ethical principles for business purposes.[6] Each of his speeches has impacted legal training and practice. The growing emphasis in law school on legal ethics, the amendments to the Code of Professional Responsibility, the expansion of clinical programs, and pro bono requirements can all be seen as addressing the issues raised by the Chief Justice.

Chief Justice Burger was born on September 17, 1907, in St. Paul, Minnesota, where he spent his childhood.[7] Raised by Swiss-German parents of modest means, Chief Justice Burger took various jobs throughout his high school years to help support his family.[8] He also quickly earned recognition as a standout student, serving as president of the student council and editor of the school newspaper. Upon his graduation from high school, he declined a scholarship from Princeton University in order to remain at home and help

Introduction written by Andrew Todres, J.D., Class of 2014, Fordham University School of Law

1. Warren E. Burger, *The Special Skills of Advocacy: Are Specialized Training and Certification of Advocates Essential to Our System of Justice?*, 42 Fordham L. Rev. 227 (1973). As of September 2014, this has been the single most cited article in Fordham Law Review history.

2. Warren E. Burger, *The Decline of Professionalism*, 63 Fordham L. Rev. 949 (1995).

3. Douglas D. McFarland, *Chief Justice Warren E. Burger: A Personal Tribute*, 19 Hamline L. Rev. 1, 1 (1995).

4. Burger, *supra* note 1.

5. *Id.*

6. Burger, *supra* note 2, at 949–50.

7. McFarland, *supra* note 3, at 2.

8. *Id.*

support his family.[9] A life insurance salesman by day, Chief Justice Burger attended night classes at the University of Minnesota, later adding evening classes at the St. Paul College of Law (now, the William Mitchell College of Law).[10] He graduated from law school, magna cum laude, in 1931.[11]

After graduation, Chief Justice Burger began his legal career with the St. Paul law firm Faricy, Burger, Moore & Costello.[12] In 1953, he moved to Washington, D.C. to become Assistant Attorney General for the Civil Division, supervising the federal government's civil and international litigation.[13] Three years later, President Dwight Eisenhower appointed him to serve as a federal judge in the District of Columbia Court of Appeals, a position he held until his nomination to the Supreme Court.[14] President Nixon appointed Chief Justice Burger to the Supreme Court in 1969.[15] The U.S. Senate confirmed his appointment by a 74-3 vote on June 9, 1969, and he was sworn in on June 23, 1969, in advance of the 1969 Term.[16]

Chief Justice Burger served as Chief Justice of the United States Supreme Court from 1969 to 1986.[17] His seventeen years in this role made him the longest-serving chief justice in the twentieth century.[18] Chief Justice Burger made many contributions to American law and the American judicial system. For example, he wrote the majority opinion limiting the ability of Congress to override actions of the executive branch in *Immigration and Naturalization Serv. v. Chadha*,[19] focusing on the balance of power between the executive and legislative branches. In that decision, the Court held that Congress could not review or veto an immigration decision made by the Attorney General in a deportation case, effectively striking down legislative vetoes.[20] In the wake of the Watergate scandal, Chief Justice Burger delivered a unanimous opinion in *United States v. Nixon*,[21] holding that a president was not entitled to absolute unqualified immunity under Article II of the U.S. Constitution, thus compelling President Richard Nixon to comply with the Watergate special prosecutor and turn over tape recordings of his conversations in office.[22]

Chief Judge Burger led the Court in *Swann v. Charlotte-Mecklenburg Board of Education*,[23] where the Court approved of busing as a means of enforcing *Brown v. Board of Education*.[24] He also joined in the majority decision in *Roe v. Wade*, the abortion rights case.[25] He was a

9. *Id.*
10. *Id.*
11. *Id.* at 3.
12. *Id.* The firm is now Moore, Costello & Hart.
13. *See id.*
14. *Id.*
15. *Id.*
16. *Id.* at 3–4.
17. McFarland, *supra* note 3, at 1.
18. *Id.*
19. 462 U.S. 919 (1983).
20. *See generally id.*
21. 418 U.S. 683 (1974).
22. *See id.*
23. 402 U.S. 1 (1971).
24. 347 U.S. 483 (1954).
25. 410 U.S. 113 (1973).

proponent of women's rights in *Reed v. Reed*, wherein the Court overturned an Idaho statute that gave preference to men over women as appointed executors of estates.[26] Writing for the Court, Chief Justice Burger, in this landmark ruling, found that the statute violated the rights of women under the Equal Protection Clause of the Fourteenth Amendment.[27] Finally, Chief Justice Burger was a leader in the area of judicial administration, promoting projects involving the administration of the Circuit Courts.[28]

In 1985, President Ronald Reagan appointed Chief Justice Burger to serve as Chairman of the Commission on the Bicentennial of the Constitution of the United States.[29] After he resigned as Chief Justice, Chief Justice Burger worked on this project full time, his responsibilities culminating in 1991 with the bicentennial of the ratification of the Bill of Rights.[30]

On June 25, 1995, Chief Justice Burger died of congestive heart failure.[31] He is buried at Arlington National Cemetery.[32]

1973 Sonnett Lecture

This occasion is one on which friends of John F. Sonnett undertake to pay tribute to him as a person, as an outstanding advocate and as a distinguished public servant. It seems an appropriate occasion, therefore, to raise for the consideration of our profession a problem of large scope and profound importance to all judges, to all lawyers, to the public and, of course, to law schools. I believe that John Sonnett, as a skillful advocate and one deeply committed to our system of justice in all its manifestations, would have shared some of the anxieties I express concerning the quality of advocacy in our courts.

To say we have a "crisis" in the availability of adequate legal services may go too far, but sober, careful, and responsible observers of the legal profession have posed the need in almost precisely those terms.[1] My objective in this discussion is not to canvass the swiftly growing need for all kinds of legal services, but to discuss narrowly the need for skilled courtroom advocacy with a special emphasis on the administration of criminal justice. I submit that we can deal with this critical situation if we direct our attention to the causes and think imaginatively about a remedy. We will not lack patterns or precedents.

26. 404 U.S. 71 (1971).
27. *Id.*
28. *See* Circuit Court Executive Act of 1971, 28 U.S.C. § 332 (e)–(f) and judicial training.
29. McFarland, *supra* note 3, at 4.
30. *Id.*
31. *Id.*
32. *Id.*

1. H. Packer & T. Ehrlich, New Directions in Legal Education 6 (1972).

What I will propose later in this discussion is that some system of certification for trial advocates is an imperative and a long overdue step. Beyond any particular system, however, is the fundamental fact that how lawyers are trained—during and after law school—will determine their skills as advocates and ultimately the quality of our justice. That fundamental fact is nowhere better revealed than in the English experience.

Although our system is a child of the common law, the legal profession has developed in ways that do not parallel England's. Our wide expanses of territory, our heterogeneous and turbulent diversity, and our more than fifty jurisdictions with 150 accredited law schools would make it impossible to transplant the English system here, and I do not suggest it by any means. But simply because we cannot adopt the English system does not mean that we cannot learn much from its operation.

Several aspects of the English legal profession stand out clearly when we look for causes of effective advocacy:

1. England separates its trial lawyers—the barristers—into a separate branch of the profession and they engage exclusively in trial work.[2]
2. Of the 30,000 lawyers in England, 3,000 are barristers.
3. England has about 65 lawyers per 100,000 population; the United States has about 160 lawyers per 100,000 population.
4. All English barristers are trained in a centuries-old school conducted by the four Inns of Court. After training in this school of advocacy, a barrister must spend a period of "pupilage," or apprenticeship, with an established barrister.
5. The four Inns of Court occupy quarters in or near the Royal Courts of Justice, and barristers' offices are situated in the same area, thus creating a unique professional community. I will not try to compare a barrister's productivity with that of an American trial lawyer. That would be unfair in part because the methods and procedures in English courts are generally conducive to speedier justice than we manage to deliver.

Every qualified observer of the English system with whom I have discussed this subject makes the same observation that I have made, drawing on twenty years of rather close contact with the British system, namely, that their trials are conducted in a fraction of the time we expend in the United States for comparable litigation. This is a generalization that has a solid basis and can be readily documented. At once I must note another difference in that, except for libel, fraud and a few other kinds of cases that arise infrequently, civil cases in England are tried without a jury, and judgment is almost invariably rendered forthwith at the close of trial. Appeals are the exception and are only by leave.

2. Although the majority of barristers are primarily experts in advocacy, there is a good deal of further specialization within their ranks. There are those who confine their practice to the Chancery Division or the Family Division or who do nothing other than criminal work. In addition to these, there are the smaller specialist bars that confine their practice, for example, to taxation, patents, company law, planning, or building contracts. A considerable part of the work of members of the smaller specialist bars is concerned with advising on matters that do not result in litigation.

Another difference is that judges of trial courts of general jurisdiction are selected entirely from the ranks of the ablest barristers. Thus, there is little or no on-the-job learning for trial judges as is all too often the case in the United States courts, both state and federal. Only the highest qualifications as a trial advocate enter into the selection of English judges. As a result, an English trial is in the hands of three highly experienced litigation specialists who have a common professional background. Each advocate has also served an intensive "apprenticeship" before he or she is permitted to appear in court as lead counsel.[3]

The English training in advocacy places great stress on ethics, manners, and deportment, both in the courtroom and in relations with other barristers and solicitors. The effectiveness of this training is reflected in their very high standards of ethics and conduct. Discipline is strict, but disciplinary actions for misconduct average about three a year for the three thousand barristers in England. My own personal observation, based on forty years of professional exposure, is that in any multiple-judge American courthouse, there are numerous daily offenses that would bring severe censure if committed by an English barrister. How many serious errors of counsel are made in trials, I would not venture to say.[4]

I have heard it said occasionally by critics of the English legal system that it tends to be "clubby" and "establishment-oriented."[5] For twenty years, I have watched advocates conduct trials in more than a dozen countries, and nowhere have I seen more ardent, more effective advocacy than in the courts of England. English advocacy is generally on a par with that of our best lawyers. I emphasize that their best advocates are no better than our best, but I regret to say that our best constitute a relatively thin layer of cream on top while the quality of the English barristers is uniformly high, albeit with gradations of quality inescapable in any human activity.

What, then, can we learn from the English legal profession? We should first recognize three implicit and basic assumptions about legal training that permeate their system. First, lawyers, like people in other professions, cannot be equally competent for all tasks in our increasingly complex society and increasingly complex legal system in particular; second, legal educators can and should develop some system whereby students or new graduates

3. It is widely accepted by England's bench and bar that these factors provide more expeditious determinations without impairing fair and just results. Whether a nonjury system for civil cases would be feasible in a geographically large and diverse country with a heterogeneous society like ours is open to serious question. There is no significant pressure to adopt the English nonjury system and I do not advocate it.

4. *See generally* ABA Special Comm. on Evaluation of Disciplinary Enforcement, Problems and Recommendations in Disciplinary Enforcement (Final Draft 1970); and ABA, Report of Special Committee for National Coordination of Disciplinary Enforcement (Aug. 1973).

5. At one time, there was concern among England's solicitors over the exclusivity of the barrister profession, but this has dissipated since transfer from solicitor to barrister was made possible. A prime example is found in the present Lord Chief Justice of England, John Widgery—incidentally the son of a working man—who was a solicitor for many years before transfer to the ranks of barrister, from which he was appointed to the Bench.

who have selected, even tentatively, specialization in trial work can learn its essence under the tutelage of experts, not by trial and error at clients' expense; and third: ethics, manners, and civility in the courtroom are essential ingredients and the lubricants of the inherently contentious adversary system of justice; they must be understood and developed by law students beginning in law school.

These three basic assumptions are sound and sensible, whether applied to the English system or to our own. Simply because we cannot implement the assumptions in the same manner as the English have done does not mean we cannot recognize their validity. Even though we cannot have, and most emphatically do not want, a small elite, Barrister-like class of lawyers does not mean we cannot take positive steps to promote qualified courtroom advocacy skills in those attorneys who choose to specialize in trial advocacy. Indeed, our failure to do so has helped bring about the low state of American trial advocacy and a consequent diminution in the quality of our entire system of justice. The high purposes of the Criminal Justice Act[6] will be frustrated unless *qualified* advocates are appointed to represent indigents.

For centuries, most societies have used performance standards for entry into certain human activities that affect large numbers of people.[7] Standards, varying in effectiveness, have long been used in an attempt to assure qualified teachers, doctors, lawyers, electricians, and a host of others essential to a modern society. Yet, in spite of all the bar examinations and better law schools, we are more casual about qualifying the people we allow to act as advocates in the courtrooms than we are about licensing our electricians. We have no testing or licensing process designed to assure that those engaged to protect and vindicate important rights by trial advocacy are genuinely qualified for their crucial role in society. This is a curious aspect of a system that prides itself on the high place it accords to the judicial process in vindicating peoples' rights.

I

Our failure to inquire into advocates' qualifications—as is done, for example, in separating surgeons from doctors generally—reveals itself in the mounting concern of those who see the consequences of inadequate courtroom performance and look for its causes.

First, and perhaps overriding other causes, is our historic insistence that we treat every person admitted to the bar as qualified to give effective assistance on every kind of legal

6. 18 U.S.C. § 3006A (1970).

7. For example, in the era of sailing vessels, masters and mates were licensed or certified on the basis of their skills in the very difficult task of navigating a ship. The measuring process was quite primitive but highly pragmatic. The traveling public wanted basically the same kind of assurance that we want about today's commercial airline pilots. Today we have more sophisticated and orderly processes to measure the total skills of an airline pilot—his coordination, poise, emotional stability and, of course, technical capacity. The care used as to airline pilots is illustrated by the fact that a graduate of the U.S. Air Force Academy would be required to meet FAA standards before being allowed to operate commercial aircraft. Qualifications are not taken for granted.

problem that arises in life, including the trial of criminal cases in which liberty is at stake, civil rights cases in which human values are at stake, and myriad ordinary cases dealing with important private personal interests. It requires only a moment's reflection to see that this assumption is no more justified than one that postulates that every holder of an M.D. degree is competent to perform surgery on the infinite range of ailments that afflict the human animal.

There is no parallel in any other area of life's problems having serious consequence to our naive assumption that every graduate of a law school is, by virtue of that fact, qualified for the ultimate confrontation in a courtroom.[8] No other profession is as casual or heedless of reality as ours.

We know, however, that the successful law firms do not expose their clients to on-the-job training: they operate their own private "apprentice" or "intern" systems in which the young lawyer who is to engage in litigation is trained by assisting a partner in preparing cases for trial and then by assisting in the second or third chair. If these law firms were to allow the very bright, but inexperienced, young lawyers to roam at large in the courts without close supervision, they would soon lose clients in droves. But, we need shed no tears for the large law firms: necessity has long since forced them to develop their own in-house training comparable to that used in England for Barristers.

So, we see that clients who can afford such lawyers—in the big firms or in the many excellent medium-size firms or indeed among this country's skilled sole practitioners—are well served by lawyers. But this is because those lawyers are not assigned tasks beyond their reach—something that happens regularly on both sides of the table in criminal cases today.

We must acknowledge, I submit, that good advocates are made, much as good airplane pilots are made—by study, by observation of experts, and by training with experts. To pursue that analogy, an aspiring pilot who can fly a Piper Cub has learned something about flying, but he is surely not ready to fly large commercial planes or a modern jet airliner. The painful fact is that the courtrooms of America all too often have "Piper Cub" advocates trying to handle the controls of "Boeing 747" litigation. (I should add that by no means are all the "Piper Cub" advocates recent law graduates.)

A second cause of inadequate advocacy derives from certain aspects of law school education. Law schools fail to inculcate sufficiently the necessity of high standards of professional ethics, manners, and etiquette as things basic to the lawyer's function. With few exceptions, law schools also fail to provide adequate and systematic programs by which students may focus on the elementary skills of advocacy. I have now joined those who propose that the basic legal education could well be accomplished in two years, after which more concrete and specialized legal education should begin. If the specialty is litigation,

8. Too few lawyers acknowledge the great difference between trial and appellate advocacy as does one leading American trial lawyer who engages a specialist in appellate work to conduct appeals in his cases. On another occasion, I hope to discuss the declining quality of appellate advocacy. For now, I note that approximately two-thirds of the lawyers who currently appear before the Supreme Court of the United States are there for the first time—and most of these for the last.

the training should be prescribed and supervised by professional advocates cooperating with professional teachers, for both are needed. A two-year program is feasible once we shake off the heritage of our agricultural frontier that the "young folks" should have three months' vacation to help harvest the crops—a factor that continues to dominate our education. The third year in school should, for those who aspire to be advocates, concentrate on what goes on in courtrooms. This should be done under the guidance of practitioners along with professional teachers. The medical profession does not try to teach surgery simply with books; more than eighty percent of all medical teaching is done by practicing physicians and surgeons. Similarly, trial advocacy must be learned from trial advocates.

After the third year, those who wish to be advocates should begin a pupilage period, assisting and participating in trials directly with experienced trial lawyers.

Today we spend on the education of a lawyer only a fraction of what is devoted to educating a doctor. If we want an adequate system of justice, we must be prepared to spend more for it—and we cannot train truly effective advocates without spending more.

We know that in the past few years much of what I am suggesting has had small beginnings in some law schools. So-called clinical programs have been developing rapidly, as reflected by the recent survey by the Council on Legal Education for Professional Responsibility. Many of these programs focus on trial advocacy. Recent rules, adopted by a number of state courts and some federal courts, allow students to appear in court as aides to lawyers.[9]

Another development is the growing number of law schools that are finally offering courses in trial advocacy. These are most effective when they provide training which students then use in so-called "clinical" programs. The National Institute for Trial Advocacy has, for the past two summers, offered an intensive training program in trial advocacy designed to channel effective laboratory techniques into law schools as well as into professional circles.[10] The law school, however, is where the groundwork must be laid.

We do not disparage the law as a profession when we insist that, like a carpenter or an electrician, the advocate must know how to use the tools of his "trade." Regrettably the development of these small beginnings in teaching elements of advocacy in law schools is offset somewhat when we see the subject of evidence become an *elective* rather than a *required* course. We might, with as much justification, try to make a lawyer without teaching contracts and wills as to omit the law of evidence.

9. For clinical programs, see Council on Legal Education for Professional Responsibility, Inc. (CLEPR), *Survey of Clinical Legal Education 1972–1973*, May 15, 1973. For recent rules permitting student practice in court, see CLEPR, State Rules Permitting The Student Practice of Law: Comparisons and Comments (Including Selected Federal Rules) (2d ed. 1973).

10. The National Institute for Trial Advocacy is sponsored jointly by the American Bar Association, American College of Trial Lawyers, and the Association of Trial Lawyers of America. The American Bar Association Project on Standards for Criminal Justice has promulgated *Standards Relating to The Prosecution Function and The Defense Function* (Approved Draft 1971) and the American College of Trial Lawyers has developed a *Code of Trial Conduct* (Jan. 1963). These are valuable resources to form the basis for training advocates in professional conduct.

The third cause is the inevitable inability of prosecutor and public defender offices to provide the same kind of apprenticeships for their new lawyers as, for example, the large law firms provide. The prosecution offices and public defender facilities have neither the wealthy clients nor consequent financial resources of the large law firms to enable them to develop whatever skills they need to carry out their mission. Prosecutors and public defenders often learn advocacy skills by being thrown into trial. Valuable as this may be as a learning experience, there is a real risk that it may be at the expense of the hapless clients they represent public or private. The trial of an important case is no place for on-the-job training of amateurs except under the guidance of a skilled advocate.

II

Time does not allow a recital of the myriad points of substantive law and procedure that an advocate in criminal cases should know in order to perform his or her task. Suffice it to say that in the past dozen or more years a whole range of new developments has drastically altered the trial of a criminal case. To give adequate representation, an advocate must be intimately familiar with these recent developments, most of them deriving from case law. Whether we measure the recent changes in terms of one decade or three, we see that the litigation volume, particularly in criminal cases, has escalated swiftly. The Criminal Justice Act[11] and the Bail Reform Act,[12] the extension of new federal standards to state courts, rising population, increased crime rates, creation of new causes of action and expanded civil remedies have contributed to the literal flood of cases in state and federal courts.

Whatever the legal issues or claims, the indispensable element in the trial of a case is a minimally adequate advocate for each litigant.[13] Many judges in general jurisdiction trial courts have stated to me that fewer than twenty-five percent of the lawyers appearing before them are genuinely qualified; other judges go as high as seventy-five percent.[14] I draw this from conversations extending over the past twelve to fifteen years at judicial meetings and seminars, with literally hundreds of judges and experienced lawyers.[15] It would be safer to pick a middle ground and accept as a working hypothesis that from one-third to one-half of the lawyers who appear in the serious cases are not really qualified to render fully adequate representation. The trial of a "serious" case, whether for damages or for

11. 18 U.S.C. § 3006A (1970).

12. *Id.* §§ 3146–52.

13. Burger, *Foreword* to L. Patterson & E. Cheatham, The Profession of Law, at v (1971).

14. One former colleague of mine on the Court of Appeals, Judge Edward A. Tamm, puts the figure at two percent. Tamm, *Advocacy Can Be Taught-the N.I.T.A. Way*, 59 A.B.A.J. 625 (1973).

15. A Sick Profession, Address by then Judge Burger, Winter Convention of the American College of Trial Lawyers, in Hollywood Beach, Fla., Apr. 11, 1967, in 27 Fed. B.J. 228 (1967), 5 Tulsa L.J. 1 (1968), and 42 Wis. B. Bull., Oct. 1969, at 7.

infringement of civil rights, or for a criminal felony, calls for the kind of special skills and experience that insurance companies, for example, seek out to defend damage claims.[16]

Let me try to put some flesh on the bones of these generalizations concerning the function and quality of the advocates. I will try to do this by way of a few examples observed when I sat by assignment as a trial judge, while serving on the U.S. Court of Appeals:

1. The thousands of trial transcripts I have reviewed show that a majority of the lawyers have never learned the seemingly simple but actually difficult art of asking questions so as to develop concrete images for the fact triers and to do so in conformity with rules of evidence.
2. Few lawyers have really learned the art of cross-examination, including the high art of when not to cross-examine.
3. The rules of evidence generally forbid leading questions, but when there are simple undisputed facts, the leading-questions rule need not apply. Inexperienced lawyers waste time making wooden objections to simple, acceptable questions, on uncontested factual matters.
4. Inexperienced lawyers are often unaware that "inflammatory" exhibits such as weapons or bloody clothes should not be exposed to jurors' sight until they are offered in evidence.
5. An inexperienced prosecutor wasted an hour on the historical development of the fingerprint identification process discovered by the Frenchman Bertillon, until it finally developed that there was no contested fingerprint issue. Such examples could be multiplied almost without limit.

Another aspect of inadequate advocacy—and one quite as important as familiarity with the rules of practice—is the failure of lawyers to observe the rules of professional manners and professional etiquette that are essential for effective trial advocacy.

Jurors who have been interviewed after jury service, and some who have written articles based on their service, express dismay at the distracting effect of personal clashes between the lawyers. There is no place in a properly run courtroom for the shouting matches and other absurd antics of lawyers sometimes seen on television shows and in the movies. From many centuries of experience, the ablest lawyers and judges have found that certain quite fixed rules of etiquette and manners are the lubricant to keep the focus of the courtroom contest on issues and facts and away from distracting personal clashes and irrelevancies.[17]

16. The techniques of advocacy in appellate courts—before regulatory agencies including tax tribunals, workmen's compensation tribunals, and others—present separate and distinct subjects and should not be treated in a discussion of trial advocacy, which usually involves a lay jury.

17. For two hundred years in this country (and in other civilized countries for much longer), all deliberative processes—the legislative in particular—have recognized that certain rules and formalities must be observed. Indeed, Thomas Jefferson, hardly one to restrain free speech, wrote the original manual of etiquette and behavior for the United States Congress, drawing on the tradition

A truly qualified advocate—like every genuine professional—resembles a seamless garment in the sense that legal knowledge, forensic skills, professional ethics, courtroom etiquette, and manners are blended in the total person as their use is blended in the performance of the function.

There are some few lawyers who scoff at the idea that manners and etiquette form any part of the necessary equipment of the courtroom advocate. Yet, if one were to undertake a list of the truly great advocates of the past one hundred years, I suggest he would find a common denominator: they were all intensely individualistic, but each was a lawyer for whom courtroom manners were a key weapon in his arsenal. Whether engaged in the destruction of adverse witnesses or undermining damaging evidence or final argument, the performance was characterized by coolness, poise, and graphic clarity, without shouting or ranting, and without baiting witnesses, opponents or the judge. We cannot all be great advocates, but as every lawyer seeks to emulate such tactics, he can approach, if not achieve, superior skill as an advocate.

What is essential is that certain standards of total advocacy performance be established and that we develop means to measure those standards, to the end that important cases have advocates who can give adequate representation. Law school students are adults who can contribute once they are persuaded of the need for training in this area. Rather than being "lectured" on ethics, they should be invited to discuss with the faculty and the best advocates the ethical element in the practice of law so as to impress them with the reality that courtroom ethics and etiquette are crucial to the lawyer's role in society—and indispensable to a rational system of justice. Woven into the seamless fabric of effective advocacy, professional ethics and professional manners are no less important than technical skills.

Lawyers are—or should be—society's peacemakers, problem solvers, and stabilizers. The English historian Plucknett suggests that England and America have been largely spared cataclysmic revolutions for two centuries, in part because the common law system lends itself to gradual evolutionary change to meet the changing needs of people. Lawyers can fulfill that high mission only if they are properly trained.

III

The focus on the inadequacies of advocates has tended to center on the criminal process, and it is plainly correct that this be given close attention and high priority. The first

---

of the English Parliament. *See* The Necessity for Civility, Address by Chief Justice Burger, ALI Opening Session, in Washington, D.C., May 18, 1971, *in* 52 F.R.D. 211, 216–17 (1971).

From time to time, a Member of the English Parliament or the House or Senate of the United States violates the rules and traditions of those bodies, and when that has happened, various sanctions can be directed against the offending Member. His colleagues may subject him to public scolding on the floor of the house in which he sits, or he may be formally censured after hearings before a committee. These things do not occur often, but frequently enough to remind Members that there are certain lines which may not be crossed with impunity. Unfortunately, in the courts today, for the most part, lines are crossed often and with impunity except in rare instances.

conviction of an accused person may be a determinant that shapes his entire future. Some convicted criminals do not need confinement in prison; neither they nor society can genuinely benefit from it. Effective advocacy can sometimes lead to other alternatives for a first offender—such as a suspended sentence or deferred prosecution.[18]

The contemporary literature tends to focus on the plight of the defendant and the inadequacy of defense counsel. For all too long we grossly neglected the needs of defendants, but the inadequacy of defense counsel is not by any means the whole story. Since we are discussing the problems of a system of justice, it is important to bear in mind that criminal justice is not a one-way street. Judge J. Edward Lumbard observed in a speech about ten years ago that the public is also entitled to due process and justice and that a just conviction is as important to the public interest as a just acquittal.[19]

The enormous demands on criminal courts naturally reflect themselves in the burdens on prosecutors' offices. I observed this in terms of one large prosecution office where the legal staff doubled in five years. The records in appeals handled by that prosecution office, confirmed by personal observations of the judges and experienced trial lawyers, strongly suggested that there was a steady decline in the prosecutors' performance before and after the increase in staff. Countless times in that jurisdiction, a prosecutor, on coming into the courtroom, would ask for a ten-minute recess so he could review a file he had never seen.

In some places, it is the observation of judges that the Criminal Justice Act has not brought about improvement in the general quality of criminal defense and that performance has not been generally adequate—neither by assigned private counsel nor by the public defender office. I am sure that the situation varies from place to place, and the observation of other judges is that the institutionalization of defense work in defender offices holds the best promise for the future. For my part, it is probably too early to reach firm conclusions on the subject, but a choice may be compelled before long.[20]

We have long since institutionalized the prosecution of criminal cases because it best serves the public interest to discharge the function in that way, and the public interest in adequate defense representation is of equal order. Fifteen or twenty years ago, some otherwise sensible people tended to regard the idea of a public defender office as a form of "creeping socialism," but I am confident that attitude no longer has significant acceptance.

18. As the ABA Committee on the Standards for Criminal Justice emphasized, the most important role and the most unsatisfactory performance of advocates may be at sentencing. *See* ABA Project on Minimum Standards for Criminal Justice, Standards Relating to Sentencing Alternatives and Procedures (Approved Draft 1968).

19. Judge Lumbard stressed this point repeatedly in speeches at the time. *See in particular The Administration of Criminal Justice*, *3S* N.Y. St. BJ. 360 (1963); *The Responsibility of the Bar for the Performance of the Courts*, 34 N.Y. St. B.J. 169 (1962); *The Lawyers' Responsibility for Due Process and Law Enforcement*, 12 Syracuse L. Rev. 431 (1961).

20. A detailed overview of this problem is found in Bazelon, *The Defective Assistance of Counsel*, 42 U. Cin. L. Rev. 1 (1973). We know much less than we should about the comparative quality of assigned and public-defender-office lawyers. An American Bar Foundation sponsored comparison is L. Silverstein, Defense of the Poor in Criminal Cases in American State Courts (1965).

However, even placing the defense of indigents largely if not entirely in the jurisdiction of a staff of career public defenders with the necessary auxiliary facilities does not in itself guarantee adequate advocacy skills. In fact, at present, the rapid expansion of both the prosecution offices and public defender facilities has been accompanied by a trend to use either of these functions—or both—as a means for young lawyers to learn how to try cases. It would be instructive to assemble the data on the tenure of staff lawyers in prosecution and public defender offices. To have bright young men and women "flit" in and out of these offices for two- or three-year apprenticeships may possibly be useful to them and their future clients, but it is a high price to pay if it results in inadequate performance for either side of a criminal trial. It is a matter of history that some prosecution offices—of which New York is a notable example—have been a proving ground for some of our most outstanding advocates, so I do not disparage the idea of a tour of duty as a prosecutor or as a public defender.

In our proper concern for criminal justice, we must not forget that the rights and interests of civil litigants should not be brushed under the rug. In nearly eighteen years on the bench and more than twenty years of general practice, I have had occasion to review literally thousands of records—civil, criminal and administrative—and I have observed as many miscarriages of justice in civil cases from inadequacy of counsel as in criminal cases. To borrow some lines from Gray's "Elegy," the injustice in some civil cases becomes part of "the short and simple annals of the poor."[21] In some of those cases, the human tragedy was very real to the principals.

IV

If there is substantial validity to this analysis of the problem, what should we do about it?

Some system of specialist certification is inevitable and, as we know, it has been discussed in legal circles for a generation or more. Dean Robert B. McKay of New York University Law School has observed that the legal profession has "marched up the hill of specialist certification only to march right down again in the face of opposition from practitioners not discontent with the absence of regulation."[22] Our commitment to the public and to the system of justice must not let us be marched down that hill any longer.

I see nothing for lawyers, litigants, or courts to fear; on the contrary I see a great potential gain, by moving toward specialist certification to limit admission to trial practice, beginning in courts of general jurisdiction where the more important claims and rights are resolved. When we have succeeded in that limited area we can then examine broader aspects of specialization. Furthermore, while the legal profession must obviously lead in this effort, the interests of the public dictate that the views of practitioners who are affected cannot be controlling any more than we allow the automobile or drug industry to

21. The Complete Poems of Thomas Gray 38 (H. Starr & J. Hendrickson eds. 1966).

22. *Role of Graduate Legal Education in the Development of the Legal Specialist*, Dec. 10, 1970, at 2 (paper prepared for symposium of ABA Special Committee on Specialization, New Orleans) (footnote omitted).

have complete control of safety or public health standards. There are more than two hundred million potential "consumers" of justice whose rights and interests must have protection, and it is the duty of the legal profession to provide reasonable safeguards—unless lawyers prefer regulation from the outside.

Our traditional assumption that every lawyer, like the legendary Renaissance man, is equipped to deal effectively with every legal problem probably had some validity in the day of Jefferson, Hamilton, John Adams, and John Marshall, but that assumption has been diluted by the vast changes in the complexity of our social, economic, and political structure.

The experience of the medical profession affords some guidance in its first step in specialty certification. That step was identifying those doctors genuinely competent to perform serious surgery and limiting access to the operating room to such doctors. Obviously, there are and probably always will be sparsely populated areas in which some doctors and lawyers must be jacks-of-all-trades. But, the fact that this is a necessity imposed in some areas of the country by geography and population density does not mean that in the metropolitan centers where courts deal with thousands of cases we need or should tolerate ineffective representation.

The American Bar Association has wisely cautioned that in undertaking certification programs, "it is not desirable for a large number of states to embark upon even experimental programs in specialization before uniform standards can be established lest unnecessarily divergent programs become prematurely crystallized."[23] The ABA committee, however, is carefully monitoring pilot or experimental programs commencing in California and Texas, among others. Those states certify three specialties, and quite appropriately, the one they have in common is criminal law.[24]

23. 95 A.B.A. Rep. 329 (1970). The ABA's Special Committee on Specialization in its 1973 Annual Report cited the avalanche of state projects and once again urged states yet to undertake pilot programs to refrain from doing so until there has been an opportunity to evaluate those already in existence. ABA Report of Special Committee on Specialization 3, 6 (Aug. 1973).

24. On November 20, 1973, the first 1,182 certificates of specialization were awarded by the State Bar of California under its pilot program in legal specialization. The specialties were divided as follows: criminal law, 391; workmen's compensation, 311; and taxation, 480. The first three certificates, one in each specialty, were issued by ABA President Chesterfield Smith.

One innovative attempt to assure adequate counsel for criminal defendants is under way in the United States District Court for the Southern District of New York, which has started to certify informally those defense attorneys considered eligible for appointment by the court under the Criminal Justice Act, 18 U.S.C. § 3006A (1970). A program of certification may not have been intended when this plan was initiated, but it in fact appears to be an important first step toward the certification of trial advocates. Accompanying the court's power to certify Criminal Justice Act attorneys is the power to decertify attorneys for lack of qualifications or refusal to accept three consecutive appointments. The Southern District Committee on the Criminal Justice Act Panel, composed of judges, has established a subcommittee of lawyers to conduct interviews, evaluate applicants' credentials, and then make a recommendation to the committee and to the Chief Judge. The applicants whose paper credentials are sufficient but who lack adequate trial experience are encouraged to serve as assistants to approved Criminal Justice Act attorneys and Legal Aid attorneys

It is in this spirit of cautious progress that I urge that we should concentrate where, in the view of most judges, the greatest need exists. For the initial stage, moreover, we should limit ourselves to certification of trial advocates until we learn more about the problems of evaluation and selection. There is danger, as the ABA report stated, in trying to do too much too soon, without knowing enough about the pitfalls. The limited step of certifying trial advocates first will be a large enough task to tax our best efforts. Given the difficulty in terms of dealing with fifty separate state systems, perhaps the prudent thing to do is to begin with the United States District Courts. After experimenting in several representative federal districts and in state courts, the Judicial Conferences in the several circuits should consider this problem.

PROPOSAL

What I propose is a broad, four-point program as a first step in specialist certification. We should:

1. Face up to and reject the notion that every law graduate and every lawyer is qualified, simply by virtue of admission to the bar, to be an advocate in trial courts in matters of serious consequence.
2. Lay aside the proposals for broad and comprehensive specialty certification (except where pilot programs are already under way) until we have positive progress in the certification of the one crucial specialty of trial advocacy that is so basic to a fair system of justice and has had historic recognition in the common law systems.
3. Develop means to evaluate qualifications of lawyers competent to render the effective assistance of counsel in the trial of cases.
4. Call on the American Bar Association, the Federal Bar Association, the American College of Trial Lawyers, the American Association of Law Schools, the Federal Judicial Center, the National Center for State Courts and others to collaborate in prompt and concrete steps to accomplish this first step in a workable and enforceable certification of trial advocates.

The fate of this proposal, as with any relating to progress in our profession, depends on the members of that "great partnership" of the law made up of lawyers, judges, and law teachers—and I have great confidence in that partnership.

---

for one year and then reapply for certification. This may also be true for those who have the threshold knowledge of criminal litigation but lack trial experience. I am informed by Chief Judge David N. Edelstein that competition for these assignments is rigorous and, interestingly enough, one finds many alumni of the United States Attorney's Office in their ranks.

The Decline of Professionalism

Chief Justice Warren E. Burger

1995 Sonnett Lecture

The first time I came to Fordham University to deliver the Sonnett lecture, more than twenty years ago, I spoke about the developing "'crisis' in the availability of adequate legal services" and, in particular, about the need for skilled courtroom advocacy.[1] That need, while still acute today, has been overtaken by a more fundamental and more urgent problem facing the legal profession. The bedrock of our profession from Blackstone's day has been *the professional ideal:* the lawyer as an officer of the court, compelled as such to maintain a standard of conduct that rises above the standard we would expect from a tradesman engaged in what many now call "the business of law." The law is not and never has been a "business." But we are well on the way to making it less than a profession.

A serious decline in professionalism in any of the learned professions is inevitably injurious to the society in which they function. In order to evaluate the seriousness of such a decline, we must examine the setting in which that decline occurs. We must ask whether it is isolated and peculiar to one profession, or whether there is also a decline in other professions and other human activities.

I see disturbing evidence that there has been a broad decline in professionalism over the past twenty to twenty-five years, not only in the three so-called learned professions—

1. Warren E. Burger, *The Special Skills of Advocacy: Are Specialized Training and Certification of Advocates Essential to Our System of Justice?*, 42 Fordham L. Rev. 227, 227 (1973).

the clergy, medicine, and the law—but also in many other important activities. For example, those who serve in the money markets—including Wall Street, banks, and savings and loan institutions—have inflicted severe damage on the public. Some have called this period a Greed Era. The decline of professionalism, especially in the law, has taken on epidemic proportions. I do not make such a statement lightly. John J. Yanas, President of the New York State Bar Association, recently stated: "Greed and avarice seem to permeate every facet of life in this country and the practice of law has not proven to be immune."[2] He then went on to state:

> Within our profession we now condone advertising and solicitation of clients, activities that were formerly unethical and unprofessional. Our young lawyers are judged by their billable hours. . . . One wonders whether we will continue to move away from our established traditions and canons of professional ethics.[3]

Two books sharply critical of lawyers have been published recently—*The Betrayed Profession* by Sol Linowitz[4] and *The Lost Lawyer* by Anthony Kronman.[5] I commend them to your attention.

The legal profession has indeed moved away from long-established traditions and canons of professional ethics. In 1970, a report from an American Bar Association committee, chaired by my late colleague Justice Tom Clark, found that bar associations' disciplinary action in response to lawyers' professional misconduct was "practically nonexistent."[6] As a result of the marked increase in attorney misconduct and the failure of the organized bar to discipline violations, the standing of the legal profession is perhaps at its lowest ebb in this century *and perhaps at its lowest in history*. Anyone who scans the writings of lawyers and judges on this subject and looks at the outrageous advertising of lawyers on television, on billboards, and in print will find abundant reason for this low standing.

Some—but I believe this to be a relatively small fraction of the legal profession—brush off this evaluation as a manifestation of the "historic contempt" for lawyers. "Lawyer bashing" they call it, and they support their position by quoting out of context the Shakespeare character who said: "The first thing we do, let's kill all the lawyers."[7] Of course, because the legal profession deals with contention and conflict, it cannot achieve the kind of benign acceptance accorded one's family physician or favorite clergyman or Sunday School teacher. Recently, however, anyone who makes a credible case for legal reform is likely to be charged with "lawyer bashing." I do not intend to bash lawyers today. There are a vast number of competent, ethical lawyers practicing law. But the organized bar's

2. John J. Yanas, *The President's Message*, N.Y. St. B.J., May 1990, at 3.

3. *Id.*

4. Sol M. Linowitz & Martin Mayer, The Betrayed Profession: Lawyering at the End of the Twentieth Century (1994).

5. Anthony T. Kronman, The Lost Lawyer: Failing Ideals of the Legal Profession (1993).

6. ABA Special Comm. on Evaluation of Disciplinary Enforcement, Problems and Recommendations in Disciplinary Enforcement 1 (1970).

7. William Shakespeare, The Second Part of King Henry the Sixth act 4, sc. 2.

failure to maintain high standards of ethics and professionalism certainly warrants criticism. "Bar association bashing" would be a more accurate description of what I have engaged in, because I have previously and will again tonight explain how the organized bar's failure to set and maintain high ethical standards for the legal profession has caused much of the decline in professionalism among lawyers and the corresponding decline in the public esteem of lawyers.

The "established traditions" of the law to which John Yanas referred began to emerge at least six hundred years ago in England when legal advocacy began to emerge as a profession. Even in England, the profession has had its ups and downs since that time; its present level of esteem there crystallized only in the past two hundred or three hundred years to produce in England what is, at once, the most vigorous and yet the most strictly regulated bar in the world. Regarding the English legal profession, the historian Professor Odgers wrote nearly a century ago:

> Of all the mighty changes that have taken place in the nineteenth century, the greatest change has been in the tone of the administration of both the civil and the criminal law. The manners of our law courts have marvelously improved. Formerly judges browbeat the prisoners, jeered at their efforts to defend themselves, and censured juries who honestly did their duty. Formerly, too, counsel bullied the witnesses and perverted what they said. Now the attitude and temper of Her Majesty's judges toward parties, witnesses, and prisoners alike has wholly changed, and the [members of the] Bar too behave like gentlemen. . . . The moral tone of the Bar is wholly different from what it was . . . . [T]hey remember that it is their duty to assist the Court in eliciting the truth. This is due partly to the improved education of the Bar; partly no doubt to the influence of an omnipresent press; but still more to Her Majesty's judges. If counsel for the prosecution presses the case too vehemently against a prisoner; if counsel cross-examining in a civil case pries unnecessarily into the private concerns of the witness; a word, or even a look, from the presiding judge will at once check such indiscretion.[8]

Remember that Odgers wrote about the English legal profession of a hundred years ago.

Of course, England's problems with respect to the legal profession are less complex than ours. We have fifty states and the District of Columbia, Puerto Rico, and the Virgin Islands, each charged with the admission, regulation, and discipline of its bar. In England, the Four Inns of Court in London govern the profession of the barristers—the "trial lawyers"—and that category consists of about five thousand men and women for the entire country. The solicitors—whom we would call "office lawyers"—are similarly limited and strictly self-regulated. Changes are in progress even there, but they are not directly related to our subject. What are the factors that explain or account for the low public esteem of our profession? I will confine my discussion to the three examples of unethical conduct in the legal profession that disturb me the most.

8. W. Blake Odgers, *Changes in the Common Law and in the Law of Persons, in the Legal Profession and in Legal Education*, *in* A CENTURY OF LAW REFORM 1, 41–42 (Roy M. Mersky & J. Myron Jacobstein eds., 1901).

I

In recent years, we have seen a gradual increase in the number of lawyers "trying their cases"—and I put that phrase in quotation marks—on the courthouse steps to newspaper and television reporters. When defense lawyers did this in criminal cases, it was not too great a cause for alarm; if they received any media attention, people shrugged and figured, "That is what defense lawyers are paid to do." But in recent years, when prosecutors joined in this activity, it has become a different matter. When prosecutors speak, it is the *State*—the government, the people—speaking, and the public naturally listens. What is the purpose of engaging in such conduct over and beyond the ego trip the lawyer enjoys from the publicity? Sometimes it is to influence public opinion and perhaps the views of jurors not yet selected. This inevitably complicates the process of jury selection and is, in my view, a plain violation of a lawyer's duty as an officer of the court. Judges ought to put a stop to this, and because they have not, judges must share the blame for it.

No prosecutor—including the Attorney General of the United States, an Assistant United States Attorney, a State Attorney General, an Assistant District Attorney, or especially that new creature of the law, the "Special Prosecutor"—should ever, except in the most unusual circumstances, make out-of-court statements about a pending investigation or a pending case. And we cannot blame the media for reporting what they see and hear on the courthouse steps. That is what a free press is for. I would have thought that by now the media's focus on this phenomenon would have stimulated the organized bar to act. But it has not. Of course, we have in recent times seen glaring examples of lawyers trying their cases in the media.

Some judges, but all too few, have moved on this subject. Recently, the *New York Times* reported that United States District Judge Kevin Duffy of New York had issued strict orders—to the prosecution, to the defense attorneys, and to all law enforcement officials involved in the massive case involving the explosion at the World Trade Center—to make no trial-related statements to reporters.[9] Judge Duffy announced that he would impose fines beginning at $200 for each violation of his order and that later violations would be mathematically squared so that the second violation would be subject to a $40,000 fine and the third to a fine of $1.6 billion! "The next time I pick up a paper and see a quotation from any of you, you best be prepared to pay some money," Judge Duffy told prosecutors and defense attorneys.[10] Although the order was overturned on appeal, Judge Duffy's effort to control out-of-court statements by attorneys should be commended.[11]

9. Mary B.W. Tabor, *As Trial Is Set in Explosion, Hunt Widens; A Gag Order Is Issued Covering Trial Figures*, N.Y. Times, Apr. 2, 1993, at B1.

10. *Id.*

11. The defendants challenged Judge Duffy's order, claiming that it prevented them from responding to government leaks to the news media. Regardless of what has happened in that case, such charges would lack credibility had not out-of-court statements and leaks by both sides become so common.

As Judge Duffy explained, the judiciary should be interested in keeping the trial *in court.* "The trial [and] the evidence," he said, "belong in the courtroom, nowhere else."[12]

II

Next in my Bill of Particulars is the so-called Rambo Lawyer, whose idea of counsel's function may have been influenced by the clownish performances seen on television programs. Here the judges are also in control—or at least they should be. When even a few judges tolerate the Rambo Lawyer's misconduct, the administration of justice suffers, and it leads to repetition of that conduct by other lawyers. Lawyers should not act like "hired guns." Civility is imperative in the courtroom: it is an essential element of the fair administration of justice. If we as a profession tolerate such an attitude among some of our practitioners, we cannot expect greater respect from the public. Lawyers, as officers of the court, should be problem-solvers, harmonizers, and peacemakers—the healers, not the promoters, of conflict. In the words of Abraham Lincoln: "As a peace-maker the lawyer has a superior opportunity of being a good man. There will still be business enough."[13] Here we see the necessity for civility.

III

Finally, something that is possibly even worse in its long-range impact than courtroom misconduct—because most courtroom misconduct does not reach the public—is the outrageous breach of professional conduct we see in the huckster advertising of some attorneys. Perhaps "huckster" is not strong enough a word. "Shyster" is more appropriate, but I find on consulting the dictionary that even "shyster" is not strong enough. Tonight, I will settle for "huckster shyster" advertising.

We in the legal profession have no ancient oath or creed like the Hippocratic Oath governing the medical profession, but we have long accepted the idea that certain conduct is prohibited—for example, our rules against champerty and maintenance. But assuming for the moment that the Constitution *permits* a lawyer to finance a client's lawsuit, surely professional standards prohibit it. Similarly, even if we read the First Amendment to permit a lawyer literally to stand on the comer of a busy street, handing out cards like a political candidate—along with a booklet or brochure telling how good he is—we may still ask if such conduct is conceivably compatible with the ethical standards of one of the three great learned professions.

Of course, this shyster element of the bar—even if it is a small fraction of our profession—will argue that "The Supreme Court has said advertising is OK." One would expect that answer from shyster lawyers inclined to do anything and everything to secure clients. We

12. *Id.*

13. Abraham Lincoln, *Notes for a Law Lecture (July 1, 1850), in* The Life and Writings of Abraham Lincoln 327–28 (Phillip Van Doren Stern ed., 1940).

see today, however, that the organized bar, especially the American Bar Association, has—sadly—taken the same view. Yet the Supreme Court's decision in *Bates v. State Bar of Arizona*,[14] on which these lawyers and the ABA rely, tells us only that the Constitution *allows* commercial advertising by lawyers—and by implication other kinds of client solicitation. But the Court's holding that lawyer advertising is protected by the First Amendment in no sense inhibits the legal profession from clearly stating that such advertising is unprofessional. Indeed, if the idea of a profession means anything, it means that a profession must adhere to standards that are above the minimum commands of the law. For centuries that is what has marked the difference between a profession and a trade.

Lawyers, like doctors, must be more than just skilled technicians. Not too many years ago, Roscoe Pound observed that if lawyers are to be an educational and professional elite, they should not stoop to common commercialization.[15] Strict regulation of all lawyer conduct is imperative to protect the public. Since the *Bates* case, the Supreme Court has acknowledged that "the absence of any standardization in the [legal] 'product' renders advertising for professional services especially susceptible to abuses."[16]

We in the law must never forget that the legal profession has a monopoly on the practice of law. It is an article of faith in America that monopolies must be strictly regulated to protect the public interest. We should emulate the British bar with its self-regulation before legislatures apply the cudgel to lawyers.

Unfortunately, the shyster conduct in solicitation and advertising is no longer limited to the "ambulance chasers." Today we see television ads, yellow pages ads, and (believe it or not) ads on billboards forty feet wide and fifteen feet high, touting a lawyer or law firm reaching out for clients. With such ads, lawyers usually emphasize that the "First Conference Is Free." Doesn't this have the ring of "Come into my parlor, said the spider to the fly?"

It is sheer nonsense to say that the public needs lawyer advertising for people to have effective access to the judicial system. Finding a competent, affordable attorney may sometimes be a difficult task in a large metropolitan area, and there is no question that people need a lawyer to ensure access to justice. But that task can be accomplished through a greater emphasis on pro bono work and especially through lawyer referral services provided by local bar associations. Many local bar associations have long placed periodic ads in local newspapers inviting the public to call their Lawyer Referral Service, which will provide the names of three or four lawyers qualified for the particular need described by the caller. And in fact, advertising is of little help to those looking for a lawyer. Recent consumer surveys have found that on average only one out of ten people who hire a lawyer find that lawyer through advertising.[17] With greater development of referral services, it would be absurd to claim that advertising is necessary.

14. 433 U.S. 350, 363 (1977).

15. Roscoe Pound, The Lawyer from Antiquity to Modern Times 12 n.3 (1953).

16. *In re* R.M.J., 455 U.S. 191, 202 (1982).

17. ABA Comm'n on Advertising, Yellow Pages Lawyer Advertising: An Analysis of Effective Elements 13 (1992) (citing ABA Consortium on Legal Services and the Public, Two

Nor is it a justification to assert that there is a long history of advertising. One nationally advertised firm—apparently sensing that its television commercials would strike the public as huckster-shyster advertising—mentioned in its commercials that Abraham Lincoln advertised. Today's slick advertising campaigns bear no resemblance—absolutely none—to what Lincoln did. Even professional cards are in some sense advertising, but they have long been acceptable, provided that they were used in a professional manner. Similarly, in many rural communities, there is a long history of inserting one's professional card or an announcement of a partnership in a local newspaper. But virtually every other form of advertising was resoundingly condemned.[18] A court in the late nineteenth century held: "The ethics of the legal profession forbid that an attorney should advertise his talents or his skill, as a shopkeeper advertises his wares."[19] What has our profession done about the disgraceful problem of huckster-shyster advertising? It would be bad enough if the answer were "practically nothing." But the answer is worse—because, in an apparent effort to accommodate certain elements of the bar, the American Bar Association, which ought to define the standards, has instead compromised our professional integrity. Of course, the ABA has no authority to admit lawyers to the practice of law or to discipline them for misconduct, but it has a duty to prescribe professional standards in keeping with centuries of experience, not a standard that says a lawyer can do anything the law allows. With its 400,000 or more members, the ABA is one of the most powerful professional associations in the world, and as such it has heavy public responsibilities. I raise the question whether it has properly met those responsibilities in formulating the "professional standard" set out in its recent Model Rules of Professional Conduct. We find this in the Rules:

> A lawyer shall not make a false or misleading communication about the lawyer or the lawyer's services. A communication is false or misleading if it:
>
> (a) contains a material misrepresentation of fact or law, or omits a fact necessary to make the statement considered as a whole not materially misleading;
>
> (b) is likely to create an unjustified expectation about the results the lawyer can achieve, or states or implies that the lawyer can achieve results by means that violate the Rules of Professional Conduct or other law; or
>
> (c) compares the lawyer's services with other lawyers' services, unless the comparison can be factually substantiated.[20]

Can this combination of words honestly be called "*professional* standards?" These alleged professional standards make no real distinction between what is *legal* and what is *professional.*

NATIONWIDE SURVEYS: 1989 PILOT ASSESSMENT OF THE UNMET LEGAL NEEDS OF THE POOR AND OF THE PUBLIC GENERALLY, F. MAGID, ATTITUDES AND OPINIONS OF FLORIDA ADULTS TOWARD DIRECT MAIL ADVERTISING BY ATTORNEYS (1987); REPORT OF FINDINGS: NEVADA LAWYERS' ADVERTISING SURVEY, LITIGATION TECHNOLOGIES (Feb. 1990)).

18. *See* GLEASON L. ARCHER, ETHICAL OBLIGATIONS OF THE LAWYER 238–48 (Fred B. Rothman & Co. 1981) (1910); GEO. W. WARVELLE, ESSAYS IN LEGAL ETHICS §§ 90–99 (2d ed. 1920).

19. People v. MacCabe, 32 P. 280, 281 (Colo. 1893).

20. MODEL RULES OF PROF'L CONDUCT r. 7.1 (1983).

Worse still is the ABA's Model Creed of Professionalism. Purportedly an attempt to set aspirational goals for lawyers, it does nothing of the kind. In regard to advertising it states: "I will be mindful of the need to protect the image of the legal profession in the eyes of the public and will be so guided when considering methods and content of advertising."[21] Does this provide any guidance to lawyers? It requires only that the lawyer think about—in the Creed's words, "be mindful" of—what he or she is doing before doing it, and the emphasis is on image rather than on ethical conduct.

Several years ago, I was invited to appear before an ABA committee considering standards for lawyer advertising. I was asked what I thought the ABA should tell the public regarding advertising by lawyers. My answer was that what we should say adds up to this: "Never, *never, never* engage the services of a lawyer who *finds it necessary* to advertise in order to get clients."

If the ABA were to ask me today what should be done about all this, I would respond that the whole subject of professional standards needs another look, focusing on lawyers, especially prosecutors, trying their cases on courthouse steps; on the matter of Rambo-type conduct in the courtroom; and on the sickening practice of huckster-shyster advertising. We must remember that if lawyers are to continue to claim status as a *profession*, we must proclaim and enforce standards that are compatible with those of a profession.

Now we must acknowledge that some members of the judiciary have not set a high standard of professional conduct. Judicial misconduct in recent years is most disturbing. From 1789 through 1980, six members of the federal judiciary—Article III judges—were either removed from office or resigned following impeachment for serious misconduct.[22] In just the past fifteen years, however, five Article III judges have been indicted and four have been convicted of serious felonies. Three of these have been impeached and removed from office.[23] As for the other two, one has resigned rather than face impeachment,[24] and one

21. Laws. Man. on Prof. Conduct (ABA/BNA) No. 67, at 01:403 (Aug. 31, 1988).

22. District Judge John Pickering of New Hampshire was impeached by the House of Representatives and convicted (removed) by the Senate in 1804; District Judge West H. Humphreys of Tennessee was impeached and convicted in 1862 after deserting his post to aid the Confederacy; Circuit Judge Robert W. Archbald of Pennsylvania was impeached and convicted in 1913; and Judge Halsted L Ritter of the District of Florida was impeached and convicted in 1936. District Judges Mark W. Delahay of Kansas and George W. English of Illinois were impeached in 1873 and 1926, respectively; each resigned before he could be tried by the Senate. ELEANORE BUSHNELL, CRIMES, FOLLIES, AND MISFORTUNES: THE FEDERAL IMPEACHMENT TRIALS (1992).

23. Judge Harry E. Claiborne of the District of Nevada was indicted in 1983 for tax evasion, convicted in 1984, and impeached and removed in 1986; Judge Alcee L. Hastings of the Southern District of Florida (who now sits in the House of Representatives as a Democrat from Florida) was indicted in 1981 for bribery and related offenses and acquitted in 1983, but he was nevertheless impeached and removed in 1989; and Chief Judge Walter L. Nixon Jr. of the Southern District of Mississippi was convicted in 1986 of lying to a grand jury and was impeached and removed in 1989. *Id.*

24. Judge Robert Collins of the Eastern District of Louisiana was convicted in 1981 of receiving and soliciting bribes; he resigned from office in 1993. United States v. Collins, 972 F.2d 1385 (5th Cir. 1992), *cert. denied*, 113 S. Ct. 1812 (1993); Judges of the United States District Courts, 821 F. Supp. vii, xiii (1993).

has not reached the end of the appellate process.[25] A footnote on this subject is important: in many cases the fact of conviction on impeachment did not lead to disbarment by the relevant state supreme court. Ponder this: Article III judges, removed from office by the two Houses of Congress for grave criminal conduct, are allowed by the states to return to the practice of law.

I have been a member of the bar for more than sixty years, with twenty-three of them in active practice and more than thirty-one years as an Article III judge. I am proud of my profession and the historic role attorneys have played as officers of the courts and as servants of the public in the administration of justice and democratic government. From the very beginning of our nation more than two hundred years ago, lawyers have been relied on by their fellow citizens, and we should remember that thirty-one of the fifty-five delegates who met in Philadelphia and drafted the greatest charter of government ever written were lawyers. Historically, lawyers have been public leaders, not merely advocates for clients. Would our profession measure up today to the lawyers among the Founding Fathers?

It is not merely the right but the duty of members of the bar to challenge the failure of the leadership of the organized bar to set high standards and the failure of local bar associations to enforce the same high standards. You, as students of law, have an especially heavy burden in this regard. This is a heavy legacy that we pass on to you. We hope that you will live up to it.

25. Judge Robert Aguilar of the Northern District of California was convicted in 1990 of illegally disclosing a wiretap and endeavoring to obstruct justice. The Supreme Court recently granted certiorari to review the Ninth Circuit's judgment overturning those convictions. United States v. Aguilar, 115 S. Ct. 571 (1994), *granting cert. to* 21 F.3d 1475, 1487 (9th Cir. 1994) (en banc).

Because of this lag between criminal conviction and impeachment, federal judges collect their judicial salaries while in prison. Legislation has been introduced in Congress to avoid this problem by suspending the pay of any judge convicted of a felony, but even if it is enacted, such legislation would be subject to constitutional challenge. In any event, the need for such legislation is a telling indication of the decline in professionalism within the legal profession.

The Compleat Advocate

Rt. Hon. Lord Widgery

The Rt. Hon. Lord Widgery delivered the fifth Sonnett lecture, entitled *The Compleat Advocate*, on January 7, 1975.[1] John Passmore Widgery was knighted in 1961 and became Lord Chief Justice of England, the highest judicial appointment in Britain, ten years later in 1971.[2] Born in South Molton, England in 1911, Lord Widgery attended Queen's College, a public boarding school, in Taunton.[3] Unlike his judicial colleagues, Lord Widgery began his career as a solicitor at the age of twenty-two and joined a firm of law tutors, Gibson & Welldon.[4] He practiced for six years until he enlisted in the Royal Artillery as a private at the start of World War II.[5] Within three years of his enlistment, he had risen to lieutenant colonel.[6]

After the war, Lord Widgery returned to the law, rising swiftly in the British judicial system.[7] He became a judge in 1959, a High Court judge in 1961, and a Lord Justice of Appeal in 1968.[8] In 1971, he was named Lord Chief Justice.[9]

Some of his most significant judgments on the appeals court involved freedom of the press.[10] In 1974, the literary executors of Richard Crossman, a recently deceased British cabinet minister, published his diaries, which included some information from confidential cabinet meetings.[11] The case came before Lord Widgery when the British government sought to block the publication on the grounds it would not be in the public interest.[12] Lord Widgery rejected the Government's request, concluding that he was "far from convinced that [the Attorney General] made out a case that the public interest requires

Introduction written by Kathleen A. Zink, J.D., Class of 2015, Fordham University School of Law.

1. Rt. Hon. Lord Widgery, *The Compleat Advocate*, 43 FORDHAM L. REV. 909 (1975).

2. Sarah Ganderup, *How White Was the Wash?: Bloody Sunday, 1972, and Memory in the Creation of the Widgery Report*, 2 CHAP. U. HIST. REV. 29, 31 (2010); *Lord Widgery is Dead at 70; Top British Judge Until 1980*, N.Y. TIMES, July 28, 1981, at B8 [hereinafter *Lord Widgery*].

3. Ganderup, *supra* note 2, at 30.

4. *Id.*

5. *Lord Widgery*, *supra* note 2.

6. *Id.*

7. *Id.*

8. *Id.*

9. *Id.*

10. *Id.*

11. Bernard Weinraub, *Press in Britain Wins Major Test: Judge Rebuffs Move for Ban on Diaries of Crossman*, N.Y. TIMES, Oct. 1, 1975, at 1.

12. *Id.* at 4.

such a draconian remedy when due regard is had to other public interest, such as freedom of speech."[13]

Lord Widgery is principally known for presiding over an inquiry into the events surrounding the so-called Bloody Sunday events of January 30, 1972, in which twenty-seven civil rights marchers were killed or injured in Northern Ireland when British soldiers opened fire.[14] In his report, Lord Widgery largely exonerated the British army of blame.[15] The report stated that there would have been no deaths if the illegal march had not created a highly dangerous situation in which a clash between demonstrators and the soldiers became almost inevitable.[16] However, Lord Widgery questioned some of the tactics of the troops, stating their firing "bordered on the reckless."[17]

In January 1998, Tony Blair announced a new inquiry into the killings of Bloody Sunday, criticizing Lord Widgery's failure to personally read eyewitness accounts and take evidence from those wounded.[18] The resulting Saville Report overturned Lord Widgery's assertions that the British soldiers had been justified in killing and wounding twenty-seven civilians on Bloody Sunday.[19]

Lord Widgery retired in 1980 and died a year later.[20] After his death, Lord Elywyn-Jones described him in the House of Lords as having "graced the Bench as Lord Chief Justice, as a Lord Justice of Appeal, and High Court judge with the qualities in high degree of fairness, integrity, courtesy, economy and clarity of expression, and above all of sound common sense."[21]

Delivered from the unique perspective of British trial lawyer and judge, Lord Widgery's Sonnett lecture, *The Compleat Advocate*, commented on the declining quality of trial lawyers. In discussing how to improve the standard of the trial lawyer, Lord Widgery examined the essential characteristics a trial lawyer should display, and how far senior members of the bar could encourage and develop these characteristics. Lord Widgery also discussed that shaping effective trial lawyers requires learning "first principles" in law school and gaining experience after graduation. Finally, Lord Widgery noted that lawyers could learn from the medical profession in their search for an ideal environment in which to produce competent, "complete" trial lawyers.

---

13. *Id.*
14. *Id.*
15. *See* Ganderup, *supra* note 2.
16. *Id.*
17. *Id.*
18. Colin Brown & David McKittrick, *'Compelling Evidence' Forces New Bloody Sunday Inquiry*, INDEPENDENT (Jan. 30, 1998), http://www.independent.co.uk/news/compelling-evidence-forces-new-bloody-sunday-inquiry-1141632.html.
19. David McKittrick, *Saville Pins the Blame for Blood Sunday on British Soldiers*, INDEPENDENT (June 16, 2010), http://www.independent.co.uk/news/uk/home-news/saville-pins-the-blame-for-bloody-sunday-on-british-soldiers-2001669.html.
20. Ganderup, *supra* note 2, at 31.
21. 423 PARL. DEB., H.L., (5th ser.) (1981) 656 (U.K.), *available at* http://hansard.millbanksystems.com/lords/1981/jul/28/supreme-court-bill-hl#column_657.

1975 Sonnett Lecture

In our adversary system of justice, the judge is at the mercy of the advocate. A captive audience of one (more, of course, in appellate courts), he is required to sit patiently day by day whilst advocates pass in a constant stream before him. Some speak at length, some are limited by the rules to a merciful fifteen to twenty minutes, some come with the flush of youthful exuberance, some come with the disillusion of middle age. Some are helpful, some time-consuming. All must be heard.

Small wonder that the judges are the first to praise or criticize the quality of the advocacy that is served up before them. The last Sonnett Memorial Lecture[1] was delivered by Chief Justice Warren Burger,[2] who devoted much of his address to a consideration of the quality of the present generation of trial lawyers in America and found that quality was wanting. In particular, he attacked the assumption (not peculiar to America) that the obtaining of a diploma from law school should qualify the recipient to argue his client's case in court, and in a particularly telling phrase he described the result as "'Piper Cub' advocates trying to handle . . . 'Boeing 747' litigation."[3]

A few weeks after the Chief Justice had delivered this lecture, his motion received a seconder, as it were, from no less an authority than Judge Kaufman.[4] Speaking at a dinner of the New York County Lawyers Association, Judge Kaufman referred to the vast increase in caseloads which had occurred in recent years, and said that as a result "it will be tempting for lawyers to expend less effort and do their jobs less skillfully than before, relying on judges to put in the extra finishing touches necessary to get the result as perfect as it formerly was. In short, there is a natural inclination to have judges do lawyer's [*sic*] work."[5]

In that last remark, Judge Kaufman surely puts his finger on one of the root causes of disquiet about the conduct of litigation at the present day. Trial lawyers (including for present purposes those who assist the advocate in preparing his case) are invariably overworked. Some are nevertheless able, by taxing their own strength, to maintain their standards, and do so. Others lack the ability or the dedication to do this, and insufficiently prepared cases are the inevitable result.

Where this occurs, the judge himself is in a dilemma. Many of my predecessors in England would have found no difficulty. They would have thrown the case back at the advocate and told him to go away and do better. Judges do not do that today; they have too much concern for the lay client who is in danger of being let down by his lawyer, and too much concern for the image of justice to have an open confrontation of this kind.

1. Address by Chief Justice Warren Burger, Fourth Annual John F. Sonnett Memorial Lecture, Fordham University School of Law, Nov. 26, 1973.

2. Burger, *The Special Skills of Advocacy: Are Specialized Training and Certification of Advocates Essential to Our System of Justice?*, 42 FORDHAM L. REV. 227 (1973).

3. *Id.* at 232.

4. *See* 170 N.Y.L.J., Dec. 7, 1973, at 5, col. 1. *See also* Kaufman, *Advocacy as Craft-There is More to Law School than a "Paper Chase,"* 28 Sw. L.J. 495 (1974).

5. 170 N.Y.L.J., Dec. 7, 1973, at 5, col. 2.

Instead, as Judge Kaufman claims, the judge will do his best to make good the deficiencies of the advocate's presentation.[6]

We all suffer from this. In England in the last few years, we have built up somewhat complex rules governing the admission for settlement in England of citizens from the old Commonwealth, for example, from India and Pakistan.[7] The resulting litigation normally comes to my Court, and I have had no choice but to learn these rules. This is not so for lawyers who have not been concerned with this type of business. The other day a charming young man arose in my Court to move for habeas corpus on behalf of an Indian who had been refused admission to England and had been detained at Heathrow Airport. With commendable frankness, the young man said, "My Lord, I have been endeavoring since my client's arrest yesterday to discover the relevant statutes and decisions which govern his case. I have not succeeded in doing this in the time available but I know that Your Lordship is expert in this subject and will not require assistance on the law from me." What can we do? I told him the answer and disposed of the case, but only a few years ago, no counsel would have dared to make such an approach, and would literally have stayed up all night to find the answer for himself. That the bench should have to help out occasionally may not be too serious a matter, but the quality of the product is bound to suffer if there is any general tendency to rely on the judge to make good counsel's deficiencies.

I recollect another example of this kind of thing that may entertain you. When in 1898, an accused man was first allowed to give evidence on his own behalf, the statute provided that if he took advantage of that right, he could not be asked questions tending to show that he was of bad character, unless he had attacked the character of a witness for the prosecution.[8] It follows that where a defendant has a bad record, his counsel is inhibited from suggesting that a police witness has been fraudulent, or planted evidence, lest this will let in a boomerang in the shape of evidence of the defendant's own bad character.

At the particular trial to which I refer, a young woman barrister was defending a man with a criminal record as long as your arm. He had, nevertheless, instructed his counsel that on the present occasion he had been the victim of a wicked plant by the police witness. Convinced of her client's innocence, and warming to her work, Miss *X* was cross-examining the first police witness. The trial judge was soon alerted to what was taking place. He could see that the allegation of a plant was only a few questions away, and, knowing the prisoner's record, he realized that a tactical disaster was imminent. He cleared his throat: "Miss *X*, do you really want to pursue this line of questioning?" "Of course, My Lord," said Miss *X*. "Don't you think you have gone as far as you can usefully go?" "Not at all, My Lord," said Miss *X*. The judge leaned forward in his seat. "Miss *X*, be so good as to look at paragraph 1529 of Archbold[9] (this is our standard textbook on criminal procedure) and read it quietly to yourself," said the judge. With ill-concealed impatience Miss

6. *Id.* at 5, cols. 2–3. Judge Kaufman points out, however, that judicial assumption of the advocate's role "will be at the expense of practicing [the] craft of judging." *Id.* at 5, col. 3.

7. *See* Immigration Act 1971, c. 77.

8. Criminal Evidence Act of 1898, 61 & 62 Vict. 35, c. 36, § 1(f)(ii).

9. J. Archbold, Pleading, Evidence & Practice in Criminal Cases (38th ed. 1973).

X looked at the paragraph in question. And then her face lit up, a dazzling smile for the judge, and a simple summation of it all: "Oh, silly me," said Miss X.

It was after having had this kind of experience himself and having heard the views expressed by the Chief Justice, that Judge Kaufman suggested that there should be a continuing dialogue within the legal profession to see in what ways, and by what means, the standard of advocacy could be improved.[10] I hope that which I say tonight may help that dialogue along.

But there is already another contestant in the list. Chief Justice Burger had mentioned certain respects in which he thought that the British system produced a better trial lawyer than did the American,[11] and this has inspired Dean Monroe H. Freedman to publish a paper in the *New York Law Journal* under the heading of "The Myth of British Superiority."[12] I have been generously told that I may comment on this paper either as advocate or arbitrator, but I am going to resist that temptation. The dialogue that I wish to join is that which is concerned with improving the standard of the trial lawyer. It would be strange if, at this stage in our respective developments, the British system were not superior to the American in certain respects, and vice versa. It is where we can learn from each other that a useful dialogue begins.

I would like to turn now to consider what are the essential characteristics that the trial lawyer should display, and how far we can encourage and develop these characteristics.

I suggest that there are four of these characteristics. First, like any other attorney, the trial lawyer must be learned in the law. Second, he must know the ground rules which govern the litigation game—that is to say, he must know the rules of evidence and procedure, and use them with the craftsman's touch which only experience can give. Third, he must be independent in mind and in fact, he must be able to do what his conscience tells him is right without fear of antagonizing the court or being overborne by his client. Finally, he must have integrity in the pursuit of justice, recognizing his responsibility to the court and his opponent, and rejecting alike the desire to win at all costs and the temptation to take an unfair advantage of such pieces of forensic luck that come his way.

That an advocate must be learned in the law is obvious, but it is idle to suppose that he can have the accumulated learning of a university professor, or that such knowledge would be of practical value if he possessed it. The practitioner in the law needs a sound knowledge of first principles. With this he can go anywhere, using the books to amplify his knowledge of the particular subject in the particular case. I believe that in America the method of implanting this basic knowledge is a three years' course at a law school, and this is a method now widely adopted in England as well. But in England we have had for many years a traditional alternative in the form of apprenticeship. Until recently, the majority of those wishing to become solicitors in England have entered into a five years' apprenticeship with a practicing solicitor. They have worked in the office of the principal,

10. 170 N.Y.L.J., Dec. 7, 1973, at 5, col. 1.

11. Burger, *The Special Skills of Advocacy: Are Specialized Training and Certification of Advocates Essential to Our System of Justice?*, 42 Fordham L. Rev. 227, 228 (1973).

12. Freedman, *The Myth of British Superiority*, 172 N.Y.L.J., Aug. 28. 1974. at 1, col. I.

picking up law and practical experience as they go.[13] It has, of course, long been recognized that this is too haphazard a method for providing the new entrant with a balanced knowledge of the substantive law, and apprenticeship has always been coupled with a system of written examinations for which the entrant could prepare himself in his own way, with or without professional teaching. It is common enough in England today to find solicitors of distinction who have had virtually no formal teaching in the law but have qualified by serving their apprenticeship and studying the books in their spare time so as to be able to pass the written professional examinations.

But tonight we are concerned with trial lawyers, which, in English terms, means that we are thinking of English barristers rather than English solicitors. Most barristers do attend a full three-years' university course, but the obtaining of a degree is not an automatic license to practice because for this purpose a further examination, set by the authorities controlling the practicing bar, must also be passed. It is as though a graduate from Fordham were required to take a further examination set by the American Bar Association. The reason for this is that the university graduate may have read law for two years, or only for one, or, indeed, may have read no law at all. The purpose of the professional examination is to ensure that either by formal teaching or private study he has acquired the necessary basic knowledge of the substantive law.

In recent years our thinking on this subject has been moving markedly towards your own, and it is now generally accepted that the right place to read law is in a law school and that satisfactory completion of the prescribed course should suffice to qualify the candidate so far as his basic, theoretical knowledge is concerned.[14] We have been slow to come to this view because until thirty years ago entry to the universities was largely restricted to the comparatively well-to-do, and the bar would have been the loser if we had excluded those who studied in a garret with a candle and meanwhile washed dishes as a means of livelihood. The first requisite, then, for an effective corps of trial lawyers is that our law schools and universities should be open to suitable entrants without prohibitive economic obstacles.

What sort of syllabus is required for this basic legal training? As I have already said, the object, in my opinion, must be to instill a really sound knowledge of first principles, and it is a waste of time to do more. In my experience those principles will provide the answer in nine cases out of ten, and we must give the student confidence that this is so, and not allow him to think that a simple dispute arising out of the sale of goods really requires a week's research into the opinions handed down by the Supreme Court of the United States.

Herein lies a danger touched upon by Judge Kaufman when he describes the three-year students as spending their time reading appellate decisions.[15] Given a small chance, this is

13. *See* T. DANIELL, INNS OF COURT (1972). *See also* A. Green, *Bibliography on British Legal Education* (West Chester State College, Dep't of Business and Economics, Research Paper No. I, 1973).

14. *See* SWEET & MAXWELL'S GUIDE TO A CAREER IN THE LAW 69–81 (7th ed. 1971). *See also* A. Green, *supra* note 13.

15. 170 N.Y.L.J., Dec. 7, 1973, at 5, cols. 4–5.

exactly what they will do. Arguing abstruse points of law is as good a mental exercise as you will find, but if a young man can spare three years of his time to attend a university, he can surely find time for other disciplines as well.

The story is told of a distinguished lawyer whose bookshelves in his chambers were full of works of history and English literature. Asked why this should be so, he replied that these were the textbooks to the study of life, and that no lawyer could meet the requirements of his profession without consulting these sources. Without history and literature, said the sage, a lawyer is a mere mechanic. Only by a study of these works can he become a craftsman. In planning the education of our embryo trial lawyer, should we not see that he learns something about the people whom the law is to serve, and that he does not forget that in dedicating himself to a life in the law he is also dedicating himself to the people who depend upon him?

When our potential trial lawyer emerges from his university or law school, the next requirement is that he should be taught the practical skills upon which his livelihood will depend. In other words, he must gain experience. This is, perhaps, the most difficult operation of all.

I think that we can begin by taking a close look at the profession of medicine to see how the doctors deal with this sort of problem. The transition from student to practitioner is certainly as great in medicine as it is in advocacy, and we must admire the medical profession for the way in which it introduces the young man or woman to real patients with a minimum of disaster. How is it done?

First, the overall period of training is much longer than ours. This is inevitable because the doctor, unlike the lawyer, cannot rely on a knowledge of first principles, supplemented by reference to books from time to time. All too often the doctor has to act at once, and he must have a wider and deeper knowledge of his subject than we achieve. We have to accept the fact that three years' study is now a maximum.

Second, medical schools tend to be closely integrated with the hospitals themselves, and are often contained in the same ring fence. The students have a sense of belonging to the hospital from the beginning, and they see the famous consultants and leaders of the profession walking about in their midst. More important still, from a comparatively early stage the student walks the wards in company of the great men to watch them at work, and either at the bedside or on leaving the ward the consultant requires the student to make a diagnosis and suggest treatment, and he is roundly corrected if he gets it wrong. This is practical training at its optimum because it is the real thing done with real people by a teacher who is acknowledged to be in the top class as a *practitioner*, and, not least, there is a sense of fraternity which links all together as part of "our hospital." Actual contact with sick people creates a sense of urgency and reality, which is lacking in the law library.

Third, when the advanced student is fit to begin to treat patients there will always be other doctors about who can keep an eye on him and to whom he can turn. He will not find himself standing alone in the middle of a courtroom like a matador facing his first bull and probably profoundly wishing that he had taken his father's advice to become an automobile salesman.

There is much here for us to learn if we set our minds to it.

It so happens that the layout of legal London gives the bar an opportunity to organize itself on the lines of a large teaching hospital. Many of you will have the scene in your own minds. In the Strand[16] we have the Royal Courts of Justice with some fifty courtrooms, which house the appellate courts and provide for the judges who are trying the heavy civil work which arises in the southern half of England. A mile away we have the Old Bailey with twenty-two courtrooms, which deal with the serious criminal cases from the greater London area. In between we have the four Inns of Court,[17] which, if I may be allowed to say so, are areas of considerable charm and which are the home of the bar. These contain both the offices (or chambers) from which the barristers carry on their practice and also the main law libraries. There are also halls in which bench and bar meet at lunch and dinner and from which the profession is controlled.[18] The analogy with medicine is clear. The two main court buildings are the hospital, and the Inns of Court are the medical school. The whole area is steeped in the law, and talking lawyers' shop is a basic recreation. Nor is this dialogue confined to students talking with students, or judges with judges. In chambers, at lunch, and in the library, bench and bar, senior and junior, meet as members of one family, and teach each other the standards, the etiquette and the code of behavior which the bar has always adopted. The groundwork for this was laid more than a century ago when the would-be barrister was first required to "eat his dinners" before he could qualify.[19] The requirement is maintained to the present day, and literally obliges the student to dine in the hall of his Inn on a specified number of occasions.[20] Some of our friends poke fun at us for maintaining this ritual, and they may be right, but the Inns must not be dismissed as mere dining clubs. They hum with activity all through the working day, and it is beyond doubt that what Chief Justice Burger describes as the ethics, manners, and deportment of the English bar are produced and nurtured in the fraternal atmosphere of the Inns.[21] I cannot put it better than in the words of a distinguished judge (Mr. Justice Hilbery) who—when asked how one who intended coming into the profession might discover where this code of conduct was to be found, and how it was to be learnt—said: "The answer to the first question is in the traditions of the profession. The answer to the second is in the Schools of the profession, its ancient craft guilds, called the Inns of

16. *See* F. Morrison, Courts and the Political Process in England 37–57 (1973). For a topographical sketch illustrating the proximity of the Law Courts, Old Bailey, and the Inns of Court, see R. Megarry, Inns Ancient and Modern, frontispiece (1972).

17. The four Inns of Court are Lincoln's Inn, The Inner Temple, The Middle Temple and Gray's Inn. H. Hanbury, English Courts of Law 140–41 (4th ed. 1967).

18. *See* R. Jackson, The Machinery of Justice in England 329–35 (6th ed. 1972). *See also* H. Hanbury, English Courts of Law 140–41 (4th ed. 1967); F. Morrison, Courts and the Political Process in England 60–61 (1973).

19. F. Morrison, Courts and the Political Process in England 60 (1973); *see* Cowper, *The Inns of Court-Lincoln's Inn*, 1 Anglo-Am. L. Rev. 537, 542 (1972).

20. The Consolidated Regulations of the Honourable Societies of Lincoln's Inn. The Inner Temple, The Middle Temple and Gray's Inn (1970).

21. *See* Burger, *The Specialized Skills of Advocacy: Are Specialized Training and Certification of Advocates Essential to Our System of Justice?*, 42 Fordham L. Rev. 227, 229–30 (1973).

Court, where all matters of professional conduct are freely and daily discussed, and where the transgressor is answerable for his misconduct."[22]

Although the concentration of the courts, bench, and bar into an area little more than one square mile has given us great opportunities to teach advocacy, we have been slow to take advantage of them. Until the end of World War II the English bar merited many of Professor Freedman's strictures. It was a profession in which family and social class counted for more than they should, and above all where money mattered since a newly called barrister might have to wait for years before he acquired a practice big enough to support him. It did, however, have the advantage that, during these years of waiting, the barrister would be in the courts and in chambers every day "devilling," as it is called, for other and more senior barristers. He would thus get experience in looking up the law, reading the case papers, and sitting beside the senior barrister in court while the case was conducted. Five or six years of this meant that when his own work began to flow in he was well prepared for it.

In the last twenty years, we have seen great changes. The amount of work for the bar has increased by over 50 percent, and a young man who is any good at all can make a living in his first year and enjoy a sharply rising income thereafter.[23] Here lies the danger—it is all too easy—we can no longer rely on competition to drive out the inadequate, and we have been forced to provide organized instruction in the professional skills of the advocate.

In doing this we have again drawn upon the experience of the teaching hospitals. I feel very strongly that the duty to train the new entrant in the skill and traditions of our profession is a duty which falls on the profession as a whole and, in particular, that it is one from which the judges cannot claim exemption.

Therefore, in addition to the moot and mock trials, which have a purpose limited by their lack of reality, we try to take our advanced students round the courts to take as active a part as possible in real-life litigation. They can read the pleadings, follow the argument, and, when the case is over, meet the judge in his room and discuss the points of the case as seen through the judge's eyes. It is, of course, imperative that the student should hear the case from start to finish. Looking in from time to time is worse than useless.

I must come in a moment to a consideration of the remaining characteristics of the compleat trial lawyer, but before I do so may I briefly return once more to the analogy of the medical profession. We have in England a legal profession that is divided into barristers and solicitors. There are 3,000-odd barristers and 25,000-odd solicitors.[24] The relevance of this for present purposes is merely that since all the trial lawyers properly so called are barristers, they are all part of the relatively small community based on the Inns of Court which I have endeavored to describe.

22. M. Hilbery, Duty and Art in Advocacy 7 (1946).

23. For a discussion of the increase and its effect on the legal profession, see R. Jackson, The Machinery of Justice in England 341–43 (6th ed. 1972).

24. Zander, *English Legal Aid System at the Crossroads*, 59 A.B.A.J. 368 (1973).

Although I am wholly committed to the view that this division of the profession is beneficial in a small and highly populated island like England, I would not like to mislead you into thinking that everybody at home shares this view. On the contrary, no year passes without someone writing to the newspapers advocating the "fusion," as it is called, of the two parts of the profession, and thus provoking others to write to extol the virtues of the status quo.[25] Dean Freedman has joined the "fusionists," and adopts, amongst other arguments, the contention that our system is wasteful because a barrister cannot be directly instructed by the client, who must approach him through a solicitor. "[T]wo lawyers for one . . . litigation,"[26] thunders the Dean—but is this really so? Look back for a moment at the doctors.

Doctors are divided into general practitioners and consultants. If you are unwell you go to your general practitioner, and if he cannot treat you adequately he sends you to a consultant who specializes in your particular malady. In the end, you pay two doctors, but is this wasteful? How could you have diagnosed your complaint, and selected the specialist, without the assistance of the general practitioner?

When applied to the English legal profession, this analogy is absolute. The solicitors are the general practitioners, and the barristers the specialist consultants. The principal specialty is advocacy, but there are barristers specializing in corporation law, antitrust law, family law, and land transfer, to name only a few. This means a client who has a particularly abstruse or difficult problem can take it to any solicitor in the country with the knowledge that he can thereby be put in touch with the top man practicing in that line. This is not wasteful duplication, but a means of ensuring that the client has prompt access to the advice most suited to his problem, and, moreover, has all the experts in the country to choose from.

But now I really must return to the remaining qualities that are essential in the compleat advocate. I can put them into two words—independence and integrity.

These last are qualities of mind and character, which cannot be taught or manufactured. Their seeds are sown in childhood and, indeed, they may be partially hereditary, but their development can be immensely influenced by environment and example.

It is no mere coincidence that these are also qualities required of the bench. Indeed, it is idle to suppose that we can have an independent bar without an independent bench, and in our search for the ideal environment in which to produce the compleat trial lawyer we must not ignore the methods of selecting and appointing judges.

I do not find it easy to contemplate the appointment of a judge who is not already an experienced trial lawyer. There are many men on both sides of the Atlantic who have a generous endowment of the necessary intellect and temperament for judicial office, but unless they have actually tried cases at the bar they cannot know the tricks of the trade. When I emerged nervously to take my seat on the bench for the first time, I was sustained

25. *See, e.g.*, Q. JOHNSTONE & D. HOPSON, LAWYERS AND THEIR WORK 385–98 (1967); Lawlon, *The Role of the Advocate in English Society*, 22 OKLA. L. REV. 396, 413–20 (1969). *See also* Boulton, *The Barrister. Advocate at the English Bar*, 57 A.B.A.J. 255, 258 (1971).

26. Freedman, *The Myth of British Superiority*, 172 N.Y.L.J., Aug. 28, 1974, at 3, col. 2.

by the knowledge that I would not have been considered for the appointment had I not first established myself as a trial lawyer in fair competition with those who were now to appear before me. The advocate who loses a case is always ready to blame the judge, and there is no more stinging criticism than that the judge is not really a professional in his courtroom. No advocate will be tempted to pull a fast one if he knows that the judge is at least his equal in the craft.

If I am right in this premise, and proficiency as an advocate should be regarded as a necessary qualification for judicial office, it follows that the machinery of appointment must somehow provide for the voice of the profession to be heard.

In England, this is easily arranged. Although new High Court judges are nominally appointed by the Queen, the appointment is made on the advice of the Lord Chancellor,[27] who is both a politician and a leading lawyer. Years ago, politics, family, class, or "knowing the right people" may have played an undue part in the Lord Chancellor's choice, but this is not so today. Successive Lord Chancellors have made it clear that the sole criterion is "who is the best man for the job," and if the Lord Chancellor wants advice on this subject he can consult senior judges and senior members of the bar. Indeed, when a vacancy occurs, informal gossip in the Inns of Court will soon narrow the likely choice down to two or three names, and the Lord Chancellor will be well aware of this. It is still true that a majority of our eighty-odd High Court judges come from the middle class and were educated at schools which you sensibly call "private," and we confusingly call "public," but they include the sons of a miner, prison officer, and a trade unionist, to mention only a few.

I believe that in recent years the American Bar Association has increased its influence over the making of judicial appointments,[28] and if this is so I would regard it as a matter for congratulation. The bench would become hopelessly inbred if judicial appointments depended on the profession alone, but it is neither fair to the appointee, nor conducive to seeing justice done, if no regard is paid to the professional standing of the appointee amongst his peers.

In the matters upon which I have touched so far, I do not believe that there is any fundamental difference between the views of an American lawyer and those of an English barrister. Each is seeking the same ends, and the differing means to those ends have been dictated by considerations of politics, history, and geography. It is when we come to the attitude of the bar toward its potential clients that we find deep and significant differences. I approach this part of the subject with hesitation and, I hope, with due humility because it is hardly credible that in these matters either of us should be wholly right, and the other wholly wrong. If, on another occasion, an opportunity is found to continue our dialogue, these are matters suitable for a study in depth. They certainly go to the root of the independence and integrity of the bar, and in England they are expressed in rules, which are treated with a reverence normally reserved for the Holy Writ.

27. R. Jackson, The Machinery of Justice in England 365, 367 (6th ed. 1972).
28. J. Grossman, Lawyers and Judges 49–81 (1965).

It is a constant source of amazement to us that you manage perfectly well without them. These are the rules:

> First. The trial lawyer must be remunerated by a fee which is fixed in advance, and is entirely independent of the outcome of the litigation. His written instructions for the case must be legibly endorsed with the amount of the agreed fee, and it is a serious professional offence to go into court with papers not so marked.
>
> Second. The trial lawyer cannot pick his clients. If he is invited to undertake a case within the field in which he holds himself out to practice, and he is paid an appropriate fee, he *must* take the case, however much he dislikes his client, and whatever his revulsions to his task.

The former rule is designed to prevent the trial lawyer from being personally involved in the outcome of the case, and to give him the sense of detachment without which we think it difficult for him to recognize his duty to the court, as well as his duty to his client. Of course, every trial lawyer wants to win. His reputation is built on success, but the temptation to win at any price must surely be increased if he has a financial stake in the result. The fact that you manage perfectly well without imposing this restriction is of great interest at the present time because it means that in this country a plaintiff with a good case should never lack a lawyer prepared to act for him on a contingency basis. In England, an indigent plaintiff who is not allowed to offer his lawyer a share of the spoils must look to the free legal aid system to pay his lawyer's fee, and although this often provides a satisfactory answer, it does not always do so.

The rule that a lawyer cannot pick his client is sometimes called the "cab rank" rule.[29] A taxi driver plying for hire must take any commission that is offered to him, and so must the trial lawyer. The purpose of the rule is, of course, to ensure that a person is not denied the advantage of legal representation merely because of his personal unpopularity or his bad reputation. It is for the court to decide the defendant's guilt, and this decision is not to be preempted by a refusal of the bar to act for him. The classic dictum on this point comes from Lord Erskine,[30] who, when at the bar, accepted the defense of the notorious Tom Paine[31] and was mercilessly criticized by public opinion for having done so. When the trial began Erskine put his views beyond doubt. He said:

> I will forever, at all hazards, assert the dignity, independence, and integrity of the English bar, without which impartial justice, the most valuable part of the English constitution, can have no existence. From the moment that any advocate can be permitted to say that he will or will not stand between the Crown and the subject arraigned in the court where he daily sits to practice, from that moment the liberties of England are at an end. If the advocate refuses to defend from what he may think of the charge or of the defense, he assumes the character of the judge; nay, he assumes it before the hour of judgment; and in

29. R. Jackson, The Machinery of Justice in England 360 (6th ed. 1972).

30. For a biography of Thomas Erskine, see L. Stryker, For the Defense (1947).

31. Lord Erskine defended Thomas Paine in a libel action arising out of the publication of "Rights of Man." *See* The Trial of Thomas Paine (1792).

> proportion to his rank and reputation, puts the heavy influence of perhaps a mistaken opinion into the scale against the accused, in whose favor the benevolent principle of English law makes all presumptions, and which commands the very judge to be his counsel.[32]

These are strong words and, no doubt, they contain an element of exaggeration. They represent the pent-up feelings of a man who had been widely criticized, and who was grasping an opportunity to justify himself. I would not put the case in those terms today, but the point remains a valid one, at all events, when applied to conditions prevailing in England. You will know, I expect, that we have just completed, or have pending, a large number of trials in which the accused are charged with killing by explosives planted in the supposed interests of the Irish Republican Army. One may well ask what would happen to these defendants in the absence of the "cab-rank" principles. Could the bar turn its back on them because of its revulsion against such activities, and allow them to go undefended? This is surely unthinkable. Nor is a solution to be found by leaving them in the hands of those members of the bar who may have sympathy with their cause, because even if sufficient counsel were to be found on that basis, they would lack the detachment which seems to us to be so important.

One interesting by-product of the "cab-rank" rule is that our trial lawyers do not associate themselves exclusively with prosecution or with defense, but tend to appear for either side according to the instructions that they receive. I think that on the whole this is a good thing, which broadens the advocate's outlook, makes him more conscious of the difficulty of the other side, and gives him a more responsible attitude to the work of the courts. I know that Professor Freedman found room for criticism here because he says that counsel appearing for defendants tend to pull their punches lest they antagonize the prosecution authorities and get no more work from that quarter.[33] This, I confess, is a new one on me, and I am not persuaded that it is true. After all, any experienced trial lawyer knows that the best way to get a new client is to give him a good drubbing in a case where he is represented by someone else. A young man who makes his mark when defending will be the more sought after by the prosecution. It is all summed up in the adage, "If you can't lick 'em, join 'em."

If I may attempt to summarize my contribution to our dialogue, I would put it thusly: The quality of the trial lawyer is not primarily dependent on his basic training in law school, or on his having an exceptionally high intelligence quotient. The essential requirements are discipline and dedication. The means by which these qualities are nurtured will vary enormously with local conditions, but the one indispensable teacher is the example set by senior members of the profession. The burden upon us as senior members of the profession is enormous, but so is the prize to be won.

May we continue to pursue it together.

32. L. Stryker, For the Defense 217 (1947), quoting Lord Erskine.

33. Freedman, *The Myth of British Superiority*, 172 N.Y.L.J., Aug. 28, 1974, at 3, col. 2.

Minnesota Plan: Mandatory Continuing Legal Education for Lawyers and Judges as a Condition for the Maintaining of Professional Licensing

Hon. Robert J. Sheran and Laurence C. Harmon

On December 9, 1975, Minnesota Chief Justice Robert Sheran delivered the sixth Sonnett lecture focusing his remarks on Minnesota's decision to become the first state to require continuing legal education for all Minnesota-licensed attorneys and judges.[1] A Minnesota native, Chief Justice Sheran graduated in 1936 from St. Thomas College,[2] where he was a national debate champion.[3] He earned his L.L.B. from the University of Minnesota Law School in 1939,[4] and had an accomplished career in both public service and private practice prior to his appointment to the bench. During World War II, Chief Justice Sheran was an FBI special agent, guarding secrets of the Manhattan Project, and from 1947 until 1949, he served in the Minnesota House of Representatives.[5] In private practice, Chief Justice Sheran was a trial lawyer with the firm Gallagher, Farrish, Sheran & Zimmerman in Mankato, Minnesota, and later with Lindquist & Vennum PLLP in Minneapolis.[6] From 1993 to 1994, Chief Justice Sheran served as the interim dean of Hamline University School of Law in St. Paul.[7]

A member of Minnesota's Democratic Farmer-Labor Party (DFL), Chief Justice Sheran was first appointed as an Associate Justice to the Supreme Court of the State of Minnesota by Republican Governor Elmer L. Andersen in 1963.[8] In his memoir, Governor Andersen recounts how he "took the heat" from his party for appointing a DFLer to the court, while also praising Sheran as "one of the most notable jurists in state history."[9]

At the time of his appointment, Supreme Court justices received a salary of approximately $20,000 per year.[10] With five children to put through college, then-Justice Sheran

Introduction written by Molly Ryan, J.D., Class of 2015, Fordham University School of Law.

1. Robert J. Sheran, *Minnesota Plan: Mandatory Continuing Legal Education for Lawyers and Judges as a Condition for the Maintaining of Professional Licensing*, 44 Fordham L. Rev. 1081 (1976).

2. *Legislators Past & Present: Sheran, Robert J.*, Minn. Legis. Ref. Libr., http://www.leg.state.mn.us/legdb/fulldetail.aspx?ID=14766#otherinfo (last visited Mar. 30, 2014).

3. Abby Simons, *Brilliant Jurist Remembered as a Great Listener*, Star Trib., Jan. 27, 2012, at B1.

4. *Legislators Past & Present*, *supra* note 2.

5. *Id.*

6. Obituary, *Sheran, Former Chief Justice Robert J*, Star Trib., Jan. 27, 2012, at B5.

7. *Id.*

8. Elmer L. Andersen, A Man's Reach 222–23 (Lori Sturdevant ed. 2000).

9. *Id.*

10. Simons, *supra* note 3, at B5.

left the bench in 1970.[11] DFL Governor Wendell Andersen subsequently appointed him Chief Justice in 1973, a decision Andersen later described as his "best appointment."[12]

Governor Andersen remarked that as Chief Justice, "Sheran made a lasting mark not only with the quality of his decisions but with his efforts to improve the court system. He was instrumental in establishing commissions to set judicial salaries, review proposed code of judicial conduct, and recruit top candidates for the bench."[13]

Perhaps most notably, the Supreme Court of Minnesota approved, under Chief Justice Sheran's leadership, a program that instituted the first mandatory continuing legal education requirement for all licensed attorneys.[14] Nearly every other state since has followed Minnesota's lead.[15]

In his Sonnett lecture, Chief Justice Sheran emphasized the rapid pace of change in the law and the need for the profession to fulfill the Code of Professional Responsibility's call for lawyers to represent their clients competently.[16] Such concerns remain no less salient today.

This article substantially embodies the text of the sixth Annual John F. Sonnett Memorial Lecture delivered by Chief Justice Sheran at the Fordham University School of Law on December 9, 1975. For the sake of editorial convenience, the first-person singular has been retained. However, the text of the article is the joint work of the authors. The authors wish to thank Timothy Baland, Law Clerk to the Chief Justice during 1975–76, for his assistance in the preparation of this article.

1976 Sonnett Lecture

On April 3, 1975, the Supreme Court of Minnesota approved a program that requires all licensed attorneys and judges in the state to complete forty-five hours of postgraduate legal education every three years.[1] Why did we take this action? How is our plan set up? How is

11. *Id.*
12. *Id.*
13. Andersen, *supra* note 8, at 223.
14. *See generally* Sheran, *supra* note 1.
15. *See* Mandatory CLE Information by Jurisdiction, A.B.A., http://www.americanbar.org/cle/mandatory_cle/mcle_states.html (last visited Mar. 30, 2014).
16. Sheran, *supra* note 1, at 1083–83.

1. The Order of Promulgation reads as follows:

"IT IS HEREBY ORDERED, that the attached Rules for continuing professional education of lawyers admitted to practice in Minnesota are adopted, and shall be distributed to the attorneys and judiciary of this state, to be effective immediately.

IT IS HEREBY ORDERED, that the Board of Continuing Legal Education shall classify, by lot, the attorneys and judges presently licensed in the State of Minnesota in three classifications of substantially equal size, for purposes of administration of and compliance with the said Rules. The first class shall complete fifteen (15) hours of approved legal study between the dates of July 1, 1974 and June 30, 1976, inclusive. The second class shall complete thirty (30) hours of approved legal

it working so far? Questions like these need to be answered. Since Minnesota was the first state to make continuing legal education mandatory, and since other states are considering similar proposals, I welcome this opportunity to explain the origins and operation of the Minnesota Plan.

INTEREST IN MANDATORY CONTINUING LEGAL EDUCATION: NATIONAL TRENDS AND FACTORS

In recent years, a number of factors have come together to raise the issue of the postadmission competence of attorneys. Traditional wisdom tells us that a lawyer's time is his stock in trade. This maxim is true, as far as it goes, but today's attorney needs to offer both society and his clients more than his time in order to deserve the title "Counselor at Law." To serve his clients adequately, a lawyer must be able to apply specialized knowledge in a skillful and effective way. Since the law changes constantly, this is not an easy task. In Minnesota, the more highly motivated and conscientious lawyers have traditionally availed themselves of voluntary continuing legal education (CLE) course offerings and other means of keeping current. For these attorneys, the advent of mandatory CLE simply formalizes practices that had previously been self-imposed. For attorneys whose skills have been eroded by time, or those who have not stayed up to date, mandatory CLE provides the incentive for doing what the times so clearly require.[2]

I mentioned that the law changes constantly. One can name almost any field of law and point to significant developments that have occurred in the last decade. For example, we now have no-fault auto insurance and fault-free divorce in many states.[3] Criminal law and procedure are hardly what they were ten years ago; in both tax and bankruptcy law, major changes appear imminent.[4]

---

study between the dates of July 1, 1974 and June 30, 1977, inclusive. The third class shall complete forty-five (45) hours of approved legal study between the dates of July 1, 1974 and June 30, 1978. After the first period, each class shall complete the prescribed educational requirements during successive three-year periods." Rules Relating to Continuing Professional Education, Supreme Court of the State of Minnesota, no. 45298, Order of Promulgation (April 3, 1975) [hereinafter cited as April 3d Order].

Our order sparked some interesting media commentary. *See* NEWSWEEK, Jan. 12, 1976, at 71; Kurland, *Polishing the Bar*, N.Y. TIMES, Apr. 24, 1975, at 35, col. 1; Oelsner, *Decision on Schooling for Lawyers Raises Broad Questions on Competence of the Profession*, N.Y. TIMES, Apr. 8, 1975, at 19, col. 2; Oelsner, *Back-to-School Plan Weighed for Lawyers*, N.Y. TIMES, Apr. 2, 1975, at 1, col. 1.

2. While Minnesota is the first state to require continuing education for attorneys, at least ten states have made continuing education a condition of relicensing for their physicians. N.Y. TIMES, Jan. 29, 1976, at 24, col. 5.

3. At least twenty states have no-fault auto insurance. Comment, *No-Fault Automobile Insurance*, 23 U. KAN. L. REV. 141 (1974). For a recent state-by-state analysis of divorce laws, see Freed, *Grounds for Divorce in American Jurisdictions (as of June 1, 1974)*, 8 FAM. L.Q. 401 (1974).

4. The scope and dimension of the changes which have taken place in the last fifteen years in criminal law and procedure are summarized in BUREAU OF NATIONAL AFFAIRS, THE CRIMINAL LAW REVOLUTION AND ITS AFTERMATH: 1960–1972 (1973). Tax law changes are discussed in *Symposium:*

That change occurs constantly can also be statistically established. Consider these figures: in 1930, the U.S. Code contained three and one-half million words; today it contains twenty million words. In the last bi-annual session of the California Legislature (1967), 1,725 laws were enacted. In the 1973–74 annual sessions, the California Legislature produced 2,825 new laws. In Minnesota's last bi-annual session, 966 laws were passed; from 1973 to 1974, the number jumped to 1,365. Similar increases have occurred in the number of reported court decisions. In 1965, the West Publishing Company printed 208 Minnesota Supreme Court decisions. Last year, 381 decisions appeared. For all volumes in the West system, state and federal, just over 28,000 decisions were reported in 1965; by last year, the number had risen to 40,847.[5]

Ethical Consideration 6-1 of the Code of Professional Responsibility states that the lawyer "should strive to become and remain proficient in his practice and should accept employment only in matters which he is or intends to become competent to handle."[6] When one combines this precept with change of the magnitude just described, the conclusion is inescapable that some formal program of postadmission education is vitally important to the law's continued credibility as a learned profession. Additionally, unless the judicial system serves its functions adequately, others will act in our stead. In 1971, for example, a resolution was introduced in the California Senate calling for continuing education of professionals in various fields.[7] There have been similar legislative rumblings in Minnesota,[8] and Minnesota and California are hardly unique in this respect.

The need for attorney postadmission education programs has, in short, become self-evident. No one seriously suggests that our law schools—now training over one hundred thousand new attorneys[9]—can meet this need. While law school training is satisfactory for its purposes, the specific skills needed to serve the practical requirements of clients are, for the most part, learned "on the job," after admission to the bar. And the fact that we need to do a better job with our postadmission educational programs, or at least extend

Federal Tax Reform, 26 NAT. TAX J. 309 (1973) and Freeman & Baland, *The Rich Get Richer and the Poor Get Taxes: Toward a Democratic Theory of Tax Reform*, 2 HAST. CONST. L.Q. 681 (1975). Proposed changes in the Federal bankruptcy laws are now pending before Congress and have been the subject of thorough study. *See* Report of the Commission on the Bankruptcy Laws of the United States, H.R Doc. No. 137, 93d Cong., 1st Sess. (1973).

5. The statistics in this paragraph were provided by West Publishing Co., St. Paul, Minnesota.

6. ABA Code of Professional Responsibility EC 6-1 (1975).

7. Calif. S. Res. No. 211, introduced in the California Senate on October 18, 1971, by Senator George Deukmejian.

8. Between February and May 1975, eleven bills affecting the legal profession were introduced in the Minnesota State Legislature. *See* the recommendations and report of the Commission on Legal Services, Minnesota State Bar Association, Oct. 4, 1975, 32 BENCH AND BAR OF MINNESOTA no. 4, 21–23 (Oct. 1975).

9. 110,713 students were enrolled in ABA-approved law schools in the fall of 1974. White, *Is That Burgeoning Law School Enrollment Ending?*, 61 A.B.A.J. 202 (1975).

their reach and coverage, is attested to by rising malpractice claims against attorneys.[10] As in the medical field, there is no longer reluctance on the part of consumers of legal services to make claims for damages where the efforts of the attorney prove unsatisfactory. The fact that attorneys are now potentially liable for the nondisclosure of material information in S.E.C. registration cases is but one recent development in this area.[11]

When one adds up all these factors-the Code's precepts, legislative intervention, increasing malpractice claims, high-volume legislative and judicial production coupled with rapid change-the question becomes not whether we should have formalized postadmission attorney education programs, but rather what form such programs should take. Many different proposals have been suggested.[12] A discussion of the various alternatives to mandatory continuing legal education is beyond the scope of tonight's lecture, but before leaving the topic I would at least like to list some of the possibilities that were considered in Minnesota. We looked into postadmission plans based upon: (1) systematized peer review, (2) voluntary self-assessment testing, (3) mandatory periodic testing as a basis for recertification, (4) specialization by a method of certification, as in California, or by representation of special competence, as in New Mexico, and (5) improvement of instructional techniques, standards, and course offerings in voluntary programs.

In concluding this portion of my remarks, let me remind you that Chief Justice Burger, in this same lecture series two years ago,[13] decried the low state of trial advocacy and called for some system of certification of trial lawyers. The Chief Justice argued that advocates owe a duty of competence to their clients and to the courts. If this obligation exists for trial advocates, then it exists for all attorneys.[14] In Minnesota, we concluded that mandatory continuing legal education is the best practical means to help insure that this duty is fulfilled.

10. *See* Blaine, *Professional Liability Claims: An Increasing Concern for Lawyers!*, 59 Il. B.J. 302 (1970); King, *Legal Malpractice: The Coming Storm*, 50 Calif. St. B.J. 362 (1975).

11. See the complaint filed by the S.E.C. in S.E.C. v. National Student Marketing Corp., [1971–72 Transfer Binder] CCH Fed. Sec. L. Rep. 93,360 (D.D.C. 1972), dismissal of complaint denied, [1972–73 Transfer Binder] CCH Fed. Sec. L. Rep. 93,820 (D.D.C. 1973). Many law review articles on the expanding obligation of attorneys to disclose corporate fraud in SEC cases have appeared. *See, e.g.*, Lowenfels, *Expanding Public Responsibilities of Securities Lawyers: An Analysis of the New Trend in Standard of Care and Priorities of Duties*, 74 Colum. L. Rev. 412 (1974); Myers, *The Attorney Client Relationship and the Code of Professional Responsibility: Suggested Attorney Liability for Breach of Duty to Disclose Fraud to the Securities and Exchange Commission*, 44 Fordham L. Rev. 1113 (1976).

12. See Parker, *Periodic Recertification of Lawyers: A Comparative Study of Programs for Maintaining Professional Competence*, 1974 Utah L. Rev. 463.

13. Burger, *The Special Skills of Advocacy. Are Specialized Training and Certification of Advocates Essential to Our System of Justice?*, 42 Fordham L. Rev. 227 (1973).

14. As David Brink has written: "In today's more complex, demanding, and consumer-oriented society, what are the true priorities for action by the organized bar? In other times some principal priorities were for social and fraternal purposes or to resist incursions by less responsible and skilled groups. while these may continue as proper goals, today's legitimate bar association activities can best be ascertained in terms of the lawyer's duties. These are, in decreasing order of importance, duties to the public, duties to the profession, duties to the organized bar, and duties to the individual." Brink, *Who Will Regulate the Bar?*, 61 A.B.A.J. 936, 938 (1975). Mr. Brink, a member

INTEREST IN MANDATORY CONTINUING LEGAL EDUCATION: MINNESOTA DEVELOPMENTS

These various national developments and pressures—all spotlighting the need for more systematic approaches to the matter of attorney competence—took concrete shape in Minnesota during 1971. In that year, members of an advisory committee to Minnesota's voluntary CLE program read a *New York Times* article, which told of several physicians in Oregon who lost their licenses to practice when they failed to comply with a mandatory continuing education program.[15] This article suggested to the committee that it was time for serious investigation of ways to ensure the continuing competence of attorneys practicing in Minnesota. A special Study Committee was established to investigate mandatory CLE and other alternatives. Special attention was given to what other professional organizations were doing. A consensus gradually developed that mandatory continuing legal education was the best solution for Minnesota. The preliminary report of the Study Committee was a major topic of discussion at the 1973 State Bar Convention. Out of that convention came a resolution that 1974 would be a "year of communication" on the subject. As a result, approximately twenty meetings between committee members and local bar groups were held all across the state. At the July 1974 State Bar Convention, the delegates voted overwhelmingly to approve the committee's proposed rule instituting a mandatory CLE program. Hearings were held that fall and winter at the Minnesota Supreme Court; judges as well as attorneys were brought within the ambit of the rule, and on April 3, 1975, Minnesota became the first state to adopt mandatory continuing legal education.

The fact that the initiative for a mandatory program had come from the State Bar Association and the fact that there was substantial support for such a program throughout the bar, weighed heavily in the court's decision to adopt mandatory CLE.

Another important consideration was the fact that in Minnesota there existed strong voluntary CLE programs for both attorneys and judges.[16] Courses for attorneys in the state had been conducted since 1965 by Minnesota Continuing Legal Education, a cooperative program of the Minnesota State Bar Association and the Continuing Education and Extension Office of the University of Minnesota. In terms of the state's attorney population of about 7,500, Minnesota CLE is probably the most active state organization.

---

of the Board of Governors of the American Bar Association, is a Minneapolis attorney who was instrumental in the creation of the Minnesota plan.

15. N.Y. Times, Jan. 9, 1972, at 63, cols. 6–8.

16. *See Final Report of the Study Committee on Continuing Professional Competence, Minnesota State Bar Association, Mar. 16, 1974*, 30 Bench and Bar of Minnesota no. 9, 21 (Mar. 1974), where the following comment appears in response to the Committee's rhetorical question as to why Minnesota should be the first state to mandate continuing education for lawyers: "[The existing voluntary] program of continuing legal education in Minnesota is an excellent one. On a per capita lawyer basis, the Minnesota program ranks favorably nationally. The availability of this excellent existing program makes Minnesota a logical candidate for the introduction of mandatory continuing legal education." *Id.* at 24.

From 1974 to 1975, for example, it sponsored thirty-seven different courses, for which more than 7,100 individuals registered.

Judges and other court personnel in Minnesota have been offered individualized educational programs since 1973 under the auspices of the Office of Continuing Education for State Court Personnel. The office, unique in the nation, offers courses and a forum for professional interchange among judges, clerks, court administrators, prosecutors, defense counsel, and law enforcement personnel. Recent programs have ranged from seminars on the new Minnesota Rules of Criminal Procedure to a session on judicial writing cosponsored with the Wisconsin Supreme Court's Judicial Education Center. Another important factor leading to the institution of mandatory CLE was the developing legislative interest in the area. During the 1975 session of the Minnesota Legislature, eleven different bills were introduced affecting matters of interest to attorneys.[17] Among the bills were measures that would have: (1) permitted specialization identification, (2) repealed the attorney's lien law, (3) required attorneys to post fees, (4) barred attorneys from serving in the legislature, (5) permitted lay persons and corporations to practice law, (6) segregated attorneys into solicitor and barrister classifications, and (7) allowed the director of consumer affairs to investigate charges against attorneys.

The bills were wide-ranging in their potential impact; moreover, they were introduced by one of the state's most influential senators during a period when fallout from Watergate and a heightened sense of consumerism had combined to create a potentially volatile atmosphere in the legislature. I believe the bar in Minnesota took the position that a mandatory educational program under the control of the judiciary was preferable to one that might be imposed by the legislature, and the initiative of the bar in the matter was a natural consequence of that position.[18]

Also of interest was the fact that the State Medical Association in Minnesota had formally approved a program that conditions association membership on attendance at educational sessions. Minnesota dentists have operated under statutory competency requirements since 1969; legislation requiring continuing education for nurses in Minnesota was passed in 1975.[19]

I mention these developments to give you a sense of the situation that existed during the fall and winter of 1974–75 when our court was considering this matter. Though we were the first court to order mandatory CLE, our decision is not altogether remarkable

17. *See supra* note 8.

18. Even if it had been the legislature which mandated continuing legal education, the enactment would no doubt have been subject to strong constitutional challenge. *See Sharood v. Hatfield*, 296 Minn. 416, 423, 210 N.W.2d 275, 279 (1973), which held that legislation affecting the right of the Minnesota Supreme Court to regulate the practice of law in the state was an unconstitutional usurpation of powers reserved to the judicial branch.

19. 11 Minn. Stat. Ann. § 150A.09(2) (1970) requires dentists in the state to take at least twenty hours of continuing education course instruction every five years. Minn. Session Laws, ch. 240 (1975) provides for a program of mandatory continuing education for nurses in the state. Rules and regulations affecting the nurses are to be ready for legislative review by January 1, 1977; the program becomes effective January 1, 1978.

considering the circumstances that I have outlined. Yet, at the same time, we were cognizant of the pioneering aspects of our decision, and I personally was always aware that we ought not to make mandatory that which could be achieved as well, or almost as well, voluntarily. In the end, we adopted mandatory continuing legal education, but it was not an easy decision.

THE MINNESOTA PLAN IN OPERATION

On the basis of our experience to date with mandatory continuing legal education, it appears that the critical factor in its success is the work of the Board in supervising the operation of the program. The Minnesota State Board of Continuing Legal Education is a thirteen-member agency composed of a chairperson, three laymen and nine lawyers, including one judge of general jurisdiction. The Supreme Court appoints the chairperson and all members of the Board, as well as an Executive Director who serves as the administrator of the program. The Board has general supervisory authority over the operation of the rules.[20]

The Executive Director initially determines whether courses submitted to the Board should be accredited and, if so, for how many hours. The Board thereafter reviews course approvals and disapprovals and may elect to overrule the Executive Director's decisions.[21]

20. *See* April 3d Order, *supra* note 1. Supreme Court Rule 2 reads in pertinent part as follows:

There is hereby established a State Board of Continuing Legal Education, to be appointed by this Court, consisting of 12 members and a chairperson. Three of the members of the Board other than the chairperson may be persons who are not members of the Bar of this state. Each other member of the Board, with the exception of one who shall be a District Judge, shall be a member of the Bar of this state who practices in Minnesota with his principal office located in this state. . . . The chairperson of the Board shall be appointed by this Court for such time as It shall designate and shall serve at the pleasure of this Court.

The Board shall have general supervisory authority over the administration of these rules. The Board shall accredit courses and programs which will satisfy the educational requirements of these rules and shall discover and encourage the offering of such courses and programs.

The Board shall at all times be subject to the direction and supervision of this Court in all matters.

21. Rule 108, Rules of Minnesota Board of Continuing Legal Education (adopted and effective Nov. 6, 1975) [hereinafter Board Rules], reads as follows:

(a) Determinations. The Executive Director shall, in response to written requests for approval of courses, awarding of credit for attending of or teaching in approved courses, waivers, extensions of time deadlines, or interpretation of these Rules, make a written response giving appropriate reasons for the determination. The Executive Director may seek a determination of the Board before making a response. At each Board meeting the Executive Director shall report to the Board on all determinations made since the Board's last meeting together with observations and comments relating to other matters under the Board's jurisdiction.

(b) Review. The Board shall review any adverse determination of the Executive Director. The lawyer or sponsoring agency affected may present information to the Board in writing or in person or both. If the Board finds that the Executive Director has incorrectly interpreted the facts or the Rules it may take such action as may be appropriate. The Board shall advise the lawyer or sponsoring agency of its findings and any action taken.

The Board's decisions are made in light of written standards.[22] Chief among them is a requirement that the course relate primarily to the practice of law or the lawyer's professional responsibility. Other standards urge the sponsoring agency to provide an atmosphere conducive to a sound educational experience. Ideally, all courses are offered in well-lighted, comfortable facilities. Each participant should have a writing surface. Typically, each course is accompanied by carefully prepared written materials that are distributed to the participants no later than at the time of registration. The faculty must be well qualified by education and experience to teach the subjects covered.

So far, the Board has approved 750 courses. Sponsors range from large, well-known organizations such as the Practicing Law Institute, American Law Institute, and Minnesota Continuing Legal Education, to small, recently organized groups such as the Minnesota Practice Institute, a for-profit private offshoot of Minnesota Bar Review, Inc. In between, one finds courses sponsored by local bar associations. "In-house" training seminars for attorneys in larger law firms have also been accredited.[23]

Most of the courses submitted to the Board have been approved, although revisions have sometimes been made in the number of credit hours allowed. Courses have been rejected when they were oriented more toward business than legal considerations or were not sufficiently keyed to legal practice. For example, a course on accounting and real estate trans-

22. Rule 101, Board Rules, *supra* note 21, reads as follows:

The following standards shall be met by any course for which credit or approval is sought:

a. The course shall have significant intellectual or practical content.

b. The course shall deal primarily with matter directly related to the practice of law or to the professional responsibility or ethical obligations of the participants.

c. Each faculty member shall be qualified by practical or academic experience to teach the subject he or she covers. Legal subjects should normally be taught by lawyers.

d. While written materials need not be distributed for every course, thorough, high quality, readable, carefully prepared written materials should be distributed to all participants at or before the time the course is offered whenever practicable.

e. Participants shall attend courses in a suitable classroom or laboratory setting devoted to the educational activity of the program. No course will be approved which involves solely TV viewing in the home, correspondence work or self-study. Video, motion picture or sound tape presentations may be used provided a faculty person is in attendance at all presentations to comment and answer questions.

f. Ordinarily credit will not be given for speeches given at luncheons or banquets.

g. A list of all participants shall be maintained by the sponsoring agency and transmitted to the Board following the presentation of the course.

h. Credit shall be awarded on the basis of one hour for each 60 minutes actually spent in attendance at an approved course.

i. A lawyer shall not receive credit for any course attended before being admitted to practice law in Minnesota, but one so admitted may receive credit of one hour for each 60 minutes actually spent in attendance, for attending for credit or as an auditor of a regular course offered by a law school approved by the American Bar Association.

23. The information in this paragraph was provided by The Office of the Executive Director, Minnesota State Board of Continuing Legal Education. This information represents the situation in Minnesota as of January 1, 1976.

actions was not accredited. A television series on the subject of bankruptcy was refused approval because it was not conducted in an academic setting.

Course offerings coupled with social occasions are also disfavored under the rules, although the last convention of the bar association did feature four seminars totaling twenty hours of course work. These sessions were conducted in facilities separated from the convention itself.

Courses certified by the State Board differ in scope, as well as subject matter, from those subjects traditionally taught in law schools. Law school instruction typically provides in-depth analysis of legal problems and trends. The CLE programs are primarily refresher courses in relatively narrow areas of the law, which are designed to update the participant on subjects with which he has some familiarity; only about twenty percent of the sessions present information that is completely new to the average practitioner.

Approved courses fall into two basic categories: about ninety percent are refresher courses designed to bring participants up to date in specific areas; the remainder emphasize performance techniques rather than information. Within these two categories, the range of courses is impressive. Recent Minnesota CLE offerings, for example, have included courses on Basic Securities Law, Professional Responsibility, and a seminar on Advising the Client in Tax Fraud Cases. A legislative wrap-up seminar and a course on the new Minnesota Probate Code were among the courses offered at the last State Bar Convention; a Patent and Trademark seminar is scheduled for early 1976.

Since mandatory continuing legal education went into effect, the number of course offerings and registrations has risen dramatically. Minnesota CLE presented eighteen courses in the first four months of its last fiscal year; in the corresponding period this year, twenty-seven courses have been offered, a fifty percent increase. Registrations have jumped from 3,370 in the first four months last year to 5,900 during the same period this year; if one counts some 1,200 registrations which were not accepted because courses were oversubscribed, then *total* registrations in the first four months of this fiscal year already equal the number achieved in all of the 1974–75 period.[24]

Attorneys who do not wish to fulfill the requirements of our mandatory plan can choose "restricted status." An attorney so classified can still represent certain close relatives or a single employer in Minnesota. The Board can grant a waiver of the rules or an extension of time in which to comply in cases of hardship or in other extenuating circumstances. Absent restricted status or hardship, noncompliance results in an investigation and hearing conducted by the Board, followed by a report to the Supreme Court, where "appropriate disposition" is to be made.[25]

24. These statistics were provided by John B. Wirt, Director, Minnesota Continuing Legal Education.

25. Restricted status is provided for by Rule 3, April 3d Order, *supra* note 1. Supreme Court Rule 3 in pertinent part reads as follows:

A restricted attorney shall not be required to maintain the educational requirements provided by these rules. Other than himself, he may not represent any person in any legal matter or proceedings within the State of Minnesota except a full-time employer, spouse, son, daughter, father,

THE STATUS OF MANDATORY CONTINUING LEGAL EDUCATION IN OTHER STATES

Minnesota is the only state with a mandatory CLE program presently in operation; Iowa joins us in January. The Wisconsin Supreme Court has approved in principle a mandatory plan similar to Iowa's, and in North Dakota a proposed rule based upon Minnesota's has the unanimous backing of the North Dakota State Bar Association and is about to be submitted to that state's Supreme Court for consideration. The Supreme Courts of New Mexico, Utah, and Washington also have proposals for mandatory CLE under consideration.[26]

In a handful of other states—California, Idaho, Kansas, and Maryland—final drafts of plans are pending before the State Bar Associations. In Kansas, a mandatory system won Kansas Bar Association Executive Council approval a year ago. Since then, a motion by the Association asking the State Supreme Court to adopt mandatory CLE has been made and then tabled; the future of the project depends upon what kind of consensus develops.

In California, legislative pressure relative to lawyer competence dates back to 1971. The Board of Governors of the California Bar Association has now approved in principle a proposal that calls for the periodic relicensing of attorneys conditioned upon either their accumulation of approved educational credits or their professional reexamination. California's tentative plan calls for sixty credits every five years, with a certain minimum number of credit hours to be devoted to specific subject areas, including ethics. Alternatively,

---

mother, brother, sister, father-in-law, mother-in-law, brother-in-law, or sister-in-law. Judges, referees, judicial officers, or magistrates of any court of record of the State of Minnesota, or attorneys serving as legal counsel in any governmental unit of the State of Minnesota, are not eligible to apply for restricted status until they retire or leave their position.

Rule 3 also provides for waivers and extensions: "In individual cases, the Board may grant waivers or extensions of the minimum educational or the reporting requirements." Rule 4 covers noncompliance procedures:

If an active attorney fails to complete the minimum educational or the reporting requirements to the satisfaction of the Board, the Board shall report such failure to the Supreme Court for appropriate disposition.

The Board of Continuing Legal Education, before reporting any matter to the Court, shall investigate the facts in order to make a report on the reasons for noncompliance including affording the lawyer involved a hearing, upon his request, in accordance with the principles of the due process of law. The Board shall, however, before reporting any noncompliance to the Court, attempt to resolve all matters on a confidential basis.

The Board has adopted rules to carry out the directives of the Court's April 3d Order. *See* Board Rule 109, *supra* note 21.

26. The facts stated in this paragraph and throughout the balance of this section come from letters received by the Chief Justice during October and November 1975 in response to state-by-state inquiries on his part as to the current status of continuing legal education in each state. Responses were received from all jurisdictions, including Puerto Rico and the District of Columbia. Information in this section relative to the current situation in Wisconsin, Iowa, and North Dakota was confirmed by phone conversation in December 1975. *See also* Parker, *supra* note 12, at 484–86.

an attorney could maintain his license to practice by successfully passing a state bar examination within the two years preceding the expiration of his license.[27]

Wisconsin's experience with mandatory CLE is worth mentioning in more detail. The Wisconsin Supreme Court held a public hearing on the matter in March 1975. In May, it announced its support for the principle of compulsory CLE, even though only four of the seven justices voted to adopt the resolution, which committed the court to adopting rules instituting mandatory CLE within a reasonable time. Also in May, again by a 4-3 decision, the Wisconsin Supreme Court ordered that an advisory referendum on the issue of mandatory CLE be held, with all active lawyers in the state (about 7,700) eligible to vote. The results of the referendum are now in, with 3,905 ballots in favor of mandatory CLE and 1,551 against.[28] Whether the court would have backed away from its resolution to adopt a mandatory system had the results of the referendum been-less one-sided is an open question. Also of interest is the 4-3 vote and the decision to issue a statement lending the prestige of the court to the concept of mandatory CLE when the members of the court were themselves split on the merits of such action.

Sixteen states are not actively considering mandatory continuing legal education at present. New York and New Jersey are in this group. In twenty-six other states the subject of mandatory postadmission education is under study by bar associations or committees, and it can be expected that the experiences of the states that already have mandatory CLE will be instructive. In Michigan, for example, an entire issue of the *State Bar Journal* was devoted to a discussion of the topic.[29] Hearings are being scheduled around that state, much as was done in Minnesota, so that a consensus might develop before any action is taken.[30]

OBJECTIONS TO MANDATORY CONTINUING LEGAL EDUCATION

Numerous objections to mandatory continuing legal education have been raised.[31] They fall into two main categories: (1) that one or another of the various alternatives

27. Letter from James H. Kovacs, Program Director, California Board of Legal Specialization, to Chief Justice Robert J. Sheran of Minnesota, October 8, 1975.

28. Letter from Chief Justice Horace W. Wilkie of Wisconsin, to Chief Justice Robert J. Sheran of Minnesota, October 2, 1975.

29. *Mandatory Continuing Legal Education—What, Where, How, When, Why, Why Not, and Whether*, 54 Mich. St. B.J. 760 (1975).

30. *Id.* at 761.

31. The most widely available compilation of the objections to mandatory continuing legal education appears in Wolkin, *A Better Way to Keep Lawyers Competent*, 61 A.B.A.J. 574 (1975) and Wolkin, *More on a Better Way to Keep Lawyers Competent*, 61 A.B.A.J. 1064 (1975). Criticisms of mandatory CLE also surface at conferences on the topic. *See, e.g.*, Bingaman, *Lawyers' Competence: Mandatory Continuing Legal Education*; Carroll, *The Economics of Continuing Legal Education.* These latter two papers were included in materials made available to participants at the A.B.A. sponsored National Conference on Continuing Legal Education, held November 10–12, 1975, in Chicago. Parker also mentions various objections to mandatory CLE. Parker, *supra* note 12,

to mandatory CLE is more likely to insure professional competence, and (2) that mandatory plans like Minnesota's are either misguided or not sufficiently rigorous in what they require.

I have already referred in passing to some of the main alternatives to mandatory CLE, and I have outlined the reasons why Minnesota decided as it did. A more complete analysis of the merits and disadvantages of the alternatives to mandatory CLE is beyond the scope of this lecture. I would, however, like to comment briefly on some of the criticisms in the second category.

It has been suggested, for example, that lawyers attending mandatory postadmission educational courses should be tested to determine whether they have assimilated the course material. Some argue that the programs are excessively lenient in permitting the lawyers to prove attendance at mandatory educational courses merely by stating the time and place of the course attended. It has been suggested that some authority other than the lawyer himself should determine his needs and prescribe the courses necessary to answer them. It seems to me that these are not arguments against the idea of mandatory education as such, but are, instead, arguments that its principles should be extended farther than has so far been considered advisable. If experience proves that testing, monitoring, and course prescription are needed and will serve a useful purpose, there is nothing in the concept of mandatory education that will prevent use of these additives.

The claim has been made that mandatory programs will dilute the healthy educational impact of voluntary programs. The point is made that an attorney who voluntarily attends a course does so because he is highly motivated and that motivation is the key to the learning process. It does not follow, however, that the advent of compulsory CLE means the end of motivation. On the contrary, it would appear that lawyers who are presently attending continuing legal education courses voluntarily will be even more likely to go back to school under a mandatory system because, in effect, the importance of what they have been doing all along has been officially recognized.

Another argument is that mandatory CLE emphasizes appearance at the expense of reality—that the result achieved is "cosmetic" rather than substantive. Mandatory CLE is seen as an overreaction to "consumer demands" upon the profession. But, in my view, we should expect that the public will approve a plan requiring refresher education for attorneys. At a time when the legal profession is so often criticized and misunderstood, a program should not be rejected simply because it is responsive to public demand. To the extent that lawyers accept mandatory educational programs purely for the sake of the appearance of things, the solution, it seems to me, is to make the fact conform with the appearance rather than to reject the program out of hand.

What about costs? Won't mandatory CLE be inordinately expensive? In Minnesota, the budget for the administrative operation of the program is estimated at $35,000 per annum. We have raised this money by adding an extra $5.00 to each attorney's annual

---

at 477. The sources listed in this note provide the basic research material for this section of this article.

registration fee.[32] For courses that are locally sponsored and presented, the cost of a day's instruction (five and one-half to six and one-half credit hours) averages about $40.00, or $8.00 an hour. This means that an attorney who receives fifteen credits per year would spend about $120 to $150 each year in course registration fees. To this, of course, must be added any travel expenses and the cost of time away from the office, but, however one adds up the figures, it is difficult to conclude that mandatory CLE is inordinately expensive or likely to work financial hardship on most attorneys.

It is argued that a mandatory program imposes hardships on certain lawyers—for example, the aged practitioner, or legal scholars and judges who, by the nature of their work, are already involved in a postadmission educational process far more rigorous than that prescribed by a mandatory plan of continuing legal education. The "hardship" argument is also raised in connection with corporate counsel or military legal personnel whose responsibilities or assignments require them to locate in states other than where they are admitted to practice. It is my impression that these cases are exaggerated. To the extent that they are real, methods of accommodating any problems that occur can be easily enough employed. In Minnesota, for example, an attorney may choose "restricted status" and still represent certain close relatives or a single employer.

The idea that mandatory CLE somehow infringes upon an attorney's independence or freedom of choice is an often-voiced, but to me unconvincing, objection to mandatory CLE. To become an attorney, one must graduate from an accredited law school and, in most states, pass a bar examination. Once admitted, an attorney is constrained by the Code of Professional Responsibility as adopted in his state. Chief Justice Burger has suggested that attorneys not be admitted to practice in the federal courts unless they first satisfy certain minimal requirements of experience and competence, and the Second Circuit is studying proposed rules to this effect.[33] No matter how independent they may be, lawyers will accept regulation when the need is dear.

Other arguments sometimes encountered are these: that mandatory CLE emphasizes the quantity rather than the quality of course offerings; that mandatory CLE will not provide courses for lawyers who have particular, specialized needs; that lawyers will not be discriminating in their selection of courses under a mandatory CLE program; that

32. Minnesota had 7,484 registered attorneys as of December 31, 1975. This information was provided by the Minnesota Supreme Court Office of Attorney Admissions and Registrations.

33. *See New Admission Rules Proposed for Federal District Courts*, 61 A.B.A.J. 945 (1975), which discusses a report on this topic prepared by the Judicial Conference of the Second Circuit. *See also* Ehrlich, *A Critique of the Proposed New Admission Rules for District Courts in the Second Circuit*, 61 A.B.A.J. 1385 (1975); Kaufman, *A Response to Objections to the Second Circuit's Proposed District Court Admission Rules*, 61 A.B.A.J. 1514 (1975); N.Y. Times, Nov. 23, 1975, § 4, at 11, col. 1. Commentary has also appeared in the *New York Law Journal. See* Frankel, *Ill-Advised Rules for Bar Admission*, 174 N.Y.L.J., Dec. 31, 1975, at 1, col. 4. Judge Frankel's speech drew strong criticism from Chief Judge Irving R. Kaufman of the Second Circuit Court of Appeals. Chief Judge Kaufman was joined in his criticism by Simon H. Rifkind, a member of Paul, Weiss, Rifkind, Wharton & Garrison. 175 N.Y.L.J., Jan. 7, 1976, at 1, col. 3.

mandatory CLE will place greater stress on exposition than participation and that therefore the educational exchange will be less effective.

On the latter point, I don't believe that a mandatory program will have any effect on the ratio of expository to participatory courses. Competition among sponsors should ensure quality as well as quantity in course offerings. Specialized courses are in fact regularly offered in Minnesota. And it seems to me that a lawyer who spends his time and money to attend legal seminars will, out of self-interest alone, be careful in his selection and alert in his participation.

Obviously, there are risks in mandating a program where experience is as limited as is the case with postadmission legal education. On the other hand, it may be that many of the apprehensions voiced with respect to mandatory CLE have been overstated. In any event, in Minnesota, we decided that the need, coupled with the prospect of success, was worth the risk of disappointment. At worst, we should be able to improve our programs in light of practical experience.

CONCLUSION: THE SYMBOLIC ASPECTS OF MANDATORY CONTINUING LEGAL EDUCATION

There is a measure of symbolism involved in the mandatory continuing legal education movement. Those who oppose mandatory CLE see it as a symbol of unjustified interference with an attorney's independence, on the theory that the lawyers should be left free to determine for themselves an ongoing course of study. This reasoning is troublesome. First, it assumes a measure of independence for attorneys that does not exist. Second, we know from experience that the freedom to prescribe one's own course of study too often results in little being done to maintain professional competence. Of course, the sensitivity of the legal matters with which lawyers and judges deal requires that they have a certain amount of autonomy in arriving at their professional judgments. But their freedom must necessarily be circumscribed, if required in the public interest. Events in Minnesota brought us to the conclusion that the public interest and the good of the profession required action on the issue of maintaining professional competence; mandatory continuing education was the result.

Those who favor mandatory continuing legal education also find it symbolic. To them it symbolizes a commitment to the proposition that the lawyer has a duty to remain competent for the duration of his practice. The importance of this obligation cannot be overemphasized, for unless he remains competent, an attorney cannot hope to satisfactorily perform his duties to the public, the profession, his clients, or himself. The Minnesota Plan reflects our judgment that an obligatory process is a timely and effective means for achieving this crucial objective.

The Most Lustrous Branch: Watergate and the Judiciary

Leon Jaworski

Leon Jaworski delivered the seventh Sonnett lecture, entitled *The Most Lustrous Branch: Watergate and the Judiciary*, on February 15, 1977.[1] Jaworski served as the second Special Prosecutor assigned to the Watergate case, which involved the illegal activities of President Nixon and some of his staff, and led to Nixon's resignation as President of the United States.[2] Jaworski prevailed in the landmark case of *United States v. Nixon*,[3] wherein the Supreme Court refused to quash a subpoena issued to President Richard Nixon for the tape recordings of conversations relating to the Watergate scandal. These tapes became one of the primary bases for impeachment proceedings. The landmark case limited the power of the President to invoke executive privilege in order to withhold access to information that could be relevant to criminal proceedings involving the executive branch.

Born in Waco, Texas, Jaworski graduated from Baylor University Law School.[4] Jaworski began his career at the law firms of Dyess, Jaworski & Strong and Fulbright, Crooker, Freeman & Bates.[5] While serving in the United States Army Judge Advocate General's department at the end of World War II, Jaworski prosecuted Nazi war criminals during the Nuremburg trials.[6] He later represented Lyndon B. Johnson, successfully litigating Johnson's right to run for both a Senate seat and Vice President in 1960, and was appointed to several commissions when Johnson became President in 1963.[7]

In 1973, Jaworski was appointed Special Prosecutor of the Watergate scandal, shortly after President Nixon ordered the firing of Jaworski's predecessor after the predecessor subpoenaed the President's taped conversations.[8] Initially believing President Nixon was not involved in the scandal, Jaworski eventually learned of the President's possible

Introduction written by Muriel Raggi, J.D., Class of 2015, Fordham University School of Law.

1. Leon Jaworski, *The Most Lustrous Branch: Watergate and the Judiciary*, 45 Fordham L. Rev. 1267 (1977).

2. *Leon Jaworski, 77, Dies in Texas; Special Prosecutor for Watergate*, N.Y. Times, Dec. 10, 1982, at B20 [hereinafter *Special Prosecutor for Watergate*].

3. 418 U.S. 683 (1974).

4. *Jaworski, Leon*, Tex. State Hist. Ass'n, http://www.tshaonline.org/handbook/online/articles/fja31 (last visited Mar. 15, 2014).

5. *Id.*

6. *Id.*; *Special Prosecutor for Watergate*, *supra* note 2.

7. Tex. State Hist. Ass'n, *supra* note 4.

8. Michael Flaherty, *Watergate Scandal—40 Years Ago—November 1, 1973 Leon Jaworski Appointed Special Prosecutor*, Flaherty Luvara Law Group LLP (Nov. 1, 2013), http://flahertyluvaralaw.com/watergate-scandal-40-years-ago-november-1-1973-leon-jaworski-appointed-special-prosecutor/.

involvement and issued a subpoena for sixty-four tape-recorded conversations that took place in the Oval Office between President Nixon and his staff members.[9]

When President Nixon refused to comply with the subpoena, citing executive privilege and asserting that the Special Prosecutor could not sue the Office of the President, Jaworski prevailed in the district court.[10] The Supreme Court, upon request of both parties, granted a writ of certiorari.[11] The Supreme Court held that a generalized assertion of executive privilege must yield to the need for evidence in a pending criminal trial and reasserted its role as the final interpreter of the Constitution.[12] The Court refused to grant the broad privilege sought by the President, holding that "it is the province and duty of this Court 'to say what the law is' with respect to the claim of [executive] privilege."[13] The implications of Nixon's tape-recorded statements forced him to resign in 1974, the only president to do so.[14]

Jaworski was also charged with deciding whether to indict Nixon on obstruction of justice charges.[15] While he believed there was sufficient evidence for a grand jury to issue an indictment, Jaworski opted not to, given the low probability of Nixon receiving a fair trial.[16] Jaworski went on to serve as special counsel to a House Ethics Committee investigating the so-called Koreagate scandal and to author several books about his experiences.[17]

Jaworski's Sonnett lecture, *The Most Lustrous Branch: Watergate and the Judiciary*, focused on his decisions as Special Prosecutor and his reverence for the supremacy of the judiciary in deciding constitutional issues implicating the separation of powers.[18] The emphasis Jaworski placed on the "oath of office" and "responsibilities assumed by an officer of the court" transcends the confines of time and legal matters.[19] The consideration Jaworski placed on protecting Nixon's constitutional rights, while performing his special prosecution duties, serves as a mandate to all prosecutors to enforce and uphold the guarantees of the Constitution without regard to an individual's "despised" or "scorned" character.[20] Jaworski's "salute to the [j]udiciary" continues to serve as a reminder of the important and unique role the court plays in decisively disposing of issues, particularly in the constitutional context.[21]

The legacy of judicial supremacy over executive branch claims of executive privilege and the importance of *United States v. Nixon* continue to impact our political system. In

9. *Id.*; *Special Prosecutor for Watergate*, *supra* note 2.
10. Flaherty, *supra* note 8; *Special Prosecutor for Watergate*, *supra* note 2.
11. 418 U.S. 683 (1974).
12. *Id.* at 713 (1974); *see Special Prosecutor for Watergate*, *supra* note 2.
13. 418 U.S. at 705.
14. Flaherty, *supra* note 8; *Special Prosecutor for Watergate*, *supra* note 2.
15. *Special Prosecutor for Watergate*, *supra* note 2.
16. *Id.*
17. Flaherty, *supra* note 8.
18. *See generally* Jaworski, *supra* note 1.
19. Jaworski, *supra* note 1, at 1267.
20. *Id.*
21. *Id.* at 1280.

Clinton v. Jones,[22] the Supreme Court, relying upon *United States v. Nixon*, rejected the broad claims of executive privilege asserted by President Clinton in connection with the claims brought against him by Paula Jones.[23]

1977 Sonnett Lecture

I *covet* the privilege of being with you on this occasion. I have long admired your institution, its prestige, and its accomplishments. There is a more special and singular reason for embracing the high prerogative of joining you this evening. I refer to the cherished memories of John F. Sonnett, with whom I had discussions touching on problems of our profession from time to time, and with whom I labored in the vineyard of the American College of Trial Lawyers.

Jack Sonnett, to me, was not a seeker of headlines. Still, his achievements in the field of advocacy were great. He was a solid, able gladiator in the courtroom, both trial and appellate, and ever mindful of his obligations as an officer of the court. Beyond this, he served his country with marked distinction.

I will have some comments to make this evening on some of the legal problems presented in the Watergate era. At this point, I should like to allude generally to the obligations and responsibilities the Special Prosecutor faced, which frequently were in conflict with those urged by some organizations, some editors, and even some lawyers. Unlike their status, I had taken an oath of office and I labored under the responsibilities assumed by an officer of the court. It appeared to me that some who urged courses of action different from those followed by the Prosecution Force often lost sight of the constitutional rights of individuals who had fallen from public grace, were despised by many and even scorned. But, regardless of public disillusionment, their rights under the Constitution remained the same, and my responsibilities of office remained the same. When, in the face of these conditions, I had decisions to make, I found comfort in the examples set by such illustrious advocates as John F. Sonnett.

I said a few years ago, in discussing the "Unpopular Cause," that "when entering the profession, a lawyer does not engage in a popularity contest, but he does assume a special creed"—as the late Mr. Justice Jackson put it—"to safeguard every man's right to a fair trial." Obviously, this "special creed" needed to be applied to Watergate defendants—to Richard Nixon—and to all others who, under our Constitution, were entitled to the rights it protects.

When, in retrospect, we think of Jack Sonnett, I hope that you will permit me to reiterate a comment I made some years ago: "The greatest reward that flows to a lawyer is not

22. 520 U.S. 681 (1997).
23. *See id.*

measured in riches, social position or popularity. Rather, it comes as an unseen, intangible inner satisfaction that emanates from the faithful discharge of duty. This is truly the lawyer's highest form of compensation."

I think that Jack Sonnett, were he with us today, would approve of my reviewing the difficult decisions in Watergate and the stellar performance of our judiciary under strained and complex circumstances. So believing, I will address myself to this subject.

Historically, Watergate cannot be swept under the rug. Whether the legal aftermaths of this tragic saga have contributed to the undergirding of our institutions for this nation's future welfare, history will determine in due course of time. The legal actions that were taken are recorded in judicial annals and someday will be judged, without the emotion and the bias and the prejudice that ruled the views of many critics at the time of decision. One of the historic decisions that faced the Special Prosecutor involved the question of whether the then President of the United States should be indicted, along with the others accused in the Watergate cover-up. It is one about which much has been written and said—some of it fairly accurately and some of it quite inaccurately.

One of the leading newspapers in this city, for instance, repeatedly and blindly has continued to distort the basic issue involved and the treatment accorded it. It has failed correctly to project the views of the staff, as well as the conclusions and actions of the Special Prosecutor.

After all of the evidence assembled in the investigation relating to the Watergate cover-up had been presented to the grand jury, the moment of decision as to what action to take with respect to the then-President was at hand. Bear in mind we are now talking about a date early in March 1974. This issue had been studied for some time. I had discussed it with some of my principal assistants, had considered their memoranda, and had undertaken to assess the question from the standpoint of what was legally sound and particularly what might be acceptable to our highest court. For the purpose of the discussion that follows, let us assume that the evidence involving the former President was sufficient to support an indictment for obstruction of justice.

Because it is now generally known that I considered indictment not to be the proper course, the reasons for my conclusion properly may be stated: There was substantial doubt that a sitting president was indictable for the offense of *obstruction of justice*, and, considering the dire consequences of an act of such doubtful validity, the returning of such an indictment, under all of the circumstances, seemed insupportable. While legally an indictment could be returned against a sitting president for the offense of murder, by way of example, there was serious doubt that the United States Supreme Court would have permitted an indictment of a sitting president for obstruction of justice, *especially when the House of Representatives' Committee on the Judiciary was then engaged in an inquiry into whether the President should be impeached on that very ground.* The proper constitutional process appeared to us to be that of letting the House Judiciary Committee proceed first with its impeachment inquiry. I should add parenthetically that in my judgment, had an indictment been returned, the then-President would not have resigned, which meant that our country would have been burdened with a beleaguered President who could not have been brought to trial for a substantial period of time. It seemed that the trauma the nation would suffer in the interim would be awesome.

A solution to the problem, it appeared to us, was that of sending to the House Judiciary Committee all of the evidence that had been assembled by the grand jury bearing on the former President's involvement in the alleged obstruction of justice. This conclusion was concurred in by the members of the staff concerned with this problem, and inferences that there existed a diversity between them and the Special Prosecutor are baseless.

Such action, of course, was without legal precedent, but it seemed to be legally proper and would induce an expediting of the situation relating to the President. Accordingly, there was prepared a detailed report of the evidence that had been presented to the grand jury involving the actions of the President pertaining to the alleged offense of obstruction of justice. This grand jury report was presented to Judge Sirica, along with the indictments of the defendants in the *United States v. Mitchell* case (the cover-up case). Litigation followed, attacking the legality of transmitting such a report, and you will recall that the courts upheld the Special Prosecutor's contention.[1] Thus, the House was enabled to begin its proceedings much sooner than otherwise and move along with greater celerity. The significance of this stratagem largely has been overlooked. It ranks in importance with the Supreme Court decision ordering a turning over to the Special Prosecutor of the tapes that were under subpoena.[2] Without the grand jury data transmitted to the House Judiciary Committee, the latter was helpless to proceed with meaningful hearings. It is my belief, as well as that of those aware of the facts, that the House Judiciary Committee, without the benefit of the grand jury proceedings, would have foundered in progressing effectively in the pending impeachment proceedings.

There is still another facet to the matter. The then-President was entitled to his constitutional rights to a fair trial, whether it be an impeachment proceeding or a criminal proceeding. For both processes to have undertaken to function contemporaneously may have meant a denial of the right to a fair trial. It may even have caused a stalemate for a long period of time.

If you wonder whether I would make the same decision today as I did then—the answer is yes.

During the Watergate days, the subject of plea bargaining was highlighted. It is a subject in the administration of our criminal justice system much discussed these days; it is a subject misunderstood by many and even distorted by some. Its importance cannot be overemphasized.

In recent years, the American Bar Association released a volume on its approved Standards of Criminal Justice.[3] This monumental work, begun in 1965, was completed in 1973 when approval was given to the final set standards. The Special Committee in charge of

1. *In re* Report & Recommendation of June 5, 1972 Grand Jury, 370 F. Supp 1219 (D.D.C.), writ of mandamus denied sub nom. Haldeman v. Sirica, 501 F.2d 714 (D.C. Cir 1974).

2. United States v. Nixon, 418 U.S. 683 (1974).

3. ABA Standards Relating to the Administration of Criminal Justice, Compilation (1974).

this project was composed of eminent jurists, outstanding members of the bar, including both defense counsel and prosecutors.[4]

One of the topics to which these standards address themselves is that of plea discussions, often referred to as "plea bargaining." An advisory Committee on Criminal Trials—composed of distinguished judges, lawyers, and law professors—was assigned this subject for special consideration.[5] The following excerpt is particularly enlightening.

> Trials, however, by no means represent the major activity of a prosecutor in the administration of criminal justice in the United States. The vast majority of criminal cases are disposed of without trial as the result of guilty pleas and, if the system as a whole is working properly, *this is as it should be*. . . . The process of plea discussion serves important social interests and . . . is one of the *most important functions of both prosecution and defense counsel*. . . . Properly conducted, plea discussion may well produce a result approximating closely, but informally and more swiftly, the result which ought to ensue from a trial, while avoiding most of the undesirable aspects of that ordeal. Disposition without trial of course provides a substantial cost saving to the accused and to the public in terms of the time of lawyers and all other participants. *Although the cost saving alone would not be an appropriate justification for abridging the legal process if it were achieved at the expense of fairness or equal justice, from the standpoint of the objectives of the criminal law, a fair and just disposition of a case without trial is obviously preferable to its disposition by trial, as is true in civil litigation.* The speed and certainty of a disposition by plea promotes *deterrence*, a *basic* goal of criminal justice.[6]

In my humble judgment, there is nothing wrong with upright plea bargaining. Of course, as is true in the performance of any official function, it is subject to abuse by one who does not approach it with fairness for the rights of all concerned. A prosecutor has dozens of ways to fail in the proper performance of the prosecutorial function, and thus I wonder why critics should show any more concern in regard to the procedure of plea bargaining than any of the other duties that the prosecutor performs. The whole matter gets back to the prosecutor's proper, fair, and just performance of duty. My predecessor, Archibald Cox, believed in plea discussions; I believe in them; my successors, Henry Ruth and Charles Ruff, believe in them; and I am not aware of an instance in which the practice was abused in the Special Prosecutor's Office.

Before the government witnesses in the cover-up case were permitted to plea-bargain, they had to agree to plead guilty to a felony carrying at least a five-year maximum sentence; they also had to agree to testify to the truth under penalties of perjury. Is there anything unfair in such an arrangement either to society or to the individual? What is important to remember is that among the Watergate accused, there are men who have paid their debt to society by serving time in prison and who are now free to pursue their rehabilitation because of proper plea bargaining; there are others who have been and are being brought to the halls of justice because of appropriate plea bargaining, who otherwise

4. *Id.* at 467–70.
5. *See* Pleas of Guilty, in *id.* at 295.
6. *Id.* at 78–79 (emphasis added).

would have escaped the processes of the law.[7] The American public has demanded that the story of Watergate be known, and through the processes of justice under law, the story has been made known. And I can assure you that had it not been for perfectly fair and just plea discussions, the full story of the break-in and the cover-up would never have been known.

What will sustain our basic system of criminal justice is the fairness of its administration. Once the fairness fails, the system itself will be in jeopardy. The administration must be fair to society, but it must also be fair to the individual.

Next let me treat the subject of a clash between the constitutional forces of fair trial and free press, which could have created a dilemma. My topic pertains to one factual situation of historical significance and without precedent, and let us hope that there will never be another like it. The dilemma I want to discuss with you is hypothetical but it could have been real. Suppose President Ford had not pardoned Richard Nixon, and an indictment of him had been returned. Could he have received a fair trial? If so, under what circumstances?

The problem, of course, was created by the exercise of the constitutional guarantee of freedom of the press and the public's right to know. The right, in fact, the obligation to report to the American people the events that preceded the pardon were fulfilled properly, effectively, and certainly, with perhaps a few exceptions, responsibly. But what I want to examine with you is the consequence of the discharge of that right and that responsibility on Richard Nixon's constitutional right to a fair trial, had the pardon not been granted and an indictment had been returned. In short, the press, in this setting, had the right to exercise its constitutional guarantee and Richard Nixon had the right to stand on his constitutional guarantee. Therein lies the dilemma.

A brief resume of some events that transpired prior to the pardon should be helpful in the consideration of this problem.

The House Judiciary Committee sitting in inquiry on impeachment began its hearing with many of the sessions publicized—not only in the press but on live television and radio as well. Wide coverage was given the proof that indicated Nixon's involvement. The sessions not public created a number of stories of alleged evidence adduced which were, rightly or wrongly, attributed to members of the Committee or staff, and these were widely circulated. To cap the climax, when the tape recording of June 23, 1973, was made public, numerous Republican members of the House impeachment inquiry committee, who had previously defended Nixon, went on live television, not only to say that they were changing their vote but also flatly to state that they had concluded Nixon was guilty of obstruction of justice.[8] Then followed a few days of headlines on whether Nixon would resign (with various Congressmen and others calling on him to resign[9]) and the Committee in the meantime stood thirty-eight to nothing in favor of Articles of Impeachment on the

7. For a summary of the indictments, guilty pleas and outcomes of the trials of the Watergate defendants, see L. Jaworski, The Right and the Power 280 (1976).

8. N.Y. Times, Aug. 6, 1974, at 1, col. 8.

9. *See, e.g.*, N.Y. Times, Aug. 7, 1974, at 1, cols. 4–8.

charge of obstruction of justice. When Nixon resigned, the nation was told from shore to shore that in a move to avoid certain impeachment, the President gave up his office. The columns and the airwaves were filled with inculpatory comments regarding Nixon's guilt, ignominy, and disgrace, and of the story's historically unprecedented nature. The news media did a thorough job, exercising its First Amendment rights to the fullest extent and making certain that every American willing and able to read, or willing and able to listen, knew of Nixon's predicament and his resignation. Surveys indicated that an estimated ninety-two million persons viewed the televising of the Judiciary Committee proceedings.

Typical of editorial comments was the observation that President Nixon had for all practical purposes admitted criminal wrongdoing. The damaging tape records spoke for themselves.

Such was the background. What if Nixon—now no longer a sitting president—were to be indicted for obstruction of justice? What about his constitutional right to a fair trial? Like any other citizen, and regardless of his resignation and the unprecedented accusations of guilt, he was presumed to be innocent in the eyes of the law until proven guilty according to judicial process. Then followed the days when indictment had to be considered. But where does the prosecutor go after indictment, if there cannot be had a fair trial under the Constitution?

President Ford held his first news conference and the initial questions propounded—as well as some subsequently—related to the subject of whether President Ford was considering granting Nixon a pardon. The answers were somewhat ambivalent.[10] Not long after, I received a request from the President's counsel that I inform the President of the period of time, in my judgment, that would need to elapse, in the event of indictment, before he could receive a fair trial. I made such an estimate, pointing out, however, that the situation was unprecedented and that "the complexities involved in the process of selecting a jury and the time it will take to complete the process, I find difficult to estimate at this time."[11]

A decision on whether or not to indict was not a pressing matter at the moment because, had the decision been to indict, action would not have been taken until after the jury had been selected and sequestered in the *Mitchell, et al.* cover-up case, then set for the last day of September, because otherwise any indictment of Nixon would have meant an indefinite delay in that trial. While the matter was being studied, President Ford moved to pardon former President Nixon.

But suppose the pardon had not been granted, and an indictment had been considered proper. Then the prosecution would have come face to face with the dilemma to which I have alluded.

There is the First Amendment and the public's right to know on the one hand, and then there is former President Nixon's constitutional right to a fair trial under the Sixth and other amendments on the other hand. Had the unprecedented news media coverage of the events that transpired so influenced and subjugated the minds of prospective jurors

10. N.Y. Times, Aug. 29, 1974, at 20, col. 4.
11. L. Jaworski, The Right and the Power 241 (1976).

that a fair trial could not have been accorded Nixon for a year, for two years, or three years? And how does one accord a fair trial, under a presumption of innocence, to a defendant sitting in the dock as a resigned president who left office under the pressure of impeachment proceedings charging criminal wrongdoing?

Of course, there were those whose views were spawned in prejudice and hatred, who had piously spoken and written of constitutional rights and safeguards in the past, who could find no cause for concern regarding Nixon's constitutional rights in this setting. Some editorials indicated a complete lack of understanding of or concern for the constitutional problems involved. But it must be remembered that constitutional safeguards apply to *all*, and if they are to be glossed over when the scorned are involved, by easy stages their erosion is sure to follow.

May I, at this point, make it clear that I have not and am not now taking a position on whether President Ford should have granted the pardon. This is not within my province to do. I did take the position that it was within his constitutional power to grant a legal pardon, and having done so, it was a final and conclusive act. A few months after my decision was made, and in another case, the Supreme Court, on December 23 in what is known as the *Schick* case, held that any limitation to the pardoning power must be found in the Constitution—and there is none.[12]

In a poll conducted by West Publishing Company among lawyers of our nation to select the great milestones of law during the two centuries of America's existence,[13] *United States v. Nixon* received the third largest number of votes.[14] And why? Because it so pointedly and unmistakably affirms the doctrine that no one is above the law, not even the President. And in the *Nixon* case, as it did in *Marbury v. Madison* (which received the largest number of milestone votes),[15] the Supreme Court assumed the responsibility of becoming the ultimate guardian of the Constitution.

Professor Alexander Bickel of Yale authored an interesting volume fifteen years ago discussing the Supreme Court at what he termed the "Bar of Politics." He gave it the title *The Least Dangerous Branch*.[16] In selecting the title, Professor Bickel drew from the words of Alexander Hamilton, in the *78th Federalist*, "the judges as guardians of the Constitution."[17]

I doubt that the judiciary of our nation has been put to a severer test, since its early history, than it faced in this generation, culminating in the tragic episodes at the seat of our government in the past few years.

12. Schick v. Reed, 419 U.S. 256, 266 (1974).

13. *See* J. Lieberman, Milestones (1976).

14. 418 U.S. 683 (1974).

15. 5 U.S. (1 Cranch) 137 (1803).

16. A. Bickel, The Least Dangerous Branch: The Supreme Court at the Bar of Politics (1962).

17. The Federalist No. 78, at 517 (P. Ford ed., 1898). Although the primary theme of the *78th Federalist* is indeed "the judges as the guardians of the Constitution," Hamilton's exact words were: "[it] would require an uncommon portion of fortitude in the judges to do their duty as faithful guardians of the Constitution."

I wish on this occasion to rename Professor Bickel's title selection, based on Alexander Hamilton's observation. With pride and reverence, I wish to refer to it as "The Most Lustrous Branch." As I retrospectively review the performance of this third branch of government in times of stress and crises, I feel confident that this renaming can be justified. I do not base my judgment on the bold and unwavering performance of the judiciary in the matters spawned in Watergate alone, but as well in the response of the courts to the challenges our free society faces in modern times.

I doubt that there are any among us who fully conceive the effect of the judiciary's actions on the attitudes and resolves of this generation's young. I hope that you will believe my assurance that the youth of today follow more closely the labors of our courts than fifty years ago—yes, even more so today than a decade ago. Of this I am fully convinced, and the volume of correspondence I received during my days in Washington from young people—and the multitude of letters I have since—bear out this conviction.

Prime Minister Disraeli told us that the youth of a nation are the trustees of posterity.[18] This admonition is easy to understand and to accept. If we embrace this truism and give it proper regard, it follows that the youth of our nation are our society's most precious possession. If they are to become disenchanted with our institutions of government—if they are to lose faith in our judicial system—then posterity will not be served by fiduciaries of confidence and faith and trust in our courts; rather posterity then will be served by trustees of disenchantment and indifference, leading perhaps to radical changes from a system which, fundamentally, today is unexcelled in basic fairness and justness.

Let me return to the reactions of the youth of this nation to the recent tragedy in Washington. Here is a girl, from Colorado, who writes:

> I am 11 years old and am very interested in our country and its history and government. The Watergate days were not very good times for the country but now that they are over I think we are a better and stronger nation and everything was done within our Constitutional idea.

Then she added: "I sure bet you're glad to be back in Houston." (This last comment was the understatement of the year.)

A student at Duke University wrapped it up in these words: "Hopefully the court proceedings will teach us that no man is above the law and that all of us must answer for our actions."

Finally, let me share this one with you from a young lady in high school in California, who put it this way: "In the inspiring and refreshing search for truth and justice, there has been provided a sterling example for the young of my generation. There has been erased some of our cynicism towards government and that's a lot to accomplish!"

I could go on and on, but this is a fair, albeit meager, sampling of what runs through the minds of young America, and I trust that you will find these expressions as meaningful as have I.

18. Sybil, *Book VI*, ch. 13, in R. Blake, Disraeli 205 (1966).

Last year, I stood in the hallowed room in Independence Hall in Philadelphia, where the Declaration of Independence was signed, and eleven years later, after four months of debate, deliberation, study, and prayer, our Constitution was drafted. There were vast differences of opinions and a great contrariety of views permeating these extensive sessions on the Constitution, yet in the end dissents were largely resolved by an understanding approach to opposing views of the participants and the acceptance of sincereness and good faith on the part of all. The eventual result was a monumental document that has stood the test of time and has enabled us daily to enjoy the freedoms and the individual rights it guarantees.

As I contemplated the setting in Independence Hall, as it existed almost two hundred years ago, there crossed my mind, more deeply than ever before, the hardships, the sacrifice, and above all else, the selflessness of these great patriots who gave so much to earn for generations to come the freedoms that are ours today. They risked being captured, regarded as traitors and being put to death. And as I walked away from this historic place, there returned afresh the eloquent expressions of dedication and devotion that meant so much to them and which they hoped would be as fervently embraced by us. To remind me—almost to haunt me—came the recollections of immortal words they penned: "that all men are created equal"; "life, liberty and the pursuit of happiness"; and, finally, the pledge to each other of "our lives, our fortunes and our sacred honor." Then I paused to wonder: are these just empty phrases to many of us today, or are they still as radiant, as inspirational, and as binding in our pursuits as they were to these great founders of freedom and seekers of justice? I could not stop with these musings. What tortured my thinking was the undivided and unquestioned integrity and probity of these patriots—their trustworthiness and guilelessness, as contrasted with the shams and deceits and corruptions perpetrated by some of their successors of modern times.

What were the characteristics of the Founders who gave birth to this nation? And of the framers who cast our Constitution? Were they self-serving and greedy? Or were they men and women who loved freedom and justice and placed on the altar of sacrifice their fortunes—even their lives—to attain these ends? We gain some semblance of understanding of what plagues us today when we compare their sacrificial dedication to the conduct of some of our people in government today. But as we deplore their disgraceful conduct, let us applaud and never forget the exemplary and dedicated labors of so many of our nation's public servants.

Still fresh on my mind is the sadness of seeing one of the great tragedies of modern history—men who once had fame in their hands sinking to infamy—all because eventually their goals were of the wrong dreams and aspirations. The teaching of right and wrong had been forgotten, and little evils were permitted to grow into great evils, small sins to escalate into big sins. How did Alexander Pope put it? "Unblemished, let me live or die unknown. Give me an honest fame or give me none."[19]

19. Paraphrased from *The Temple of Fame*, *in* The Complete Poetical Works of Pope 52, 59 (Cambridge ed. 1931).

The Founders of this nation would have been shocked at the Watergate revelations. Then they would have concluded that despite the failures, shortcomings and wrong-doings on the Washington scene, they still had faith and optimism in the determination and dedication of this and future generations to carry forth the spirit of America and to attain the American ideal.

When I pause to contemplate the evil of tampering with the administration of justice, of obstructing it and prostituting it, I think of Saint Thomas More who breathed life into one of the greatest of all obligations of man—that of unswerving loyalty to the ends of justice. Not justice for the affluent and the powerful alone, not justice for the admired and the favored alone, not justice alone for those whose views and beliefs are shared, but justice as well for the weak, for the poor, and even for the despised and the scorned.

Saint Thomas More is best known in history for his courageous and sacrificial resistance of the evil demands of his King, whom he served as Lord Chancellor. He placed his conscience above life itself. It has been aptly said that he "reverenced the goodness of authority but reverenced even more the authority of goodness." Do you recall his last words on the scaffold? "I die the King's good servant, but God's first."

In eloquent terms and with lustrous integrity, this great man in history made his point in clear and unmistakable terms: You do not follow an obviously corrupt and evil leader.

Nothing leaves me with such a lack of faith and confidence in aspirants to public office and spokesmen of political parties than to hear them wail about some of the problems of today, without saying one word of the need of foundations of truth, justice, and honor in public affairs. The question naturally arises: Do they just assume them to be there, or do they even care?

In my own home state, I was saddened to read the appeal of a man interested in his own political future. He was urging his listeners to elect three men to Congress belonging to a certain political party. He did not consider it necessary for them to have any other qualifications than to be members of that particular party. Whether they were men of honor and trust seemed to be beside the point—what was important to him was having three bodies voting the straight party line. This is precisely what America does not need.

There was an English statesman named Shaftesbury—perhaps you never heard of him—who spoke words that should be embraced by us all and never forsaken by those who serve in government. He put it thusly: "[T]he most natural beauty in the world is honesty and moral truth."[20]

I always admired Henry L. Stimson, a great public servant, who inspired confidence in his devoted service. It was he who said: "The sinfulness and weakness of man are evident to anyone who lives in the active world. But men are also great, kind and wise. Honor begets honor; trust begets trust; faith begets faith; and hope is the mainspring of life."[21]

20. 1 A. Cooper, Earl of Shaftesbury, Characteristics of Men, Manners, Opinions, Times 94 (Robertson ed. 1964).

21. H. Stimson & McG. Bundy, On Active Service in Peace and War 672 (1948).

Public officials face many trials and tribulations; many face great temptations. When they have come to grips with their responsibilities and have dealt with the issues inherent in their duty to God and to fellow man, let us hope that they can say, as did Abraham Lincoln at the end of the Civil War: "I have felt His hand upon me in great trials."

I would add these thoughts. Shortcomings and failures notwithstanding, we should be proud of America and evidence that pride with acclaim and enthusiasm. There is no other country like ours in the entire world. We can and must keep America great, not only for ourselves, but as well for the leadership our nation gives to the rest of the world.

I would say that insofar as concerns our judiciary, after the passage of two hundred years, the operation of our government under law would have brought forth expressions of pride and plaudits from the framers. After this long passage of time, we find that indeed the Constitution does work in times of the severest of stresses and strains. Contemplate with me for just a moment how superbly this document has preserved freedoms and established justice. And during the Watergate years it was interpreted again to leave no doubt that no one, absolutely no one, is above the law.

Well, just what was it that our courts did in the Watergate days to counteract cynicism of the young and to keep the respect of the older generation? There was a trial judge, Judge Sirica, who would not accept distortions of truth and the obstruction of justice. He sought the truth and he found it. There was an appellate court ready to meet the first challenge of the President to the release of the tape recordings.[22] It acted with dispatch and decisiveness. The same trial court and the same appellate court, without delay and with a direct approach, decided that a crucial grand jury report should be transmitted to the House Judiciary Committee.[23] The final test of the courts as a "lustrous branch" came when the trial court overruled the President's claim of executive privilege in response to a subpoena duces tecum in a situation involving criminal wrongdoing.[24] The Supreme Court, in the interest of expediting justice, bypassed the court of appeals in granting certiorari,[25] and then boldly and unwaveringly and with a minimum of delay laid to rest the troublesome problems that beset the nation.[26]

It was perhaps the American judiciary's finest hour. Suppose the trial judge had been indifferent to his full responsibilities. Suppose the court of appeals had not come to grips forthrightly with the unprecedented question posed in the transmission of the grand jury report to the House Judiciary Committee. And suppose the Supreme Court had not measured up courageously and judiciously to the traumatic issues that confronted all three branches of government and the nation as a whole. I dread the thought. The result would

22. *In re* Grand Jury Subpoena Duces Tecum Issued to Richard M. Nixon, 360 F. Supp. 1 (D.D.C.), *modified in part sub nom.* Nixon v. Sirica, 487 F. 2d 700 (D.C. Cir. 1973).

23. *In re* Report & Recommendation of June 5, 1972 Grand Jury, 370 F Supp. 1219 (D.D.C.), *writ of mandamus denied sub nom.* Haldeman v. Sirica, 501 F. 2d 714 (D.C. Cir. 1974).

24. United States v. Mitchell, 377 F. Supp. 1326 (D.D.C.), *aff'd sub. nom.* United States v. Nixon, 418 U.S. 683 (1974).

25. United States v. Nixon, 417 U.S. 927, 960 (1974).

26. United States v. Nixon, 418 U.S. 683 (1974).

have been a chapter in our history books charging that our courts were ineffective and indolent. Respect for the administration of justice, at a time when suspicion lurked in the minds of the young, would have received a serious setback. Men in high places, whose sentences have become final, would have escaped the arm of the law. Had the grand jury report not been transmitted, the House Judiciary Committee hearings on the Articles of Impeachment would have been so slow in proceeding and perhaps so long delayed that efforts to arrive at effective action could well have been temporized and eventually frustrated. Finally, had not the Supreme Court of the United States fearlessly and stalwartly met the issues on the subpoenaed tape recordings, there would have been no end to the ordeal burdening the nation, and the scars of doubt and disillusion would have been deepened. The question naturally arises: how would this have affected the faith and the credence of the trustees of posterity in our institutions of government, especially the Judicial Branch?

Let us make no mistake about it—this salute to the Judiciary lies not in who won or lost—it rests on the record of the courts putting into operation the judicial process as it should work, with reasonable dispatch, meeting the issues squarely and disposing of them decisively. This brings to mind Lord Erskine's declaration in 1820, at the time of the trial of Queen Caroline: "[T]here is something so beautiful and exalted in the faithful administration of justice, and departure from it is so odious and disgusting."[27]

Daniel Webster lived from 1782 to 1852. He labored in the field of law with great devotion and never failed to champion the supremacy of the law. On one occasion, he eloquently affirmed that justice is man's great interest on earth. He would stoutly assert, were he speaking to us today, that the judicial process is a mighty fortress, and that we must not ever let it be weakened. And then he would remind us, as he once did in the prime of his illustrious career: "The Law: It has honored us, may we honor it."

27. 8 Lord Campbell, Lives of the Lord Chancellors of England 264 (Mallory ed., 1875).

The Attorney General: The Federal Government's Chief Lawyer and Chief Litigator, or One Among Many?

Griffin B. Bell

Former U.S. Attorney General Griffin Bell delivered the eighth Sonnett lecture, entitled *The Attorney General: The Federal Government's Chief Lawyer and Chief Litigator, or One Among Many?*, on March 14, 1978.[1]

Judge Bell, as he was referred to both before and after serving as Attorney General, was born in Americus, Georgia, in 1918.[2] After graduating from Georgia Southwestern College, Bell was drafted by the Army in 1941, serving as a company commander during World War II.[3] After the war, he graduated from Mercer University's Law School in Macon, Georgia.[4] Judge Bell then joined the Atlanta law firm of King & Spalding, where he became managing partner.[5]

President John F. Kennedy appointed Bell to the Fifth Circuit Court of Appeals in 1961,[6] leading Judge Bell to sit on the court at the height of the Civil Rights Movement. Perhaps most notably, after the decision in *United States v. Hinds County School Board*,[7] Judge Bell was assigned the task of overseeing the development and implementation of desegregation plans in thirty-three Mississippi school districts.[8] Judge Bell returned to King & Spalding in 1975.[9]

After being nominated by President Carter on January 25, 1977, Judge Bell was confirmed in the Senate as the seventy-second U.S. Attorney General.[10] As the Attorney General, Bell is credited with bringing independence and accountability to the Department of Justice (DOJ), and helping to restore the Department's image after the Watergate

Introduction written by Scott Silverman, J.D., Class of 2014, Fordham University School of Law.

1. Griffin B. Bell, *The Attorney General: The Federal Government's Chief Lawyer and Chief Litigator, or One Among Many?*, 46 Fordham L. Rev. 1049 (1978).

2. *Id.*

3. Stephen Louis A. Dillard, 1 Great American Judges: An Encyclopedia 55 (John R. Vile ed., 2003).

4. *Griffin Boyette Bell*, The United States Department of Justice, http://www.justice.gov/ag/bio/bell-griffin-boyette (last visited Mar. 5, 2014).

5. *Id.*

6. *Id.*

7. 417 F.2d 852 (5th Cir. 1969).

8. Dillard, *supra* note 3.

9. *Bell*, *supra* note 4.

10. *Id.* Judge Bell was confirmed by more than a three to one margin. *Id.*

scandal.[11] He also played a crucial role in creating federal policy supporting affirmative action.[12]

Following his resignation in 1979, Bell returned to King & Spalding where his work included representing Eugene Hasenfus, whose capture exposed the Iran-Contra scandal.[13] Judge Bell passed away in 2009 at the age of ninety due to complications with pancreatic cancer.[14]

Judge Bell's Sonnett lecture focused on the importance of clarifying the position and role of the Department of Justice.[15] Specifically, he believed that the Department of Justice and the Attorney General should exercise a review and supervisory function in an effort to bring uniformity to the government's legal positions.[16] Judge Bell thought one of the best ways to accomplish this was to have the Justice Department represent all executive branch departments and agencies.[17] Judge Bell's advocacy of greater DOJ control of federal litigation continues to be the subject of favorable comment in scholarly articles.[18]

Judge Bell also discussed The Freedom of Information Act (FOIA) in his lecture, emphasizing the importance of government-wide coordination to provide uniform application of the law.[19] This vision culminated with the issuance of government-wide guidance on a range of FOIA implementation issues by current U.S. Attorney General Eric Holder, providing for greater transparency and more efficient administration.[20]

During Judge Bell's tenure as Attorney General, the Department of Justice was composed of roughly 3,800 attorneys.[21] Today, that number has surpassed 10,000,[22] making the need for a uniform position and consistent enforcement more important than ever before.

---

11. Patrick J. Lyons, *Griffin B. Bell, Carter's Attorney General, Is Dead*, N.Y. Times, (Jan. 5, 2009).

12. *Griffin Bell (1918–2009)*, New Georgia Encyclopedia, http://www.georgiaencyclopedia.org/articles/government-politics/griffin-bell-1918–2009 (last visited Mar. 5, 2014).

13. Lyons, *supra* note 11.

14. *Id.*

15. Bell, *supra* note 1, at 1049.

16. *Id.* at 1058.

17. *Id.* at 1059.

18. *See* Neal Devins & Michael Herz, *The Uneasy Case for Department of Justice Control of Federal Litigation*, 5 U. Pa. J. Const. L. 558, 578 n.78 (2014); James R. Harvey III, *Loyalty in Government Litigation: Department of Justice Representation of Agency Clients*, 37 Wm. & Mary L. Rev. 1569, 1573 n.18 (1996).

19. Bell, *supra* note 1, at 1063.

20. *Accomplishments*, Department of Justice, http://www.justice.gov/accomplishments/#s5 (last visited Mar. 5, 2014).

21. Bell, *supra* note 1, at 1049.

22. *Office of Attorney Recruitment and Management*, The United States Department of Justice, http://www.justice.gov/oarm/ (last visited Mar. 5, 2014).

1978 Sonnett Lecture

I became Attorney General with fixed expectations about the Department of Justice. Despite its size and recent history, I expected to find a strong Department with a clear understanding of its place in the nation's government and a confident vision of its future.

After only a few weeks on the job I began to question my expectations. Now, well into my second year, I believe I fully appreciate the realities of the Department of Justice.

The truth is that the Department of Justice is strong. But it is a strength born solely of the outstanding individuals who comprise it. The Department as a whole draws little strength or stability from a clear conception, either within the Department or elsewhere, of the role that the Department should play in our federal government. Least of all is there a clear course charted for the future of the Department.

As Attorney General I am unavoidably caught up in several great issues: the investigation of Korean influence-buying in Congress, the investigation of past abuses in the Federal Bureau of Investigation, the national effort to develop a response to the influx of undocumented aliens, and several others. But these headline-grabbing issues will pass, many to become mere footnotes to history. As much as possible without shortchanging sensitive matters of the immediate moment, I am focusing on the Department of Justice as a whole—past, present, and future. It is my firm belief that clarifying the position and role of the Department of Justice in the order of government is of first importance to the long-range interests of the nation.

Tonight I want to share some of what I have learned about the Department, some of my perceptions of its current problems, and some tentative views on its proper place in our system.

The Department of Justice today has 54,528 employees, including 3,806 attorneys (2,008 in the Justice Department and 1,798 in the United States Attorney's Offices).[1] About ninety-two percent of our attorneys are involved in the trial and appeal of lawsuits. The other 300 attorneys supervise divisions or offices, render legal advice, consult with Congress or other departments and agencies regarding legislation, and—to a quite limited extent—draft and interpret rules and regulations.

Shortly after I took office, the President asked me to determine the total number of lawyers in the government and their functions. I learned that such information had not been gathered in several years, so we started an inventory of every department and agency in the government. We discovered 19,479 lawyers who are performing "lawyer-like" functions—litigating, preparing legal memoranda, giving legal advice, and drafting statutes, rules, and regulations. These lawyers are distributed throughout the departments and agencies, and practically no agency is too small to have its own "General Counsel."

Some of the 15,673 federal lawyers in government agencies outside the Department of Justice are handling litigation themselves; some are involved in direct support of the Justice Department's litigation efforts. Others are involved in other administrative law

1. *See* U.S. Dep't of Justice, Legal Activities 2 (1977).

functions within their agencies. About one-fourth of all the federal government's lawyers, 5,247 to be exact,[2] are in the Department of Defense and the military services where they administer a totally separate court-martial system under the Uniform Code of Military Justice.

Although I am the chief legal officer in the executive branch, I have learned that I have virtually no control or direction over the lawyers outside the Department of Justice, except indirectly in connection with pending litigation.

AUTHORITY OF THE ATTORNEY GENERAL AND THE DEPARTMENT OF JUSTICE

History

It may come as a surprise to many of you, as it did to me, to learn that the Department of Justice is little more than a century old. For over eighty years the nation had only an Office of the Attorney General. This fact alone, and the reasons for it, go far to explain the absence of strong traditions and clearly defined roles to undergird the present Department.

The first Congress created the office of Attorney General in the Judiciary Act of 1789,[3] at the same time it created the federal court system. The Act called for "a meet person, learned in the law, to act as attorney-general for the United States,"[4] but gave him little power. He was to do nothing more than represent the United States before the Supreme Court and, upon request, to give opinions on matters of law to the President and heads of departments.[5] Congress also clearly intended the Attorney General to rank below the heads of the three departments—War, Foreign Affairs, and Treasury—which existed at the time. First, it ranked the Attorney General behind them for succession and protocol purposes. Whereas the salary for the heads of the Treasury and Foreign Affairs Departments was set at $3,500, that of the Attorney General was only $1,500.[6] And, whereas the department heads were given ample staff and quarters, the Attorney General received nothing beyond his salary—no funds to hire a clerk, purchase office supplies, or provide for heat or light. He was required to pay all his expenses himself.

Historians have discerned two motives behind Congress's treatment of the office of Attorney General. The first was frugality; the new nation was unsound financially and Congress had to cut corners wherever possible.[7] But the second and perhaps more important motive for our purposes was fear of a strong Attorney General.[8] Those early representatives vividly remembered the tyranny that could result from strong central enforcement of laws, and they hesitated to create machinery in the executive branch that possibly could

2. This figure includes 3,739 lawyers in uniform.
3. Ch. 20, § 35, 1 Stat. 93 (corresponds to 28 U.S.C. § 503 (1970)).
4. *Id.*
5. *Id.* (corresponds to 28 U.S.C. §§ 511–12 (1970)).
6. J. Easby-Smith, The Department of Justice 5 (1904)
7. *See* L. Huston, The Department of Justice 9–10 (1967),
8. *See id.* at 7–8.

serve as an engine of oppression. Nowhere was this concern more evident than in the arrangement for the enforcement of penal law and the representation of the federal government in civil litigation at the trial level. The Judiciary Act gave the Attorney General no role in either matter, vesting both powers exclusively in the thirteen United States attorneys,[9] then called district attorneys, who were totally independent of the Attorney General.

The first Attorney General, Edmund Randolph, made his first report to the President in 1791. In it he sought redress of the very handicaps that Congress had intentionally placed upon him. He requested authority to participate in litigation in the inferior courts, in order to have some input into making the records in cases that he eventually would have to argue in the Supreme Court. He requested authority to supervise the district attorneys because they already had shown tendencies toward uneven enforcement of the laws. And he requested a clerk to help him with the simple mechanical chores of his office. President Washington endorsed all three requests and transmitted them to Congress—where they got nowhere.[10]

The congressional snub of Randolph's recommendations in 1791 established a pattern that was to persist for decades. Seven Attorneys General had succeeded Randolph before Congress in 1818 finally appropriated funds for the hire of a clerk.[11] Despite renewed recommendations by President Jackson in 1829 and 1830, by President Polk in 1846, and by President Pierce in 1854. It was not until 1861—a full seventy years after the first request by Randolph and Washington—that Congress finally gave the Attorney General some measure of authority over the district attorneys.[12]

The congressional opposition to these requests by successive administrations illustrates the persistence throughout much of the nineteenth century of the fear of a strong Attorney General. As the federal government grew, its legal business grew along with it. There were periodic attempts by some administrations and some members of Congress to gain support for the idea of a centralized law department to handle that legal business. The unfailing reaction of Congress to each new increment, however, was to create a law officer, usually known as a Solicitor, in the department generating the legal issues, and put him in control of the resulting litigation with no duty to answer to the Attorney General. The first Solicitor was created in the Treasury Department in 1830.[13] The next forty years witnessed a steady stream of such officers—Solicitors for the Navy, for the War Department, for the State Department, for the Post Office, for Internal Revenue.

As for the Attorney General, Congress was perfectly willing to add piecemeal to his duties; for instance, placing him on the Patent Board, making him a member of the Sinking Fund Commission, whatever that was, and rerouting executive clemency petitions from the State Department to him. But Congress refused to authorize any enlargement

9. Ch. 20, § 35, 1 Stat. 92 (1789) (no longer in force).

10. J. Easby-Smith, The Department of Justice 6–7 (1904).

11. W. Seymour, United States Attorney 21 (1975).

12. *Id.* at 22.

13. *See* A. Langeluttig, The Department of Justice of the United States 5 (1927).

of his legal domain. And it was careful to keep the Attorney General's staff just large enough—some would say too small—to assist him with his duties already assigned, so there was no chance of his augmenting his power by asserting de facto control over legal business where Congress had refused him de jure authority. In fact, in debates over how to handle increasing federal litigation, those who opposed the creation of a law department invariably cited the overworked state of the Attorney General as proof that the new business could not be lodged with him.

At some point, of course, the fear of centralized authority had to dissipate as the memories of legal oppression from the Old World receded and the federal government increased in power without becoming more prone to abuses of the states or individuals in the process. Added to that development was a growing belief that centralization of the legal activity of the federal government would be more efficient and thus cheaper than the system of Solicitors and relatively independent district attorneys. That system had effectively broken down under the continuing press of new business in the 1860s, resulting in the hiring of numerous outside counsel at considerable expense.

The conjunction of these two threads—acceptance of the idea of centralization and a desire for economy—helped to create the Department of Justice in 1870. The debates in Congress at the time evidence a third reason for the move—the need to insure that the federal government spoke with one voice in its view of and adherence to the law. Senator Jenckes of Rhode Island, in explaining the proposal to the Senate, addressed himself to the existing Solicitors and expressly spelled out this purpose:

> I need not dwell upon the manner in which these officers have performed their duties. I have no doubt they have performed them to the best of their ability and honestly in every case. But we have found that there has been a most unfortunate result from this separation of law powers. We find one interpretation of the laws of the United States in one Department and another interpretation in another Department. . . .
>
> . . .
>
> . . . It is for the purpose of having a unity of decision, a unity of jurisprudence, if I may use that expression, in the executive law of the United States, that this bill proposes that all the law officers therein provided for shall be subordinate to one head.[14]

The Act establishing the Department of Justice sought to remedy the problem of divergent executive branch legal views by giving the Attorney General supervision over the several departmental Solicitors as well as the district attorneys and any outside counsel employed on behalf of the United States.[15] The position of Solicitor General was created as an assistant to the Attorney General, as were two positions of Assistant Attorney General.[16] The Act also gave the Attorney General and the Department of

14. Cong. Globe, 41st Cong., 2d Sess. 3036 (1870).

15. Act of June 22, 1870, ch. 150, §§ 3, 15–16, 16 Stat. 162, 164 (corresponds to 28 U.S.C. §§ 518–519, 543 (1970)).

16. *Id.* § 2, 16 Stat. 162 (corresponds to 28 U.S.C. §§ 505–506 (1970)).

Justice control of all criminal and civil litigation in which the United States was interested.[17]

On its face, the Act of 1870 seemed to presage preeminence for the new Department of Justice and a new era of economy and harmony in the legal business of the federal government. But two serious oversights by Congress at the time effectively doomed from the outset this attempt to consolidate and rationalize federal legal activity. First, Congress failed to repeal or modify the statutes establishing the various Solicitors as independent legal officers and defining their duties. The 1870 Act did state that they now were subject to "supervision" by the Attorney General,[18] but that is a vague term and the Solicitors continued to claim their same pre-1870 powers and independence. The second oversight greatly compounded the difficulties caused by the first. Congress gave the new Department no building or other quarters where all of the attorneys under the Attorney General's supervision could concentrate their offices. The Solicitors stayed in the buildings housing their old departments, where they were subject to continuing supervision by the heads of those departments rather than their nominal new boss, the Attorney General.

Congress was exhibiting a curious ambivalence about the role of the Attorney General and the Department of Justice, appearing to give them total control over the nation's legal business on the one hand but failing to take action necessary to make that control effective on the other. Within five years of creating the Department of Justice, Congress took three steps that showed it had not been serious about centralizing all legal activity under the Attorney General. In 1871 and 1872 it created two new Assistant Attorney General positions, but expressly assigned them to the Interior and Post Office Departments where they were subject to supervision by the heads of those departments rather than the Attorney General. And in 1874 Congress reenacted all of the old laws defining the roles of the Solicitors, with no attempt to modify their powers so as to subject them to more effective attorney general control.

The creation of the first independent regulatory agency, the Interstate Commerce Commission, in 1887,[19] with the express congressional intent that it not be under the control of the President or the executive branch, added a new dimension to what Congress intended the role of the Department of Justice to be. There is some evidence that the Commission handled most of its cases in the lower courts from the beginning, and that it cooperated with the Solicitor General in the presentation of its cases to the Supreme Court. In any event, in 1910 President Taft sent a special message to Congress recommending that all litigation affecting the government be under the control of the Department of Justice and specifically objecting to the practice of the Interstate Commerce Commission in employing its own attorneys who, "while subject to the control of the Attorney-General, act upon

17. *Id.* § 5, 16 Stat. 162–63 (corresponds to 28 U.S.C. §§ 514–519 (1970)).
18. *Id.* § 3, 16 Stat. 162 (no longer in force).
19. Act of February 4, 1887, ch. 104, § 11, 24 Stat. 383 (current version at 49 U.S.C. § 11 (1970)).

the initiative and under the instructions of the commission."[20] After a vigorous debate in Congress—centering largely on whether the Department of Justice would have the authority to second-guess the Commission on the merits—Congress enacted legislation allowing the Commission to intervene as a party and, as such, to be represented by its own attorneys. Justice Department attorneys could therefore oppose the Commission's attorneys in court, and indeed, that has happened on a number of occasions, although the Commission and the Solicitor General have cooperated to file joint briefs in the Supreme Court in most cases.

During most of the pre–World War I period, however, the Attorney General was nominally the head of all federal legal activity, but the Solicitors and their offices retained their actual independence. The Labor, Commerce, and Agriculture Departments were created, each with its own Solicitor. And at the Attorney General's suggestion the two Assistant Attorneys General in the Post Office and Interior Departments were made Solicitors in acknowledgment of their real independence from him.

There was one bright spot for the Attorney General during this period. In 1886 the last vestige of the earlier concern with downgrading the Attorney General was removed when the Attorney General was restored to the fourth rank among Cabinet positions for protocol and succession purposes. Previously he had ranked behind all other heads of departments, even those created after the office of Attorney General.[21]

At the outset of World War I many new agencies were created in the federal government to meet the emergency situation. Following the lead of the older departments, these agencies all insisted on their own legal counsel and authority over their own litigation. Their demands created enough confusion that the question of the lack of centralized litigating authority was brought to President Wilson's personal attention. The result was an executive order under which all Solicitors and other law officers were directed to submit to the Attorney General's authority, and the Attorney General's legal opinions were made binding on all executive departments.[22] But this executive order *was* promulgated under an act giving the President temporarily expanded powers for the war effort, and it expired along with the act six months after the armistice. The predictable result was an almost immediate return to the status quo ante, with all Solicitors and other legal officers reasserting their independence from the Attorney General.

In 1920, the Interstate Commerce Commission attorneys were granted statutory authority to appear for the Commission "in any case in court,"[23] and the United States Shipping Board was authorized to employ attorneys to "represent the board in any case in

20. Special Message of the President of the United States on Interstate Commerce and Antitrust Laws and Federal Incorporation, H.R. Doc. No. 484. 61st Cong. 2d Sess. 5 (1910).

21. J. Easby-Smith, The Department of Justice 4–5 (1904).

22. Exec. Order No. 2877 (May 31, 1918), *reprinted in* Key, *The Legal Work of the Federal Government*, 25 Va. L. Rev. 165, 190 n.94 (1938).

23. Transportation Act, 1920, ch. 91, § 428, 41 Stat. 492 (current version at 49 U.S.C. § 16(11) (1970)).

court."[24] In 1921 a Veterans Bureau was established, and its attorneys were given control over all veterans' litigation.

Before long, different parts of the government again were making different interpretations of the same laws and again taking inconsistent positions before the courts. In 1928, the Attorney General in his Annual Report likened the situation to that which had existed prior to the creation of the Department of Justice in 1870. He noted that only 115 of the 900 legal positions in the executive departments and agencies in Washington were even nominally under his control.[25] The Attorney General recommended that serious consideration again be given to consolidating all legal activities under the chief law officer of the government.[26]

A few months into his administration, President Franklin Roosevelt issued an executive order centralizing all litigating authority in the Department of Justice and giving the Attorney General the exclusive right to supervise United States attorneys.[27] Roosevelt's action, like that of the Congress in 1870 and President Wilson in 1918, resulted from a perception that decentralized control of the government's legal affairs had led to chaos and excessive expense.

Roosevelt's effort met the same fate as the two before it. The trend away from centralized responsibility started again almost immediately. The Securities and Exchange Commission was established in 1934[28] and the National Labor Relations Board in 1935,[29] and both were given the power to conduct their own litigation. The cycle of disintegration and reform had continued.

The exceptions to centralized litigation authority that were created during the next thirty-five years mostly involved new independent regulatory agencies, although one executive department, the Department of Labor, also received some independent litigating authority. Agencies such as the Federal Communications Commission, the Federal Power Commission (now the Federal Energy Regulatory Commission), the Federal Maritime Commission, the Atomic Energy Commission (now the Nuclear Regulatory Commission), and the Equal Employment Opportunity Commission were granted at least some degree of independent litigating authority. Since about 1969/1970, new grants of independent litigating authority have literally seemed to explode, with authority not only going to independent agencies such as the Consumer Product Safety Commission, the Commodity Futures Trading Commission, and the International Trade Commission, but also to some executive branch agencies such as the Environmental Protection Agency. Today, some thirty-one separate federal governmental units have or exercise authority to conduct at least some of their own litigation.

24. Act of June 5, 1920, ch. 250, § 3, 41 Stat. 990 (repealed 1936).

25. Compared to 3,806 of the 15,740 federal civilian lawyers today.

26. [1928] Att'y Gen. Ann. Rep. 1–2, 347.

27. Exec. Order No. 6166, § 5 (June 10, 1933), *reprinted in* 77 Cong. Rec. 5707–08 (1933).

28. Securities Exchange Act of 1934, ch. 404, § 4, 48 Stat. 885 (current version at 15 U.S.C. § 78d (1976)).

29. Act of July 5, 1935, ch. 372, § 3(a), 49 Stat. 451 (current version at 29 U.S.C. § 153(a) (1970)).

The Present

The basic statutory scheme today is the same as in 1870: except as otherwise authorized by Congress, the conduct of litigation in which the United States or an agency or officer thereof is a party, or is interested, is reserved to officers of the Department of Justice, under the direction of the Attorney General. The problem is the number of exceptions authorized by Congress. Professor John Davis has aptly characterized the situation as follows:

> a continuing effort by Attorneys General to centralize responsibility for all government litigation in Justice, a continuing effort by many agencies to escape from that control with respect to civil litigation, and a practice by Congress of accepting the positions of the Attorneys General in principle and then cutting them to pieces by exceptions.[30]

Prosecution of all criminal violations is controlled by the Department of Justice, and I do not understand that authority to be seriously challenged; but there is no consistent or rational statutory scheme applicable to agencies in civil litigation. The curious patchwork of civil litigation authority cannot be explained in terms of a congressional conception of the role of the Justice Department. Some grants of separate litigating authority seem to have been enacted simply because of loud and persistent complaints from the agencies seeking such authority. Others seem designed to increase the control of particular congressional committees or subcommittees over particular agencies or programs. Neither a congressional body that works closely with an agency, nor the agency itself, wants the Justice Department making decisions counter to its desires. Fiefdoms have been created, and the Justice Department's efforts to ensure uniformity in government litigating postures can constitute a real threat to them.

Some recent grants of independent litigating authority have occurred in strange ways. For example, the litigating authority of the Federal Trade Commission was significantly enlarged in 1973 by an amendment on the floor of the Senate tacked onto the Act authorizing the Trans-Alaska oil pipeline,[31] thereby avoiding veto.

I recognize that Congress intended some regulatory agencies and government corporations to be independent of the executive branch and the President. That independence has extended to independence from the Department of Justice in legal matters, including litigation. The price of such independence is high, as it can and sometimes does result in two sets of government lawyers opposing each other at taxpayer expense. More importantly, it requires the judicial branch to decide interagency disputes that might be resolved more easily and better through the mediation of the Department of Justice.

I do not favor the independence of these regulatory agencies and government corporations in legal matters. I think it is unseemly for two government agencies to sue each other. It requires the judicial branch to decide questions of government policy, a role never

30. Davis, Department of Justice Control of Agency Litigation 17 (Report to the U.S. Administrative Conference Aug. 14, 1975).

31. Act of Nov. 16, 1973, Pub. L. No. 93–153, § 408. 87 Stat. 591–92 (1973) (current version at 15 U.S.C. §§ 45(1), 46, 53(b), 56 (1976)).

envisioned by our country's Founding Fathers. It is time-consuming and expensive. I believe it would be possible to preserve the independence of these bodies even if they were represented by the Justice Department. Such a system would be more efficient and would reduce the amount of judicial intrusion into intragovernmental disputes. The Department of Justice can exercise a review and supervisory function in an effort to bring uniformity to government legal positions and still recognize the independence of the regulatory agencies' enforcement efforts.

My predecessors as Attorney General have shared my view that the Justice Department should represent the regulatory agencies. To date, however, Congress has been willing to pay the price of independent litigating authority for those agencies.

If separate litigating authority is going to continue for independent regulatory agencies and government corporations, then we should at least devise a rational system for the conduct of such litigation. One agency's case often will affect other regulator, agencies or executive branch departments. At the least, an agency should be required to alert the Justice Department in such cases so that the views of the executive branch could also be presented to the court. If a case could affect the entire government, such as an employment discrimination claim or a Freedom of Information Act complaint, the Justice Department should have control of the litigation rather than the single agency that is party to the case. The position taken by a single agency on a question of general concern should not bind the entire federal government.

It is my view that the Justice Department should represent all executive branch departments and agencies. The Department must, of course, work closely with its clients in a cooperative effort, recognizing the peculiar expertise and abilities of agency lawyers and delegating authority to agency lawyers in certain circumstances, but always retaining final control in the Justice Department.

A study of federal legal offices in 1955 found that the absence of lines of authority from agency general counsels to the Attorney General contributed to the diversity of legal positions in the federal government. The report of that study strongly supported centralized litigation authority in the Department of Justice.

President Carter last August directed his Reorganization Project to study the way the government's lawyers are used, stating that he considers "the effective use of legal resources to be a vital part of . . . [the] Administration's effort to improve the performance of the Federal Government. . . ." The President hopes that better use of these resources will enable the federal government better to comply with its own rules and regulations and thus prevent unnecessary litigation and administrative delay. The President stated that he also hoped to improve the procedures for conducting government litigation in order to ensure more uniform application of the law.[32]

32. In addition to studying the proper allocation of litigation authority, the President's Reorganization Project is examining several other issues that touch on the future role of the Justice Department. These include the flow of information between government lawyers, the hiring and retention of lawyers, and their training.

Plans for the Future

The President's Reorganization Project is completing its study and will forward its recommendations to the President in the next few weeks. This seems a particularly appropriate time to discuss the proper role of the Department of Justice in the future.

It is clear that the Solicitor General must continue to perform his current function of representing all the executive departments and the independent regulatory agencies before the Supreme Court. As counsel for the federal government, the Solicitor General is responsible for presenting cases to the Supreme Court in the manner that will best serve the overall interests of the United States. He is also responsible for deciding whether lower court decisions adverse to the government should be appealed and whether the government should file amicus curiae briefs in cases to which it is not a party. During the past term, the government filed or supported petitions for writs of certiorari in 107 cases, seventy-six percent of which were granted.[33] That percentage should be compared to the percentage of all petitions granted—six percent. This reflects the Solicitor General's careful screening of the government's cases, and his skillful advocacy in presenting the government's views in an accurate and balanced manner. Last year was not exceptional; over the past decade, the Supreme Court has reviewed only six to ten percent of the cases presented to it but taken sixty to seventy percent of the government's cases.[34]

The United States is involved in about one-half of the cases decided on the merits by the Supreme Court each year.[35] The Solicitor General's overview of all these cases is critical to avoiding inconsistencies in the government's positions. His responsibility to the entire government helps him avoid litigating a significant legal issue with government-wide impact in a case that, because of its factual or procedural context, is a poor vehicle. An agency often does not see this broader picture; vindication in the pending case is often more important to it than the long-range interests of the United States. Solicitor General Erwin Griswold made that point in this way:

> The Solicitor General's client in a particular case cannot be properly represented before the Supreme Court except from a broad point of view, taking into account all of the factors which affect sound government and the proper formulation and development of the law. In providing for the Solicitor General, subject to the direction of the Attorney General, to attend to the "interests of the United States" in litigation, the statutes have always been understood to mean the long-range interests of the United States, not simply in terms of its fisc, or its success in the particular litigation, but as a government, as a people.[36]

33. [1977] Solicitor Gen. Ann. Rep. 2.

34. *See* Statement of Solicitor General Erwin N. Griswold Concerning Securities Exchange Act H.R. 5050 Before the Subcomm. on Commerce and Finance of the House Comm. on Interstate and Foreign Commerce, 93d Cong., 1st Sess. 5 (June 7, 1973).

35. *See* [1977] Solicitor Gen. Ann. Rep. table I.

36. The Office of the Solicitor General—Representing the Interests of the United States Before the Supreme Court 12, Address by Solicitor General Erwin N. Griswold, University of Missouri Law School (Mar. 14, 1969) (footnote omitted).

The Solicitor General's screening function is an aid to the Supreme Court itself because of the large volume of cases filed there. The Court recognizes and supports this role. Chief Justice Burger sent a letter to Congress in 1971, on behalf of a unanimous Court, in response to a congressional inquiry whether the Securities and Exchange Commission should be empowered to conduct its Supreme Court litigation independently of the Solicitor General's Office. The Chief Justice noted the Solicitor General's "highly important role in the selection of cases to be brought here"[37] and predicted that diluting the Solicitor General's authority would very likely increase the workload of the Supreme Court.

The various Solicitors General have been careful in the exercise of their authority, and the Office is well respected by other departments and agencies for its expertise, independence, and objectivity. Although Congress has authorized several agencies[38] independently to file petitions for writs of certiorari in certain categories of cases, such separate petitions have been relatively infrequent, presently averaging one or two a year. The Solicitor General's Office recognizes that control over the government's litigation is not intended to transform the Department of Justice into a superagency sitting in judgment on the policy decisions of other departments or agencies. With a few notable exceptions, such as the antitrust and the civil rights laws and the Freedom of Information Act, Congress has committed elsewhere the primary responsibility for most of the policy decisions in the government.

It is my belief that all 3,800 lawyers in the Justice Department can perform with the same degree of independence, objectivity, and litigation expertise as the twenty attorneys in the Solicitor General's Office. Agency lawyers are enmeshed in the daily routine of a specific government agency and cannot be expected to litigate cases with the broad perspective and objectivity that ensures proper representation of the best interests of the entire government—and therefore of the people. Justice Department lawyers have the perspective and objectivity, but they must take care not to interfere with the policy prerogatives of our agency clients. An agency's views should be presented to a court unless they are inconsistent with overall governmental interests, or cannot fairly be argued.

Agency lawyers are often experts in their own regulatory, and enforcement programs and statutes, and are often deeply involved in their agency's programs. Justice Department lawyers and United States attorneys are litigation experts, and perform a critical function in translating the agency's programmatic expertise into effective briefs and arguments for

37. Statement of Solicitor General Erwin N. Griswold Concerning Securities Exchange Act H.R. 5050 Before the Subcomm. on Commerce and Finance of the House Comm. on Interstate and Foreign Commerce, 93d Cong., 1st Sess. 11 (June 7, 1973).

38. These include the Federal Communications Commission, the Nuclear Regulatory Commission, the Interstate Commerce Commission, the Federal Maritime Commission, the Maritime Administration, and the Secretary of Agriculture (under the Packers and Stockyards Act, 1921, ch. 64, § 316, 42 Stat. 168 (current version at 7 U.S.C. § 217 (1976)), and the Perishable Agricultural Commodities Act, 1930, ch. 436, § 11, 46 Stat. 535 (current version at 7 U.S.C. § 499k (1976)). In addition, the Tennessee Valley Authority has in some cases represented itself before the Supreme Court.

judges who deal with an almost bewildering variety of cases and problems involving the federal government.

I recognize that our lawyers must better utilize the expertise of our client agencies. Since taking office I have recognized that we need to improve our day-to-day working relationships with other agencies. We have taken new steps to ensure advance consultation with client agencies before cases can be settled, and to ensure that our client agencies are properly informed of the progress of pending cases. In short, we have tried to develop a new sensitivity to treating our client agencies as any private lawyer would treat a client. To help nurture this sensitivity, we are devising a new system of evaluating the performance of our lawyers, which will include consideration of comments from the agencies they have represented.

We are considering other steps to more effectively and better serve our client agencies. A number of agencies feel that the Justice Department has not devoted sufficient effort to affirmative enforcement of their programs because of the demands of an increasingly heavy civil defensive caseload. One way to meet this problem may be the establishment of a group of attorneys who would litigate only affirmative agency cases.

Overburdened and strained resources continue to be a problem for the Justice Department, just as they were during our early history. We are examining ways to better manage the resources we have, including a better system of dividing civil cases between Washington and the field. We also have to work with our client agencies to make the most effective use of our attorneys. For example, every case does not need an agency lawyer in the field, an agency lawyer in Washington, a Justice Department lawyer in Washington, and an assistant United States attorney to review and agree to the filing of each pleading. More sensible delegations of responsibility simply have to be worked out. As a first step, we are considering significantly increasing the authority of United States attorneys to settle monetary claims against the government without first getting approval from Washington. In keeping with our concern for the views of our client agencies, however, if the client agency objects to the proposed disposition we will require review of the matter at a supervisory level of the Justice Department in Washington.

I would like to speak for a moment to another issue related to the Justice Department's role of representing agencies in litigation. I believe Justice can and should play a greater role in prelitigation counseling of other departments and agencies. After all, one of the principal functions of a lawyer is to "keep all clients out of court"—that is, to advise him or her how to accomplish objectives without leaving him or her vulnerable to suit. This legal counseling role for government agencies is now generally performed by their own general counsels. Functioning as a lawyer independent of the agency, the Department of Justice can provide the agency with a dispassionate view of legal problems associated with policy objectives. Moreover, as chief litigator for the government, the Department is able to apply the knowledge and experience it gains in that arena to anticipate potential legal difficulties presented by agency activities.

A good example of how that experience has been put to use is in the area of agency affirmative action efforts. The Department has probed this complex area of the law through its experience in formulating a position in the *Bakke* case,[39] as well as in representing the Department of Commerce in extensive litigation over the minority business enterprise provision of the Public Works Employment Act of 1976.[40] By gaining familiarity with the issues common to all affirmative action programs, we are able to advise departments or agencies of potential legal problems. Thus, the experience gained in filing a brief amicus curiae on behalf of the United States and in representing the Department of Commerce might be utilized in advising the Department of Defense or representing the Labor Department.

Because the Department has become familiar with potential problems in the affirmative action area, I have brought those questions to the attention of the various departments and have offered the services of the Department in advising them on the establishment of such programs. For example, the Department has taken the position that an affirmative action program is legally justified if necessary to remedy the effects of past public and private discrimination. Articulation of such a purpose will aid a court in evaluating the legality of a program if it is later challenged. Moreover, we can advise agencies how to tailor their programs to accomplish their remedial objectives. In this way, we hope to establish a uniform position throughout the government, to enable agencies to better accomplish their goals and to avoid litigation.

The Freedom of Information Act is another example of a set of legal principles and public policies which pertain to all federal activities and which should be interpreted and respected throughout the government with a fair degree of uniformity.[41] There is a clear need for effective government-wide coordination to avoid conflicting interpretations by various government agencies. In 1977 the Justice Department consulted with other federal agencies over four hundred times on Freedom of Information Act questions not then in litigation, and we feel these efforts make an important contribution to securing a uniform application of the law.

OPINIONS OF THE ATTORNEY GENERAL: THE STRUGGLE FOR POLITICAL INDEPENDENCE

Since 1789, the Attorney General has been charged by statute with responsibility for providing the President and the heads of departments with his opinion on questions of law.[42] With regard to the President, this responsibility was extended in 1870 to the giving of the Attorney General's "advice" as well as his opinion on legal questions.[43]

39. Bakke v. Regents of the Univ. of Cal., 18 Cal. 3d 34, 553 P.2d 1152, 132 Cal. Rptr. 680 (1976), *cert. granted*, 429 U.S. 1090 (1977).

40. Pub. L. No. 94–369, § 207, 90 Stat. 1007–08 (current version at 42 U.S.C.A. § 6727 (West Supp. 1978)).

41. 5 U.S.C. §§ 552–559 (1976).

42. *See* Judiciary Act of 1789, ch. 20, § 35, 1 Stat. 93 (corresponds to 28 U.S.C. §§ 511–12 (1970)).

43. Act of June 22, 1870, ch. 150, § 14, 16 Stat. 164 (corresponds to 28 U.S.C. § 511 (1970)).

Most opinions are rendered on questions that will not ultimately be resolved by the courts in litigation. Attorneys General have traditionally declined to render formal legal opinions on questions then in litigation. These opinions of the Attorney General are generally regarded as authoritative within the executive branch, and they may often have the salutary effect of avoiding litigation by acting as a check on executive conduct that may not be in accord with the law.

Historically, Attorneys General have personally approved and signed their opinions. Until 1950, preparation of those opinions was vested generally in the Solicitor General or the Assistant Solicitor General. In 1950, the latter position was abolished and the opinion preparation function was transferred to what is now the Office of Legal Counsel, headed by an Assistant Attorney General. In addition to preparing his formal legal opinions, that Office, acting for the Attorney General, renders legal advice and opinions to the executive branch and agencies on a daily basis under the same rules as are followed with respect to formal opinions of the Attorney General.[44]

The increased complexity of our society and the government's relationship to it over the past several decades is reflected in the opinion-giving functions performed by the Attorney General and his subordinates. Today, the subject matter encompassed by that function is as broad as the activities of the government itself. It is not overstatement to say that, in this complex society, the need for sound legal advice in advance of governmental action has become particularly acute. There is no substitute for doing something right the first time.

Another important objective—and one perhaps more difficult to achieve—furthered by the opinion function is ensuring that the many diverse agencies of government speak with one voice on the main legal issues that cut across the responsibilities of more than one department or agency. In the past, the reconciling of interagency disputes regarding questions of law arising in litigation has often not taken place until specific cases were brought to the attention of the Solicitor General after a decision by a federal district court on the question involved. Where no litigation is involved, the opinion function may serve and has served to harmonize diverse legal opinions and to ensure that the government acts legally.

As we examine what the role of the Department of Justice should be in the future, we must consider the fact that in recent years there has been a frequent voicing of the idea of an "independent" Attorney General. This concept encompasses the entire Department of Justice and contemplates some kind of formal measures to insulate it from executive branch pressures in carrying out its law-defining and law-enforcing responsibilities. The currency of this "independence" movement is partly due to the Watergate experience. Many people called not only for a cleansing of the Department, but for the removal of the potential for abuse forevermore. In 1976, President Carter made the subject one of national debate by proposing during his campaign that the Attorney General be appointed for a term of

44. Formal opinions of the Attorney General have been published in the past. We are now preparing for publication the first volume which will contain the separate opinion letters and memoranda of the Office of Legal Counsel as well as the formal Attorney General opinions.

between five and seven years, with removal occurring only upon congressional and presidential approval.

Discussions about the role of the Attorney General and his need for independence from policy matters are not new to the political scene. From the inception of the office of the Attorney General in the Judiciary Act of 1789,[45] there has been ambiguity about the role, and disagreement about the independence, of the Attorney General. The Judiciary Act described the functions of the office in terms seemingly without relation to the policy-making, politically rooted tasks of the rest of the executive branch:

> to prosecute and conduct all suits in the Supreme Court in which the United States shall be concerned, and to give his advice and opinion upon questions of law when required by the President of the United States, or when requested by the heads of any of the departments, touching any matters that may concern their departments.[46]

The opinion-giving responsibility of the Attorney General was for "questions of law" only. Moreover, President Washington's letter to Edmund Randolph urging him to become Attorney General indicates he was seeking a skilled, neutral expounder of the law rather than a political adviser:

> The selection of the fittest characters to expound the laws, and dispense justice, has been the invariable object of my anxious concern. I mean not to flatter when I say that considerations like these have ruled in the nomination of the attorney general of the United States, and that my private wishes would be highly gratified by your acceptance.[47]

Notwithstanding those noteworthy independent beginnings, our Attorneys General soon came to know the tensions created when the independence of their deliberations came in conflict with the policy preferences of the presidency. Senator George H. Williams, who himself later became Attorney General, described such a clash during the controversy in 1830 over the national bank:

> Consulting with his Attorney General, [President Jackson] found that some doubts were entertained by that officer as to the existence of any law authorizing the Executive to [designate certain banks to be depositories of U.S. funds], whereupon Old Hickory said to him, "Sir, you must find a law authorizing the act or I will appoint an Attorney General who will."[48]

This tension between the Attorney General's role as one who dispassionately defines the legal limits of executive action and the presidential desire to receive legal advice facilitating certain policy decisions has been manifested in modern administrations as well.

45. Ch. 20, § 35, 1 Stat. 93 (corresponds to 28 U.S.C. § 503 (1970)).

46. *Id.* (corresponds to 28 U.S.C. §§ 509, 511 (1970)).

47. L. Huston, A. Miller, S. Krislov & R. Dixon, Roles of the Attorney General of the United States 44 (1968).

48. *Id.* at 51. There is some doubt as to whether this incident actually occurred. *See* H. Cummings & C. McFarland, Federal Justice 109–10 (1937).

In 1940, President Roosevelt determined to provide the British with fifty destroyers in exchange for long-term leases on British territory in the Western hemisphere. However, the United States had in 1939 proclaimed its neutrality, which potentially barred such an exchange. As a result, three legal questions were posed to then Attorney General Robert H. Jackson:

> (a) Could the President acquire the leases by an executive agreement between himself and the British Prime Minister, or must the agreement be submitted to the Senate as a treaty . . . ? (b) Did the President have the authority to dispose of the 50 destroyers, and if so, on what conditions? (c) Did the statutes of the United States forbid delivery of such war vessels by reason of the belligerent status of Great Britain?[49]

Although each of these issues was difficult, Jackson stated in an opinion issued on August 27, 1940, that the President could make the exchange without seeking Senate approval,[50] and the exchange was made. But a respectable, though by no means unanimous, body of legal opinion in the United States thought that Jackson had gone too far in accommodating the law to the exigencies of politics.

A somewhat different example of limited independence of an Attorney General is reported in Francis Biddle's account of the internment of American Japanese in World War II. Biddle, Attorney General under Roosevelt, stated that at the time of the internment proposal he thought the program "ill-advised, unnecessary, and unnecessarily cruel."[51] However, he did not so advise the President, and the Justice Department subsequently defended the action successfully before the Supreme Court. Biddle explained that he "was new to the Cabinet, and disinclined to insist on my view to an elder statesman [Secretary of War Stimson] whose wisdom and integrity I greatly respected."[52]

A final illustration of the pressures on an Attorney General when a President seeks a legal opinion on a course of action he deems to be necessary occurred during the 1962 Cuban missile crisis. President Kennedy had decided to take action, but there was concern as to whether a detention and search of Soviet ships carrying arms to Cuba would be interpreted as a blockade, an act of war. If the ship searches could be considered a quarantine, they would qualify as a legitimate defensive measure. Because of time pressures, the opinion was hammered out in oral discussions between Justice and State Department lawyers. Notwithstanding serious questions of international and constitutional law, the opinion was favorable to the President's wishes.[53]

This difficulty regarding independence is due in part to the multifaceted nature of the Attorney General's job. The Attorney General has a variety of responsibilities: to prosecute violations of federal law; to represent the United States in judicial proceedings, either

49. L. Huston, A. Miller, S. Krislov & R. Dixon, Roles of the Attorney General of the United States 57 (1968).

50. *Id.* at 57–58.

51. *Id.* at 55.

52. *Id.* at 56.

53. *Id.* at 59.

as lawyer for client agencies and departments or as amicus in cases of national importance; to provide legal opinions on questions submitted by other departments and agencies; to provide requested comment on pending legislation; to propose and steer Justice Department legislation through the Congress; and to advise the President on the appointment of federal judges and prosecutors. These tasks and responsibilities require varying degrees of contact and coordination with the executive branch on the one hand, and independence from the executive branch on the other. Thus, the independence of the Attorney General has only a general and uneven tradition to support it, and a complexity that resists easy resolution.

The executive branch inevitably encounters legal questions arising out of its policy formulation and implementation alternatives. As a matter of good government, it is desirable generally that the executive branch adopts a single, coherent position with respect to the legal questions that arise in the process of government. Indeed, the commitment of our government to due process of law and to equal protection of the laws probably requires that our executive officers proceed in accordance with a coherent, consistent interpretation of the law, to the extent that it is administratively possible to do so. It is thus desirable for the president to entrust the final responsibility for interpretations of the law to a single officer or department. The Attorney General is the one officer in the executive branch who is charged by law with the duties of advising the others about the law and of representing the interests of the United States in general litigation in which questions of law arise. The task of developing a single, coherent view of the law is entrusted to the President himself, and by delegation to the Attorney General. That task is consistent with the nature of the office of Attorney General.

Moreover, with a few rather significant exceptions, the Attorney General is removed from the policymaking and policy implementation processes of government, and this is especially true when he deals with legal questions that arise in the administration of departments other than his own. It makes sense to assign the task of making definitive legal judgments to an officer who is not required, as a general matter, to play a decisive role in the formulation of policy. Such an officer enjoys a comparative advantage over policymakers in the discharge of the law giving function.

Therefore, some have suggested that the independence of the Attorney General should be increased and secured institutionally, within the limits imposed by the Constitution. It has been suggested that an executive order could be issued that would endorse the concept that the Attorney General must be free to exercise independent judgment in his litigating function and in his counseling function, subject only to the constitutional prerogatives of the President. Such an order could provide that the Attorney General's opinions on questions of law, as opposed to questions of policy, would be binding in certain circumstances. It could establish removal procedures that would require the President to justify the removal of an Attorney General because of differences of opinion over questions of law. It might also include an expiration provision, terminating the order on the inauguration of President Carter's successor, but the order could be a model for future administrations. I haven't reached any conclusions as to whether I would recommend to President Carter that he issue such an executive order. However, as we discuss and decide the future role of the Department of Justice, careful consideration must be given to this problem.

In the *Bakke* case and in some other instances,[54] I have played an important role as a buffer between our truly independent litigating lawyers in the Department of Justice, including the Solicitor General and his staff, and other government officials outside the Department of Justice. In these specific instances, I think I have been successful in preserving the independent positions taken by our Justice Department lawyers. A refined definition of the Attorney General's role in such disputes is something that is clearly needed as we decide our charter for the future.

CONCLUSION

I have mentioned several important questions tonight that deserve careful consideration as we reexamine what the roles of the Attorney General and the Department of Justice should be in the future. Although our client is the government, in the end we serve a more important constituency: the American people. As the President seeks to make our increasingly complex federal government more responsive to the needs of the people, we must improve the performance of the government's lawyers, including those in the Department of Justice. I hope we can do that in part by developing a clear concept of just what the roles of the Attorney General, the Justice Department, and indeed, the government lawyer, should be.

We covered a lot of history tonight. I don't know if you've been as fascinated listening to the history of the Department as I have been in researching it and telling the story. I must share one little tidbit with you as an aside. I was very pleased to learn that the Attorney General when the Department of Justice was created, A. T. Akerman, was from Georgia. I admit that I subsequently discovered that he was born in New Hampshire, but he moved to Georgia at an early age and grew up there. While that rather significant fact doesn't have much to do with tonight's speech, it was an important discovery for an amateur Georgia historian. His lack of fame in Georgia is no doubt the result of his having been appointed Attorney General by President Grant shortly after what we in the South sometimes call the War of Northern Aggression.

54. Bakke v. Regents of the Univ. of Cal., 18 Cal. 3d 34, 553 P.2d 1152, 132 Cal. Rptr. 680 (1976), *cert. granted*, 429 U.S. 1090 (1977).

Selected Bibliography

The following bibliography is supplemental to those materials cited in footnotes.

Bell, *Federalism in Current Perspective*, 1 GA. L. REV. 586 (1967).

Cohen, *Justice Report: Richardson Moves to Assert His Control of Watergate-Shaken Justice Department*, 5 NAT'L J. REP. 1011 (1973).

Cohen, *Justice Report: U.S. Attorneys Push Wide-Ranging Study to Gain Larger Role in Law Enforcement Policy*, 5 NAT'L J. REP. 1785 (1973).

Comm. on Organization of the Executive Branch of the Government, Final Report to the Congress (June 1955) (2d Hoover Comm.).

EISENSTEIN, J., COUNSEL FOR THE UNITED STATES (1978).

HOROWITZ, D., THE JUROCRACY (1977).

Key & LeSourd, *The Struggle of the Attorney General to Retain His Powers* (undated, unpublished paper in Department of Justice Library).

Learned, *The Attorney-General and the Cabinet*, 24 POLITICAL SCI. Q. 444 (1909).

NAVASKY, V., KENNEDY JUSTICE (1970).

Note, *Government Litigation in the Supreme Court: The Roles of the Solicitor General*, 78 YALE L.J. 1442 (1969).

Note, *Judicial Resolution of Administrative Disputes Between Federal Agencies*, 62 HARV. L. REV. 1050 (1949).

Stern, *"Inconsistency" in Government Litigation*, 64 HARV. L. REV. 759 (1951).

Swisher, *Federal Organization of Legal Functions*, 33 AM. POLITICAL SCI. REV. 973 (1939).

Cruel and Unusual Punishments: The Proportionality Rule

Hon. William Hughes Mulligan

The Honorable William Hughes Mulligan, former dean of the Fordham University School of Law, delivered the ninth Sonnett lecture on January 30, 1979.[1] Judge Mulligan, who left Fordham after his 1971 appointment to the United States Court of Appeals for the Second Circuit,[2] resigned from the bench in 1981. He then joined Skadden, Arps, Slate, Meagher & Flom, where he worked until his retirement in 1991.[3]

Born in the Bronx, New York, on March 5, 1918, Judge Mulligan remained close to his roots for his education and much of his legal career.[4] He graduated cum laude from Fordham University in 1939, and again received cum laude honors when he graduated from Fordham University School of Law in 1942.[5] After serving in the United States Army as a Special Agent in the Counter-Intelligence Corps during World War II, Judge Mulligan returned to Fordham as a law professor, where he spent the next twenty-five years.[6] He served as assistant dean from 1954 to 1956 and as dean from 1956 to 1971, and was named the Wilkinson Professor of Law in 1961.[7] In recognition of his significant impact on the Fordham community, the moot court team named its summer intramural competition in his honor.

During his tenure as dean, Judge Mulligan spearheaded both the significant growth in the school's prestige and its relocation to Lincoln Center. He simultaneously served the greater New York community: he was a member of the New York Law Revision Commission under Governors Averell W. Harriman and Nelson A.

Introduction written by Scott Silverman, J.D., Class of 2014, Fordham University School of Law.

1. The Hon. William Hughes Mulligan, *Cruel and Unusual Punishments: The Proportionality Rule*, 47 Fordham L. Rev. 639 (1979).

2. *History of the Federal Judiciary*, Fed. Judicial Ctr., http://www.fjc.gov/servlet/nGetInfo?jid=1713&cid=999&ctype=na&instate=na (last visited Mar. 17, 2014).

3. Wolfgang Saxon, *William Hughes Mulligan, 78, Judge and Dean of Law School*, N.Y. Times (May 14, 1996), http://www.nytimes.com/1996/05/14/nyregion/william-hughes-mulligan-78-judge-and-dean-of-law-school.html.

4. *See supra* note 2.

5. William Hughes Mulligan, Jr., *Eulogy to William Hughes Mulligan St. Joseph's Church*, 65 Fordham L. Rev. 27, 28 (1996).

6. *Id.*

7. *See* Saxon, *supra* note 3.

Rockefeller.[8] Governor Rockefeller also named him to lead a seven member committee to study reapportionment of the Legislature.[9] Finally, he served as a trustee of St. Patrick's Cathedral, Catholic Charities of the Diocese of New York, and Fordham University.[10]

Though he authored numerous significant opinions while he sat on the Second Circuit, Judge Mulligan was also renowned for his jovial nature and "Celtic wit."[11] In his final opinion, *United States v. Byrnes*, in which Judge Mulligan considered rare bird smuggling offenses, he concluded: "the judgment of conviction is affirmed, justice has triumphed, and this is *my* swan song."[12] Judge Mulligan was also a gifted public orator, often delivering humorous remarks throughout his serious speeches to bar associations and civic groups. A collection of Judge Mulligan's speeches was published by the Fordham University Press under the title *Mulligan's Law: The Wit and Wisdom of William Hughes Mulligan*.[13]

While Judge Mulligan was known for his wit, his Sonnett lecture, *Cruel and Unusual Punishments: The Proportionality Rule*, tackled a serious constitutional issue. Focusing on one aspect of the "cruel and unusual punishment" clause of the Eighth Amendment to the United States Constitution, Judge Mulligan considered whether terms of imprisonment could be excessively disproportionate to an offense so as to be considered "cruel and unusual." In noting that the Eighth Amendment prohibition is evolutionary in nature, Judge Mulligan considered whether the proportionality test, which requires a court to (1) determine the gravity of the offense in question, (2) compare the sentence under review with those imposed in the same jurisdiction for more serious crimes, and (3) compare the challenged sentence with those imposed in other jurisdictions, is an effective way to evaluate whether punishment violates the Eighth Amendment. In his analysis, Judge Mulligan appropriately weighed the different roles of the judiciary and the legislature—as many scholars still do[14]—as he explained and critiqued the proportionality test. Recognizing each branch's limitations, he ultimately concluded that the proportionality rule was a required outgrowth of the Eighth Amendment and called for judicial restraint to achieve the eighth amendment's purpose: the effective and fair administration of justice.

---

8. *See supra* note 2.
9. *See supra* note 2.
10. *See* Saxon, *supra* note 3.
11. *See generally* Joseph M. McLaughlin, *In Memoriam: William Hughes Mulligan*, 65 Fordham L. Rev. 15 (1996).
12. 644 F.2d 107, 112 (2d Cir. 1981) (emphasis added).
13. *See Mulligan Jr.*, *supra* note 5, at 28.
14. The Proportionality Rule continues to be the subject of scholarly and judicial debate. *See* Solem v. Helm, 463 U.S. 277 (1983); Note, *The Eighth Amendment, Proportionality and the Changing Meaning of "Punishment,"* 122 Harv. L. Rev. 960 (2009); Schneider, *Sentencing Proportionality in the States*, 54 Ariz. L. Rev. 241 (2012).

1979 Sonnett Lecture

The Eighth Amendment to the United States Constitution provides in the usual stark and unadorned constitutional prose: "Excessive bail shall not be required, nor excessive fines imposed, nor cruel and unusual punishments inflicted."[1] The constitutional restriction binds both the legislative and judicial branches of the federal government and through the Fourteenth Amendment is applicable to the states as well.[2] While both branches are governed by the constitutional limitation, our system of judicial review provides an enormous potential power for the federal judiciary to strike down sentences presumably fixed by state legislatures as appropriate sanctions reflecting the judgment of their constituencies as to the seriousness of particular criminal offenses.

This paper is primarily concerned with only one aspect of the "cruel and unusual" clause—the so-called proportionality principle. Simply expressed, the principle dictates that a punishment which is grossly or excessively severe in relation to the gravity of the crime charged must be struck down by the courts as violative of the Eighth Amendment. Even before Gilbert and Sullivan's *Mikado*,[3] an article of popular faith had been that the punishment fit the crime. In American jurisprudence, however, responsibility is deemed to be on the legislature which created the crime and fixed the sanction. Only recently has it become recognized that punishment grossly in excess of the gravity of the offense may offend the Constitution of the United States. I will briefly review the history of the principle and the test which has been developed to apply it. I will suggest some inherent weaknesses and dangers in the test and indicate the balancing of principles which must be employed in applying it lest it become a device for the imposition of judicial concepts of criminal punishment in the guise of constitutional interpretation.

1. U.S. Const. amend. VIII. As with most constitutional language, "[t]he words [the judge] must construe are empty vessels into which he can pour nearly anything he will." Hand, *Sources of Tolerance*, 79 U. Pa. L. Rev. 1, 12 (1930).

2. U.S. Const. amend. XIV. The cruel and unusual punishments clause has been applied to the states, *Robinson v. California*, 370 U.S. 660, 664, 666–67 (1962), but the Supreme Court has not expressly incorporated the excessive bail and excessive fines restrictions into the fourteenth amendment. This incorporation would seem to be implicit, however, in the fourteenth amendment per se. *See* Schilb v. Kuebel, 404 U.S. 357, 365 (1971) (dictum); Tate v. Short, 401 U S. 395, 398–401 (1971). In O'Neil v. Vermont, 144 U.S. 323, 332 (1892), the Court had indicated that the Eighth Amendment was not binding on the states.

3. "My object all sublime/I shall achieve in time—To let the punishment fit the crime—The punishment fit the crime." W. Gilbert & A. Sullivan, *Mikado*, *in* The Complete Plays of Gilbert and Sullivan 331 (W. Norton ed. 1976).

CRUEL AND UNUSUAL PUNISHMENT: AN EVOLVING CONCEPT

The history of the cruel and unusual punishment clause has been set forth in several law review articles[4] and in expansive judicial opinions.[5] There is no need to present it in detail here.

The phrase itself, "cruel and unusual punishments," first appeared in the English Bill of Rights of 1689 which prohibited such sanctions. Historians generally have perceived the prohibition to be a reaction to the treason trials of 1685—the "Bloody Assize" caused by the abortive rebellion of the Duke of Monmouth. The penalty for treason involved hanging by the neck, being cut down while still alive, and then being disemboweled, beheaded, and quartered.[6] (I omit some of the grislier details.) That the methods of punishment employed by the English then and later were cruel and barbarous by today's standards is quite apparent.

There is another view which has gained some acceptance that the phrase "cruel and unusual punishments" was inserted in the English Bill of Rights not simply as an interdiction of barbarous methods of punishment, but also to prohibit sentences which were disproportionate to the gravity of the crime committed. One theory is that the conviction of the infamous Titus Oates for perjury in 1685 and his subsequent sentence support the proposition that a sentence disproportionate to the crime was cruel and unusual within the meaning of the Bill of Rights. In 1679, Oates swore that he was present at a meeting where a group of influential Catholic laymen and Jesuit priests plotted to murder the Protestant King Charles II and to place his brother James, a Catholic, upon the throne. Oates, who had a vivid imagination, provided certain lurid details—the Jesuits were to kill the King with silver bullets and, if that failed, four Irish ruffians were to stab him to death. As a result of the alleged "Popish Plot," panic prevailed in London and, as a result of Oates's testimony, a score of innocent Catholics were executed in the manner heretofore described. James II eventually did ascend the throne, evidence of Oates's perjury became overwhelming, and in 1685 he was convicted of perjury, sentenced to prison for life, severely flogged, fined, placed in a pillory four times a year, and defrocked as a minister of

4. *E.g.*, Granucci, *"Nor Cruel and Unusual Punishments Inflicted:" The Original Meaning*, 57 CAL. L. REV. 839 (1969); Comment, *The Eighth Amendment, Beccaria, and the Enlightenment: An Historical Justification or the Weems v. United States Excessive Punishment Doctrine*, 24 BUFFALO L. REV. 783 (1975).

5. *E.g.*, Furman v. Georgia, 408 U.S. 238, 316–22 (1972) (Marshall, J., concurring); Carmona v. Ward, 576 F.2d 405, 425–27 app. (2d Cir. 1978) (Oakes, J., dissenting), *cert. denied*, 99 S.Ct. 874 (1979); People v. Broadie, 37 N.Y.2d 100, 119–30 app., 332 N.E.2d 338, 347–54 app., 371 N.Y.S.2d 471, 483–92 app., *cert. denied*, 423 U.S. 950 (1975).

6. Granucci, *supra* note 4, at 854. Nor were the Stuarts the first English monarchs to arouse public anger by inflicting a penalty commonly believed to be disproportionate to the offense. In 1579, Queen Elizabeth incurred public wrath by having the right hand of an author, John Stubbs, and his printer, William Page, hacked off for publishing an attack on a marriage match that the aging queen desired with a French nobleman. Elizabeth was not unmoved by the public dissent; she did not stay the sentence but did send her personal physician to attend to the wounds of the criminals. R. BERLETH, THE TWILIGHT LORDS 26–27 (1978).

the Church of England.[7] After the revolution of 1688, the flight of James II and the ascension to the throne of William and Mary of Orange, Oates was not only pardoned but even given a lifetime pension.[8]

An influential law review article, which has espoused the view that "cruel and unusual punishments" should be equated with the disproportionality of the sentence and not simply the barbarity of the method of punishment, argued that Oates's sentence was cruel and unusual not because of the flogging and pilloring, which were normal methods of punishment in those days, but because a term of life imprisonment was disproportionate to the crime of perjury.[9] This argument, in my view, is unpersuasive both logically and historically. Oates's perjury led directly to the barbaric execution of some twenty-one innocent people, including seven Jesuits, one of whom was the provincial of the English Society.[10] Winston Churchill, hardly an Anglophobe, in his discussion of the Popish Plot, describes Oates as "being as wicked as any man who ever lived."[11] The usual punishment for perjury at the time included "branding or tongue-boring, or both."[12]

Oates's sentence, viewed in the light of contemporary penological practices, was neither cruel nor unusual. His eventual release and reward by William of Orange was not the result of any belief that he had been subjected to cruel and unusual punishment but, as described by a modern biographer of Oates, it was "an act of gratitude by William of Orange . . . who knew his friends and recognized the instruments which helped him attain the throne of England."[13] While Titus Oates was a fascinating as well as frightening character, I do not believe his sentence casts any light upon the meaning of the phrase "cruel and unusual punishments" nor does it support the proportionality principle.

In 1791, the same phrase "cruel and unusual punishments" was adopted with little debate as part of the eighth amendment of the United States Constitution. It is quite clear that the framers intended to outlaw barbarous punishments. The first Eighth Amendment cases to come before the Supreme Court established that punishments involving lingering death or torture, which were acceptable to our Anglo-Saxon legal forbearers, were cruel and unusual under the interdiction of the eighth amendment.[14] In *In re Kemmler*,[15] however, the Court held that death by electrocution was not cruel and unusual under the United States Constitution.

7. Granucci, *supra* note 4, at 857–58.

8. T. Macaulay, The History of England 355 (1889).

9. Granucci, *supra* note 4, at 859–60; *see* Carmona v. Ward, 576 F.2d 405, 425 n.4 (2d Cir. 1978) (Oakes, J., dissenting), *cert. denied*, 99 S.Ct. 874 (1979). *See also* Furman v. Georgia, 408 U.S. 238, 318, 319 n.14 (1972) (Marshall, J., concurring).

10. G. Clark, The Later Stuarts 90 (1949).

11. W. Churchill, A History of the English Speaking Peoples 61 (1965).

12. E. Dakers, Titus Oates 319 (1949).

13. *Id.* at 329.

14. *See, e.g.*, Wilkerson v. Utah, 99 U.S. 130 (1878).

15. 136 U.S. 436, 447 (1890).

The question as to whether a term of imprisonment could be so excessively disproportionate to the offense so as to be within the eighth amendment was not addressed in the Supreme Court until 1892 and then only in dicta in a dissenting opinion. In *O'Neil v. Vermont*,[16] the defendant, who was licensed to sell liquor in New York, had been sentenced to 19,914 days (over fifty-four years) for conviction on 307 counts of illegal sale of liquor shipped to Vermont. The majority did not reach the question of whether the penalty violated the Eighth Amendment since that point had not been raised as error.[17] In his dissenting opinion Mr. Justice Field, however, considering the fact that the penalty was harsher than could have been imposed for burglary or manslaughter, concluded, "It was one which, in its severity, considering the offences of which [the defendant] was convicted, may justly be termed both unusual and cruel."[18]

In 1910, the Supreme Court decided *Weems v. United States*,[19] which is now regarded as the seminal case with respect to the proportionality principle. The defendant, an official of the Philippine government, was convicted of falsifying public records and was sentenced under the Penal Code of the Philippines, then a United States territory, to fifteen years of hard and painful labor, with a chain at the ankle hanging from the wrists. He was stripped of the right of parental authority, guardianship of person or property, participation in the family council, marital authority, administration of property, and the right to dispose of his property. He was placed under surveillance by the state for the rest of his life, could not vote, hold office, receive retirement pay, or even change his residence without permission.[20] Only six Justices participated in this decision and two, White and Holmes, dissented. The majority found that this punishment was "cruel in its excess of imprisonment and that which accompanies and follows imprisonment. It is unusual in its character. Its punishments come under the condemnation of the bill of rights, both on account of their *degree and kind*."[21] The Court was repulsed by the nature of the penalty as well as its lack of proportion to the seriousness of the underlying crime. Thus, the Court compared the punishment of the defendant to those imposed in the same jurisdiction for crimes which the Court considered to be more serious than the one for which the defendant had been convicted.[22] It also compared the punishment under attack with those imposed in other

16. 144 U.S. 323 (1892).

17. *Id.* at 331. The majority also opined that the Eighth Amendment did not apply to the states, *id.* at 332, but this view was expressly rejected in 1962. *See supra* note 2 and accompanying text.

18. 144 U.S. at 339 (Field, J., dissenting). It is interesting to note that Mr. Justice Field accepted "whipping for petty offences" as a form of punishment within the state's power. *Id.* at 340 (Field, J., dissenting).

19. 217 U.S. 349 (1910). The Court was construing the Philippines' Bill of Rights which contained a cruel and unusual punishment clause identical to the language of the Eighth Amendment. *Id.* at 365, 367.

20. *Id.* at 364–66.

21. *Id.* at 377 (emphasis added).

22. *Id.* at 380.

jurisdictions for the same crime.[23] These two steps have become major parts of the contemporary proportionality test.[24]

While the language of *Weems* arguably does support the doctrine of proportionality, it must be remembered that the Court was considering not simply a fifteen-year prison term, but one accompanied by "painful labor" in chains, lifetime supervision, and civil interdiction. It is difficult, indeed, to believe that the Supreme Court would have held a fifteen-year term of imprisonment unconstitutional had it not been for the barbarous terms which had accompanied and, indeed, followed its service.[25]

Weems is an important decision in any event because of its affirmation of two principles of jurisprudence, the first of which is indeed basic and the second almost obvious. The first is as the Court stated:

> [T]here is a certain subordination of the judiciary to the legislature. The function of the legislature is primary, its exercises fortified by presumptions of right and legality, and is not to be interfered with lightly, nor by any judicial conception of their wisdom or propriety. They have no limitation, we repeat, but constitutional ones, and what those are the judiciary must judge.[26]

The second is that the Eighth Amendment prohibition is evolutionary in nature.[27] This principle was succinctly formulated by Chief Justice Warren: "The Amendment must draw its meaning from the evolving standards of decency that mark the progress of a maturing society."[28] I believe that there may well be some question as to whether we Americans have, in general, espoused higher standards of decency and whether our society is becoming more instead of less mature. Nonetheless, in the context of criminal sanctions, no one can seriously contest the proposition that the human physical and mental torture, degradation, and loss of personal dignity acceptable to Sassenach or the Sioux, have long since been rejected, at least in democratic societies. Hence, it is beyond doubt that what was an acceptable sanction at the time of the adoption of the Constitution is hardly permissible today and forms no basis for judicial inquiry to determine present constitutional criteria.

What is significant is that since *Weems* was decided in 1910, there has been no opinion in the Supreme Court which has struck down a noncapital punishment on proportional-

23. *Id.* at 380–81.

24. *E.g.*, Hart v. Coiner, 483 F.2d 136, 141–42 (4th Cir. 1973), *cert. denied*, 415 U.S. 983 (1974); People v. Broadie, 37 N.Y.2d 100, 112, 332 N.E.2d 338, 342, 371 N.Y.S.2d 471, 476, *cert. denied*, 423 U.S. 950 (1975); *see* 44 Fordham L. Rev. 637 (1975).

25. *Weems* was not followed in Davis v. Davis, 585 F.2d 1226, 1229–30 (4th Cir. 1978), where the issue was solely the length of sentence unaccompanied by barbarous conditions. *Accord*, Carmona v. Ward, 576 F.2d 405, 408 n.5 (2d Cir. 1978), *cert. denied*, 99 S.Ct. 874 (1979). *Contra*, *id.* at 420–21 (Oakes, J., dissenting).

26. 217 U.S. at 379.

27. *Id.* at 378.

28. Trop v. Dulles, 356 U.S. 86, 101 (1958).

ity grounds. Indeed, since then there has been only one other case in which a majority of that Court found that a noncapital penalty violated the cruel and unusual punishment clause. In *Robinson v. California*,[29] as noted by Chief Judge Kaufman in a prior Sonnett lecture,[30] the Court ruled that a person could not be convicted of a crime simply because he suffered from the condition or status of being addicted to a narcotic drug.[31] Although the two are often confused, whether a certain act should be a crime and whether the punishment should fit the crime are entirely separate inquiries.[32]

Throughout the present decade the Supreme Court has struggled with the apparently intractable problem of capital punishment.[33] A judge must be careful in applying these precedents which involve the ultimate irrevocable sanction, and in which a majority opinion is rare, to cases involving much different considerations because of the lesser penalties involved.[34] Two propositions are clear, however, from the opinions in the death penalty cases. One is that the Supreme Court now accepts the principle of proportionality as constitutionally mandated.[35] The other is that there is a strong presumption that the legislative penalty is valid because "the constitutional test is intertwined with an assessment of contemporary standards and the legislative judgment weighs heavily in ascertaining such standards."[36]

Whether the proportionality concept was within the "cruel and unusual punishments" clause of the Bill of Rights of 1689 or in the minds of the founding fathers when the Eighth Amendment was adopted is academic. It has now been espoused in principle by the

29. 370 U.S. 660 (1962).

30. Kaufman, *Prison: The Judge's Dilemma*, 41 FORDHAM L. REV. 495, 502 (1973).

31. 370 U.S. at 667.

32. H.L.A. HART, LAW, LIBERTY AND MORALITY 36 (1963). *See also* E. VAN DEN HAAG, PUNISHING CRIMINALS 4 (1975). In Trop v. Dulles, 356 U.S. 86 (1958), a plurality of the Court concluded that denationalization for wartime desertion was cruel and unusual punishment. Although the rationale of the decision is not entirely clear, the Court explicitly rejected any argument that the punishment was excessive in relation to the gravity of the crime. *Id.* at 99.

33. *E.g.*, Coker v. Georgia, 433 U.S. 584 (1977); Gregg v. Georgia, 428 U.S. 153 (1976); Furman v. Georgia, 408 U.S. 238 (1972).

34. "Death is irrevocable; life imprisonment is not. Death, of course, makes rehabilitation impossible; life imprisonment does not. In short, death has always been viewed as the ultimate sanction, and it seems perfectly reasonable to continue to view it as such." Furman v. Georgia, 408 U.S. 238, 346 (1972) (Marshall, J., concurring).

35. Coker v. Georgia, 433 U.S. 584, 592 (1977) (plurality opinion of White, J., in which Stewart, Blackmun, and Stevens, JJ., concurred); Ingraham v. Wright, 430 U.S. 651, 667 (1977); Gregg v. Georgia, 428 U.S. 153, 173 (1976) (plurality opinion of Stewart, J., in which Powell and Stevens, JJ., concurred); Furman v. Georgia, 408 U.S. 238, 279 (1972) (Brennan, J., concurring). *Id.* at 331 (Marshall, J., concurring).

36. Gregg v. Georgia, 428 U.S. 153, 175 (1976) (plurality opinion of Stewart, J., in which Powell and Stevens, JJ., concurred); *accord*, Furman v. Georgia, 408 U.S. 238, 383 (1972) (Burger, C.J., dissenting); *see id.* at 465–70 (Rehnquist, J., dissenting).

Supreme Court[37] and the New York Court of Appeals,[38] as well as a large number of other state courts.[39]

THE PROPORTIONALITY TEST

The cases have developed a generally accepted three-pronged test to determine whether a sentence is so excessively disproportionate to the crime that it violates the Eighth Amendment. The three steps are: first, a judgment by the court of the gravity of the offense; second, a comparison of the sentence under review with that imposed in the same jurisdiction for other crimes which the court considers to be more serious; and third, a comparison of the challenged sentence with those imposed in other jurisdictions for the same crime.[40] There is even authority that the comparison can include the penalties imposed by foreign nations.[41]

The aim of the test is to reduce the input of judicial subjectivity in Eighth Amendment jurisprudence. While a three-pronged test facially phrased in objective terms is not to be lightly discarded (and I suppose must be viewed with more respect than a two-pronged test), I am frankly becoming less and less convinced that the proportionality rubric is of any real value in cases where the only claim is that the Eighth Amendment has been violated simply because of the length of the term imposed.[42] There is no case, in fact, in either the Supreme Court, the Second Circuit, or the New York Court of Appeals where a sentence has ever been set aside for this reason, even though the test has been accepted.[43] This is

37. *See* cases cited *supra* note 35.

38. People v. Broadie, 37 N.Y.2d 100, 111, 332 N.E.2d 338, 341, 371 N.Y.S.2d 471, 475, *cert. denied*, 423 U.S. 950 (1975).

39. 44 FORDHAM L. REV. 637, 638–44 (1975). Indeed, even prior to *Weems*, Massachusetts had recognized the principle of proportionality. McDonald v. Commonwealth, 173 Mass. 322, 328, 53 N.E. 874, 875 (1899), *aff'd*, 180 U.S. 311 (1901).

40. Carmona v. Ward, 576 F.2d 405, 409 (2d Cir. 1978) (collecting sources), *cert. denied*, 99 S.Ct. 874 (1979).

41. Coker v. Georgia, 433 U.S. 584, 596 n.10 (1977).

42. This discussion does not purport to encompass those instances in which a challenge under the cruel and unusual punishment clause is made to brutal treatment or harsh deprivations inflicted upon inmates during their confinement. *See, e.g.*, Sostre v. McGinnis, 442 F.2d 178, 190–94 (2d Cir. 1971) (en banc), *cert. denied*, 405 U.S. 978 (1972). *See also* Kaufman, *supra* note 30, at 509–12.

43. Downey v. Perini, 518 F.2d 1288 (6th Cir.), *vacated and remanded on other grounds*, 423 U.S. 993 (1975), is the only Circuit Court case striking down a sentence for a term of years solely because of its length. In *Downey*, the defendant received a sentence of thirty to sixty years' imprisonment for his first offense of possession and sale of a small amount of marijuana. *Compare* Rummel v. Estelle, 568 F.2d 1193 (5th Cir. 1978) (as applied to petitioner, a Texas statute mandating life imprisonment upon third conviction for any felony held violative of Eighth Amendment) *and* Hart v. Coiner, 483 F.2d 136 (4th Cir. 1973) (mandatory life sentence for third felony conviction unconstitutional where crimes were perjury, passing $50 check with insufficient funds, and transporting $140 worth of bad checks across state lines), *cert. denied*, 415 U.S. 983 (1974) *with* Roberts v. Collins,

because *Weems* itself has emphasized the great deference which must be paid to the state legislature. As Chief Justice Marshall pointed out in 1820, "[i]t is the legislature, not the court, which is to define a crime, and ordain its punishment."[44] Mr. Justice Stewart has recently emphasized that "a heavy burden rests on those who would attack the judgment of the representatives of the people."[45]

The first prong of the test requires the Court to make a judgment as to the seriousness of the crime charged and this of course invites the substitution of the subjective views of the judge for those of the legislature.[46] The concern here is both constitutional and practical. We must observe the doctrine of separation of powers as well as federalism.[47] This emphasizes the need for judicial restraint. A practical consideration, of course, is the institutional limitation on judicial fact-finding. The legislature, acting through commissions and committees with funds for counsel and staff and public hearings, is patently better equipped than the judiciary to make the factual and social determinations which underlie any decision as to the gravity of a crime.[48] It is also more attuned to contemporary community standards and can best judge the public's concern about particular criminal activity.[49]

The second prong of the test is even more vulnerable since it calls for a comparison by the judicial branch of the statutory sentence imposed for the crime committed with those imposed for more serious offenses in the same jurisdiction. The problem of determining the gravity of a particular crime is difficult enough without having to make judgments

---

544 F.2d 168 (4th Cir. 1976) (setting aside on Eighth Amendment grounds five years of a twenty-year sentence for simple assault to comport with the maximum for assault with intent to murder, of which simple assault is merely a lesser included offense), *cert. denied*, 430 U.S. 973 (1977). *See In re* Foss, 10 Cal.3d 910, 519 P.2d 1073, 112 Cal. Rptr. 649 (1974); *In re* Lynch, 8 Cal.3d 410, 503 P.2d 921, 105 Cal. Rptr. 217 (1972) (collecting cases); People v. Lorentzen, 387 Mich. 167, 194 N.W.2d 827 (1972).

44. United States v. Wiltberger, 18 U.S. (5 Wheat.) 76, 95 (1820).

45. Gregg v. Georgia, 428 U.S. 153, 175 (1976).

46. *See* Carmona v. Ward, 576 F.2d 405, 410–12 (2d Cir. 1978), *cert. denied*, 99 S.Ct. 874 (1979); Rummel v. Estelle, 568 F.2d 1193, 1201 n.3 (5th Cir. 1978) Thornberry, J., dissenting); Note, *Criminal Procedure-Eighth Amendment Proportionality Analysis in Its Infancy*, 52 N.C L. Rev. 442, 452–53 (1973). *See also* 1976 Wis. L. Rev. 655, 667–69.

47. It is often said, as it was recently by United States District Judge Frank M. Johnson, Jr., that "[t]he power of the federal judiciary to review and to decide matters involving the legislative and executive branches of government is circumscribed by two basic constitutional doctrines"—separation of powers and federalism. Johnson, *The Role of the Judiciary with Respect to the Other Branches of Government*, 11 Ga. L. Rev. 455, 463 (1977). As Judge Johnson seems to realize, however, the effectiveness of these principles as a check on judicial power depends on self-restraint. *See id.* at 466. Where the judiciary is concerned, the appropriate question is indeed, "*Quis custodiet custodes?*"

48. *See* Chayes, *The Role of the Judge in Public Law Litigation*, 89 Harv. L. Rev. 1281, 1296–98 (1976).

49. *See* Gregg v. Georgia, 428 U.S. 153, 175–76 (1976); 2 J. Stephen, A History of the Criminal Law of England 81–82 (1883). Even the legislature, however, can be slow in sensing the public judgment. *See* J. Wilson, Thinking About Crime 22–23 (1975).

about other crimes. It is rather simple to make a decision that smoking in the subway is not as serious as rape. But comparing the crimes of and punishments for arson and kidnapping, automobile larceny and drunken driving, requires the digestion of a vast amount of penological and sociological data not usually available to the jurist. The comparisons cannot be mechanically applied and the danger of the judiciary's substitution of its judgment on a social issue for that of the legislature charged with the responsibility of making the decision initially is apparent.

The third step of the proportionality test requires the court to compare the sentence under review with those imposed in other jurisdictions for the same crime. This is the least susceptible to misuse as a tool facilitating the substitution of individual judicial policy views for those of the legislature. At the same time, it is flawed and is basically antagonistic to the principles of federalism. The Supreme Court has recognized, for example, that there is no national standard for obscenity and that the courts are to apply local community standards.[50] Yet this leads to the anomaly that while a jury is required to apply local standards in determining whether an act is criminally obscene, consideration of national standards is encouraged in determining whether the punishment is constitutional. The rationale supporting the distinction of using local standards to determine whether a first amendment violation has occurred, but a national standard to decide whether an Eighth Amendment infraction has transpired, is not at all clear.

The use of the standards of foreign nations to determine the constitutionality of punishment seems to be generally of little or no help. Aside from differing moral, social, and cultural values, I would suspect that a few years in a dungeon in some foreign climes can hardly be compared with incarceration in most modern American penal institutions.

In any event, a state may be faced with a particularly virulent type of criminal activity and I submit it should have some latitude in determining a strategy to combat that crime; one means may be the imposition of a longer sentence. In *Carmona v. Ward*,[51] the most recent case in our circuit to challenge a prison term as unconstitutional because of its length, we held it to be significant, as had the New York Court of Appeals, that New York had a particularly acute drug problem.[52] The state legislature in 1967 had embarked upon a penal law approach which emphasized treatment of the addict and not incarceration. Six years and over one billion dollars later, the legislature determined that the program was not successful and adopted admittedly stern measures with lifetime maximum prison terms.[53] It is not for the courts to determine the wisdom or effectiveness of the program. It has engendered criticism and it may well not be working, but the legislature has already made changes and is clearly in the best position to make more.[54] We held the drug statute

50. Miller v. California, 413 U.S. 15, 30 (1973).

51. 576 F.2d 405 (2d Cir. 1978), *cert. denied*, 99 S.Ct. 874 (1979).

52. *Id.* at 412.

53. *Id.* at 413.

54. *Id.* at 415–16 & n.19; *cf.* N.Y. Times, Jan. 18, 1979, § A, at 20, col. I (criticizing the harshness of the statute).

not to be violative of the Constitution and the Supreme Court subsequently denied certiorari in a seven-to-two decision.[55]

CONCLUSION

In conclusion, I would point out that a prison term so disproportionate in length in comparison with the gravity of the crime as to shock the conscience should be held to be cruel and unusual under the Eighth Amendment of the Constitution. This is so neither because it was in the minds of the framers of the English Bill of Rights in 1689, nor because of the Bloody Assize or the trial of Titus Oates, nor even because the founding fathers had it in mind in adopting the language of the prior act. What books Jefferson may have read hardly support the inference that he believed the maxim "let the punishment fit the crime" was of constitutional dimension. Nor do I believe that a lone dissent in *O'Neil* or the majority opinion in *Weens* (which involved barbarous treatment) necessarily preordained acceptance of the proportionality principle. I see no reason to strain or struggle with doubtful historical or judicial precedent to establish the point. Unless the Eighth Amendment is to become totally moribund in a sentencing context and the phrase simply a shibboleth, since barbarous methods of punishment have generally disappeared, it must apply to extraordinarily excessive terms. This I accept because, as I have indicated, the clause is evolutionary in character, not because the founding fathers had the principle in mind.

At the same time, I believe that state legislatures usually do not act aberrantly and are normally responsive to and reflect community standards. Unlike federal judges who serve for life, the legislator must answer to his constituency after relatively brief terms of office. The deference we must pay the legislative determination is due not only to constitutional concepts of separation of powers and federalism, but also because of the institutional difficulty of the judiciary making the social, moral, and penological decisions inherent in the test which has been constructed. I believe it is of some significance that in the most recent federal case in point, the Fourth Circuit, which had initially employed the proportionality test,[56] has now refused to apply it at least where the sentence is for a term of years. It will set aside such a term which is within the state's statutory maximum only where there are "extraordinary and special circumstances."[57]

So-called judicial activists, of course, will maintain that the refusal to set aside admittedly harsh sentences constitutes an abdication of the constitutional mandate, but this requires an understanding of what our constitutional mandate really is. From the foregoing discussion, I submit that our responsibility is narrow indeed. The role of the federal judiciary becomes even less active where the state courts have already upheld the constitutionality of the statute against the same attack. The state court judges have sworn to uphold the same Constitution as the federal judiciary.

55. Carmona v. Ward, 99 S.Ct. 874 (1979).
56. *See* Hart. v. Coiner, 483 F.2d 136, 139–40 (4th Cir. 1973), *cert. denied*, 415 U.S. 983 (1974).
57. Davis v. Davis, 585 F.2d 1226, 1233 (4th Cir. 1978).

I think the significant factor is judicial restraint. I recall to you Mr. Justice Frankfurter's elegant articulation of the point: "[T]here is not under our Constitution a judicial remedy for every political mischief, for every undesirable exercise of legislative power. . . . In a democratic society like ours, relief must come through an aroused popular conscience that sears the conscience of the people's representatives."[58]

58. Baker v. Carr, 369 U.S. 186, 270 (1962) (Frankfurter, J., dissenting).

Intelligence Gathering and the Law: Conflict or Compatibility?

Benjamin R. Civiletti

Former United States Attorney General Benjamin R. Civiletti delivered the tenth Sonnett lecture, entitled *Intelligence Gathering and the Law: Conflict or Compatibility?*, on January 15, 1980.[1] The winner of the 2009 *American Lawyer* Lifetime Achievement Award,[2] Mr. Civiletti was born in Peekskill, New York, on July 17, 1935.[3] He obtained his bachelor's degree from Johns Hopkins University in 1957 and his law degree from the University of Maryland School of Law in 1961.[4] Upon graduation, he clerked for the Honorable W. Calvin Chestnut of the United States District Court for the District of Maryland.[5] His early career was split between the Baltimore firm, Venable, Baetjer & Howard, and various positions in the U.S. Department of Justice.[6]

Civiletti served as the seventy-third United States Attorney General from 1979 to 1981.[7] During that time, he appeared in front of the International Court of Justice to argue on behalf of the Americans being held captive during the Iran Hostage Crisis.[8] Notably, during his tenure, Mr. Civiletti was the first Attorney General to opine that the

Introduction written by Michael A. Hardin, J.D., Class of 2014, Fordham University School of Law.

1. Benjamin R. Civiletti, *Intelligence Gathering and the Law: Conflict or Compatibility?*, 48 Fordham L. Rev. 883 (1980). This article is adapted from the Tenth Annual John F. Sonnett Memorial Lecture, delivered by the Attorney General at the Fordham University School of Law on January 15, 1980. The article was prepared with the assistance of several attorneys in the Department of Justice, particularly Kenneth B. Reisenfeld of the Office of Intelligence Policy and Review.

2. Press Release, Venable LLP, Venable Partner Ben Civiletti Named *American Lawyer* Lifetime Achievement Award Winner for 2009 (Aug. 7, 2009), http://www.venable.com/NEP/pressreleases/NewsDetail.aspx?news=595dcc7b-e789-4849-acbe-e68245b2c840 [hereinafter Press Release].

3. *Benjamin Richard Civiletti*, U.S. Dep't Justice, http://www.justice.gov/ag/aghistpage.php?id=72 (last visited Mar. 17, 2014) [hereinafter DOJ Biography].

4. *Id.*

5. *Benjamin R. Civiletti: Profile*, Venable LLP, http://www.venable.com/Professionals/Bio.aspx?Bio=130f638b-d85c-4bd7-a5ec-81c9dfa426fc (last visited Mar. 17, 2014).

6. *See* DOJ Biography, *supra* note 3.

7. *Id.*

8. Press Release, Venable LLP, *supra* note 2.

Antideficiency Act[9] requires government agencies to cease operations if Congress does not pass a budget on time.[10] He is also known for having the Justice Department promulgate open trial guidelines and report on protocols regarding how white collar crime is investigated and prosecuted.[11]

Now a retired partner at Venable LLP,[12] Mr. Civiletti served the firm previously as Managing Partner and then firm Chairman.[13] His successful practice focused on commercial litigation and corporate governance.[14]

Civiletti's Sonnett lecture came in the middle of the Iran Hostage Crisis, while he was still serving as the Attorney General.[15] But even in the face of international conflict, he advocated for balancing the needs of the intelligence community with the constitutional freedoms that government owes to the American people.[16] He explained that, although legally and historically separate, the government functions of law enforcement and foreign intelligence were converging,[17] which raised novel issues under the First and Fourth Amendments.[18] Tracing the development of "intelligence law," law that checks government's ability to conduct surveillance, Mr. Civiletti noted the challenge of crafting comprehensive legislation to this end, while expressing optimism that it could be done.[19] He also called for more internal review and self-regulation across agencies within the Executive Branch to prevent them from overstepping their authority.[20]

Perhaps most prophetically,[21] Mr. Civiletti repeatedly stressed that rapid advances in surveillance technology would require the Executive Branch to self-regulate without much useful guidance from past court opinions.[22] His recommendation rings true in an era of American concern over NSA surveillance, as the Supreme Court continues to grapple with the best way to evaluate new technology under old precedent.[23]

---

9. 31 U.S.C. § 1341 (2012).

10. Denver Nicks, *The Man Who Invented the Government Shutdown*, Time Swampland (Oct. 9, 2013), http://swampland.time.com/2013/10/09/the-man-who-created-the-government-shutdown/.

11. Press Release, Venable LLP, *supra* note 2.

12. *Benjamin R. Civiletti: Profile*, *supra* note 5.

13. Press Release, Venable LLP, *supra* note 2.

14. *Id.*

15. Civiletti, *supra* note 1, at 883.

16. *See generally id.*

17. *Id.* at 884–89.

18. *Id.* at 893–903.

19. *Id.* at 889–93.

20. *Id.* at 893, 896.

21. The surveillance and related issues and investigations regarding the 2016 Presidential election can learn much from Mr. Civiletti's lecture.

22. *Id.* at 899–902, 906.

23. *See, e.g.*, United States v. Jones, 132 S. Ct. 945, 954–57 (2012) (Sotomayor, J., concurring).

1980 Sonnett Lecture

These are troubled times for international legal order. A band of terrorists has seized the American Embassy in Tehran and holds United States diplomats hostage.[1] The International Court of Justice[2] considered this international outrage and ruled unanimously that the hostages must be freed.[3] The Court declared that "[there is no more fundamental prerequisite for the conduct of relations between states than the inviolability of diplomatic envoys and embassies," a principle of international law so well established that "throughout history nations of all creeds and cultures have observed reciprocal obligations for that purpose."[4] Iran refused to comply with the Court's order to release the hostages. With similar disdain for international law, Soviet armed forces have invaded a sovereign nation and installed a puppet government.[5] Following a Soviet veto of a Security Council resolution,[6] the United Nations General Assembly overwhelmingly condemned the actions of the Soviet Union and declared that the invasion—and occupation of Afghanistan is deplorable and inconsistent with the principles of the United Nations charter.[7]

Iran's continuing defiance of the very foundations of international law demonstrates the fragility of the law as a means of ordering human behavior. The action of the Soviet Union damages the rule of law even more significantly because its action cannot be rationalized as an aberrational act by revolutionary terrorists. Indeed, the Soviets claim shamelessly that their invasion was required by a mutual defense treaty with Afghanistan.[8] Both events illustrate that international law is not self-executing, and that our ability to enforce the law through peaceful means is limited. When the law is broken with apparent impunity, the ensuing frustration may result in a willingness to reject the very concept of law itself and a temptation to engage in acts we would otherwise condemn. There are indications that such feelings are astir within our nation today. Nevertheless, we must not permit our frustration to result in the abandonment of recently developed legal strictures on the intelligence-gathering activities of the United States.

1. N.Y. Times, Nov. 5, 1979, § A, at 1, col. 4; *id.*, Apr. 8, 1980, § A. at 1, col. 3.

2. The International Court of Justice (ICJ) is the "principal judicial organ of the United Nations." U.N. Charter art. 92, 59 Stat 1031, 1051 (1945), T. S No. 993. at 21. The ICJ consists of fifteen members, each from different nations, who serve for nine-year terms. Statute of the International Court of Justice, June 26, 1945, arts. 3, 13, 59 Stat. 1055, 1055–56, T.S. No. 993, at 25–26. Member states of the United Nations may unilaterally invoke the ICJ's jurisdiction in several situations, including a dispute involving "any question of international law [and] the existence of any fact which, if established, would constitute a breach of an international obligation." *Id.*, art. 36, 59 Stat. at 1060, T.S. No. 993. at 30.

3. United States Diplomatic and Consular Staff in Tehran, United States v. Iran, I.C.J. (Order of Dec. 15, 1979).

4. *Id.* at 16.

5. N.Y. Times, Dec. 27, 1979, § A, at 1, col. 6; *id.*, Dec. 31, 1979, § A, at 1. col 4.

6. N.Y. Times, Jan. 8, 1980, § A, at 1. col. 2.

7. G.A. Res. ES-6/2 (Jan. 14, 1980).

8. N.Y. Times, Dec. 31, 1979, § A, at 1, col. 1.

This article focuses on the evolving relationship between the rule of law and the intelligence-gathering activities of our government. The collection and utilization of intelligence information are essential ingredients of foreign policy and national security, and the dramatic increase in international tensions emphasizes our country's crucial need for timely and accurate foreign intelligence. Nevertheless, past excesses in the conduct of intelligence activities indicate that such operations cannot be implemented without careful regard for the rule of law.[9] The following analysis considers the complexities of developing a rule of law that comports with the genuine need of our government to engage in foreign intelligence activities and preserves the civil liberties and privacy interests of our citizens.[10]

THE NATURE AND ROLE OF INTELLIGENCE GATHERING

In the past, the line between foreign and domestic intelligence gathering often was not clearly drawn.[11] The Executive Branch, however, is now careful to distinguish these

9. Several congressional committees and executive commissions have thoroughly investigated instances of misconduct by the intelligence agencies. *E.g.*, S. Rep. No. 755, 94th Cong., 2d Sess. (1976) [hereinafter cited as the Church Committee Report]; *United States Intelligence Agencies and Activities: Performance of the Intelligence Community: Hearings Before the House Select Comm. on Intelligence*, 94th Cong., 1st Sess. (1974); *Domestic Intelligence Operations for Internal Security Purposes: Hearings Before the House Comm. on Internal Security*, 93rd Cong., 2d Sess. (1974); Staff of Subcomm. on Constitutional Rights of the Senate Comm. on the Judiciary, 92nd Cong., 2d Sess., Report on Army Surveillance of Civilians: A Documentary Analysis (1972); Commission on CIA Activities within the United States, Report to the President (June 1975), [hereinafter cited as the Rockefeller Commission Report].

10. Several authors have grappled with the evolving rule of law in the area of national security. *E.g.*, Theoharis & Meyer, *The "National Security" Justification for Electronic Eavesdropping: An Elusive Exception*, 14 Wayne L. Rev. 749 (1968); *Developments in the Law—The National Security Interest and Civil Liberties*, 85 Harv. L. Rev. 1130 (1972); Comment, *Privacy and Political Freedom: Applicability of the Fourth Amendment to "National Security" Investigations*, 17 U.C.L.A. L. Rev. 1205 (1970); Note, *Foreign Security Surveillance and the Fourth Amendment*, 87 Harv. L. Rev. 976 (1974).

11. The difficulty of distinguishing between domestic and foreign intelligence-gathering operations has partially resulted from an inability to define clearly the terms applicable to various types of surveillances. The confusion has generally been clarified as case law and statute have increasingly abandoned or defined the term national security. For example, in Katz v. United States, 389 U.S. 347 (1967), the Court reserved decision on the question of the applicability of the Fourth Amendment warrant requirement to national security electronic surveillance. *Id.* at 358 n.23.

In *United States v. United States Dist. Court (Keith)*, 407 U.S. 297 (1972), the Court analyzed the domestic aspects of national security but once again reserved "the issues which may be involved with respect to activities of foreign powers or their agents." *Id.* at 322 (footnote omitted); *see* United States v. Smith, 321 F. Supp. 424, 429 (C.D. Cal. 19711 (applicability of warrant requirement to *foreign* national security surveillance not decided, although warrant mandated for *domestic* security surveillances). *Keith* may have added to the confusion surrounding the meaning of national security. The opinion emphasizes that it is often difficult to distinguish between domestic and foreign threats to the nation's security. 407 U.S. at 309 n.8. The Court acknowledged that Title III of the Omnibus Crime Control and Safe Streets Act of 1968, 18 U.S.C. §§ 2510–2520 (1976), uses the term national security to refer only to the activities of foreign powers. *Id.* § 2511(3). Nevertheless,

two concerns. Thus, intelligence is defined to include only foreign intelligence and counterintelligence,[12] both of which, in turn, are defined as information relating to "*foreign* powers, organizations or persons."[13] Recent bureaucratic reorganizations and the promulgation of rules, regulations, and guidelines have also reflected this sharp domestic/foreign distinction.[14] In the Federal Bureau of Investigation (FBI), for example, criminal and intelligence investigations are handled by two separate divisions.[15] Similarly, the President's Executive Order on Intelligence Activities specifically provides that it does not "apply to or interfere with any authorized civil or criminal law enforcement responsibility of any department or agency."[16]

---

the Court continued to apply the term national security to both domestic and foreign intelligence operations. 407 U.S. at 309 n.8.

In *Zweibon v. Mitchell*, 516 F.2d 594 (D.C. Cir. 1975) (en banc), *cert. denied*, 425 U.S. 944 (1976), the court extended *Keith* and the warrant requirement to a wiretap of a domestic organization that is neither the agent of, nor acting in collaboration with, a foreign power, even if the surveillance is undertaken in the name of foreign intelligence gathering. The court, in a very long footnote, attempted to distinguish between "internal security" or "domestic security" and "foreign security." *Id.* at 613 n.42. The court's efforts failed, however, when it concluded: "'National security' will generally be used interchangeably with 'foreign security,' except where the context makes it clear that it refers to both 'foreign security and 'internal security.'" *Id.* On remand, the district court established its own categorization and distinguished "domestic security," "domestic national security," and "foreign security" surveillances. Zweibon v. Mitchell, 444 F. Supp. 1296, 1299 n.3 (D.D.C. 1978), *rev'd in port and remanded on other grounds*, 606 F.2d 1172 (D.C. Cir. 1979). Although these classifications appear to correlate roughly with the distinctions provided in Exec. Order No. 12036, 3 C.F.R. 112 (1979), the terminology used may foster continued confusion.

12. Exec. Order No. 12036, § 4-206, 3 C.F.R. 112, 133 (1979).

13. *Id.* §§ 4-202, 205, 3 C.F.R. 112, 133 (1979) (emphasis added). Foreign intelligence is defined as "information relating to the capabilities, intentions and activities of foreign powers, organizations or persons," *id.* § 4-205, 3 C.F.R at 133, and counterintelligence is defined as "information gathered and activities conducted to protect against espionage and other clandestine intelligence activities, sabotage, international terrorist activities or assassinations conducted for or on behalf of foreign powers, organizations or persons." *Id.* § 4-202, 3 C.F.R at 133. Intelligence organizations have not always had the benefit of such specific definitions. Sherman Kent, former chairman of the CIA's Board of National Estimates, described intelligence in his pivotal book as comprising three definitional subjects: knowledge that our nation must have regarding other nations to assure itself that planning and decision-making will not be conducted in ignorance; an organization structured to obtain, centralize, and evaluate that knowledge; and the activity of gathering such knowledge. S. Kent, Strategic Intelligence For American World Policy ix (1949).

14. Although many of the regulations and guidelines are not available in published form, they can be obtained from the agency which they govern. Requests should be made in the same manner as requests under the Freedom of Information Act.

15. All foreign intelligence and counterintelligence investigations are handled by the Intelligence Division (Division 5), and all domestic security and international terrorism investigations are within the purview of the Criminal Investigation Division (Division 6). *See supra* note 14.

16. Exec. Order No. 12036, § 4-107, 3 C.F.R. 112, 133 (1979).

This distinction between foreign intelligence and domestic law enforcement reflects not only the attitude of the courts[17] and the legislature,[18] but also the present belief of the Executive Branch that the purposes of intelligence gathering are fundamentally different from those of domestic law enforcement and, therefore, require different regulations. Law enforcement is intended to discover and punish acts which society deems unacceptable. Intelligence activities are intended to acquire information so that the President and his advisors can make informed decisions in conducting international diplomacy, foreign relations, and national security affairs.[19] In counterintelligence, however, there are some areas in which intelligence and domestic law enforcement interests overlap. This intersection is particularly apparent when the government attempts to monitor clandestine information gathering by foreign agents in the United States because many forms of foreign espionage conducted within our nation's borders are crimes under federal law.[20] The need to observe

17. *See supra* note 11.

18. *See infra* notes 49–59 and accompanying text.

19. Positive foreign intelligence surveillances differ markedly from those in criminal investigations. For example, a foreign intelligence surveillance may be undertaken without probable cause to believe a crime has been committed, and may be of considerable duration and scope. United States v. Humphrey, 456 F. Supp. 51, 56 (E.D. Va. 1978). Its purpose is to gather information about the intentions and capabilities of a foreign government, not to obtain admissible evidence of a crime. *Id. But see* United States v. Stone, 305 F. Supp. 75, 82 (D.D.C. 1969) (foreign intelligence wiretap used as evidence in criminal trial); United States v. O'Baugh, 304 F. Supp. 767, 763 (D.D.C. 1969) (wiretap of embassy used as evidence in criminal proceeding). Foreign counterintelligence activities more closely parallel law enforcement activities. Nevertheless, while it is true that many activities of the targets of counterintelligence surveillances may be criminal, *see, e.g.*, 18 U.S.C. § 641 (1976) (relating to unauthorized use of government property); *id.* §§ 792–799 (relating to espionage); *id.* §§ 2151–2157 (relating to sabotage); *id.* §§ 2381–2391 (relating to treason, sedition, and subversive activities), the primary objective of the surveillance is not preparation for prosecution. *But see*, United States v. Humphrey, 456 F. Supp. at 56 (distinguishing between foreign intelligence surveillance and domestic surveillance and stating that: "It would seem rare that the government would engage in domestic electronic surveillance without some plans to prosecute *at some time*."); Zweibon v. Mitchell, 516 F.2d 594, 648 (D.C. Cir.) (en banc) (claiming it is a "myth to characterize national security surveillance as purely non-prosecutorial in the criminal sense"), *cert. denied*, *425* U.S. 944 (1976). The objective of a counterintelligence surveillance is to identify, isolate, and prevent breaches of security in the foreign intelligence and national defense apparatus. The distinction between certain intelligence surveillances and law enforcement activities was carefully set forth in the Senate Report accompanying the Foreign Intelligence Surveillance Act. S. Rep. No. 604, 95th Cong., 1st Sess. 4–7 (1977), *reprinted in* [1978] U.S. Code Cong. & Ad. News 3904, 3905–9.

20. *See supra* note 19. There has been some concern regarding the adequacy of the espionage statutes in certain circumstances. *See Espionage Laws and Leaks: Hearings Before the Subcomm. on Legislation of the House Permanent Select Comm. on Intelligence*, 96th Cong., 1st Sess. (1979). *See generally* Edgar & Schmidt, *The Espionage Statutes and the Publication of Defense Information*, 73 Colum. L. Rev. 929 (1973); Nimmer, *National Security Secrets v. Free Speech: The Issues Left Undecided in the Ellsberg Case*, 26 Stan. L. Rev. 311 (1974).

the activities of agents of foreign powers and to defend against their operations demands considerable caution.[21]

Intelligence activities, which, as presently defined, pertain only to foreign affairs and national security issues,[22] must be kept strong and effective. The government needs to obtain the best information available concerning the intentions and activities of foreign powers. The ability of the United States to react to events in foreign lands is limited under any circumstances. Without timely and accurate information, the ability to react constructively is eliminated. Moreover, obtaining critical intelligence is exceedingly difficult. Although it may be virtually impossible, given today's technology, for any country to conceal substantial troop movements, the transfer of funds and arms and the strategies of foreign governments are not as readily detectable. Unless we possess current, accurate knowledge about the actions a foreign power is likely to take, our information base is limited; and the more limited our information base, the more speculative are our analyses, and the greater the danger to our security. Secrecy, however, is an essential element of effective intelligence gathering. Even if we are able to gain information concerning a hostile foreign nation, our success will be short-lived if we disclose the facts of our success. Further, if we reveal the information obtained, we will not only lose our advantage and risk changes in the acquired plans, but we will also jeopardize or perhaps destroy our sources and methods of gathering information.[23]

21. Only a small percentage of all counterintelligence cases can be considered for successful criminal prosecutions, and investigations of foreign intelligence agents are seldom conducted from the outset as they would if eventual prosecution were expected. Many counterintelligence professionals believe that criminal prosecutions should never be brought against hostile agents because doing so may only result in their replacement by other, unknown agents of whose activities we may not be aware. Moreover, criminal proceedings may not only confirm the accuracy of classified information that has been passed to a foreign power, but may also reveal at least some of the material to a far wider audience. This problem is known as "graymail." *See* Senate Select Comm. on Intelligence, 95th Cong., 2d Sess., Report on National Security Secrets and the Administration of Justice (Comm. Print 1978). Graymail problems, however, are not insurmountable. For example, in *United States v. Kampiles*, 609 F.2d 1233 (7th Cir. 1979), the trial court's procedures and judgment avoided the graymail problem. The trial court prevented classified information from being introduced at trial by issuing a protective order after in camera, ex parte proceedings in which the government presented evidence of the sensitive document that was passed to the Soviets and of the FBI's counterintelligence investigation into the document's disappearance. *Id.* at 1248. The court of appeals upheld the espionage conviction based upon the defendant's confession that he had met with and sold a classified document to a Soviet intelligence officer and upon sufficient other evidence to corroborate the reliability of the defendant's confession. *Id.* at 1238. The Administration has introduced legislation to resolve the graymail problem and to establish a workable and fair procedure for handling classified information in criminal cases. *See infra* note 102.

22. *See supra* note 13 and accompanying text.

23. There is continuing debate concerning the need for and scope of legitimate government secrecy. *Compare* Snepp v. United States, 100 S. Ct. 763, 765 n.3 (1980) (stating "[t]he Government has a compelling interest in protecting both the secrecy of information important to our national security and the appearance of confidentiality so essential to the effective operation of our foreign intelligence service") *and* Colby, *Intelligence Secrecy and Security in a Free Society*, INT'L SECURITY 3

What makes these seemingly self-evident observations controversial is that intelligence activities can come perilously close to intruding upon our most basic statutory and constitutional rights.[24] This inherent danger is increased by the highly sophisticated technological advances, commonly used throughout the world today, that widen the range of possible intelligence-gathering activities. The necessity of secrecy, however, often prohibits any judicial review of questionable intelligence activities.[25] The Executive Branch, therefore, is required to redouble its efforts to ensure that intelligence activities are not exempted from all responsible checks and balances.[26] The need to create durable mechanisms to regulate and review intelligence activities has led to the evolution of intelligence law.

(Fall 1976) (setting forth a conceptual framework for limiting unnecessary government disclosures) *with* Church Committee Report, *supra* note 9, (Bk. I) at 16 (recognizing the dangers of excessive secrecy to a democracy) *and* M. Halperin & D. Hoffman, Top Secret: National Security and the Right to Know (1977) (arguing that the secrecy veil of the intelligence community needs to be pierced). *See generally Investigation of Publication of Select Comm. On Intelligence Report: Hearings Before the House Comm. On Standards of Official Conduct*, 94th Cong., 2d Sess. (1976).

24. *See infra* section "Illustrative Constitutional Problems in Intelligence Gathering".

25. The Foreign Intelligence Surveillance Act of 1978, 50 U.S.C.A. §§ 1801–1811 (West Supp. 1979), does provide judicial review of certain intelligence activities. *See infra* note 48. The proposed National Intelligence Act of 1980, S. 2284, 96th Cong., 1st Sess., 126 Cong. Rec. S1307 (daily ed. Feb. 8, 1980) [hereinafter cited as S. 2284], would expand the scope of judicial review to cover physical searches as well as electronic surveillance both within the United States and abroad. *Id.* § 801.

26. Executive Order 12036 and its implementing regulations create an effective structure for oversight of intelligence activities within the Executive Branch. The duty to identify, inspect, and report unlawful or improper activity is placed upon senior officers throughout the intelligence community. Exec. Order No. 12036, § 1-7, 3 C.F.R. 112, 119–20 (1979). This obligation is reinforced and monitored by the Inspectors General and General Counsel for each agency. *Id.* § 3-2, 3 C.F.R. at 131. These officers are required to investigate and report to the Intelligence Oversight Board any activities that raise questions of legality or propriety. *Id.* The executive order also gives the Attorney General substantial oversight and review responsibilities. *Id.* § 3-3, 3 C.F.R. at 131. For example, the Attorney General is empowered to establish and approve procedures for each agency which will ensure compliance with law and protection of constitutional rights and privacy. *Id.* § 3-305, 3 C.F.R. at 131. To advise and assist the Attorney General in connection with his intelligence-related responsibilities, the Office of Intelligence Policy and Review was established. 45 Fed. Reg. 13729 (1980) (to be codified in 28 C.F.R. § 0.33). This office is currently staffed by ten attorneys and is under the direction of the Counsel for Intelligence Policy. The Executive Branch oversight apparatus also includes the President's Intelligence Oversight Board (IOB), which is composed of three individuals appointed by the President. Exec. Order No. 12036, § 3-1, 3 C.F.R. at 130. The IOB periodically reviews the oversight procedures and guidelines of each intelligence agency, forwards reports of illegality to the Attorney General, and informs the President of its findings and any serious questions of legality or propriety. *Id.* § 3-102, 3 C.F.R. at 130–31. This comprehensive system of oversight within the Executive Branch is supplemented by extensive review in Congress. *See infra* note 104.

THE DEVELOPMENT OF INTELLIGENCE LAW

Although both law enforcement and intelligence activities have existed in this country since before the creation of the Republic,[27] they have developed largely along separate tracks because of their conflicting natures. Law enforcement emphasizes openness, stability, and a balancing of interests; its concerns are domestic and its scope is comprehensive. Intelligence activities require secrecy, flexibility, and a single-mindedness of purpose; they focus on foreign developments and rapid adaptability to specific circumstances. Given these disparities, it is no surprise that law enforcement and intelligence activities did not converge in the United States until recently.

The first permanent peacetime intelligence organizations in the United States were created in the latter part of the nineteenth century.[28] These were relatively ineffective, however, and during World War I the nation relied to a great extent on the intelligence capabilities of its allies.[29] It was not until World War II that American intelligence efforts began to flourish under the Office of Strategic Services.[30] Apart from various directives dealing essentially with organizational matters, there was almost no accompanying development of law relating to intelligence activities.[31]

After World War II, a permanent Central Intelligence Agency (CIA) was created by the National Security Act of 1947.[32] This statute was the first public declaration by any nation concerning the existence and functions of its intelligence service. The Act is remarkably concise; in five short subparagraphs it instructs the CIA to collect intelligence information and to perform other related functions at the direction of the National Security Council.[33] The Act's sole express restriction is the proviso that the CIA should not have any police, subpoena, or law enforcement powers or internal security functions.[34] This limitation was as much a concession to established law enforcement agencies as it was an effort to prevent the creation of an American secret police.[35]

27. There is clear evidence that General Washington authorized and relied upon substantial intelligence activities in the conduct of the American Revolution. For an excellent account of the history and evolution of United States intelligence capabilities, see A. Dulles, The Craft of Intelligence (1963). *See also* H. Ransom, Central Intelligence and National Security (1958); Church Committee Report, *supra* note 9, (Bk. VI) at 9–15.

28. The first permanent intelligence agency was the Office of Intelligence established by the Navy in 1882. Church Committee Report, *supra* note 9, (Bk. VI) at 309. Three years later the Army organized its own intelligence unit, the Military Intelligence Division. *Id.*

29. A. Dulles, *supra* note 27, at 40–41.

30. H. Ransom, The Intelligence Establishment 65–76 (1970).

31. A. Dulles, *supra* note 27, at 42–44.

32. 50 U.S.C. § 403 (1976).

33. *Id.* § 403(d)(1)–(5).

34. *Id.* § 403(d)(3).

35. Rockefeller Commission Report, *supra* note 9, at 61. S. 2284, *supra* note 25, proposes to replace the National Security Act provisions governing intelligence activities. As Senator Huddleston noted when he introduced S. 2284: "The National Security Act of 1947, the current 'charter' for intelligence activities, is vague and cursory. As Clark Clifford, a primary author of that legislation,

With the exception of espionage statutes enacted originally in 1917 and subsequently amended,[36] and administrative housekeeping laws enacted to facilitate the operation of the CIA and the National Security Agency, there were no other laws expressly relating to United States intelligence activities from 1947 until the 1970s.[37] In fact, during this period laws were passed that, if taken literally, would have obstructed or prevented clearly legitimate and necessary intelligence programs.[38] Faced with an absence of particularized law or precedent and an array of general purpose laws inappropriate to intelligence endeavors, the government and its intelligence agencies understandably ignored the broad range of legal strictures that apply in other areas of governmental activity. The deference shown to intelligence matters for almost thirty years by the public, press, judiciary, Congress, executive officials, various presidents and attorneys general considerably strengthened the assumption that intelligence efforts were so different or special that modified legal standards should be applied to them.[39] Over the past few years, however, this perception has changed, and express legal principles have been specifically developed to govern intelligence activities. Although there may continue to be some confusion about how the law applies to a particular matter, there is no longer any doubt that intelligence activities are subject to definable legal standards.

The first comprehensive statement of intelligence law, which delineated various standards, authorizations, and prohibitions designed to govern our intelligence operations, was

---

told this committee, that act was considered interim legislation that would be replaced once the Executive and Congress better knew what was required. [In S. 2284] we have given the intelligence community authority to do what needs to be done." 126 Cong. Rec. S1305 (daily ed. Feb. 8, 1980).

36. 18 U.S.C. §§ 792–794 (1976).

37. A key aspect of the present structure and functioning of the intelligence community is that of all the organizations engaged in foreign intelligence, only the CIA has been created by legislation. The National Security Agency, the FBI, and the Defense Intelligence Agency have been operating without legislative charters.

38. For example, there are a variety of statutes which, if applied literally, would limit the ability of the FBI to engage in undercover investigative operations for the collection of foreign intelligence or counterintelligence. *E.g.*, 31 U.S.C. § 484 (1976) (restricting the use of proceeds from government operations); *id.* § 521 (restricting the deposit into banks of proceeds from government operations); *id.* § 869 (restricting acquisition or creation of proprietary corporations or business entities). In recent years, Congress has used the Department of Justice Appropriation Authorization Act to provide an annual waiver from these requirements for intelligence operations. *See, e.g.*, Dep't of Justice, Appropriations Act, Fiscal Year 1980, P.L. 96–132, § 7(a), 93 Stat. 1040, 1045–46, *reprinted in* [1979] U.S. Code Cong. & Ad. News.

39. It was not until 1972 that the Supreme Court acknowledged the Executive Branch did not have full discretion to undertake intelligence operations to protect national security. United States v. United States Dist. Court (Keith), 407 U.S. 297, 316–17 (1972). In fact, the Justice Department declined prosecution of individuals involved in two large-scale mail opening programs operating between 1953 and 1973 because of the ambiguity of the law as it related to intelligence operations during that period. DEP'T OF JUSTICE, REPORT CONCERNING ITS INVESTIGATIONS AND PROSECUTORIAL DECISIONS WITH RESPECT TO CENTRAL INTELLIGENCE AGENCY MAIL OPENING ACTIVITIES IN THE UNITED STATES (1977). Since *Keith*, however, the courts have attempted to define the constitutional limits of intelligence investigations. *See supra* note 11.

announced by President Ford on February 18, 1976.[40] After two years of experience with President Ford's order, President Carter issued his own executive order which broadens and strengthens the controls over the intelligence community.[41] For example, this order requires that various procedures be developed, subject to the approval of the Attorney General, to govern the complete range of collection and dissemination practices by all intelligence agencies when the information collected or disseminated pertains to persons entitled to the protection of the United States Constitution.[42] The United States is the only country that has issued such a comprehensive statement.

President Carter also ordered that the government's document classification system be changed.[43] This new executive order officially embraces the principle that even a properly classified document should sometimes be declassified if the public interest in disclosure outweighs the damage to national security that might reasonably be expected from disclosure.[44] The order also creates an administrative mechanism, complete with disciplinary sanctions, designed to eliminate any abuses of the system,[45] such as the unnecessary classification of documents.[46]

Congress has also played an important role in the development of intelligence law. In 1978, Congress enacted the Foreign Intelligence Surveillance Act (FISA),[47] which mandates judicial review of certain proposals from intelligence agencies regarding the conduct of intelligence-related electronic surveillance in the United States.[48] Moreover, the Attorney General retains sole authority to approve agency-certified surveillance applications

40. Exec. Order No. 11905, 3 C.F.R. 90 (1977).

41. Exec. Order No. 12036, 3 C.F.R. 112 (1979). For example, President Carter's order goes well beyond President Ford's order in specifying the preconditions for targeting United States persons for electronic surveillance. *Compare id.* § 2-202, 3 C.F.R. at 126 *with* Exec. Order No. 11905, § 5(b)(2), 3 C.F.R. 90, 100 (1977). President Carter's order also governs, for the first time, television and movie surveillance, Exec. Order No. 12036, § 2-203, 3 C.F.R. at 126, and covert procurement and contracting. *Id.* § 2-303, 3 C.F.R. at 129.

42. Exec. Order No. 12036, § 2-201, 3 C.F.R. 112, 126 (1979).

43. Exec. Order No. 12065, 3 C.F.R. 190 (1979).

44. *Id.* § 3-303, 3 C.F.R. 190, 197 (1979).

45. *Id.* § 5, 3 C.F.R. 190, 201–04 (1979).

46. *Id.* § 1-3 to 1-6, 3 C.F.R. 190, 193–95 (1979).

47. Foreign Intelligence Surveillance Act of 1978, Pub. L. No. 95–511, 92 Stat. 1783 (codified at 50 U.S.C.A. §§ 1801–1811 (West Supp. 1979)).

48. FISA directs the Chief Justice to "publicly designate seven district court judges from seven of the United States judicial circuits who shall constitute a court which shall have jurisdiction to hear applications for and grant orders approving electronic surveillance anywhere within the United States." 50 U.S.C.A. § 1803(a) (West Supp. 1979). The Chief Justice is also directed to designate three judges "who together shall comprise a court of review which shall have jurisdiction to review the denial of any application made under this Act." *Id.* § 1803(b). The Attorney General, rather than the Court, is authorized to approve electronic surveillance of certain communications transmitted by means of communications used exclusively between or among foreign powers and of technical intelligence from property under the open and exclusive control of a foreign power. *Id.* § 1802(a)(1)(A)–(B). The Attorney General must advise the Court of his actions. *Id.* § 1802(a)(3).

before they are submitted to the court.[49] This judicial and executive review process helps ensure that only necessary and carefully considered electronic surveillances will be initiated.[50] Governing standards for intelligence operations are also provided by the Case-Zablocki Act, which requires that Congress be advised of any international agreement to which the United States is a party, including agreements between intelligence services.[51] Both the Senate and the House of Representatives have created independent committees with primary responsibility for overseeing the activities of the intelligence agencies.[52] The Freedom of Information Act[53] and the Privacy Act[54] have also had a significant effect on the information collection, dissemination, and storage practices of the intelligence agencies.

For the past three years, Administration and Congressional representatives have endeavored to develop comprehensive charter legislation that would delineate proper and improper intelligence activities.[55] This goal, however, has proved far more elusive than many had anticipated. Intelligence agencies are called upon to operate in societies with vastly different cultures, most of which we do not fully understand, and to provide services in an atmosphere of international political tension and volatility. The effort to reach agreement on a charter that gives the agencies sufficient flexibility to meet changing situations to protect our security, without delegating virtually unlimited discretion, has been herculean.

On February 8, 1980, Senators Huddleston, Mathias, Bayh, and Goldwater introduced the very complex and comprehensive National Intelligence Act of 1980 (S. 2284).[56] With few exceptions, S. 2284 represents a consensus of the Executive Branch and the Senate Select Committee on Intelligence concerning the principles governing United States intelligence activities.[57] S. 2284 carefully balances the practical need for an intelligence

49. *Id.* § 1804.

50. Experience has demonstrated that our intelligence agencies are functioning well under FISA. The record refutes the argument that congressional consideration of such statutes would undermine the entire intelligence apparatus of the United States. *See generally* S. Rep. No. 379, 96th Cong., 1st Sess. (1979).

51. 1 U.S.C. § 112(b) (1976 & Supp. II 1978).

52. The Senate Select Committee on Intelligence was created by S. Res. 400, 94th Cong., 2d Sess., 122 Cong. Rec. 14673–75 (1976). The House Permanent Select Committee on Intelligence was established by H. R. Res. 658, 95th Cong., 1st Sess., 123 Cong. Rec. H7104–6 (daily ed. July 14, 1977).

53. 5 U.S.C. § 552 (1976).

54. *Id.* § 552a.

55. One of the purposes of the Church Committee was to create a record to serve as a foundation for drafting such legislation. Church Committee Report, *supra* note 9.

56. S. 2284, *supra* note 25.

57. President Carter stated there was "virtually complete agreement [between the Executive Branch and the Senate Select Committee on Intelligence] on the organization of the intelligence community and on the authorizations and restrictions pertaining to intelligence collection and special activities." 126 Cong. Rec. S1307 (daily ed. Feb. 8, 1980). He continued, however, to state that "a few issues remain to be resolved." *Id.* One of the primary disagreements between the Administration and the authors of S. 2284 relates to prior reporting to Congress of covert operations and sensitive collection operations. *See infra* note 105.

apparatus with the guarantees provided by the Constitution and other relevant laws, and, for the first time, legislatively defines and authorizes the activities and conduct of the entire intelligence community. S. 2284 also provides workable standards for the initiation of activities concerning United States persons,[58] by providing a clear hierarchy of responsibility and oversight, and by prohibiting certain activities that are anathema to American democracy.[59] Regardless of whether S. 2284 becomes law, however, its formulation and consideration by the Senate has had the positive effect of focusing attention on the policy choices required to be made in conducting our intelligence activities and on the structural tools available for implementing those choices. As long as we continue to examine objectively the legal guidelines for our intelligence operations, I am confident we will neither abandon our progress nor retreat from what we have gained.

ILLUSTRATIVE CONSTITUTIONAL PROBLEMS IN INTELLIGENCE GATHERING

The basic tension in intelligence-gathering activities exists between the government's legitimate need for information and the individual's right to privacy.[60] Although federal law protects United States persons[61] from excessive or improper intrusions into their

58. *See infra* note 61.

59. For example, S. 2284, *supra* note 25, prohibits assassination, *id.* § 131, covert domestic propaganda, *id.* § 133; covert contracting with educational institutions. *id.* § 134. and accomplishing indirectly what cannot be done directly, *id.* § 135.

60. Fortunately for all Americans, the vast preponderance of the information our government seeks comes from foreign persons and organizations, most of them located outside the United States. In *all* cases, the federal government collects the information this country needs without intentionally violating United States law. United States law contains few limitations on the collection of intelligence from foreign sources. *See, e.g.*, 50 U.S.C.A. § 1802(a)(1)(A)(i) (West Supp. 1979) (electronic surveillance directed at communications exclusively between or among foreign powers may be approved by the Attorney General without court order); Exec. Order No. 12036, § 2-208, 3 C.F.R. 112, 128 (1979) (restricting only the collection of nonpublicly available information concerning United States persons).

61. A United States person is defined in Executive Order 12036 as "a citizen of the United States, an alien lawfully admitted for permanent residence, an unincorporated association organized in the United States or substantially composed of United States citizens or aliens admitted for permanent residence, or a corporation incorporated in the United States." Exec. Order No. 12036, § 4-214, 3 C.F.R. 112, 135 (1979). FISA uses a similar definition. 50 U.S.C.A. § 1801(i) (West Supp. 1979). S. 2284, *supra* note 25, however, provides a more limited definition of United States person. *Id.* § 103(21). For example, it excludes corporations incorporated in the United States and unincorporated associations organized in the United States which are "openly acknowledged by a foreign government or governments to be directed and controlled by such foreign government or governments." *Id.* One's status as a United States person is, in general, not determined by one's location. Thus, a United States citizen abroad remains a United States person for intelligence law purposes, while a foreign visitor to this country does not automatically become a United States person upon entry into this country. There are several restrictions in the law which protect foreign visitors from unwarranted intelligence activities in this country, but those limitations are significantly different from the ones applicable to United States persons. For example, Executive Order 12036

private affairs in the name of national security,[62] intelligence activities aimed at collecting information not publicly available[63] inevitably involve some incursion into the privacy of individuals or organizations. The rights which may be affected by intelligence activities directed against nonconsenting United States persons arise from the Constitution, particularly the First and Fourth Amendments. Because our government does not exist as an end unto itself, but as a means of preserving certain precious freedoms for each of us, we cannot allow a need to protect the nation to become an excuse to violate the very rights the government was instituted to protect. Nevertheless, we cannot ignore the government's legitimate need for intelligence information which may at times affect the freedoms guaranteed by the Constitution.

First Amendment Issues

United States persons may acquire their knowledge of foreign governments in the course of political activities protected by the First Amendment, and courts are often required to balance these First Amendment rights with the government's need for intelligence information.[64] It is generally recognized that, in certain circumstances, the government can

---

protects United States persons and foreign visitors alike from unregulated covert electronic or mechanical monitoring, physical searches, mail surveillance in the United States, and from unlawful physical surveillance by the FBI. Exec. Order No. 12036, §§ 2-202 to 2-206, 3 C.F.R. at 126–27. The protections provided for foreign visitors, however, are far more limited than those mandated for United States persons. *See, e.g., id.* § 2-208, 3 C.F.R. at 128.

62. *See, e.g.*, Exec. Order No. 12036, §§ 2-1 to 2-3, 3 C.F.R. 112, 125–30 (1979).

63. The collection, retention, and dissemination of publicly available information is not regulated by Executive Order 12036 or by the procedures for the various intelligence agencies which were approved by the Attorney General pursuant to this order. Exec. Order No. 12036, § 2-201, 208, 3 C.F.R. 112, 126, 128 (1979). Consequently, the definition of publicly available information is a threshold consideration to the application of legal standards to intelligence gathering. The procedures for the CIA and the Department of Defense define the term publicly available similarly. The Defense Department's definition provides: "'Available publicly' means information that has been published or broadcast for general public consumption, is available upon request to a member of the general public, could lawfully be seen or heard by any casual observer, or is made available at a meeting open to the general public." *See supra* note 14. S. 2284, *supra* note 25, fails to define what information is publicly available but provides the following standard for the collection and use of publicly available information: "Publicly available information concerning any United States person may be collected by an entity of the intelligence community when such information is relevant to a lawful function of that entity, and may be retained and disseminated for lawful governmental purposes." *Id.* § 211(c).

64. The First Amendment freedoms of association and of expression are implicated whenever the government compels an individual to delineate his political affiliations before a legislative committee, *e.g.*, Eastland v. United States Servicemen's Fund, 421 U.S. 491, 509 (1975); Gibson v. Florida Legislative Investigation Comm., 372 U.S. 539, 544–46 (1963); Sweezy v. New Hampshire, 354 U.S. 234, 249–50 (1957), or a grand jury, *e.g.*, Branzburg v. Hayes, 408 U.S. 665, 690–91 (1972); Bursey v. United States, 466 F.2d 1059, 1085–86 (9th Cir. 1972); *In re* Wood, 430 F. Supp. 41, 45–46 (S.D.N.Y. 1977); *In re* Verplank, 329 F. Supp. 433, 437–38 (C.D. Cal. 1971), or to identify his politi-

compel a person to disclose information about such protected activities.[65] The courts have adopted an exacting standard to analyze the encroachment that a compelled disclosure imposes on First Amendment freedoms. The governmental interest in disclosure must be substantial. Also, courts have required that there be a "relevant correlation"[66] or "substantial relation"[67] between the governmental interest and the specific information to be revealed, and that the direct and indirect burdens on an individual's or group's associational rights be carefully scrutinized.[68] A final factor that weighs in the balance is the government's ability to pursue its goal in a manner less intrusive on fundamental personal liberties.[69]

Utilizing this balancing standard, courts have held it constitutional for the United States to compel private citizens to disclose their contributions to presidential campaigns,[70] to

---

cal beliefs as a condition of exercising First Amendment rights, *e.g.*, Lamont v. Postmaster Gen., 381 U.S. 301, 305–07 (1965); NAACP v. Alabama, 357 U.S. 449, 462 (1958), or of obtaining government employment, *e.g.*, Shelton v. Tucker, 364 U.S. 479, 487–88 (1960). *See generally* L. Tribe, American Constitutional Law § 12-2, at 581–82 (1978).

65. There are, however, severe limits on the government's right to compel information. For example, it is unconstitutional for a state to compel a private political organization to furnish its membership list to the state where the effect of doing so would be to subject the organization's members to economic reprisal, loss of employment, or physical coercion. *E.g.*, Louisiana *ex rel.* Gremillion v. NAACP, 366 U.S. 293, 295–96 (1961) (upholding temporary injunction restraining enforcement of statute requiring certain not-for-profit organizations to file membership lists); Bates v. City of Little Rock, 361 U.S. 516, 527 (1960) (invalidating occupational license tax statute which required membership list); NAACP v. Alabama, 357 U.S. 449, 466 (1958) (reversing civil contempt judgment against NAACP for refusing to disclose its membership list in violation of foreign corporation registration statute). These foreseeable consequences would dramatically chill the individual's freedom of expression and of private political association.

66. Bates v. City of Little Rock, 361 U.S. 516, 525 (1960).

67. Gibson v. Florida Legislative Investigation Comm., 372 U.S. 539, 546 (1963).

68. Buckley v. Valeo, 424 U.S. 1, 64–68 (1976) (per curiam). Exacting "scrutiny is necessary even if any deterrent effect on the exercise of First Amendment rights arises, not through direct government action, but indirectly as an unintended but inevitable result of the government's conduct in requiring disclosure." *Id.* at 65 (citing NAACP v. Alabama, 357 U.S. 449, 461 (1958)).

69. Lamont v. Postmaster Gen., 381 U.S. 301, 310 (1965) (Brennan, J., concurring); Shelton v. Tucker, 364 U.S. 479, 488 (1960). This ad hoc balancing test has been criticized for being "so unstructured that it can hardly be described as a rule of law at all." T. Emerson, The System of Freedom of Expression 16 (1970). Nevertheless, the Supreme Court in *Buckley v. Valeo*, 424 U.S. 1 (1976) (per curiam), used the balancing test and acknowledged that the governmental interest in disclosure must be weighed against not only the damage to the individuals involved but also the injury suffered by the public at large. *Id.* at 64–68. *Buckley*, however, made it more difficult to prove a constitutional abridgement by requiring evidence of such probable harassment resulting from disclosure as was found in NAACP v. Alabama, 357 U.S. 449, 462 (1958). 424 U.S. at 72. According to Chief Justice Burger, this increased evidentiary burden on litigants challenging compelled disclosure marks a departure from the "historic safeguards guaranteed by the First Amendment." *Id.* at 238 (Burger, C.J., concurring in part and dissenting in part).

70. In Buckley v. Valeo, 424 U.S. 1 (1976) (per curiam), the Supreme Court upheld the requirement of the Federal Election Campaign Act of 1971, 2 U.S.C. §§ 431–456 (1976), that political

require private lobbyists for foreign governments to register,[71] and to require citizens acting as agents of a foreign power to disclose the details of their agency and their activities.[72] The law is less settled, however, when the government obtains information about an individual's activities without his consent, and under circumstances in which that person is not subject to legislative, judicial, or administrative compulsion. Judicial opinions indicate that it is not unconstitutional for an undercover agent in a law enforcement investiga-

---

committees record and transmit to the government the names of individuals contributing in excess of ten dollars to political committees or independent candidates. The Court considered the substantial governmental interest in maintaining the integrity of the electoral process to be of such magnitude as to outweigh the possibility of First Amendment infringements. 424 U.S. at 66–68. The Court upheld the ten-dollar minimal threshold reporting requirement based upon a finding that it was not irrational. *Id.* at 83. This deference to a complex congressional judgment represents the Court's hesitation to substitute its judgment for that of the legislature. *See* Shelton v. Tucker, 364 U.S. 479, 490 (1960) (Frankfurter, J., dissenting); *cf. id.* at 488 ("legislative abridgment [of First Amendment freedoms] must be viewed in the light of less drastic means for achieving the same basic purpose" [footnote omitted]).

In a slightly different context, *Shelton's* least restrictive alternative test has been more stringently applied. In Pollard v. Roberts, 283 F. Supp. 248 (E.D. Ark.), *aff'd per curiam, 393* U.S. 14 (1968), the district court enjoined a quasi-grand jury investigation which had subpoenaed essentially the contributor list of the Arkansas branch of the National Republican Party. The prosecutor issued the subpoena in the course of his investigation of possible election law violations. The court, relying on the principles of *Shelton*, held that "even if a [s]tate can legitimately compel a limited disclosure of individuals affiliated with a group, it does not follow that the [s]tate can compel a sweeping and indiscriminate identification of all of the members of the group in excess of the [s]tate's legitimate need for information." *Id.* at 257.

71. The reporting requirements of the Foreign Agents Registration Act of 1938, as amended, 22 U.S.C. §§ 601–621 (1976), were upheld against a First Amendment challenge in Attorney Gen. v. Irish N. Aid Comm., 346 F. Supp. 1384, 1389–91 (S.D.N.Y.), *cert. denied*, 409 U.S. 1080 (1972). The court found that the disclosure of defendant's activities bore a substantial relation to a legitimate government interest—informing the government and the public as to sources of foreign propaganda—and that the government interest outweighed "any possible infringement of the First Amendment rights of the defendant's members or contributors." *Id.* at 1391. The court was careful to emphasize the vital governmental interest in safeguarding our political process from unacknowledged foreign influences and, on the basis of these concerns and the foreseeable complications with United States foreign policy, rejected the First Amendment claim. *Id.*

72. There are three basic statutes requiring the registration of individuals or organizations that serve as spokesmen or agents for, or receive money from, foreign governments. First, 22 U.S.C. § 612 (1976) provides that anyone who acts as an agent of a foreign principal must file a registration statement with the Attorney General. The registration statement must contain a thorough description of the registrant's business and employees, the agency relationship, and the activities performed for the principal. Second, 18 U.S.C. § 951 (1976) requires that anyone who acts as an agent of a foreign government must notify the Secretary of State. Third, 18 U.S.C. § 2386 (1976) provides that organizations which accept support from foreign governments must register with the Attorney General if they engage in activities designed to forcibly control or overthrow the United States government, or if they engage in activities constituting military training. This statute has been successfully challenged under the Fifth Amendment. *See* Albertson v. Subversive Activities Control Bd., 382 U.S. 70, 77–78 (1965).

tion to obtain information that a person is willing to disclose, even though that disclosure is induced by some form of deception.[73] Nevertheless, when the information disclosed concerns political activities and is gathered by a law enforcement agency for purposes other than criminal prosecution the practice may be unconstitutional.[74]

Although these decisions are helpful, they do not specifically address the different considerations that exist when the information is sought by an intelligence agency for intelligence-gathering rather than law-enforcement purposes.[75] If the government can compel agents of foreign powers to register and describe their political activities, is it unconstitutional to place covert domestic agents in those same foreign agent groups to obtain information?[76] Case law indicates there is no absolute answer and that each situation

73. The use of informers or infiltrators in a criminal investigation does not give rise to any violation of the First or Fourth Amendments. Handschu v. Special Servs. Div. 349 F. Supp. 766, 769 (S.D.N.Y. 1972). For Fourth Amendment purposes, a person assumes the risk that any known party to a conversation concerning criminal conduct is an undercover police agent. *E.g.*, Hoffa v. United States, 385 U.S. 293, 300–03 (1966); Lewis v. United States, 385 U.S. 206, 211 (1966). The Fourth Amendment, however, does restrict the scope of permissible activities of an undercover agent. *See, e.g.*, Gouled v. United States, 255 U.S. 298. 304–6 (1921) (informant overstepped constitutional bounds when he obtained entry into business office of suspect by deception and secretly ransacked office and seized incriminating documents). Infiltration for law-enforcement purposes into a political organization or rally which might dampen the exercise of First Amendment rights of the participants has also been upheld. Socialist Workers Party v. Attorney Gen., 419 U.S. 1314, 1319–20 (1974); United States v. McLeod, 385 F.2d 734, 750 (5th Cir. 1967). Nevertheless, because of the inherent danger that First Amendment activities may be significantly impaired, undercover investigations in university classes or political organization meetings will be sustained only if there is a substantial government interest to justify the probable impairment of First Amendment rights. White v. Davis, 13 Cal. 3d 757, 768–73, 533 P.2d 222, 229–32, 120 Cal. Rptr. 94, 101–4 (1975) (in bank); *see* Socialist Workers Party v. Attorney Gen. 419 U.S. at 1319.

74. *Compare* White v. Davis, 13 Cal. 2d 757, 773, 533 P.2d 222, 232, 120 Cal. Rptr. 94, 104 (1975) (en banc) (reversing demurrer of plaintiff's complaint and finding that police undercover surveillance on university campus, which gathered information that pertained to no illegal activity, was a prima facie violation of First Amendment rights) *with* Fifth Ave. Peace Parade Comm. v. Gray, 480 F.2d 326, 332–33 (2d Cir. 1973) (affirming dismissal of complaint and finding police surveillance of a large antiwar demonstration to be a perfectly lawful method of preserving public safety and deterring violence), *cert. denied*, 415 U.S. 948 (1974) *and* Anderson v. Sills, 56 N.J. 210, 229–31, 265 A.2d 678, 688–89 (1970) (reversing injunction of widespread police surveillance program and holding that, absent proof of bad faith or arbitrariness, the Executive Branch should perform "detectional and preventive" functions and gather any information reasonably believed to be necessary without judicial interference). *See generally* Note, *Domestic Intelligence Informants, the First Amendment and the Need for Prior Judicial Review*, 26 Buffalo L. Rev. 173 (1976); Note, *Governmental Investigations of the Exercise of First Amendment Rights: Citizens' Rights and Remedies*, 60 Minn. L. Rev. 1257 (1976).

75. *But cf.* United States v. United States Dist. Court (Keith), 407 U.S. 297, 320 (1972) (extending Fourth Amendment to domestic security electronic surveillances); Zweibon v. Mitchell, 516 F.2d 594, 611–13 (D.C. Cir. 1975) (en banc) (extending Fourth Amendment to national security electronic surveillance), *cert. denied*, 425 U.S. 944 (1976).

76. There is very little case law in this area because of the difficulty of proving sufficiently specific injuries to overcome the threshold case and controversy standing requirement as articulated

must be carefully considered, balancing both the need of the government and the effect on the individual.[77]

The Executive Branch has tried to provide some guidance in this area. President Carter's Executive Order on United States Intelligence Activities generally prohibits an intelligence agency from covertly placing agents in any organization in the United States unless the organization is acting on behalf of a foreign power and is primarily composed of individuals who are not United States persons,[78] or unless the infiltration is undertaken on behalf of the FBI as part of a lawful bureau investigation.[79] The order also permits agencies to have employees participate in organizations, without disclosure of their intelligence affiliation, in certain narrow circumstances under publicly available guidelines approved by the Attorney General.[80] The CIA, for instance, is not required to disclose participation by agency employees in domestic organizations for the purpose of developing individual associations and credentials needed to substantiate a cover employment.[81]

---

in Laird v. Tatum, 408 U.S. 1 (1972). Mere allegations of a subjective chilling impact of government surveillance on First Amendment activities is not an adequate basis for justiciability. *Id.* at 12–13. Allegations of disruption, harassment, or bad faith are generally required before one can litigate First Amendment rights when intelligence activities are involved. *E.g.*, Berlin Democratic Club v. Rumsfeld, 410 F. Supp. 144, 149–51 (D.D.C. 1976).

77. In Buckley v. Valeo, 424 U.S. 1 (1976) (per curiam), the Court refused to grant a blanket exemption from the federal contributor reporting requirements for all minor parties and independent candidates. *Id.* at 74. Instead, the Court established a case-by-case procedure which allows each such party to prove that disclosure of contributor lists would substantially impair its members' constitutional rights. *Id.* Since *Buckley*, political parties have had varying success in the lower courts. *Compare* Wisconsin Socialist Workers 1976 Campaign Comm. v. McCann, 433 F. Supp. 540, 548–49 (E.D. Wis. 1977) (injunction issued relieving party from complying with Wisconsin Campaign Financing Act) *and* Partido Nuevo Progresista v. Hernandez Colon, 415 F. Supp. 475, 482–83 (D.P.R. 1976) (per curiam) (injunction issued prohibiting the use of government inspectors to enforce Puerto Rico's political contribution and disclosure statute) *with* Oregon Socialist Workers 1974 Campaign Comm. v. Paulus, 432 F. Supp. 1255, 1259–60 (D. Or. 1977) (injunction denied where Oregon Campaign Disclosure Act was found to have minimal impact on First Amendment rights of party).

78. *See supra* note 61.

79. Exec. Order No. 12036, § 2-207(a), 3 C.F.R. 112, 127 (1979).

80. Executive Order 12036 and the procedures adopted pursuant to it have established formal controls over this sensitive form of information gathering. Exec. Order No. 12036, § 2-207, 3 C.F.R. 112, 127 (1979). Guidelines have been approved thus far for the CIA, the Department of Defense, and the FBI. *See supra* note 14. *But see* Wisconsin Socialist Workers 1976 Campaign Comm. v. McCann, 433 F. Supp. 540, 548 (E.D. Wis. 1977) (prior to adoption of Executive Order 12036 and public procedures, the court expressed skepticism that harassment of dissident political groups had been terminated).

81. The CIA guidelines authorize undisclosed participation in organizations in the United States "to develop associations and credentials to be utilized for purposes relating to foreign intelligence as for example by joining an organization to which an employee would ordinarily be expected to belong if his cover employment were his true employment." Such undisclosed participation is also permitted "to obtain training or education relevant to CIA employment . . . to obtain publications of organizations whose membership is open to the general public . . . to maintain or enhance the

Approval of such undisclosed participation must be given by an appropriate CIA senior official, and all such approvals are subject to review by the Attorney General.[82] These procedures go considerably beyond the requirements of any existing statute or judicial decision. They reflect an awareness of the chilling effect that undisclosed government involvement may have on the exercise of First Amendment freedoms and privacy. Thus, the procedures attempt to balance the competing interests of the individual and the government by defining categories of permissible participation and by requiring appropriate review in each case.

Fourth Amendment Issues

Another constitutional provision often at issue in intelligence gathering is the Fourth Amendment's prohibition against unreasonable searches and seizures.[83] Intelligence techniques involve traditional searches as well as the utilization of new technology that has not yet been considered by the courts. The FISA[84] requires that a court order be obtained for most traditional forms of wiretapping or eavesdropping conducted within the United States.[85] Such a warrant is also required before the government employs most surveillance devices in the United States to gather information under circumstances where there is "a reasonable expectation of privacy and a warrant would be required for law-enforcement purposes."[86] For example, consider the instrument known as a beeper. This device is attached to a vehicle and emits periodic radio signals which enable the person monitoring the device to determine the location of the vehicle. The FISA does not require a court order before a beeper can be used to determine the location of a foreign agent's car unless, under

qualifications of CIA employees, and to make it possible for them to stay abreast of developments in their fields of professional expertise . . . to maintain the cover of CIA personnel, programs, and facilities which are not publicly acknowledged as such by the United States Government . . . to utilize individuals on a witting or voluntary basis who are members of an organization within the United States to develop persons of foreign nationality as sources or contacts for purposes related to foreign intelligence . . . to place employees in an organization within the United States to identify and develop persons of foreign nationality as sources or contacts for purposes related to foreign intelligence [and] to protect the degree of CIA interest in a particular foreign intelligence subject matter, but limited to participation in an organization that permits such participation by government employees in their official capacities." *See supra* note 14.

82. Exec. Order No. 12036, § 2-207, 3 C.F.R. 112, 127 (1979).

83. U.S. Const. amend. IV.

84. *See supra* notes 47–50 and accompanying text.

85. 50 U.S.C.A. §§ 1801–1804 (West Supp. 1979).

86. *Id.* § 1801(f)(1), (4). *See supra* note 48. The drafters of FISA relied on the Supreme Court's decision in Katz v. United States, 389 U.S. 347 (1967), and intended the statute to reflect evolving concepts of the Fourth Amendment as interpreted by the courts. Thus, the legislative history of FISA manifests Congress' intention to incorporate the *Katz* standard for constitutionally protected privacy interests into the definition of electronic surveillance, which serves to activate the statute's requirements. S. Rep. No. 604, 95th Cong., 1st Sess. 4–18 (1977), *reprinted in* [1978] U.S. Code Cong. & Ad. News 3904, 3905–20.

applicable decisions, a court order would be required if the FBI used such a device to locate a bank robber. Thus, while the Fourth Amendment's applicability to the use of beepers is not yet completely clear, these devices have been involved in numerous criminal cases and there is some judicial precedent to which intelligence agencies can turn for guidance.[87]

The rapid development of technology, however, permits intelligence agencies to use surveillance devices that have never had the benefit of judicial review. As each new technique is considered, the Department of Justice must determine whether it is necessary to seek court approval before using the device. The FISA thus poses a problem. The court's jurisdiction under the Act is limited to issuing orders for electronic surveillance as defined in the Act.[88] Yet the definition of electronic surveillance itself requires consideration of judicial interpretations of the Fourth Amendment, and there may not be any precedent covering a particular new technology. For example, case law indicates that a court order must be obtained before a microphonic surveillance device is used to intercept a private conversation

87. Most circuits have recognized that the use of beepers to trace airplanes or automobiles on public thoroughfares does not implicate the Fourth Amendment primarily because there is no reasonable expectation of privacy in activities that are readily observable in public. *E.g.*, United States v. Bruneau, 594 F.2d 1190, 1197 (8th Cir.) (airplane), *cert. denied*, 100 S. Ct. 94 (1979); United States v. Curtis, 562 F.2d 1153, 1156 (9th Cir. 1977) (airplane), *cert. denied*, 439 U.S. 910 (1978); United States v. Hufford, 539 F.2d 32, 33–34 (9th Cir.) (automobile), *cert. denied*, 429 U.S. 1002 (1976). *But see* United States v. Holmes, 521 F.2d 859, 864 (5th Cir. 1975) (automobile) (holding use of beeper to track vehicles impinges upon reasonable expectation of privacy), *aff'd en banc by equally divided panel*, 537 F.2d 227 (5th Cir. 1976) (per curiam). Subsequent decisions, however, indicate that the original panel decision in *Holmes* is not the settled law of the Fifth Circuit. United States v. Conroy, 589 F.2d 1258, 1263 & n.5 (5th Cir.), *cert. denied*, 100 S. Ct. 60 (1979); United States v. Cheshire, 569 F.2d 887, 888 (5th Cir.), *cert. denied*, 437 U.S. 907 (1978). The First Circuit has concluded that although the use of a beeper to track an automobile constitutes a search within the meaning of the Fourth Amendment, the lessened expectation of privacy associated with an automobile justifies the use of a beeper without a warrant. United States v. Moore, 562 F.2d 106, 111–12 (1st Cir. 1977), *cert. denied*, 435 U.S. 926 (1978). Similarly, the placement of a beeper inside contraband is not a search within the meaning of the Fourth Amendment because there can be no objectively justifiable expectation that the possession of an illicit item or stolen good will not be traced by government authorities. E.g., United States v. Pringle, 576 F.2d 1114, 1119 (5th Cir. 1978), (beeper placed in contraband mail); United States v. Emery, 541 F.2d 887, 889–90 (1st Cir. 1976) (beeper placed in contraband package); *see* United States v. Dubrofsky, 581 F.2d 208, 211–12 (9th Cir. 1978) (beeper placed in contraband package); United States v. Bishop, 530 F.2d 1156, 1157 (5th Cir.) (beeper inserted in stolen bait money), *cert. denied*, 429 U.S. 848 (1976). The placement of a beeper in a lawfully possessed item, however, is a search within the meaning of the Fourth Amendment and requires a warrant, particularly when it can trace a person's movement within a home United States v. Moore, 562 F.2d 106, 112–13 (1st Cir. 1977) (beeper placed in noncontraband package. *cert denied*, 435 U.S. 926 (1978)); United States v. Bailey, 465 F. Supp. 1138, 1141 (E.D. Mich, 1979) (beeper placed in noncontraband package). *But see* United States v. Perez, 526 F.2d 859, 862 (5th Cir.) (beeper placed in television set received in exchange for contraband). *cert denied*, 429 U.S 846 (1976). *See generally* Marks & Batey, *Electronic Tracking Devices. Fourth Amendment Problems and Solutions*, 67 Ky. L.J. 987 (1978–79); Note, *Tracking Devices and the Fourth Amendment*, 13 U.S.F. L. Rev. 203 (1978); Note, *Tracking Katz: Beepers, Privacy and the Fourth Amendment*, 86 Yale L.J. 1461 (1977).

88. 50 U.S.C.A. § 1801(f) (West Supp. 1979).

if the communicant has a reasonable expectation of privacy.[89] The cases, however, do not clearly define the limits of such an expectation. Placing such a listening device in a home, office, or other private location requires a warrant.[90] Using a tape recorder to record a conversation that can be heard by an individual lawfully in an adjacent room does not require a warrant.[91] Use of a parabolic microphone, such as those used by television crews to enhance the entertainment value of professional football, may well require a warrant.[92] It is often difficult, therefore, to determine when a particular surveillance technique requires a warrant. For instance, suppose an intelligence agency is able to use a normal, readily available tape recorder to listen to sounds that are discernible, though not intelligible, to the human ear without any physical intrusion, and then subject that recording to audio enhancement to render the sounds intelligible. Is that activity one which would require a warrant if undertaken for law enforcement purposes? The answer is not clear.[93]

Consider a similar issue. No one would suggest that the FBI must obtain a warrant before reading the daily newspaper. The FBI may act on the basis of information contained in the paper without the slightest suggestion that it has undertaken a search. If members of a criminal conspiracy decide to use the classified advertisement section of the paper to communicate their plans, an FBI agent may certainly read that same section and, if clever enough, discover the conspiracy. The situation is undoubtedly the same if the advertisement is published in a foreign language. Suppose, however, the conspirators believe their advertisement is completely indecipherable by outsiders because it is written in a complicated mathematical code generated by a computer that is beyond the state of the art. Assume further that the FBI is able to break that code by using an even more sophisticated computer. Surely most people would agree that the FBI has not undertaken a search within the meaning of the Fourth Amendment. The answer, however, is uncertain. It is, of course, possible to argue that the conspirators had a reasonable expectation that their communications were secret. Nevertheless, the decision to put those communications in the public domain, even though in cryptic form, may justify the conclusion that their privacy expec-

89. Katz v. United States, 389 U.S. 347 (1967) is the seminal case prohibiting the warrantless use of electronic surveillance devices when the target has a reasonable expectation of privacy. Title III of the Omnibus Crime Control and Safe Streets Act of 1968. 18 U.S.C. §§ 2510–2520 (1976), imposes criminal penalties, *id.* § 2511, and authorizes recovery of civil damages. *Id.* § 2520, for the warrantless use of bugs or wiretaps in certain circumstances.

90. *See* Berger v. New York, 388 U.S. 41 (1967) (bringing eavesdropping within the purview of the Fourth Amendment).

91. United States v. Carroll, 337 F. Supp. 1260 (D.D.C. 1971) (using a tape recorder no more sensitive than the human ear, defendant recorded a conversation, which he could hear without assistance or contrivance from his adjacent hotel room).

92. See Lopez v. United States, 373 U.S. 427, 465–66 (1963) (Brennan, J. dissenting) (highlighting danger which modern electronic surveillance devices pose to privacy interests and personal security); United States v. Kim, 415 F. Supp. 1252, 1255–56 (D Hawaii 1976) (suggesting there might be a technological limit to reasonable government searches) *See generally* Westin, *Science, Privacy, and Freedom: Issues and Proposals for the 1970's* (pts. 1–2), 66 Colum. L. Rev. 1003, 1205 (1966).

93. *See supra* note 92.

tation is not one that the courts are prepared to protect from governmental surveillance. This analysis rests, in part, on reported cases which indicate that one who broadcasts a message on a radio, a public communications medium, does not have an expectation of privacy,[94] and in part, on cases which permit police, without a warrant, to take trash from outside a person's home and subject it to chemical analysis to determine whether any drugs have been discarded.[95]

These First and Fourth Amendment issues, many of which involve attempts to apply case law in novel contexts, are typical of those presented to the Department of Justice. The precedents developed and rules promulgated by the Justice Department, however, are often not subject to judicial review or public comment. Thus, the American principle of checks and balances can be eviscerated when it comes to intelligence activities. It is extremely important, therefore, that we institutionalize in the Executive Branch a process for obtaining a multiplicity of views on the fundamental legal issues arising from intelligence activities.[96] For example, in the Justice Department, the Attorney General receives advice on these matters from former CIA employees, members of the American Civil Liberties Union, and the Department's Office of Intelligence Policy and Review. It is likewise important for intelligence agencies to encourage meaningful in-house criticism of their proposals. The ability to argue against his client's project is one of the most difficult, but most important, skills a lawyer must acquire if his practice is to meet minimal standards of social responsibility.[97] This is particularly true in the government. This process of debate, consideration of conflicting opinions, and careful review will help ensure that intelligence decisions are properly and legally made. Although this process may not always result in perfect legal decisions, it will at least guarantee that the legal issues are considered, the appropriate questions asked, and reasonable conclusions reached.

THE FUTURE OF INTELLIGENCE LAW

The evolution of the law applicable to intelligence activities is directly influenced by world conditions. The current emphasis on legal guidelines for intelligence operations is a result of past excesses which were disclosed during a period in our history when a President was forced out of office and an unpopular war was prolonged despite vigorous public dissatisfaction.[98] Current events, however, may provoke a different analysis. Some may now

94. United States v. Hall, 488 F.2d 193, 198 (9th Cir. 1973) (holding there is no reasonable expectation of privacy in a radio-telephone conversation that could be received by generally available radio-reception equipment); United States v. Hoffa, 436 F.2d 1243, 1247 (7th Cir. 1970) (holding there is no reasonable expectation of privacy in a telephone conversation from a mobile telephone unit that can be received by an ordinary commercial FM radio receiver), *cert. denied*, 400 U.S. 1000 (1971).

95. United States v. Crowell, 586 F.2d 1020, 1024–25 (4th Cir. 1978), *cert. denied*, 440 U.S. 959 (1979).

96. *See supra* note 26 and accompanying text.

97. *See* ABA Canons of Professional Ethics No. 5.

98. *See supra* note 9 and accompanying text.

argue that attempts to regulate intelligence activities are futile and self-destructive. Others may seriously question the costs and benefits of regulation in view of the enormity of hostile acts abroad. While such reexamination is necessary and constructive, it should not cause us to lose sight of the past. Watergate did happen. CHAOS and COINTELPRO were actual programs.[99] Those abuses had their beginnings in action which appeared necessary and reasonable to the officials who began them. As the programs grew, however, the justifications expanded and responsibility disappeared.

The proliferation of law governing intelligence activities has not been entirely without cost. It has limited some of the flexibility and ease of action formerly enjoyed by intelligence officials.[100] We have gained, however, much more than we have lost. Intelligence agencies now operate under the most lucid statements of authority, and limitations thereon, ever available. The protection of individual rights and liberties from infringement by intelligence activities is at a high point. At the same time, there are few, if any, cases in which it has proved impossible under the law to collect truly vital intelligence information. Rather, intelligence officials think more carefully and answer more precisely before proposing or authorizing particular activities. Nevertheless, there is still more work to be done in this area. Existing law provides inadequate protections to the people who serve our nation as intelligence officers. They need, and deserve, better protection against those who would intentionally disclose their secret mission and jeopardize their safety by revealing their identities. Although public comment and criticism of intelligence activities and specific operations is proper, exposing the identities of particular intelligence personnel and thereby placing them in danger serves no legitimate purpose. Our proper concern for individual liberties must be balanced with a concern for the safety of those who serve our nation in difficult times and under dangerous conditions.[101] We must also adopt legal

99. *See* Church Committee Report, *supra* note 9, (Bk. II).

100. *See, e.g., Hearings on H.R. 5129 Before the Subcomm. on Government Information and Individual Rights of the House Government Operations Comm.*, 96th Cong., 1st Sess. (1980) (statement of Frank Carlucci, Deputy Director of Central Intelligence, CIA) (reporting detrimental impact of Freedom of Information Act on security and efficiency of intelligence analysis process and on intelligence gathering from foreign intelligence services and sources, and recommending that CIA be relieved from certain of FOIA's provisions).

101. Several proposals have been introduced in Congress to criminalize disclosure of an intelligence agent's or source's identity. *E.g.*, S. 2284, *supra* note 25, tit. VII; Intelligence Reform Act of 1980, S. 2216, 96th Cong., 2d Sess., 126 Cong. Rec. S366, 369–70 (daily ed. Jan. 24, 1980) [hereinafter cited as S. 2216]; S. 191, 96th Cong., 1st Sess., 125 Cong. Rec. S431 (daily ed. Jan. 23, 1979); H.R. 3762, 96th Cong., 1st Sess., 125 Cong. Rec. H2383 (daily ed. Apr. 26, 1979); H.R. 1068, 96th Cong., 1st Sess., 125 Cong. Rec. H187 (daily ed. Jan. 18, 1979). Another proposal that has received considerable attention is the Intelligence Identities Protection Act, H.R. 5615, 96th Cong., 1st Sess., 125 Cong. Rec. H9324–25, 9331 (daily ed. Oct. 17, 1979). This bill seeks to restrict the disclosure of information identifying any covert intelligence agent, employee, or source by persons who presently have or formerly had authorized access to classified government information concerning covert identities. *Id.* § 501(a). The bill would also prohibit the disclosure of identifying information by any person, regardless of previous government service or access to classified information, who discloses it with an "intent to impair or impede the foreign intelligence activities of the United States."

procedures to resolve the problem of graymail, where criminal defendants who have had access to classified information escape punishment by threatening to disclose secret information during a criminal trial.[102] Although it is not impossible to prosecute such cases,[103] the court's ability to protect legally irrelevant secret information from unnecessary disclosure must be strengthened.

Further protection for the intelligence community could also be achieved by a change in the Hughes-Ryan Amendment, which requires the timely reporting of covert action to seven congressional committees.[104] This cumbersome procedure disseminates knowledge of intelligence operations to such a large number of persons that the secrecy essential to their success becomes doubtful. A carefully crafted amendment to the statute should require reporting only to the Senate and House intelligence committees.[105] This would give Congress the information it needs without unduly jeopardizing intelligence projects.

Id. § 501(b). The House Permanent Select Committee on Intelligence has held hearings on this proposal. The Administration supports an alternative proposal which would (a) prohibit the knowing disclosure of identifying information by any person acting with knowledge that the disclosure is based on classified information, and (b) prohibit current and former government employees, who have had access to information concerning covert identities in the course of their employment, from making any disclosure concerning the identity of agents or sources to unauthorized persons, even if the particular disclosures were based purely on speculation or publicly available information. *See* Hearings on S. 2284 Before the Senate Select Comm. on Intelligence, 96th Cong., 1st Sess. (1980). This alternative would balance the need to protect the identities of covert agents and sources with the public's right to free and open discussion of intelligence policies and activities.

102. There are several outstanding legislative proposals to resolve the graymail problem and to prevent the disclosure of classified information during a criminal proceeding. *E.g.*, Classified Information Criminal Trial Procedures Act, H.R. 4736, 96th Cong., 1st Sess. 125 Cong Rec. H5780 (daily ed. July 11, 1979). H.R. 4736 is a complex legislative proposal which, *inter alia*, creates a procedure for securing pretrial rulings to determine whether classified information may be disclosed at pretrial or trial proceedings, and authorizes the government to take interlocutory appeals from adverse district court orders relating to the disclosure of classified information. The proposal also provides for appropriate protective orders to safeguard classified information disclosed to defendants. H.R. 4736 is strongly supported by the Justice Department.

103. *See supra* note 21.

104. The Hughes-Ryan Amendment, 22 U.S.C. § 2422(a) (1976), requires that Presidential findings be made with regard to each proposed covert action operation of the CIA, and that notice of these findings be provided "to the appropriate committees of the Congress, including the Committee on Foreign Relations of the United States Senate and the Committee on Foreign Affairs of the United States House of Representatives." *Id.* Currently such reports are also made to the intelligence committees of both houses, the Senate and House appropriations committees, and the Senate Armed Services Committee, under arrangements between the CIA and these committees.

105. S. 2284, *supra* note 25, and S. 2216, *supra* note 101, propose to repeal the Hughes-Ryan Amendment and replace it with a requirement that only the House and Senate intelligence committees be notified of proposed covert operations. S. 2284, however, would require that Congress receive prior notice of all covert operations. S. 2284, *supra* note 25, §§ 103(18), 125. This contrasts with the requirement of the Hughes-Ryan Amendment to report all such operations in "a timely fashion" to appropriate House and Senate committees. 22 U.S.C. § 2422(a) (1976). S. 2284 would

While we pursue legislative solutions to these problems, the process of self-regulation in the Executive Branch must continue. Many of the regulations are publicly available,[106] and as they gain wider review we will all benefit from the analysis and critical comment of others.[107] The need for governmental self-regulation, however, will increase as modern technology grows ever more sophisticated. The state of the art is already so advanced as to bear little relation to traditional Fourth Amendment analysis, and will continue to outstrip the development of decisional law for the foreseeable future. Although these technological advances will benefit national security by providing increased efficiency of intelligence gathering, they will also increase the responsibility for fashioning proper safeguards in intelligence law. The interpretation of constitutional provisions, statutes, executive orders, and procedures affecting intelligence gathering will evolve in response to changing perceptions and new experiences. While we must guard against the adoption of an overly pliant construction of our self-imposed rules, I am confident that, in the light of experience, we can continue to devise new standards which do not compromise our essential liberties and which support a strong intelligence community equal to its critical mission.

---

also codify requirements that the intelligence agencies furnish any information requested of them by the intelligence committees, and report to these committees information relating to illegal or improper intelligence activities. *Id.* § 142(a). The prior notice provision of S. 2284 might unduly jeopardize the safety and security of some covert operations which require the utmost secrecy. When the Hughes-Ryan Amendment was originally enacted, Congress specifically rejected the language of the Senate bill, which clearly required prior reporting of covert operations. *Compare* Conference Report on Foreign Assistance Act of 1974, H.R. Rep. No. 1610, 93rd Cong., 2d Sess. 12, 42–43, *reprinted in* [1974] U.S. Code Cong. & Ad. News 6734, 6744–45, *with* S. Rep. No. 1299, 93rd Cong., 2d Sess. 43, 90–91, *reprinted in* [1974] U.S. Code Cong. & Ad. News 6674, 6707. The language adopted by Congress requires only timely reporting of covert operations. Experience under the Amendment has proven the wisdom of that decision. Although prior notice is, as a rule, compatible with national interests, there are occasions where prior notice would jeopardize the safety of individuals involved in the activity or impair the effectiveness of an activity that reasonable people would clearly support. In such cases, timely notice comports with the constitutional role of the President to execute the laws and of Congress to inform itself in order to legislate. Prior notice is not essential to the legislative or oversight process, and subsequent timely notice may be critical to the successful execution of a covert operation.

106. *See supra* note 14.

107. The entire corpus of unclassified rules, regulations, and statutes that is emerging as the substantive field of intelligence law needs to be carefully reviewed by the academic community. Such examination and evaluation is critical to the continued evolution of intelligence law.

Waste Not, Wait Not: A Consideration of Federal and State Jurisdiction

Hon. Lawrence H. Cooke

Judge Lawrence H. Cooke delivered the eleventh Sonnett lecture, entitled *Waste Not, Wait Not—A Consideration of Federal and State Jurisdiction*, on February 24, 1981.[1] Judge Cooke was elected to the New York Court of Appeals, New York State's highest court, in 1974 and appointed Chief Judge by Governor Hugh L. Carey in 1979.[2] During his tenure on the Court, Judge Cooke championed several reform endeavors and wrote a series of momentous decisions.

Judge Cooke was born in Monticello, New York in 1914, graduated from Georgetown University, cum laude, at the age of twenty, and then completed his legal education at Albany Law School.[3] He started his own practice soon after being admitted to the bar and began his judicial career in 1953 as a Sullivan County Surrogate and Children's Court Judge, where he remained until he was elected to the New York State Supreme Court, Third Judicial District in 1961.[4] One of Judge Cooke's hallmarks was concluding his trials by personally writing letters to the sitting jurors, thanking them for their service and expressing his hope that their experience had been a positive one.[5]

Judge Cooke was intimately dedicated to the principle that "fairness is just a synonym for justice,"[6] a prevalent theme in many of his decisions. For instance, in *People v. Isaacson*, Judge Cooke drafted a powerful opinion in defense of due process when dismissing an indictment obtained through "reprehensible police action."[7] In *Isaacson*, Judge Cooke explained that "[t]he administration of justice must be above reproach,"[8] a concept evident

Introduction written by Meaghan Millan, J.D., Class of 2014, Fordham University School of Law.

1. Lawrence H. Cooke, *Waste Not, Wait Not—A Consideration of Federal and State Jurisdiction*, 49 Fordham L. Rev. 895 (1981).

2. William H. Honan, *Lawrence H. Cooke, 85, New York Chief Judge, Dies*, N.Y. Times (Aug. 19, 2000), http://www.nytimes.com/2000/08/19/nyregion/lawrence-h-cooke-85-new-york-chief-judge-dies.html.

3. *Id.*; Joyce Adolfsen & Lou Adolfsen, *Lawrence Henry Cooke*, New York Unified Court System, available at http://www.nycourts.gov/history/legal-history-new-york/luminaries-court-appeals/cooke-lawrence.html.

4. Judith S. Kaye, *Dedication, An Open Letter to my Colleague and Friend on the Occasion of His Seventieth Birthday*, 53 Fordham L. Rev. 147, 147 (1984); Adolfsen, *supra* note 3.

5. Adolfsen, *supra* note 3.

6. John Conway, *Driving Judge Cooke: A Conversation with Judge Lawrence Cooke*, Sunday Record (Troy, NY), Aug. 26, 1990, at 3, 6.

7. 378 N.E.2d 78, 79 (N.Y. 1978).

8. *Id.* at 85.

in his proclamation of a bright-line rule regarding the right-to-counsel of defendants in *People v. Rogers*.[9]

Judge Cooke was also seen as a champion of freedom of the press. In *Beach v. Shanley*,[10] Judge Cooke held that the New York State Shield Law protects journalists from disclosing their sources to a body as powerful as a grand jury, even though the source's disclosure may have, in itself, been a criminal act.[11] His penchant for fairness resonated in civil decisions as well. In *Sharrock v. Dell Buick-Cadillac, Inc.*,[12] Judge Cooke struck down provisions of the Lien Law as improperly contradicting the due process provisions of the State Constitution.[13]

To combat the recent increase in litigation, Judge Cooke implemented a system of temporarily assigning judges to the Supreme Court civil parts within New York City to reduce congestion.[14] This system was soon expanded to both civil and criminal parts.[15] Judge Cooke was also in tune with women's rights matters; in a 1974 interview with *Good Housekeeping Magazine*, Judge Cooke explained that in the context of rape, "women are outside the effective protection of the law and criminals know it."[16] Judge Cooke urged that the prosecution of rape cases be allowed to proceed without corroboration of the victim's account.[17] This standard became the law and remains so today. Further, Judge Cooke created the New York State Task Force on Women in the Courts, and this work led him to be selected as an honorary member of New York State Women's Bar Association.[18]

When Judge Cooke reached the age of mandatory retirement in 1984, he entered private practice, mediated commercial disputes, taught at Pace Law School for several years, and was a founding board member of two journals at Albany Law School.[19] In 1997, the Sullivan County courthouse was renamed the Lawrence H. Cooke Sullivan County Courthouse.[20] Judge Cooke expressed that although this courthouse bore his name, "the courts belong to the people."[21] Judge Cooke died on August 17, 2000.[22]

9. 48 N.Y.2d 154, 385 N.E.2d 612, 412 N.Y.S.2d 574 (1978); *see also* People v. Skinner, 52 N.Y.2d 24, 417 N.E.2d 511, 436 N.Y.S. 2d 207 (1980) (discussing right to counsel; People v. Settles, 46 N.Y.2d 154, 385 N.E.2d 612, 412 N.Y.S.2d 874 (1978)).

10. 62 N.Y.2d, 465 N.E.2d 304, 476 N.Y.S.2d 765 (1984).

11. *Id.*

12. 45 N.Y.2d 152, 379 N.E.2d 1169, 408 N.Y.S.2d 39 (1978).

13. *Id.*

14. Adolfsen, *supra* note 3. Judge Cooke's extensive reforms led him to even become a litigant in his own court. *See* Morgenthau v. Cooke, 56 N.Y.2d 24, 436 N.E.2d 467, 451 N.Y.S.2d 17 (1982).

15. Adolfsen, *supra* note 3.

16. *Id.*

17. *Id.*

18. *Id.*

19. *Id.*; Vincent Martin Bonventre, *Dedication, Tribute to Chief Judge Lawrence H. Cooke 1914–2000*, 64 Alb. L. Rev. 1, 2 (2000).

20. Adolfsen, *supra* note 3.

21. *Id.*; *see also* Warren Burger, *Dedication, Lawrence H. Cooke: A Tireless Judicial Administrator*, 53 Fordham L. Rev. 147, 147 (1984) ("Lawrence Cooke has recognized that the courts . . . are not ends in themselves but a means to an end—a tool—and the end is the proper administration of justice.").

22. Adolfsen, *supra* note 3.

Judge Cooke's Sonnett lecture discussed the "avalanche of litigation" that struck the U.S. judiciary during the 1980s.[23] In concert with his reputation for recognizing that courts service the American people, Judge Cooke lamented that "prompt and well-considered justice is not being delivered to substantial segments of society as claimed largely because of insufficient judicial person-power and resources."[24] He then discussed the current dilemma of overloaded courts due to increased litigation—an increase of almost twenty percent in federal courts,[25] and over forty percent in many state courts[26]—and the "blurring" of jurisdiction between state and federal courts.[27] Judge Cooke reviewed several of the proposed solutions to the issue, and emphasized that through a solution remedying the overlap of jurisdiction and "repetition of effort" between state and federal courts, "delay in the delivery of justice will be reduced to a minimum. We can then say, 'waste not, wait not.'"[28] Decades later, Judge Cooke's words still ring true.[29]

1981 Sonnett Lecture

A paradox of our time is legal scarcity amidst plenty. It is consistent with other incongruities such as momentous scientific advances and an apparent dearth of natural resources, shocking rises in violent crime in a society better educated than ever before, and an inflationary spiral during economic recession. The rubber band between demand and supply in almost any field—in the halls of government, in the commercial marketplace, and in the circles of culture—is now stretching in both directions. The recitation of parallels could be almost endless.

I have always considered my Father as the personification of virtue. He was a man of common sense and logic-with his feet always solidly on the ground. A cobbler's son, he earned his way through life and frequently referred to those who lived beyond their means as having a "champagne appetite and a beer income."[1] He frequently recited a jingle that went something like "eat it up, clean it up, sew it up, use it up" and ended with the proverb

23. Cooke, *supra* note 1, at 895.
24. *Id.* at 901.
25. *Id.* at 896.
26. *Id.* at 899.
27. *Id.* at 898 (citation omitted).
28. *Id.* at 902.
29. *See* Martin H. Redish, *Reassessing the Allocation of Judicial Business Between State and Federal Courts*, 78 Va. L. Rev. 1769 (1992). Legislation continually adjusts the allocation of cases between the federal and state courts. *See, e.g.*, Class action Fairness Act of 2005, 28 U.S.C §§ 1711–1715 (2005).

1. This is an American variant of "Beggar's person and Emperor's mouth," 2 J. Doolittle, A Vocabulary and Hand-Book of the Chinese Language, Romanized in the Mandarin Dialect 189 (1872), also corrupted to "a beer salary and champagne appetite."

of "waste not, want not." Having realized the inability of our material cornucopia to send forth an endless supply and the futility of an economy of extravagance, our mentality moves from expectations of profusion to those of moderation to provide even the physical necessities of life. The same course is generally outlined for government, in which programs and appropriations are slashed at random, and the shadows of Propositions 13 and 2 1/2 cast their pall over budgetary councils.[2] For the judiciary in particular, there is an analogous imbalance. A constant avalanche of litigation at the instigation of an endless horde of suitors seriously threatens to engulf every apparatus of justice—the physical facilities, the judicial and nonjudicial personnel, the tested methods and protections, and indeed, the system of justice itself.

In June 1980, Chief Justice Warren Burger, in welcoming remarks to the American Law Institute (ALI), stated that "[i]t is surely plain by now that both federal and state courts share the burdens of what has been called 'the litigation explosion.'"[3] He then added that "[s]ome thoughtful observers tell us that this enormous expansion of litigation is a result of the failure of the political processes to meet the peoples' expectations."[4] Eleven years earlier, the ALI made a study of allocation of jurisdiction and reported that "the present inquiry has a special urgency because of the continually expanding workload of the federal courts and the delay of justice resulting therefrom."[5] In the state courts of Minnesota, litigation has doubled in the last ten years, but the number of judges has remained constant.[6] Although the number of dispositions rose because of efforts of the judges, the filing of indictments increased last year by 19.1% in New York City; the statewide increase was 13.3%.[7] Recently, Laurence H. Tribe, Professor of Constitutional Law at Harvard, wryly observed that "[i]f court backlogs grow at their present rate, our children may not be able to bring a lawsuit to a conclusion within their lifetime."[8] President Carter expressed his concern to the Los Angeles County Bar Association over this "interminable delay especially when delay itself can often mean victory on one side."[9]

2. In a newspaper article, it is stated that "[f]or the first time since Proposition 2 1/2 was approved in November amid predictions of fiscal chaos, city officials and leaders of the banking and financial community here are talking openly about bankruptcy for the city." Knight, *Boston Prepares to Retrench as Tax Cut Drains Treasury*, N.Y. Times, Feb. 16, 1981, § A, at 10, col. 1. The plights of cities such as New York and Cleveland are recalled.

3. Address by Chief Justice Warren E. Burger, American Law Institute (June 10, 1980), reprinted in 126 Cong. Rec. S8964, S8965 (daily ed. June 30, 1980) [hereinafter cited as Burger Speech].

4. *Id.*

5. ALI, Study of the Division of Jurisdiction Between State and Federal Courts 1 (1969).

6. Address by Hon. Robert J. Sheran, Chief Justice of the Minnesota Supreme Court, State/Federal Judicial Council Meeting in Brainerd, Minnesota (Aug. 19–21, 1980).

7. State of N.Y. Office of Court Administration, Press Release (March 18, 1981).

8. Time, Aug. 20, 1979, at 48, 51.

9. Address by President Jimmy Carter, Los Angeles County Bar Association, 100th Anniversary Luncheon (May 4, 1978), reprinted in 64 A.B.A.J. 840, 842 (1978).

In September 1980, Senator Strom Thurmond, now Chairman of the Senate Judiciary Committee, introduced a bill to establish a Federal Jurisdiction Review and Revision Commission.[10] The Commission would study federal and state court jurisdiction, including problems of substantive law, civil and criminal procedure, workload of the courts, and case processing.[11] Senator Thurmond stated that he was introducing the legislation because of his "belief that our legal system is drifting into a posture of blurring the jurisdiction between the State and Federal courts" and that "[i]ncreasing caseloads in the Federal courts reveal a trend which could eventually lead to a total breakdown of traditional federalist principles as we know them."[12] Quoting Chief Justice Burger, he pointed out that in the past decade Congress has enacted no less than seventy new statutes enlarging the jurisdiction of federal courts; many of these statutes expand federal jurisdiction to cover relief already available in state courts.[13]

Any survey of federal and state court jurisdiction requires an examination of the historical roots of our judicial systems and a recognition of the interrelationship of the federal and state governments. When the delegates to the Constitutional Convention gathered at Philadelphia in 1787, they came from thirteen self-governing and sovereign states. Each state had its own courts, structured with a jurisprudence similar to that of England and flavored by a variety of colonial prescriptions. There was no preexistent federal superstructure or dual pattern of government such as the one that evolved from the men at Philadelphia—"[m]ost of [whom] had been warned before [leaving] home that they had no right to do more than amend the Articles of Confederation."[14]

The face of government changed with the adoption of the Constitution. There emerged the intriguing concept of dual sovereignty, federal and state, as applied to the central federal union and the component states. The system was described as an "indestructible Union, composed of indestructible States."[15] The judicial article of this new Constitution provided for "one supreme Court, and . . . such inferior Courts as the Congress may from time to time ordain and establish"[16] and specified the cases to which the judicial power extends.[17] Therefore, a federal judicial system was erected alongside, or atop, the individual state courts.

Another landmark was reached with the passage of the Judiciary Act of 1789,[18] by which Congress immediately exercised its power to create inferior federal courts. The federal courts are courts of limited jurisdiction, empowered to hear only such cases as are within the judicial power of the United States as defined in the Constitution and entrusted to

10. S. 3123, 96th Cong., 2d Sess., 126 Cong. Rec. S12768 (daily ed. Sept. 17, 1980).
11. *Id.*; *see* 126 Cong. Rec. S12767 (daily ed. Sept. 17, 1980) (remarks of Sen. Thurmond).
12. 126 Cong. Rec. S12767 (daily ed. Sept. 17, 1980) (remarks of Sen. Thurmond).
13. *Id.* (quoting Burger Speech, *supra* note 3. at S8965).
14. 1 D. Perkins & G. Van Deusen, The United States of America: A History 191 (1962).
15. Texas v. White, 74 U.S. (7 Wall.) 700, 725 (1868).
16. U.S. Const. art. III, § I.
17. *Id.* § 2.
18. Judiciary Act of 1789, ch. 20, 1 Stat. 73.

them by a jurisdictional grant by Congress. In contrast, each state has courts of general jurisdiction, and these courts enjoy a presumption of jurisdiction over a particular controversy that may be overcome only by a strong showing to the contrary. Chief Justice Burger, in reference to the ALI's study of the jurisdiction of state and federal courts,[19] has observed that "[u]narticulated, but implicit, in the Institute's study was that the state courts of this country are the basic instrument of justice under our system, and this, of course, is the heart of what we call federalism."[20]

Perhaps Senator Thurmond, in his observations on the "blurring" of jurisdiction,[21] determined that the line of demarcation was becoming indistinct. From the tenor of his remarks, it is fair to assume that he, like others, is disturbed by this trend. Others sense a de facto "merging" and attempt to assess the consequences. The perimeters of the expression "merger of state and federal courts" have not been demarked. In the context employed, an "organizational merger" is not suggested, but "merger" seems to imply that more and more the state and federal courts, using similar methods, are plowing over the same ground. In a 1977 address, Professor Dan Meador, then Assistant Attorney General in the Office of Improvements in the Administration of Justice, posed the question: "Are we heading for a merger of federal and state courts?"[22] In intimating bases that might elicit an affirmative response, Professor Meador cited "the opening of the federal trial courts to some business which had always been handled exclusively by the state courts"[23] and a "growing uniformity in the law being applied by both and in the rules of procedures being used."[24] Similarly, a 1979 report to the Conference of Chief Justices from the Task Force on a State Court Improvement Act mentioned "the Federal-State Partnership in the Delivery of Justice."[25]

Awareness of the possibility of merger has not been confined to these comments. Proposed changes in federal diversity jurisdiction have inspired intense differences. State appellate judges have been known to fume as determinations of their highest courts have been invalidated at the hands of a single United States district court judge. Federal judges have occasionally rankled when required to preside over garden-variety tort and contract disputes instead of nationally significant legal issues.

Consideration of whether state-federal judicial merger, viewed by some as gradual but definite, is a reality reveals the dearth of satisfactory empirical data on this subject.[26]

19. *See* ALI, *supra* note 5, at 7–8.

20. Burger, *To Weaken Our State Courts Is to Destroy Federalism*, 17 Judges' J., 11, 12 (1978).

21. *See* notes 10–13 *supra* and accompanying text.

22. Meador, *Are We Heading for a Merger of Federal and State Courts?*, 17 Judges' J., 9 (1978).

23. *Id.* at 46.

24. *Id.* at 47.

25. Hearings on S. 2387 Before the Subcomm. on Jurisprudence and Governmental Relations of the Senate Comm. on the Judiciary, 96th Cong., 1st & 2d Sess. 151 (1979–80) [hereinafter cited as Hearings].

26. Burger Speech, *supra* note 3, at S8965. *See also* Fischer, *Institutional Competency: Some Reflections on Judicial Activism in the Realm of Forum Allocation Between State and Federal Courts*, 34 Miami L. Rev. 180 (1980).

Information would be required to determine if merger exists and, as a preface, the notion of merger must be defined to permit the experiential analysis to proceed. If merger were found, a diagnosis could be made to determine whether it is a problem, a blessing, or a mere phenomenon. Designs for judicial or legislative treatment or surgery would follow. In any event, the gathering of information would serve a propitious purpose either in activating the highly motivated or in allaying their fears.

A fairly recent report of a Department of Justice Committee on Revision of the Federal Judicial System broadcast the distress signal that those courts "now face a crisis of overload, a crisis so serious that it threatens the capacity of the federal system to function as it should. . . . [I]t is therefore a crisis for the nation."[27] As for state courts, in the twenty states providing full information for the decade ending in 1976, there was an average caseload increase of forty-three percent in the trial courts of general jurisdiction.[28] In those same states, the average appellate caseload doubled during the same period.[29]

Obviously, this recital does not warrant complacency in approach or inefficiency in operation. More money could provide more courtrooms and more judicial personnel, but solid reliance on this possibility is not warranted in the face of projected cuts in the federal budget of over forty-one billion dollars and sizeable reductions in federal aid to the states.[30] "[T]he 1980s [will be] a decade of limited resources for courts."[31] Certainly waste can never be justified, and it is submitted that there are certain areas in the jurisdictional allocation between federal and state courts in which savings in time and effort can be accomplished.

The framers of the Constitution drew a design in which the state courts would be the primary guarantors of constitutional rights.[32] By virtue of the federal supremacy clause,[33] state courts were obliged to apply federal law when applicable, but there was little to apply in the early years. For the better part of the first century, the only significant federal incursion into state court affairs was the infrequent review by the United States Supreme Court of determinations by a state's highest judicial body.

The Civil War and the subsequent Reconstruction aroused an intense spirit of nationalism and produced demands for an expansion of federal authority. From this atmosphere came the opening of the federal nisi prius courts to judicial matters previously handled exclusively by the state courts. In the late 1860s, Congress enacted legislation that expanded

27. U.S. Dep't of Justice, The Needs of the Federal Courts, Report of the Committee on Revision of the Federal Judicial System 1 (1977).

28. National Center of State Courts, State Court Caseload Statistics: Annual Report, 1976, at 133–38 (1980).

29. *Id.* at 50–51.

30. N.Y. Times, Feb. 22, 1981, § 1, at 1, col. 6.

31. Steelman, *Options for Reducing Civil Volume and Delay: A Review and Analysis for the 1980's*, 4 State Ct. J., 9, 10 (1980).

32. *See generally* Hart, *The Power of Congress to Limit the Jurisdiction of Federal Courts: An Exercise in Dialectic*, 66 Harv. L. Rev. 1362 (1953).

33. U.S. Const. art. VI, § 2.

the category of diversity cases that could be removed to the federal courts,[34] and, for the first time, authorized writs of habeas corpus for persons detained by the states.[35] The Fourteenth Amendment was adopted, imposing upon the states as a matter of federal law the responsibility for ensuring the rights of equal protection and due process. In the succeeding decade, Congress granted to federal trial courts the jurisdiction to entertain suits arising under federal law;[36] Congress also enacted section 1983 of the Civil Rights Act of 1871.[37] The full impact of these measures was realized, not in their infancy, but in more recent years, and because of these measures an enormous flood of cases has poured into the federal trial system. Vast numbers of state criminal cases have been pervasively reviewed and, as a result of Ex parte Young,[38] numerous state office holders have been enjoined in the performance of official duties.

The concurrent jurisdiction enjoyed by both systems has long aroused judicial and legislative concern. Proposals to reduce duplications of jurisdiction include sharply limiting the scope of the diversity jurisdiction of federal courts[39] and eliminating the federal question jurisdiction of state courts. The underlying bases of these suggestions have been the obvious merit of jurisdictional clarity and the overriding desire to channel genuinely federal causes to federal courts and genuinely state causes to state courts. Thus far, however, the proclivity of attorneys for a choice of forum, a luxury we can no longer afford, has prevailed over judicial efforts to secure jurisdictional precision.

The most incessant abrader of judicial feelings may be the overturn of the deliberative judgment of the highest court of a state by a single federal trial court judge. The distinguished Chairman of the Conference of Chief Justices, Robert J. Sheran, recently voiced the opinion that such overturns not only incur the resentment of the Conference members, but also are not in the interest of the system as a whole.[40] Certain United States magistrates, with the consent of the parties and when authorized by the district court in which he or she serves, may even conduct any or all proceedings in civil matters including habeas corpus and order the entry of judgment in the cases.[41] One proposal has been that all proceedings concerning state criminal cases containing federal issues be routed to the United States Courts of Appeals to avoid federal trial court review.

Once it has been determined that there should be a redistribution of the caseload, the most difficulty will be encountered in isolating those cases that should be diverted from their present situs. The allocation should be based on sound reasoning. Judge Henry

34. Act of July 27, 1866, ch. 288, 14 Stat. 306 (current version at 28 U.S.C.§ 1441 (1976)).

35. Act of Feb. 5, 1867, ch. 28, § 1, 14 Stat. 385 (current version at 28 U.S.C. § 2241(c)(3) (1976)).

36. Act of March 3, 1875, ch. 137, 18 Stat. 470 (current version at 28 U.S.C. § 1331 (1976)).

37. Act of April 20, 1871, ch. 22, § 1, 17 Stat. 13 (codified at 42 U.S.C. § 1983 (1976)).

38. 209 U.S. 123 (1908).

39. H.R. 2202, 96th Cong., 1st Sess. (1979).

40. Remarks of Hon. Robert J. Sheran, Chief Justice of the Supreme Court of Minnesota, National Center for State Courts and Marshall-Wythe School of Law Seminar on State Courts and Federalism in the 1980s, Williamsburg, Virginia (Jan. 24, 1981).

41. 28 U.S.C. § 636(c) (Supp. 1979).

Friendly, a member of the United States Court of Appeals for the Second Circuit, would remove from federal forums not only diversity jurisdiction, but also "state prisoner habeas corpus cases, numerous criminal cases, and much federal question litigation such as environmental protection, personal injury actions created by federal statutes, and most section 1983 suits."[42] Although some view these proposals as too drastic, the recommendations emanate from a respected authority and deserve serious consideration. Moreover, it should be noted that there are more than ten times as many general jurisdiction state judges as there are federal district judges,[43] and state courts handle well over ninety percent of the cases filed in any given year.[44]

If our federal and state court dockets are as heavily laden as reported, and if our systems are being taxed so that prompt and well-considered justice is not being delivered to substantial segments of society as claimed largely because of insufficient judicial person power and resources—and I do not doubt these premises—then the day has arrived when there must be a survey of the systems and an updated allocation of the jurisdiction between the federal and state courts. This is not the time to tolerate a haphazard pattern of jurisdiction that by its very intricacy breeds litigation with festering procedural nuances. We can ill afford unnecessary duplication of judicial effort. We are haunted by the specter of criminal cases that run the full gamut of state trial and appellate levels only to start anew up the ladder of federal courts and then perhaps somewhere along the line return to the beginning of the obstacle course. The process may take many years.

In 1959, Chief Justice Warren said that "[i]t is essential that we achieve a proper jurisdictional balance between federal and state court systems, assigning to each system those cases most appropriate in light of the basic principles of federalism."[45] In his speech to the ALI, Chief Justice Burger raised for consideration the question "whether the time [had] come for a broader reappraisal of the allocation of jurisdiction" than that included in the 1969 ALI report.[46] History furnishes instances of disdain for state judiciaries. For this attitude, there is no longer any justification. Recent years have seen extraordinary efforts toward improvement. These include the establishment of the National College for the Judiciary, the institution of state training courses for judges, such as in New York State where yearly training of five days is mandatory for all judges of courts of record, the requirement of minimum qualifications in most states for judges serving in courts with significant responsibilities, the initiation of training in modern management methods provided by the Institute for Court Management, the provision of technical assistance and support programs by the National Center for State Courts, and highly motivated efforts of both the American Judicature Society and the American Bar Association.

42. Sheran & Isaacman, *State Cases Belong in State Courts*, 12 Creighton L. Rev. 1, 23–24 (1978).

43. Burger, *supra* note 20, at 12.

44. Hearings, *supra* note 25, at 140.

45. Burger, *supra* note 20, at 11 (quoting Address by Chief Justice Earl Warren, American Law Institute (May 1959)).

46. Burger Speech, *supra* note 3, at S8966.

People are looking for leadership, but those who seek a different and more efficient utilization of judicial resources should expect reaction ranging from confrontation to "no-holds-barred" opposition. In the words of Arthur T. Vanderbilt, "[m]anifestly judicial reform is no sport for the shortwinded or for lawyers who are afraid of temporary defeat."[47] The responsibility for providing justice must be divided between the federal and state court systems so they might realize their maximum potential by utilizing their full capacity as efficaciously as possible. As American citizens, we live under a government committed "to establish justice," and a malfunction of our judicial apparatus anywhere is reason for the disquiet of all of us. If we allot spheres of jurisdiction in such a way as to avoid overlap and to free judicial components from repetition of effort, then we will not squander our judicial substance, and delay in the delivery of justice will be reduced to a minimum. We can then say, "waste not, wait not."

There is much to be gained from the uniformity and stability generated from a central authority. There is also advantage in dispersed authority that can operate with more accommodation. We can alter our structures, by modernization, by an infusion of capital, and by innovation, but in the end, the ultimate test is whether we have afforded the citizenry a vehicle guided by competent and impartial judges for the prompt and just resolution of their disputes, under prevailing law applicable to all in equal measure.

47. E. Gerhart, Arthur T. Vanderbilt, The Compleat Counsellor iii (1980).

Barristers and Judges in England Today

Rt. Hon. Sir Robert Megarry

In 1982, the distinguished British Justice Robert E. Megarry delivered the twelfth Sonnett lecture, entitled *Barristers and Judges in England Today.*[1] Judge Megarry was a distinguished teacher and author, as well as a judge for over twenty-nine years. He is regarded as a profound learner and the most "hard-working Judge of his time."[2]

Judge Megarry was born in Crydon, England, to a family with deep legal roots.[3] He studied at Trinity Hall, Cambridge, and after being admitted as a solicitor, taught courses in equity for the bar at the Counsel of Legal Education.[4] Judge Megarry continued his career as a teacher and academic when he served as a lecturer at the Faculty of Law at Cambridge from 1939 until 1940.[5] Further, Judge Megarry served as an assistant editor of the academic journal, the *Law Quarterly Review*, from 1944 to 1967.[6]

Judge Megarry was appointed to the chancery bench in 1956 and became vice chancellor of the chancery division in 1983, two years before he retired from the bench in 1985.[7] He is known for presiding over *St. Edmundsbury and Ipswich Diocesan Board of Finance v. Clark*,[8] a case that saw him become the first judge to sit outside London in order to observe a contested night in Iken, Suffolk.[9] A mock funeral was conducted to test if it was possible to carry a coffin along an alleged right of way—a disputed key question in the case.

In addition to being a beloved teacher and judge, Judge Megarry wrote several books. Along with coauthor Sir William Wade, he wrote and created the series of law textbooks entitled *The Law of Real Property*,[10] which provides a comprehensive explanation of land and property law in England and Wales. The first edition, published in 1957, was followed

Introduction written by Kristen White, J.D., Class of 2015, Fordham University School of Law.

1. Rt. Hon. Sir Robert Megarry, *Barristers and Judges in England Today*, 51 Fordham L. Rev. 387 (1982).

2. Nicholas Merriman, *Sir Robert Megarry: Long-lived Judge of Profound Learning and Epigrammatic Wit*, Independent (Oct. 25, 2006), http://www.independent.co.uk/news/obituaries/sir-robert-megarry-6230441.html.

3. *Id.*

4. *Id.*

5. *Id.*

6. Louis Bloom-Cooper, *Sir Robert Megarry: Senior Judge Who Took the Side of the Individual in His Rulings and Writings*, Guardian (Oct. 18, 2006), http://www.theguardian.com/news/2006/oct/19/guardianobituaries.mainsection.

7. Merriman, *supra* note 2.

8. [1973] 1 WLR 1572.

9. *Sir Robert Megarry*, Telegraph (Oct. 17, 2006), http://www.telegraph.co.uk/news/obituaries/1531581/Sir-Robert-Megarry.html.

10. Robert Edgar Megarry & Sir William Wade, The Law of Real Property (1957).

by seven subsequent editions, the latest of which was published in 2012.[11] Judge Megarry also wrote and created a series of handbooks entitled *The Rent Acts*, which provided explanations of the statutory provisions that control residential tenancies and licenses in England and Wales.[12]

Not only did Judge Megarry publish law textbooks, but he also wrote *A New Miscellany-at Law*,[13] which exemplifies his wonderful sense of humor. The three editions of *A New Miscellany of Law* gather accounts of strange and remarkable cases, anecdotes from the courtroom, and wise and witty remarks from the viewpoint of the bench.

Judge Megarry's Sonnett lecture focused on the structures of the British bar that ensure British lawyers continue their legal education and sustain their skills.[14] Judge Megarry explained that although the members of the English bar have doubled, the quality standards to which barristers are held have been maintained because, from the beginning of a barrister's career, "the barrister finds himself enveloped in a system of continuous professional assessment, correction, and encouragement."[15] This message of encouragement and structure for members of the bar is still pertinent today as the American Bar Association continues to promote the benefits of continuing legal education.

1982 Sonnett Lecture

It is indeed an honor to be invited to deliver the twelfth annual John F. Sonnett lecture at Fordham University. It is also somewhat intimidating to be following in the footsteps of my eleven highly distinguished predecessors, including, as they do, Chief Justices of the United States, of England, and of Ireland. At one stage I began to fear that I would be struck dumb; but I am a lawyer, and I was comforted by the well-known rule of medical diagnosis in your country. This is that you can always tell the state of a lawyer's health by looking at his mouth: if it is shut, he is dead. I hope that I am not.

The careers of my predecessors in office, and that of John F. Sonnett himself, suggested that my subject should be professional rather than academic in nature, and so I shall speak of barristers and judges in England today. The main problem, of course, is not what to say but what to omit; for the subject is vast. The question that I ask and shall seek to answer is this: With all the changes in society and social attitudes since 1945, how are the bar and

11. Charles Harpum, Stuart Bridge & Martin Dixon, Megarry & Wade: The Law of Real Property (8th ed. 2012).

12. Robert Megarry, The Rent Acts (1939).

13. R.E. Megarry, A New Miscellany-At-Law: Yet Another Diversion for Lawyers and Others (2005).

14. *See generally* Megarry, *supra* note 1.

15. *Id.* at 388.

the judiciary in England faring, both individually and in relation to each other? From time to time on your side of the Atlantic there are flattering references to the high general standards of advocacy in England; but are they deserved today? I propose, therefore, to attempt something of a progress report on the forensic process in England and Wales. Scotland and Northern Ireland have their own separate legal systems and legal professions, and so I shall say nothing of them. Limitations of time mean that I must generalize, so that to most of what I say there will be unspoken exceptions and qualifications; and my emphasis will be on the bar.

I must begin with a short prelude on scale. By comparison with the United States, everything in England and Wales is so small. My figures are very approximate, for in such matters detail tends to stultify. The area of England and Wales is less than 60,000 square miles, in contrast with your 3.5 million; and our population is not quite 50 million, as against your figure of over 225 million. Thus although our population is some twenty-two percent of the size of yours, it is crammed into less than two percent of your area. Moreover, very few live more than 250 miles from London, where there is a heavy concentration of lawyers. Our legal profession is also relatively very small. We have some 500 judges for a population of nearly 50 million. The judges with unlimited jurisdiction (comprising the High Court, Court of Appeal, and House of Lords) number a little over 100; and there are less than 350 circuit judges, exercising a limited jurisdiction. If one adds a number of lawyers whom we do not call judges but who exercise full-time judicial functions and would probably be called judges in your country, there is a total of 500, or not much more. This compares with some 30,000 judges in the United States. Then we have some 4,500 practicing barristers and about 45,000 practicing solicitors, so that, including the judges, there are some 50,000 lawyers for nearly 50 million people. I do not know how many lawyers there are in the United States. I have heard it estimated that before very long there will be nearly a million of them; and I know that in 1979 there were over a quarter of a million members of the American Bar Association. In the year 1978, I believe that some 36,500 new lawyers were admitted to the various bars in the United States; and this alone is equal to nearly three-quarters of the entire legal profession in England and Wales.

The accuracy of the figures does not matter much. What does matter is the broad effect of the comparison. Nobody in a vast country such as yours can hope to understand how the English legal profession works without appreciating to the full how small and compact it is by comparison with yours. Even so, it is now far larger than it was in 1939 or 1945. Since then, in broad terms, the profession has doubled in numbers; and in some respects it has more than doubled. The great surge in crime and divorce, and the extensive provision of legal aid, have seen to that. So how are the standards of the profession faring? Has more meant worse? Any answer must be very much a matter of impression; but I think that the general view is that for the most part, with some unhappy exceptions, standards have been maintained. Certainly, I would assert this for the Chancery Bar, which I know best, though I believe that there are fields in which my common-law brethren are less happy.

Let me assume this to be so, and let me address myself to the bar. Why is this the case? How is it done? In attempting to answer these questions I must express my thanks to those who founded this series of lectures for forcing me to attempt some analysis of what it is all too easy to assume and take for granted. After due reflection, I can put my answer in a single but not very short sentence. From the outset of his career at the English bar, a barrister finds himself enveloped in a system of continuous professional assessment, correction and encouragement, and this directs and sustains his career in accordance with the established standards of the bar.

That is my proposition. It rests on six major factors. Let me list them, before turning to look briefly at each of them. They are: (1) the pupillage system; (2) the chambers system; (3) the Inns of Court; (4) the institution of silk; (5) the influence of the bench; and (6) the judgment of solicitors. You will observe that I have not included legal education. In the course of teaching much law and some professional skills, legal education contributes something, and there have been many improvements over the last twenty years; but I cannot see it as being a major factor in my thesis. I do not suggest that the six factors that I list form part of any overall plan or design. Each grew up separately, and each has been refined and improved from time to time; yet however haphazard, the team works. In a word, it is very English. Let me take each of the six heads in turn.

THE PUPILLAGE SYSTEM

Nobody may practice at the English bar without first becoming a pupil of an approved practicing barrister for a year or more. A rule of this sort had been customary for very many years; but not until 1959 was it made binding. In order to ensure that the pupil-master is sufficiently experienced, that he has a good reputation, and that he has enough work to make the pupillage valuable to the pupil, the pupil-master must have been continuously in practice at the English bar for at least five years, and he must be on his Inn's list of approved pupil-masters. He must also be a junior (that is, a barrister, of whatever age, who is not a Queen's Counsel), so that he will have work of the type that the pupil will hope to do when his pupillage ends.

The pupil has a seat in his pupil-master's chambers, and he tries his hand at any or all of his pupil-master's work. He goes to court with him, makes notes of the evidence and arguments, fetches textbooks and law reports when a new point suddenly emerges, and generally assists his pupil-master. In chambers, he drafts opinions and pleadings, makes notes on points of law and practice for his master, and attends conferences with solicitors and clients. A valuable part of this education lies in the pupil seeing how far his master alters or rejects what the pupil has drafted; and his master will explain to him why this has been done. Another valuable part of his education is learning what his master, and others in chambers, regard as being proper to do, and how best to do it.

For the first six months of his pupillage the pupil, despite being a barrister, is not allowed to address a court; but after that, his pupil-master, if he thinks him fit, may give him some relatively simple work to do, such as making a plea in mitigation of sentence in a minor case, or appearing before a master in chambers on some small procedural point. The pupil may also, under the guidance of his master, accept work on his own account, if he is fortunate enough to get any. The essence of the pupillage, however, is for the pupil to see everything from the inside, living in the highly professional atmosphere of barristers' chambers, and seeing how experienced and reputable advocates behave. Until some ten years ago the pupil paid his pupil-master a customary fee of 100 guineas (i.e., £105). This had been unchanged since it was first fixed in about 1780; but now there is no payment, either by or to the pupil. There is a system of scholarships, bursaries, and loans to help in meeting the financial problems of the pupillage year.

A pupillage is wonderfully revealing. Within a few months the pupil-master will know whether or not the pupil has any real aptitude for the bar. The pupil's academic record may be outstanding or modest or dismal; but success at the bar depends upon many other factors, and these begin to emerge during the pupillage. The pupil, too, knows that his future largely depends upon his performance during his pupillage. The bar is competitive and crowded, and when a pupillage ends, the pupil will have to find a set of chambers willing to accept him as a member. If he has shown outstanding qualities, his pupil-master's chambers, however pressed for space, will somehow find room for him; for all concerned will do everything possible to keep up the standards of their own chambers. If the pupil is merely good, and there is no room for him in his pupil-master's chambers, the master will at least speak well of him when other chambers enquire. But a pupil who has been found to be lazy, stupid, self-important, untrustworthy, or a dozen other things, will have small prospects of obtaining a seat in any save the dreariest of chambers. Careers at the bar begin with the pupillage; and some end there. Yet a pupillage is not merely a time of trial; it is an essential part of the training for those who will succeed at the bar. The beginner must be caught at the outset of his career and set upon the right lines. Early habits and attitudes tend to endure.

THE CHAMBERS SYSTEM

No barrister may practice at the bar unless he does so from a set of chambers. Physically, chambers consist of a number of rooms containing other barristers (usually from about eight to twenty of them, some sharing rooms) and a barristers' clerk, with typists and other staff. The rent and other expenses are shared by all the barristers in the chambers. In London, where about three-quarters of the barristers practice, nearly all the chambers are in one of the four Inns of Court. The clerk is a sort of business manager for each barrister in his chambers, and his functions include fixing and collecting their fees.

An essential difference between barristers' chambers and solicitors' offices is that every barrister is independent and practices on his own. He is not in partnership with the other members of chambers or anyone else; partnerships at the bar are prohibited. Often two members of the same chambers will be on the opposite sides in a case, assailing each other in court with all the added zest of being stablemates, and often close personal friends. This is particularly the case in some of the specialist chambers. Apart from the broad division between Chancery chambers and common-law chambers, there are sets of chambers that specialize in company law, or taxation, or landlord and tenant, and so on. In these chambers, the chances of opposing solicitors each briefing a different member of the same chambers is high. In such cases, the clerk of the chambers is a happy man; for most clerks work on the basis of a percentage of the earnings of each of his barristers.

Despite these prospects of diversity, there is a strong corporate spirit in a set of chambers. One of the senior members will be the Head of Chambers, responsible for paying the rent and other outgoings, and for collecting (through the clerk) a fair share from each of the other members of chambers. It is to the Head of Chambers that junior members will turn for advice and assistance when confronted with some problem of ethics or propriety. It is the Head of Chambers who will utter warning words to any member of chambers whose conduct appears to require them. He shares with all the other members of chambers a common concern that the chambers should maintain their high standing in the eyes of the bench, the rest of the bar, and solicitors. Standards can be maintained much more readily by personal and informal words within a small unit than by an impersonal and formal disciplinary process, a process which must of necessity be reserved for major delinquencies and cannot so well supply a warning word in time.

There is also a strong tradition at the bar for senior members to help beginners; and this flourishes in the atmosphere of chambers. It is in chambers that beginners get started at the bar. Sometimes a busy and overpressed practitioner will divert some small work to a beginner in chambers whom he trusts; and there is also a process known as "devilling." The overworked practitioner will ask a not-so-busy beginner to draft an opinion or statement of claim for him, or to write a note on the law, much as the beginner did when he was a pupil. The difference is that the devil will usually be paid for his work. If the work is good and can be used without much alteration, he may expect to get at least half the fee received by the principal. As with a pupillage, this process is highly educational; and a devil may work for any or all in his set of chambers, or, indeed, outside.

THE INNS OF COURT

The four Inns of Court are Lincoln's Inn, Inner Temple, Middle Temple, and Gray's Inn, to put them in their traditional order. They are as closely similar in substance as they are pleasantly diverse in detail. They are all close to the Royal Courts of Justice in London and to each other. Nobody can be called to the bar without joining one of them. Indeed, it is the Inns of Court alone, and not the courts, that can call a person to the bar; and it is the Inns of Court alone that, subject to an appeal to the judges as Visitors to the Inns, can suspend or disbar a barrister. Each Inn is managed by its bencher (above) who belongs to the Inn, some forty of the senior Queen's Counsel of the Inn, and perhaps ten of the senior juniors. There are also a number of distinguished persons, some of them not members of the Inn, or indeed, lawyers, who have been elected honorary benchers. I give the numbers of my own Inn, Lincoln's Inn, the Inn in which Thomas More held office over 450 years ago. Today we have about 130 benchers, including many who have retired and twenty honorary benchers. The main body of active benchers is about sixty or seventy strong.

One essential of being a bencher is to recognize that within the Inn all benchers are treated as being equal, regardless of any judicial or other office that they hold. The one exception is the treasurer, who during his year of office is the Head of the Inn. This rule of equality is good for the judges, doing much to prevent them from becoming too pompous and self-important. Much of the work of the Inn is done by standing committees. Nobody would be surprised to find a junior presiding over a committee in which a proposition that is strongly supported by a Lord Justice, a High Court judge and a junior is being opposed by three Queen's Counsel and a master, and is ultimately defeated by a large majority. There is also easy conversation between all benchers round the lunch table (most benchers sitting or appearing in the Law Courts lunch in their Inn), though counsel who are appearing before a judge who is a fellow-bencher will usually avoid sitting next to him. This easy mixing does much to avoid the "them" and "us" syndrome. In addition to being undeniably pleasant, it also plays a real part in the formation and maintenance of professional standards, and in diminishing the avoidable asperities of conflict in the courtroom. It was Tranio who advised: "Do as adversaries do in law / Strive mightly, but eat and drink as friends."

The civilizing effect of habitual communal lunching is not, of course, confined to benchers, but applies to all members of the Inn. Any temptation to indulge in sharp practice becomes less acute if the victims will be those whom you have met, and will meet, at the lunch table of your Inn. In addition, the hope of becoming a bencher in due time plays its part, even if only subconsciously; for election as a bencher is by the benchers, and none save those of good repute will be elected.

THE INSTITUTION OF SILK

Taking silk is indeed an important step in a career at the English bar. Norman Birkett, who became Sir Norman, and then Lord Birkett, once told me that he always regarded it as the most important and pleasurable step of all, outstripping appointment as a judge or promotion. Out of a practicing bar of some 4,500, about ten percent are, more formally, "Masters of the Bench." These consist of all the judges of the High Court (and are silks, or "Queen's Counsel"). The term "silk" comes from the gown. When appointed a Queen's Counsel you become entitled to wear a silk gown in place of the cotton gown of juniors, and you wear a tailcoat of a particular design instead of an ordinary jacket. On formal occasions (and they are few), you wear knee breeches and a wig with long flaps on each side, like a bloodhound's ears (a "full bottomed wig"), in place of the short wig that you wear on ordinary occasions, and juniors wear on all occasions. You also put "Q.C." after your name; and this is known, both inside the law and out, as an official recognition of your high standing as counsel. Despite the name, today there is no special position for Queen's Counsel in relation to working for the Crown.

The effect of becoming a Queen's Counsel is that you have to give up doing some of the less important kinds of work, leaving them for juniors, and you expect to spend your time on the more important and difficult cases. Broadly, you will be paid more money for doing less work, though it will be work of greater responsibility. Some juniors come to accept that silk is beyond their reach, while others hesitate to accept the responsibility, preferring to be "led" by a Queen's Counsel in the important cases. Yet the great majority of juniors hope to reach the plateau of silk, and reach it as early in their careers as they safely can. Needless to say, nobody has any prospect of being given silk unless he is of good repute.

The process of taking silk begins with an application to the Lord Chancellor, made by December 31 in any year. It is usually futile to apply for silk until you have been in practice for at least ten years; fifteen or twenty years is more normal. With your application, you send details of your career and your earnings at the bar, and you name two High Court judges as referees. The referees will in due course send the Lord Chancellor their views on your abilities as an advocate, and your conduct and repute; and they will be very frank. Usually the views of other judges will be available as well.

The Lord Chancellor then holds a meeting to consider the list of applicants, summoning the four Heads of Division, namely, the Lord Chief Justice (for the Queen's Bench Division), the Master of the Rolls (for the Court of Appeal), the President (for the Family Division), and the Vice-Chancellor (for the Chancery Division). All of these are, of course, practicing judges, sitting every day in court. The Lord Chancellor himself is no mere Minister of Justice, but is a working judge who often sits as such, presiding over the House of Lords for the hearing of appeals. Among those at the meeting, there is likely to be at least one with a firsthand knowledge of each applicant for silk; and all will know the judges who have expressed their views about the applicants. There will be a frank exchange of opinions, particularly about those thought to be marginal, and ultimately the Lord Chancellor will decide upon a list of the successful. In recent years, the list has tended to include not much more than a quarter of those who have applied. The list is now much longer than it once was. In 1956, I was one among eleven, whereas today there are a little over fifty each year. But even this is very different from Canada, where in a single year one province alone may create double our number for a population less than one-sixth our size.

In England, the institution of silk is thus vigilantly guarded. Great care is taken to ensure that, as far as possible, every silk is truly silkworthy. The list will often include one or two who are not practicing barristers, such as a distinguished academic lawyer, or the holder of some important governmental legal position; but all the others will be appointed on purely professional grounds. Yet despite every care, there will be occasional mistakes. One New York lawyer visiting the Law Courts in London heard a dreary and incompetent lawyer addressing the court. On being told that the advocate was a Queen's Counsel, the American said: "Now I know why you say 'God save the Queen.'"

As you might expect, there are some pleasant formalities when new silks are appointed. Each year, the list of the successful is published just before Easter; and some ten days later, on the first day of the next term, the new silks will put on their formal dress and be sworn in before the Lord Chancellor at the House of Lords. They will then come to the Law Courts to be "called within the bar" by each of the Heads of Division; for silks sit in the front row in court. Between the front row and the second row, where juniors sit, there is a notional "bar," represented in many of the courtrooms by a little wooden gate at each side of counsel's rows. When the new silks come to my court, I interrupt the case that I am hearing, and say to the first of the new silks: "John Arthur Smith" (or whatever his name is), "Her Majesty having been pleased to appoint you one of her counsel learned in the law, you will take your seat within the bar accordingly." Mr. Smith will then advance through the little gate, stand in the middle of the front row, bow to me, to the other silks and to the juniors, and then sit down. Whereupon I say: "Mr. Smith, do you move?" He then rises, bows to me (which is the courteous way of saying "No, I have no motions to move"), and then leaves the court. *E da capo al fine.*[1]

There are, of course, variations. When asked: "Mr. Smith, do you move?", one obese new silk replied: "With difficulty, my Lord." Whether he rivalled Chief Justice Taft, I do not know; at times Taft weighed well over three hundred pounds. Mr. Justice Brewer once reported, as an instance of Taft's innate courtesy, that he had seen him give up his seat in a street car to three ladies. When the future Lord Morton of Henryton took silk, Lord Justice Scrutton, who shared Morton's love of the golf course, was presiding over a Court of Appeal before which Morton had made the requisite three bows. As Morton was leaving the court, Scrutton called out "fore," by way of friendly greeting; but Morton heard it as "four," and returned to make an extra bow.

THE INFLUENCE OF THE BENCH

The influence of the bench is twofold; for the bench is both a goal and a guardian. It is a goal in that most practicing barristers—not all, but the great majority—hope that one day they will be offered a seat on the High Court bench. Such an offer will be made only to those of the highest professional standing and integrity. The attractions are various. The work, though demanding, is interesting and important. Although there are now seventy-seven High Court judges in place of the twenty-eight of 1939, their standing in the community remains very high. They are always knighted on appointment, so that Mr. John Smith becomes "Sir John Smith" and his wife "Lady Smith," a feature not to be ignored. The salary is much less than earnings at the bar (when I was appointed it meant a reduction to about one-third), but there is an assured income, and a pension which can be taken after fifteen years of service. The salary today is about $75,000; but few are appointed until they are over fifty, when they have passed the worst financial stresses of educating their children. (The youngest appointments to the High Court bench this century were the future Lord Hodson and the future Lord Devlin, each appointed when forty-two; but they were exceptional.) To those in their mid-fifties, wondering how long they will be able to maintain their full vigour as advocates and withstand the competition of younger rivals, and lacking any partners to sustain them, a seat on the bench has obvious attractions. They will bear in mind that an offer, once rejected, is unlikely to be repeated, and that with a compulsory retiring age of seventy-five, and with fifteen years of service required to qualify for a full pension, as the age of sixty approaches and is passed the offer of an appointment will become less and less likely.

The process of appointment is simple enough. The appointment is made by the Queen on the advice of the Lord Chancellor, after he has made such consultations as he thinks

1. "And this is repeated until the end."

fit. These consultations always include the Heads of Division, much as on the appointment of silks, though on a more intensive scale. The sole criterion is to find the most suitable man or woman for the job. Politics, though once a factor, have ceased to play any real part in appointments to the bench. The time of the change may be pinpointed. For a very long time the Attorney General of the day was regarded as having a strong claim to the Lord Chief Justiceship, when it fell vacant. Yet when Viscount Caldecote, a former Attorney General, resigned the Chief Justiceship on January 21, 1946, while a Labour government was in office, the new Chief Justice was not the Attorney General but was Lord Goddard, a Law Lord with no more than a trace of politics in his youth, and that not on the Labour side. When he resigned in 1956, Lord Justice Parker took his place. In 1971 he was succeeded by Lord Justice Widgery, who as Lord Widgery, the Lord Chief Justice, delivered the John F. Sonnett Lecture in 1974. In 1980, he was succeeded by Lord Lane, a Law Lord. All these were nonpolitical career lawyers; and in each case the Conservative government that was in power at the time followed the lead given by the Labour government in 1946.

This nonpolitical attitude has percolated downward. Not for many years has a Member of Parliament been regarded as having, as such, any claim to a vacant judgeship, or, for that matter, to appointment as a Queen's Counsel. Any preferment must be based on professional standing rather than political affiliations. At most there may be an occasional suspicion that in a marginal case politics may have tipped the balance.

Another feature of the past that has disappeared is the appointment to the Court of Appeal or House of Lords of anyone who has not first become a High Court judge. I do not say that such leaps have become impossible; but the climate of opinion makes them improbable. A few years on the High Court bench may do much to demonstrate the suitability (or unsuitability) of a judge for a seat in the Court of Appeal; and those few years are also likely to give greater understanding and depth to the exercise of the appellate function. Nor has the appointment of academic lawyers to the bench come any nearer. As a former president of the Society of Public Teachers of Law (which roughly corresponds to the Association of American Law Schools), I suppose that I am about the nearest approach to an academic lawyer on the English bench. But my road to the bench, like everyone else's, was through practice at the bar. That is now the only road. A modern development, introduced by the Courts Act 1971, is that many senior Queen's Counsel are now appointed to sit as Deputy High Court judges once or twice a year, for two, three, or four weeks at a time. The primary object is to make inroads on the backlog of cases waiting to be heard; but a valuable secondary consequence is that the process is usually revealing about the silk's suitability for appointment to the bench.

I turn from the bench as a goal to the bench as a guardian. Every barrister realizes that the judges play a large part in whatever standing and recognition he has, especially as the numbers of judges and practicing barristers are so relatively small. The impact of counsel and judge upon each other in court is also great. Except in serious criminal cases and in defamation, for all practical purposes every case is decided by the judge alone, without any jury. On appeal, there are no briefs in your sense of the word. The whole forensic process, both at trial and on appeal, is one of oral communication between counsel and judge.

All is direct, man to man, or woman to woman, or as the case may be. In the bound and rebound of ideas between bench and bar, the stress of argument is wonderfully revealing.

There are no formal time limits, even on appeal. Chief Justice Hughes, I am told, was so punctilious a time-keeper in your Supreme Court that he was able to stop a Wall Street lawyer in the middle of the word "if." In England, the courts subscribe to the proposition that one of the first duties of a judge is to make it disagreeable for counsel to talk nonsense; and usually the judges apply the skills that they have acquired in this process to prolixity as well, though their success is not uniform. The Court of Appeal once vainly attempted to stem the flow from a barrister notorious for his ability to make ten words do the work of one. On and on he went, and finally, as he was going round the course for the third time, he made a new complaint about the trial judge: "And when I tried to put that point, my Lord, the judge stopped me." The presiding judge saw his chance: "Tell us, Mr. Smith, just *how* did he do that?" The reply was prompt and indignant: "By falsely pretending to be in my favor, my Lord." In another appeal, counsel began to cite a number of cases in support of elementary propositions of law. Soon the presiding judge gently observed: "Mr. Jones, I think that you may assume that this court has *some* knowledge of the law." "My Lord," replied Mr. Jones, grimly, "that was the mistake that I made in the court below."

THE JUDGMENT OF SOLICITORS

In England, no barrister can appear in court as counsel unless he has been instructed by a solicitor. The livelihood of a barrister is thus wholly dependent upon solicitors and what they think of him. Solicitors are the judges of the bar; they brief the good and ignore the bad. The judgment of forensic ability is made not by laymen, who too often think that storm and fury make good advocacy, even when empty of content. It is made by solicitors, lawyers who are skilled in litigation and well accustomed to appreciating quiet and effective competence, and to discounting froth, however impressively uttered. They can recognize the budding skill of a beginner, perhaps on the other side in a case, who, though losing, proves to be resourceful and tenacious; and for the next case that they have of the same kind, they may well brief that beginner in preference to counsel whose win was unimpressive. From counsel's point of view, the ultimate triumph may lie not in winning the case but in winning the solicitors on the other side for future cases. In a word, counsel are the subject of continuous assessment by the general body of solicitors, all of whom have the commendable aim of getting for their clients the best possible value for money.

CONCLUSION

Those, then, are my six major factors. I have set out my prelude, stated my theme, and deployed my six variations; and so I come to my coda. From the outset, a barrister is enveloped in a system of continuous professional assessment, by his pupil-master, by his fellows, by judges, and by solicitors. His progress depends on their judgment of how good a barrister he is. Politics play little or no part, whether party politics or the politics of any bar association or other body; nor do the views of laymen count. The whole atmosphere is professional. The barrister is set on the right lines by his pupillage, sustained by the chambers system and the fellowship of his Inn, continuously assessed, aided, and corrected by solicitors, his fellows and the judges, and encouraged throughout by the goal of silk and ultimately the bench. Is it any wonder, then, that, set in this climate, so many barristers attain and maintain high standards? Instead, it would be surprising if they did not. There are, of course, failures, quite apart from those who are found to lack the qualities necessary for practice at the bar, and who, weeded out by the system, depart for other fields of endeavor. There are a few whom no system will tame, just as there are many who in any event would instinctively go right. But for those at neither extreme, the system does much—very much—to bring out the best and discourage the worst. It is also very pleasant. The barrister's Inn is a social club in which the real brotherhood of the law flourishes. This emphasizes one of the defects of the system. Today, a quarter of the bar mainly practice outside London; and for them, the Inns, from geographical necessity, can provide so little. There are other defects, too; I certainly am not suggesting that the rose has no thorn. But even after allowing for all qualifications and exceptions and blemishes, I assert that the system as a whole plays a very large part in maintaining high standards at the English bar. Perhaps I may end by saying something of my own Inn. When a bencher dies, the great bell of Lincoln's Inn, brought back from Cadiz in 1596, is slowly tolled from 12:30 PM until 1:00 PM. For many years, barristers in the Inn, hearing the bell, have sent their clerks to find out who it is that has been gathered to his fathers; and this continues to this day. When the bell was still newly hung in the chapel, the great Dr. John Donne was Preacher to the Inn; he held office from 1616 until 1622. In 1624 his *Devotions Upon Emergent Occasions* was first published; and in it there is a well-known passage which may have had its origin in the brotherhood of the law that Donne found in the Inn. I like to take it as extending also to the brotherhood of the law that knows no national boundaries. In modern orthography, it runs as follows:

> No man is an island, entire of itself; every man is a piece of the continent, a part of the main; if a clod be washed away by the sea, Europe is the less, as well as if a promontory were, as well as if a manor of thy friend's or of thine own were; any man's death diminishes me, because I am involved in mankind; and therefore never send to know for whom the bell tolls; it tolls for thee.

The Supreme Court of the United States: Managing Its Caseload to Achieve Its Constitutional Purposes

William T. Coleman Jr.

William T. Coleman Jr. delivered the thirteenth Sonnett lecture, entitled *The Supreme Court of the United States: Managing Its Caseload to Achieve Its Constitutional Purposes*, on May 9, 1983.[1] Born in Germantown, Pennsylvania, in 1920, Coleman graduated summa cum laude from the University of Pennsylvania in 1946.[2] Mr. Coleman served on the editorial board for the *Harvard Law Review* and graduated magna cum laude from Harvard Law School in 1945.[3]

After graduating, Coleman clerked for Judge Herbert F. Goodrich of the U.S. Court of Appeals for the Third Circuit.[4] He became the first African-American clerk for the U.S. Supreme Court, clerking for U.S. Supreme Court Justice Felix Frankfurter.[5] However, he was not welcomed by the large New York and Philadelphia law firms until Justice Frankfurter intervened with the Paul Weiss firm on his behalf.[6]

After his clerkship, Coleman entered private practice, where he was a key legal strategist and coauthored the legal brief for plaintiffs in *Brown v. Board of Education*,[7] which held racial segregation in schools to be unconstitutional in 1954.[8] In 1982, Coleman successfully argued before the Supreme Court to ban tax exemptions for private schools that denied black students admission.[9]

Introduction written by Elizabeth Langton, J.D., Class of 2015, Fordham University School of Law.

1. William T. Coleman, Jr., *The Supreme Court of the United States: Managing Its Caseload to Achieve Its Constitutional Purposes*, 52 Fordham L. Rev. 1 (1983).

2. *See* Todd C. Peppers, *William Thaddeus Coleman, Jr.: Breaking the Color Barrier at the U.S. Supreme Court*, 33 J. Sup. Ct. Hist. 353, 355 (2008).

3. *Id.* at 355, 357.

4. *Id.* at 358; *see also William T. Coleman Jr. Awarded Harvard Medal* (May 28, 2013), *available at* http://www.naacpldf.org/news/william-t-coleman-jr-awarded-harvard-medal.

5. *See* Peppers, *supra* note 2, at 362; *see also William T. Coleman Jr. Awarded Harvard Medal*, *supra* note 4. While clerking, Mr. Coleman and his fellow clerk, Elliot Richardson, spent one hour each day reading Shakespeare, a unique daily activity that has become lore among Supreme Court law clerks. *See* Peppers, *supra* note 2, at 359–60.

6. William T. Coleman, Jr., Counsel for the Situation (Brookings Institution, 2010).

7. 347 U.S. 483 (1954).

8. *See* Rich Barlow, *William T. Coleman, Jr., to Be Honored at Commencement*, BU Today (May 12, 2010), http://www.bu.edu/today/2010/william-t-coleman-jr-to-be-honored-at-commencement/.

9. *Bob Jones University v. United States*, 461 U.S. 574 (1983); Barlow, *supra* note 8.

In 1975, President Gerald R. Ford appointed Coleman Secretary of Transportation.[10] Coleman oversaw the launch of the National Highway Traffic Safety Administration's car testing center in Ohio and the creation of pipeline safety and hazardous material regulations.[11]

Coleman is an accomplished author, publishing his memoir, *Counsel for the Situation: Shaping the Law to Realize America's Promise*, in addition to numerous scholarly articles.[12] He has received several awards, including the Congressional Medal of Freedom, presented by President Bill Clinton in 1995, and the Thurgood Marshall Lifetime Achievement Award, awarded by the NAACP Legal Defense and Education Fund in 1997.[13]

Mr. Coleman's Sonnett lecture, *The Supreme Court of the United States: Managing Its Caseload To Achieve Its Constitutional Purposes*, focused on the effect of the Supreme Court's excessive caseload on the quality of judicial decision-making.[14] This rising workload affects the Court's ability to fulfill its goal of maximizing individual freedoms, erodes the quality of decision-making, deflates the Court's influence, and reduces collegiality.[15] His lecture is as timely today as it was thirty years ago.[16]

Mr. Coleman examined the solutions that have been proposed, such as the establishment of a national appellate court or a rotating panel of judges from the appellate courts.[17] He ultimately rejected these solutions, however, as they would alter the core responsibilities of the Court and fail to fully address the workload problem.[18] Mr. Coleman concluded his address by proposing four reforms: (1) make the Court's mandatory appellate jurisdiction discretionary, except for constitutional cases involving fundamental human rights that may cause nationwide divisiveness; (2) allow inter-circuit conflicts to be resolved among the affected circuits without the Court's intervention; (3) limit the Court's review to only issues of fundamental national importance; and (4) discourage unnecessary litigation through judicial restraint, collegial deference, and disciplined opinion writing.[19]

William T. Coleman Jr. died from complications of Alzheimer's disease at his home in Alexandria, Virginia, on March 31, 2017, age ninety-six.

---

10. *See* Barlow, *supra* note 8; *see also* WILLIAM T. COLEMAN JR., *supra* note 6.
11. *See* Barlow, *supra* note 8.
12. *See* WILLIAM T. COLEMAN JR., *supra* note 6.
13. *Id.*
14. *See generally* Coleman, *supra* note 1.
15. *See id.* at 1–2.
16. *See, e.g.*, EDWIN CHERMERINSKY, THE CASE AGAINST THE SUPREME COURT (2014). Professor Chermerinsky proposes various reforms to address the greater fractiousness on the Court. Proposals commonly discussed include an eighteen-year term limit on service on the Court, and some of the proposals set forth by Mr. Coleman in his Sonnett lecture.
17. Coleman, *supra* note 1, at 2, 12–16.
18. *Id.*
19. *Id.* at 16–32.

1983 Sonnet Lecture

In his persistent and innovative efforts to improve the administration of justice, Chief Justice Burger has invited public debate about the effect of the Supreme Court's rising caseload on the quality of judicial decision-making.[1] Because Justice Holmes once reminded us that justice and high judicial performance require the company of the bench and the bar acting in concert,[2] commentary from a practicing member of the bar seems appropriate. Thus, in the spirit of the Chief Justice's invitation, I will (1) discuss the Supreme Court's excessive workload, (2) survey solutions that have been proposed, primarily by other Justices, and (3) suggest an alternative that may be more consistent with the Court's historic traditions and basic constitutional purposes. This issue transcends the workload question itself; it goes to the essence of the Supreme Court's responsibilities during the next two hundred years of our constitutional democracy. The solution chosen will affect the quality of the Court's contribution to efficient but fair justice and to economic growth with enhanced productivity. Indeed, it will determine how successfully the Court can fulfill the constitutional goal of maximizing, as Justice O'Connor said in *Kolender v. Lawson*, "individual freedoms within a framework of ordered liberty."[3]

The Court's excessive workload presents an immediate and serious problem which, if not resolved, will erode the quality of decision-making of the nation's highest tribunal. More importantly, it will deflate the Court's leavening influence in this diverse, vibrant, and contentious democracy. Many of the solutions being discussed, however, would unnecessarily alter the core responsibilities of the Supreme Court. Establishment of a national appellate court,[4] for example, would unwisely delegate the Supreme Court's final authority to decide certain cases or, equally troubling, to select cases for Supreme Court review. Similarly, the selection of a rotating panel of judges from the thirteen federal appellate courts to review conflicts among the circuits[5] would interpose a new level of review and address only part of the problem.

The alternative I propose consists of four interrelated reforms, each of which would strengthen the Court's ability to identify and decide legal issues of fundamental national importance while optimizing the use of its valuable time. The reforms would: (1) make the Court's appellate jurisdiction entirely discretionary except in certain rare instances where a constitutional challenge involves the denial of fundamental human rights in a way

1. Chief Justice Burger, *Annual Report on the State of the Judiciary*, 69 A.B.A.J. 442, 446 (1983) [hereinafter cited as *Annual Report*].

2. Address by Justice Holmes, Suffolk Bar Association Dinner (February 5, 1885), *reprinted in* M. Lerner, The Mind and Faith of Justice Holmes 29–31 (1943); *see* P. Freund, On Understanding the Supreme Court 78–79 (1950).

3. Kolender v. Lawson, 103 S. Ct. 1855, 1858 (1983).

4. *See infra* notes 35–41 and accompanying text.

5. *See infra* notes 42–44 and accompanying text.

that is the cause of nationwide divisiveness,[6] (2) resolve most inter-circuit conflicts without any Supreme Court involvement in the process, (3) limit Supreme Court review to issues of fundamental national importance, and (4) reinvigorate the traditions of judicial restraint, disciplined opinion writing, and deferential collegiality epitomized by the contributions to prior Courts of, among others, Chief Justice Hughes, and Justices Holmes, Frankfurter, and Brandeis.

These reforms would not only reduce the pressures of the Court's burgeoning caseload but would also regenerate the principal source of its strength—the ability to fashion collegially, with the power of reason alone, the fabric of a just and free society. In this sense, the Supreme Court is a microcosm of a diverse and dynamic populace, the fragile unity of which rests on respect for law and the resolution of disputes through reason. It is the legal system that avoids bitter fractionalization by transforming the tensions of a pluralistic society into creative progress toward a more workable civilization. The Court must resolve—or justify—the disparate perspectives of its members through reason and explain its evolving consensus with clarity, force, and detached analysis. Review of some facts and history regarding the Supreme Court's workload will place the issue in perspective and explain why the alternative proposed herein is fully consistent with both the Court's traditions and its constitutional mandate.

FACTS AND HISTORY REGARDING SUPREME COURT CASELOAD

Statistical Analysis

The increasing burden of the Supreme Court's workload is amply demonstrated by various statistical analyses cited by the Justices themselves.[7] The Chief Justice, for

6. Cases reviewable under such jurisdiction would involve rights such as those presented in Roe v. Wade, 410 U.S. 113 (1973) (abortion), and Brown v. Board of Educ., 347 U.S. 483 (1954) (equal educational opportunity). The precise definition of this narrow right of mandatory appeal will require further research, debate, and refinement.

7. Justice Brennan recently noted that during the 1981 term, the Supreme Court "granted review in 210 cases, which is 26 more than the Term before and 56 more than two Terms ago." Brennan, *Some Thoughts on the Supreme Court's Workload*, 66 JUDICATURE 230, 230 (1983) (quoting Justice White) [hereinafter cited as Brennan I]. The Justice noted that "for more than 15 of [his] 26 terms starting in 1956, the Court averaged about 100 opinions per term . . . . But since the 1970 term that number has inexorably crept up, first to the high 120's, then to the 130's and last term to 141 signed [opinions] plus 9 per curiam [opinions]." *Id.* In his assessment of the workload crisis facing the federal judiciary, Justice Powell observed that "[c]ivil rights filings in federal district courts have increased from about 270 in 1961 to some 30,000 in fiscal year 1981." Powell, *Are the Federal Courts Becoming Bureaucracies?*, 68 A.B.A.J. 1370, 1371 (1982). Justice O'Connor has noted that in the 1935 term there were 983 new filings, by 1951 the number had grown to 1,234, and during the 1981 term there were 4,422 new filings in the Supreme Court. O'CONNOR, COMMENTS ON SUPREME COURT'S CASE LOAD, JOINT MEETING OF THE FELLOWS OF THE AMERICAN BAR FOUNDATION & THE NATIONAL CONFERENCE OF BAR PRESIDENTS, at 7 (Feb. 6, 1983) [hereinafter cited as Comments of Justice O'Connor] (available in files of *Fordham Law Review*).

example, recently noted that in 1953, the first year of Chief Justice Warren's tenure, the Court had 1,463 cases on its docket and issued 65 signed opinions.[8] In the term ending July 1982, the Supreme Court had 5,311 cases on its docket and issued 141 signed Court opinions.[9] This amounts to a docket increase of 270 percent and more than a doubling of signed opinions.[10] In the term ending July 6, 1983, the Court issued 151 signed opinions.[11]

During Chief Justice Burger's tenure, Congress has created over one hundred new statutory causes of action.[12] The Court itself, although to a lesser extent, has also created new causes of action.[13] Further evidence of the growing litigiousness of the American public lies in the number of licensed attorneys, which has almost doubled since the early 1970s, and the number of federal judges, which has increased over the past thirty years from 279 to 647.[14] It is these attorneys and judges who "produce the grist for the

8. *Annual Report*, *supra* note 1, at 42. "Signed" opinions do not include concurring, dissenting or per curiam opinions. *Id.* at 443 n.1; *see infra* note 17.

9. *Id.* at 442. Some commentators have pointed out that "the statistical rise in applications does not create a proportionate rise in demand on the Justice's time in reviewing applications." Alsup, *A Policy Assessment of The National Court of Appeals*, 25 HASTINGS L.J. 1313, 1320 (1974). This is because the increase in applications is largely due to *in forma pauperis* cases which are often readily identifiable as frivolous. *Id.* at 1320–21; Brennan, *The National Court of Appeals: Another Dissent*, 40 U. CHI. L. REV. 473, 476–77 (1973) [hereinafter cited as Brennan II]; Gressman, *Much Ado About Certiorari*, 52 GEO. L.J. 742, 745–46 (1964); Comment, *The National Court of Appeals: Composition, Constitutionality, and Desirability*, 41 FORDHAM L. REV. 863, 864–65 (1973) [hereinafter cited as *Composition, Constitutionality, and Desirability*]; *see* Poe, Schmidt & Whalen, A *Dissenting View*, 67 NW. U.L. REV. 842, 846 (1973).

10. *Annual Report*, *supra* note 1, at 442. Of course, it is the lower federal courts, as well as the states' court systems, that fuel the oversized Supreme Court docket. Justice Rehnquist recently illustrated this by noting that in 1937 there were 155 federal district court judges and 46 judges of the federal courts of appeals. Remarks by Justice Rehnquist, Mac Swinford Lecture, University of Kentucky, at 10 (Sept. 23, 1982) (available in files of *Fordham Law Review*). Today there are 515 federal district court judges and 132 federal appellate judges. Annual Report of the Director of the Administrative Office of the United States Courts 1982, at 77, 96 [hereinafter cited as Administrative Office Report].

11. See Appendix, Chart II. Nearly one-third of these opinions were issued during the final three weeks of the Term. N.Y. TIMES, July 10, 1983, § 1 at 1, col. 2.

12. WASH. POST, Feb. 7, 1983, at A12, col. 1.

13. *Annual Report*, *supra* note 1, at 442–443; *see, e.g.*, Cannon v. University of Chicago, 441 U.S. 677, 689–709 (1979) (implied right of action for injunctive relief under § 901(a) of Title IX of the Education Amendments of 1972); Bivens v. Six Unknown Fed. Narcotics Agents, 403 U.S. 388, 389 (1971) (implied damage action under the fourth amendment). For a discussion of the recent developments in the area of implied rights of action, see Hazen, *Implied Private Remedies Under Federal Statutes: Neither a Death Knell Nor a Moratorium—Civil Rights, Securities Regulation, and Beyond*, 33 VAND. L. REV. 1333 (1980); Note, *Implied Private Rights of Action Under Federal Statutes: Congressional Intent, Judicial Deference, or Mutual Abdication?*, 50 FORDHAM L. REV. 611 (1982).

14. WASH. POST, Feb. 7, 1983, at A12, col. 1.

Supreme Court 'mill,'"[15] yet the number of Supreme Court Justices has remained at nine since 1869.[16]

Other statistics, not as commonly cited, tell a different story. There actually has not been an increase over the long term in the total number of opinions of the Court. In 1882, for example, there were 260; in 1932, there were 168; and in 1982, there were 151.[17] There has been a dramatic increase, however, in the number of concurring opinions—4 in 1882, 4 in 1932, and 70 in 1982; and the number of dissenting opinions—17 in 1882, 24 in 1932, and 144 in 1982.[18] Stated another way, in 1882, there were 242 unanimous decisions (93.08% of the total); in 1932, there were 133 (79.64% of the total); and in 1982, there were 34 (22.52% of the total).[19] Since the advent of the Warren Court in 1953, the total number of opinions per term, including concurring and dissenting opinions, has risen from 138 to 361.[20] Dissension among the Justices contributes to the workload problem not only by spawning separate opinions but also by inspiring prospective litigants to seek to catapult concurring or dissenting views into majority opinions.

15. *Annual Report*, *supra* note 1, at 443.

16. Comments of Justice O'Connor, *supra* note 7, at 4. Increasing the number of Justices on the Supreme Court would arguably create more problems than it would solve by exacerbating the already difficult task of reaching a consensus.

17. *See* Appendix, Chart I. The 1882 figure, however, is somewhat misleading. As Chief Justice Burger has said recently, "[i]f the Court had been authorized to exercise discretionary certiorari jurisdiction in 1882, probably half of what were described in 1882 as 'cases' would have been denials of certiorari," and hence orders rather than opinions. *Annual Report*, *supra* note 1, at 443. Moreover, the figures cited here include only signed opinions and not per curiam opinions, which currently constitute a larger percentage of total opinions than in the Court's earlier years. *See* Appendix, Chart I.

18. *See* Appendix, Chart I. Between 1948 and 1970, "the court wrote an average of 218 opinions annually; after 1970 it averaged 354. There was not a huge change, however, in the number of 'opinions of the court': they rose from 107 annually to 145. The real rise was in dissents (from 78 to 134) and in separate concurrences (from 33 to 76)." Barone, *Our Overworked Justices Should Fire Some Law Clerks*, WASH. POST, Nov. 24, 1982, at A17, col. 1.

19. *See* Appendix, Chart I.

20. *See* Appendix, Charts II and III. The number of opinions issued during the 1953 term, however, represented "the smallest number of cases decided on the merits in . . . fourteen years." *The Supreme Court, 1953 Term*, 68 HARV. L. REV. 96, 187 (1954). The number of opinions rose in later years to 200 in 1958, 218 in 1963, 267 in 1968, 339 in 1973, 353 in 1977, and 361 in 1982. *See* Appendix, Charts II and III.

Whether relevant or not, the increase in the number of separate opinions corresponds to the increase in the number of law clerks. Years ago, some Justices hired one clerk; by the 1950s, most Justices hired two; by 1970, the Justices were allowed three; and in 1978, most had four law clerks. Barone, *supra* note 19, at A17, col. 1; *see* Kester, *The Law Clerk Explosion*, 9 LITIGATION 20, 61 (Spring 1983) ("With rising case loads, pressure to expand judges' staffs will grow. For any bureaucratic difficulty, bureaucrats prescribe more bureaucracy. But law clerks are not part of the solution; they are part of the problem.").

History of Reform

Concern over the Court's workload is as old as the Court itself. Soon after the Judiciary Act of 1789[21] established a six-Justice Supreme Court, thirteen single-judge district courts, and three circuit courts, consisting of one district judge and two Supreme Court Justices "riding circuit,"[22] it became apparent that the Court's workload was overwhelming. Congress directed President Washington's Attorney General, Edmund Randolph, to devise a solution. Recognizing that the quality of judicial contemplation was essential to the performance of the Court's function, Randolph reported in 1790: "Sum up all the fragments of their time, hold their fatigue at naught, and let them bid adieu to all domestic concerns, still the average term of a life, already advanced, will be too short for any important proficiency."[23]

Congress's response in subsequent years was to eliminate the circuit-riding duties and increase the size of the Supreme Court.[24] In 1891, Congress established nine circuit courts of appeals and did away with the mandatory right of appeal in some subject areas by introducing the concept of discretionary review by writ of certiorari.[25] Mandatory review was retained in only clearly defined areas.[26] Nevertheless, by the 1923 Term the Supreme Court

21. Ch. 20, 1 Stat. 73.

22. *Id.* at 73–75. The Supreme Court's appellate jurisdiction was limited by this Act to two types of cases: (1) appeals from circuit court decisions in civil cases involving sums of more than $2,000; and (2) appeals from final state court rulings upholding a state law against a challenge that it conflicted with the Constitution, federal laws or federal treaties. Congressional Quarterly, Guide to the U.S. Supreme Court 263 (1979). The Supreme Court was not granted appellate jurisdiction in capital criminal cases until 1889. Act of February 6, 1889, ch. 113, 25 Stat. 655, 656. Shortly thereafter the Court's jurisdiction was extended to "infamous crime[s]." Circuit Court of Appeals Act of 1891, ch. 517, 26 Stat. 826, 827; *see* P. Bator, P. Mishkin, D. Shapiro & H. Wechsler, Hart and Wechsler's The Federal Courts and the Federal System 32–49 (2d ed. 1973) [hereinafter cited as Hart & Wechsler]; F. Frankfurter & J. Landis, The Business of the Supreme Court 109 (1927).

23. F. Frankfurter and J. Landis, *supra* note 23, at 15 (quoting Rep. Atty. Gen. 1).

24. Judiciary Act of 1875, ch. 137, 18 Stat. 470. This Act broadened the Supreme Court's jurisdiction "almost to the full extent of the constitutional authorization." Hart & Wechsler, *supra* note 22, at 39. Although Congress had, in the meantime, reduced the Justices' circuit-riding duties and raised the number of Justices from six to nine, the 1875 Act dramatically increased the number of cases entering the Court's docket. *See* Comments of Justice O'Connor, *supra* note 7, at 5.

25. Circuit Court of Appeals Act of 1891, ch. 517, 26 Stat. 826. This Act constituted the first major restructuring of the federal judicial system. It granted the circuit courts of appeals jurisdiction over appeals from district courts in virtually all diversity, admiralty, patent, revenue, and noncapital criminal cases. Supreme Court review of circuit court decisions was made mandatory only upon the appellate court's certification of a case to the high court. The Supreme Court also retained discretionary review of courts of appeals decisions by writ of certiorari. Direct appeal to the Supreme Court was reserved by the Act only for cases involving constitutional questions, matters of treaty law, jurisdictional questions, capital crimes, and conflicting laws. *See* Congressional Quarterly, Guide to the U.S. Supreme Court 265 (1979).

26. *See supra* note 24.

was more than one year behind in its docket.[27] This delay was intolerable to Chief Justice Taft, who sponsored a committee of Justices to draft legislative reforms.[28] With uncharacteristic speed, and without the modern congressional tendency to engage in "elegant variation," Congress adopted the Justices' draft in the Judges' Bill of 1925.[29] The bill further narrowed the mandatory jurisdiction of the Supreme Court to a few categories, including appeals from federal court decisions holding state statutes unconstitutional or invalid under federal law or treaties, and state court decisions upholding state statutes against federal constitutional attack.[30] The framework established by the Judges' Bill of 1925 persists today, giving the Supreme Court great flexibility in choosing its cases for review. For, instead of narrowing the Court's jurisdiction, Congress chose, in more and more instances, to delegate to the Court the responsibility for determining which federal issues are of sufficient national importance to warrant Supreme Court review.[31] The process of issue selection, therefore, has become an increasingly crucial part of the review function. While Congress, in 1976, eliminated the right of direct appeal from three-judge district courts in most cases,[32] there have not been any significant statutory changes in the Supreme Court's jurisdiction since 1925.[33]

27. Frankfurter & Landis, *The Business of the Supreme Court of the United States—A Study in the Federal Judicial System*, 40 Harv. L. Rev. 834, 836 & n.7 (1927). Congress had never, in the past, taken steps to relieve the Court of its workload until there was evidence of a backlog. There was a backlog of a few years prior to the 1891 Act, which established the circuit courts of appeals. Alsup, *supra* note 9, at 1324–25; *see* Gressman, *The National Court of Appeals: A Dissent*, 59 A.B.A.J. 253, 254 (1973).

28. F. Frankfurter & J. Landis, *supra* note 23, at 259–60; *see* Blumstein, *The Supreme Court's Jurisdiction—Reform Proposals, Discretionary Review, and Writ Dismissals*, 26 Vand. L. Rev. 895, 898–99 (1973).

29. Ch. 229, 43 Stat. 936.

30. *Id.* at 937, 939. Direct appeals to the Supreme Court remained available, *inter alia*, in cases under antitrust or interstate commerce laws; appeals by the federal government under the Criminal Appeals Act of 1907; suits to halt enforcement of state laws or official state actions; and suits to halt Interstate Commerce Commission orders. In the 1970s most of the direct appeal jurisdiction was eliminated, except for appeals from a federal district court holding a federal statute unconstitutional, 28 U.S.C. § 1252 (1976), and appeals from a decision of a panel of three district judges, convened pursuant to an act of Congress or in reapportionment cases. 28 U.S.C. § 2284(a) (1976). Congressional Quarterly, Guide to the U.S. Supreme Court 265 (1979).

31. *See* Blumstein, *supra* note 29, at 903. *See supra* notes 26–31 and accompanying text.

32. Pub. L. No. 94–381, § 1, 90 Stat. 1119 (1976) (repealing 28 U.S.C. § 2282 (1976)).

33. President Franklin Roosevelt, of course, tried and failed to increase the number of Justices in his "court-packing" reorganization plan of 1937, but his motives were to outnumber the conservative majority. Some scholars believe, however, that the mere threat had an effect on the decision-making process. L. Baker, Felix Frankfurter 187–91 (1969); *see* M. Parrish, Felix Frankfurter and His Times 272 (1982). In addition, the Federal Courts Improvement Act of 1982, Pub. L. No. 97164, § 127(a), 96 Stat. 37, (current version at 28 U.S.C.A. § 1295 (West Supp. 1983)), transferred the duties of the Court of Claims and Court of Customs and Patent Appeals to the new Court of Appeals for the Federal Circuit, thereby eliminating Supreme Court review of appeals from the previously existing courts. Although decisions of the Court of Appeals for the Federal

The rising case load, nevertheless, has continued to stimulate discussion.[34] In 1971, the Chief Justice appointed a seven-member study committee, chaired by Professor Paul Freund of the Harvard Law School. The Freund Committee recommended the establishment of a National Court of Appeals to screen all certiorari petitions and appeals, referring approximately four hundred to the Supreme Court and denying the rest.[35] Of the cases referred to it, the Supreme Court would decide either to grant or deny certiorari, or to remand the case to the National Court of Appeals for decision.[36] If the National Court of Appeals did not refer a case to the Supreme Court, there would be no procedure by which the Court could review such a decision. Thus, had this proposal been adopted, many issues would never have come to the attention of the Supreme Court in any form, and the choice of factual context in which the issues presented to the Court are reviewed would have been severely restricted.

In 1972, Congress established a commission headed by Roman Hruska. This commission also recommended the establishment of a National Court of Appeals.[37] This proposed National Court, however, would not have screened certiorari petitions, but rather would have heard cases referred to it by the Supreme Court or transferred to it by a court of appeals.[38] The Supreme Court would thus have been forced to expend its time reviewing which cases should go to the National Court of Appeals. The Freund and Hruska proposals generated a flurry of scholarly comment, both favorable and unfavorable.[39] Some critics

Circuit are reviewable under the same statute which governs Supreme Court review of other court of appeals decisions, 28 U.S.C. § 1254 (1976), the Act's legislative history suggests that the creation of the new court was inspired at least in part by a desire to relieve the Supreme Court of some of its burdensome workload. *See* S. Rep. No. 275, 97th Cong., 2d Sess. 3, *reprinted in* 1982 U.S. Code Cong. & Ad. News 11, 13.

34. For a thoughtful analysis of the Supreme Court's caseload see G. Casper & R. Posner, The Workload of the Supreme Court (1976); F. Frankfurter & J. Landis, *supra* note 23; Douglas, *The Supreme Court and Its Case Load*, 45 Cornell L. Q. 401 (1960). For a delightful essay on the workload issue, see Kurland & Hutchinson, *The Business of the Supreme Court, O.T. 1982*, 50 U. Chi. L. Rev. 628 (1983).

35. Federal Judicial Center, Report of the Study Group on the Caseload of the Supreme Court 47 (1972) [hereinafter cited as Report of the Study Group]. *See* Freund, *A National Court of Appeals*, 25 Hastings L.J. 1301, 1305–9 (1974).

36. Report of the Study Group, *supra* note 36, at 47. The Freund committee also recommended the substitution of certiorari for the Court's mandatory appellate jurisdiction, the elimination of the three-judge district courts (which has been accomplished for the most part, *see supra* note 33), and the establishment of a nonjudicial panel to investigate and report on prisoner complaints. *Id.* at 47–48.

37. Commission on Revision of the Federal Court Appellate System, Structure and Internal Procedures: Recommendations for Change 5, 30 (1975) [hereinafter cited as Recommendations for Change].

38. *Id.* at 32.

39. *See, e.g.*, A. Bickel, The Caseload of the Supreme Court and What, If Anything to do About It (1973); Black, *The National Court of Appeals: An Unwise Proposal*, 83 Yale L.J. 883 (1974); Brennan II, *supra* note 9; Freund, *Why We Need a National Court of Appeals*, 59 A.B.A.J. 247 (1973); Gressman, *supra* note 28; Warren & Burger, *Retired Chief Justice Warren Attacks, Chief Justice*

thought the proposals would be an unconstitutional delegation of authority vested in "one supreme Court"[40] and, more importantly, would deprive the Court of essential functions and information in the selection and resolution of fundamental national issues.[41]

The most recent proposal—currently on the congressional agenda[42]—was made by the Chief Justice at the American Bar Association meeting in New Orleans in February of 1983. The Chief Justice advocates, as an interim step, the establishment of a five-year temporary special panel of the new United States Court of Appeals for the Federal Circuit. The special panel would have the narrow jurisdiction to decide all inter-circuit conflicts.[43] Two judges would be designated from each circuit, creating a pool of twenty-six judges. A panel of seven to nine judges would be drawn from the pool for six months to a year to hear and decide all inter-circuit conflicts and, possibly, a defined category of statutory interpretation cases. The panel could remove thirty-five to fifty cases a year from the argument calendar of the Supreme Court, which would, however, retain certiorari jurisdiction over these cases.[44] The Chief Justice views his proposal as only an interim and partial solution and, therefore, further consideration of a permanent National Court of Appeals is not entirely moot.

In addition to proposals for reform, the Supreme Court has attempted to alleviate its workload over the last two decades through self-help measures. These include shortening the time for oral argument to half an hour; assigning additional law clerks to the Justices; dispensing with records on petitions for certiorari; and, in some cases, pooling law clerk resources.[45] Despite these efforts, the workload problem persists.

In recent months, most of the Associate Justices have begun to speak out on the workload problem, offering a variety of solutions on the following subjects:

Burger Defends Freund Study Group's Composition and Proposal, 59 A.B.A.J. 721 (1973); *Composition, Constitutionality, and Desirability*, *supra* note 9.

40. U.S. CONST. art. III, § 1.

41. Black, *supra* note 40, at 885–87; Warren, *supra* note 40, at 729; *Composition, Constitutionality, and Desirability*, *supra* note 9, at 873–85.

42. Five bills, S. 381 through S. 385, were introduced by Senator Heflin on February 2, 1983, covering such subjects as the establishment of a National Court of Appeals, provision for mandatory Supreme Court review in certain areas, and creation of a Federal Courts Study Commission. 129 Cong. Rec. S892–94 (daily ed. Feb. 2, 1983). These bills were consolidated, amended slightly, and reintroduced as a single bill, S. 645, on March 1, 1983. 129 Cong. Rec. S1845 (daily ed. March 1, 1983). Senator Dole was the primary sponsor of the new bill. The Subcommittee on Courts, Civil Rights and Administration of Justice reported favorably on S. 645 on June 29, 1983. 1983–1984 Cong. Index (CCH) 21,013. Two portions of the Senate legislation—the National Court of Appeals ("Intercircuit Tribunal") and mandatory jurisdiction provisions—were separately introduced in the House by Congressman Kastenmeier on March 8, 1983. 129 Cong. Rec. H940 (daily ed. March 8, 1983). The two bills, H.R. 1968 and H.R. 1970, were considered at hearings held by the Subcommittee on Courts, Civil Liberties, and the Administration of Justice on April 27, 1983. 1983–1984 Cong. Index (CCH) 35,015.

43. *Annual Report*, *supra* note 1, at 447.

44. *Id.*

45. Freund, *supra* note 36, at 1304.

Mandatory Jurisdiction. All the Justices who have spoken publicly agree that the remaining mandatory appellate jurisdiction of the Supreme Court should be eliminated.[46]

Screening Certiorari Petitions. Justice Stevens has recommended that the function of screening certiorari petitions be delegated to a new National Court of Appeals.[47] If a new National Court of Appeals is not created, however, Justice Stevens has suggested that five instead of four votes be required in order to grant certiorari.[48]

Inter-circuit Conflicts. Justice White has suggested that a federal court of appeals be required to hold a hearing en banc before it takes a position on the interpretation of a statute that differs from that of another court of appeals.[49] The first en banc decision would be binding on all the other circuits and reviewable only by the Supreme Court.[50] Justice Stevens has recommended that Congress establish a standing committee to decide between two conflicting judicial readings of a given statute.[51] The committee would propose a statutory revision to resolve the conflict.[52] Justice Brennan has taken issue with Justice Stevens's suggestion because "it overlooks the role of compromise in the legislative process."[53] As previously noted, Chief Justice Burger recommends that inter-circuit conflicts be resolved by a special temporary panel of the new United States Court of Appeals for the Federal Circuit.[54]

Limitations on Jurisdiction. Justices Powell, Rehnquist, and O'Connor have suggested a number of limitations on federal courts' diversity, habeas corpus, and Section 1983 jurisdiction[55] that would reduce the flow of cases to the Supreme Court.[56] Justice Powell has noted that the number of civil rights

46. Brennan I, *supra* note 7, at 235; Powell, *supra* note 7, at 1371; Stevens, *The Life Span of a Judge-Made Rule*, 58 N.Y.U. L. Rev. 1, 21 (1983) [hereinafter cited as Stevens I]; Proceedings of the Forty-Second Annual Judicial Conference of the District of Columbia Circuit, 93 F.R.D. 153, 162 (1981) (remarks of Chief Justice Burger) [hereinafter cited as Remarks of Chief Justice Burger]; Comments of Justice O'Connor, *supra* note 7, at 12.

47. Stevens, *Some Thoughts on Judicial Restraint*, 66 Judicature 177, 182 (1982) [hereinafter cited as Stevens II].

48. Stevens I, *supra* note 47, at 21.

49. Brennan I, *supra* note 7, at 232 (quoting Justice White).

50. *Id.*

51. Stevens II, *supra* note 48, at 183.

52. *Id.*

53. Brennan I, *supra* note 7, at 233.

54. *Annual Report*, *supra* note 1, at 4.

55. *See* Powell, *supra* note 7, at 1372 ("[T]hese three sources of federal court jurisdiction provided nearly 40 per cent of the total district court civil filings.").

56. Justices Powell and O'Connor would require exhaustion of administrative remedies prior to bringing a Section 1983 lawsuit and recommend study of possible elimination or limitation of the diversity jurisdiction of the federal courts. Comments of Justice O'Connor, *supra* note 7, at 14; Powell, *supra* note 7, at 1371–72. Justice Powell would modify further the habeas corpus jurisdiction of

actions filed in federal courts has increased from approximately 270 to 30,000 over the last twenty years.[57] Approximately half of the over 30,000 civil rights suits filed in 1981 were filed by state prisoners under Section 1983.[58] Justice Powell, therefore, would limit the habeas review to "cases of manifest injustice in which the issue is guilt or innocence."[59]

Greater Selectivity. Other Justices have advocated greater selectivity on the part of the Supreme Court in deciding what cases to take. Justices Stevens and Brennan, among others, would minimize the Supreme Court's role in correcting lower court errors and in the review of cases at an interlocutory stage.[60]

Reforms recommended by the Justices and others fall into three general categories: delegation of Supreme Court authority to another court to select or decide cases,[61] further statutory limitations on the jurisdiction of the Supreme Court or on federal courts in general,[62] and the exercise of greater judicial restraint and discipline by the Supreme Court itself in its selection of issues for review.[63] All three approaches merit serious study and debate. Emphasis, however, should be placed on the third, with the addition of a fourth that will be advanced with great temerity at the end of this article.[64] The preferred approaches would concentrate on the fulfillment of the Supreme Court's constitutional mandate to construct a legal consensus on a few issues of fundamental national significance.

---

federal courts, *see* 28 U.S.C. § 2254 (1976), to create finality of federal review or a statute of limitations, and would make the court of appeals' jurisdiction over certain categories of cases (for example, administrative agency actions) discretionary. Powell, *supra* note 7, at 1371–72. Justice Rehnquist would have Congress review statutes that create a federal cause of action to determine whether access to the federal courts through these statutes should be limited or eliminated. *See* Remarks of Justice Rehnquist, *supra* note 10, at 30.

57. Powell, *supra* note 7, at 1371.

58. *Id.* According to Justice Powell, "no other system of justice [is] structured in a way that assures no end to the litigation of a criminal conviction" the way our system does through unnecessarily repeated use of the federal habeas statute. *Id.*

59. *Id.* at 1372.

60. Brennan I, *supra* note 7, at 231; Stevens II, *supra* note 48, at 180.

61. *See Annual Report*, *supra* note 1, at 447; Stevens II, *supra* note 48, at 182; Recommendations for Change, *supra* note 38, at 30–39; Report of the Study Group, *supra* note 36, at 47.

62. *See* Powell, *supra* note 7, at 1371–72; Comments of Justice O'Connor, *supra* note 7, at 14; Remarks of Justice Rehnquist, *supra* note 10, at 30.

63. Brennan I, *supra* note 7, at 231; Stevens II, *supra* note 48, at 180. Several Justices also have suggested procedural changes to expedite the resolution of some cases. Chief Justice Burger has proposed establishing a grievance procedure in the prison system to reduce the need for prisoners' litigation. Remarks of Chief Justice Burger, *supra* note 47, at 165. Justice O'Connor advocates the institutionalization of alternative forms of dispute resolution outside the court system. Comments of Justice O'Connor, *supra* note 7, at 14. Although opposed to the proposition, Justice Brennan has mentioned that "there is sentiment among some of [his] colleagues" to reduce or eliminate oral argument in certain Supreme Court cases. Brennan I, *supra* note 7, at 232.

64. *See infra* section "Collegial Analysis: Reaching a Consensus."

ANALYSIS

Proposals for an Intermediary Court

Delegation of the Supreme Court's case selection authority to an intermediary supercourt of appeals seems contrary to the Constitution's provision for "one supreme Court."[65] Constitutional considerations apart, however, delegation of the Supreme Court's power to screen cases would significantly alter the function of the Supreme Court in shaping constitutional law. The power to select cases is a fundamental part of the power to define the issues and trends in the development of constitutional and statutory interpretation.[66]

Life-tenured Supreme Court Justices bring to the issue-selection process a variety of backgrounds—judicial, political, and academic[67]—an experienced ear attuned to monitoring the heartbeat of a living Constitution, and a reasoned interaction of diverse philosophies and interests.[68] Because most Justices are assimilated gradually during extended intervals, the Court provides continuity, knowledge of trends, and collective perspective that simply could not be replicated in a panel of rotating judges with more limited functions and purposes.[69] In selecting cases for review, Justices must weigh not only the importance of the issues presented, but the timeliness of their review, the appropriateness of the factual context in which they arise, the adequacy of representation by counsel, the likely views of the other Justices on the merits, the reasons why on previous occasions they may have avoided the issues, and the relationship of the issues presented to issues in other pending cases and doctrinal developments.[70]

As Justice Brennan has stated:

> In my experience over more than a quarter century, the screening process has been, and is today, inextricably linked to the fulfillment . . . of the Court's unique mission. . . .
>
> The choice of issues for decision largely determines the image that the American people have of their Supreme Court. The Court's calendar mirrors the everchanging concerns of

65. U.S. CONST. art. III, § 1; *see* Black, *supra* note 40, at 885–87.

66. *See* Black, *supra* note 40, at 891 (quoting Hoadly's sermon preached before the King, March 31, 1717) ("Whoever hath an absolute authority to control the nature and scope of questions to be decided is to all intents and purposes controller over the process of decision."); Blumstein, *supra* note 29, at 907.

67. *See infra* note 112 and accompanying text.

68. Justice Brennan once commented: "I expect that only a Justice of the Court can know how inseparably intertwined are all the Court's functions, and how arduous and long is the process of developing the sensitivity to constitutional adjudication that marks the role." Brennan II, *supra* note 9, at 484.

69. In fact, throughout the nation's history only 103 Justices have served on the Supreme Court. Indeed, there are more judges sitting on the circuit courts today—132—than have served on the Supreme Court since its establishment. *See* Administrative Office Report, *supra* note 10, at 77.

70. Justice Frankfurter often remarked that his *personal* reading of the petitions for certiorari and jurisdictional statements was the most important judicial function he performed. *See* L. Baker, *supra* note 34, at 215 (1969). This fortunately relieved his law clerks from having to write thirty or more bench memos each week on certiorari petitions and jurisdictional statements.

> this society with ever more powerful and smothering government. The calendar is therefore the indispensable source for keeping the Court abreast of these concerns. Our Constitution is a living document and the Court often becomes aware of the necessity for reconsideration of its interpretation only because filed cases reveal the need for new and previously unanticipated applications of constitutional principles. . . . [T]o limit the Court's consideration to a mere handful of the cases selected by others would obviously result in isolating the Court from many nuances and trends of legal change throughout the land.
>
> The point is that the evolution of constitutional doctrine is not merely a matter of hearing arguments and writing opinions in cases granted review. . . . The screening function is an indispensible and inseparable part of the entire process and it cannot be withdrawn from the Court without grave risk of impairing the very core of the Court's unique and extraordinary functions.[71]

The selection of the appropriate time and factual context in which to address—or readdress—an issue of constitutional or societal importance is uniquely a function of the Supreme Court. The decision to grant the petition for certiorari in *Baker v. Carr*[72] would not inevitably have been the choice of an intermediary supercourt of appeals, given the Supreme Court's clear direction in *Colegrove v. Green*[73] that legislative apportionment was a political matter beyond the province of the Court.[74] Nor is it clear whether an intermediary supercourt of appeals would have considered the question of school desegregation in *Brown v. Board of Education*[75] worthy of the Supreme Court's attention, or whether the doctrine of "separate but equal" in *Plessy v. Ferguson*[76] would have resolved the matter conclusively. Moreover, three years after the Court had held in *Rummel v. Estelle*[77] that the Eighth Amendment's prohibition of "cruel and unusual punishment" could not be invoked to shorten the length of a sentence, it is equally doubtful that an intermediary court would have thought the Court would again be interested in reviewing the sentence issue. In *Solem v. Helm*,[78] however, the Court held that the Eighth Amendment proscribes a life sentence without the possibility of parole for a seventh nonviolent felony.[79]

Another example of the dangers presented by separating the screening process from the decisional process is *Gideon v. Wainwright*.[80] During the 1962 term, many petitions raising the issue of right to counsel were presented and rejected[81] before the Court seized

71. Brennan I, *supra* note 7, at 235.
72. 369 U.S. 186 (1962).
73. 328 U.S. 549 (1946).
74. *Id.* at 552; *see* Black, *supra* note 40, at 889–91.
75. 347 U.S. 483 (1954).
76. 163 U.S. 537 (1896).
77. 445 U.S. 263 (1980).
78. 103 S. Ct. 3001 (1983).
79. *Id.* at 3013, 3016.
80. 372 U.S. 335 (1963).
81. *See* Alsup, *supra* note 9, at 1334.

upon *Gideon* as a proper vehicle for carrying out its intention to overrule *Betts v. Brady.*[82] Under the proposed system, not all of those petitions would have been presented to the Court and, as a result, the Court's "menu of vehicles" for reviewing the issue would have been limited, making it less likely that an appropriate case would have been found.[83] Had the Supreme Court been denied access to these and other cases, the shape of constitutional law today would have been drastically altered.[84]

Efforts to restrict the jurisdiction of the Supreme Court by statute or to delegate specific issues for final resolution by an inferior court—either a permanent new court or a rotating panel of judges—present additional public policy problems. Lower court judges may not have the stature or detachment required to address the highly explosive social and economic issues of which the Supreme Court is the ultimate arbiter. Justices who reach the pinnacle of the judicial system bring with them, acquire, or have "thrust upon them" (by virtue of their unreviewable, life-tenured authority) an aura of detached wisdom. Such proposals misapprehend the unique function that the Supreme Court plays in our constitutional democracy.[85] The Supreme Court is not the final court of errors and appeals. In the words of the Freund Committee:

> The cases which it is the primary duty of the Court to decide are those that, by hypothesis, present the most fundamental and difficult issues of law and judgment. . . . To maintain

82. 316 U.S. 455 (1942), *overruled*, Gideon v. Wainwright, 372 U.S. 335 (1963); *see* Alsup, *supra* note 9, at 1334.

83. Alsup, *supra* note 9, at 1334.

84. For other cases that might not have been chosen by an intermediary supercourt of appeals because strong precedent existed, consider: Flast v. Cohen, 392 U.S. 83, 102–3 (1968) (taxpayers have standing to challenge spending programs on the ground that they exceed "specific constitutional limitations imposed upon the exercise of the congressional taxing and spending power"), in light of Frothingham v. Mellon, 262 U.S. 447, 488 (1923) (absent direct injury, taxpayer lacks standing to challenge Acts of Congress); Yates v. United States, 354 U.S. 298, 318 (1957) (abstract advocacy of government overthrow not actionable under Smith Act absent incitement to action), in light of Dennis v. United States, 341 U.S. 494, 516–17 (1951) (advocacy of future government overthrow actionable under the Smith Act); and New York Times Co. v. Sullivan, 376 U.S. 254, 279–80 (1964) (establishing "actual malice" requirement for recovery by a public official in a libel action), in light of Near v. Minnesota, 283 U.S. 697, 715 (1931) (libelous statements are not protected by first amendment). *See* Black, *supra* note 40, at 888–90 (1974).

Other cases might well have been judged too trivial for Supreme Court review. It is hard to imagine that the proposed intermediary court would have referred to the Supreme Court the "Shuffling Sam" case, Thompson v. City of Louisville, 362 U.S. 199 (1960), in which a loitering conviction was overturned on due process grounds for lack of evidentiary support. Similarly, Cohen v. California, 403 U.S. 15 (1971), would almost certainly have been a casualty of an intermediary supercourt of appeals. How many judges on such a court would have found the First Amendment right to wear a jacket bearing the words "Fuck the Draft" into a courthouse consequential enough to merit the Supreme Court's attention? *See* Alsup, *supra* note 9, at 1313.

85. As Professor Black aptly remarked, "[t]he authors of [the Report of the Study Group] are recommending amputation of the right arm as a cure for overweight" when they suggest that vesting the screening function in another court will cure the Supreme Court's caseload problem. Black, *supra* note 40, at 891.

> the constitutional order the Court must decide controversies that have sharply divided legislators, lawyers, and the public. And in deciding, the Court must strive to understand and elucidate the complexities of the issues, to give direction to the law, and to be as precise, persuasive, and invulnerable as possible in its exposition.[86]

The issue is not whether there should be limitations on access to the Supreme Court; obviously there must be. As the number of cases increases, the percentage which can be reviewed in the Supreme Court correspondingly diminishes. The Supreme Court, however, need not foreclose its power to make important judgments in certain jurisdictional areas. Rather, it should retain the discretion to choose the issues worthy of its review in the broadest possible jurisdictional environment. An inferior court simply cannot bring to significant national issues the experience of collegial interaction and moral authority necessary to sustain the independence of its actions. Nor should a national appellate court be established merely to correct the errors of other appellate courts. If this were its function, the ultimate effect would be an erosion of respect for the federal appellate courts—courts which historically have attracted jurists of great distinction. It is one thing for a great jurist like Learned Hand to be overruled by the Supreme Court; it would be quite a different matter for him to be overruled by a rotating panel of judges. The primary responsibility for correcting errors should rest with the circuit courts. A solution to the Supreme Court's workload problem is needed, however, which both preserves and enhances the ability of the Court to perform its core constitutional responsibilities.

An Alternative Proposal

The Supreme Court must be freed from the illusion that it has a duty to correct every error and resolve every conflict. At the same time, the Court needs to identify and resolve legal issues of fundamental national significance in a clear and consistent manner. The proposal outlined below achieves these goals and consists of four interrelated parts.

1. The Supreme Court's remaining mandatory appellate jurisdiction should be limited to constitutional cases in which fundamental human rights raising an issue of nationwide divisiveness are involved.[87] The Court should be the guardian of its docket and not be forced by statute to take for argument and decision any case which it otherwise would determine is not of prime national importance.
2. Conflicts among the circuit courts that do not involve issues worthy of Supreme Court review should be resolved by the affected circuits without any involvement of the Court.

86. Report of the Study Group, *supra* note 36, at 1.

87. Rather than eliminating mandatory jurisdiction, it is preferable to limit it to narrower circumstances. *See* American Law Division (Congressional Research Service), Report on Mandatory Appellate Jurisdiction of the Supreme Court of the United States 62 (Preliminary Draft June 18, 1982) (available in files of *Fordham Law Review*).

3. The Supreme Court should be highly selective in choosing for review only issues of fundamental national significance.
4. The Supreme Court should reduce the pressure on its caseload by discouraging unnecessary litigation (and invitations to unfocused arguments on the part of the bar) through the exercise of greater judicial restraint, collegial deference, and disciplined opinion writing by the Justices.

The first and second parts of the proposal are intended to reduce the flow of cases that the Supreme Court now feels obligated to review even though they do not involve issues of prime national importance.

Reducing the Number of Cases Presented for Review It has been estimated that mandatory appeals constitute about 25 percent of the Court's caseload.[88] Enactment of H.R. 1968[89] and S. 645[90] would replace the Court's remaining mandatory appellate jurisdiction with discretionary review, thus reducing the number of cases the Court *must* review each year. Elimination of mandatory jurisdiction, except in truly rare situations, is necessary[91] to complete the conversion of the Supreme Court—started by the Act of 1891[92] and accelerated by the Judges' Bill of 1925[93]—from a final court of errors and appeals to the ultimate judicial authority on issues of fundamental national significance. The one exception to the total elimination of mandatory jurisdiction, necessary to preserve the core constitutional responsibility of the Court, would be to mandate review of those cases in which a lower court has upheld the constitutionality of a state or federal statute denying fundamental human rights of a truly divisive national character. Because the Supreme Court is the ultimate vindicator of such rights under the Constitution, it would not be consistent with the Court's constitutional responsibility to avoid such issues through the discretionary denial of review. History teaches that the ability to avoid an issue may be too facile a solution to a politically uncomfortable situation—a solution too readily available and too often seized by the legislative and executive branches of government. Mandatory judicial review has forced some of the great civil rights gains of the past.[94]

88. Comments of Justice O'Connor, *supra* note 7, at 12. For an even higher estimate of cases arising out of mandatory appeals see H.R. Rep. No. 824, pt. I, 97th Cong., 2d Sess. 92 app. B. (1982) (36.2%).

89. H.R. 1968, 98th Cong., 1st Sess. (1983).

90. S. 645, 98th Cong., 1st Sess. (1983).

91. The Subcommittee on Courts, Civil Liberties and the Administration of Justice received a letter from all nine Supreme Court Justices recommending that H.R. 6872, a bill curtailing the mandatory appellate jurisdiction of the Supreme Court, be adopted. H.R. Rep. No. 824, pt. I, 97th Cong., 2d Sess. 4 (1982).

92. Circuit Court of Appeals Act of 1891, ch. 517, 26 Stat. 826.

93. Ch. 229, 43 Stat. 936.

94. *See, e.g.*, Roe v. Wade, 410 U.S. 113 (1973); Brown v. Board of Educ., 347 U.S. 483 (1954).

Alternatives for Resolving Inter-Circuit Conflicts The second part of the proposal also reduces the number of cases that require Supreme Court review. It simply is not necessary, in the fulfillment of its constitutional responsibilities, for the Supreme Court to act as an arbitrator among conflicting circuit courts unless the issues are of fundamental national significance. Justice O'Connor has estimated that 23.7% of the Supreme Court's decided cases during her first term involved "interpretation[s] of statutes on which the lower courts had reached conflicting decisions."[95] Professor Schaefer has concluded that there are more than one hundred conflicting statutory interpretations among circuit court decisions each year.[96] In a recent term, of the 149 cases in which the Supreme Court granted plenary review, 26 involved conflicts among the circuits on the issue presented.[97] There is a growing consensus that another mechanism is needed to resolve these conflicts. Suggested mechanisms range from the Chief Justice's proposal for a temporary national panel[98] to Justice White's proposal for a mandatory en banc hearing.[99]

The approach suggested in this article is a variation on these proposals, which is designed to augment the underlying theme of these reforms: the resolution of legal conflict through collegial reason and the search for consensus. Whenever a circuit renders a decision that is in conflict with a prior decision of another circuit, the losing party should be allowed to petition the court issuing the conflicting opinion for a rehearing before a panel of seven judges, three from each of the two circuits which gave rise to the conflict, and a seventh to be assigned from another circuit by the Chief Justice.[100] Judges from the two circuits in conflict thus would participate in an en banc rehearing to resolve the conflict.[101] The decision of the en banc panel would constitute binding precedent on all circuits, subject only to discretionary review by the Supreme Court if an issue of fundamental national importance is presented. Should a third circuit fail to follow the precedent established by the inter-circuit en banc hearing,[102] the petitioner could request an

95. Comments of Justice O'Connor, *supra* note 7, at 13.

96. Schaefer, *Reducing Circuit Conflicts*, 69 A.B.A.J. 452, 454 (1983).

97. Wallace, *The Nature and Extent of Intercircuit Conflicts: A Solution Needed for a Mountain or a Molehill?*, 71 Calif. L. Rev. 913, 938 (1983).

98. *See Annual Report*, *supra* note 1, at 447.

99. *See* Brennan I, *supra* note 7, at 232 (quoting Justice White). It has also been suggested that reducing the number of circuit courts could reduce the number of inter-circuit conflicts. Wallace, *supra* note 98, at 940.

100. The Chief Justice is authorized to "assign temporarily any circuit judge to act as circuit judge in another circuit." 28 U.S.C. § 291(a) (1976).

101. Circuit judges are authorized by 28 U.S.C. § 46(c) (1976) to sit en banc within a single circuit, but the statute makes no reference to inter-circuit en banc hearings. Hence, legislation would be required to effect this portion of the proposal.

102. The decision of the inter-circuit en banc court would be binding precedent for all other circuits. It is therefore hoped that the need for the further procedure set forth above would be rare indeed.

en banc hearing by seven judges, two from each of the three circuits that had addressed the issue and one assigned by the Chief Justice. While this approach would require legislation,[103] it is preferred to the alternatives that have been proposed because:

1. it avoids the creation of a new court or the enlargement of the new Federal Circuit Court by a special panel of twenty-six judges;
2. it promotes judicial efficiency and consistency because the issue has already been briefed and argued before at least three of the judges conducting the rehearing;
3. it forces the judges who disagree with their peers to confront, discuss and, it is hoped, resolve their differences;
4. it does not elevate a group of circuit court judges to a special panel to sit in judgment on their peers;
5. it avoids involving the Supreme Court except for the Chief Justice's strictly administrative task of designating one of the circuit judges; and
6. it does not create the public impression of a "supercourt," without the attributes of the Supreme Court, that would undermine public respect for the circuit courts.

The long-term effect of bringing the differing circuit judges together would be a greater respect on the part of federal appellate judges for the precedents of other circuits. Indeed, such respect should be encouraged by the Supreme Court through its rules and decisions. There are no inherent geographic or political reasons why federal judges in the thirteen circuits should apply federal statutes differently in response to local circumstances.[104] The argument that circuit conflicts help sharpen the issues for Supreme Court review or provide a testing ground for various interpretations is, in a word, foolish. In any event, such an argument is far outweighed by the injustice, chaos, and burden of litigation caused by conflicting statutory interpretations. The words of Eighth Circuit Judge Lay in *Aldens Inc. v. Miller*[105] are instructive:

> As an appellate court, we strive to maintain uniformity in the law among the circuits, wherever reasoned analysis will allow, thus avoiding unnecessary burdens on the Supreme Court docket. Unless our . . . courts of appeals are thus willing to promote a cohesive network of national law, needless division and confusion will encourage further splintering and the formation of otherwise unnecessary additional tiers in the framework of our national court system.[106]

103. While "[t]he Supreme Court and all courts established by Act of Congress may from time to time prescribe rules for the conduct of their business" under the authority of 28 U.S.C. § 2071 (1976), nowhere are they given express authority to hold inter-circuit en banc hearings. The Court cannot alter its own jurisdiction.

104. *See* Schaefer, *supra* note 97, at 454.

105. 610 F.2d 538 (8th Cir. 1979), *cert. denied*, 446 U.S. 919 (1980).

106. *Id.* at 541.

These two proposals—if the earlier cited estimates of conflict and mandatory jurisdiction cases are correct—could reduce the number of cases argued before the Court by up to 47 percent.[107]

Concentrating Supreme Court Decision-Making The third suggestion is, in large measure, an acknowledgment of what has become a reality. Since Congress enacted the Judges Bill of 1925,[108] the Supreme Court has not been expected to take on the "function . . . of primarily—or even largely—correcting errors committed by other courts."[109] The value of Supreme Court decision-making is not in how many individual disputes are resolved, but rather in the clarity and cohesiveness of the legal guidance it provides the highest courts of the various states, the lower federal and state courts and the political branches of government.

As Congress reacts to media events and special interest pleas, and as the executive branch is consumed by "crisis-coping" and "fire-fighting," the importance of a third and independent branch, committed to reflective reasoning and to a rational search for sometimes elusive constitutional values increases. As Justice Holmes once said:

> The best defense for leaving fundamental responsibilities to this Court came from Brandeis . . . that constitutional restrictions enable a man to sleep at night and know that he won't be robbed before morning—which, in days of legislative activity and general scheming, otherwise, he scarcely would feel sure about.[110]

Individuals selected to fulfill this constitutional mandate need not necessarily be judges by experience, although Justices Holmes and Stewart, among others, demonstrated that appointments from the judiciary often function superbly. Some of the greatest Justices—to speak only of those no longer on the bench—have come from academic halls (Frankfurter), from the practicing bar (Brandeis and Harlan), and from the political process (John Marshall, Warren, and Black).[111] Justice Frankfurter once wrote that a Justice must have "poetic sensibilities" and the "gift of imagination."[112] He must "pierce the curtain of the

107. See *supra* notes 89, 96 and accompanying text (25% of the caseload are cases arising out of mandatory jurisdiction and 23.7% involve inter-circuit conflicts).

108. Ch. 229, 43 Stat. 936.

109. Stevens II, *supra* note 48, at 180. "It is far better to allow the state supreme courts and federal courts of appeals to have the final say on almost all litigation than to embark on the hopeless task of attempting to correct every judicial error that can be found." *Id.*

110. Letter from O.W. Holmes to Felix Frankfurter, Holmes Papers, Harvard Law School (April 20, 1921) (quoted in A. Bickel, The Supreme Court and the Idea of Progress 28 (1970)) [hereinafter cited as A. Bickel I].

111. Prior to his service on the Supreme Court, Justice Frankfurter was a professor at the Harvard Law School. Congressional Quarterly, Guide to the Supreme Court 851. Justices Brandeis and Harlan were in private practice. *Id.* at 842–43, 859. Justice John Marshall served in the Virginia House of Delegates, as minister to France, and as a member of the U.S. House of Representatives. *Id.* at 804. Chief Justice Warren served both as attorney general and governor of California. *Id.* at 858. Justice Black was a member of the U.S. Senate. *Id.* at 849.

112. F. Frankfurter, *Of Law and Men* 39 (1956) (quoted in A. Bickel I, *supra* note 111, at 38).

future . . . and give shape and visage to mysteries still in the womb of time."[113] To enable each Justice to contribute a unique perspective and reasoned insight requires "ample time," again in the words of Justice Frankfurter, "and freshness of mind for private study and reflection in preparation for discussion at Conference."[114] As Professor Thomas Reed Powell of the Harvard Law School wrote, "[t]he logic of constitutional law is the common sense of the Supreme Court of the United States."[115]

No Plimsoll line can be established which helps the Court to discharge its difficult responsibilities. With many of the issues with which it deals—for example, due process, just compensation, equal protection—the Court is left with the need for intuitive judgment. According to Justice Powell, however, simply coping with the rising caseload may require a Justice during the busy opinion writing months of May and June to work "twelve to fifteen hours a day, six days [a] week."[116] Such a schedule simply is not conducive to quiet reflection or sound judgment.[117] The answer is not to relegate the Justices, like too many senators and cabinet officers, to the role of managers of an ever-expanding staff.[118] Rather, the Court should limit the number of cases that it decides on the merits each year to a manageable number, allowing sufficient time for discussion, common sense reflection, and clarity of presentation. As Justice Stevens has noted, the Supreme Court's caseload could be reduced significantly by stricter adherence to the doctrine of judicial restraint.[119] Very simply, if it is not necessary to decide the issue—if the issue is not ripe for review—the Court should not undertake to decide it, for as Alexander Bickel said, "[n]o answer is what the wrong question begets."[120] There are, moreover, some issues that the Court simply need not address. In *Sakraida v. Ag Pro, Inc.*,[121] the Supreme Court granted certiorari to decide the validity of respondent's patent covering a water flush system to remove cow manure from the floor of a dairy barn. The Court's holding that the system "did not produce a 'new or different function' . . . within the test of validity of combination patents"[122] was certainly helpful to the litigants involved but hardly an issue of prime national importance.

113. *Id.*

114. Dick v. New York Life Ins. Co, 359 U.S. 437, 458 (1959) (Frankfurter, J., dissenting).

115. Powell, *The Logic and Rhetoric of Constitutional Law*, 15 J. Phil. Psychology & Sci. Method 645, 646 (1918) (quoted in A. Bickel I, *supra* note 111, at 20).

116. Powell, *supra* note 7, at 1372.

117. Hart, *The Supreme Court, 1958 Term—Forward: The Time Chart of the Justices*, 73 Harv. L. Rev. 84, 99–100 (1959).

118. Justice Brandeis once observed: "The reason the public thinks so much of the Justices of the Supreme Court is that they are almost the only people in Washington who do their own work." C. Wyzanski, Whereas—A Judge's Premises 61 (1965) (remark of Justice Brandeis) (quoted in Remarks of Justice Rehnquist, *supra*, note 10, at 27).

119. Stevens II, *supra* note 48, at 180; *see* Ashwander v. Tennessee Valley Authority, 297 U.S. 288, 341, 345–48 (1936) (Brandeis, J. concurring).

120. A. Bickel, The Least Dangerous Branch 103 (1962).

121. 425 U.S. 273 (1976).

122. *Id.* at 282 *(quoting* Anderson's Black Rock v. Pavement Salvage Co., 396 U.S. 57, 60 (1969)).

Justices Brennan and Stevens have publicly cited the school library case, *Board of Education v. Pico*,[123] as an example of the type of case the Supreme Court should not take.[124] The issue there was whether the First Amendment restrained the school board in the removal of books from a school library.[125] After the district judge granted the school board summary judgment,[126] the Second Circuit reversed on the ground that the case presented a genuine issue of fact as to the school board's motivation.[127] Further proceedings by the trial court would have clarified the constitutional issue and perhaps mooted the entire case.[128] Yet the Supreme Court took the case at the interlocutory stage, disposed of it by affirming the remand for trial and filed seven separate opinions, none of which commanded the votes of a majority. The Supreme Court addressed a constitutional issue prematurely, and in such a confusing and ambiguous manner that it undoubtedly will stimulate a great deal of litigation in search of a clearer set of guiding principles. As Justice Marshall, one of only two Justices who did not write a separate opinion in *Pico*, commented, "it may be pretty difficult for the lower courts, or anyone else, to figure out exactly what the decision stands for."[129] Perhaps when the Court took the case for review it thought that a consensus could be achieved, but after briefing and argument that consensus proved impossible. The Court then should have considered a summary remand.

Another type of case that the Supreme Court need not review involves issues limited to a specific geographical area. In *Watt v. Alaska*,[130] for example, the Supreme Court reviewed a dispute between Alaska and one of its counties over the division of mineral leasing revenues[131]—a dispute that could only arise in the Ninth Circuit. While there may have been an error by the court below, this was not a sufficient reason for Supreme Court review of a decision that did not have any implications beyond Alaska.

Cases that are factually unique also need not be reviewed. In *Oregon v. Kennedy*,[132] for example, five Justices volunteered a new double jeopardy doctrine[133] even though the Oregon Court of Appeals had misapplied the doctrine to a peculiar set of facts unlikely to be duplicated elsewhere.[134] The Supreme Court's pronouncement was totally unnecessary

123. 457 U.S. 853 (1982).

124. Brennan I, *supra* note 7, at 231; Stevens II, *supra* note 48, at 180.

125. 457 U.S. at 855–56.

126. *See id.* at 859.

127. *Id.* at 860–61.

128. Brennan I, *supra* note 7, at 232.

129. Remarks of Justice Marshall, Second Circuit Judicial Conference, at 2 (Sept. 9, 1982) (available in files of *Fordham Law Review*).

130. 451 U.S. 259 (1981).

131. *Id.* at 263.

132. 456 U.S. 667 (1982).

133. *Id.* at 679.

134. Stevens II, *supra* note 48, at 180.

to the resolution of the specific case. Moreover, the Oregon court was free to reinstate its prior judgment by relying on Oregon rather than federal law.[135]

135. *Id.* Another example of the Court's lack of judicial restraint may be found in Snepp v. United States, 444 U.S. 507 (1980) (per curiam). There the court below had held that Snepp's publication of a book about Vietnam had violated his secrecy agreement with the CIA. *Id.* at 508. The government opposed Snepp's petition for certiorari and filed a conditional cross-petition, praying that if the Court granted Snepp's petition it also should consider whether the remedy ordered by the lower court was adequate. *Id.* at 524 (Stevens, J., dissenting). The Supreme Court granted both petitions, but summarily dismissed Snepp's claim, *id.*, and without hearing argument on the merits, issued a per curiam opinion ordering that a constructive trust be imposed on the book's earnings even though there was neither a statutory nor a contractual basis for this novel remedy. *Id.* at 517–18 (Stevens, J., dissenting). Since the government had not even asked the Court to review the remedy issue unless it granted Snepp's petition, this was a clear example of the Court's unnecessary exercise of power. Stevens II, *supra* note 48, at 181. Another example is Michigan v. Long, 103 S. Ct. 3469 (1983), in which the Supreme Court reversed and remanded a decision by the Michigan Supreme Court because the lower court had given too restrictive an interpretation to federal constitutional law. *Id.* at 3478–82. The Court, notwithstanding similar provisions in the Michigan Constitution, held that absent clear evidence in the lower court opinion of adequate state law grounds, the Court will presume that the decision is based on federal law. *Id.* at 3476. Justice Stevens dissented, not only because of the Court's adoption of "presumptive jurisdiction" but because the Court should not be concerned with a state court decision which provides greater protection to a citizen than is required by the Constitution. *Id.* at 3489–90. Justice Stevens wrote:

> Even if I agreed with the Court that we are free to consider as a fresh proposition whether we may take presumptive jurisdiction over the decisions of sovereign states, I could not agree that an expansive attitude makes good sense. It appears to be common ground that any rule we adopt should show "respect for state courts, and [a] desire to avoid advisory opinions." . . . And I am confident that all members of this Court agree that there is a vital interest in the sound management of scarce federal judicial resources. All of those policies counsel against the exercise of federal jurisdiction. They are fortified by my belief that a policy of judicial restraint—one that allows other decisional bodies to have the last word in legal interpretation until it is truly necessary for this Court to intervene—enables this Court to make its most effective contribution to our federal system of government.
>
> The nature of the case before us hardly compels a departure from tradition. These are not cases in which an American citizen has been deprived of a right secured by the United States Constitution or a federal statute. Rather, they are cases in which a state court has upheld a citizen's assertion of a right, finding the citizen to be protected under both federal and state law. The complaining party is an officer of the state itself, who asks us to rule that the state court interpreted federal rights too broadly and "overprotected" the citizen.
>
> Until recently we had virtually no interest in cases of this type. . . . Sometime during the past decade . . . our priorities shifted. The result is a docket swollen with requests by states to reverse judgments that their courts have rendered in favor of their citizens. I am confident that a future Court will recognize the error of this allocation of resources. When that day comes, I think it likely that the court will also reconsider the propriety of today's expansion of our jurisdiction.

Id. at 3490–91 (Stevens, J., dissenting) (footnotes omitted).

These cases clearly illustrate the need for more disciplined case selection and opinion writing. Each decision of the Supreme Court should be a uniquely crafted work of art; even the dissenting views, like contrasting colors and offsetting shadows, should contribute to the clarity and vitality of the whole. It is hoped the Court's archetypes would tend more toward the harmony of Monet and clarity of Rembrandt than the harried spontaneity of Pollock or discordance of Kandinsky.

Collegial Analysis: Reaching a Consensus The most significant opportunity to reduce the Supreme Court's caseload may ultimately be through disciplined opinion writing and collegial deference in the rendering of decisions. In selecting cases for review, the Court should consider whether members of the Court are prepared to work together to clarify and advance the state of the law. The subtle judgments and mutual deference involved in this process spring from the Court's deeply embedded traditions and the practical wisdom of its finest members. One such great exemplar was Justice Brandeis, of whom his former law clerk, Paul Freund, has written:

> For Brandeis almost the paramount quality of a good judge was the capacity to be reached by reason, the freedom from self-pride that without embarrassment permits a change of mind. It was this quality of open-mindedness which made Justice Pitney, who was in many respects poles apart from Brandeis, an especially respected colleague. The constructive influence of Brandeis in the councils of the Court owed much to his high boiling point, his self-control which, when excessively taxed, was able to convert the fire within him into the heat of dry ice.[136]

The unpublished opinions of Justice Brandeis, as analyzed by Alexander Bickel, provide useful insight into the collegial decision making of past Courts and the judgment involved in deciding whether to dissent.[137] Brandeis had been assigned to write the Court's opinion in *St. Louis Iron Mountain & Southern Railway Co. v. Starbird*,[138] concerning the question whether the Supreme Court had jurisdiction to review a state court's decision if a federal right had not been expressly asserted in the state court below. Brandeis wrote a draft opinion denying jurisdiction, but several months later Justice Day issued a unanimous opinion for the Court finding jurisdiction and addressing the merits. Why did Brandeis not dissent? Bickel asserts that Brandeis "suppressed his dissenting views on questions which he considered to be of no great consequence."[139] Similarly, although Brandeis disagreed with the majority in *Gooch v. Oregon Short Line Railroad* Co.,[140] he refrained from dissenting on the grounds that the issue presented—whether a railroad pass

136. Freund, *Introduction* to A. Bickel, The Unpublished Opinions of Mr. Justice Brandeis at xx (1957).

137. *See* A. Bickel, The Unpublished Opinions of Mr. Justice Brandeis *passim* (1957) [hereinafter cited as A. Bickel II].

138. 243 U.S. 592 (1917).

139. A. Bickel II, *supra* note 138, at 28.

140. 258 U.S. 22 (1922).

condition restricted a personal injury claim—was "not important enough to warrant dissent." [141]

In *Starbird*, it is also likely that Brandeis wished to find a more effective context in which to articulate his jurisdictional views, and that he further recognized that a dissent could have focused more sharply the holding with which he differed. As Professor Frankfurter once said: "[T]he scope of a Supreme Court decision is not infrequently revealed by the candor of dissent." [142] Brandeis "suppressed dissents for tactical reasons" [143] and often "referred to Holmes' reluctance to dissent again after he had once had his say on a subject." [144] The Court has often performed magnificently in adjusting the views of its members to avoid dissension on great public issues, particularly when unanimity was important to gain public acceptance. The nation should greatly admire and appreciate the effort, time, and talent which was expended in fashioning a single Court opinion in, inter alia, *Brown v. Board of Education*,[145] *Brown v. Board of Education II*,[146] *Cooper v. Aaron*,[147] *Swann v. Charlotte-Mecklenburg Board of Education*,[148] *United States v. Nixon*,[149] and in achieving near-unanimity (eight to one) in *Bob Jones University v. United States*.[150]

While these cases demonstrate that the Court sometimes has struggled mightily for consensus, there is little public indication that the traditional spirit of collegial deference pervades the Court today. Indeed, as the statistics cited earlier indicate,[151] unanimous decisions may be becoming an "endangered species." Carefully crafted and sparingly used dissents can contribute to the sharpness of the Court's message and even foreshadow its future direction.[152] In some instances, a clear and forceful opinion of the Court accom-

141. A. Bickel II, *supra* note 138, at 28.

142. F. Frankfurter, The Commerce Clause under Marshall, Taney and Waite 106 (1937) (quoted in A. Bickel II, *supra* note 138, at 29).

143. A. Bickel II, *supra* note 138, at 18. Occasionally, however, a dissent may be used tactically to attempt to narrow the precedential value of a decision. Justice Brennan's recent dissent in Brown v. Thomson, 103 S. Ct. 2690 (1983), offers a not too subtle illustration: "Although I disagree with today's holding, it is worth stressing how extraordinarily narrow it is, and how empty of likely precedental value. . . . Hence, although in my view the Court reaches the wrong result in the case at hand, it is unlikely that any future plaintiffs challenging a state reapportionment scheme as unconstitutional will be so unwise as to limit their challenge." *Id.* at 2700 (Brennan, J., dissenting).

144. A. Bickel II, *supra* note 138, at 18.

145. 347 U.S. 483 (1954). The case was first argued on December 9, 1952 but was not decided until May 17, 1954. *Id.* at 483.

146. 349 U.S. 294 (1955).

147. 358 U.S. 1 (1958).

148. 402 U.S. 1 (1971).

149. 418 U.S. 683 (1974).

150. 103 S. Ct. 2017 (1983).

151. *See supra* note 19 and accompanying text.

152. *E.g.*, Plessy v. Ferguson, 163 U.S. 531, 552 (1896) (Harlan, J., dissenting); *see* Brennan, *Justice Brennan Calls National Court of Appeals Proposal "Fundamentally Unnecessary and Ill Advised,"* 59 A.B.A.J. 835, 838 (1973). Justice Brennan's concern that he may not be able to suggest through dissent from a denial of certiorari that substantial issues are presented, *id.*, is countered by Justice

panied by equally lucid and scholarly concurring and dissenting opinions can provide both clarity and realism in evaluating the underlying societal tensions. The Chief Justice's eloquent opinion for the Court in *Immigration & Naturalization Service v. Chadha*,[153] Justice Powell's lucid concurring opinion, and Justice White's scholarly dissent each contribute to public understanding of the legislative veto issue and the true tensions inherent in any future attempt at a legislative solution.

The Court, however, must confront "that 'great difficulty of all group action'—when to dissent, and when to concede and be silent."[154] While concurring opinions may contribute to the development of the law, concurrences such as the one filed by Justice O'Connor in *Commissioner v. Tufts*[155] do little to sharpen the Court's holding. After reciting at length from Professor Barnett's amicus brief, Justice O'Connor concluded: "Persuaded though I am by the logical coherence and internal consistency of this approach, I agree with the Court's decision not to adopt it judicially."[156] Such persistent fragmentation of views and lack of cohesion erode the Court's moral authority, befuddle the beneficiaries of its guidance, and—most relevant here—invite further pressure on its workload.

The confusion begat by fragmentation can be illustrated by the Court's recent decision on the Fourth Amendment's protection against illegal search and seizure in *Florida v. Royer*.[157] Mr. Royer had purchased an airline ticket to New York City at Miami Airport under the name "Holt" and had checked two suitcases bearing this appellation.[158] In the airport concourse, a nervous Royer was approached by two detectives who had observed him and believed that he fit the so-called "drug courier profile."[159] Upon request, but without *oral* consent, Royer produced his airline ticket and driver's license, the latter of which bore his correct name.[160] The detectives then informed Royer that they were narcotics investigators and they suspected he was transporting narcotics.[161] Without returning his ticket or license, they asked him to accompany them to a small room adjacent to the concourse where they retrieved his luggage and requested his consent to search it.[162] Royer did not *orally* consent but provided a key that unlocked one of the suitcases in which marijuana was found.[163]

Stevens' contention that the Supreme Court "shouldn't waste scarce time and energies writing dissents when it denies petitions for review." Wash. Post, Dec. 5, 1978, at A12, col. 1.

153. 103 S. Ct. 2764 (1983).

154. A. Bickel II, *supra* note 138, at 21.

155. 103 S. Ct. 1826, 1836 (1983) (O'Connor, J., concurring).

156. *Id.* at 1837 (O'Connor, J., concurring).

157. 103 S. Ct. 1319 (1983).

158. *Id.* at 1322.

159. *Id.* at 1321–22.

160. *Id.* at 1322.

161. *Id.*

162. *Id.*

163. *Id.*

This is not a unique set of circumstances. Last year, in the Detroit Airport alone, drugs were found in 77 out of 141 searches.[164] Because narcotics smuggling is a serious national problem, clear Supreme Court guidance would be helpful to law enforcement officials and to the lower courts.

It is instructive, therefore, to examine the "guidance" the Court provided through its five separate opinions.[165] In a plurality opinion, Justice White concluded that Royer's detention in the airport concourse was legal, but that his removal to the small room constituted an illegal detention.[166] Thus, although Royer *consented* to the search of his luggage, the consent was tainted by the illegal detention, and therefore ineffective to justify the search.[167] Justice Powell concurred, but concluded that in the "small, windowless room—described as a 'large closet'"[168] Royer's mere surrender of his luggage key did not constitute consent.[169] Concurring in the result, Justice Brennan concluded that the initial stop of Royer in the airport concourse was illegal and that everything thereafter was therefore tainted.[170] Justice Blackmun dissented, arguing that society's interest in the detection of drug traffickers is so great that the detectives did not need to have "probable cause" to detain Royer.[171] Justice Rehnquist, joined by the Chief Justice and Justice O'Connor, also dissented, concluding that under the circumstances the two detectives did have "probable cause" to arrest Royer and that the transfer to a small room and interception of the luggage were consistent with the Fourth Amendment's "reasonableness test."[172]

Despite the five opinions, a law enforcement officer, prosecuting or defense attorney, or lower court has no clear answer to many important questions. For instance, should the law enforcement officers have requested permission to search the suitcases in the open public concourse rather than transferring Royer to a small room? If the room had been large and spacious, rather than small and windowless, would the officers' conduct have been reasonable? If the officers had returned Royer's ticket and driver's license, would the encounter have been consensual? If Royer had orally agreed to open the suitcase, would this have been sufficient?

The Supreme Court's resolution of the *Royer* case, some might say, represents the intellectual jousting of a debating society, each Justice spinning his own web of procedural distinctions from the Court's esoteric Fourth Amendment jurisprudence.[173] It fails to exhibit any collegial attempt at consensus on basic principles. It is devoid of real guidance

164. *Id.* at 1339 n.6 (Rehnquist, J., dissenting).

165. Florida v. Royer, 103 S. Ct. 1319 (1983) (plurality opinion of White, J., at 1321; concurring opinion of Powell, J., at 1329; concurring opinion of Brennan, J., at 1330; dissenting opinion of Blackmun, J., at 1332; dissenting opinion of Rehnquist, J., at 1336).

166. *Id.* at 1326.

167. *Id.* at 1326–27.

168. *Id.* at 1330 (Powell, J., concurring).

169. *Id.*

170. *Id.* at 1331–32 (Brennan, J., concurring).

171. *Id.* at 1332. (Blackmun, J., dissenting).

172. *Id.* at 1337 (Rehnquist, J., dissenting).

173. *See* Will, *Justice Squints*, Wash. Post, Mar. 31, 1983, at A23, col. 5.

for officers and lawyers, and invites further litigation to resolve the ambiguities it has created. Furthermore, having upheld a similar airport drug search in 1980 in *United States v. Mendenhall*,[174] the Supreme Court was not under any compulsion to revisit the issue.[175]

The Supreme Court should have denied certiorari in *Royer*. If it did not become apparent until after certiorari was granted that the case did not present the best opportunity to revisit the issue of airport drug searches, the Supreme Court could have disposed of the case summarily in a per curiam affirmance of the judgment below (perhaps stating that an opinion would not be written because there was no consensus on the issue). Alternatively, the Court should have admitted its mistake in granting certiorari and reversed the grant. The Court's action in *Illinois v. Gates*,[176] for example, despite criticism from the press,[177] was clearly correct. The Justices simply announced that the Court would not rule on the controversial law enforcement questions presented because "[t]hey had picked the wrong case."[178]

A month after *Royer*, the Supreme Court, in a similar display of fragmentation, applied the "plain view" doctrine to a police officer's seizure of a drug-filled green party balloon from respondent's automobile.[179] Justice Rehnquist—joined by Chief Justice Burger, Justice White, and Justice O'Connor—maintained that seizure of the balloon did not constitute a violation of the Fourth Amendment.[180] Justice Powell, joined by Justice Blackmun, concurred, arguing that the plain view doctrine articulated in *Coolidge v. New Hampshire*[181] was dispositive of the issue presented.[182] Justice Stevens, joined by Justices Brennan and Marshall, wrote a separate concurring opinion pointing out that the state would have to justify opening the balloon without a warrant before the balloon's contents could be used as evidence.[183] In a one-paragraph concurrence, Justice White noted his continued disagreement with the views of four Justices in *Coolidge* that plain view seizures

174. 446 U.S. 544 (1980).

175. Subsequent to *Royer*, the Supreme Court again granted certiorari in an airport drug seizure case. In United States v. Place, 103 S. Ct. 2637 (1983), six Justices were able to agree that detaining a suspect's luggage for over ninety minutes was not reasonable in the absence of probable cause. In contrast to *Royer*, this case is a good example of the type of clear guidance a more cohesive opinion can provide.

176. 103 S. Ct. 2317 (1983). The issue in *Gates* was whether the exclusionary rule should be modified to allow the introduction of illegally obtained evidence, when that evidence was obtained in the good faith belief that the search and seizure in question complied with the requirements of the Fourth Amendment. *Id.* at 2321. The Court declined to decide this issue because it had not been presented to or decided by the Illinois Court. *Id.*

177. *See, e.g.*, Barbash, *High Court Feared Issuing the Right Ruling in the Wrong Case*, WASH. POST, June 10, 1983, at A7, col. 1.

178. *Id.*

179. Texas v. Brown, 103 S. Ct. 1535 (1983).

180. *Id.* at 1541–44.

181. 403 U.S. 443 (1971).

182. Texas v. Brown, 103 S. Ct. 1535, 1544–45 (1983) (Powell, J., concurring).

183. *Id.* at 1547 (Stevens, J., concurring).

are only valid if inadvertent.[184] Although there were no dissents, the four separate opinions, none of which reflected the views of a Court majority, completely diffused the practical value of any guidance provided by the Court.

Perhaps the classic example of fragmentation occurred in *Regents of the University of California v. Bakke*.[185] Two different five-to-four majorities decided the two main issues in the case,[186] resulting in six separate opinions.[187] Even though Justices Marshall, White, and Blackmun joined Justice Brennan in his opinion, they each also wrote their own separate opinions.[188] The resultant 156 pages left the law regarding affirmative action in medical school admissions in a state of reasoned ambiguity.

The substantial increase in the number of separate opinions in cases such as *Royer*, *Brown*, and *Bakke* adds fuel to the flames of a litigious population by inviting litigants throughout the federal system to press for particular points of view that have some support on the Court.[189] As the statistics recited earlier[190] suggest, there is less cohesion and unity of purpose on today's Court. Some of this dissension may be explained by the diversity of backgrounds and perspectives on the present Court, the increased complexity of the social and technical issues that are presented to the Court today (in contrast to the Courts on which Hughes, Holmes, and Brandeis sat), and the tendency of Congress to "punt" on too many controversial issues. But the outside observer sees too little evidence of a genuine effort by the Justices to work out their differences in conference rather than spell them out in separate opinions.[191] Ironically, the Supreme Court, as Justice Frankfurter reminded us, derives its authority not from the exercise of power or control of the purse, but through

184. *Id.* at 1544 (White, J., concurring).

185. 438 U.S. 265 (1978).

186. *Id.* at 271–72; *see* Tribe, *Comment, Perspectives on Bakke: Equal Protection, Procedural Fairness, or Structural Justice?*, 92 Harv. L. Rev. 864, 864 (1979).

187. Regents of the Univ. of Cal. v. Bakke, 438 U.S. 265 (1978) (Opinion of Powell, J., at 269; opinion of Brennan, J., Marshall, J., White, J., and Blackmun, J., concurring in part and dissenting in part, at 324; opinion of White, J., at 379; opinion of Marshall, J., at 387; opinion of Blackmun, J., at 402; opinion of Stevens, J., concurring in part and dissenting in part, at 408).

188. *See supra* note 188.

189. *See* N.Y. Times, July 9, 1982, at A1, col. 2. In the 1981 term, thirty-three cases were decided by a one-vote margin as compared to the previous term in which seventeen cases were decided by a one-vote margin. *Id.* In the 1982 term, thirty-three cases were decided by a one-vote margin. *See* Appendix, Chart I.

190. Between 1955 and 1982, the Supreme Court issued approximately "three times as many plurality decisions as were issued in the entire previous history of the Court." Wallace, *supra* note 98, at 921 (citing Note, *Plurality Decisions and Judicial Decisionmakings*, 94 Harv. L. Rev. 1127, 1127 n.1, 1147 (1981)).

191. Unless the Justices routinely employ tact and diplomacy in order to establish convincing majorities, court decisions may resemble a "restricted railroad ticket, good for this day and train only." *See* Smith v. Allwright, 321 U.S. 649, 669 (1944) (Roberts, J., dissenting). *See supra* notes 18–20 and accompanying text.

its capacity to gain the consent of the governed to a reasoned, ordered process of dispute resolution.[192]

It does little to aid the Court's image as the ultimate dispute resolver when the Justices themselves cannot refrain from engaging in attacks on one another's positions. An example of this sort of internal bickering is the 5-4 decision in *FERC v. Mississippi*.[193] Justice Blackmun, writing for the Court, referred to Justice O'Connor's "purported distinctions" as "little more than exercises in the art of *ipse dixit*."[194] Justice O'Connor, in her partial dissent, referred to Justice Blackmun's choice between the states' abandoning regulation of public utilities or complying with a federal statute as "an absurdity, for if [the] analysis is sound, the Constitution no longer limits federal regulation of state governments."[195] Justice Blackmun recently noted that on such close votes, "[y]ou're locked in combat. It's competitive to that degree. . . . But I think, clearly, this is an educational process—and I would hope that one matures as the years go by."[196]

There are, of course, times when a clear and forceful dissent contributes greatly to public understanding of the law, but dissents should be saved for such occasions. One should not advocate that the fiercely independent intellects that constitute today's Supreme Court consign themselves to the lowest common denominator of compromise. Nor should attempts at accommodation resort to intentional ambiguities like the legislative ambiguities created by House-Senate conferences. If clarity and candor are best served by dissenting opinions, then a dissent is preferable to disingenuous accommodation. Often unanimity is not obtained by scientists, even on matters subject to objective proof. One cannot expect that the Justices will always achieve harmonious consent on difficult philosophical, economic, and governmental matters. As Chief Justice Hughes stated in 1936:

> How amazing it is that, in the midst of controversies on every conceivable subject, one should expect unanimity of opinion upon difficult legal questions! In the highest ranges of thought, in theology, philosophy and science, we find differences of view on the part of the most distinguished experts,—theologians, philosophers and scientists. The history of scholarship is a record of disagreements. And when we deal with questions relating to principles of law and their application, we do not suddenly rise into a stratosphere of icy certainty.[197]

But the heritage of the law—particularly the common law—is that objective neutral principles can be applied by well-trained lawyers to reach a correct judgment. It would be less than candid not to suggest that the Supreme Court could do much to reduce the

192. *See* N. Dawson, Louis D. Brandeis, Felix Frankfurter, and the New Deal 2728 (1980).

193. 456 U.S. 742 (1982).

194. *Id.* at 762 n.27.

195. *Id.* at 781 (O'Connor, J., concurring in part and dissenting in part).

196. Jenkins, *A Candid Talk with Justice Blackmun*, N.Y. Times, Feb. 20, 1983, § 6 (Magazine), at 20.

197. *Address of Chief Justice Hughes*, 13 Proc. Am. Litigation Inst. 61, 64 (1936), *quoted in* P. Freund, *supra* note 2, at 117 n.2.

pressures of its workload if the Justices would work a little harder at reaching agreement with each other and a little less hard at writing separate opinions.

Paul Freund's description of Justice Brandeis's approach to decision-making illustrates a tradition that has much meaning for today's Court:

> Brandeis exploited to the full the resources available to a judge. . . . He was not an addict of speed in the work of the Supreme Court. Unlike a Holmes or a Cardozo, he was not impatient to turn off an opinion while the frenzy was on him so much as he was anxious that it persuade and instruct. Time for research, documentation, reflection, and the architecture of an opinion was indispensable. . . . [H]e made a practice of distributing his own drafts early in the week, holding them over if necessary lest they reach the brethren too near the time for decision. . . . What emerges from all this is the image of a judge whose strength lay in his power to blend tradition and change, to find in the heritage of the law resources adequate to the needs of the new day, if only there is imagination to see the resources and understanding to see the needs. . . .
>
> The willingness, indeed the temperamental inclination, of Brandeis to work within the received framework of the law, is a clue to his effectiveness in the collective task of decision-making.[198]

CONCLUSION

It is truly ironic for one who feels so deeply that the Court has consistently discharged its constitutional responsibility with more judgment, style, and foresight than any other institution of government to suggest any criticism whatsoever. When the President and Congress avoided the issues, the Court had the courage and foresight to end racial segregation in the public school system, to come to grips with the right of a woman to have an abortion, to recognize that sex discrimination is unacceptable in a constitutional democracy, and to insist upon a fair criminal process. Anyone who knows American history must concede that the Court has performed with a higher standard of excellence than any other institution, state or federal, in this constitutional democracy. The libraries at Oxford, Cambridge, and Harvard undoubtedly contain more critical theses about Shakespeare or Pushkin than any minor writers or poets; the Court must accept the fact that institutions that excel are the subject of continuing critical pressure to attain even greater standards of excellence—perhaps because they are the repository of so many of civilized society's aspirations. In that spirit this conclusion is written.

Much of the answer to the workload problem lies not in the establishment of new institutions but deep in the traditions of the Supreme Court. Congress should give the Court discretion to choose only those few issues of fundamental national importance for review, delegating to the circuit courts the power to resolve lesser conflicts. Like a microcosm of the larger society it reflects, the Supreme Court's success depends on it taking those limited issues and weaving the diverse strands of a complex society into a cohesive fabric. Thus,

198. Freund, *Introduction* to A. Bickel, The Unpublished Opinions of Mr. Justice Brandeis at xviii–xix (1957).

the ultimate objective in the management of the Supreme Court's caseload should be to provide the Justices with the freedom to grapple together as wise individualists in search of common principles rooted in the unfulfilled vision of our Constitution. It is a disciplined search that cautions against needless dissent and pointless contention. As Alexander Bickel has said, society "values the capacity of the judges to draw its attention to issues of largest principle that may have gone unheeded in the welter of its pragmatic doings."[199]

Chart I. Statistics: Supreme Court Opinions*

	1882	1932	1982
1. Total Court Opinions**	260	167	151
—Per Curiam	0	1	11
2. Concurring Opinions	4	4	70
—Concurrences as a percentage of total opinions	1.55%	2.39%	46.35%
3. Dissenting Opinions	17	24	144
—Dissents as a percentage of total opinions	6.58%	14.37%	95.36%
4. Total Separate Opinions	21	28	214
—Separate opinions as a percentage of total opinions	8.13%	16.76%	141.72%
5. Unanimous Decisions	242	133	34
—Unanimous decisions as a percentage of total opinions	93.08%	79.64%	22.52%
6. Five-to-Four Votes	4	3	33
—Five-to-four votes as a percentage of total opinions	1.55%	1.79%	21.85%

* Figures for 1882 and 1932 Terms were compiled by the author's staff from U.S. Reports for those Terms. Figures for the 1982 Term were obtained from the *Harvard Law Review* and will be published in *The Supreme Court, 1982 Term*, 97 HARV. L. REV.—,—(1983).

** Does not include per curiam opinions.

199. A. BICKEL I, *supra* note 111, at 177.

Chart II. United States Supreme Court: Opinions Written*

TERM	OPINIONS OF THE COURT	CONCURRENCES	DISSENTS	TOTAL
1982	151	70	140	361
1981	141	95	135	371
1980	122	91	119	332
1979	132	79	156	367
1978	130	78	122	330
1977	129	81	143	353
1976	126	91	140	357
1975	138	89	126	353
1974	123	51	101	275
1973	140	57	142	339
1972	140	67	178	385
1971	129	69	130	328
1970	106	82	115	303
1969	83	52	70	205
1968	99	67	101	267
1967	110	75	91	276
1966	100	26	97	223
1965	97	37	74	208
1964	91	46	71	208
1963	111	30	77	218
1962	110	40	76	226
1961	84	31	66	181
1960	109	42	111	262
1959	96	26	99	221
1958	98	30	72	200
1957	96	23	93	212
1956	100	18	83	211
1955	73	21	55	149
1954	78	15	47	140
1953	65	16	57	138
1952	104	32	89	225
1951	83	19	73	182
1950	91	23	60	174
1949	87	18	64	169
1948	114	37	93	244

* Source: *The Supreme Court: The Statistics*, 63–97 HARV. L. REV., November issues (1949–1983). These figures do not include per curiam opinions.

Chart III. United States Supreme Court: Number of Opinions*

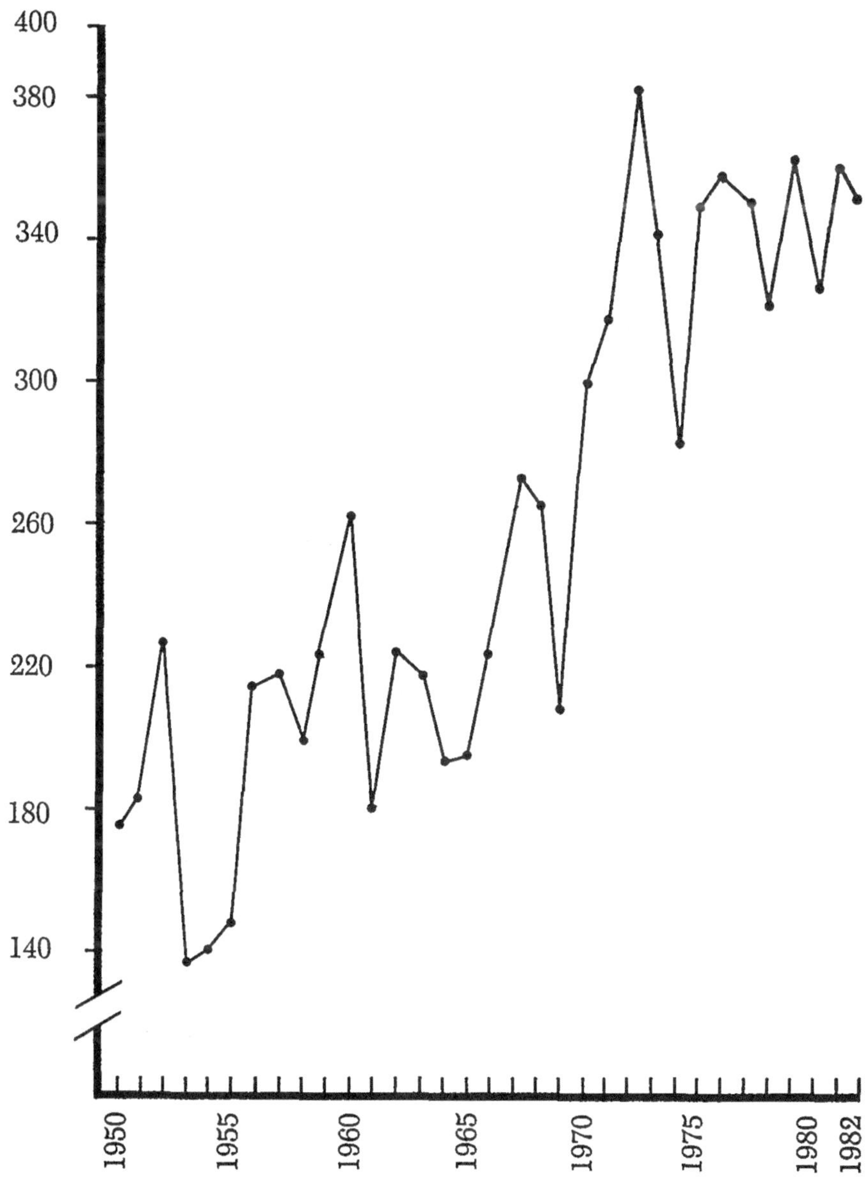

*Source: *The Supreme Court: The Statistics*, 63–97 Harv. L. Rev., November issues (1950–1983). These figures do not include per curiam opinions.

The Office of Chief Judge of a Federal Court of Appeals

Hon. Wilfred Feinberg

Judge Wilfred Feinberg delivered the fourteenth Sonnett lecture, entitled *The Office of Chief Judge of a Federal Court of Appeals*, on October 23, 1984.[1] Born in New York, New York in 1920, Judge Feinberg graduated from Columbia University in 1940.[2] After serving in the army during World War II from 1942 to 1945, Judge Feinberg received his law degree from Columbia Law School, where he was editor-in-chief of the *Columbia Law Review*.[3] Upon graduating in 1946, Judge Feinberg worked for two years as a law clerk to Judge James P. McGranery of the United States District Court for the Eastern District of Pennsylvania.[4] Judge Feinberg then returned to New York in 1949 and entered private practice, eventually joining McGoldrick, Dannett, Horowitz & Golub as a partner in 1953.[5]

Judge Feinberg joined the United States District Court for the Southern District in 1961. As a district judge, Judge Feinberg was held in high regard for his even-tempered courtroom demeanor and nuanced understanding of the law.[6]

In 1966, President Johnson nominated Judge Feinberg to a position on the United States Court of Appeals for the Second Circuit. Judge Feinberg was appointed Chief Judge of the Second Circuit in 1980.[7]

During his tenure on the Second Circuit, Judge Feinberg penned several significant decisions. For example, his opinion in *United States v. Miller*,[8] a case about the public burning of a draft card, marked an early and important contribution to First Amendment jurisprudence regarding the protection of symbolic speech. Judge Feinberg garnered renown for his views on finality and appealability. His contrasting positions in *Armstrong v. McAlpin*[9] and *American Express Warehousing, Ltd. v. Transamerica Insurance Company*[10] reflect an understanding that finality must be relaxed in some circumstances to promote

Introduction written by David Krauss, J.D. Class of 2015, Fordham University School of Law

1. Wilfred Feinberg, *The Office of Chief Judge of a Federal Court of Appeals*, 53 Fordham L. Rev. 369 (1984). The assistance of H. Geoffrey Moulton Jr. in the preparation of Feinberg's article is gratefully acknowledged.

2. Maurice Rosenberg, *Chief Judge Wilfred Feinberg: A Twenty-Fifth Year Tribute*, 86 Colum. L. Rev. 1505, 1505 (1986).

3. *Id.*

4. *Id.* 1505–06.

5. *Id.* at 1506.

6. *See* Rosenberg, *supra* note 2, at 1506.

7. *Id.*

8. 367 F.2d 72 (2d Cir. 1966), *cert. denied*, 386 U.S. 911 (1967).

9. 625 F.2d 433 (2d Cir. 1980) (en banc), *vacated*, 449 U.S. 1106 (1981).

10. 380 F.2d 277 (2d Cir. 1967).

the needs of justice.[11] Though typically reserved, his opinions sometimes showed flashes of passion, perhaps most notably in his strong dissent in *United States v. McCord*, where he forcefully argued that a conscientious objector's sentence was unjust and unfairly severe.[12]

Judge Feinberg's commitment to the law extended beyond his seat on the bench, as evidenced by his memberships on the Advisory Council for Appellate Justice, the Subcommittee on Supporting Personnel of the Committee on Court Administration of the United States Judicial Conference and the Subcommittee on Judicial Statistics, the Federal Judicial Center's Advisory Committee on Experimentation in the Law, and the American Bar Association's Task Force on Criminal Justice Standards.[13] In addition, Supreme Court Chief Justice Earl Warren appointed Judge Feinberg to the Advisory Committee on the Federal Rules of Civil Procedure in 1965 in recognition of his desire to improve judicial procedure.[14]

Judge Feinberg's Sonnett lecture, as its title suggests, focused on the position of chief judge of a federal appellate court. Judge Feinberg traced the development of the position from its humble origins (the office of "chief judge" was formally adopted in 1948 "with little fanfare") to its heightened importance in today's court structure.[15] In addition, Judge Feinberg provided an in-depth discussion of the office's duties, focusing particularly on the chief judge's role in organizing the composition of panels and appointing visiting judges,[16] administering the Criminal Justice Act (which regulates the hourly rates of compensation for court-appointed attorneys),[17] and reviewing allegations of judicial misconduct pursuant to the Judicial Councils Reform and Judicial Conduct and Disability Act.[18] Judge Feinberg also provided suggestions for change in the office of chief judge, arguing that a heavier caseload would increase collegiality amongst judges.[19]

1984 Sonnet Lecture

The office of chief judge of a federal court of appeals is a peculiar sort of job, in many ways an invisible post on an invisible court. The Supreme Court is always subject to the glare of publicity and often so are trial judges, particularly when they preside over a notorious case. But for some reason, no one outside the legal profession seems to know very

11. *See* Rosenberg, *supra* note 2, at 1510.
12. 466 F.2d 17 (2d Cir. 1972).
13. *See* Rosenberg, *supra* note 2, at 1506.
14. *Id.*
15. *See* Feinberg, *supra* note 1, at 370–73.
16. *Id.* at 375.
17. *Id.* at 379.
18. *Id.* at 380.
19. *Id.* at 384–85. *See also* 28 U.S.C. § 332 (detailing some of the myriad of duties of the Chief Judge involving the Judicial Council of the Circuits).

much about the courts of appeals, a state of knowledge often shared even by fellow lawyers. As I have noted elsewhere, this is both a blessing and a bane.[1] The blessing is that we can go about our business, relatively undisturbed by the distractions that accompany media attention. The bane is that it is important for the body politic to understand the workings of the courts, particularly those that in the federal system operate as a court of last resort in approximately ninety-nine percent of the cases they decide,[2] and are, in Judge Friendly's phrase, the "work-horses of the federal appellate process."[3]

My focus here, however, is not on the courts of appeals, as important as they are, but on the position of chief judge of one of these courts, the lead workhorse, so to speak. That job is also an invisible one. Few federal judges, let alone lawyers, can name all of the chief judges of the various federal courts of appeals. Similarly, few people are aware of what the chief judges of these courts do and of how and why they do it. Little has been written on this subject.[4] This article is designed to dispel some of that ignorance and to educate. It

1. *See* Feinberg, *The State of the Second Circuit*, 38 REC. A.B. CITY N.Y. 363, 366–67 (1983).

2. In statistical years 1981 through 1984, the courts of appeals decided a total of approximately 50,000 cases after submission of briefs. *See* Admin. Office of U.S. Courts, 1984 Annual Report of the Director of the Administrative Office of the United States Courts, A-2, table B-1 [hereinafter cited as 1984 Annual Report]; Admin. Office of U. S. Courts, 1983 Annual Report of the Director of the Administrative Office of the United States Courts 220, table B-I [hereinafter cited as 1983 Annual Report]; Admin. Office of U.S. Courts, 1982 Annual Report of the Director of the Administrative Office of the United States Courts 190, table B-i; 1981 Annual Report of the Director of the Administrative Office of the United States Courts 346, table B-1. In the same 1981–84 period, the Supreme Court decided fewer than 850 cases on certiorari from state courts and inferior federal courts. *See The Supreme Court, 1983 Term*, 98 HARV. L. REV. 1, 311–12, tables II, III (1984) (194 cases decided on certiorari); *The Supreme Court, 1982 Term*, 97 HARV. L REV. 1, 299–300, tables II, III (1983) (209 cases on certiorari); *The Supreme Court 1981 Term*, 96 HARV. L. REV. 1, 308–9, tables II, III (1982) (230 cases on certiorari); *The Supreme Court 1980 Term*, 95 HARV. L. REV. 1, 342–43, tables II, III (1981) (212 cases on certiorari).

3. Letter from Henry J. Friendly, Senior Circuit Judge, United States Court of Appeals for the Second Circuit, to A. Leo Levin, Executive Director, Commission on Revision of the Federal Court Appellate System (April 22, 1975), *reprinted in* 2 HEARINGS BEFORE THE COMMISSION ON REVISION OF THE FEDERAL COURT APPELLATE SYSTEM: SECOND PHASE 1311, 1313 (1975).

4. The creation of the office of chief judge was attended by little comment. See sources cited *infra* note 8. In early 1980, the Federal Judicial Center conducted a survey of how chief judges operated and subsequently published the results. *See* R. WHEELER & C. NIHAN, ADMINISTERING THE FEDERAL JUDICIAL CIRCUITS: A SURVEY OF CHIEF JUDGES' APPROACHES AND PROCEDURES (Federal Judicial Center (1982)). Research has uncovered no other article-length treatment of the subject. Judge J. Edward Lumbard, a former chief judge of the Second Circuit, did discuss the job in a section of his reminiscences. *See* COLUM. U. & N.Y.B. FOUNDATION, A CONVERSATION WITH J. EDWARD LUMBARD 62–79 (1980) [hereinafter cited as A CONVERSATION WITH LUMBARD]. By contrast, an interesting and provocative book-length examination of the office of the Chief Justice of the United States was published just last year. *See generally* THE WHITE BURKETT MILLER CENTER OF PUBLIC AFFAIRS AT THE U. OF VA., THE OFFICE OF CHIEF JUSTICE (1984). For a brief history of the office of chief judge of the district courts, see R. WHEELER, DESK BOOK FOR CHIEF JUDGES OF UNITED STATES DISTRICT COURTS A-I TO 5 (Federal Judicial Center (1984)).

also offers a few modest suggestions for improving the chief judge's role as court administrator.

HISTORY

General MacArthur, in his famous speech to the joint houses of Congress in 1951, said "old soldiers never die; they just fade away."[5] Not long before, the reverse effect apparently occurred with the office of chief judge; it seems to have just "faded in." The position was formally created with little fanfare by the revision of the United States Code in 1948, when the term "chief judge" in the context of a court of appeals was apparently used for the first time in a federal statute.[6] The chief reviser of the Code indicated that this was a mere change in nomenclature, like the contemporaneous change in the name of the court on which a chief judge sits, from circuit court to court of appeals.[7] Most of the few commentators who took note of the change thought it of no moment.[8]

At the time, the federal intermediate appellate bench was small. There were eleven circuit courts manned by fifty-eight circuit judges.[9] I use the word "manned" advisedly; there were no women at all on those courts, a situation that happily has changed dramatically. Today, only four courts of appeals can be so described.[10] In the text that follows, I use the masculine gender to refer to a chief judge only for convenience, not out of conviction or preference. Although it happens that the present chief judges may be so described with accuracy, that will—happily—change in the years to come.

In 1948, the largest circuit courts had an authorized complement of seven judges and the smallest had three,[11] the bare minimum to constitute a panel. Only 2,758 appeals were filed in all the circuit courts in 1948;[12] 381 of those were in the Second Circuit.[13] Criminal

5. D. MacArthur, *Saying*, in J. Bartlett, Familiar Quotations 771 (15th ed. 1980) (Address to a Joint Meeting of Congress, April 19, 1951).

6. *See* Act of June 25, 1948, ch. 646, § 45(a), 62 Stat. 869, 871 ("The circuit judge senior in commission shall be the chief judge of the circuit.").

7. Barron, *The Judicial Code: 1948 Revision*, 8 F.R.D. 439, 441 (1949).

8. *See id.*; Galston, *An Introduction to the New Federal Judicial Code*, 8 F.R.D. 201, 202 (1949). *But see* Maris, *New Federal Judicial Code: Enactment by 80th Congress a Notable Gain*, 34 A.B.A.J. 863, 865 (1948) ("The revision recognizes that an administrative head is needed in each circuit, and accordingly creates the office of Chief Judge of the Circuit, to be held by the Circuit Judge senior in commission.").

9. There were fifty-nine authorized court of appeals judgeships in 1948. *See* Act of June 25, 1948, ch. 646, § 44, 62 Stat. 869, 871. At the end of the year, apparently just one of these judgeships was vacant. *See* Judges, United States Courts of Appeals and District Courts, 168 F.2d vii–xiv (1948).

10. As of December 31, 1984, the Courts of Appeals for the First, Fourth, Seventh and Eighth Circuits had no female members.

11. Administrative Office of the United States Courts, 1948 Annual Report of the Director 118, table B-1 (1948) [hereinafter cited as 1948 Annual Report].

12. *Id.*

13. *Id.*

appeals nationally numbered only 359;[14] the Second Circuit had forty-one.[15] There was no right to assigned counsel in criminal appeals and no national mechanism for such appointments.

With numbers so small and with administrative matters for the court as a whole so few, the title of chief judge might almost have seemed out of place. The fundamental tenet of federal judges is that all members of a court are equal. In 1948, whatever privileges or precedence may have accrued because of seniority were regarded as stemming primarily from custom and tradition, regardless of statute.

Much has happened in the intervening three and one-half decades. There are now 168 judges authorized for all of the thirteen courts of appeals.[16] This figure represents the total of the twelve regional courts—including one covering the small but highly significant region of the District of Columbia—and the Court of Appeals for the Federal Circuit,[17] the newest circuit court. This court was born in 1982,[18] only a year after the Eleventh Circuit came into being as a spin-off from the Fifth.[19] The largest court of appeals, the Ninth, has twenty-eight judges authorized; the smallest, the First, has grown from three to six.[20] In the statistical year ending June 30, 1984, 31,490 appeals were filed in the circuit courts nationwide, 2,945 in the Second Circuit.[21] Appeals from convictions in criminal cases comprise a significant portion of this number,[22] and those who cannot afford to retain counsel have the right to have counsel appointed for them and paid by the federal government.[23]

The federal judicial system as a whole has become a much larger operation, of which the courts of appeals are, of course, an integral part. A sizeable infrastructure of personnel has come into being. The Administrative Office of the United States Courts was created in 1939 to assist the courts in coping with the countless problems of budget, supplies, pay scales, and personnel management that are inevitably part of a system that now employs thousands of people.[24] Another institution—The Federal Judicial Center—was created in 1967 to be a research arm and to assist in the continued education of the increasing numbers of federal judges.[25] A President in a single four-year term may now appoint over two

14. *Id.*
15. *Id.*
16. *See* 28 U.S.C.A. § 44(a) (West Supp. Sept. 1984).
17. *See id.*
18. *See* Federal Courts Improvements Act of 1982, Pub. L. No. 97–164, § 127, 96 Stat. 25, 37.
19. Fifth Circuit Court of Appeals Reorganization Act of 1980, Pub. L. No. 96–452, 94 Stat. 1994 (codified at 28 U.S.C.A. § 41 (West Supp. Sept. 1984)).
20. *See* 24 U.S.C.A. § 44(a) (West Supp. Sept. 1984).
21. 1984 Annual Report, *supra* note 2, at A-2, table B-1.
22. *See id.*
23. *See* 18 U.S.C. § 3006A (1982).
24. *See* Administrative Office Act of 1939, ch. 501, 53 Stat. 1223 (codified at 28 U.S.C. §§ 601–611 (1982)).
25. *See* Pub. L. No. 90–219, 81 Stat. 664 (1967) (codified at 28 U.S.C. §§ 620–628 (1982)).

hundred federal judges, as President Carter did; President Reagan appointed over 165 in his first term.[26]

With this quantum leap in scale and in scope, it was inevitable that the position of chief judge would change from its scarcely noted formal beginning in 1948. Indeed, had the job not existed, we would have had to create it. When a court goes from an authorized complement of six judges—as the Second Circuit was in 1948[27]—to thirteen judges, the present number,[28] plus four or five senior judges, the decisions as to who sits with whom, and when, and how the cases are distributed to these various panels become more complicated. Similarly, when a court of appeals, to help it cope with its caseload, needs to import judges who can be spared elsewhere—this is one of the little-known efficiencies of the federal judicial system—someone has to decide whom to invite and for what period. Of course, it is not written in granite that such decisions, and others like them, must be made by a judicial officer, and indeed many are not. Today's circuit executives, like yesterday's hospital administrators, constitute an important new profession.[29] But by common consent it appears to be accepted that some things, though administrative in nature, should be done by a judge. The job of chief judge had the virtue of *being there*, and into this receptacle custom and Congress have poured a potpourri of duties, which I will describe shortly.

As the position of chief judge has taken on added significance, Congress has occasionally and almost reluctantly scrutinized it and defined it more carefully. In 1958, aware of situations in which a chief judge had refused to relinquish the post although he should have,[30] Congress imposed an age limit of seventy.[31] A few years ago, there was an attempt to remove this restriction, but it was unsuccessful.[32]

In 1982, Congress created a further age limitation: no one over the age of sixty-four could become chief judge.[33] In addition, a chief judge's term was limited to seven years.[34] At

26. Telephone interview with Marian Ott, Staff Assistant to the Director, Administrative Office of the United States Courts (Oct. 18, 1984).

27. *See* Act of June 25, 1948, ch. 646, § 44(a), 62 Stat. 869, 871.

28. 28 U.S.C.A. § 44(a) (West Supp. Sept. 1984).

29. The office of circuit executive was created in 1971 by the Circuit Executive Act, Pub. L. No. 91–647, 84 Stat. 1907 (1971) (codified at 28 U.S.C. § 332(e), (f) (1982)).

30. *See* 1956 Annual Report of the Proceedings of the Judicial Conference of the United States 312 (Report of the Proceedings of a Special Session of the Judicial Conference of the United States (March 13 and 14, 1956)); S. Rep. No. 1780, 85th Cong., 2d *Sess., reprinted in* 1958 U.S. Code Cong. & Ad. News 3256, 3257–58, 3260.

31. Act of Aug. 6, 1958, Pub. L. No. 85–593, 72 Stat. 497.

32. *See* 125 Cong. Rec. 6949 (1979).

33. *See* 28 U.S.C. § 45 (a)(1)(A) (1982). This change followed a comprehensive study of the operation of the courts of appeals by a commission headed by Senator Roman L. Hruska. *See* Commission on Revision of the Federal Court Appellate System, Structure and Internal Procedures: Recommendations for Change (1975) [hereinafter cited as Hruska Commission Report].

34. *See* 28 U.S.C. § 45(a)(3)(A) (1982). The limitation of the term to seven years does not apply to chief judges serving as such on the effective date of the act (October 1, 1982). *See* Federal Courts Improvement Act of 1982, Pub. L. No. 97–164, § 203, 96 Stat. 51, 53.

the same time, Congress reaffirmed the concept that seniority determines the choice of chief judge.[35] There are problems with this, of course. Seniority and administrative skill do not necessarily accompany each other. My own judgment, to paraphrase Winston Churchill, is that seniority is the worst way to select a chief judge, except for all the other ways. Also, to my astonishment, it seems to work.[36]

DUTIES

The chief judge of a modem federal court of appeals is the head of what are essentially two institutions. First, he is the chief officer of the entire circuit, ultimately responsible for its operation. Most people do not know, or do not appreciate, that the judiciary is an institution requiring administration and that the chief judge is the chief administrator of the circuit. A number of these duties are statutory. The chief judge is also the head of the court of appeals, and many of the duties here, although not all, are governed by tradition rather than by statute. The administrative duties of a chief judge fall into three general categories: those that affect only the operation of the court of appeals itself, which may be called "internal duties"; those that relate to the functioning of the federal judicial system as a whole, which may be called "systemic duties"; and those relating to the public, which may be called "external duties." Of course, these categories tend to overlap somewhat, but they are a useful basis of description.

Internal Duties

In the Second Circuit, it is the responsibility of the chief judge to select and organize the composition of the panels of three judges. I do that twice a year, several months in advance. This allows each of us to plan well ahead of time working schedules and other professional commitments, such as attendance at judicial conference committee meetings, moot courts, and so on.

Such scheduling also has other less obvious but important benefits. For example, some time ago, after a decision in a highly controversial case, a lawyer for the unsuccessful appellant wrote the clerk of the court, sending a copy of his letter to me, questioning how it was that the case was heard by a panel that the writer obviously thought was unfriendly to his point of view. The facts were that I had designated the panel several months before without any knowledge of what cases it would hear, and that much later the clerk's office had assigned the appeal to that week and to that panel in the usual way without regard to

35. *See* 28 U.S.C. § 45(a) (1982).

36. It is interesting to note that while the Hruska Commission, *supra* note 33, initially suggested that chief judges be selected by the Chief Justice of the United States, *see* Commission on Revision of the Federal Court Appellate System, Structure and Internal Procedures: Recommendations for Change, A Preliminary Report 108–9 (1975), it ultimately recommended retaining selection by seniority. *See* Hruska Commission Report, *supra* note 33, at 147.

the composition of the panel. The clerk's response to that effect apparently ended the matter.[37]

Selecting the panels well ahead of time is not as simple as it sounds. First, we must calculate how many panels we will need to handle the probable volume. In the statistical year that ended June 30, 1984, we had fifty-one panels. Then, we attempt to have each of the judges sit with as many other judges as practicable. Also, the most senior active judge presides on each panel, and in composing the panels we try to have all the judges preside a few times. Thus, the most junior active judge can and does preside, if sitting with a senior judge of the court and a visiting judge.

Presiding, like rank, has its privileges. The presiding judge assigns the opinions, if he is in the majority. But presiding also has its burdens. The presiding judge customarily prepares the bulk of the written summary orders for the week.[38] The chief judge, who is by definition the most senior judge, always presides when he sits. Last year, in addition to writing my share of published opinions, I prepared some 110 summary orders. These are sometimes two or three single-spaced typewritten pages in length and impose a heavy burden on the presiding judge. I have had more than one of the newer judges tell me that they regard presiding much as did the fellow who was being ridden out of town on a rail and "wouldn't be doing this if it weren't for the honor of the thing!"

Moreover, scheduling requires taking into account the needs and desires of the senior judges, who literally work for nothing[39] and, by definition, should not be subjected to more stress and strain than they are voluntarily willing to assume. They are a precious resource whose welfare and health must be every chief judge's concern.

In addition, scheduling requires an estimate of how many visiting judges will be needed in the next six-month period. The chief judge, often with suggestions from his colleagues, decides whom to invite and initiates the necessary steps; if the visitors come from outside the circuit, the permission of the Chief Justice of the United States must be obtained.[40] When the visiting judges sit, it is important to obtain their perceptions, based on their different backgrounds, on how well or how poorly our court operates, as well as their suggestions for improvement. Finally, last-minute changes in the composition of a panel because of recusals, illness, or other unforeseen contingencies almost always end up with the chief judge, who may find it necessary to obtain a substitute on short notice.

Another substantial portion of a chief judge's time is devoted to monitoring the flow of cases through the appellate process. A court of appeals is like a pipeline in which the intake at one end is called a filing and the outflow at the other is called a termination. Terminations, however, are not all of the same sort. Some require the expenditure of significant

37. Letters (available in files of *Fordham Law Review).*

38. A summary order is used in the Second Circuit if the decision of the panel is unanimous, and each judge believes that an opinion would serve no jurisprudential purpose. *See* 2d. Cir. R. § 0.23.

39. Article III judges who take senior status continue to receive their full salary whether or not they continue to hear cases. *See* 28 U.S.C. § 371(a) (1982).

40. *See* 28 U.S.C. §§ 291(a), 292(d) (1982).

judicial time by panels of the court. Roughly half of our appeals fall into this category.[41] But the other half is disposed of in a number of ways: by settlement through our Civil Appeals Management Program (CAMP),[42] by dismissal for failure to meet court-imposed deadlines, by voluntary dismissal, and so on.

The pipeline in a court of appeals is quite lengthy. The median time nationally from the filing of a notice of appeal at one end of the pipeline to termination at the other is almost one year.[43] In the Second Circuit, the median time is just over six months.[44] But whether the time span is six months or one year or something in between, obviously someone must be watching carefully to make sure that the flow does not get unduly delayed at one point or another.

The responsibility for all this, in the first instance, lies with the clerk and the staff in the clerk's office. But ultimately, it rests with the chief judge. If the weekly flow of cases to the panels is not even, so that some panels receive the usual twenty-four while only fifteen are ready for the next panel, the chief judge will hear about it. If the panels do not receive the briefs in sufficient time before the argument, the chief judge will hear about that, too—in no uncertain terms. In addition, the chief judge receives and studies a number of periodic reports dealing with filings, cases routed to CAMP or to our pro se clerks, cases calendared for argument, and cases argued but not yet decided sixty days after argument—all designed to minimize undue stops and starts and delays.

This system does not always run smoothly. Nothing does! Yet, by and large, because of the hard work and dedication of the judges and staff of the court, it works tolerably well. The aim is to prevent the growth of lengthy backlogs by trying to terminate in a year approximately the same number of appeals as have been filed. In the year that ended June 30, 1984, 2,945 appeals were filed and 2,952 were terminated;[45] in the year before, the figures were slightly lower but roughly in the same proportion.[46]

There are countless other matters affecting the internal operation of the court to which a chief judge devotes time: planning for and presiding over periodic meetings of the active judges at which all of the above matters, and others, are discussed (there are approximately five of these meetings a year); supervising the filling of the most important staff positions, such as the recent selection of our new Clerk of the Court; acting as a clearing house for the inevitable suggestions (the quaint wording still persists) for a rehearing in

41. *See* 1984 Annual Report, *supra* note 2, at A-2, table B-1 (1,224 cases decided after hearing or submission; 1,399 cases disposed of without hearing or submission; remainder consolidated).

42. The general purpose of CAMP is to cull from the appellate docket those cases that might be settled without the further expenditure of judicial resources, and where settlement is not possible, to bring more closely into focus those questions needing resolution. *See generally* Kaufman, *The Pre-Argument Conference: An Appellate Procedural Reform*, 74 Colum. L. Rev. 1094 (1974).

43. Report of the Circuit Executive, United States Court of Appeals for the Second Circuit 1983, at 5, figure 2 (1984).

44. *Id.*

45. 1984 Annual Report, *supra* note 2, at A-2, table B-I.

46. *See* 1983 Annual Report, *supra* note 2, at A-2, table B-1.

banc; supervising the voting—not too frequent in our circuit—when at least one judge requests a poll on an in banc hearing and—even less frequently—shepherding the in banc hearing to its conclusion when a majority of the court votes for it.

When I look at the number of in banc hearings in other circuits, I realize how important a chief judge's position on their utility can be. The tradition in the Second Circuit, a tradition that goes back to Learned Hand, is that in bancs are not encouraged. My view, and that of my predecessor, Irving R. Kaufman, is that for the most part in bancs are not a good idea: they consume an enormous amount of time and often do little to clarify the law.[47] I firmly believe that a chief judge can play a significant role in reducing the number of in bancs.

Finally, the chief judge acts as the ultimate chief cook and bottle washer on a host of other matters that may require his intervention, such as problems arising in connection with appointment of counsel for indigents in criminal appeals, delay by court reporters in furnishing transcripts in cases on appeal, switching of sitting by judges, and allocation of chambers, present and future, a matter exacerbated at Foley Square by the need to squeeze the judges of both the Southern District and the court of appeals into one fifty-year-old building.

Although the duties I have described up to now have grown considerably with the tremendous increase in the court's filings and the not-so-tremendous increase in its judges, these duties do not differ significantly from those of four decades ago. It is in the next two categories—systemic and external duties—that enormous changes have occurred.

Systemic Duties

Each chief judge of a court of appeals is a member of the Judicial Conference of the United States and twice a year attends its meeting in Washington, D.C.[48] Each meeting ordinarily lasts two days and is now usually followed on the third day by a meeting of only the chief judges. The Conference is composed of the thirteen circuit chiefs and one district judge representative from each circuit, and is presided over by the Chief Justice.[49] The Conference sets policy on a wide variety of subjects affecting the operation of the federal judiciary nationwide and its relationship with the other branches of government.

Without going into too much detail, it is almost impossible to describe the broad range of subjects considered, most of which come to the Conference by way of an extensive committee report presented in person by the Committee chairman. Let me mention just a few taken from published reports of recent proceedings. The Report of the Committee on Court Administration proposed regulations under which district courts could determine

47. *See* Kohn, *Circuit Judges; Lawyers Fault Rehearings by En Banc Courts*, N.Y.L.J., Sept. 17, 1984, at 1, col. 1.

48. These meetings are required by statute. *See* 28 U.S.C. § 331 (1982).

49. *See id.*

whether electronic sound recordings would be a viable alternative to shorthand, stenotype, or other methods of recording trial proceedings.[50] That committee's report also addressed, among other things, various pay and personnel practices affecting court reporters and law clerks,[51] court space requirements,[52] and the procedures to be followed in evaluating the need for additional judgeships in both the district courts and the courts of appeals.[53] The Judicial Ethics Committee reported on the almost 1,900 financial disclosure reports filed by some 950 "judicial officers" and some nine-hundred "judicial employees."[54] The Advisory Committee on Codes of Conduct reported on various inquiries and responses.[55] There were also reports from the Committees on the Administration of the Bankruptcy System and the Federal Magistrates System.[56] At the meeting I attended in September 1984, there were twenty-eight agenda items and reports. One of these was a report, which received attention in the press, concerning the televising of federal court proceedings.[57]

Before the Conference, each member receives extensive, bulky committee reports and other material that will be considered at the meeting. It usually takes me a couple of days simply to read this stack of documents. Until I became wiser, it took me even longer to recover from carrying it all with me to Washington, D.C. After my second meeting, it dawned on me that duplicates of all the materials were always placed at my designated spot at the Conference table, and I learned to read it all *before I* went to the airport.

The meeting of chief judges after the Judicial Conference is devoted to matters that concern mainly the circuit courts and is a valuable way of exchanging information and learning from each other. The chief judges also form committees to follow up on the work of the semi-annual meetings.

Closer to home, we have meetings of the Second Circuit Judicial Council, the administrative mechanism for the circuit, at least twice a year. These, like the meetings of the Judicial Conference of the United States, are commanded by statute.[58] Only recently, Congress passed the Judicial Councils Reform and Judicial Conduct and Disability Act of 1980,[59] which changed the composition of the Council to require the inclusion of district as well as circuit judges.[60]

50. Report of the Proceedings of the Judicial Conference of the United States 47–49 (1983).

51. *Id.* at 49–50.

52. *Id.* at 54–55.

53. *Id.* at 61.

54. *Id.* at 63.

55. *Id.* at 64

56. *Id.* at 69–79.

57. *See Made for Television*, Nat'l L.J., Oct. 8, 1984, at 12, col. 1.

58. *See* 28 U.S.C. § 332 (1982).

59. Pub. L. No. 96–458, 94 Stat. 2035 (codified as amended in scattered sections of 28 U.S.C.).

60. 28 U.S.C. § 332(a)(1)(C) (1982).

The Second Circuit Council is now composed of all the active circuit judges and one district judge from each of the six districts in the circuit.[61] The Act required the adoption of new local rules and procedures, which were drafted and are now in effect.[62]

The Council's agenda, except for consideration of judicial misconduct complaints,[63] is a microcosm of the Judicial Conference of the United States. The Council considers such matters as the needs of the various districts in the circuit for new district judges, bankruptcy judges, and magistrates, certifying of support staff for senior judges, and approval of district court plans and procedures in compliance with various statutes, such as the Criminal Justice Act,[64] the Speedy Trial Act,[65] and the Jury Selection and Service Act.[66] The chief judge plans for the meetings, presides at them and supervises the transaction by mail of essential business between the meetings.

Other chief judge duties involve administration of the Criminal Justice Act, an enlightened statute that transforms into reality the constitutional guarantee of the right to counsel for indigent defendants in criminal cases.[67] The Act provides hourly rates of compensation to be paid by the government for court-appointed counsel in both the trial and appellate courts.[68] Unfortunately, in light of inflation, the rates have been much too low for several years.[69] The statute also fixes maximum amounts, which may be exceeded only when the appointing judge certifies that certain statutory standards have been met and the chief judge of the circuit approves.[70] Last year, over 420 vouchers were presented to me for approval; they require scrutiny and occasionally raise issues that warrant an opinion by the chief judge.[71]

In recent years, the operation of the bankruptcy system has been a constant object of the chief judge's attention. The Bankruptcy Reform Act of 1978[72] designated the chief judge as the last step in a complicated process whereby bankruptcy judges were reappointed to interim terms for a period ending in 1984.[73] After a committee, composed of local representatives of a law school, a bar association, and the practicing bar, had considered all objections and had nevertheless recommended reappointment, the chief judge still had to

61. *See* United States Court of Appeals and Judicial Council for the Second Circuit, *In re* Restructuring the Judicial Council of the Second Circuit pursuant to the Judicial Councils Reform and Judicial Conduct and Disability Act of 1980, Pub. L. No. 96–458, 94 Stat. 2035 (1980) (May 7, 1984) (modifying previous order dated March 4, 1981) (available in files of *Fordham Law Review*).

62. *See id.*

63. *See infra* notes 80–87 and accompanying text.

64. Criminal Justice Act of 1964, 18 U.S.C. § 3006A (1982).

65. The Speedy Trial Act of 1979, 18 U.S.C. §§ 3161–3165 (1982).

66. Jury Selection and Service Act of 1968, 28 U.S.C. §§ 1861–1877 (1982).

67. *See* 18 U.S.C. § 3006A(a) (1982).

68. *Id.* § 3006A(d).

69. *But see infra* notes 109–11 and accompanying text.

70. *See* 18 U.S.C. § 3006A(d)(2)–(3) (1982).

71. *See, e.g.*, *In re* Gross, 704 F.2d 670, 672–73 (2d Cir. 1983).

72. Pub. L. No. 95–598, 92 Stat. 2549.

73. *Id.* § 404, 92 Stat. at 2683.

decide whether to accept the recommendation.[74] The right to exercise such a veto power raised delicate and difficult issues.

Last summer chief judges all over the country were in the middle of the confusion over the status of bankruptcy judges occasioned by the delay in passing the Bankruptcy Amendments and Federal Judgeship Act,[75] and had to attempt to steer an intelligent course and to answer questions from judges, lawyers, and the public.[76] The new Act now vests in the courts of appeals the power to fill for new fourteen-year terms all the bankruptcy judgeships in the circuit,[77] so that the chief judge is again in the thick of it.

Finally, with overall responsibility for operation of the circuit, the chief judge watches the statistics of each of the district courts. When a district court needs additional assistance, he must approve temporary switching of judge-power within the circuit,[78] as when a Southern District judge helps by trying cases in the District of Connecticut, or he must request the Chief Justice of the United States to approve a similar inter-circuit transfer.[79]

External Duties

Finally, a chief judge has many responsibilities in dealing with those outside the judicial system proper but who use it or are concerned with it: the bar, the litigants, the public, the press. By far the largest time demands stem from the Judicial Councils Reform and Judicial Conduct and Disability Act of 1980,[80] which became effective in October 1981, and required creation and adoption of an entirely new set of local rules and procedures.[81] The Act allows any person to file a complaint charging that a judicial officer "has engaged in conduct prejudicial to the effective and expeditious administration of the business of the courts, or . . . is unable to discharge all the duties of office by reason of mental or physical disability."[82] The Act represented a compromise, after many years of controversy, between those who felt that there had been no effective way of dealing with the occasionally senile, dishonest, or ill judge and those who regarded the system in effect prior to 1981 as sufficient and appropriate for the purpose.[83]

The Act covers any complaint of misconduct against any of the some 130 judicial officers anywhere in the circuit—magistrates, bankruptcy judges, district judges, and circuit

74. *Id.* § 404, 92 Stat. at 2683–84.

75. Pub. L. No. 98–353, 98 Stat. 333 (1984).

76. *See* Wermiel & Taylor, *Makeshift U.S. Bankruptcy Court System Hobbles Along Amid Dispute About Law*, Wall St. J., Aug. 19, 1984, at 37, col. 5; Riley, *Bankruptcy Uncertainty Continues*, Nat'l L.J., July 30, 1984, at 3, col. 1.

77. *See* 28 U.S.C.A. § 152(a)(1) (West Supp. Sept. 1984).

78. *See* 28 U.S.C. § 292(b) (1982).

79. *See id.* § 292(d).

80. Pub. L. No. 96–458, 94 Stat. 2035 (codified as amended in scattered sections of 28 U.S.C.).

81. *See* 2d Cir. R. § 0.24.

82. 28 U.S.C. § 372(c)(1) (1982).

83. *See* S. Rep. No. 362, 96th Cong., 2d Sess. 1–5, 20–29, *reprinted in* 1980 U.S. Code Cong. & Ad. News 4315–19, 4333–43.

judges.[84] Each complaint, after filing, must go to the chief judge, who has limited options. First, he may dismiss the complaint as frivolous or outside the scope of the Act or as directly related to the merits of a ruling, or mark it closed because corrective action has been taken.[85] Second, if he does not take this course, he *must* convene a statutory committee, composed of equal members of district and circuit judges, and himself.[86] Such a committee, if convened, then investigates and reports to the Circuit Council, which in turn has a variety of options under the statute, ranging from dismissal of the complaint to recommendation to the Judicial Conference of the United States for impeachment.[87]

Every complaint must be treated with great seriousness. The record facts are obtained, the charge is considered with care, and, even if the complaint is dismissed, an order—actually, a short opinion—is written. By June 30, 1984, almost fifty complaints had been filed in the Second Circuit since the effective date of the Act in October 1981.[88] Each year there has been an increase in the complaints filed. Because the Act is so new, each circuit is feeling its way in devising procedures. For example, when we had a complaint filed in the Second Circuit against all of the active circuit judges, including me, the question of who would handle it immediately arose. After obtaining views from a number of knowledgeable sources, I requested and obtained the designation of a chief judge from another circuit to act as chief judge of the circuit for the purpose of handling the complaint.

In a related vein, I mention only in passing the hundreds of letters I receive every year from frustrated pro se litigants, many of whom are incarcerated or are simply unhappy with the way they have been treated by the judicial system. I usually read each one quickly in order to send it to the appropriate person for investigation. Some of the more serious require careful attention. Of course, all judges get such correspondence, but my experience has been that people suffer from the false impression that the chief judge has the power to correct all ills. Would that it were so!

Another major portion of the chief judge's time—again mandated by statute—is devoted to the convening and running of the annual Circuit Judicial Conference.[89] In the Second Circuit, the Conferences were first held in desultory fashion, starting some forty-five years ago,[90] and took their present form about fifteen years later. J. Edward Lumbard, who was chief judge for almost twelve years and happily is still carrying a substantial workload, recently recalled in a volume of his reminiscences that Chief Judge Charles E. Clark was the first "to make something" of the Circuit Conference in the Second Circuit, starting in 1955 in Hartford.[91]

84. 28 U.S.C. § 372(c)(1) (1982).

85. *Id.* § 372(c)(3).

86. *Id.* § 372(c)(4).

87. *Id.* § 372(c)(6)(B), (c)(7).

88. *See* 1984 Annual Report, *supra* note 2, at 70, table 30; 1983 Annual Report, *supra* note 2, at 78, table 30; 1982 Annual Report, *supra* note 2, at 66, table 30.

89. *See* 28 U.S.C. § 333 (1982).

90. *See* Administrative Office Act of 1939, ch. 501, § 306, 53 Stat. 1223, 1224.

91. A Conversation with Lumbard, *supra* note 4, at 62.

The Conference is an annual affair, attended now by circuit, district, and bankruptcy judges whose presence is required by statute unless excused by the chief judge,[92] and about 150 lawyers, usually with spouses, along with other interested invitees, for a grand total of some five hundred people. Usually, the Conference lasts two and one-half days and is held in an area far from the madding crowd.[93]

At the Conference an executive session of the judges is held; indeed, it is the only time each year that all the active judges in the circuit meet with one another. The subjects of the Conference vary: in the last three years, they have been, respectively, the operation of the jury system, the pretrial phase of civil and criminal cases, and the operation of the appellate process in the Second Circuit. Panels and workshops, led by judges, academics, and practicing lawyers, address aspects of the general topic. The chief judge is directly involved in the planning for and organizing of the Conference in all its phases. He also presides at it, gives an annual report to the conferees, and in recent years, has appointed a committee each year to follow up on the serious work of the Conference.

There are many other external duties that make heavy demands on a chief judge's time. Congressional committees frequently express interest in hearing the views of chief judges on matters affecting the federal courts. Last year, I testified before Congressman Kastenmeier's Subcommittee on Courts, Civil Liberties and the Administration of Justice of the Committee on the Judiciary, in opposition to the proposal for a new inter-circuit tribunal.[94] Similarly, I have often publicly advocated the elimination of diversity jurisdiction.[95] I believe it is important for Congress and those who run the national government to hear the views of those who neither work nor reside in Washington, D.C. A friend of mine who had a recent stint in the executive branch in Washington was startled by how much of his agency's daily agenda was set by the media in the Capitol and by how different his perspective became, once he got away from Washington.

In addition, it is essential for the public to know how the courts are operating. On a circuit-wide basis, this information is conveyed primarily by means of reports issued and speeches given by the chief judge. I do not refer here to news about a particular decision, which is not the responsibility of the chief judge unless a systemic problem arises, such as inability to get copies of filed opinions. I refer instead to statistical reports, to speeches (such as the talk that is the basis of this article), and to the myriad ways of letting the profession and the public know what is taking place in the various courts in the circuit, particularly in the court of appeals.

92. *See* 28 U.S.C. § 333 (1982).

93. Last year was an exception: as an experiment, the conference was again held in the urban area of Hartford, Connecticut.

94. Supreme Court Workload: Hearings on H.R. 1968 Before the Subcomm. On Courts, Civil Liberties and the Administration of Justice of the House Comm. on the Judiciary, 98th Cong., 1st Sess. 150–55 (1984) (statement of Wilfred Feinberg, Chief Judge, United States Court of Appeals for the Second Circuit).

95. *See, e.g.*, Feinberg, *supra* note 1, at 374–75.

Over the last few years, in addition to two "State of the Second Circuit" addresses before the Association of the Bar of the City of New York and talks at other annual bar association dinners, I have gone to meetings of local bar associations or their committees to discuss our procedures and problems, and in the case of our summary orders to explain and defend our practices. With regard to the latter, at times I have felt like Daniel in the den of lions![96]

Other ways of informing the public about the courts as an institution may not be immediately obvious, such as induction ceremonies usually held in the courthouse. In all of these settings the chief judge must maintain the delicate balance in the judiciary's relationship with the media by attempting to meet their legitimate requests for information and to obtain adequate publicity about the functioning of the courts while at the same time protecting confidentiality where it is essential. There are a number of other ways by which the federal courts reach out to inform and to be informed by the profession or by other courts. The state/federal councils are composed of representatives from each judicial system in the states involved.[97] A committee on Local Rules and Internal Operating Procedures of the Court of Appeals, which is mandated by statute,[98] is composed of judges, lawyers, and academics. The chief judge is directly involved in selecting the membership of these bodies and in following up on their recommendations.

I could go on with further illustrations of external duties, such as meeting with distinguished visitors, many from foreign countries, but I think that no more examples are needed.

RUMINATIONS AND SUGGESTIONS FOR CHANGE

My own ruminations about the job of chief judge are based on my experience of more than four years as chief judge and, before that, some fourteen years as a circuit judge, and four and one-half years as a district judge. I focus here only on the chief judge's role as an administrator and leader with regard to policies and problems that affect the court as a whole rather than on his role as a leader with regard to substantive legal doctrine.

The demands of the office of chief judge are great, and quite simply cannot be appreciated until you are in it. As this article suggests, I spend a great deal of time on what, for want of a better term, we call judicial administration. My rough but realistic guess is that this absorbs about fifty percent of my time. I also carry eighty percent of an active judge's usual caseload. That is, in the last few years of heavy volume, eight weeks of sitting instead of ten during the year, with approximately twenty-four appeals heard in each of those weeks. My wife has pointed out to me with some asperity that 50% plus 80% equals 130%,

96. *See supra* note 38 and accompanying text.

97. *See* Report of the Circuit Executive, Court of Appeals for the Second Circuit 1983, at 59–60 (1984).

98. *See* 28 U.S.C. § 2077(b) (1982).

an observation whose accuracy I cannot contest.[99] What this means is that briefs and various memoranda concerning administrative matters are read at night or over the weekend and in the interstices of existence: on the train, in the subway, in an automobile (while someone else is driving, I hasten to add)—literally, it sometimes seems during sitting weeks, in every spare moment.

The obvious question, of course, is whether this load is necessary. Whether, for example, a chief judge should sit in almost as many cases as his colleagues and whether his administrative burdens can, or should, be lightened, and if so, how. The first part of this question is comparatively easy to answer. I put to one side the obvious: For most federal judges, including this one, deciding cases is much more interesting than presiding at, or preparing for, meetings. Even after twenty-three years on the bench, despite the relentless flow of cases, many frivolous or inadequately argued, I still find it exciting to be a judge and to decide cases. Each year, there are still more appeals that sorely perplex me, and then engage me to the fullest in the attempt, never perfectly achieved, to reach the right result for the right reasons, explained clearly and concisely.

But it is for entirely different, institutional reasons that I believe that the caseload assumed by a chief judge should not be significantly lighter than that of the other active judges. As statutory responsibilities expand, chief judges will be hard-pressed to become more and more like full-time administrators. I suggest that this would be most unfortunate, and that the challenge will be to prevent it from happening. If administrative duties come to consume the bulk of the chief judges' time, the courts of appeals would lose the service of their most experienced members. More importantly, the model of collegial government would tend to break down; the chief judge's problems and duties would be very different from those of his colleagues on the court, and, in time, he would cease to be perceived as one of them. He would be regarded as an administrator rather than as a colleague who also happens to have additional responsibilities.

The difference in perception is subtle but significant. The essence of a smoothly functioning court is collegiality. That spirit extends to every aspect of the court's operation: the number of cases it disposes of, the speed of disposition, and the quality of the judicial work product. The effect of collegiality on the first two aspects is obvious. Court of appeals judges work very hard—over the past several years, in the face of increased filings, probably too hard. Last year, an active court of appeals judge in the Second Circuit sat, on the average, in 240 appeals. That means the judge read the briefs, heard argument except for comparatively rare submissions, and participated in the decision in 240 cases and also wrote his fair share of opinions. Increased filings have also brought an increase in the number of sitting weeks and in the number of cases heard each week. No one welcomes these additional burdens, but no one is shirking the work either, and in a collegial court, each is willing to carry the load and does so.

99. A former clerk with a mathematical bent pointed out that if 50% of my time is spent on an 80% caseload, then in fact I spend 160% of the time I would were I not chief judge. Whatever the figure, it represents a substantial amount of time.

Similarly, the Second Circuit has continued to dispose of its appeals with remarkable expedition. The median time in the Second Circuit from notice of appeal to termination has consistently been the lowest in the nation.[100] Part of this stems from our practice of summary orders, which account for about sixty percent of our dispositions of cases heard or submitted.[101]

Our low median time is also due to our CAMP program[102] and to our use of what we call "the sixty-day list" to move opinions along. This is a list of cases undecided sixty days after argument or submission. It is examined case by case at each meeting of the court of appeals. There is no criticism of anyone on the list; almost all of us, including the chief judge, are on it from time to time. But the willingness to accept it as a useful device, like the willingness to accept the burdens of preparing detailed written orders in a short period of time, stems from a spirit of collegiality in a cooperative enterprise.

Not so obvious, perhaps, is that collegiality also improves the quality of opinions and keeps down the number of separate opinions, which often create needless confusion. When members of a panel are willing to listen to the suggestions of their colleagues regarding a proposed disposition and ultimately regarding a proposed opinion, the work product usually benefits. Three heads are almost always better than one. Do not misunderstand me; appeals court judges are usually strong-minded, independent souls. They relish criticism no more than anyone else does—perhaps less—and they are willing to accept it in a cooperative spirit only up to a point. But the location of that point is affected by the collegiality of the court. Indeed, given the Article III[103] independence and the strong personalities of the judges, it is remarkable that there is so much harmony and cooperation in the Second Circuit.

I must back up a bit to clarify my thesis. I do not suggest that a chief judge alone can create such a spirit, although he could undoubtedly substantially impair it. Much more depends upon tradition, the character and personality of the judges, the indefinite chemistry when personalities meet and clash, and the panel system, which allows us to go about our business without all of us sitting with each other in each case, with the constant need to agree or disagree. But tradition may wither, and the chief judge can, by example and emphasis, help to preserve and continue valuable customs of the court, such as our voting memoranda,[104] a practice that goes back to Learned Hand and is unique, I believe, to the

100. *See supra* notes 43–44 and accompanying text.

101. *See* Report of the Circuit Executive, Court of Appeals for the Second Circuit 1983, at 7 (1984). *See supra* note 38 and accompanying text.

102. *See supra* note 42 and accompanying text.

103. U.S. Const. art. III, § 1.

104. For those cases that the panel, after argument, agrees should be decided by opinion rather than by summary order, it is customary to exchange voting memoranda. These "voting memos" set out the particular judge's vote as well as the reasons for that vote. Voting memos are extremely useful for the purpose of discussion at the voting conferences held after the cases are heard; the memos also benefit the eventual opinion writer, who weeks later has in written form valuable suggestions about the reasoning of an opinion, as well as cogent statements of a colleague's concerns.

Second Circuit. This chief judge function is particularly important when there is a large influx of new judges to the court in a short period of time.

Moreover, the chief judge can to some extent encourage collegiality in many ways through his relationships with members of the court: by building consensus, by striving to get strong-minded individuals to work together and to avoid pointless feuding, by smoothing ruffled feathers, by heading off potential crises or problems, if possible, before they arise, by emphasis on appropriate ceremonial occasions, such as inductions and memorial services in court,[105] and generally by tact and concern for the welfare and feelings of his colleagues in the performance of the various duties described earlier. Obviously, this is a tall order and no chief judge can achieve it completely. But to the extent that a chief judge is able to improve collegiality at all, the perception of him primarily as colleague rather than as administrator helps.

I therefore do not find attractive the notion that a chief judge's caseload should be very much less than that of his colleagues. Where else to turn, then, to prevent the job from becoming an impossible one? An obvious answer is to lighten the administrative burdens by delegation. For example, I have in large part delegated responsibility for running the annual Second Circuit Judicial Conference.[106] I do not know how many hours I spent in connection with the first such Judicial Conference for which I had ultimate responsibility, but they were many. Since then, because the governing statute allows leeway,[107] I have delegated the primary responsibilities for the program of the Conference to one of my colleagues, as Conference Chairman, and to the head of our Planning and Program Committee. This procedure has worked splendidly in the three subsequent Conferences. Although the chief judge still has much to do in connection with each Conference, his load has been reduced considerably.

Much can also be delegated to the Circuit Executive, a position created only because of the wisdom and perseverance of Chief Justice Burger, whose efforts on behalf of improved administration of the courts have been herculean. The Circuit Executive is a useful and indispensable aid in administering the circuit. Indeed, I shudder to think of what the job of chief judge would be without him. But the Circuit Executive's duties are predominantly circuit-wide and systemic. Even in this sphere, the chief judge has ultimate responsibility and therefore must supervise. In addition, there are duties that only the chief judge can perform even in the first instance, such as attending and participating in the Judicial Conference of the United States.

Frequently there are reasons for not delegating even when it is in theory possible. In at least one circuit, I believe, invitations to visiting judges,[108]—whether district judges from inside the circuit or judges from outside the circuit—are made by staff personnel, not by a judge. I have found that a telephone call from the chief judge is more effective and obtains a quicker response. In theory, computers can compose panels, but in practice, we

105. We have had four of the former, and sadly five of the latter since I have been chief judge.
106. *See supra* notes 89–91 and accompanying text.
107. *See* 28 U.S.C. § 333 (1982).
108. *See supra* note 40 and accompanying text.

have not yet achieved this result. I attain almost the same efficient results by working closely with an experienced staff member in meeting the various conditions, such as the number of desired panels, the need to mix up the composition of panels as much as possible, and to have all judges preside at least once and in fair proportions, the equitable spacing of sitting weeks, and so on.

No doubt there are duties now carried out by the chief judge that could be efficiently delegated to other members of the court, but there are limits there, as well. Not every judge is interested in taking on administrative, as distinguished from judicial, burdens; some, of course, are better at it than others, and all are quite busy. But even where other judges are willing and able to assume administrative responsibilities, Congress frequently has made delegation all but impossible. Under the Criminal Justice Act, for example, the chief judge is the only official authorized to approve payments in excess of the maximum amounts permitted.[109] There is simply no persuasive reason why the statute should not be amended to allow the chief judge, or another member of the court selected by him, to perform that function.[110] At the very least, the maximum amounts that trigger chief judge involvement should be raised to higher levels. Congress recently increased them somewhat, but not sufficiently.[111]

Similarly, I suggest that there is no persuasive reason to confine only to the chief judge the authority to act at the initial stage upon complaints of judicial misconduct. Regardless of whether experience will fortify the views of those who supported or those who opposed the statute, it may come to be perceived as an alternate appeal route for the disappointed or troubled litigant who, as I have pointed out elsewhere,[112] may have a grudge against the system or the world that is not amenable to any sort of legal remedy. A few months ago, I read with mounting concern a lengthy account of the hearing in open court by a statutory committee of five judges—three circuit judges, including the chief judge, and two district judges—concerning a complaint against a judge in that circuit.[113] My reaction was not based on the merits of the complaint—I have no view as to that—but on the number of judge-hours being consumed by consideration of it. In that case, a determination had already been made that the complaint was neither frivolous, nor outside the scope of the Act, nor directly related to the merits of a ruling. I therefore do not quarrel at all with the view that the chief judge should preside over and directly participate in any further proceeding. But what about complaints that *are* frivolous, or outside the scope of the Act, or directly related to the merits of a ruling, as experience has shown most so far to be? Must each of those require the personal attention of the chief judge? If Congress now trusts the

109. *See* 18 U.S.C. § 3006A(d)(3) (1982).

110. *Cf.* Pretrial Services Act of 1982, 18 U.S.C. § 3152(a) (1982) (chief pretrial services officer selected by panel including chief judge or designee).

111. *See* Comprehensive Crime Control Act of 1984, Pub. L. No. 98–473, 98 Stat. 1837, 2185 (amending 18 U.S.C. § 3006A).

112. *See* Feinberg, *Foreword* to Foundation of the Fed. B. Council, The Remarkable Hands: An Affectionate Portrait vi (1983).

113. *See* Ranii, *A Judge's Public Battles*, Nat'l L.J., July 23, 1984, at 1, col. 2.

chief judge's judgment sufficiently to make this initial determination, should it not also trust his ability to delegate fairly and wisely this function to a colleague? I submit that it should, and that the statute should be amended to allow it.[114]

Similarly, as I have already noted, in 1978 Congress created an entirely new set of responsibilities in connection with selection of bankruptcy judges.[115] In the period from 1978 to 1984, the chief judge alone was required by statute to decide whether to veto reappointment of incumbents.[116] This was clearly not necessary. In the new Bankruptcy Act,[117] the court of appeals has the responsibility for appointment of bankruptcy judges to new fourteen-year terms.[118] Putting to one side whether this power might not better rest with the district courts, who are more knowledgeable about the bankruptcy judges, it is still a step in the right direction. Of course, the chief judge will be intimately involved. But vesting the appointment power not in the chief judge alone, but in the court of appeals as a whole, was an improvement because it allows some room for delegation. Generally, the ability to delegate should be encouraged. It enhances the spirit of collegiality and it exposes future chief judges to the issues they will have to face. Someone remarked to me recently that I should be pleased because the chief judges are being given so much administrative power. My response is that a chief judge is getting so powerful, he soon won't have time to do anything!

CONCLUSION

I hope that this sketchy summary of the history of the job of chief judge of a court of appeals, his responsibilities, and some reflections of my own have added to an understanding of this rarely examined office. It is in many ways an odd sort of job. The chief judge of a circuit has ultimate responsibility for administering a large enterprise in which there may be, as in the Second Circuit, some 130 judicial officers and over a thousand employees. Yet the chief judge has little or no control over the budget for the enterprise, the judgepower and staff available to it, the space allocated to it and rates of compensation for those affiliated with it. I suppose a modem chief executive officer might question the wisdom—if not the sanity—of anyone who voluntarily assumed such a position. In addition to being a circuit-wide administrator, the chief judge is also responsible for the administration of the appellate court of which he is a member. And while serving as an administrator, he also sits as a busy appellate judge on that court. And yet, despite all of this, the job of chief judge is so interesting, the responsibilities so challenging, the relationship with colleagues so rewarding, and the intangible satisfaction simply of being the titular head of an historical institution so great, that the job is irresistible—at least for a while!

114. *See supra* note 110.
115. *See supra* notes 73–74 and accompanying text.
116. *See supra* note 74 and accompanying text.
117. 28 U.S.C.A. § 152 (West. Supp. Sept. 1984).
118. *See supra* note 77 and accompanying text.

Advocacy: Has It a Future?

Hon. Thomas A. Finlay

Chief Justice Thomas A. Finlay delivered the fifteenth Sonnet lecture, entitled *Advocacy: Has It a Future?*, on March 19, 1986. Appointed in June 1985, Justice Finlay served as the Chief Justice of the Supreme Court of Ireland until 1994.[1] Prior to serving in Ireland's court of final appeal, Justice Finlay sat for twelve years as a judge of the High Court in Ireland, where he was appointed President in 1974.[2] Before transitioning to the role of judge, Justice Finlay spent just short of thirty years working as a barrister in Ireland, including time as a Fine Gael Teachta Dála (Member of Parliament) for Dáil Éireann in the Oireachtas, the lower house of the Irish Parliament.[3]

Born in Ireland in 1922, Justice Finlay attended Clongowes Wood College, University College Dublin, and King's Inn.[4] During his time at University College Dublin, Justice Finlay was elected auditor of the University College Dublin Law Society, where he managed one of the largest student societies in Europe.[5] He was called to the bar in 1944 and to the inner bar in 1961.[6]

As Chief Justice, Justice Finlay authored numerous opinions on significant national issues, focusing specifically on the Irish Constitution and the separation of powers. He gave the leading judgment in *Attorney General v. X*,[7] in which a fourteen-year-old girl, pregnant as a result of rape by a family friend, was permitted to travel to England for an abortion in spite of the constitutional guarantee that the state would protect the unborn's right to life and prior policy allowing abortions only when the mother's life was in immediate danger.[8] He also played a leading role in *Attorney General v. Hamilton and A*,[9] in which the Supreme Court held that the confidentiality of cabinet discussions

Introduction written by Amanda Asaro, J.D., Class of 2015, Fordham University School of Law.

1. *Former Chief Justices*, The Supreme Court of Ireland, http://www.supremecourt.ie/SupremeCourt/sclibrary3.nsf/pagecurrent/B8E6388E466B6FB68025731500 5A41D3?opendocument&l=en (last visited Mar. 7, 2014).

2. *Id.*

3. *Id.*

4. *Id.*

5. William Karr, *Members of the Fifteenth Dáil—Thomas Aloysius Finlay*, The Irish Rising (Nov. 24, 2012), http://theirishrising.blogspot.com/2012/11/members-of-fifteenth-dail-thomas.html.

6. *See supra* note 2.

7. [1992] 1 IR 1 (Ir.).

8. James F. Clarity, *Irish High Court Explains Decision*, N.Y. Times (Mar. 6, 1992), http://www.nytimes.com/1992/03/06/world/irish-high-court-explains-decision.html.

9. [1993] 2 IR 250 (Ir.).

were absolute, and in *Attorney General v. Hamilton (No. 2)*,[10] in which the Supreme Court held that Teachta Dálas are not amenable to legal processes for utterances made in the Dáil.[11]

While Justice Finlay occupied a variety of roles throughout his career, there was one distinct common thread: his consistent observation of advocacy in Ireland's courts. Justice Finley's Sonnett lecture, *Advocacy: Has It a Future?*, focused on this experience to opine on the role of the judiciary, the adversarial systems of advocacy in Ireland and the United States, and whether a more inquisitorial system would provide for better advocacy opportunities. Regardless of the system, however, Justice Finlay stressed the importance of effective advocacy for achieving the ultimate goal—securing justice.

1986 Sonnett Lecture

The rather fatuous question that I personally chose as the title of this paper admits of a ready answer.

As long as there is an independent judiciary, and until such time as the first computer is appointed to the Bench, the craft of advocacy has, in some form, a very definite and important future in, I would have thought, both our legal systems. The title was chosen, however, not merely to yield this very obvious answer, but to serve the purpose that is sometimes fulfilled by a form of pleading dear to lawyers, though not quite so dear to judges, namely—that being, as we say in Ireland, as wide as a farmyard gate—it permits under its umbrella a discussion on every or any aspect of advocacy.

I have chosen the subject of advocacy for two reasons. Possibly the most important and dominant one, candidly, is that my entire experience and background as a lawyer has left me with an almost obsessional interest in advocacy.

I was for just short of thirty years what I would describe as a journeyman barrister in Ireland, not seeking to specialize in any particular branch of the law and appearing in court more regularly and for a greater proportion of my time than I spent in advisory work. Those appearances were, in criminal as well as in civil cases, daily involvement in the presentation of facts seeking, I hope with propriety, to influence both juries and judges, and making, where necessary and appropriate, legal submissions.

For a further twelve years, I sat as a judge of the High Court, which meant that, under the system which we operate, again I eschewed specialization, tried both civil and criminal cases, tried ordinary tort actions with a jury, and other actions as a judge sitting without a jury and, from time to time, exercised in two different areas an appellate jurisdiction.

10. [1993] 3 IR 227 (Ir.).
11. *See supra* note 2.

In the last fourteen months, I have had the privilege of presiding over the Supreme Court of Ireland, the court of final appeal.

For all these years, therefore, and in all those differing but not widely different occupations, advocacy has either been the constant tool of my trade or has been something which I have observed with a continued interest and to the apparent effectiveness and consequences of which I have given much thought. During that period, I think I could properly claim, not with personal but with national pride, that I had the opportunity of observing some really great advocates in the daily exercise of their skill in the Irish courts. I have often wondered what a really great advocate is, and how one should define him or her. I had to wait a considerable period for an answer to that question some twenty years ago when, at a dinner to mark the fiftieth year of practice of the late John A. Costello, a leader for most of that period of the Irish bar and twice the Prime Minister of Ireland, a speech was made in his praise. Kevin Liston, who is now the father and a leader of the Irish bar, resolutely and strenuously practicing in his eighties, made the speech. And he defined on that occasion a great advocate in a way that has always attracted me, namely, as being a barrister, or lawyer, who could win a bad case before a good judge.

The second and less personal reason why it appeared to me appropriate that I might discuss with you here, this evening, the subject of advocacy, is this: our two legal systems have much in common. We both operate a common law system, but one that is subject to the overall control of a written constitution. The common law system that we operate we inherited from the English system of law, the constitutions we took to ourselves.

For the purpose of administering both the common law and the constitutional law by which our systems are governed, we took, certainly in the case of Ireland, almost it would seem to me without question the adversarial system of advocacy peculiarly associated with and possibly peculiarly appropriate to the administration of the common law. Although I have no doubt that our styles and systems of advocacy on either side of the Atlantic may have, with the passage of time, diverged and altered, we both retain this adversarial system and that seemed to me to be another good reason why some consideration of its development might be appropriate on this occasion.

To look at the future of advocacy, it would appear necessary to look first at its past. In particular, its development and the directions it may be taking on its journey into the next century may well be affected by considerations of how it has changed in the last forty to fifty years. But here I enter a caveat.

It would seem to me to be the height of folly, and of impudence as well, for me to come here to this great law school and in this distinguished company of practicing American lawyers and lecture you in any way upon the development or standards of your advocacy in America.

I, therefore, intend merely to mention my experience of advocacy in Ireland and the changes that appear to me to have taken place in it in the hope that they may, either by their similarity or their contrast, be of interest to you reflecting on the changes in your own systems. There can be little doubt that, with us at least, much of the flamboyance, much of the theatrical, has disappeared from the art of advocacy, even in those forty years. It was probably in decline from the end of the Victorian period and into the twentieth century. One cannot conceive today one of my very treasured examples of Victorian English lawyer's advocacy, where it is recorded that an action for defamation brought in the London courts in the second half of the nineteenth century was opened by counsel with the magnificent phrase addressed to the jury: "Gentlemen, the reputation of a cheesemonger in the City of London is like the bloom upon a peach: breathe upon it and it is gone forever."

Even though this picturesque form of address had largely disappeared, there was still at the Irish bar when I first joined it a considerable element of the dramatic, particularly in the advocacy to be seen in criminal trials and in civil jury trials. It was certainly a heightening of the entertainment value of the trial of cases. The entertainment value of the trial of cases was certainly at that time a matter of very considerable importance, particularly in rural Ireland. I can remember that in country towns when the Circuit Court, dealing with both civil and criminal cases, came for a week a significant number of people who had no business there, who were not involved in any case, simply came for the pleasure of watching the unfolding drama to be seen in court. We were fortunate enough to have at that time a jovial, talkative, and entertaining judge who had no great reluctance in heightening the drama which existed. I have seen a man leaving such a country courthouse chuckling to himself after a particularly dramatic performance in some quite minor case and, somewhat similarly to an opera lover leaving the Met, saying over and over again: "Man and boy, I have been attending this court for thirty years and that's the best case I ever heard."

Second, the drama was a great satisfaction to the client in many cases. I remember one of my mentors, when I first commenced practice, advising me that an assault case about which I had sought his opinion and in which neither the facts nor the law seemed to be on my side, was a case in which all the questions should be asked in a loud and angry voice. But I wondered even then, and I wonder even more now, whether the flamboyant and in a sense the aggressive form of advocacy, which undoubtedly was then fashionable but which has diminished in popularity, was ever really as effective as either the litigants or its own proponents thought it to be. It has always seemed to me very easy indeed, by too militant a cross-examination of a witness, having regard to the obvious disparity of advantage there is between a trained lawyer and a witness to elicit, even by an apparently successful cross-examination, a significant sympathy from a jury to the witness. What probably has been an overall increase in the courtesy or communication, in every walk of life, in this century as compared to the nineteenth century, is, I think, reflected in what a jury expects in a court: the quiet, the subtle, and above all, the courteous cross-examination, in my view, before a jury, proves much more effective and has always done so, than the hectoring one. There could be no real question at all that it is significantly more effective before a judge.

Another major change which has occurred in advocacy over this period is the necessity for and development of a special style of examination of technical witnesses.

There can be no doubt that in both criminal and civil law the technical witness has come to stay and reliance is being increasingly placed upon his evidence. An attack on the credit of a technical witness seldom succeeds, though occasionally it may do so. An attack or undermining of his qualifications is less infrequent, but still, in my experience in Ireland at least, the exception rather than the rule.

The most commonly required expertise is, on the one hand, for the lawyer whose technical witness is being led on the direct, to make sure that his evidence is understandable to the judge or, if relevant, to a judge and jury. His opponent, if he is to make any headway in cross-examination of such a witness, must have the background information and knowledge to enable him to test the logic of the reasoning on which the conclusions are reached. Both lawyers, therefore, dealing with this type of technical evidence must, in the first instance at least, be themselves capable of fully understanding and following it. On the other hand, they must be able to convert that understanding on their part into a form of language and expression which is clearly understandable to the judge or, as I say, in the jury cases, to the judge and to the jury.

Here, from my own experience, might I sound a note of warning? Very few judges, in my humble opinion, have real technical knowledge. From an advocate's point of view, a judge who appears to have a facile understanding or acceptance of technical words or technical theories can be in a most dangerous situation. He will undoubtedly resent, to use a very vulgar expression, being taught by his grandmother to suck eggs. The fact that he does partly understand the technical words and phrases, however, is not an absolute guarantee that he is fully understanding the theory of a very technical witness.

Above all, a technical witness should, to the utmost possible extent, be separated from the technical jargon of his discipline. I have always enjoyed the, no doubt, apocryphal story of the doctor, learned in his profession, called to give evidence before that most unusual of animals, an irascible judge. He was a doctor of the old school and properly stuck to his Latin last, refusing to call the *os calcis* a heel bone, and refusing to acknowledge the scapula as a shoulder. This proper point of view clashed with the mood or temper of the judge, and some exchanges took place. Looking over to the jury as the learned doctor finished his evidence the judge said: "Thank you, doctor, though I greatly doubt we are as the result of your evidence much wiser," whereupon the doctor bowing and removing his papers replied courteously to the judge: "So do I, but you are certainly better informed."

I suppose the skill of presenting or testing technical evidence must, at the end of the day, be gained by experience and by imitation of those who have already acquired it. Do we, however, sufficiently recognize the necessity for that skill in the scope and format of our systems of legal education—academic, professional, and practical?

It used to be said, even up to the 1930s in Ireland, when the great bulk of litigation arose out of land, its ownership, the sale of its produce, the existence of easements over it, and perennial problems of fencing and flooding, that the proper training for a young man—and it would in those days have been a young man—seeking to become a successful Irish barrister was to spend two years on a farm and then study sufficient law to have himself called to the Irish bar.

May it be that the equivalent advice properly to be given—not only in Ireland, but conceivably also here in America as well—to a young lawyer seeking advocacy as his career would be to go and get a nodding acquaintance with the applied sciences, a sniff of the

Bunsen burner or its modern equivalent, some idea of what makes a man or a woman in a white coat tick?

The random thoughts about the development of advocacy really only deal with something that has occurred and is likely to continue as a result of what might be called market forces. These developments have not occurred as the result of any intervention by the judiciary or by the legislature. They will, I believe, continue, to a varying extent and at a varying speed without such intervention either.

I would turn, however, to a more radical question that emanates from the intervention of the judiciary, at least, and of which I am aware that there is a marked discrepancy between the practice here in the United States and the practice we observe in Ireland. I refer to the balance or proportion between oral and written submissions on questions of law, both to a court of originating jurisdiction and to an appellate court.

First, to set out the present actual position in Ireland, it is as follows.

There is not, in reality, by statute or statutory rule of court, any requirement to submit in writing legal submissions prior to a hearing, whether an originating or an appellate hearing. I say "in reality" because, while in pleading before trial the general rule is that facts but not matters of law should be pleaded, reliance upon particular statutory provisions such as, for example, a statute of limitations, or upon an identifiable legal principle, such as, for example, the doctrine of laches, must be stated, but without setting out the arguments in support of that reliance. Equally, on appeal from the High Court to the Supreme Court, which is not an appeal by way of rehearing but on a question or issue of law only, the notice of appeal would have to indicate the issues of law under which it is alleged that the trial judge in the High Court erred. But again, the reference to such is of an extremely abbreviated kind and does not constitute any submission of law. An appropriate format, for example, for a notice of appeal would be that the learned trial judge erred in law in holding that the contract for the sale of land had been sufficiently evidenced by a note or memorandum in writing within the provisions of the Statute of Frauds. But the reason why he reached that error is not, in that document, set out.

Approximately twenty years ago, I should think, the Supreme Court introduced, as a practice measure only, the requirement for submissions. It started, in my recollection, as being confined to cases where the constitutional validity of a statute of the Oireachtas was being challenged and to cases where a hitherto unrecognized constitutional right was being asserted. It was later extended to a limited number of cases in which a major question of law was being raised that either had not previously been determined by the Supreme Court of Ireland—although it might have been the subject matter of decision either in the United Kingdom or here in the United States—or in a case where it was sought to persuade the Supreme Court to reverse or vary a decision on a point of law previously reached by it. These requirements with regard to submissions are still maintained and form a consistent policy of the Court up to the moment.

The first major difference which, as I understand your procedure here, in particular in relation to the United States Supreme Court, is that the requirement for a submission of these written submissions of law in no way curtails the length of time that the court permits the succeeding oral submissions to occupy. Furthermore, in the way in which the practice has developed, the oral submissions are not additional to the written submissions but rather consist of an expansion of them. In addition, there is no rigidity that has arisen yet in practice from these submissions: the reproof or reprimand which an advocate might obtain were he subsequently in his oral submissions to seek to go outside or beyond his written document would, I think, be generally speaking, limited. Certainly there would never be a question of his being prevented from exploring an area that the court considered was relevant or helpful to it.

From my own experience, the major value of these submissions is to ensure that in addition to the court, the adversary on either side is aware of the legal arguments and submissions that they have to meet. Furthermore, it permits the court in preparation for the hearing of such an appeal, by the identity of the legal issues arising, to be prepared at the subsequent oral hearing to invite submissions on what it deems to be consequential issues or further sub-issues arising as a result of the parties' legal submissions. It avoids what can be the frustrating and disturbing experience that after a very full hearing on a question of law, the court, as would happen in Ireland, having sat down to confer and consider the issues thus arising, discover that a topic not dealt with by any of the parties may be material to its thinking and would then feel obliged, as would be our practice, to sit again, inform the parties of the issues which has not been covered and give them, on notice, an opportunity to make further submissions.

Although these advantages are clearly there, I personally have no doubt that the making of written submissions in the appropriate type of cases to which I have referred, in Ireland, has not diminished by one jot or tittle the fundamental and dominant importance of the oral submissions and, in particular, of the exchange between bench and bar on issues of law, the setting of questions and the answering of them. I am by no means certain that I would like it to have so altered that system, but that may well be the inevitable conservatism of a person of my age who, for the greater part of his practicing career, was accustomed to a different system. It may well also be that, as so many people suspect, the real gift of the Irish is in talking and not writing, and that the submissions by oral advocacy are more suited to us as a nation than alternative systems.

While I pass these rather unformed views on the system, I should point out that we have on our Eastern side, on the mainland of Europe, an interesting situation developing in which our Irish lawyers are concerned. As many of you are probably aware, the Court of the European Community carries out a very high proportion of its determination and trial of issues before it as a result of detailed written legal submissions, and the proportion there between the time occupied by the Court in the hearing of oral submissions, even in the most grave of cases, compared with the time occupied in the perusal of the written submissions, rejoinders, and replies, is very limited indeed. Irish lawyers have, as far as I can see, quite successfully taken to that different form of practice, and I personally believe that the origin of our initiation of written submissions in Ireland was probably due to the example we saw happening on the mainland of Europe.

I paid a recent visit to the Court of Luxembourg—in September of last year—and there discussed with the President of the Court and with the other members of it, including my predecessor and former Chief Justice, Tom O'Higgins, the development and situation with regard to the practice and procedure of that Court in regard to oral and written submissions. It should be recognized that with the exception of the United Kingdom and ourselves, almost all the other Member States would have systems of law wholly different from the adversarial system of the common law and would be much more accustomed, first, to the lengthy written submissions on questions of law and, second, to the limited oral submissions, and, third, to the nonintervention by the judge by way of questioning or otherwise.

As far as I am concerned, the European Court, predominantly staffed by judges with such legal backgrounds, started on the basis that it would follow the Continental European example. Possibly due to the fact that its present President is a former judge of the United Kingdom, but, I believe, more due to the fact that the judges have seen all the different systems in operation, it is now clearly recognizing the necessity for a dominant, though not a predominant, part of its deliberations to consist of oral submissions and, furthermore, for the necessity and desirability of the Court to intervene during the course of such oral submissions.

Although, therefore, some years ago, I might have said the example that we at the Irish bar would be obtaining from their intervention in the Court of the European Communities was likely to move the practice and procedure of our courts more to the written and away from the oral submissions, I am not quite so certain now that that is going to be, and I certainly would be interested in a dialogue, at judicial level and, I think, at the level of practicing advocates as well, in a serious way between ourselves and your country, in relation to the advantages and disadvantages of this system.

I next come to the much more radical question as to whether the relatively strictly adversarial nature of our systems of advocacy is likely to, or should, survive unchanged. I believe that there are significant pressures external to the legal system and lawyers, in Ireland at least, which are seeking to change from the adversarial to an inquisitorial system of advocacy and, of course, procedure. They seem to me to derive from a view that the adversarial system is somehow wasteful of manpower and time and in some way inefficient.

Businessmen, politicians, and administrators are inclined to point to the fact that when they require for the purpose of making a decision to ascertain facts, they make or cause to be made the inquiries themselves, identifying the information they require, and then proceed to a conclusion. The simple argument, therefore, runs that a judge to reach a decision should do likewise, and that if he did, the legal system would overnight become more speedy and less expensive, and that in civil cases at least litigants could probably dispense, to a very large extent, with the use of advocates.

What is possibly a more serious criticism of the adversarial system, certainly with regard to civil cases, comes from within the legal system in the sense that it represents the view of judges and lawyers working in inquisitorial and investigatory systems of advocacy. It is this: that for cases in which questions of law of general application and importance are concerned, and a fortiori for those in which the interpretation of a written constitution is concerned, that it is fundamentally unsatisfactory to be relying on the factual material established by the parties and the issues thus raised when—if the court had the right to make its own investigations as to fact and, therefore, to raise its own issues—a different conclusion or conclusions might emerge.

Before considering these individual criticisms, it is, I think, appropriate as it were to stand back and look at what the rote and functions of the courts in a free society are and should remain.

In the realm of criminal law, it is generally speaking that the executive branch undertakes the responsibility of enforcing the law by deterrent, by detection, and by punishment. It invokes the aid of the court in two contexts only, namely, (1) to obtain the decision as to whether a person has been proved to have broken the criminal law, and (2) to have decided the nature and extent of the punishment of those proved to have done so.

It would be quite inconsistent with my understanding of our constitutional principle of the separation of powers for the judiciary to become involved in the detection of crime or in the administration as distinct from the selection of punishment.

It appears to me equally impossible for it to be involved in the ascertainment or presentation of evidence. Its function in the first instance is literally to be available. To exercise its powers if, but only if and when, they are invoked by the prosecuting authority. When such powers are invoked, to permit the prosecuting authority to present the case of its choosing on the evidence of its choosing subject to the legal principles of admissibility and of due process. Thereafter, to stand independently between the prosecution and the accused, jealously guarding in particular the legal and constitutional rights of the latter. If this constitutes an accurate and relatively complete identification of the functions of the courts under our system of law in criminal cases, it seems to me of itself to leave no room for any system of advocacy other than one which is strictly an unqualified adversarial one. No consideration, even if it could be proved, of efficiency, speed, or economy, could justify an alteration of these functions. Any move, no matter how limited, to investing a judge in criminal cases with an inquisitorial or investigative role, seems to me to be a step on the road to the acceptance of the judge prosecutor whose existence in so many countries throughout the world has led and is leading to such untold injustice and misery. The retention of the adversarial system in criminal cases seems, therefore, to me at least, to be based on a bedrock of constitutional necessity.

There is, however, a form of criminal procedure—inquisitorial rather than adversarial—which exists in some of the European systems and which is preliminary to, and not part of, the actual criminal trial.

That is the preliminary investigation carried out by a judicial officer from which the file that forms the book of evidence for the actual trial is compiled. As I understand that system, or some forms of it, a magistrate sits in the presence of the accused and his lawyer; examines witnesses whose names are submitted by the prosecution; may call and examine other witnesses not thus proffered; may, in some legal systems, in a sense, confront the accused with this evidence; and ask him to comment on it, and thus by a process compiles the file of the prosecution for the trial.

Such a system clearly brings a judge into the realm of the prosecution, even though it is not the trial judge. It is inconsistent in some ways with the separation of powers. It is relevant that it exists for the most part, as I would understand the position, in legal systems where the judiciary is largely a career-structured state service and where what we would see as the necessary rigid independence of the judiciary from any part of the state service of the prosecution would not be such an obvious requirement.

Such a system has one theoretical advantage. It is a principle of our system of criminal law, and I assume I am correct in believing of your system in the United States also, that it is the obligation of the prosecution not merely to prove its case but to place before the court of trial all relevant and credible evidence within its knowledge and procurement touching on the guilt or innocence of the accused.

Such a principle is in Ireland fully accepted and in my experience of the conduct of prosecuting officers and counsel engaged on their behalf, in the main, scrupulously observed. We have not, however, devised, during the course of a trial at least, any really effective way of enforcing it. An accused aware of the failure of the prosecution to tender a witness favoring the case for an acquittal or raising a doubt against the validity of the case for conviction is usually left to the far from satisfactory remedy of calling such witness as his own witness and leaving him open to cross-examination by the prosecution.

Anything bordering on the suppression of evidence, or the conscious omission of material evidence merely because it did not fit the prosecution case would, of course, represent in our system as it would in yours, good grounds for quashing a conviction thus obtained on the basis of a violation of the accused's right, under the terms of our Constitution, to a trial in due course of law. Clear as that right in a convicted accused might be, it manifestly is a much less valuable right as a post factum remedy than would be a proper procedure preventative of the happening of such injustice. Our present system of preliminary examination, which I understand is not entirely different from yours, merely vests in a judge the task of examining the evidence tendered and submitted on behalf of the prosecution and the evidence, if any, tendered and submitted on behalf of the accused and reaching a decision as to whether, upon that evidence, a prima facie case for the prosecution has been established. He has not got, of course, any power to call for any other witnesses, other than those whose statements are submitted on either side, nor to make any investigations on his own. The judge, therefore, conducting such preliminary examination, even if he suspected or was informed that the prosecution was aware of a credible witness who cast a doubt upon the case for which they were contending would have no power to force them to call that witness, though he could, of course, permit the accused to call him.

If, therefore, his brief were extended so as to give him inquisitorial or investigatory powers, then, in such an event and provided he became aware of the existence of such a witness, it is possible to conceive of a system where he could summon him, himself examine him, and, in effect, even if the accused were being returned for trial, make him part of the evidence which the prosecution would be obliged to call.

Notwithstanding this advantage, I still believe that the total separation of the function of the judiciary from that of the prosecution is far too valuable a guarantee of a fair trial, and of the confidence of the people at large in a fair trial, to make any amendment of or invasion into it, even for the apparent purpose of obtaining a fair and complete presentation of the evidence by the prosecution, wise.

With regard to civil proceedings different considerations may apply. On the one hand, the general concept of the court being available to be called into action to the extent and for the issues only chosen by the complainant or plaintiff before it, seems, if anything, stronger in relation to civil proceedings than it is in relation to the prosecution of criminal proceedings. Litigation between parties must never be impeded, but surely it should seldom be encouraged. A very close colleague of mine at the Irish bar, Oliver Gogarty (the son of a well-known Irish literary figure at the beginning of the century, who spent a considerable time here in the United States, Oliver St John Gogarty, and not without much of his father's wit) used to be particularly aggrieved when—as, certainly in Ireland, was their habit—persons concerned with the claims departments of insurance companies used in regard to actions against them frequently recommend a course of conduct on the basis that it would help to discourage litigation. Oliver frequently said to me that this was an absolute piece of nonsense, that litigation was not something you could either encourage or discourage: it was a major calamity which occurred to you from time to time and might with luck always be avoided.

Be that as it may, certainly it is not something which should depend upon the courts to initiate it, nor should the courts ever be seen to be thought to impose litigation, either ab initio or the extent or nature of litigation upon the litigants before it.

On the other hand, except in so far as the litigation before it may consist of a contest between the individual and the state or state institutions, the same vital and fundamental questions of constitutional law and constitutional rights may not apply in civil actions as do in criminal cases.

There are many forms of advocacy acceptable to other legal systems other than the common law systems in civil cases which, while clearly an indent on the adversarial system, do not of themselves represent a departure from a fair procedure. In some systems, the court calls or summons all the witnesses. In one sense, in common law countries, with the subpoena issued under the authority of the court, this could be said to be technically so there as well. In the systems to which I am referring, what follows then is that the judge examines the witness and, having done so, leaves him or her available for cross-examination by both the parties. I understand from persons who have knowledge of the practice in some of the European countries that this in theory has been greatly watered dawn, and significantly so, by the habit of many judges to ask the witness their name; their address, if relevant, their qualifications; and possibly the manner in which they are concerned in the issues before the court. Having done so, the witness is then left to be examined by both the parties.

Leaving aside the advantages or disadvantages that may arise from the confining of counsel examining a witness on the direct to nonleading questions, such a system is not very largely different from the common law system of the calling of witnesses and does not appear to have any major advantage, nor possibly to have any great disadvantage either.

With regard to the calling of evidence, however, the power of the court to call witnesses not suggested by either of the parties is the major breakaway from the adversarial system.

I understand that this is very largely availed of in relation to the calling by the court of technical, or expert, witnesses who will be asked by the court to examine the material or location that affects the issues in dispute and then to give evidence, as the witness of the court, of those matters, subjecting himself or herself, of course, to the examination by counsel on each side. This does, undoubtedly, represent a major departure from the adversarial system. It is different from the concept of an assessor whose function, in our law at least, in Ireland, is wholly confined to interpreting the evidence of other expert witnesses and who does not become involved in the making of a technical examination, himself, nor of the expression of a technical opinion.

There are, however, many possible advantages to such a system. I have already indicated in an earlier part of this paper what I believe to be the very rapid and wide expansion of the importance of technical evidence in the resolution of civil cases. Even assuming a complete honesty on the part of expert witnesses, I suppose all our experience is that by reason of the manner in which they become involved in a case by reason of the inevitable and, again, maybe quite honest emphasis and slant of the facts of the case with which they are supplied in order to arm them, to make their scientific or technical examination, and to express an opinion, they inevitably become associated, to some extent, even if it is subconsciously, with the interest and claim of their client.

The task of resolving a contest between two honest but at the same time by now committed technical witnesses of roughly equal experience and qualifications is a massive one for a judge or for a jury. It seems to me that we should, with the extent of this development of technical evidence, be at least considering the possibility of the court employing experts for the specific purpose of examining the material at issue and expressing an opinion in the witness box, subject to cross-examination by each of the parties concerned.

It would appear logical, if one contemplates the possibility of the court employing an expert as a witness to assist in resolving issues of fact, that one should also consider as to whether in relation to the determination of issues of law which are either of a general application outside the scope of the case before the court, or concern the interpretation of constitutional provisions, that similar assistance of an independent nature emanating from the court might be contemplated.

The most obvious example of this is the use of the Advocate-General in the Court of the European Community. He is, by definition, a wholly independent officer, learned in the law and independent, not only of the parties before the Court, but, in a sense, of the Court itself. He proposes to the Court, in oral submission, in public conclusions, views, and opinions and much of what, in my experience—having had the opportunity of sitting in on a number of sessions or presentations by Advocates-General in Luxembourg—what really might be considered to be a draft judgment. As the system is there worked, he would largely be drawing his conclusions and opinions from the submissions of the parties before the Court and certainly from the factual features presented by them. It is easy to see an adaptation of his role, however, that would involve him in drawing to the attention of the Court factual matter not presented by either party, that might assist in the resolution of a major legal question, and also in having a special role to indicate to the Court the consequences of a legal decision in a particular case with regard to other cases as yet unheard or unforeseen.

For such a system there are obvious attractions and, in particular, it avoids the situation where, in relation to the construction of constitutional provisions in particular, the narrow front on which, for example, a legislative provision is either attacked or defended, may improperly affect the correctness of the overall question of its validity.

I think I should, however, indicate an experience which may favor the retention, even in these instances, of the relatively strictly adversarial system.

There is provided by the Constitution of Ireland, under Article 26, a procedure whereby the President of Ireland, who is the last chain in the legislative framework of the Constitution, may when a bill passed by both Houses of the Oireachtas has been submitted to him for his signature, of his own volition and on his own decision, submit that bill to the Supreme Court to determine the question as to its validity, having regard to the provisions of the Constitution, either in toto, or in regard to separate parts of it. When that is done, the Supreme Court nominates counsel and the solicitor to instruct them to oppose or attack the bill, and the Attorney General by himself and/or counsel engaged by him, defends its constitutional validity. No evidence is adduced. This is the only originating jurisdiction that the Supreme Court of Ireland exercises. If, with regard to a bill or a specific portion of a bill, the Supreme Court concludes that it is on a reference under Article 26 consistent with the Constitution, then the President signs it, it becomes law, and that bill, or that portion of the bill, may never again be challenged in any court by any individual.

I think it is proper for me to say, without being in any breach of the sworn fealty I owe to the Constitution of Ireland, that this particular method of testing the constitutional validity of a bill represents considerable difficulties. It is necessary for the counsel assigned by their ingenuity and for the court in so far as it may have to, by adding to that, to conceive of each and every hypothetical case that could arise under the impugned provisions of the statute so as to ensure whether the statute could yield an unconstitutional result. It is, in my experience, at least, a considerably more difficult task than is the ordinary task of the Supreme Court, which would be on appeal from the High Court, to determine an issue as to the constitutional validity of a statute already enacted in the light of the experience and consequences of that statute as proved in evidence by a person complaining of its invalidity.

In so far, therefore, as any departure from the adversarial conduct, even of the debate on legal and constitutional issues of the description that I have indicated, was to yield a sort of trial of the moot or an advisory role in the court of the facts proved before it, my experience would raise a significant query as to the value of that method of determining great issues of law or constitutional interpretation.

I am conscious that these random thoughts on the future of advocacy may have raised many more questions than they have answered and indeed that you may consider that there are many questions and answers which have not been raised at all.

Of some things, however, I am absolutely certain. To be an advocate in the practice of the law is to belong to an ancient and honorable calling. It is an exacting discipline not adapted to those of faint heart or infirm health. It can be frustrating, depressing, and stressful. It requires of its practitioners not only a shining integrity but also a fierce independence. It is a service that should, subject to certain ethical limitations, be available alike to saints and to rogues.

But it has rewards much more important and more lasting than the material rewards it may attract, which compensate for its hardships. The raw material of the craft of an advocate is human nature and, for my own part at least, that can never be dull. But there is a reward that transcends the excitement of the courtroom and even that supreme moment of satisfaction, the victory. It surely is the knowledge that by the exercise of your skill as an advocate and the maintenance of the standards required of you as such, you are taking a major part in realizing one of humanity's greatest achievements: the securing of justice.

Long may the part played by the advocate in that great task remain as it is.

Untitled (Sonnett Lecture)

Chief Judge Sol Wachtler

Judge Sol Wachtler delivered the sixteenth Sonnett lecture in 1987. Judge Wachtler was elected to the New York Court of Appeals in 1972. Governor Mario Cuomo then appointed him Chief Judge of the Court in 1985.[1] Prior to serving on the Court of Appeals, Judge Wachtler had an almost ten-year career in Long Island politics, winning a number of positions for the Republican party.[2] Born in Brooklyn, New York, Judge Wachtler attended Washington and Lee College, earning both a bachelor's degree and a law degree over the span of five years.[3] After college, Solomon Wachtler was drafted by the Army—he legally changed his name to Sol during service—then spent a brief time in private practice in Queens, New York.[4]

In *People v. Liberta*, Judge Wachtler penned one of his most noteworthy opinions.[5] The case came to the Court of Appeals over a question of whether the marital exception defense to a rape charge applied when husband and wife were separated under a court-issued order of protection.[6] Judge Wachtler discerned and resolved a more fundamental issue, finding that there was no rational basis—and therefore it was unconstitutional—to distinguish between marital and nonmarital rape, effectively removing the marital exception to rape in its entirety.[7]

Judge Wachtler's Sonnett lecture championed vigilance to the rights of individuals by noting the limitations of original intent and its potential to overrun the Ninth Amendment to the United States Constitution.[8] This express admonition is that the Bill of Rights "shall not be construed to deny or disparage other rights retained by the people." Wachtler dismissed unchecked reverence for the words and actions of the past and, instead, demanded that words are "dependent on each generation to give them a meaning and content for [their] own time and place."[9] In support of this proposal, Wachtler recalled the historical definitions and redefinitions of the meaning of the word "men,"

Introduction written by Michael D. Jenks, J.D., Class of 2015, Fordham University School of Law.

1. *See* John R. Bunker, *"You Could Look It Up": The Judicial Opinions of Sol Wachtler on the New York Court of Appeals*, 52 SYRACUSE L. REV. 847, 848 (2002).
2. *See* JOHN M. CAHER, KING OF THE MOUNTAIN, 44–50 (1998).
3. *See id.* at 34, 37.
4. *See id.* at 39–40.
5. *See* 64 N.Y.2d 152 (1984).
6. *See id.* at 159–60.
7. *See id.* at 163–64.
8. U.S. CONST. art. IX; *see generally* Sol Wachtler, Chief Judge, N.Y. State Court of Appeals, Sonnett Lecture (1987), *infra* (transcript on file with *Fordham Law Review*).
9. *Id.* at 2.

tracing a chronological progression of some of the most famous and infamous Supreme Court cases from *Dredd Scott* to *Brown v. Board of Education.*[10] In addressing the original intent approach favored by then-Attorney General Edwin Meese, Wachtler first recognized the near impossibility of applying original intent to modern-day technological issues.[11] He further cautioned against the danger of undermining the Ninth Amendment through the application of an original intent approach, resulting in governmental encroachment into the rights of individuals.[12] Those that would use original intent to "side with the government whenever the government's interests are contrary to those of the individual" could not be further from the true intent of the framers.[13] Wachtler notes that there is ample evidence in the writings of the framers that support an approach to Constitutional interpretation guided by changing social norms.[14] The charge to avoid the pitfalls of original intent construction resonate at least as strongly today as they did when Judge Wachtler delivered his Sonnett lecture; it is critical that judges, lawyers, and legislators alike heed Judge Wachtler's warnings on abuse of original intent lest another *Dredd Scott*–style decision imposes another severe stain on our great democratic experiment.

1987 Sonnett Lecture

I was in Philadelphia in September representing New York State at the bicentennial celebration. You see, Governor Cuomo recently signed into law a bill passed by our legislature appointing me the New York Chairman of the United States Constitutional Bicentennial Commission. I was flattered until I remembered that it was a similar appointment that moved Chief Justice Burger to resign—I wonder if they were trying to tell me something.

The celebration of our Constitution is not being marked by fireworks and tall ships as was the birthday of the Statue of Liberty. Instead, it is a celebration of reflection. Last July 4, we were reminded that we are the children of a nation of immigrants. That they survived—and in fact thrived—is a testament not only to their own fortitude, but also to the foresight of our constitutional forebears, and to the seeds of a just government that they planted so firmly.

We can be rightly proud of our Constitution—a Constitution written at a time when Maryland and Virginia were about to go to war over navigation rights in the Potomac River, when Massachusetts was still recovering from Shay's Rebellion, when New Jersey

10. *See id.*
11. *See id.* at 3.
12. *See id.*
13. *Id.*
14. *See id.* at 3–5.

had her own customs service, and nine of the thirteen colonies had their own navies. When, as one French writer observed of the various states, "Their political interests, their commercial views, their customs and their laws are so varied that there is no way in which these states can become a nation." And yet those men, assembled in Philadelphia during that hot summer two hundred years ago, created a nation—and a free society.

Those who came before us did their work well.

Yet we would be negligent to be satisfied with a mere celebration of the past. Celebrations are also a time for examination and resolve to consider where we are now, what the future holds in store for us, and whether the future will see the survival of this great democratic experiment.

The answer lies with each of us and a fundamental recognition of what America is all about. It is a historic past—and it is a love of country summed up in the single emotion known as patriotism and it is national defense and it is the integrity of our economy. But it is and must be much more to those of us who will be responsible for our nation's future. That responsibility, I believe, does not include an acceptance of the belief that the past has done its work for the present and that our liberty, which is the cornerstone of democracy, is guaranteed. The truth is that one generation can never protect the rights of another, and although our greatest documents—the Declaration of Independence, the Constitution and the Bill of Rights—are ideal reflections of our finest aspirations, they are not self-fulfilling chariots of justice. For all their beauty, they are only words, dependent on each generation to give them a meaning and content for its own time and place.

For example, I cannot think of words less in need of annotation than the truth so proudly declared self-evident in our Independence Declaration that: "All men are created equal." Yet, it is all too clear that while our founders wrote those words with hearts full of devotion to freedom and justice for mankind, they never once meant to include members of the black race or women. Every generation—from *Dred Scott*, where a black person could be owned, to *Plessy v. Ferguson*, where the Constitution, amended in the wake of a bloody civil war—was interpreted by different Supreme Court Justices to say that there must be equal treatment for blacks—but that equality could still be separate, to *Brown v. Board of Education*, where still different Justices of the Supreme Court, interpreting the same Constitution, held that there must be true equality between the races. And most recently, the *Santa Clara Highway Department* case, which upheld affirmative action to achieve equality for women. All of these progressive interpretations of our Constitution have given the simple words "all men are created equal" a meaning and content consistent with and reflecting *our* evolving principles, *our* morality and *our* sense of justice.

We have seen the same change and expansion of meaning occur with virtually all of our constitutional principles, and as the pace of our lives has quickened, so too has the pace of change.

Despite this, there are those, like our Attorney General, Edwin Meese, who say that "original intent is the only legitimate basis for constitutional decision." I have difficulty with that premise.

In the first place, I do not know, and I am certain that Attorney General Meese does not know, how the framers' intent would apply to the problems of pollution in the Hudson

River or whether a terminally ill patient should be removed from a life support system. A more fundamental problem arises when those who have embraced the doctrine of original intent are quick to side with the government whenever the government's interests are contrary to those of the individual. If ever there was a thought or a promise that was contrary to the original intent of the framers, that would be it. Indeed, it was the pain of despotic government that caused our founders to seek independence and to write a Constitution that would protect individual liberties from an oppressive government. For them to say, in the name of original intent, "An individual does not possess a constitutional right, unless that right is granted by the constitution"—or to suggest that such rights as "the right of privacy," not having been provided for in the Constitution, are not guaranteed—is to stand the real "original intent" of the framers on its head. Indeed, the argument overlooks the unique character and historic value of the American Constitution.

By creating a new government possessing only limited powers delegated by the people, the drafters of the Constitution felt that they would avoid the abuses of power experienced in the past and would in fact eliminate the need for a Bill of Rights. When critics of the Constitution noted the absence of a Bill of Rights, Alexander Hamilton made the point in the Federalist Papers by asking a pointed question: "Why declare that things shall not be done which there is no power to do?" The absurdity of listing all the rights retained by the people was underscored by Noah Webster, when he sarcastically suggested that there be a clause "that everybody shall, in good weather, hunt on his own land, and catch fish in rivers that are public property . . . and that Congress shall never restrain any inhabitant of American from eating and drinking, at seasonable times, or prevent his lying on his left side, in long winter's night, or even on his back, when he is fatigued by lying on his right." Alexander Hamilton went further and argued that a Bill of Rights "[is] not only unnecessary in the proposed Constitution, but would even be dangerous. Could not someone perversely read the Bill of Rights backwards to permit the government to do anything with respect to personal liberties that the Bill of Rights did not specifically prohibit the government from doing?"

Those who wanted a Bill of Rights recognized that these were legitimate concerns. That is why the Ninth Amendment was written: "The enumeration in the Constitution of certain rights shall not be construed to deny or disparage others retained by the people." If those who espouse the doctrine are looking in the Constitution for the power of the people to do certain things, I will agree with them that they will not find it there. But that does not mean that such rights do not exist. The Ninth Amendment and the concept of retained powers have rarely been addressed by the courts. In most cases the courts have been able to resolve conflicts by reference to one or more of the rights specified in the Bill of Rights. But that is becoming increasingly more difficult as we move farther away from the Eighteenth Century and confront, in the modern technological world, problems that our forbears could not have anticipated in their wildest imaginings. Thus, on occasion, and sparingly, the courts have dipped in to that vast reservoir of retained powers to protect the individual from government intrusions unknown and unimaginable in the age of King George III.

Justice Goldberg did so in his concurring opinion in *Griswold v. Connecticut*, in which the Supreme Court first recognized the right of marital privacy. More recently, in the *Richmond Newspapers* case, Chief Justice Burger relied in part on these retained powers to uphold the right of the public and the press to attend criminal trials—a right not specifically mentioned in the Bill of Rights. It is understandable that the courts would, and should, be reluctant to employ a concept so susceptible to subjective judgments. There is a need for judicial respect for the prerogatives of the executive and legislative branches under our separation of powers doctrine.

The Ninth Amendment should not be used as a roving commission to invalidate programs initiated by the people's elected representatives whenever a court feels they are ill advised. There is a place for judicial restraint. But the protection of such things as individual and privacy freedoms is a uniquely judicial obligation and responsibility. Judicial restraint should not be confused with judicial abdication.

And I don't think for a moment that our founding fathers intended for us to interpret the Constitution according to their divined intent, divorced, somehow, from contemporary understanding. As Thomas Jefferson phrased it, in a free society, "nothing is unchangeable but the inherent and unchangeable rights of man." And John Marshall, a member of the Virginia ratifying convention and later Chief Justice of the United States, spoke to this very point when he said that the Constitution "was intended to endure for ages to come and be adapted to the crises of human affairs." That Constitution, written in one hundred days, has survived for two hundred years; that Constitution, written with a quill pen, has survived to this era of the microchip precisely because we have recognized that the framers of the Constitution were not so arrogant as to suppose that they could anticipate the future. And this nation has survived because there has been, in this state and country, a recognition of our obligation to enact laws and to adapt the law to the "crises of human affairs."

The framers of the United States Constitution, remarkably, asked the most conservative of the institutions, the courts, to implement words laid down by radicals, dreamers, and idealists. Those responsible for our justice system were given the responsibility of maintaining our constitutional ideals of justice, and their success—our success—will be measured not in what we do to appease the majority, but what we do to protect the rights of the individual. As the celebration of our Constitution continues, we will hear some describe the framers as exemplars of a revolutionary idealism the likes of which we will never see again—"an assembly of demigods" as Thomas Jefferson referred to them—and others will see them more as politicians than statesmen, who struck pragmatic deals out of self-interest. There will be those who will speak of "defects," as did Justice Thurgood Marshall, and others who will insist, as does Attorney General Meese, on "original intent." But in the final analysis there will be the inevitable realization that we were given a Constitution that is nothing short of miraculous.

But, as I noted initially, this celebration must also be a time for resolve, and that must include a recognition that the primary predicate for the Constitution was the expressed need to create a society free from governmental oppression to guarantee the individual's liberty under the law. So long as we remain constant to that objective, so long as we are willing to defend in our courts those basic freedoms which are cherished by all of our citizens—even if that protection is unpopular, then we have done our part in seeing to it that the future of our Constitution is secure.

Time moves quickly, and while the present may seem eternal, all too soon future generations will be here to appraise us as we now appraise the work of our forbears. When they do, they will hopefully conclude: This was our nation—still in its youth—and we too did our work well.

The Invisible Prince

Hon. Francis T. Murphy

Justice Francis T. Murphy delivered the seventeenth Sonnett lecture, entitled *The Invisible Prince*, on November 2, 1988.[1] Serving forty years on the bench in both New York City and New York State courts, Justice Murphy has written on a wide array of issues advocating for legal and social reform.[2] He established, among other things, the New York Supreme Court Appellate Division's Committee on Child Sexual Abuse, the First Department's Committee on Juvenile Justice Dyslexia and Other Learning Disabilities, and approved the erection of a thirty-eight-foot marble Holocaust Memorial at the Appellate Division Courthouse.[3] Born in the Bronx, New York, Justice Murphy attended Fordham College, after having served in the U.S. Navy during World War II.[4] In 1952, he graduated from New York Law School.[5] Justice Murphy served as an Assistant District Attorney in Bronx County before being appointed to the bench.[6]

In 1957, Mayor Robert Wagner appointed Justice Murphy to the Municipal Court of the City of New York.[7] When the municipal and city courts merged in 1962, Justice Murphy became a judge in the Civil Court of the City of New York.[8] In that same year, Justice Murphy was elected Justice of the New York Supreme Court.[9] In 1971, he was appointed to the First Judicial Department of the Appellate Division by Governor Rockefeller.[10] Six years later, Justice Murphy was designated the Presiding Justice of the Court.[11] He presided over 63,000 appeals and held this distinguished position until he reached the mandatory judicial retirement age in 1997.[12] Upon retiring from the bench, Justice Murphy joined the law firm of Kelley Drye & Warren.[13]

Introduction written by Muriel Raggi, J.D., Class of 2015, Fordham University School of Law.

1. Francis T. Murphy, *The Invisible Prince*, Sonnett Lecture (1989) (transcript on file with *Fordham Law Review*).
2. *Francis T. Murphy*, N.Y. State App. Div. First Dep't, http://www.courts.state.ny.us/courts/ad1/centennial/Bios/ftmurphy2.shtml (last visited Mar. 8, 2014) [hereinafter First Dep't].
3. *Attorneys & Professionals: Francis T. Murphy*, Kelly Drye & Warren LLP, http://www.kelleydrye.com/attorneys/francis_murphy (last visited Mar. 8, 2014) [hereinafter *Attorneys & Professionals*].
4. First Dep't, *supra* note 2.
5. *Id.*; *Attorneys & Professionals*, *supra* note 3.
6. First Dep't, *supra* note 2.
7. *Id.*
8. *Id.*
9. *Id.*
10. *Id.* The Appellate Division is New York's intermediary appellate court.
11. *Id.*
12. *Id.*
13. *Id.*; *Attorneys & Professionals*, *supra* note 3.

Justice Murphy's contributions to legal and social reform extended to educating and assisting his fellow legal professionals. Justice Murphy coordinated with local bar associations to establish clinical advocacy programs, and directed the publication of educational newsletters for practitioners in practice areas involving criminal defense, children with learning disabilities, and family court.[14] He also established New York State Assigned Counsel Plan, Inc., which facilitates the appointment of representation to criminal appellants, as well as the Law Guardian Program, which publishes a newsletter for law guardians.[15]

Justice Murphy's Sonnett lecture, *The Invisible Prince*, advocated for reform by shedding light on the dilemma all of mankind faces in choosing among morality, power, and success.[16] Justice Murphy recognized the soundness of some of the principles enunciated in Niccolo Machiavelli's *The Prince*,[17] ultimately concluding that Machiavelli was wrong about the nature of mankind.[18] Justice Murphy asserted that humans can lead ethical lives while still attaining power and success, but to try to exist between the two is commensurate to ignoring half of one's body after a stroke.[19] Justice Murphy noted the shortcomings of law firms and law schools in failing to teach young lawyers to be interrogative of the morality of their profession and their clients' actions.[20]

He advocated for lawyers to be in better touch with the morality of their profession. Justice Murphy's suggested middle ground permits lawyers to lead an ethical life and recognize their morality while still prospering and achieving success. This solution remains relevant and provides insight into the inner workings of an individual's mind in striking that balance.

1988 Sonnett Lecture

On a December night in 1513, a poor, thin, middle-aged man of medium height, having a bony face, piercing eyes, and thin lips lining a secretive smile, entered a little house in Sant' Andrea, seven miles from Florence. For fourteen years, he had been a dedicated statesman of Florence, which he had so loved that, fourteen years later, two months before his death, he wrote to his friend, Francesco Vettori, "I love my native city more than my own soul." In August 1512, Florence had been sacked by the Medici and, in November, he was dismissed from office. In February 1513, two assassins, intent upon slaying Giuliano de'Medici, were arrested. Four days later, they were executed. In the possession of one of them, a list of about twenty names was found, among them that of our poor friend.

14. *Attorneys & Professionals*, *supra* note 3.
15. *Id.*
16. Murphy, *supra* note 1.
17. Niccolo Machiavelli, The Prince (1532).
18. Murphy, *supra* note 1, at 11.
19. *Id.* at 11–13.
20. *Id.* at 9.

He was seized and tied to a rack. Normally, four turns were the maximum torture inflicted by the rack, but our friend endured six turns, yet he would not confess. In March 1513, after having been kept handcuffed and shackled in prison, the walls of which were "full of lice so big and fat they seem like butterflies," he was released. Exiled from Florence, he returned to his five children, to whom he had been a good father, and to his wife, to whom he was constantly affectionate and constantly unfaithful. After he entered that little house that December night, he sat at his table and, in a remarkable letter to his friend Vettori, he described his impoverished, desolate life. In autumn, he wrote, he had been rising before dawn and going out with bird cages on his back in order to snare thrushes. Now, in winter, he rose with the sun and engaged in the selling of wood and in the petty arguments that accompanied it. At lunch, his family and he ate meager food. At the local inn, he spoke to travelers and played cards all day with the innkeeper, the butcher, a miller, and two bakers. With these there were many loud and offensive arguments over a few pennies. In words that, like a door flying open, suddenly reveal his soul, he told Vettori: "Caught this way among these lice I wipe the mold from my brain and release my feeling of being ill-treated by Fate: I am happy to be driven along this road by her, as I wait to see if she will be ashamed of doing so." In one of the famous passages of Italian literature, our friend told Vettori what he does at night:

> When evening comes, I return to my home, and I go into my study; and on the threshold, I take off my everyday clothes, which are covered with mud and mire, and I put on regal and curial robes; and dressed in a more appropriate manner I enter into the ancient courts of ancient men and I am welcomed by them kindly, and there I taste the food that alone is mine, and for which I was born; and there I am not ashamed to speak to them, to ask them the reasons for their actions; and they, in their humanity, answer me; and for four hours I feel no boredom, I dismiss every affliction, I no longer fear poverty nor do I tremble at the thought of death: I become completely part of them. . . . I have noted down what I have learned from their conversations, and I composed a little work . . . where I delve as deeply as I can into thoughts of this subject, discussing what a principality is, what kinds there are, how they are acquired, how they are maintained, why they are lost.

Thus, in that little house was *The Prince* written by Niccolo Machiavelli, in spirit talking as a peer to the great ancients, to Aristotle, Caesar, Cicero, and Alexander.[1]

The Prince, one of the most powerful political works ever written, was given by Machiavelli to Lorenzo de'Medici, the ruler of Florence, in the vain hope that Machiavelli would thus prove himself of value to the Medici and would be able to support his family by having a position in that world of politics that he loved with unbridled passion. Indeed, Machiavelli wrote to Vettori, "I am wearing myself away, and I cannot remain in this state

1. *See* The Letters of Machiavelli 249 (Allan Gilbert ed. and trans., Chicago, 1961); Machiavelli 69 (Peter Bondanella and Mark Musa eds. and trans, Penguin Books 1979); Roberto Ridolfi, The Life of Niccolo Machiavelli 135–38, 151–53 (Cecil Grayson trans., Chicago 1963); J. Hale, Machiavelli and Renaissance Italy (London, 1961); the painting of Machiavelli by Santi di Tito (1536–1603) in the Palazzo Vecchio, Florence.

for long without being despised for my poverty, not to mention my desire that these Medici lords begin to make use of me, even if they start me off by rolling stones."[2]

Machiavelli's writing of *The Prince* was indeed a curiously ugly gift, for by it he betrayed himself. As a servant of the Florentine republic, he had proved his absolute dedication to the ideal of freedom in a republic. Now, for the sake of a political job, for the sake of entering the political game that was his inner life, he wrote *The Prince*, a handbook for autocrats, a bedside book for those who would use the state to dominate the people. Lorenzo de'Medici, it is said, accepted Machiavelli's gift of *The Prince* with less enthusiasm than two hunting dogs that were given to him at the same time.[3] The story is told in proof of Lorenzo's intellectual insensibility. I read the story differently. Lorenzo, I suspect, knew that two hunting dogs would give him more loyalty than a politician whose principles were for sale.[4]

This slim book is one of the classics of our civilization. Like the Bible, few have read it and everyone claims to know its contents.[5] What did Machiavelli write in *The Prince* that

2. The Italian novelist, Alberto Moravia, tried his hand at a psychoanalytical interpretation of *The Prince* in *Portrait of Machiavelli*, 22 PARTISAN REVIEW 357, 369 (1955): "Machiavelli had written the *Prince* not out of conscious Machiavellianism or the conscious wish to condense into one book all that he had learned and practiced during his years as a professional in politics; nor with the instinct of a poet who observes with delight and cherishes a terrible figure in a wholly aesthetic atmosphere. Instead . . . he wrote in order to drag himself up from the mire of indifference, to prove to himself that he was alive, to hurt himself and feel the pain." There is nothing like the voice of a Freudian mystic.

3. GIUSEPPE PREZZOLINI, MACHIAVELLI ANTICRISTO (Rome, 1954), MACHIAVELLI 148 (Gioconda Savini trans., New York, 1967).

4. Machiavelli's gift of *The Prince* to Lorenzo is a collector's specimen of man's almost sublime capacity to deceive himself. Did Machiavelli, the great political realist, believe that Lorenzo de'Medici, successor of Giuliano de'Medici, would grant Machiavelli a governmental position when Lorenzo knew that (a) Machiavelli had been a suspect in a conspiracy to assassinate Giuliano, (b) the Medici's had recently treated Machiavelli to six turns on the *strappado*, (c) Machiavelli had zealously loved the republic that the Medici's had overthrown, and (d) *The Prince* itself justified Machiavelli's betrayal of Lorenzo in order to restore a republic? *See* Mary G. Dietz, *Trapping the Prince: Machiavelli and the Politics of Deception*, 80 AMERICAN POLITICAL SCIENCE REVIEW 777 (1986). Indeed, the reader might smile when he learns that, in order to write *The Prince*, Machiavelli interrupted his writing of his great work in favor of a republic, *The Discourses*. THE DISCOURSES OF NICCOLO MACHIAVELLI (Leslie J. Walker trans., New Haven, 1950). On the other hand, the reader will stop smiling when he examines arguments that the *Discourses* was begun after Machiavelli had completed The Prince. H. Baron, *Machiavelli: The Republican Citizen and the Author of* The Prince, 76 ENGLISH HISTORICAL REVIEW 217–53 (1961).

5. An extraordinary accounting of the conflicting theories that have barnacled *The Prince* is found in Eric W. Cochrane, *Machiavelli: 1940–1960*, 33 JOURNAL OF MODERN HISTORY 113–36 (1961). The bibliographical list exceeds three thousand. *See* RICHARD C. CLARK, MACHIAVELLI: BIBLIOGRAPHICAL SPECTRUM. I REVIEW OF NATIONAL LITERATURES 93–135 (1970); FELIX GILBERT, MACHIAVELLI AND GUICCIARDINI (Princeton, 1965); MACHIAVELLI: CYNIC, PATRIOT, OR POLITICAL SCIENTIST? (De Lamar Jensen ed., Boston, 1960). A major study of Machiavelli's political thought is that of J. POCOCK, THE MACHIAVELLIAN MOMENT (Princeton, 1975); *see also*, J. WHITFIELD, MACHIAVELLI (Oxford, 1947), S. ANGLO, MACHIAVELLI: A DISSECTION (London, 1969). The only

so captured the imagination that, for more than 450 years, many have read his words, celebrated their realism inwardly, yet drawn back from publicly identifying with him?[6] What in Machiavellianism made the noted twentieth-century German historian, Meinecke, say that it "was a sword thrust in the body politic of Western humanity, causing it to cry out and to struggle against itself"?[7] Why did the philosopher, Maritain, say of it that it was "the most violent mutilation suffered by the human practical intellect."[8] Yet what is it, in the face of these judgments, that makes it the rare reader who puts down *The Prince* without an inexplicable disquiet, perhaps the pain of a suppressed benevolence towards Machiavelli for appealing to that pagan desire for an amoral realism that lies deep within each of us?

What did Machiavelli write in *The Prince*? Man, said Machiavelli, desires the creation of a powerful state. However, in order to create such a state man cannot have delusions about mankind, else the truth will punish him. He must therefore closely observe reality and history, particularly the minds of antiquity, for man never changes. He is everywhere and always the same. Therefore, man must guard against those who do not look at men as they are, but who look at them as they ought to be. Statesmen of that idealistic kind do not deal with things as they are; they drag men to ruin. They commit the mortal sin of unrealism. Men are not as Jews and Christians idealize them. In the main, men are, said Machiavelli, "ungrateful, wanton, false and dissimulating, cowardly and greedy . . . arrogant and mean, their natural impulse is to be insolent when their affairs are prospering and abjectly servile when adversity hits them."[9] There is no universal scheme, no a priori method, by which one can learn about man. Men say they love liberty, when, in fact, they care little for it. The idea means more to them than its reality. Liberty means less to them than security and property. Man responds to love, but in dealing with him fear is more reliable, though the ruler should be cautious that fear does not turn into hate. As for the morals of the men in Machiavelli's ideal state, these are to be found in the clas-

---

work of Machiavelli that was published in his lifetime, apart from *Mandragola*, a comedy, and *The First Decade*, a poem, was the *Art of War* (1521). The first edition of *The Discourses* appeared in 1531 (Blado, Rome), four years after Machiavelli had died. *The Prince* and the *History of Florence* first saw print in 1532 (Blado, Rome).

6. The November 1972 interview of Henry Kissinger by Oriana Fallaci, the Italian journalist, includes this exchange: "Q: Not Machiavellian by any chance, Dr. Kissinger? A: No, not at all. Why? Q: Oh, only that, listening to you, one sometimes wonders not how much you have influenced the President of the United States, but to what extent you have been influenced by Machiavelli. A: To none whatever. There is very little of Machiavelli's one can accept or use in the contemporary world" Oriana Fallaci, *Kissinger*, The New Republic, December 16, 1972, at 17, 21.

7. Friedrick Meinecke, Machiavellism 49 (Douglas Scott trans., London, 1957) [Friederich Meinecke, Die Idee der Staatsrason in der neueren Geschichte 61 (2d, ed., Munich/Berlin, 1927)].

8. Jacques Maritain, *The End of Machiavellianism*, 4 Review of Politics 292, 294 (1942).

9. *See* Giuseppe Prezzolini, *The Christian Roots of Machiavelli's Moral Pessimisim*, 1 Review of National Literatures 26, 27 (1970).

sical societies that dominated Machiavelli's imagination. States, he says, are made great by pagan virtues—power, pride, public spirit, austerity, the pursuit of glory, and the expansion of the *patria.*

And now we come to Machiavelli's notoriously dark side. He is so candid that one can almost become fond of him. Machiavelli tells us that, in order to rule, one may have to be ruthless. Force, fraud, cruelty, treachery, and even the slaying of the innocent, may be used. If men must be governed by measures that violate Judeo-Christian morals, then so be it. And this is the heart of Machiavellianism. Machiavelli did not liberate politics from morals, or ethics, or religion. Machiavelli said that man must choose between a pagan and a Judeo-Christian life. If he chooses the Judeo-Christian life, then man chooses virtues that are insuperable obstacles to the creation of that Roman society that men want. Machiavelli does not deny that what Jews and Christians call good is actually good, and what is evil is indeed evil. He does not say that cruelty, fraud, and the slaying of the innocent are good attributes. He argues simply that it is impossible to practice Judeo-Christian virtues and enjoy a strong society. Practice Judeo-Christian virtues and you will be politically impotent, for the powerful, the clever, and the unscrupulous are waiting in the woods to overwhelm you. If you want Athens or Rome, take your eyes away from Jerusalem. This unresolved choice between two incompatible moral worlds is the secret wound that man suffers until today, and suffered before Machiavelli wrote *The Prince.* Expressing varying levels of horror, Machiavelli's commentators have given *The Prince* meanings so different that one wonders whether they have read the same text. Some say that *The Prince* is a satire.[10] Others say it is a disguised warning or cautionary tract.[11]

One thinks *The Prince* a literary performance common in the Renaissance, a "mirror for princes."[12] Others say that it is an anti-Christian piece, a defense of the pagan life.[13] Others see in him a kind of Hamlet, a humanist grieved by human vices that make evil decisions politically unavoidable; thus he separated politics from ethics.[14] Some look at Machiavelli as a technician of power, ethically and politically neutral.[15] Many identify Machiavelli as the supreme realist.[16] Among the multitude standing in the bibliographical forest, there are those who say that Machiavelli saw the state as a work of art, and so treated

10. *See* Garrett Mattingly, *Machiavelli's Prince: Political Science or Political Satire?*, 27 American Scholar 482–91 (1958).

11. Benedictus de Spinoza, *Tractus politicus*, ch. 5, sec. 7; Rousseau, *Du contrat social*, book 3, ch. 6, note; *see* I. McKenzie, *Rousseau's Debate with Machiavelli in the Social Contract*, 43 Journal of the History of Ideas 209 (1982).

12. *See* A.H. Gilbert, Machiavelli's Prince and its Forerunners (Durham 1938).

13. Prezzolini, *supra* note 3; Hiram Haydn, The Counter-Renaissance (New York, 1950).

14. *See* Benedetto Croce, Elementi di politica 62 (Bari, 1925).

15. *See* Ernst Cassirer, The Myth of the State c. 12 (London and New Haven, 1946); W.K. Hancock, *Machiavelli in Modern Dress: An Enquiry into Historical Method*, 20 History 97–115 (1935–36).

16. See De augmentis, book 7, ch.2; book 8, ch.2; The Works of Francis Bacon, vol. 5, 17, 76 (Ellis and Heath Spedding eds., London, 1857–74).

politics as an aesthetic exercise.[17] An original interpreter saw Machiavelli as a religious and national reformer who might have been for the Italians, if they had been like the Germans, what Luther, Machiavelli's contemporary, had been for Germany.[18] Whatever these views, the one commonly held of Machiavelli is that of most Elizabethan dramatists and scholars: for them, Machiavelli was called by the devil to lead men straight to hell.[19]

While opinions of Machiavelli and his origination of *The Prince* vary radically, the text of *The Prince* is fixed for those who want to judge its ethical nature. For them, Machiavellianism is an unarmed, stationary target.

Machiavelli was a radical pessimist who did not see in man the image of God, and thus anointed the forehead of totalitarianism. Of course, politics is a part of ethics. Everyone can see that Machiavelli reversed that relationship by shaping ethics for the sake of politics. Indeed, he taught that religion should be used for the state because of religion's "power as a myth in unifying the masses and cementing their morale." [20] Certainly, the true end of politics is the common good, an ethical end, while for Machiavelli the purpose of politics was conquest by power. And surely everyone knows the answers of personal ethics to political ethics, that man may never commit evil for any good of any kind, and that the common good is provided by justice and political morality.[21] Yet, while these arguments are intellectually persuasive, they do not explain why man is so drawn to Machiavelli, almost like a sightseer drawn to an abyss. It is this human fact that draws me to Machiavelli as the subject of this address, for it has led me to detect in Machiavelli the invisible Prince in our society, a society that Machiavelli never could have foreseen.

There is something in Machiavelli's brutally frank choice of evil over good that simultaneously fascinates and repels man. If *The Prince* was a mirror for princes, Machiavelli is in some way a mirror for man. The choice between good and evil, like a persistent beggar standing at the door of man's soul, demands an answer to the tormenting question of whether God exists. In writing *The Prince*, however, Machiavelli did not assume that God exists. Indeed, he showed no interest in conscience or in any theological issue, for *The Prince* is not an abstract or philosophical treatise. It is an empirical analysis of politics written independently of any philosophical construct. Machiavelli, neither a jurist nor a philosopher,

17. Jacob Burckhardt, The Civilization of the Renaissance in Italy part I, ch.7, 104 (S.G.C. Middlemore trans., London, 1929); Charles S. Singleton, *The Perspective of Art*, 15 Kenyon Review 169–89 (1953).

18. Leonhard von Muralt, Machiavellis Staatsgedanke (Basel, 1945); *see* Prezzolini, *supra* note 3, at 281, 325. In the mind of the Communist, Antonio Gramsci, Machiavelli's *The Prince* became a work advocating an antifeudal revolution by the Italian peasants. A. Gramsci, The Modern Prince and Other Writings (New York, 1957).

19. Mario Praz, *Machiavelli and the Elizabethans*, 13 Proceedings of the British Academy 49–97 (1928); Felix Raab, The English Face of Machiavelli (London, 1964); *see also*, Maritain, *supra* note 8; Leo Strauss, Thoughts on Machiavelli (Glencoe, 1958).

20. The Prince and The Discourses (The Modern Library 1940), introduction by Max Lerner, at xxxvii; trans. by Christian E. Detmold (1891). Cochrane, *supra* note 5, at 114, recommends George Bull's (Penguin) translation of *The Prince* as the more accurate version.

21. Maritain, *supra* note 8.

was free of the intellectual convictions of his age. He does not even refer to natural law, the language of which was used in his time by Christians, pagans, jurists, philosophers, and theologians. In *The Prince*, there is no sign of Platonic or Aristotelian teleology, no allusion to any ideal order, no shadow of any belief in man's place in nature. Machiavelli lays all of his cards on the table face up. He warns us that he has taken a path never before trodden by any man.

Man, however, knows that the moral nature of his life and that of the world turns upon the answer to the abstract but very real question of God's existence. And man knows the answer that ordinary man has given.

Man does not *know* whether God exists. Man, if he has given the matter any consideration, *believes* that God exists and *hopes* that good will be rewarded and evil punished in an afterlife. If this is so, if man's soul is like a frozen sea out of which he can escape only by faith, then the man of faith, just as Machiavelli has said, has much to fear, for he knows also that among the mass of mankind faith is for many, if not for most, a dry reed waiting for the first soft wind to break it. Hence, man's anxiety over Machiavellianism is rooted, on one hand, in a sense of genuine peril should he live totally in faith and, on the other hand, in a revulsion for the evil of which *he* is capable should he, in his painful, existential condition, deny God. Nor is man's sense of a Machiavellian danger limited to Machiavellianism in politics. Logically, Machiavellianism engages not only political life but the whole of human life.[22] Thus the reader of *The Prince* profoundly senses that only his faith in God separates him from Machiavelli, and that that faith, under pressure, may give way, as it

22. Maritain, *supra* note 8, at 295. Croce, however, interprets Machiavelli as granting, out of necessity, an amoral autonomy to politics. Like two stepping-stones in a brook, the amorality of politics and the morality of Judeo-Christian private life are seen as close together but forever apart, surely a weak grasp of reality, for an amoral state would inevitably infect the totality of its society. As for Machiavellianism's penetration of life, one need only scan a social sciences index. *See* M. Dingler-Duhon and B. Brown, *Self-disclosure as an Influence Strategy: Effects of Machiavellianism, Androgyny, and Sex*, 16 Sex Roles 109 (1987); S. Flynn et al., *Cheating as a Function of Task Outcome and Machiavellianism*, 121 Journal of Psychology 423 (1987); C. Poderico, *Machiavellianism and Anxiety among Italian Children*, 60 Psychology Reports 1041 (1987); J.M. Comer, *Machiavellianism and Inner and Outer Directedness: A Study of Sales Managers*, 56 Psychology Reports 81 (1985); G. Nigro and I. Galli, *On the Relationship between Machiavellianism and Anxiety among Italian Undergraduates*, 56 Psychology Reports 37 (1985); M.M. Okanes and L.W. Murray, *Machiavellian and Achievement Orientations among Foreign and American Master's Students in Business Administration*, 50 Psychology Reports 519 (1982); M. Ames and A.H. Kidd, *Machiavellianism and Women's Grade Point Averages*, 44 Psychology Reports 223 (1979); M.M. Okanes and L.W. Murray, *Manipulative Tendencies and Social Insight in a Hospital Setting*, 47 Psychology Reports 991 (1980); D.C. Martinez, *Differences among Chicano and White Students on Items of Machiavellianism Scale*, 48 Psychology Reports 433 (1981); P.B. Johnson, *Need Achievement and Machiavellianism*, 46 Psychology Reports 466 (1980). Of interest to the corporate executive might be Antony Jay's *Management and Machiavelli* (1968), and surely of interest to bench, bar, and society at large is the argument that the lawyer's role is an amoral one. *See Symposium on the Lawyer's Amoral Ethical Role*, 1986 American Bar Foundation Research Journal 613–73 (1986). For a feminist perspective of Machiavelli, *see* Hanna Pitkin, Fortune is a Woman: Gender and Politics in the Thought of Niccolo Machiavelli (Berkeley, 1984).

does whenever he violates any of his moral beliefs. Man, after all, knows nothing if he does not know his own inconstant heart. Further, if the reader of *The Prince* reflects at all upon what Machiavelli has said, he will suddenly realize that *The Prince*, written for the eyes of a prince over 450 ago, might as well have been addressed to the reader's ears for his guidance as an ordinary citizen in a modern democracy.

What one man may do, millions may do as one man. Hence, Machiavellianism may be expressed in the majoritarian rule of a democracy as well as in the person of an autocrat.[23] It may be expressed by people acting independently of their governmental structures. It may be found in private social institutions, in economic classes, behind the eyeglasses of a profession, and under the birettas of pious cardinals. Wherever power is consecrated to the preservation of an entity or of a class, there in the evening twilight sits the invisible Prince. Indeed, his residence has a chameleon character, for he always seems to be in someone else's country, never one's own. Yet, however invisible he may be, he leaves an imprint, a mark, a scar. Our nation yields examples, past and current, from which we naturally avert our eyes.

Prior to our Civil War, the legislatures of slave states showed their love of a much-professed Christianity by enacting statutes of a kind designed to sustain slavery, and hence the economy of the slave states, by stripping the black man of his humanity. Section 59 of chapter 92 of the laws of Mississippi of 1840, for example, provided:

> Sec. 59. If any negro or mulatto shall be found . . . to have given false testimony, every such offender shall, without further trial, be ordered by the . . . court, to have one ear nailed to the pillory, and there to stand for the space of one hour, and then the said ear to be cut off, and hereafter the other ear to be nailed in like manner, and cut off at the expiration of one other hour, and moreover to receive thirty-nine lashes on his or her bare back, well laid on, at the public whipping post.

Alabama's laws of 1843 thoughtfully drove the knife of slavery into that part of a black man that would never leave him in doubt about his condition: "U16. All slaves are hereby prohibited from keeping dogs, under any pretence or consideration whatsoever; and the slave or slaves so offending upon complaint thereof before any justice of the peace, shall be punished with not exceeding twenty-five stipes for every such offense." A Christian society that would not allow a man a dog would be careful about allowing him to learn of the Gospel. Accordingly, the people of Alabama provided: "If any slave . . . shall preach to . . . any . . . slaves . . . unless in the presence of five respectable slave-holders, any such slave . . . shall, on conviction before any justice of the peace, receive . . . thirty-nine lashes for the first offence, and fifty lashes for every offence thereafter." These slave statutes are not anecdotal material. They are laboratory specimens of Machiavellianism. Other historical slides may be placed under the microscope.

Our trade union movement arose out of the clash between property's self-interest and labor's demand for social justice. However, when our labor unions reached a point of equilibrium with their capitalistic managerial opponents, many unions used their members

23. *But cf.* Prezzolini, *supra* note 3, at 326.

for purposes that had little to do with social justice and much to do with the enlargement of raw union power. These union members expressed a majoritarian will for power that blinded them to the ethical character of the means they used and the ends they sought.

Law firms paying large salaries set the standard for the success of law schools. Law firms and their clients need skilled legal artisans. They do not need lawyers who will question both the morality of their professional services and the morality of their clients' businesses. Accordingly, it is not by chance that law schools do not require the study of moral philosophy, and particularly the problems of distributive justice. It is not by chance that law school catalogues read like handbooks for uncritical minds intent solely upon earning fees. The law school has thus developed as an institution less intellectually inquisitive than the university of which it is a part. In fitting itself within our economic system, the substantial material rewards of which are found neither in the middle nor the lower economic classes, it pays the price of accommodation. It has produced students whose pockets are stuffed with laws and whose minds are as distant from issues of morality as they are from problems in biochemistry.

In the main, our established religions have carefully protected their institutional popularity by accommodating themselves to things as they are, not as they ought to be. Neither the labor movement, nor the struggle of women for equality, nor the confrontation of anti-Semitism or racism, nor the peace movement of the Vietnam period[24] or the peace movement of today, can trace their leadership to steps of institutionalized religion. Notwithstanding the unconditional, ethical commitments of our religious faiths, their histories in this country have generally shown a contentment with silence when speech required courage.

Surely, the invisible Prince would have approved the silence of those churchmen in this country who for generations have known of the appalling poverty of Latin America where a feudal system, without feudalism's historical justification, enabled landowners to dominate the wretched and agonized poor upon whose backs the landowners lived.

Surely, the invisible Prince would have approved of the uncritical silence of our religious institutions following the nuclear bombings of Hiroshima and Nagasaki, to say nothing of the obliteration bombing of Dresden and other German cities, acts that violated the principle of discrimination in the conduct of warfare.

Of course, there have been activist clergymen who have engaged themselves as their consciences directed, but our characterization of them as activists distinguishes them from their churches.

24. One wonders what our young Vietnam dead would have thought had they read the recent article of Michael Vlahos, now Director of the Center for the Study of Foreign Affairs, U.S. Department of State: "Worse, the war trampled upon the old myths of America itself. In Vietnam we were fighting like a corrupted European monarchy, insensitive to the squandered blood of our young men, pursuing objectives defined by a pseudo aristocratic elite. That this war was prosecuted by the party of reform and revolution (in recent mythic terms) and that its members developed the callous theories of 'graduated response' and 'signaling' only heightened the perception of corruption. The military was fighting the war, but a sinister bank of academic and political sorcerers was pulling the strings." *The End of America's Postwar Ethos*, 66 Foreign Affairs 1091, 1100 (1988).

As to activism, one must indeed keep a sharp eye out for the invisible Prince. Consider, for example, why our college students demonstrate against apartheid in South Africa but never, never against poverty in the United States. There are about thirty-three million Americans who are poor, and another twenty to thirty million who have so little that, by any measure, they are in need. Why are college students not demonstrating for the poor in America? Is it because American college students have nothing to risk in South Africa but, in the United States, they risk much if they have to divide the economic pie with the poor?

Are American college students disciples of a materialism so hypocritical, so self-centered, that they pretend to love the black poor in Pretoria but would not give a nickel for the tears of the black poor in Detroit or the white poor in Georgia?

Ask our politicians what they actually intend to do for the millions of America's poor. You will see that love beyond family, bed, and friends has very narrow limits and that all the Bible thumping in the world, all of the praying and chanting, all of the handclapping, bowing, and singing will not move a hair on a poor man's head.

And then ask how much we are willing to deny ourselves to help the poor. If we are willing to do very little, and if we are but a few of the tens of millions of our class, then we will begin to see the silhouette of the invisible Prince defending a society's economic system by violating its religious ethics. Should we look even closer, we will see that we, the politically dominant working and middle classes, eager to compel the upper classes to share economic benefits with us, are unwilling to share our economic benefits with the lowest economic classes. Moreover, we may hold to our positions even though the limitations of our natural resources indicate that the working and middle classes in the West must make substantial sacrifices if the lowest classes are to receive a sufficiency for their human development.

What we do to our poor at home, we do to the poor abroad. Developed nations have given only one to two percent of their gross national products in assistance to underdeveloped nations. The failure to give more is traceable in great part to the refusal of middle-class electorates to reduce their own level of consumption.

In the end, Machiavelli was right. We must choose between the Rome of pagan antiquity and the Jerusalem of Judeo-Christian ideals. And Machiavelli was right in his view that the great body of mankind chooses neither Rome nor Jerusalem but instead vacillates between them, attempts to compromise, weakens, and fails. Yet, Machiavelli was fatally wrong about the nature of man. He saw in man a selfish, treacherous animal, unchangeable by time or place, whose history was worthy of study because it was bound to repeat itself. Machiavelli therefore chose Rome.

Man, however, is not the weak victim of the rules of a Platonic world of perfection. He is capable of living an ethical life while doing so with the cunning of the serpent and the innocence of the dove.[25] He is capable of living a life in which he has transcended himself by reaching out in love to others. If he lives that life, the life of the Judeo-Christian tradition,

25. Matthew 10:16.

then he will have lived a life in a dimension that has made him truly human. In the end, he will know that by love he has touched the heart of the mystery of creation.

If, however, man chooses a life in the abyss between Rome and Jerusalem, then he will have taken, in Machiavelli's words, "middle ways that are very injurious."[26] Medicine yields an appropriate analogy.

There is in neurology a curious, catastrophic condition sometimes suffered by victims of stroke. In the prose of medical understatement, it is called "neglect of the left."[27]

The patient acts as if nothing is wrong, yet he reports that his left side has disappeared. When shown his paralyzed left arm, he denies that it is his arm, asserts that it belongs to someone else, and taking hold of it may fling it aside. He looks dull, apathetic, inattentive. He is indifferent to failure and reports a feeling of "something missing." He neglects the left side of his body in dressing and grooming. He fails to shave one side of his face or to comb his hair on one side. He cannot put on eyeglasses or insert dentures, for half of him does not exist. His perception of the unity of his body, of the bodily parts to one another, has been ripped root and branch from his mind. At night, while other patients sleep, he lies in bed, repeatedly pressing his right side against a sideboard, all in search of an unreachable sense of limitation, of wholeness, of unity.

So it is with Machiavelli's conception of man. The half of him that is animalistic, that is attracted by the invisible Prince, that part remains; but the part that inclines itself to God, to "what ought to be," is abandoned and atrophies. A sense of subtle paralysis of the will intrudes and with it a sense of a lack of wholeness, of unity, a sense of the abyss. In pathology, the condition is called a morbid inertia. In theology, it is called "an oppressive sorrow that so weighs upon a man's mind that he wants not to exercise any virtue." It is the deadly sin of sloth, the sin of neglect by which we separate ourselves from humanity. It is the sin by which we open our door to the world only wide enough to take in the morning paper.

26. Discourses I 26.

27. In neurology, it is designated as unilateral asomatognosis (Anton-Babinski syndrome). Raymond D. Adams and Maurice Victor, Principles of Neurology 339–340 (3rd ed., New York, 1985).

28. *See* T.S. Eliot, *Niccolo Machiavelli*, in For Lancelot Andrewes 50 (1928): "Lord Morley . . . intimates that Machiavelli . . . saw only half of the truth about human nature. What Machiavelli did not see about human nature is the myth of human goodness which for liberal thought replaces the belief in divine grace." *See also* Prezzolini, *supra* note 9. *But cf.* Machiavelli's letter of May 17, 1521 to Francesco Guicciardini, an administrator in the papal states, a confidant of the Medici Pope Clement VII, and Renaissance Italy's leading historian, through whose friendship Machiavelli must have hoped to gain the favor of the Medici's: "When your letter arrived, I was sitting on the toilet thinking about the vanities of this world, and I was completely absorbed in constructing a preacher after my own tastes for Florence, one that would suit me perfectly. . . . It is true that I differ with my fellow citizens in this as well as in other matters, for they want a preacher to show them the way to Paradise, and I want to find one that will show them how to go to the devil. . . . I believe that the true way of going to Paradise is to learn the way to Hell in order to avoid it." Bondanella and Musa, *supra* note 9, at 73–74.

Fictions

Hon. John J. Gibbons

Judge John Joseph Gibbons delivered the eighteenth Sonnett lecture, entitled *Fictions*, in 1989.[1]

An accomplished jurist and attorney, Judge Gibbons has authored publications and received accolades too numerous to list. He is also a champion of individual liberties. Judge Gibbons led the fight in New Jersey to abolish the death penalty in the 1970s and has since participated in other states' antideath penalty movements.[2] In *Rasul v. Bush*, he challenged the Bush Administration's detention of 660 foreign nationals at the Guantanamo Bay Naval Base in Cuba.[3] More recently, he has criticized the Obama Administration's use of drones for targeted killings.[4] Judge Gibbons also founded and directs his law firm's pro bono program, the John J. Gibbons Fellowship in Public Interest & Constitutional Law.[5]

Judge Gibbons was born in 1924 in Newark and raised in nearby Belleville, New Jersey.[6] He served in the United States Navy from 1943 to 1946 and graduated from the College of the Holy Cross in 1947.[7] After receiving his law degree from Harvard Law School in 1950, Judge Gibbons spent about two decades in private practice with the Newark law firm Crummy, Gibbons & O'Neill.[8]

In 1969, President Richard M. Nixon nominated Judge Gibbons to succeed Gerald McLaughlin on the U.S. Court of Appeals for the Third Circuit.[9] He was confirmed by the Senate and received his commission in December 1969.[10] Judge Gibbons was elevated to Chief Judge in 1987, a position he held until retiring from the judiciary on

Introduction written by Alexander J. Callen, J.D., Class of 2014, Fordham University School of Law

1. John J. Gibbons, *Fictions*, Sonnett Lecture (1989) (transcript on file with *Fordham Law Review*).

2. John J. Gibbons, Attorney Biography, Gibbons P.C., http://www.gibbonslaw.com/biographies/attorney_biography.php?attorney_id=78 (last visited Mar. 6, 2014).

3. 542 U.S. 466 (2004).

4. John J. Gibbons, *War on Terror: Life, Death and Drones*, L.A. Times, July 19, 2013, http://articles.latimes.com/2013/jul/19/opinion/la-oe-gibbons-targeted-killings-drones-20130719.

5. Gibbons, Attorney Biography, *supra* note 2.

6. John J. Gibbons, *Biography of Directory of Federal Judges, History of the Federal Judiciary*, Fed. Judicial Ctr., http://www.fjc.gov/servlet/nGetInfo?jid=844&cid=999&ctype=na&instate=na (last visited Mar. 6, 2014) (hereinafter Fed. Judicial Ctr.).

7. Gibbons, Attorney Biography, *supra* note 2; Fed. Judicial Ctr., *supra* note 6.

8. Gibbons, Attorney Biography, *supra* note 2.

9. Fed. Judicial Ctr., *supra* note 6.

10. *Id.*

January 15, 1990.[11] Upon retirement, Judge Gibbons returned to private practice with the law firm Gibbons P.C. in Newark and became a professor at Seton Hall Law School.[12]

Judge Gibbons's Sonnett lecture commemorated the bicentennial of the United States' social contract—the Constitution and, especially, its Bill of Rights. In *Fictions*, Judge Gibbons traced the evolution of the various legal fictions Anglo-American regimes have employed to validate their sovereignty, from notions of monarchical divine mandates to our own theory of republican popular consent.

Judge Gibbons began with David Hume's observation that all governments depend upon the good opinion of those governed. Maintaining such legitimacy requires cloaking the reality that sovereignty derives from military strength, which English governments accomplished through legal fictions, such as the divine right of kings, social compacts, and virtual representation.

Judge Gibbons contrasted the circumstances fostering these English fictions with those in the early American colonies, where the king and his army were far away, an abundance of land permitted dissatisfied colonists to relocate freely, and there was very little government beyond the local level. As Judge Gibbons observed, "[w]hen government was almost completely unobtrusive upon individuals the stimulus for speculation about the sources of its authority were largely lacking."

Instead, a natural rights theory filled the void. Indeed, the American Revolution marks the conversion from a trickle-down legal fiction, in which rulers grant liberties to individuals, to a trickle-up, in which governments, at least theoretically, require permission before curtailing "self-evident" or "inalienable" individual rights.[13]

Although a popular sovereignty theory legitimizes our government, Judge Gibbons admonishes us to guard against the dangers of representatives who treat their authority as irrevocable and suppress dissension—even when a majority dissents. As Judge Gibbons cautioned, "[o]ur only guarantee that our own government will not become tyrannical lies in the constant insistence that individual rights entrenched in the Bill of Rights are living realities, not fictions." The issue of individual rights entrenched in the Bill of Rights continues to be the subject of debate and evolving jurisprudence.[14]

---

11. *Id.*

12. *Id.*

13. *See* The Declaration of Independence para. 2 (U.S. 1776).

14. *See, e.g.*, Town of Greece v. Galloway, 134 S. Ct. 1811 (2014); United States v. Sterling, 724 F.3d 482 (4th Cir. 2013) (reporter's privilege claim denied); E. Berger, *Individual Rights, Judicial Deference, and Administrative Law Norms in Constitutional Decision Making*, 91 B.U. L. Rev. 2029 (2011); William M. Carter, *A Thirteenth Amendment Framework For Combating Racial Profiling*, 39 Harv. Civ. Liberties L. Rev. 17 (2004); Donna Lieberman, *Infringement on Civil Liberties After 9/11*, 56 N.Y.L. Sch. L. Rev. 1121 (2012); Neal Kumar Katyal, *Stochastic Constraint*, 126 Harv. L. Rev. 990 (2013) [reviewing Jack Goldsmith, Power and Constraint: The Accountable Presidency After 9/11 (2012)].

1989 Sonnett Lecture

The amendments to the Constitution of the United States, to which we commonly refer as the Bill of Rights, were proposed by Congress on September 25, 1789, and became part of that Constitution on December 15, 1789. It was upon that ratification that the American Revolution finally was completed; the amendments made explicit in the Constitution the premises of that revolution. The key terms in the previous two sentences are *Constitution*, *revolution*, and *Bill of Rights*. Because we are celebrating political events that occurred in the last quarter of the eighteenth century, we should try to use those terms in the same sense that they were used at that time. The terms *Constitution*, *revolution*, and *Bill of Rights* had meanings for educated Americans in that quarter century that are not necessarily the same as the meanings with which we use those terms today.

Take the word *revolution*. Most of us think of the American Revolution as a war that commenced at Lexington, Massachusetts, on April 19, 1775, and ended at Yorktown, Virginia, when General Cornwallis surrendered on October 19, 1781. That was not the eighteenth-century usage of the word *revolution* among educated people. At that time, it primarily meant a change in the established order of things. True, most such changes in the established order of things were accompanied by—probably even caused by—a war. The term *revolution*, however, referred not to the military outcome, which might simply have put the victor in charge of the same old structure of relationships in society, but to the new structure in those relationships.[1]

Take the term *Constitution*. Most of us, when we hear that term, think of the American written Constitution enforced by the courts as law. In 1787 the term had been in use, however, for several hundred years to refer to something entirely different, namely, the appropriate boundaries, often vague, between the sovereign and his subjects.[2] In 1787, when the American written national Constitution was drafted, Englishmen had been struggling with the appropriateness of their constitution for several centuries, during which England underwent several revolutions. Americans, who had lived on this side of the Atlantic Ocean for a century and a half, had largely been spectators of those revolutionary events, rather than participants in them. Their happy situation as spectators, however, did not mean that they were ignorant of the issues of sovereignty that were being fought out in the British Isles.

Take, finally, the phrase *Bill of Rights*. The eighteenth-century use of this term was both specific and generic; it was specific in the sense that it originated as a reference to a specific English statute passed in 1689. It was generic in the sense that it referred, by 1789, to a theory of sovereignty that the 1689 statute was thought to reflect.[3] When, during the ratifying debates on the 1787 constitution, the Anti-Federalists rallied under the banner

1. *See* Compact Edition of the Oxford English Dictionary 2533 (2d ed. 1971).

2. *See* B. Bailyn, The Ideological Origins of the American Revolution 175–84 (1967).

3. *See* G. Wood, the Creation of the American Republic 1776–1787, at 266 (1969); 1 J. Reid, Constitutional History of the American Revolution; The Authority of Rights 69–70 (1986).

of a bill of rights and forced the Federalists to propose one, they were less interested in the specific than the generic usage. It is that usage I propose to explore.

SEVENTEENTH-CENTURY SOURCES OF LEGITIMACY

In 1758, David Hume observed that all governments, whether despotic and military or free and popular, depend upon the good opinion of the governed.[4] Hume made this profound observation at a time when government on the western side of the Atlantic had been, relatively speaking, both free and popular for seven generations. During those same seven generations, the British Isles, in contrast, underwent periods of despotism and of civil war, which tested the limits of public acceptance of the legitimacy of traditional theories of sovereignty. Appreciation of the uses in North America of late eighteenth-century political vocabulary demands putting one's self in the position of those happy spectators who watched from afar the turmoil in the mother country.

Modern government came to England with the Norman Conquest.[5] The title "William the Conqueror" tells us the real source of Norman authority to impose such government.

Norman political power came from the possession of superior force.[6] As Hume later observed, however, an elite minority could not in the long run maintain its ascendancy in the face of opposition from those governed. Thus, opposition to the Norman kings and their successors continued, culminating in the faceoff at Runnymeade on June 15,1215, when King John, the Roman Catholic Bishops, and the Barons worked out a complicated set of legal fictions which served to legitimize royal sovereignty.

One legal fiction was that the monarch's right to govern had been confirmed by the Pope, as Christ's vicar on earth. Royal power to govern was legitimized by association with a source of power that, in the popular imagination, was more significant than force of arms. This fiction assumed that all rights were derived from the same spiritual source. The Magna Carta, after first acknowledging the special position of the Roman Catholic Church, continued with the statement that "[w]e also have *granted* to all the freemen of our kingdom, for us and our heirs for ever, all the underwritten liberties, to be had and holden by them and their heirs, of us and our heirs for ever."[7] The use of the language "we also have granted" confirms the fiction. Although King John used this rhetorical form, the reality was that the Bishops and Barons at Runnymeade commanded sufficient physical power to

4. D. HUME, ESSAYS AND TREATISES ON SEVERAL SUBJECTS OF FIRST PRINCIPLE OF GOVERNMENT (1758).

5. A comparatively sophisticated central government existed under the Anglo-Saxon kings which the Normans expanded and refined. *See* V. GALBRAITH, THE MAKING OF DOMESDAY BOOK (1961); DOMESDAY BOOK: A REASSESSMENT (P. Sawyer ed., 1985).

6. William did in fact have a legitimate claim to the English throne. *See* D. DOUGLAS, WILLIAM THE CONQUEROR: THE NORMAN IMPACT UPON ENGLAND 169 (1964). Nonetheless, it took a military triumph for that claim to become reality. *See id.* at 176–77.

7. Magna Carta, cap. 2 (1215), *reprinted in* N.J. STAT. ANN CONST. (West 1971) (emphasis added).

confront that of their Norman sovereign and assented to John's continuance in office on terms which they dictated. The Bishops and Barons, themselves a small minority in England, willingly embraced the fiction because their own special positions were also thereby legitimated. The Magna Carta says as much, putting in King John's mouth the following words: "All the aforesaid customs and liberties, which we have granted to be holden in our kingdom, as much as it belongs to us, towards our people of our kingdom, as well clergy as laity shall observe, as far as they are concerned, towards their tenants."[8] The Magna Carta is a remarkably detailed code of laws on various subjects, all wrapped up in the fiction that the source of those laws is the king's exercise of authority of divine origin, confirmed by the Church of Rome.[9] The fiction was not that God had created man with rights with which the sovereign could not interfere, but that God's vicar on earth recognized the sovereign's authority to grant or withhold rights. In theory, the king was the source of all law, and even the Bishops and Barons, having empirically disproved the theory, continued to acknowledge the fiction.

By the late sixteenth century, when Englishmen began colonizing in the Western Hemisphere, disputes between the king and the church had seriously eroded the effectiveness of the Roman connection as a useful fiction for the legitimation of authority. The charters granted to various explorers and entrepreneurs by Henry VII, Elizabeth I, James I, and Charles I, authorizing colonization in their names, all commenced with the familiar announcement that each was sovereign by the Grace of God. Like the Magna Carta, colonization charters were couched in the form of grants of rights from a monarch exercising such dispensing spiritual authority.[10] Thus, the very titles of the leaders of colonial America to their positions of authority, like the titles of the Bishops and Barons at the time of the Magna Carta, depended on the same fiction. In England, however, by the early seventeenth century the fiction had been refined to accommodate the new reality that the forces aligned with Rome and the forces aligned with the English king opposed each other. For the Stuart kings in particular, the refinement eliminated the Roman connection in favor of an assertion that their authority to rule was derived directly from God. It was from monarchs asserting this fiction that English colonial charters were received.[11] Thomas Hobbes was perhaps the leading expositor of a theoretical justification for the new fiction in which the king, freed from the supposed constraints of the Roman church, became head of both church and state. Asserting that the Church of Rome was nothing more than the old Holy

8. *Id.* at cap. 60.

9. *Id.* at cap. 60.

10. *See, e.g.*, 7 The Federal and State Constitutions, Colonial Charters, and Other Organic Laws 3783–89 (F. Thorpe ed. 1909) [hereinafter Federal and State Constitutions] (First Charter of Virginia in 1606); 3 Federal and State Constitutions 1846–60 (Charter of Massachusetts Bay in *1629); id.* at 1677–86 (Charter of Maryland granted to Lord Baltimore in 1632).

11. The Political Works of James I (C. McIlwain 2d ed. 1918); J.N. Figgis, The Divine Right of Kings 66–106,137–76 (2d ed. 1965). *See generally* E. Morgan, Inventing the People: The Rise of Popular Sovereignty in England and America 19–37 (1988) [hereinafter Inventing the People] (discussing the elevation of kings by the governing elites to the status of spokesmen for the divinity).

Roman Empire in disguise, he justified subjugation of the church to the nation-state, a state in which the fictional sources of all rights, in matters even of religion, were derived from a king who spoke directly for God.[12]

When the American colonists received their charters, the English Parliament had not yet emerged as a locus of sovereignty. In theory, it was no more than a collection of wise counselors, called at the king's pleasure to consult with him and propose laws that only he could promulgate, and to agree on behalf of the places they represented to grant him revenue. During the reign of James I, however, when colonization in North America was in its infant stages, the reality and the theory of the role of Parliament began to separate. While the king still proclaimed himself as the source of all rights and the authority for all law, he became increasingly dependent upon the members of Parliament in maintaining the good opinion of the country upon which his actual ability to govern depended.

Two new fictions were developed in the early seventeenth century to achieve that end.

The first fiction was that members of Parliament were representatives of the people rather than counselors to the king.[13] The second fiction was that the king, as God's lieutenant, could do no wrong, although his ministers, bailiffs, or judges might occasionally misperceive the king's will.[14] In their representative capacity, the members of Commons could claim to speak for all subjects, although Commons was far from truly representative. But the representation fiction and the fiction that the king could do no wrong permitted the assertion, in the Petition of Right of 1628, that the king's subjects could not be taxed or confined by his ministers without "common consent by act of [P]arliament" and without "the process of law."[15] The fictions were carried a step further about that time when Commons began the practice of presenting to the House of Lords bills of impeachment of the king's ministers. Still, however, the source of all rights was God's lieutenant. Parliament merely began to assert that in some instances it knew the king's will better than he did.

The king's response to the assertion of rights, which his ministers must recognize even though he did not, was to refuse to convene a Parliament from 1630 to 1640. In the latter years, the necessity for restoring the good opinion of the country required that one be convened, and soon after it convened the parliamentarians forced the king to accept a Triennial Act which provided that Parliament would sit every three years whether he called them or not. By the device of impeachment, the self-proclaimed representatives of the people could, at least triennially, punish his ministers for misunderstanding his will. Thus,

12. *See* I. Hobbes, Leviathan: Parts I and II 79–80, 241, 326–27 (1960).

13. F. Morgan, Inventing the People, *supra* note 11, at 38–51.

14. *Id.* at 53. A famous exchange between Charles II and Lord Rochester captured the distinction in a more lighthearted fashion. As a royal epitaph, Rochester once suggested: "Here lies our sovereign lord the King/Whose promise none relies on;/He never said a foolish thing./Nor ever did a wise one." Oxford Dictionary of Quotations 407 (2d ed. 1955). To which Charles replied, "This is very true, for my words are my own, and my actions are my ministers." *Id.* at 136.

15. 3 Car. 1, ch. 4 (1628) *reprinted in* Sources of Our Liberties (R. Perry & Cooper ed. 1978).

the first step was taken toward transferring accountability of governmental ministers from king to Parliament.

Lord Coke summarized the new fictions in the oft-quoted aphorism "non sub homine sed sub Deo et lege." Coke has sometimes been associated with the assertions of a natural law jurisprudence but, if so, his jurisprudence still depended on the fiction of the divine authority for the exercise of sovereignty.[16]

The religious civil wars in England in the mid-seventeenth century placed enormous pressure on the fiction of divine origin of the sovereign's authority as the source of legitimation of the regime. They also exposed the fiction of representation, because when a Protestant Parliament came into being it simply stayed on from 1640 to 1653, carrying on a civil war against the nominal source of its authority to govern. Gradually purging 110 dissidents from its ranks and, thus, depriving of representation the geographic areas that had designated those dissidents, the Long Parliament first raised an army and eventually in 1649 deposed and beheaded their heretical king.[17] Interestingly, neither in the Long Parliament nor during the Commonwealth did the parliamentarians advance what we would today call a democratic justification for their actions. Issues like toleration of Roman Catholics would not be decided by majority vote of the people, but by their self-appointed and self-perpetuating representatives. In justification for their actions, the roundheads relied upon still another fiction. The newest fiction was that William the Conqueror's authority and that of his successors depended, not on conquest (which was the truth) and not on his legitimation by the Vicar of Christ (the older fiction), but on a contract between him and the people's representatives. If the king breached that contract, the people's representatives had a duty to depose him. If there was a people, it was the Parliament's so-called "New Model Army."[18] The roundheads' true source of authority, like that of William the Conqueror, was success in arms. But like William's successors on the throne, the roundheads needed more than this to persuade the mass of the population to submit to their government. There were obvious flaws in the roundheads' reliance on the sovereignty of the people, for if the people were sovereign they could depose Parliament, and it is likely that an actual majority in the kingdom had favored the king.[19]

An effort by the Levellers to promote an actual rather than fictional social compact—a proposed agreement of the people to be signed by every Englishman who agreed to transfer to his representatives specified but limited powers of movement—was finally rejected by the House of Commons as seditious. The roundheads' position was that once the fictional people conferred authority upon their fictional representatives in Parliament that authority was irrevocable. The representatives of the people thus could suppress heresy

16. *See* C. Tite, Impeachment and Parliamentary Judicature in Early Stuart England 88–110 (1974).

17. *See* D. Underdown, Pride's Purge (1985); B. Warden, The Rump Parliament (1974).

18. So argued, among others, the influential parliamentary leader Sir Henry Vane. See H. Vane, A Healing Question (1656).

19. *See* Morgan, Inventing the People, *supra* note 11, at 70–83.

even if a majority in the kingdom was heretical. Oliver Cromwell did so, passionately and ferociously.[20]

The Leveller contractarians were soon put down. In 1653 Cromwell unilaterally dissolved the remnants of the Parliament elected in 1640 and proclaimed a new Instrument of Government, pursuant to which elections were held for a unicameral Parliament with a strictly limited franchise. Seeking a way to legitimate itself, this body created a new House of Lords and urged the restoration of a monarchy. The king, however, would be chosen by Parliament rather than by the hereditary hand of God. Cromwell accepted the kingly powers tendered, but declined the title.[21]

After Cromwell died in 1658, the surviving members of the Long Parliament, who first had been called to Westminster by the king eighteen years before and dismissed by Cromwell five years before, reassembled there. They struggled for two years to find a way to govern a country increasingly dissatisfied with the excesses of military dictatorship. In 1660, the Rump members restored those members of the 1640 Parliament who had been purged, and that body dissolved itself in favor of a Convention that it summoned into existence.

The Convention promptly restored Charles II to the throne. It also passed bills that confirmed the Magna Carta and the Petition of Right.[22] This reconfirmation, however, merely restored the fiction that the king alone was the locus of sovereignty and the source of rights.

When Charles II called a new Parliament in 1661, the fiction of representation was temporarily interred. Its members disclaimed any legislative authority apart from the king, emasculated the Triennial Act, and restored the national Church of England with the king as its head. Charles II and his successor, James, failing to understand what Hume later explained, acted as if the fiction of their direct relationship with God was fact, and soon ran into trouble in dealing with their parliamentary counselors. Religious bigotry was the dominant opinion driving these English elects, and they reacted with alarm when Charles displayed a sympathetic attitude toward Catholics. Their alarm, however, did not immediately produce a resurrection of the fiction that Parliament represented the people. It would have been hard to make much use of that fiction as a way of assuring favorable opinion because the members of Parliament did not face an election from 1661 to 1679. Faced with the prospect that his Catholic brother might succeed to the throne, the Parliamentarians sought to change the succession, but Charles II would not agree, and between 1679 and 1681 he dissolved four Parliaments. It was in this climate that Algernon Sidney, who was hanged for treason in 1683, and John Locke, who escaped to Holland in 1682, began to develop a refined version of a fiction of representation. Locke's influential *Two Treatises of Government*, first published in 1698, but written earlier, was at bottom a justification for parliamentary exclusion from the throne of Charles II's Roman Catholic brother, James.

20. *Id.* at 20.

21. *See* Leveller Manifestos of the Puritan Revolution (D. Wolfe 2d ed. 1967), The Leveller Traces (W. Haller & G. Davies eds., 1944).

22. 3 Cat., ch. 1 (1828), 7 Statutes at Large, 317–20 (1763).

Charles's steps in gerrymandering Parliament were so successful, however, that when he died in 1685 James succeeded to the throne, challenged only by an abortive rebellion led by the Duke of Monmoth, Charles's bastard son.[23]

Unfortunately for James, his daughter Mary was married to William of Orange, who, like William the Conqueror and Oliver Cromwell, had the real rather than fictional source of sovereignty—an army with a proven record of success. Mary was next in line for the throne when a son was born to her father. The opponents of a king, sympathetic to Roman Catholics, encouraged William to spread the story that the child had not been born to the Queen, but had been smuggled into her bed. Acting on the fiction that he had to preserve God's true hereditary successions, William demanded that a new parliament, elected on the old apportionment plan, be called to determine the succession.[24] This ultimatum caused James to flee to France without calling a new parliament.

With the king out of the country, a "Convention" chosen in the manner William of Orange demanded, convened and, acting in the name of the people, declared that James had breached his fictional contract with it.[25] After declaring the throne vacant, this corporate embodiment of the people came up with an unusual blend of fictions, when it offered the throne not to Mary alone, who had a hereditary, and thus a divine claim, but to William as well. Therefore, the Convention attempted to blend in the throne both the fiction of the divine right of kings and the fiction that kings were selected by a social compact with the people. It was the government compact fiction which was most relied upon, however, because in offering the throne to William and Mary the Convention laid down conditions to which they had to assent.

William and Mary accepted those conditions and ascended to the throne. Once they were in place, the Convention declared itself to be a parliament, and presented their conditions as a bill for the king's assent.[26] King William signed the bill on December 16, 1689, making it a statute.[27] That statute is the Bill of Rights, to which so many subsequent references were made in North America in the following century. The Bill of Rights, therefore, is the first physical manifestation of the theretofore entirely mystical, and even then entirely fictional, government compact.

The next year Locke's influential book, written earlier, was published.[28] His purpose seems to have been to legitimate a new constitution—a new order of things—in which

23. *See* J. Jones, Country and Court: England 1658–1711 (1978). J. Jones, The First Whigs: The Politics of the Exclusion Crises, 1678–83 (1961).

24. *See* The Eighteenth-Century Constitution 1688 1815 (F. Williams ed. 1970).

25. I use the pronoun "it," rather than "them," because this assertion of the new civil compact refers not to individual rights held by real persons, but to rights held collectively by the artificial construct, an elite group, one house of which was elected by a narrow and unequal franchise, embodying in its corporate self the ultimate source of sovereignty.

26. 1 W. & M., ch. 2 (1689). 9 *Statutes at Large*, 67–73 (1689).

27. *Id. See also* Appendix A (reprinting England's Bill of Rights).

28. *See supra* note 23. For an examination of the parallels between William and Mary's 1689 Bill of Rights and John Locke's second treatise of government see Appendix A. [J. Locke, Two Treatises of Government 45–46 (P. Laslett, 2d ed. 1967)]

king and parliament shared sovereignty. Locke wrote provocatively of man in a state of nature entering into a social compact, but made it quite clear that the dissolution of the government, which had occurred with disturbing frequency during the religious wars, did not restore that natural state. Society continued, the social compact continued, and representative elites who had power could undertake to act on behalf of all, including Jews and Catholics, women, children, and servants, who had never had a voice in the selection of those representatives. Moreover, members of those groups had no individual rights that the representatives of the fictional people in their collective sense were obliged to recognize. And while kings formerly were restrained in theory, at first by their theoretical subservience to Rome and later by their own perceptions of God's will, the representatives of the people were never theoretically restrained in either manner. The fiction of the government compact was no more than a justification for the all-powerful parliamentary state. As the Levellers had earlier discovered, efforts to act as if the fiction of the social compact was fact were suppressed as treason. Although the issue was later debated, the fiction of representation of the people in parliament was never carried so far as to require that members of Commons vote in conformity with the instructions of their borough or county constituencies.[29] For the vast number of disenfranchised persons, including overseas colonists, the fiction of representation was refined further. Although members of Commons were elected from specific boroughs or counties, each member became a representative of the entire people of the Empire, and thus the disenfranchised were virtually represented even though they had no voice in the selection of an all-powerful parliament.[30] The protection of individual persons from the fictional corporate people depended not upon recognition of individual rights, but upon the structure of government, a doctrine of separation of powers developed somewhat vaguely by Locke in his *Second Treatise*.[31]

That the fictional social compact was what the government rested on can be appreciated from the ambiguity of the title "Bill of Rights," for the term "bill" in eighteenth-century usage was roughly the equivalent of "petition;" a petition could become a statute, and thus a law, only when a sovereign granted or approved it.[32] Thus this most famous manifestation of the Glorious Revolution, while embracing the fictions of the original government compact and of virtual representation, schizophrenically embraced as well the competing fiction of a divine origin through God's lieutenant, or positive law. And, while the Bill of Rights restated some of the provisions of the Magna Carta, it did not entrench them for future generations. Indeed, by 1969 subsequent British parliaments had repealed thirty-three of the Magna Carta's sixty-two clauses.[33]

29. *See* Morgan, Inventing the People, *supra* note 11 at 174–208.
30. *Id.* at 242–44.
31. J. Locke, *supra* note 23, at 143–44, 146–48, 151, 153, 159.
32. *See* S. De Smith, Constitutional and Administrative Law, 280–87 (1971).
33. A. Pallister, Magna Carta: The Heritage of Liberty, at 32,37–38, 73, 89 (1971).

LEGITIMACY AND THE COLONIES

The fiction that the parliament of England was the present corporate embodiment of the people who made the social compact in the dim and distant past was irrelevant to the North American situation in the seventeenth century. As noted earlier, English colonization began there on the authority of charters, which originated from the queen or king alone. Those granted to Sir Walter Raleigh in 1584,[34] to the Virginia Company in 1606, 1609, 1612,[35] to the Massachusetts Bay Colony in 1629,[36] to Lord Baltimore in 1632,[37] to the Duke of York in 1664,[38] and to William Penn in 1681[39] all antedated the emergence of the fictions of social compact and virtual representation. No act of parliament authorized them and no parliament, before or after their issuance, ever invited a colony to send representatives to it. Each conferred governmental authority as a grant from a sovereign purporting to be divinely endowed with authority to do so. There were differences in form among these charters, but all were essentially feudal. Indeed, the charter to Lord Baltimore was modeled after the charter of the Durham palatinate, a crown fiefdom.[40]

Reference is occasionally made to the Mayflower Compact of 1620 as a manifestation of the social compact. Certainly the forty-one males who signed it at Cape Cod in November 1620 were more or less in the state of nature. The document they subscribed, however, clearly is no acknowledgment of the sovereignty of the people, individually or collectively. Rather it is an acknowledgment of the authority of the church in civil matters, which in turn acted on the authority of a king who claimed to be God's lieutenant: a reconfirmation of the representations of loyalty and orthodoxy made to King James I, two years earlier, in hopes of obtaining from the Virginia Company or the crown a patent for colonization.[41] It was nine years before King Charles accommodated the Mayflower survivors with such a patent.

Still, the fiction of the divine right of a king as God's lieutenant was not very useful as a source of legitimation of governmental authority west of the Atlantic. The king was a long way off and had no army close by to enforce his perception of the divine will. Proprietors

34. 1 Federal and State Constitutions, *supra* note 10, at 53–57 (Charter to Sir Walter Raleigh granted in 1584).

35. See 7 Federal and State Constitutions, *supra* note 10, at 3783–89 (First Charter of Virginia in *1606. See also id.* at 3790–3802 (Second Charter of Virginia in 1609); *id.* at 3802–10 (Third Charter of Virginia in 1612).

36. *See* 3 Federal and State Constitutions, *supra* note 10, at 1846–60 (Charter of Massachusetts Bay in 1629.

37. *See id.* at 1677–86 (Charter of Maryland granted to Lord Baltimore in 1632).

38. *See* 2 Foundations of Colonial America 793–96 (K. Kavenagh ed. 1973) (Charter of New York From Charles II to Duke of York in 1664).

39. *See* 5 Federal and State Constitutions, *supra* note 10, at 3035–44 (Charter for the Province of Pennsylvania granted in 1681).

40. *See* C. Hall, The Lords Baltimore and the Maryland Palatinate 32–34 (1902).

41. Mayflower Compact, *reprinted in*, Sources of Our Liberties, *supra* note 15, at 60, *see* 1 C. Andrews, The Colonial Period of American History 249–99 (1934). The Leyden Agreement, *reprinted in* Documents of American History 14 (H. Commager ed. 1946).

like Lord Baltimore, capitalistic adventurers like the owners of the Virginia Company, or zealous clerics like the leaders of the Massachusetts Bay Colony thus were at least as dependent upon the good opinion of the populace as was the government in England; perhaps more so. Not surprisingly, all of the charter grantees devised representative assemblies. By the time of the Glorious Revolution every English colony west of the Atlantic has some form of such an assembly. These functioned until the late 1760s with little effort made on either side of the Atlantic to define their relationship to Parliament.

The Privy Council in England and the royally appointed governors in America exercised a veto power over colonial legislation,[42] but in theory this power was consistent with the older fiction that God is the source of all governmental authority. Moreover, the use of the veto proved ineffective. The Privy Council itself used the power sparingly.[43] The royal governors in contrast did make regular use of the veto which was just part of an arsenal that included powers to prorogue and dissolve assemblies and to remove judges at pleasure. In the wake of the Glorious Revolution, not even the crown enjoyed such powers in relation to Parliament. Yet practical factors, including the governors' high turnover rate, their limited discretion in light of binding instructions from London, and most of all, their lack of patronage insured that these inflated, paper powers remained just that.[44] For a century and a half prior to the 1760s each colony governed itself.

There was little occasion during that century and a half for serious speculation west of the Atlantic about sovereignty and rights. Unlike crowded England, white persons dissatisfied with the government of the place in which they found themselves, because of the abundance of land, were free to relocate. Thus, for example, dissenters from the theocratic government of the Massachusetts Bay colony moved to Providence, Rhode Island, and to Hartford, Connecticut, where they established theocratic governments more to their liking.[45] To the extent that a fictional justification for governmental authority over individuals was required, the older divine source of that authority served their purpose. There was in fact, however, very little need to resort to fictions, because government in all the North American colonies, except at the local level, was minimal. The North Americans, until the French and Indian War, were mostly spectators rather than participants in the wars of the European powers and the threat to external security posed by the Indian Nations did not require major governmental revenue. There were, it is true, occasional disputes over religious toleration,[46] but none that produced the kind of civil wars of the English seven-

42. B. Bailyn, The Origins of American Politics 67 (1967).

43. For a detailed discussion of how the Privy Council would disallow a colonial measure *see* 1 J. Goebel, The Oliver Wendell Holmes Devise History of the Supreme Court of the United States 67–71 (1971).

44. Bailyn, *supra* note 42, at 59–105.

45. *See* E. Morgan, The Puritan Dilemma: The Story of John Winthrop (1958).

46. The Glorious Revolution produced a wave of anti-Catholic sentiment in Maryland in particular. Initially directed at the colony's Catholic elite, the movement soon became a rebellion that resulted in measures barring Catholics from holding office, worshipping publicly or educating children under Catholic school masters. See L. Carr & D. Jordan, Maryland's Revolution of Government 1689–92 (1974).

teenth century. When government was almost completely unobtrusive upon individuals the stimulus for speculation about the sources of its authority were largely lacking.

EMERGENCE OF IMPERIAL LEGISLATIVE SUPREMACY

The development of British constitutional theory between the Glorious Revolution and the Stamp Act crisis is beyond the scope of this article. It suffices to note that when Parliament decided in 1764 that the North Americans should bear a fair share of the cost of their external security and the North Americans resisted, the contractarian fiction in England has passed out of favor, while the virtual representation fiction had become dominant. Parliament had come to claim, first for Ireland in 1720,[47] and eventually for the entire Empire, an unlimited sovereignty.

The assertion of parliamentary supremacy involved two aspects: one structural or federal, the other individual. Both aspects emerged in the dispute, in 1761 in Massachusetts, over the enforcement of general warrants or writs of assistance authorized by acts of Parliament.[48] James Otis Jr. made a structural argument against those statutes upon which the customs collector relied, urging that because the people of North America were not represented in Parliament that body could not bind them by legislation. He also contended, however, that even in England a law authorizing general warrants was void because no act of Parliament could establish such a writ in violation of so fundamental a right as the freedom of one's house.[49] Otis's federalist arguments in favor of local control over economic issues would not recur in North America until the Civil War.[50] In the short run, capsulized in the phrase "no taxation without representation," it became a rallying cry for the emerging movement toward independence. In that form, it was a rejection by the Americans of the fiction of virtual representation. Otis's individual rights point, which asserted that even for Englishmen who were represented in Parliament there were fundamental rights which could not be interfered with, was an argument which, if not entirely original, was at least a new variation of the older fiction that God's lieutenant would not act immorally.

By enacting the Sugar Act[51] and the Stamp Act[52] Parliament resoundingly rejected both Otis's federalist argument and his individual rights argument. Parliament not only im-

47. 6 Geo., ch. 10 (1719); *see* Note, *The Empire Strikes Back:* Annesley v. Sherlock *and the Triumph of Imperia I Parliamentary Supremacy*, 87 COLUM L. REV. 595 (1987).

48. 8 Will. III, ch. 22 para. VI (1696); 3 *Statutes at Large* 586 (1696); 11 Will. III, ch. 3 (1699).

49. *See, e.g.*, M. SMITH, THE WRITS OF ASSISTANCE CASE (1978); J. Adams, *"Abstract" of the Argument in the Writs of Assistance Case* (1761), *reprinted in* S. PRESSER & J. ZAINALDIN, LAW AND AMERICAN HISTORY: CASES AND MATERIALS 66–71 (1980).

50. Indeed, it has resurfaced quite recently. *Compare* Garcia v. San Antonio Metro. Transit Auth. 469 U.S. 528 (1985) (Congress has the power to regulate a local government's governmental functions so long as it affects interstate commerce) *with* National League of Cities v. Usury, 426 U.S. 8833 (1976) (Congress has not the power to regulate areas of traditional local government concern even though it might affect interstate commerce).

51. 4 Geo. III, ch. 15, (1763); 26 Statutes at Large, 33 (1764).

52. 5 Geo. III, ch. 12 (1765); 26 Statutes at Large, 179 (1765).

posed taxes on the colonies, but shifted the burden of proof to defendants in enforcement proceedings, provided for nonjury trials, and conferred official immunity on customs officials from the traditional common law remedies against them for exceeding their authority. Thus, issues both of structural legitimacy and of individual rights were presented by their enactments. The Massachusetts legislature, on Otis's motion, sent a circular letter to other North American legislative assemblies, inviting them to consult together on the circumstances of the colonies. In the fall of 1765, nine colonies responded by sending delegates to the Stamp Act Congress in New York.[53]

When Parliament learned of North America's resistance to the Stamp Act it lacked, for the time being, the physical power of enforcement. Yielding to expediency, however, Parliament simultaneously asserted what had become in England the reigning virtual representation orthodoxy of total legislative supremacy by enacting the Declaratory Act of March 18, 1766.[54] This pronouncement rejected both Otis's federalist and structural arguments against virtual representation of Americans in Parliament and his individual rights argument that there were zones of individual autonomy that no legislature could invade.[55] Not only could Parliament legislate for the colonies; it could "bind the colonies and people of *America* . . . in all cases whatsoever."[56] The fiction of virtual representation applied not only to the disenfranchised residents of geographic areas represented in Parliament, but also to residents of geographic areas which had never sent a representative to Westminster. Moreover, the social compact restored by the Glorious Revolution and embodied in the Bill of Rights, was not entrenched for future generations. It bound the king, perhaps, but not the "representative" branch of government.

Thus, by 1766, those in control of English parliamentary government had embraced the same totalitarianism that Thomas Hobbes had once advanced in defense of absolute monarchy.

Attenuation of the fiction of virtual representation, coupled with abandonment of the fiction of an entrenched social compact, resulted in the loss by Parliament of the favorable opinion upon which, in David Hume's view, its ability to govern North America depended. The fiction that a member of the House of Commons from some obscure rotten borough in a remote comer of England acted as a representative for the residents of Philadelphia or Boston was simply too implausible to be useful, especially when Parliament recognized

53. See E. Morgan & H. Morgan, The Stamp Act Crises; Prologue to Revolution 21–70 (1955).

54. 6 Geo. III, ch. 11 (1766). *See* Appendix B.

55. Virtual representation served as the chief justification for the Sugar and Stamp Acts in the preceding Anglo-American debate. *See* T. Whately, The Regulations Lately Made Concerning the Colonies and the Taxes Imposed Upon Them, Considered 100–14 (1765).

56. Ironically, the phrase "in all cases whatsoever" had originally been inserted in the Declaratory Act of 1766 in lieu of a specific assertion of the authority to tax. The Rockingham ministry did so in part to placate the colonies' great colonial champion, William Pitt. Pitt, however, objected to the vaguer formula as well. In consequence, the "in all cases whatsoever" language, which has been intended to keep Parliament's claims designedly vague, was taken as an assertion of both a general power to legislate and a specific power to tax. E. Morgan & H. Morgan, *supra* note 54, at 277–79.

no limitations whatsoever on its powers over those residents. The combination of positions asserted by Parliament in the Declaratory Act made a revolution very likely, if not inevitable.

JUSTIFYING REVOLUTION

While the Sugar, Stamp, and Declaratory Acts deprived parliament of the good opinion of most North Americans, their local leaders had not, in 1766, developed either a substitute theory that would legitimate government, or a substitute governmental framework. The franchise was more widely shared in the colonies than in England, and thus, sovereignty of the people was an attractive fiction. Yet it was plain that neither a continent nor a single colony could be governed by actual participation, as in the New England town meetings. Thus, some sort of principle of representation was a necessary corollary to the fiction of sovereignty of the people. At the same time, however, the evolution in Parliament of the fiction of a virtual representation that produced the abolition of the jury trial and the enforcement of general warrants suggested that some limitation on that corollary was also necessary.

What emerged was the principle that certain rights were entrenched against the government, not by virtue of a fictional social compact entered into by a mythical people in the dim and distant past, but because those rights were inherent in the human condition. The Declaration and Resolves of the First Continental Congress used the words, "by the immutable laws of nature."[57] That 1774 document, before listing those statutes which must be repealed in order to restore harmony, set forth a ten-paragraph "bill of rights" which demonstrated familiarity with the 1689 version. The case for a natural rights justification for entrenching the specifics referred to should not be overstated, for Congress relied also upon "the principles of the English Constitution and the several charters or compacts."[58] The document is an interesting mixture of inconsistent themes. Its first resolve, however, sets forth the contention that "they are entitled to life, liberty, and property, and they have never ceded to any sovereign power whatever, a right to dispose of either without their consent.[59] This resolve, thus, rejected the fiction that by a social compact in the dim and distant past the people collectively surrendered to their virtual representatives the powers which parliament now claimed. The fourth resolve repeated the rejection of virtual representation in Parliament and disclaimed any interest in actual representation. The second, third, and fifth resolves dealt with the extent to which colonial emigrants brought with them the protections of an entrenched English common law, particularly with respect to trials in local vicinages and by local jurors. The sixth resolve contended that the colonists were entitled to the benefit of such English statutes as existed at the time of colonization "and which they have, by experience, respectively found to be applicable to

57. 1 Journals of the Continental Congress 67 (W. Ford ed. 1904) [hereinafter Journals].
58. *Id.*
59. *Id.*

their several local and other circumstances."[60] What parts of the English statutory Constitution applied in North America was, in other words, a matter of local autonomy.

The Declaration and Resolves of 1774 is a brief against the principle of parliamentary supremacy asserted in the Declaratory Act. As propaganda associating the Americans with the spirit of the Glorious Revolution, it probably was an effective justification for a similar "revolution." The charge that Parliament violated the English Constitution was, after all, the same charge made against James II and earlier against Charles I. The new idea, however, was that a proper constitution rested not on a fictional conformity with a social compact, but upon "the immutable laws of nature."[61] Before this new idea could be explored in any depth, events overtook discourse. On April 19, 1775, General Gage's attempt to remove military stores from the control of local authorities—a sensible precaution considering the assertion in the Declaration and Resolves of the "right" to be free from coercion by a standing army—resulted in the Battle of Lexington and Concord. As a consequence of this action, the Continental Congress when it reconvened in Philadelphia on May 10, 1775, began by necessity to function as a de facto national government before its members could more fully develop a theoretical justification for its existence. Without practical experience in central government, the delegates governed to the extent that a minimum amount of government was necessary for their revolutionary situation. Having no leisure to grapple with the new and difficult questions of government they were facing, and divided by religious, class, and economic differences, the delegates proceeded for a year pragmatically.[62] Function preceded form. It was not until June 1776 that the Continental Congress addressed the latter, when it appointed a committee to prepare a "plan of confederation."[63] Simultaneously, however, it appointed a committee to prepare a Declaration of Independence, which has since become our most revered state paper.

That great state paper is rather ambiguous on the question of whether the Continental Congress spoke for the fictional people of a single nation, or merely as an agent for thirteen fictional peoples joined by a treaty.[64] This paper is not concerned, however, with structural or federalist issues. What is significant for present purposes is the reference to the "self-evident [truth] that all men are created equal, that they are endowed by their Creator with certain inalienable rights, that among these are Life, Liberty, and the pursuit of Happiness."[65] It is "to secure these rights," Jefferson continued, that "governments are

60. *Id.* at 69.

61. *See supra* note 58 and accompanying text.

62. See R. Middlekauff, The Glorious Cause: The American Revolution 1765–1789, at 312–32 (1982).

63. The Lee-Adams resolution of June 7, 1776 provided: "That these United Colonies are, and of right ought to be free and independent States, that they are absolved from all allegiance to the British Crown, and that all political connection between them and the State of Great Britain is, and ought to be, totally dissolved./That it is expedient forthwith to take the most effectual measures for forming foreign Alliances./That a plan of confederation be prepared and transmitted to the respective Colonies for their consideration and approbation." 5 Journals, *supra* note 58, at 425.

64. *See* E. Morgan, The Challenge of the American Revolution 211–28 (1976).

65. The Declaration of Independence para. 2 (U.S. 1776).

instituted among Men, deriving their just power from the consent of the governed."[66] When a government becomes "destructive of these ends," he urges, the people must abolish it.[67]

Read in the context of late eighteenth-century political thought, these few sentences are remarkably illuminating. Rights, proclaimed Jefferson, are not dependent upon a social compact. They are inherent to the human condition. Social compacts are entered into only for the purpose of securing them. There is an acknowledgment of the fictional sovereignty of the people in the reference to the consent of the governed. But the reference to certain rights being "inalienable," is a rejection of the parliamentary assertion of virtual representation "in all cases whatsoever." Thus, Jefferson elegantly expresses the natural rights position of James Otis, of the Declaration and Resolves of 1774, and of many

66. *Id.*

67. *Id.* Regardless of other influences on Jefferson, the parallels between the Declaration and Locke's second treatise are striking. *See, e.g.*, G. Wills, Inventing America: Jefferson's Declaration of Independence (1978). Locke wrote:

The Reason why Men enter into Society, is the preservation of their Property; and the end why they chuse and authorize a Legislative, is, that there may be Laws made, and Rules set as Guards and Fences to the Properties of all the Members of the Society, to limit the Power, and moderate the Dominion of every Part and Member of the Society. For since it can never be supposed to be the Will of the Society, that the Legislative should have a Power to destroy that, which everyone designs to secure, by entering into Society, and for which the People submitted themselves to the Legislators of their own making; *whenever the Legislators endeavor to take away, and destroy the Property of the People*, or to reduce them to Slavery under Arbitrary Power, they put themselves into a state of War with the People, who are thereupon absolved from any farther Obedience, and are left to the common Refuge, which God hath provided for all Men against Force and Violence. Whensoever therefore the *Legislative* shall transgress this fundamental Rule of Society; and either by Ambition, Fear, Folly or Corruption, *endeavor to grasp* themselves, *or put into the hands of any other an Absolute Power* over the Lives, Liberties, and Estates of the People, By this breach of Trust they *forfeit the Power*, the People had put into their hands, for quite contrary ends, and it devolves to the People, who have a right to resume their original Liberty, and, by the Establishment of a new Legislative (such as they shall think fit) provide for their own Safety and Security, which is the end for which they are in Society. What I have said here, concerning the Legislative, in general, holds true also concerning the *Supreame Executor*, who having a double trust put in him, both to have a part in the Legislative, and the supreme Execution of the Law, Acts against both, when he goes about to set up his own Arbitrary Will, as the Law of the Society.

Great mistakes in the ruling part, many wrong and inconvenient Laws, and all the *slips* of humane frailty will be *born by the People*, without mutiny or murmur. But if a long train of Abuses, Prevarications, and Artifices, all tending the same way, make the design visible to the People, and they cannot but feel, what they lie under, and see, whither they are going; 'tis not to be wonder'd, that they should then route themselves, and endeavor to put the rule into such hands, which may secure to them the ends for which Government was at first erected; and without which, ancient Names, and specious Forms, are so far from being better, that they are much worse, than the state of Nature, or pure Anarchy; the inconveniences being all as great and as near, but the remedy farther off and more difficult.

J. Locke, *supra* note 93, 430–33 (emphasis in original).

other Americans who were speculating about the relationship between men and their government.[68]

It is, of course, true that the Declaration of Independence proceeds to list specific grievances, most of which can be related either to the federalist dispute over the status of Parliament vis-a-vis the colonies, or to specific provisions of the English Bill of Rights. Thus, one cannot dispute that colonial grievances were in part structural.[69] They were not solely structural, however, for the Declaration of Independence is quite explicit in rejecting, with respect to any government, the fictions of an open-ended social compact resulting in virtual representation on all subjects whatsoever.

THE NEW STATE CONSTITUTIONS

The Declaration of Independence justified revolution—change—but did not seriously address the consequences for government of the principles on which it relied for that justification. The process of developing new governments, however, had already begun before the Continental Congress formally proposed independence. By the end of 1775, three colonies had already sought from that body advice respecting the establishment of new governments replacing those dependent upon the crown.[70] Those colonies and Virginia were advised to call representatives of the people to form interim governments pending resolution of the dispute with Great Britain. Rhode Island unilaterally cut its ties with the crown on May 4, 1776, opting to retain its existing charter as a constitution. Less than a week later the Continental Congress resolved to recommend to the respective charter governments and colonial conventions that where none had yet been established, new governments should be, which would suppress the exercise of any authority under the crown.[71] It was in the local conventions or legislative assemblies, therefore, that serious discussions of the nature, purpose, and limits of government took place. Structure was a major concern, and in the written constitutions that emerged great concessions were made to the theory and practice of separation of powers among independent branches of

68. On the eve of the fighting, Adams, writing under the pseudonym "Novanglus" set out his views at length in a celebrated newspaper debate with the loyalist Daniel Leonard who wrote as Massachusettinsis. For the latest edition of these exchanges, *see* The American Colonial Crisis: The Daniel Leonard—John Adams Letters to the Press 1775–1775 (B. Mason ed. 1972).

69. For a comprehensive revisionist view that colonial grievances leading to the Revolution rested solely on Parliament's infringement of distinctively English common law rights and precedents, see J. Reid, Constitutional History of the American Revolution (1986).

70. Wood, *supra* note 3, at 130.

71. The resolution read: "*Resolved*, That it be recommended to the respective assemblies and conventions of the United Colonies where no government sufficient to the exigencies of their affairs have been hitherto established, to adopt such government as shall, in the opinion of the representatives of the people, best conduce to the happiness and safety of their constituents in particular, and America in general." 4 Journals, *supra* note 58, at 357–58. *See* 1 Debates in the Several State Conventions on the Adoption of the Federal Constitution (1. Elliot ed. 1947); Wood, *supra* note 3, at 132.

any government.[72] Many constitution makers did not, however, rely solely for the protection of republican freedom upon this Whig idea of a self-policing, internally balanced state. Five states in 1776—Virginia, Pennsylvania, Maryland, Delaware, and North Carolina—included separate bills of rights that entrenched against legislative change explicit rights deemed to be fundamental.[73] New Jersey that same year included explicit guarantees in the text of its 1776 Constitution.[74] New York, South Carolina, and Georgia did likewise in 1777. Vermont in 1777 and Massachusetts in 1780 included in their constitutions separate bills of rights. Only the two charter states, Connecticut and Rhode Island, which were already republican in form, did not do so.[75]

Constitutionalism as we know it today is tied fundamentally to the public perception of judicial review. That innovation had only just begun to develop in this early period.[76] Thus, the distinction we now recognize between statutory and constitutional law was not as clear then as it later became. Nevertheless, the constitution makers of the early years of independence plainly intended that the entrenchment of bills of rights in their fundamental laws would be binding on future legislatures,[77] even if they had not yet refined that unique American contribution to government—judicial review. This paper does not address the development of early American thought on the superiority of constitutions over legislation, the generic problem of entrenchment. What it does address is the distinction between the entrenchment of a structure of government and the entrenchment of individual rights, which that government was not free to transgress. The inclusion of such provisions in all eleven of the new constitutions adopted in response to the May 15, 1776, instruction from the Continental Congress is weighty evidence of the popularity of the natural rights position expressed in the Declaration of Independence.[78] In these constitutions, the abstraction of the Declaration of Independence became an accepted principle of government.

72. Wood, *supra* note 3, at 125–56.

73. *Id.* at 271–72. New Hampshire established its bill of rights in 1783. N.H. Rev. Stat. Ann. Const., art. 1 (1955).

74. N.J. Stat. Ann. Prior Constitutions, 599 (West 1971).

75. Wood, *supra* note 3 at 226–78.

76. *Id.* at 453–63. Judicial review had begun to develop in several important state cases in the years leading up to the Federal Convention. *See, e.g.*, Rutgers v. Wadington, (New York 1781). Trevett v. Weedon (Rhode Island 1786). Bayard v. Singleton, 1 N.C. 5 (1787).

77. *See, e.g.*, B. Gale, Brief, Decent, but Free Remarks and Observations, on Several Laws Passed by the Honorable Legislature of the State of Connecticut, Since the Year 1775 (1782): The Federalist No. 49 (J. Madison), Ackerman, *The Stars Lectures: Discovering the Constitution*, 93 Yale L.J. 1013 (1984).

78. Virginia was an exception to this pattern where the first state constitution was adopted by the legislature rather than by a convention. Thomas Jefferson responded to this deficiency by advocating the entrenchment of fundamental rights against the caprice of subsequent legislatures, ultimately through a ratifying convention and "council of revision." Jefferson's Bill for Establishing Religious Freedom" his "Notes on the State of Virginia" and his 1783 draft for a new Virginia Constitution all reflect his concern for the protection of individual natural rights. *See* Wood, *supra* note 3 at 275–76.

The state bills of rights were largely, although not exclusively, derived from the Bill of Rights of 1689, which after all was only a statute. In the late eighteenth century, however, symbolically it was a good deal more. It was the manifestation, in law, of the fruits of what for English Protestants was the critical constitutional event of British history.[79] Many of the provisions that were borrowed deal with matters of procedure or process rather than what today we refer to as substantive due process rights. That does not in any way detract from the late eighteenth-century American insistence that those rights were entrenched, that the Declaratory Act was, therefore, unconstitutional, and that their new constitutions must entrench certain individual rights against future governments.

THE ERROR OF THE 1787 CONVENTION

The *de facto* national government which had invited the adoption of new state constitutions technically committed suicide when, on November 15, 1777, it sent to the states for ratification the Articles of Confederation in which it acknowledged that each state was now totally sovereign.[80] A treaty model for the government of North America was not successful and, as we know, the Philadelphia Constitutional Convention of 1787 was called to rectify the error of 1777. That convention primarily addressed structural issues including the distribution of political power between the state and the national government, and the separation of powers among the three branches of the latter. Whether by design or as a result of fatigue, there was very little discussion in the convention of a bill of rights and, except for such textual provisions as the *ex post facto* clause, the reference to jury trials in Article III, and the habeas corpus clause, none of the specific guarantees of individual rights were included, which by 1787 were common in state constitutions.[81]

The Anti-Federalists seized upon the absence of a bill of rights as a reason for opposing ratification.[82] The Federalists urged that none was necessary because the new government was one of limited specified powers and because separation of powers would prevent excesses.[83]

What is significant in the ratification debates is not the dispute over whether there was a need for a bill of rights in the federal constitution. The significant point is rather that

79. It is probably still so regarded by Northern Ireland Protestants. *See* K. Boyle & T. Hadden, Ireland: A Positive Proposal 54–55 (1985).

80. Article II of the Articles of Confederation stated that "[e]ach state retains its sovereignty, freedom, and independence, and every power, jurisdiction and right, which is not by this confederation expressly delegated to the United States, in Congress assembled." Articles of Confederation, art. II (1781). The suicide this clause represented, however, was more apparent than real. Congress continued to exercise substantial central powers, including the power to make war and peace, enter into treaties, assert admiralty jurisdiction, and compel national allegiance. R. Morris, The Forging of the Union 1781–1787, at 55–110 (1987).

81. *See id.* at 267–97, C. Rossiter, 1787, The Grand Convention 159–273 (1966).

82. Wood, *supra* note 3 at 536–43; *see* The Complete Antifederalist (H. Storing ed. 1981).

83. The Federalist No. 84 (Hamilton); *see* Pennsylvania and the Federal Constitution 1787–1788, at 143–49, 313–14 (J. McMaster & F. Stone ed. 1942).

Federalists and Anti-Federalists alike acknowledged the centrality in the American Revolution—the change from one status to another—of the idea that real individual persons, not a fictional corporate "people," had rights which no government, whether monarchical or republican, could transgress.

Ratification was a close thing, achieved in part because of the expectation that the federal constitution would be amended to include what most state constitutions already had—a bill of rights reflecting those principles.[84]

True to his word while electioneering, James Madison undertook in the first Congress the task of proposing the amendments we now call the Bill of Rights. Like their state constitution precursors, they borrow heavily from the Bill of Rights of 1689. Their ratification completed the American Revolution, for it was only when the national constitution explicitly included the principle that certain individual rights were entrenched even against republican majorities that our Constitution—our order of things—conformed to the major premise of the revolution set forth in the Declaration of Independence.

CONCLUSION

The divine right of kings, the social compact, and virtual representation were all, I have suggested, fictions devised from time to time by governing elites to help maintain the consent of the governed. Is the natural rights premise of an entrenched bill of rights simply more of the same? Is the personhood of rational human animals, as Hans Kelsen argued, nothing more than a construction of juristic thinking?[85] The legal positivists pose a difficult question that might better be addressed to ontologists than to lawyers. Certainly, the Bill of Rights has had at various times great utility as a symbol useful for preserving the consent of the governed. Equally certain is that there have been periods in our history when, despite the principle that some individual rights are entrenched against the government, many individuals were deprived of them. The American experience with slavery is, of course, the most graphic illustration of this paradox.[86] It is also the American experience which best illustrates Hume's point that governors depend for support on the favorable opinion of the governed, for it was over that issue that the government was effectively overturned. On balance, however, measured against other societies, it seems to me that our constitutionalizing of a philosophy of government based upon the premise that all men are "created equal and endowed by their Creator with certain inalienable rights" has produced more than a substitute for the fictions we rejected in 1776. In the world's history God's lieutenants often became tyrants. Our only guarantee that our own government will not become tyrannical lies in the constant insistence that individual rights entrenched in the Bill of Rights are living realities, not fictions.

84. *See* Onuf, *Reflections on the Founding: Constitutional Historiography in Bicentennial Perspective*, 46 Wm. & Mary Q. 341, 370–72 (1989).

85. *See* H. Kelsen, Pure Theory of Law 168–92 (M. Knight trans. 1967).

86. *See, e.g.*, E. Morgan, American Slavery American Freedom: The Ordeal of Colonial Virginia (1978).

APPENDIX A

Bill of Rights[87]
December 16, 1689

An Act declaring the rights and liberties of the subject, and settling the succession of the crown.

WHEREAS the Lords Spiritual and Temporal and Commons assembled at Westminster, lawfully, fully, and freely representing all the estates of the people of this realm, did upon the thirteenth day of February in the year of our Lord one thousand six hundred eighty-eight, present unto their Majesties, then called and known by the names and stile of William and Mary, prince and princess of Orange, being present in their proper persons, a certain declaration in writing made by the said Lords and Commons, in the words following, viz.

WHEREAS the late King James the Second, by the assistance of divers evil counsellors, judges and ministers employed by him, did endeavour to subvert and extirpate the Protestant religion, and the laws and liberties of this kingdom.

1. By assuming and exercising a power of dispensing with and suspending of laws, and the execution of laws, without consent of Parliament.
2. By committing and prosecuting divers worthy prelates, for humbly petitioning to be excused from concurring to the said assumed power.
3. By issuing and causing to be executed a commission under the great seal for erecting a court called, The Court of Commissioners for Ecclesiastical Causes.
4. By levying money for and to the use of the Crown, by pretence of prerogative, for other time, and in other manner, than the same was granted by Parliament.
5. By raising and keeping a standing army within this kingdom in time of peace, without consent of Parliament, and quartering soldiers contrary to law.
6. By causing several good subjects, being protestants, to be disarmed, at the same time when papists were both armed and employed, contrary to law.
7. By violating the freedom of election of members to serve in parliament.
8. By prosecutions in the court of King's bench, for matters and causes cognizable only in Parliament; and by divers other arbitrary and illegal courses.
9. And whereas of late years, partial, corrupt and unqualified persons have been returned and served on juries in trials, and particularly divers jurors in trials for high treason, which were not freeholders.

87. 1 W. & M. ch. 2 (1689), *reprinted in* Sources of Our Liberties, *supra* note 15, at 245 (emphasis in original).

10. And excessive bail hath been required of persons committed in criminal cases, to elude the benefit of the laws made for the liberty of the subjects.
11. And excessive fines have been imposed; and illegal and cruel punishments inflicted.
12. And several grants and promises made of fines and forfeitures, before any conviction or judgment against the persons, upon whom the same were to be levied.

All which are utterly and directly contrary to the known laws and statutes, and freedom of this realm.

And whereas the said late King James the Second having abdicated the government, and the throne being thereby vacant, his Highness the prince of Orange (whom it hath pleased Almighty God to make the glorious instrument of delivering this kingdom from Popery and arbitrary power) did (by the advice of the Lords Spiritual and Temporal, and divers principal persons of the Commons) cause letters to be written to the Lords Spiritual and Temporal, and divers principal persons of the Commons) cause letters to be written to the Lords Spiritual and Temporal being Protestants; and other letters to the several counties, cities, universities, boroughs and cinque-ports, for the choosing of such persons to represent them, as were of right to be sent to Parliament, to meet and sit at Westminster upon the two and twentieth day ofJanuary in this year one thousand six hundred eighty and eight, in order to such an establishment, as that their religion, laws, and liberties might not again be in danger of being subverted: upon which letters, elections having been accordingly made.

And thereupon the said Lords Spiritual and Temporal, and Commons, pursuant to their respective letters and elections, being now assembled in a full and free representative of this nation, taking into their most serious consideration the best means for attaining the ends aforesaid; do in the first place (as their ancestors in like case have usually done) for the vindicating and asserting their ancient rights and liberties, declare;

1. That the pretended power of suspending of laws, or the execution of laws, by regal authority, without consent of Parliament, is illegal.
2. That the pretended power of dispensing with laws, or the execution of laws, by regal authority, as it hath been assumed and exercised of late, is illegal.
3. That the commission for erecting the late court of commissioners for ecclesiastical causes, and all other commissions and courts of like nature are illegal and pernicious.
4. That levying money for or to the use of the crown, by pretence of prerogative, without grant of Parliament, for longer time, or in other manner than the same is or shall be granted, is illegal.
5. That it is the right of the subjects to petition the King, and all commitments and prosecutions for such petitioning are illegal.
6. That the raising or keeping a standing army within the kingdom in time of peace, unless it be with consent of parliament, is against law.

7. That the subjects which are Protestants, may have arms for their defence suitable to their conditions, and as allowed by law.
8. That election of members of Parliament ought to be free.
9. That the freedom of speech, and debates or proceedings in Parliament, ought not to be impeached or questioned in any court or palace out of Parliament.
10. That excessive bail ought not to be required, nor excessive fines imposed; nor cruel and unusual punishments inflicted.
11. That jurors ought to be duly impanelled and returned, and jurors which pass upon men in trials for high treason ought to be freeholders.
12. That all grants and promises of fines and forfeitures of particular persons before conviction, are illegal and void.
13. And that for redress of all grievances, and for the amending, strengthening and preserving of the laws, Parliaments ought to be held frequently.

And they do claim, demand, and insist upon all and singular the premises, as their undoubted rights and liberties; and that no declarations, judgments, doings or proceedings, to the prejudice of the people in any of the said premisses, ought to any wise to be drawn hereafter into consequence or example.

To which demand of their rights they are particularly encouraged by the declaration of his highness the prince of Orange, as being the only means for obtaining a full redress and remedy therein.

Having therefore an entire confidence, That his said Highness the prince of Orange will perfect the deliverance so far advanced by him, and will still preserve them from the violation of their rights, which they have here asserted, and from all other attempts upon their religion, rights, and liberties.

II. The said Lords Spiritual and Temporal and Commons, assembled at Westminster, do resolve, that William and Mary prince and princess of Orange be, and be declared, King and Queen of England, France and Ireland, and the dominions thereunto belonging, to hold the crown and royal dignity of the said kingdoms and dominions to them the said prince and princess during their lives, and the life of the survivor of them; and that the sole and full exercise of the regal power be only in, and executed by the said prince of Orange, in the names of the said prince and princess, during their joint lives; and after their deceases, the said crown and royal dignity of the said kingdoms and dominions to be to the heirs of the body of the said princess; and for default of such issue to the princess Anne of Denmark, and the heirs of her body; and for default of such issue to the heirs of the body of the said prince of Orange. And the Lords

Spiritual and Temporal, and Commons, do pray the said prince and princess to accept the same accordingly.

III. And that the oaths hereafter mentioned to be taken by all persons of whom the oaths of allegiance and supremacy might be required by law, instead of them; and that the said oaths of allegiance and supremacy be abrogated.

I, A.B., do sincerely promise and swear, That I will be faithful, and bear true allegiance, to their Majesties King William and Queen Mary: So help me God.

I, A.B., do swear, That I do from my heart abhor, detest, and abjure as impious and heretical, that damnable doctrine and position, That princes excommunicated or deprived by the pope, or any authority of the see of Rome, may be deposed or murdered by their subjects, or any other whatsoever. And I do declare, That no foreign prince, person, prelate, state or potentate hath, or ought to have any jurisdiction, power, superiority, pre-eminence, or authority ecclesiastical or spiritual, within this realm: So help me God.

IV. Upon which their said Majesties did accept the crown and royal dignity of the kingdoms of England, France, and Ireland, and the dominions thereunto belonging, according to the resolution and desire of the said lords and commons contained in the said declaration.

V. And thereupon their Majesties were pleased, That the said lords Spiritual and Temporal, and Commons, being the two Houses of Parliament, should continue to sit, and with their Majesties royal concurrence make effectual provision for the settlement ofthe religion, laws and liberties of this kingdom, so that the same for the future might not be in danger again of being subverted; to which the said Lords Spiritual and Temporal, and Commons, did agree and proceed to act accordingly.

VI. Now in pursuance of the premisses, the said Lords Spiritual and Temporal, and Commons in Parliament assembled, for the ratifying, confirming and establishing the said declaration, and the articles, clauses, matters, and things therein contained by the force of a law made in due form by authority of Parliament, do pray that it may be declared and enacted, That all and singular the rights and liberties asserted and claimed in the said declaration, are the true, ancient, and indubitable rights and liberties of the people of this kingdom, and so shall be esteemed, allowed, adjudged, deemed and taken to be, and that all and every the particulars aforesaid shall be firmly and strictly holden and observed, as they are expressed in the said declaration; and all officers and ministers whatsoever shall serve their Majesties and their successors according to the same in all times to come.

VII. And the said Lords Spiritual and Temporal, and Commons, seriously considering how it hath pleased Almighty God, in his marvelous providence, and merciful goodness to this nation, to provide and preserve their said Majesties royal persons most happily to reign over us upon the throne of their ancestors, for which they render unto him from the bottom of their hearts their humblest thanks and praises, do truly, firmly, assuredly, and in the sincerity of their hearts think, and do hereby recognize, acknowledge and declare, That King James the Second having abdicated the government, and their Majesties having accepted the crown and royal dignity as aforesaid, their said Majesties did become, were, are and of right ought to be, by the laws of this realm, our sovereign liege lord and lady, King and Queen of England, France, and Ireland and the dominions thereunto belonging, in and to whose princely persons the royal state, crown, and dignity of the said realms with all honours, stiles, titles, regalities, prerogatives, powers, jurisdictions and authorities to the same belonging and appertaining, are most fully, rightfully and entirely invested and incorporated, united and annexed.

VIII. And for preventing all questions and divisions in this realm, by reason of any pretended titles to the crown, and for preserving a certainty in the succession thereof, in and upon which the unity, peace, tranquility, and safety of this nation doth, under God, wholly consist and depend, The said Lords Spiritual and Temporal, and Commons, do beseech their Majesties that it may be enacted, established and declared, That the crown and regal government of the said kingdoms and dominions, with all and singular the premisses thereunto belonging and appertaining, shall be and continue to their said Majesties, and the survivor of them, during their lives, and the life of the survivor of them: And that the intire, perfect, and full exercise of the regal power and government be only in, and executed by his Majesty, in the names of both their Majesties during their joint lives; and after their deceases the said crown and premises shall be and remain to the heirs of the body of her Majesty; and for default of such issue to her royal highness the Princess Anne of Denmark, and the heirs of her body; and for default of such issue to heirs of the body of his said Majesty; And thereunto the said Lords Spiritual and Temporal, and Commons, do, in the name of all the people aforesaid, most humbly and faithfully submit themselves, their heirs and posterities for ever; and do faithfully promise, That they will stand to, maintain, and defend their said Majesties, and also the limitation and succession of the crown herein specified and contained, to the utmost of their powers, with their lives and estates, against all persons whatsoever, that shall attempt anything to the contrary.

IX. And whereas it hath been found by experience, that it is inconsistent with the safety and welfare of this Protestant kingdom, to be governed by a popish prince, or by any King or Queen marrying a papist; the said Lords Spiritual and Temporal, and Commons, do further pray that it may be enacted, That all and every person and persons that is, are or shall be reconciled to, or shall hold communion with, the see or church of Rome, or shall profess the popish religion, or shall marry a papist, shall be excluded, and be for ever incapable to inherit, possess, or enjoy the crown and government of this realm, and Ireland, and the dominions thereunto belonging, or any part of the same, or to have, use, or exercise any regal power, authority, or jurisdiction within the same; and in all and every such case or cases the people of these realms shall be, and are hereby absolved of their allegiance; and the said crown and government shall from time to time descend to, and be enjoyed by such person or persons being protestants, as should have inherited and enjoyed the same, in case the said person or persons so reconciled, holding communion, or professing, or marrying as aforesaid, were naturally dead.

X. And that every King and Queen of this realm, who at any time hereafter shall come to and succeed in the imperial crown of this kingdom, shall on the first day of the meeting of the first Parliament, next after his or her coming to the crown, sitting in his or her throne in the house of peers, in the presence of the Lords and Commons therein assembled, or at his or her coronation, before such person or persons who shall administer the coronation oath to him or her, at the time of his or her taking the said oath (which shall first happen) make, subscribe, and audibly repeat the declaration mentioned in the statute made in the thirtieth year of the reign of King Charles the Second intituled, An act for the more effectual preserving the King's person and government, by disabling papists from sitting in either house of parliament. But if it shall happen, that such King or Queen, upon his or her succession to the crown of this realm, shall be under the age of twelve years, then every such King or Queen shall make, subscribe, and audibly repeat the said declaration at his or her coronation, or the first day of the meeting of the first parliament as aforesaid, what shall first happen after such king or queen shall have attained the said age of twelve years.

XI. All which their Majesties are contented and pleased shall be declared, enacted, and established by authority of this present parliament, and shall stand, remain, and be the law of this realm for ever; and the same are by their said Majesties, by and with the advice and consent of the Lords Spiritual and Temporal, and Commons, in Parliament assembled, and by the authority of the same, declared, enacted, and established accordingly.

XII. And be it further declared and enacted by the authority aforesaid, That from and after this present session of parliament, no dispensation by non obstante of or to any statute, or any part thereof, shall be allowed, but that the same shall be held void and of no effect, except a dispensation be allowed of in such statute, and except in such cases as shall be specially provided for by one or more bill or bills to be passed during this present session of parliament.

XIII. Provided that no charter, or grant, or pardon, granted before the three and twentieth day of October, in the year of our Lord one thousand six hundred eighty-nine shall be any ways impeached or invalidated by this act, but that the same shall be and remain of the same force and effect in law, and no other than as if this Act had never been made.

APPENDIX B

An Act for the better securing the dependency of his Majesty's Domains in America upon the Crown and Parliament of Great Britain.[88]

Whereas several of the Houses of Representatives in his Majesty's Colonies and Plantations in America, have of late, against Law, claimed to themselves, or to the Governed Assemblies of the same, the sole and exclusive right of imposing Duties and Taxes upon his Majesty's Subjects in the said Colonies and Plantations; and have, in pursuance of such Claim, passed certain Votes, Resolutions, and Orders, derogatory to the Legislative Authority of Parliament, and inconsistent with the Dependency of the said Colonies and Plantations upon the crown of Great Britain: May it therefore please your most excellent Majesty, that it may be declared; and be it declared by the King's most excellent Majesty, by and with the Advice and Consent of the Lords Spiritual and Temporal, and Commons,

88. 6 Geo. III, ch. 11 (1766) (emphasis in original).

in the present Parliament assembled, and by the Authority of the same, That the said Colonies and Plantations in America have been, are, and of Right ought to be, subordinate unto, and dependent upon, the Imperial Crown and Parliament of Great Britain; and that the King's Majesty, by and with the Advice and Consent of the Lords Spiritual and Temporal, and Commons of Great Britain, in Parliament assembled, had, hath, and of Right ought to have, full Power and Authority to make Laws and Statutes of sufficient Force and Validity to bind the Colonies and People of America, Subjects to the Crown of Great Britain, in all Cases whatsoever.

II. And it be further declared and enacted by the Authority aforesaid, That all Resolutions, Votes, Orders and Proceedings, in any of the said Colonies or Plantations, whereby the Power and Authority of the Parliament of Great Britain, to make Laws and Statutes as aforesaid, is denied or drawn into questions, are, and are hereby declared to be, utterly null and void to all Intents and Purposes whatsoever.

Legal Remedies for the Failure of European Community Institutions to Act in Conformity with EEC Treaty Provisions

Hon. Ole Due

Judge Ole Due delivered the nineteenth annual John F. Sonnett lecture, entitled *Legal Remedies for the Failure of European Community Institutions to Act in Conformity with EEC Treaty Provisions*, on November 1, 1990.[1] Born in 1931,[2] Judge Due served as a civil servant, teacher, judge, and President of the Court of Justice of the European Communities ("Court of Justice").[3]

Judge Due began his career in the Danish Ministry of Justice in 1955.[4] He served twenty years with the Ministry and was involved in the Hague conference on private international law and Community law.[5] Prior to Denmark joining the European Communities in 1972, Ole Due served as secretary, and later president, of the Commission to adapt Denmark's law.[6] As a permanent delegate to the conferences, he played a key role in adjusting Community measures.[7] He also drafted the legal provisions of the Treaty of Accession and the Danish law of accession, which was praised as a model of clarity and simplicity.[8] It later served as the basis for the accession laws of other Nordic countries that joined the European Union.[9] In 1978, he also became legal adviser to the Court of Appeal in Copenhagen.[10]

In 1979, Judge Due was appointed to the Court of Justice,[11] and became President of the Court of Justice in 1988, a position he held until 1994.[12] In addition to improving the

Introduction written by Elizabeth Langton, J.D. Candidate, Class of 2015, Fordham University School of Law.

1. Ole Due, *Legal Remedies for the Failure of European Community Institutions to Act in Conformity with EEC Treaty Provisions*, 14 FORDHAM INT'L L.J. 341 (1990).

2. Press Release, European Union, Death of Ole Due, Former President of the Court of Justice of the European Union (Jan. 26, 2005), http://europa.eu/rapid/press-release_CJE-05-9_en.htm?locale=en.

3. Gil Carlos Rodríguez Iglesias, *Dedication to Ole Due*, 19 FORDHAM INT'L L.J. 841, 841 (1995).

4. *Id.*

5. *Id.*

6. *Id.*

7. *Id.*

8. *Id.*

9. *Id.*

10. Press Release, European Union, *supra* note 2.

11. *Id.*

12. *Id.* Judge Due has been remembered as a "lawyer's lawyer" and "a master of the principle of collegiality, combining his good Scandinavian pragmatism, humor, and common sense with an astute perception for equality and justice." Iglesias, *supra* note 3, at 842.

efficiency and accessibility of the Court of Justice, he oversaw the establishment of the Court of First Instance in September 1989, and the subsequent transfers of jurisdiction to this new court.[13]

Judge Due taught lawyers at various institutions around the world, including Fordham University School of Law, the University of Copenhagen, and the University of Stockholm.[14] He authored numerous books and articles.[15]

Judge Due's Sonnett lecture, *Legal Remedies for the Failure of European Community Institutions to Act in Conformity with EEC Treaty Provisions*, discussed the case law of the Court of Justice.[16] More specifically, Judge Due focused on judicial activism and case law by which the Court of Justice had tried to compensate for political inaction by the Ministers of the European Communities (Council).[17] From a procedural viewpoint, he examined the legal remedies employed against the Council's inaction.[18] Judge Due confined his inquiry to the European Economic Community (EEC) and its governing instrument, the Treaty Establishing the European Economic Community (EEC Treaty).[19] He found that the EEC Treaty indicates that the best method to address inactions is the action for failure to act.[20] Judge Due reviewed the range of effect procedural weapons to combat the Council's failure to act before discussing why the action for failure to act has been of such little importance.[21] He concluded that the action for failure to act was so innocuous that it had been largely abandoned, and it should be primarily regarded as measure of last resort.[22]

1990 Sonnett Lecture

Any discussion of the case law of the Court of Justice of the European Communities (the "Court" or the "Court of Justice") will sooner or later touch upon what is commonly called the judicial activism of the Court.

A European Community member state lawyer's attitude toward judicial activism normally depends on the relations between the judicial and legislative powers within his country. This relationship varies from member state to member state, ranging from the very

13. Iglesias, *supra* note 3, at 842.
14. *Id.* at 843.
15. *Id.* He was also the creator and substantial contributor to EU Karnov (Danish Community Law Commentary). *Id.*
16. *See generally* Due, *supra* note 1.
17. *Id.* at 342.
18. *Id.* at 343.
19. *Id.*
20. *Id.*
21. *Id.*
22. *Id.* at 358.

cautious approach of the French and Danish courts to the extensive control exercised by the German court, the "Bundesverfassungsgericht." As expected, the Court of Justice has placed itself somewhere in the middle of these extremes.

A U.S. lawyer will normally try to compare the case law of the Court of Justice with that of the U.S. Supreme Court, trying to distinguish between periods in which the tendency to promote integration has been more or less pronounced. Indeed, the Court of Justice's activism and role as intermediary between legislative and executive arms of the European Economic Community (the "EEC" or the "Community") and between national authorities and the institutions of the Community has led some to compare the Court to the U.S. Supreme Court under Chief Justice Marshall.

In fact, differences in the Court's jurisprudence may be observed over time. However, contrary to the situation in the United States, developments in the Court's jurisprudence are difficult to relate to changes in its composition. While in the United States, it is perfectly acceptable for the executive branch to seek to influence future case law by making appointments to the federal courts, this is less common in the member states of the EEC. I am not aware of any nomination to the Court of Justice aimed at changing the Court's attitude toward European integration.

Therefore, the different trends in the case law of the Court of Justice should probably be seen more as reactions to changes in the political environment. In periods where centrifugal tendencies have dominated the political scene, the Court has tried to defend treaty objectives against such tendencies. In certain periods, the political institutions, first and foremost the Council of Ministers of the European Communities (the "Council"), have found it hard to live up to the aims of the treaties, whether because of the need for unanimity in a decision of the Council or because of the political currents in some of the major member states. During these periods, we may find a tendency to compensate for this lack of legislative activity by basing Court decisions directly on the treaty provisions. On the other hand, during periods of great political activity aimed at a strengthening of the Community, we may find the Court of Justice more reluctant to commit itself.

I shall concentrate on that part of the case law by which the Court has tried to compensate for the inaction of the political institutions. I shall examine this case law from a procedural viewpoint. My purpose is to find out which procedural weapons the Court has made use of.

That formulation might seem odd. Like other courts, the Court has no right to take initiatives itself. It must confine itself to dealing with the cases brought before it. It is thus up to the plaintiff to select the weapon that will best achieve the sought after objectives by way of the legal procedure used.

It is, however, clear that by means of its case law the Court has an important influence on that choice. By accepting a certain form of legal procedure as the appropriate form to achieve the plaintiff's objective, the Court can sharpen the weapon so that the procedure constitutes an attractive choice for future plaintiffs. Conversely, the Court can limit the effectiveness of a form of legal procedure so that recourse to that weapon will be made only when no other is available. It is this interplay between the plaintiff and the Court that I wish to examine.

My examination will be confined essentially to the legal remedies employed against the Council's inaction. However, since the Council consists of representatives of the member states, I shall to some extent have to look also at the inaction of the member states themselves.

I shall, moreover, confine myself to the EEC and its governing instrument, the Treaty Establishing the European Economic Community (the "Treaty" or the "EEC Treaty").[1] Euratom[2] has little practical significance in this respect. Further, even though the Treaty Establishing the European Coal and Steel Community[3] raises certain interesting parallels, it chiefly concerns the relationship between undertakings and the Commission of the European Communities (the "Commission").

The EEC Treaty appears to indicate that the best weapon for confronting inaction should be the action for failure to act.[4] Apparently, this type of action constitutes the proper means of forcing the institution in question to fulfill its duty to act. Experience shows, however, that quite different weapons have been effective.

I shall first run through the forms of procedure which have in practice proved to be the most appropriate before going on to examine why the action for failure to act has been of so little significance.

The most important innovation in the section of the EEC Treaty that deals with the Court is Article 177.[5] This rule deals with the right, and in certain cases, the duty, of national courts to refer questions to the Court *for a preliminary ruling* on the interpretation and validity of Community rules. The aim of the provision is to ensure uniform interpretation and application of Community law in the member states, but it has proven to offer other possibilities, especially in the area with which we are concerned. In fact, no other weapon against inaction on the part of the member states and the organs of the Community has been hardened and sharpened to such a degree by the Court's case law.

The process has involved several stages. First, the Court recognized that Community rules which impose clear and unconditional duties on the member states create rights in favor of citizens and undertakings which they can rely on before national courts (direct effect).[6] Subsequently, the Court mandated that such Community rules oblige the authorities of the member states to set aside any conflicting national provisions (precedence of Community law).[7] Finally, the Court emphasized that a decision on the relevance of a preliminary ruling to a case pending before the national court is to be left to that national

1. Mar. 25, 1957, 1973 Gr. Brit. T.S. No. 1 (Cmd. 5179–11), 298 U.N.T.S. 3 (1958) [hereinafter EEC Treaty].

2. Treaty Establishing the European Atomic Energy Community, Mar. 25, 1957, 1973 Gr. Brit. T.S. No. 1 (Cmd. 5179-II), 295 U.N.T.S. 259 [hereinafter Euratom Treaty].

3. Apr. 18, 1951, 1973 Gr. Brit. T.S. No. 2 (Cmd. 5189), 261 U.N.T.S. 140.

4. EEC Treaty, *supra* note 1, art. 175.

5. *Id.* art. 177.

6. The first clear decision in that respect is the judgment of Van Gend & Loos, Case 26/62, 1963 E.C.R. 1, Common Mkt. Rep. (CCH) 8008.

7. The precedence of Community law was first established in the judgment of Costa v. ENEL, Case 6/64, 1964 E.C.R. 585, Common Mkt. Rep. (CCH) 8023. The principle found its clearest

court. Such a decision cannot be challenged by the member states or the EEC institutions in their observations before the Court of Justice.[8]

Thus hardened and sharpened, the preliminary ruling procedure became an effective weapon for the enforcement of the Treaty's standstill provisions.[9] Subsequently, the procedure was useful in attaining the free movement of goods, persons, and services by the end of the transitional period on January 1, 1970, although some implementing provisions had still not been adopted by the Council.[10] Finally, the preliminary ruling procedure gave effect to clear directive provisions that had not been correctly transposed into national law within the mandated time.[11]

In a broad range of circumstances, the case law of the Court under Article 177 has led simply to the relinquishment, by the Commission, of legislative initiatives as superfluous after a decision by the Court. Such was the case with the implementing provisions in the spheres of establishment and services that had yet to be adopted at the end of the transitional period. It was also the direct conclusion drawn by the Commission after the so-called "Cassis de Dijon" line of cases,[12] developed by the Court on the basis of references for a preliminary ruling. The Commission concluded from that case law that as a principal and overriding rule, it was a breach of the prohibition in Article 30 of the Treaty to limit, for technical or commercial reasons, the marketing in its territory of goods that were lawfully produced and marketed in another member state.[13] That view led temporarily to an almost complete halt to the Commission's legislative initiatives with regard to the harmonization of the technical requirements of the member states with respect to goods. The Commission was clearly convinced that traders would presumably know how to avail themselves of the means offered by the Court in order to remove such obstacles to trade.

Although the preliminary ruling procedure is an effective weapon against failure to act, its aim is not very accurate. It can be used to demolish barriers in the form of national provisions, but not to build up common rules, however desirable those rules might be. Fortunately, the Commission has now embarked on a more balanced harmonizing policy, and the Single European Act[14] has created a legal basis that appears to provide an appropriate foundation for such a policy.

---

expression in the judgment of Simmenthal, Case 106/77, 1978 E.C.R. 629, Common Mkt. Rep. (CCH) 8476.

8. *See* Salgoil, Case 13/68, 1968 E.C.R. 453, Common Mkt. Rep. (CCH) 8072.

9. Van Gend & Loos, Case 26/62, 1963 E.C.R. 1, Common Mkt. Rep. (CCH) 8008.

10. *See* Reyners, Case 2/74, 1974 E.C.R. 631, Common Mkt. Rep. (CCH) 8256; Van Binsbergen, Case 33/74, 1974 E.C.R. 1299, Common Mkt. Rep. (CCH) 8282; Charmasson, Case 48/74, 1974 E.C.R. 1383, Common Mkt. Rep. (CCH) 8291. The transitional period was the period within which the Common Market should be established. *See* EEC Treaty, *supra* note 1, art. 8.

11. Becker, Case 8/81, 1982 E.C.R. 53, Common Mkt. Rep. (CCH) 8789.

12. *See* Rewe-Zentral, Case 120/78, 1979 E.C.R. 649, Common Mkt. Rep. (CCH) 8543.

13. EEC Treaty, *supra* note 1, art. 30 (regarding measures having effect equivalent to quantitative restrictions between member states).

14. O.J. L 169/1 (1987), Common Mkt. Rep. (CCH) 21,000.

The Court's decisions in certain areas have thus rendered superfluous legislative initiatives already underway. However, the Court's decisions have also contributed to encouraging legislative initiatives in other areas. Moreover, national courts' application of Article 177 in cases between undertakings or private persons and national authorities continues to be an effective way of exerting influence over the implementation of Community rules by the member states and of motivating the Council to adopt common rules. The cases on the application of the Treaty's competition rules to air transport are some of the most recent examples on this point.[15] The Court held that the area of air transport is covered by the rules on competition. In addition, the Court attributed direct effect to the prohibition in Article 86[16] of abuse of a dominant position in the member states, despite the absence of implementation provisions. As a result of the Court's holding, common legislation in the area became an absolute necessity to avoid chaos. The Court was thus giving a decisive push in the direction of the long-awaited Community rules.

As a rule, however, the application of Article 177 is limited to cases where there are clear and unconditional duties of abstention or action. Admittedly, national courts are increasingly referring questions regarding the proper interpretation of a directive to the Court of Justice, on the assumption that the national legislature has intended to implement the directive correctly. Thus, the Article 177 procedure acquires a significance, independent of any direct effect the Community provision might have. However, this development has thus far been primarily limited to the national courts' application of national provisions that are designed to implement a specific directive. The private person's participation in bringing Community institutions' inactivity to an end thus remains, generally speaking, subject to the relevant Community provision being clear and unconditional.

Instead of referring to the private person's "participation" it would perhaps be more correct if I spoke of the private person's "initiative." In Article 177 cases, the Commission always avails itself of the right accorded to the institutions and member states to submit written observations, and the Commission always appears at the hearings. By means of its observations and pleadings, the Commission has made a decisive contribution to molding the preliminary ruling procedure into an appropriate weapon against the inactivity of the Council. A recent example of the Commission's activity involved a reference for a preliminary ruling intended to clarify whether the Netherlands' rules on value-added tax ("VAT") on trade in secondhand goods were compatible with Community law. Pursuant to article 32 of the Sixth VAT Directive,[17] the member states should have adopted common rules in that area by the end of 1977. In its written observations before the Court, the Commission argued that national rules which deviated from the VAT system's prohibition of principle against double taxation should now be regarded as a breach of Community law.

15. *See* Asjes, Joined Cases 209 to 213/84, 1986 E.C.R. 1425, Common Mkt. Rep. (CCH) 14,287 (known as the *Nouvelles Frontières* case); Ahmed Saeed, Case 66/86, 1989 E.C.R. 803, Common Mkt. Rep. (CCH) [1989] 2 CEC 654.

16. EEC Treaty, *supra* note 1, art. 86.

17. Council Directive No. 77/388, O.J. L 145/1 (1977), Common Mkt. Rep. (CCH) 9947.

The Commission argued that such a finding should be regarded as a consequence of more than ten years' inactivity in the VAT area. In that case the Court did not agree with the Commission.[18] Notably, that case concerned a VAT on trade in second-hand goods within a single member state and thus did not bear upon obstacles to trade between member states. In an earlier decision,[19] the Court had held that Article 95 of the EEC Treaty[20] obliged the member states to deduct the residual part of the VAT[21] when levying a VAT on the importation by a private person of second-hand goods. Thus, the Court went further than the Commission had suggested. The Court thereby brought about a legislative initiative on the Commission's part concerning the establishment of more detailed rules in respect of such deduction.

In addition to its contribution to Article 177 cases, the Commission has another effective weapon at its disposal, namely *an action against the member states for infringement of the Treaty* pursuant to Article 169.[22] It is quite clear that that form of procedure is a suitable means of putting an end to a member state's inactivity. It is, however, surprising that it is also effective in reactivating a Commission proposal that has run aground in the Council. There are a considerable number of examples on point. Two examples will suffice to demonstrate the technique.

The cases on the taxation of alcoholic beverages,[23] like the case on the light tax on Danish fruit wine,[24] formed part of an attempt on the part of the Commission to arouse the member states' interest in adopting the Commission's proposals for the harmonization of tax on alcoholic beverages. By obtaining a ruling that the existing taxation system in a number of member states was protectionist and therefore in breach of Article 95 of the Treaty, the Commission hoped to remove the main cause of the member states' resistance to tax harmonization in the area of alcoholic beverages.

The attempt was successful because in most cases the Court upheld the Commission's argument that the national tax system favored national beverages in a way that infringed Article 95. However, the Commission did not achieve its main objective. Even if some national systems are weighted in favor of their national products, they are primarily part of a general taxation policy pursuing fiscal and health ends which do not *per se* infringe Community law. The Commission therefore also had to include the area of alcoholic beverages in its general program for tax harmonization in preparation for the completion of the internal EEC market in 1992.

18. *See* ORO Amsterdam Beheer, Case 165/89, 1989 E.C.R. 4081.

19. *See* Schul, Case 15/81, 1982 E.C.R. 1409, Common Mkt. Rep. (CCH) 8831.

20. EEC Treaty, *supra* note 1, art. 95.

21. The residual part of the VAT is reflected in the value of the goods at the time of initial purchase in the exporting member state.

22. EEC Treaty, *supra* note 1, art. 169.

23. *See* Commission v. France, Italy and Denmark, Cases 168, 169 & 171/78, 1980 E.C.R. 347, 385 & 447, Common Mkt. Rep. (CCH) 8647, 8648 & 8649.

24. *See* Commission v. Denmark, Case 106/84, 1986 E.C.R. 833, Common Mkt. Rep. (CCH) 14,315.

An additional reason for the Commission's lack of success in the series of cases dealing with tax harmonization of alcoholic beverages was the Court's observance of the delineation of tasks between the legislature and the judiciary. In the case against the United Kingdom concerning the relationship between wine and beer taxation,[25] the Commission had hoped to force the Court to choose one of the criteria that the parties had suggested (tax calculation based on either volume, alcoholic strength, or pretax price). The Court, however, left the choice between those criteria to the legislature and confined itself to a finding that the wine was too heavily taxed regardless of the criterion applied.

On that particular point, the Commission was more successful in the actions it brought against the member states' restrictions on the rights of foreign insurance companies to contract for risk insurance without setting up branches or agencies. In the case against Germany,[26] the Commission managed to isolate the questions on which the member states disagreed and which had thus blocked the adoption of the directive on services in the area. For its part, the Court succeeded in finding a solution to these questions by balancing the Treaty's general rules on free exchange of services against the special consumer protection considerations governing the insurance area. The directive could thus finally be adopted a year after the judgment was delivered.

An Article 169 action is especially effective against failure by the Council to act in areas where it is necessary to create new rules but where the Community alone has competence.

For example, as a consequence of lack of unanimity in the allocation of fishing quotas, the member states sought, in the late 1970s, to protect the disappearing fishery resources by means of national rules. The Court, however, held that competence had irrevocably passed to the Community and the member states could therefore act solely as *negotiorum gestores*[27] and then only with the Commission's consent.[28] On the other hand, the Court has not until now accepted the notion that in such a situation the Commission can, on grounds comparable to necessity, exercise the power conferred by the Treaty on a paralyzed Council.[29]

A third form of procedure which has been used successfully by the Commission to prevent blocking in the Council is the *action for annulment* under Article 173 of the EEC

25. *See* Commission v. United Kingdom, Case 170/78, 1980 E.C.R. 417, Common Mkt. Rep. (CCH) 8651, *case reopened*, 1983 E.C.R. 2265.

26. *See* Commission v. Germany, Case 205/84, 1986 E.C.R. 3755, Common Mkt. Rep. (CCH) 14,339.

27. *Black's Law Dictionary* defines a negotiorum gestor as, *inter alia*, "one who, without any mandate or authority, assumes to take charge of an affair or concern for another person, in the latter's absence, but for his interest." Black's Law Dictionary 1036 (6th ed. 1990).

28. *See* Commission v. United Kingdom, Case 804/79, 1981 E.C.R. 1045, Common Mkt. Rep. (CCH) 8752.

29. *See* Kingdom of the Netherlands v. Commission, Case 326/85, 1987 E.C.R. 5091; *see also* Pluimveeslachterij, Joined Cases 47 & 48/83, 1984 E.C.R. 1721, Common Mkt. Rep. (CCH) 14,087 (offering possible suggestion that Commission is entitled to act on ground of necessity).

Treaty.[30] In such cases the Council has in fact been active, but has, in the Commission's opinion, perhaps not gone far enough. For example, the Commission brought an action for annulment in a case where the Council had chosen to establish tariff quotas in the form of national quotas instead of Community quotas.[31]

That form of procedure has, however, been used by the Commission primarily as a weapon against the Council's tendency to base a legal measure on a provision of the Treaty that requires unanimity rather than on a provision that merely requires a qualified majority.[32] In such cases, the Commission has generally not objected to the substance of the rules adopted. Rather, its challenge to the legal measure has been aimed solely at precluding any future blocking in the Council of the matter. The Court has admitted this type of action.

As is well known, the Single European Act has made it possible for the Council to adopt more decisions by a qualified majority. It has, however, also conferred new powers on the Community, for example in environmental matters, where unanimity is required. There is consequently little chance that the Court will, in the near future, be able to avoid these cases, which often appear very formalistic but can have considerable impact on the balance of power between the institutions.

As a provisional conclusion it may thus be said that, according to the actual circumstances, references for preliminary rulings, actions for infringement of the Treaty, and even actions for annulment may constitute appropriate weapons against failure to act on the part of the Council.

Of the important forms of procedure under the Treaty, only the action for failure to act and the action for damages have not been mentioned. Both have been tried, but have met with little success.

It is clear from the text of the EEC Treaty that an action for failure to act brought by an undertaking or a private person against the Council is unlikely to be admissible. Under the third paragraph of Article 175, natural or legal persons may only complain in the case of a failure to address an act "to that person."[33] Apart from its relationship to its servants, the Council does not issue acts addressed to individual persons or undertakings. The expression "to that person" has been extended, by analogy with Article 173 on actions for annulment, to encompass acts that are not addressed to the applicant but concern him directly and individually.[34] Even then, it is difficult to imagine any action for failure to act

30. EEC Treaty, *supra* note 1, art. 173.

31. *See* Commission v. Council, Case 51/87, 1988 E.C.R. 5459.

32. *See, e.g.*, Commission v. Council, Case 45/86, 1987 E.C.R. 1493; *cf.* United Kingdom v. Council, Case 68/86, 1988 E.C.R. 855, Common Mkt. Rep. (CCH) 14,475 (known as the Hormones judgment and brought by member state); United Kingdom v. Council, Case 131/86, 1988 E.C.R. 905, Common Mkt. Rep. (CCH) 14,494 (known as the Battery Hens judgment and brought by member state).

33. EEC Treaty, *supra* note 1, art. 175.

34. *See, e.g.*, Holtz and Willemsen v. Council, Case 134/73, 1974 E.C.R. 1, Common Mkt. Rep. (CCH) 8255 (known as the Holtz and Willemsen I judgment).

brought by an undertaking or a private person against the Council that would not be dismissed, because the case law of the Court on Article 173 is so strict.

Here the action for damages provided for in Article 178[35] offers, in principle, better prospects. The Court has held that even if an action for damages can lead to a result similar to that of an action for failure to act, this may not *per se* lead to its being dismissed.[36] Moreover, the award of compensation for a failure to act will certainly, as a general rule, presume infringement of a duty to act. The infringement will be, in turn, indirectly established thereby. But if the Court is not exacting in regard to formal requirements for an action for damages, it has, however, mandated strict substantive conditions which must be fulfilled before it will recognize liability for damages in connection with the Community's law-making activity. In practice, the Court therefore will be able to find in favor of the Community without expressly adopting a position on the question whether there was a formal duty to act.

Any undertaking or private person seeking the Court's assistance against the Council's failure to act is thus in fact obliged to use a roundabout approach. The undertaking or private person must persuade a national court to refer a question to the Court for a preliminary ruling under Article 177.

There is no such limitation on the right of so-called "privileged applicants," the member states and the other Community institutions, to bring an action for failure to act. While there are odd examples of actions for failure to act brought by a member state against the Commission,[37] thus far no member state has itself brought an action for failure to act against the Council. That might, of course, be explained by the general disinclination of the member states to seek the Court's assistance in resolving disputes between them. That disinclination cannot, however, explain why the Commission has brought only one action for failure to act against the Council.[38]

The restraint of the privileged applicants may therefore be a result of the weak effect of a judgment establishing failure to act. Whereas a declaration of nullity brings to an end the existence of a legal measure challenged, usually even with retrospective effect, the failure to act remains as such after a judgment pursuant to Article 175. The Court cannot itself promulgate the desired legal measure. Under Article 176,[39] the duty to comply with the judgment supplements the preexisting duty to act found in the judgment. However, it is still up to the political authorities to adopt the legal measure in accordance with the

35. EEC Treaty, *supra* note 1, art. 178.

36. *See, e.g.*, Holtz and Willemsen v. Council, Case 153/73, 1974 E.C.R. 675, Common Mkt. Rep. (CCH) 8277 (known as the Holtz and Willemsen II judgment).

37. *See, e.g.*, Germany v. Commission, Case 84/82, 1984 E.C.R. 1451, Common Mkt. Rep. (CCH) 14,090; Germany v. Commission, Case 44/81, 1982 E.C.R. 1855, Common Mkt. Rep. (CCH) 8,839 (attempting to invent non-existent action for payment); Asteris and Others and Hellenic Republic v. Commission, Joined Cases 97, 99, 193 & 215/86, 1988 E.C.R. 2181, Common Mkt. Rep. (CCH) 14,502 (holding that action for failure to act was changed to action for annulment of earlier express decision that refused to issue desired measure).

38. *See* Commission v. Council, Case 383/87, 1988 E.C.R. 4051.

39. EEC Treaty, *supra* note 1, art. 176.

general rules of legislative procedure. A direction to the legislature regarding the detailed content of the legal measure may only be ordered if the unfulfilled duty to act is described precisely in the EEC Treaty. Due to the Treaty's character as a framework instrument, the Treaty will seldom provide such a clear description.

In a case concerning the absence of a transport policy,[40] in which the Commission intervened in favor of the applicant European Parliament (the "Parliament"), the Court even held that it could find a failure to act only if the Treaty indicated at least the aim of the required measure. In the transport policy area, this condition was fulfilled only with regard to the liberalization of services. And even in this respect, it must be admitted that the judgment has not, in practice, provided the Community legislation with the desired momentum.

In reality, the Commission and the member states have an evident interest in an action for failure to act only if the duty to act is set out in a clear and unconditional manner in the Treaty. Only in such instances can the Court declare *obiter* that the Treaty provision has direct effect regardless of the Council's failure to act. The Netherlands government sought such a holding by the Court with regard to liberalization of services when it intervened in the transport policy case. On that point the Court wisely exercised restraint. It did not regard the requirement of freedom to provide services in the area of transport as having become directly effective once the transitional period had expired. The Council was entitled to a reasonable period to work out rules on the matter as part of the Community's transport policy and it was not necessary to adopt a position with regard to the consequences of possible continued failure to act on the part of the Council. Nevertheless, that circumspect hint in the judgment might very well give rise to a fresh action for failure to act if the plans for a gradual liberalization of cross-border road transport are not implemented in 1992.

Apart from the possibility of such obiter dicta, an action for failure to act does not give the member states or the Commission a weapon against the Council's failure to act which is more effective than their political means as participants in the legislative process or their legal arsenal described above. As far as the Commission is concerned there is, however, an exception to this rule, namely the budget procedure. Budgetary authority is shared between the Council and the Parliament. The Commission is more or less detached from the procedure once it has transmitted its preliminary draft budget to the Council. From then on it may exert its influence only indirectly and its best ally is then the Parliament. The Commission thus has an interest in whether the Council timely adopts its budget proposals and forwards those proposals to the Parliament. Even though a budget is necessary for the Community's continued work, there is no possibility that failure to act might create a ground of necessity for the Commission. The consequence of absence of a budget is in fact expressly spelled out in Article 204 of the Treaty, the so-called "one-twelfth rule."[41]

40. *See* Parliament v. Council, Case 13/83, 1985 E.C.R. 1513, Common Mkt. Rep. (CCH) 14,191.

41. EEC Treaty, *supra* note 1, art. 204. Article 204 provides in part: "If at the beginning of a financial year, the budget has not yet been voted, a sum equivalent to not more than one-twelfth of the budget appropriations for the preceding financial year may be spent each month." *Id.*

Also, an action for annulment is an inappropriate means of dealing with a budget that has been adopted too late.

Therefore, in the absence of better weapons, the Commission might have an interest in challenging the Council's failure to act in its capacity as budgetary authority by way of an action under Article 175. It has in fact done so once, in 1987, when the Council did not transmit the budget proposals to the Parliament in time.[42] The action brought by the Commission and the corresponding action brought by the Parliament[43] were regarded by the Court as being devoid of purpose once the Council, albeit after a long delay, had fulfilled its duty to act; the actions had nonetheless fulfilled their function as a means of exerting pressure.

The Community institution that has the greatest interest in the possibilities of bringing an action for failure to act is the Parliament. Even though its political powers have been considerably extended in relation to the original treaties, first as regards the budget and most recently in the Single European Act in legislative matters, it has still not been granted the power to initiate action in these areas. The Parliament may thus avail itself of its budgetary and legislative powers only if the requisite proposal is submitted to it.

It was therefore natural for the Parliament to bring an action in the already mentioned case against the Council concerning the absence of a transport policy and for it to bring proceedings with the Commission in 1987, when the Council had not timely transmitted the draft budget for the coming year.

The Parliament has an even greater interest in the right to bring an action for annulment against an act of the Council when the Council has not sufficiently considered the Parliament's wishes. Although the Parliament now has the last word in the budget negotiations, the Council makes the final decisions in the legislative area. Even where the Treaty provides for the use of the cooperation procedure that was introduced by the Single European Act, the most the Parliament can do is to force the Council to comply with the requirement of unanimity if the Council disagrees with the position of the Parliament. Over the last year the Parliament has therefore fought to win the right to bring an action for annulment. It failed at its first attempt, but now in the last round it has won a partial victory.

The difficulty is that the Parliament is not among the institutions mentioned in the first paragraph of Article 173, conferring the right to bring an action for annulment. During the negotiations for the Single European Act, the question whether the Parliament should be incorporated into the text was raised, but no solution was reached. This rested in part on the ground that the Parliament had already raised the question before the Court in the so-called "Comitology" case.[44]

True, the second paragraph of Article 173, referring to "any natural or legal person" gives a limited right to bring an action. However, it does not seem natural initially to ex-

42. *See* Commission v. Council, Case 383/87, 1988 E.C.R. 4051.

43. *See* Parliament v. Council, Case 377/87, 1988 E.C.R. 4017.

44. Parliament v. Council, Case 302/87, 1988 E.C.R. 5615, Common Mkt. Rep. (CCH) [1990] 2 CEC 139.

clude the Parliament from the rule concerning the institutions in the first paragraph and then to let that institution in through the back door as a "legal person," an expression which hardly covers the Parliament. Moreover, the requirement in the second paragraph that the applicant must be directly and individually concerned by the legal measure is not an adequate representation of the Parliament's interest in bringing an action.

It is therefore not so surprising that the Court in the "Comitology" judgment did not think it could interpret Article 173 as giving the Parliament the right to bring an action for annulment.

If the "Comitology" judgment has met with strong criticism, that is primarily because the judgment simultaneously sought to show that the Parliament was not without any legal safeguard against the disregard of its prerogatives on the part of the Council. The judgment states in particular that as guardian of the Treaty, the Commission has the responsibility for ensuring that the Parliament's prerogatives are respected and for bringing such actions for annulment as might prove necessary. The judgment also indicated that the Parliament itself has a right to bring an action for failure to act under Article 175, which refers to all the institutions of the Community.

In this respect, the judgment states that the right to bring an action for failure to act is not extinguished merely because the institution that is requested to act refuses the request, unless that refusal can be regarded as putting an end to the failure to act. That statement is not completely in accordance with earlier case law.[45] Previously, the Court was inclined to regard such a refusal as a definition of position that excluded an action for failure to act. However, the refusal could be challenged as a corollary issue by way of an action for annulment. The statement can therefore be construed as an indication that the Court would have been more sympathetic to an action for failure to act brought by the Parliament, because this institution was barred from bringing an action for annulment. Thus the judgment may be understood as indirectly encouraging the Parliament to explore the avenue of an action for failure to act.

The Parliament did not pursue an action for failure to act, but instead persisted in the fresh action for annulment which had already been brought before the "Comitology" judgment. The Parliament's course was surely due primarily to the remarks in the judgment concerning the Parliament's other legal safeguards. In the "Comitology" case, the other legal safeguards were actually *obiter dicta*, but they were highly relevant to the new case because in the Parliament's view the circumstances clearly showed that the other safeguards were inadequate.

In the "Comitology" case the Parliament had principally challenged the content of the Council's measure which differed substantially both from the original Commission proposal and from the Parliament's suggested amendments. The new case was directed against a Council regulation mandating maximum permitted levels of radioactive contamination of foodstuffs and of feedingstuffs following a nuclear accident. The Parliament challenged

45. *See, e.g.*, Nordgetreide v. Commission, Case 42/71, 1972 E.C.R. 105, Common Mkt. Rep. (CCH) 8174.

the fact that the Council, in accordance with the Commission's proposal, had based its legal measure on a provision in the Euratom Treaty which requires merely that the Parliament be consulted.[46] The Parliament argued that the measure should have been based on a provision in the EEC Treaty which requires that the more extensive cooperation procedure be applied.

It was clear that the Commission, which agreed with the Council on the basis chosen, could not appear as the Parliament's champion. Moreover, there was very little sense in bringing an action for failure to act against the Council, because the Council had already adopted the final act.

In addition, there was the fact that the Court, in cases brought by private plaintiffs, had previously stated that a tacit refusal to revoke a legal measure may not be challenged pursuant to Article 175. Such a challenge would constitute a circumvention of the restrictions in Article 173.[47] The Court had also held that Article 175 is aimed at failure to make a decision, and is not directed at the adoption of an act other than that desired by the applicant.[48]

In its recent judgment,[49] the Court recognized that the "Comitology" judgment was too uncompromising in its rejection of the Parliament's right of action. The Court maintained its view that the Parliament is covered by neither the first nor second paragraph of Article 173. However, the Court inferred a limited right of action pursuant to the Court's duty to ensure observance of the institutional balance provided for by the Treaty. This principle, however, is limited to cases where the action is intended to safeguard the Parliament's special prerogatives. Moreover, the action must be based on grounds which relate to the alleged disregard of those special prerogatives. Because the case before it did in fact lie within those bounds, the Court admitted the case for a decision on its merits.

The most recent judgment on this issue, discussed immediately above, does not exclude the Parliament's right to bring an action for failure to act in an appropriate situation as soon as the Parliament notices that the Commission is basing its proposal on a provision that does not give the Parliament the desired influence. However, it is clear that the judgment does diminish the Parliament's interest in such a course of action. As stated, an action for annulment is an extremely strong weapon and in an initial phase, the Parliament will presumably prefer to exercise its political influence, now reinforced by some appropriate legal "saber-rattling."

In sum, it may be stated that the Court's case law has developed a range of very effective weapons to be used against the Council's failure to act. This has resulted in various forms of procedure which, from a superficial reading of the Treaty, might appear com-

46. Euratom Treaty, *supra* note 2, art. 31.

47. *See* Eridania v. Commission, Joined Cases 10 & 18/68, 1969 E.C.R. 459, Common Mkt. Rep. 8099.

48. *See* Deutscher Komponistenverband v. Commission, Case 8/71, 1971 E.C.R. 705, Common Mkt. Rep. (CCH) 8143; Irish Cement v. Commission, Joined Cases 166–220/86, 1988 E.C.R. 6973.

49. *See* Parliament v. Council, Case 70/88 (Judgment of May 22, 1990), 1990 E.C.R. (known as the "Post Tchernobyl-judgment").

pletely unsuited for the purpose. On the other hand, the ostensibly appropriate weapon, the action for failure to act, has proved to be so innocuous that it has been largely abandoned in favor of those procedures developed later. For a short time, it appeared that the action for failure to act might be resuscitated as the Parliament's only legal remedy to safeguard its prerogatives in the legislative procedure. However, after the most recent judgment on this issue, the action for failure to act has also lost its real significance as a legal remedy for the Parliament. Henceforth the action for failure to act may be primarily regarded only as a measure of last resort.

The Advocate: Should He Speak or Write?

Rt. Hon. Lord Mackay

The Honorable Lord Mackay gave the twentieth Sonnett lecture on April 3, 1991, entitled *The Advocate: Should He Speak or Write?*[1]

James Peter Hymers Mackay was born the son of a railway signalman. He was born on July 2, 1927 in Edinburgh, Scotland.[2] After completing his studies at the University of Edinburgh in math and natural philosophy, Mackay accepted a lectureship at the University of St. Andrews in its math department.[3] Mackay went on to pursue a scholarship to study mathematics at Trinity College, Cambridge, where he attained his B.A. in mathematics.[4] At this point, Mackay took his studies in a different direction, returning to the University of Edinburgh, where he earned his LL.B. with distinction.[5]

Upon completing his studies in 1955, Mackay was admitted to the Faculty of Advocates, the bar association of Scotland, and began trying civil and criminal cases.[6] Mackay held leadership positions within the Faculty of Advocates, culminating in his election as Dean of the Faculty in 1976.[7] In 1979 Mackay was appointed Lord Advocate, the most senior legal position in Scotland, and accepted the title of Baron Mackay of Clashfern.[8] Over the next eight years Lord Mackay served as a Senator of Scotland's College of Justice and Lord of Appeal in Ordinary, until Margaret Thatcher appointed him as Lord Chancellor of the United Kingdom on October 27, 1987.[9] As part of Lord Mackay's role as Lord Chancellor, he served as President of the House of Lords, as the head of the judiciary, responsible for many judicial appointments and a member of the Cabinet.[10] After ten years in this position, Lord Mackay assumed the role of Chancellor of Heriot-Watt University of Edinburgh.[11]

Lord Mackay has received countless honors during his tenure, including election as a Fellow of the Royal Society of Edinburgh, the Royal Medal of the Royal Society of

Introduction written by Christie Falco, J.D., Class of 2015, Fordham University School of Law.

1. The Rt. Hon. Lord Mackay, *The Advocate: Should He Speak or Write?*, 60 FORDHAM L. REV. 953 (1992).
2. J.J. O'Connor & E.F. Robertson, *James Peter Hymers Mackay* (Apr. 2006), http://www-history.mcs.st-and.ac.uk/Biographies/Mackay.html.
3. *Id.*
4. *Id.*
5. *Id.*
6. *Id.*
7. *Id.*
8. *Id.*
9. *Id.*
10. *Id.*
11. *Id.*

Edinburgh, and election as an Honorary Fellow of both Trinity College, Cambridge and Girton College, Cambridge.[12]

In his Sonnett lecture, Lord Mackay explored the traditions of oral and written advocacy in Scotland and England, the two jurisdictions in which he primarily spent his career. As a young advocate, Mackay relied on the books of two practitioners, Frederic Wottesley and J. H. Munkman, whose guides to effective advocacy focus only on spoken advocacy.[13] In Scotland and England, the role of oral advocacy is much greater than in American judicial proceedings, where attorneys submit substantial written filings.[14]

In Scotland, written filings were a staple of judicial proceedings throughout the eighteenth century.[15] However, by the end of the nineteenth century, oral advocacy had recommenced as the primary form of advocacy in Scotland, after various attacks on the written pleading tradition.[16] On the other hand, there has been a strong and consistent tradition of oral advocacy in England and Wales, until recent years, when written advocacy has played a larger role in civil appeals.[17] This shift has been largely in response to increasing judicial caseloads, and the backlogs and delays they have caused.[18]

Lord Mackay's analysis of the benefits and costs of oral and written advocacy continue to have relevant implications today. American litigants face ever-increasing delays, as the courts grapple with vacant judicial seats and backlogs.[19] Lord Mackay correctly drew attention to the role written advocacy may have on these delays, possibly even mitigating them to some extent.[20] A self-reflective, cost-benefit analysis of the use of written and oral advocacy in the American judicial system may be worthwhile to understand the inefficiencies of, and potential improvements to, the American court system.

1991 Sonnett Lecture

President, Dean, Boris Koztclenatz—a working lawyer—Distinguished Guests, Ladies and Gentlemen. I am both pleased and honored to be here in New York tonight to give the

12. *Id.*

13. *See generally* Mackay, *supra* note 1, at 955–56 (citing Sir F.J. Wrottesley, The Examination of Witnesses in Court (1910); J.H. Munkman, The Technique of Advocacy (3d ed. 1951)).

14. *Id.*

15. *Id.* at 962–64.

16. *Id.* at 964.

17. *Id.*

18. *Id.*

19. *See, e.g.*, Gary Martin, *Vacancies, Backlogs Plague Federal Judiciary*, Houston Chronicle (Mar. 1, 2013), http://www.chron.com/news/politics/article/Vacancies-backlogs-plague-federal-judiciary-4321484.php.

20. Mackay, *supra* note 1, at 955–56.

Twentieth Annual John F. Sonnett Lecture at Fordham University School of Law. The list of previous lecturers is indeed a distinguished one, including former Chief Justices of Ireland and England; your own Chief Justice of the Supreme Court, Warren E. Burger; and other distinguished American judges and lawyers.

John F. Sonnett, as most of you here will know better than I, had a distinguished career in law, both in public and private service. He served as an Assistant Attorney General and Chief of the Antitrust Division of the United States Department of Justice before returning to private practice and establishing an international reputation for trial and appellate advocacy. He was a graduate of the School of Law at Fordham University. The university itself was founded in 1841, and thus celebrates its 150th anniversary this year. The Law School is, however, a little younger, having been founded in 1905. It has developed to provide a wide-ranging curriculum and has produced a number of distinguished graduates.

When I received the invitation to give this lecture, the only indication I received as to its subject was that it should be "advocacy-related." After some reflection, I have chosen the title "The Advocate: Should He Speak or Write?" My choice of subject owes much to Professor Robert Martineau of the University of Cincinnati, Professor Michael Zander of the London School of Economics, and to the heavy snow we experienced in London earlier this year. The connections between the three, I am sure, will not be immediately obvious to you.

Owing to the very heavy snow, I spent a rather long time one Friday sitting in the airport lounge and on board a plane, waiting for takeoff. This provided the opportunity for a more thorough perusal of the daily press than time usually permits. One of the articles I read with great interest was a review by Michael Zander of a book by Professor Martineau called "Appellate Justice in England and the United States: A Comparative Analysis."[1] Professor Zander wrote of Professor Martineau's conclusion that the problems of dealing with high workloads and growing backlog experienced by appellate courts in England, Wales, and the United States were more easily tackled in the United States because of the use of written briefs supplemented by minimal oral advocacy.[2] This made me think about the use of oral or written advocacy in all our courts and if there were conclusive reasons for adopting one rather than the other. I decided to examine this by using examples from England, Wales, Scotland, and the United States.

A number of people have helped me with this lecture. I have already mentioned the indirect help of Professor Martineau, and I have had the opportunity of discussing with Professor Zander his article. I am also indebted to Lord Griffiths; Lord Donaldson, Master of the Rolls; Professor Ian Scott of the University of Birmingham; James Wolffe, the Legal Assistant to the Lord President of the Court of Session; and, above all, to my Private Secretary, Jenny Rowe. Responsibility for any errors or weaknesses in the lecture is, however, entirely mine.

1. Zander, *Kindly Get to the Point, My Learned Friend*, Independent, Feb. 8, 1991, at 19.
2. *See id.*

It was Francis Bacon who said, "Reading maketh a full man; conference a ready man; and writing an *exact* man." The English tradition, however, is one of predominantly oral advocacy, although the English dictionary to which I referred defined an advocate as a person who pleads on behalf of another, especially in a court of law—a person who *speaks or writes* in support of some cause, argument, or proposal.[3]

Although the dictionary definition allows for advocacy to be either written or spoken, few people in the English tradition, until comparatively recently, would have laid much emphasis on the art of written advocacy. Lord Birkett, in his presidential address to the Holdsworth Club in the University of Birmingham in 1956, defined the advocate's art in a way that clearly assumed an advocacy that was exclusively oral:

> It is clear that advocacy is made up of many elements. There is first of all, [I repeat], the importance of the advocate himself. He should count himself exceedingly fortunate if he has been endowed with a good voice. But he must use it. He must speak so that he can be heard, and he must articulate clearly. He must try to acquire tone and modulation, so that his every sentence is pleasant to the ear. To the advocate, the spoken word is the breath of his life, and it is quite astonishing to me that so little thought is given to it. . . . A commanding presence is a great asset, but if nature has been careless about this, the advocate must do the best he can by making up for it in other directions. . . . It is well if the advocate is possessed of a quick mind, alert to seize the unexpected opportunity, to adapt himself to the sudden changes which occur in the conduct of a case, and to be ready to deal with any interventions from the Bench, whether they be disconcerting or helpful. But more important than the quick mind is the understanding heart, the insight into human nature, the natural sympathy with all sorts and conditions of men, the intuitive recognition of what the particular situation demands. . . . But whether the advocate possesses all or any of these qualities, there are certain desirable things which it is in the power of all advocates to do. . . . In the conduct of any case the advocate must have made himself master of all the facts; he must have a thorough understanding of the principles and rules of law which are applicable to the case and the ability to apply them on the instant; he must gauge with accuracy the atmosphere of the court in which he pleads and adapt himself accordingly; he must be able to reason from the facts and the law to achieve the end he desires, and he must above all have mastered the art of expressing himself clearly and persuasively in acceptable English.[4]

I learned my advocacy principally at the Scottish bar. In my view, the best training for oral advocacy is to appear before a really good, well-controlled court, presided over by judges of high caliber. I was very fortunate in this respect; when I went to the bar, there was a great deal of rating work available. It was conducted, at first instance, before local committees of laymen, and there was an appeal from these local committees to the Lands Valuation Appeal Court. This court consisted of three judges, two from the Inner House of the Court of Session, which as I shall explain later is the appellate part of that Court,

3. *See* The Random House Dictionary of the English Language (2d ed.).

4. Lord Birkett, *Presidential Address to the Holdsworth Club at the University of Birmingham* (1956) (source available at Fordham Law Review).

and the third the senior judge of the Outer House, the first instance section of the Court. All three were judges of acute mind, rigorous legal intellect, and a courtesy that was most encouraging to those who were prepared and devastating to the unprepared. Because of their intellectual rigor, their judgments were highly consistent and it was, therefore, possible for a young advocate, as I was, to forecast with remarkable precision what the result of any particular appeal would be. This gave one reputation and confidence. I found myself appearing before them a great deal, and I believe their testing of my preparation and of the logic of my argument helped me greatly to develop a style, at least for appellate work, which was much better than I could have attained without their help.

But it is also possible to learn about advocacy from the written experience and analysis of others. In order to prepare this lecture, I tried to remember how I prepared myself to advocate. I am greatly indebted to two notable practitioners of the art of advocacy: Frederic Wrottesley, latterly a Lord Justice of Appeal, in his book *The Examination of Witnesses in Court*;[5] and Munkman, in his book *The Technique of Advocacy*.[6]

It says something about how old I am that I had great difficulty in getting my hands on copies of these books. Both are books to which I referred frequently during my early time at the bar, and they are still valuable guides to any advocate. Munkman takes a similar line to Birkett. Wrottesley writes from the point of view of a specialist in civil rather than criminal matters during the first quarter of this Century, when most civil trials in England still took place before a jury. Some of his comments may, therefore, with due allowance for passage of time, be particularly relevant to an American audience where the jury still plays such an important part in civil as well as criminal cases. Wrottesley makes his own personal view of the strengths of oral advocacy very plain at an early stage:

> No better mode of ascertaining the truth of a past transaction will probably ever be devised by human ingenuity than the present method of *viva voce* examination of witnesses, conducted as it is in open court, in the sight of the public and in the presence of the parties, their counsel, and of the judge and jury, who all have an opportunity of observing the intelligence, demeanor, inclination, bias or prejudice of the witnesses. In this way every man is given a fair and impartial trial, and his rights cannot be abridged, nor can he be deprived of the inestimable blessings of life, liberty, or property, without the concurrence of judge and jury.[7]

Wrottesley then goes on to set out what might be described as a plan of attack for the advocate, which is very similar to the technique propounded by Munkman. Counsel must first take great care in the introduction of his evidence, ensuring that any documentary evidence is proved and that he takes every lawful advantage of his adversary to ensure that documents are disclosed.[8]

5. Sir F.J. Wrottesley, The Examination of Witnesses in Court (1910) [hereinafter Wrottesley].

6. J.H. Munkman, The Technique of Advocacy (3d ed. 1951) [hereinafter Munkman].

7. Wrottesley, *supra* note 5, at 16.

8. *See id.* at 12–13.

Turning to the actual examination of his witnesses the advocate should, in nearly every case, put his most intelligent and honest witness in the box first.[9] This allows him to make as good an impression as possible upon the Court and jury at the earliest possible moment. Furthermore, because that witness is likely to have to undergo the sharpest cross-examination, it is important that he be well able to cope with it. If the first witness is weak, he may do incalculable harm to the advocate's client. Witnesses should then be introduced in a logical and sequential manner, so that evidence on a particular subject is introduced as a whole, rather than in a fragmented fashion.[10] It is also suggested that a strong witness be retained until the end of the case, once again to increase the impact upon the court and jury. While the theory is sensible, this does assume you have sufficient witnesses to organize them in this way.

Wrottesley states what may be a self-evident truth, certainly for oral advocacy, that "[n]o lawyer can be successful in the highest sense of the term unless he is a master of the difficult art of examining witnesses. It requires a greater combination of qualities than almost any other branch of advocacy, the most important of which are patience, coolness, courage, and tact."[11] He goes on to say that it is difficult to lay down any rules that would govern this, but that certain precepts can be gained from the writings of others on this subject.[12] Wrottesley gives in full the eleven golden rules set out by the American attorney, David Paul Brown. I think I can do no better than he by quoting those rules in full.

> *First.* If your own witnesses are bold, and may injure your cause by pertness or forwardness, observe a ceremony and gravity of manner towards them which may be calculated to repress their assurance.
>
> *Second.* If they are alarmed or diffident and their thoughts are evidently scattered, commence your examination with matters of a familiar character, remotely connected with the subject of their alarm, or the matter in issue, as for instance: "Where do you live?" "Do you know the parties?" "How long have you known them?" and the like. When you have restored them to composure, and the mind has gained its equilibrium, proceed to the most essential features of the cause being careful to be mild and distinct in your approaches, lest you may trouble the fountain again from which you are to drink.
>
> *Third.* If the evidence of your own witnesses be unfavorable to you—which should always be guarded against—exhibit no want of composure: for there are many minds that form opinions of the nature or character of testimony chiefly from the effect which it may appear to produce upon the counsel.
>
> *Fourth.* If you see that the mind of the witness is imbued with prejudices against your client, hope but little from such a quarter—unless there be some facts which are essential to your client's protection, and which that witness alone

9. *See id.* at 13.
10. *See id.* at 14.
11. Wrottesley, *supra* note 5, at 35.
12. *See id.*

can prove; either do not call him, or get rid of him as soon as possible. If the opposite counsel see the bias to which I referred he may employ it to your own ruin. In judicial inquiries, of all possible evils the worst and the hardest to resist is an enemy in the disguise of a friend. You cannot impeach him—you cannot disarm him; you cannot even indirectly assail him; and if you exercise the only privilege that is left to you, and call other witnesses for the purpose of an explanation, you must bear in mind that instead of carrying the war into the enemy's country, the struggle is between sections of your own forces, and in the very heart, perhaps, of your own camp. Avoid this by all means.

Fifth. Never call a witness whom your adversary will be compelled to call. This will afford you the privilege of cross-examination. Take from your opponent the small privilege it thus gives you, and, in addition thereto, not only render everything unfavorable said by the witness doubly operative against the party calling him, but also deprive that party of the power of counteracting the effect of the testimony.

Sixth. Never ask a question without an object—nor without being able to connect that object with the case if objected to as irrelevant.

Seventh. Be careful not to put your questions in such form that, if opposed for informality, you cannot sustain it, or at least produce strong reasons in its support. Frequently failures in the discussion of points of evidence enfeeble your strength in the estimation of the jury, and greatly impair your hopes in the final result.

Eighth. Never object to a question put by your adversary without being able and disposed to enforce the objection. Nothing is so monstrous as to be constantly making and withdrawing objections; it indicates either a want of correct perception in making them, or a deficiency of reason, or of moral courage in not making them good.

Ninth. Speak to your witness clearly and distinctly, as if you were awake, and engage in a matter of interest, and make him, also, speak distinctly and to your question. How can it be supposed that the Court and jury will be inclined to listen, when the only struggle seems to be whether the counsel or the witness shall first go to sleep?

Tenth. Modulate your voice as circumstances may direct. "Inspire the fearful and repress the bold."

Eleventh. Never begin before you are ready, and always finish when you have done. In other words, do not question for question's sake—but for an answer.[13]

I see no reason to dissent from any of these rules except for the fifth. In my time as an advocate, I have disobeyed that rule, so as to give myself two opportunities to question a witness. The initial examination of an unsuspecting witness can prove an invaluable means

13. *Id.* at 38–39.

of eliciting information the witness may be reluctant to give, leaving the jury to draw its own conclusion.

The sixth rule, "never ask a question without an object," is of absolutely vital importance. This includes care in choosing the right words and the emphasis you give to the words you have chosen, so that the answers you receive do little damage, and as much good, as possible to the case you are presenting. Munkman takes two admirable examples from the Arran murder case where Graham Murray (later Viscount Dunedin) was examining for the prosecution.

The body of a man had been found on a mountainside on the beautiful Island of Arran—I know of no better viewpoint, if I may insert a tourist plug. His companion was charged with murdering him. The defense was suggesting (among other things) that the place was dangerous and death might have been caused by an accidental fall.

> MURRAY: "Was there anything in the character of the ground which would make it *specially* dangerous?"
> WITNESS: "No."[14]

Later in the same case it appeared that the police, for some mysterious reason, had not kept the boots of the dead man, and the defense used this to raise vague suspicions. Graham Murray, examining a police witness, asked him:

> MURRAY: "It *seems* that you afterwards buried a pair of boots that were on the body?"
> WITNESS: "Yes, on the seashore at Corrie."[15]

In each case the introduction of a single word, *specially* and *seems*, has a very important effect. Without *specially*, the answer received would have been completely the opposite. The introduction of the word *seems* in the second example tended to undermine the idea that it was a deliberate action.

Of course, while the skilled advocate is putting all of these principles into practice, his opponent should not be idle. He should pay close attention to the questions put by his opponent and the answers they elicit. He should ensure that each question is properly put, according to the rules of evidence, and also endeavor to see what its bearing is on the case and the unfolding plan of his opponent. He is well advised, as we have seen in the eleven golden rules, against the making of unnecessary interventions and objections during examination in chief. But an objection in the right place can seriously weaken your opponent's case, as Wrottesley says:

> If you watch closely the examination of witnesses, in a trial where an experienced advocate is on the one side and an inexperienced one on the other, you will see the practiced man putting question after question and eliciting facts most damaging to the other side which his adversary might have shut out by a prompt objection to them, but which he permits to pass without protest.[16]

14. MUNKMAN, *supra* note 6, at 46.
15. *Id.* at 47.
16. WROTTESLEY, *supra* note 5, 42.

Does the technique vary on cross-examination? Sir James Scarlet once said of a Mr. Topping, an eminent leader on his Circuit, that his idea of cross-examination was putting over again every question asked in chief in a very angry tone.[17] That is, perhaps, a fault from which advocates are not entirely free even today. Courts and juries may be apt to give credit to an advocate for delicacy of feeling in cross-examination; a jury is apt to sympathize with a witness who is unjustly attacked and their verdict may unconsciously be influenced by the impression gained.

There are four aims for cross-examination: the first is to obtain some new information which will be helpful to the party cross-examining; the second is to destroy the material parts of the evidence in chief; the third is to weaken the evidence, where it cannot be destroyed; and the fourth is to undermine the witness or shake his credit by showing that he cannot be trusted to tell the truth or that he is speaking of matters of which he has no real knowledge. Wrottesley further suggests that the advocate has two courses open to him in cross-examining a witness. He may demonstrate his distrust of the witness by his manner, look, or tone of voice; or he may examine him as though he thought him an honest witness.[18] Both courses have their advantages in different circumstances, and whichever is adopted may very well depend upon the circumstances of the case. The witness who is patently not believed by counsel may well lose credit with the judge or jury, while the witness who thinks that he has been believed may well become careless and reveal inconsistencies in his testimony. I always found the most sensible course was not to betray to the witness anything about my own feelings. The experienced cross-examiner should not take the statements of honest witnesses for granted, but should investigate them thoroughly and endeavor to show that they are mistaken as to what they think they heard or saw and seek to show that the witness who is genuinely saying what he believes he saw or heard cannot be relied upon because of the surrounding testimony or the inherent unreasonableness of his story. The simple fact that a witness is honest does not mean that you cannot qualify his evidence. A young advocate, wishing to learn about cross-examination, can do little better than look at examples such as the cross-examination of Oscar Wilde by Sir Edward Carson. It is so short and yet so effective that it is worth reminding ourselves of it.

Carson had evidence of Wilde's books, some of which might convey immoral implications; personal letters; and actual association with a series of young men for immoral purposes. He set out his facts in that order but by way of an opening gambit confronted Wilde with facts that proved him to be a liar at the very start.[19]

CARSON: "You stated that your age was thirty-nine. I think you are over forty. You were born on 16 October 1854?"

WILDE: "I have no wish to pose as being young. I am thirty-nine or forty. You have my certificate and that settles the matter."

17. *See id.* at 64.
18. *See id.* at 71.
19. *See* MUNKMAN, *supra* note 6, at 71.

CARSON: "But being born in 1854 makes you more than forty?"
WILDE: "Ah! very well."[20]

Carson then went on to examine specific passages from several of Wilde's works. Wilde defended himself by stating that none of the passages had a personal relevance.[21] Carson then brought to bear private letters addressed to Lord Alfred Douglas that expressed sentiments of great affection.[22] Wilde was forced to admit that this represented "a tender expression of my great admiration for Lord Alfred Douglas. It was not, like the other, a prose poem."[23] Having gradually backed Wilde away from his originally detached position, Carson then delivered the final blow questioning Wilde about this relationship with a young man called Walter Grainger:

CARSON: "Did you ever kiss him?"
WILDE: "Oh, dear no. . . . He was, unfortunately, extremely ugly."
CARSON: "Was that the reason why you did not kiss him?"
WILDE: "Oh, Mr Carson, you are pertinently insolent."
CARSON: "Did you say that in support of your statement that you never kissed him?"
WILDE: "No. It is a childish question."
CARSON: "Why did you mention his ugliness?"
WILDE: "It is ridiculous to imagine that any such thing could have occurred under any circumstances."
CARSON: "Then why did you mention his ugliness, I ask you?"
WILDE: "Perhaps because you insulted me by an insulting question."
CARSON: "Was that a reason why you should say the boy was ugly?"[24]

At this point Wilde became inarticulate and unable to answer.[25]

This was a classic example of a confrontational technique of cross-examination destroying both the opposing side's case and the witness's credibility. Nevertheless, an advocate should never become an instrument of vengeance at the hands of his client. An injudicious attack upon a witness may well harm an advocate's case. Understatement is a wise thing. If the advocate allows his professional judgment to be overruled by that of his client then he will lose the power to direct both the cross-examination and the case in the most suitable way.

There is, however, perhaps more difficulty in deciding whether or not the character or past history of a witness should be attacked. Wrottesley strongly advises against this, saying that someone who is trying to live an honest life now should not have their offenses brought back to them,[26] but I am sure that many of you will recall cases where the

20. *Id.* at 71–72.
21. *See id.* at 72.
22. *See id.* at 73.
23. *Id.*
24. *Id.* at 74.
25. *See id.*
26. *See* WROTTESLEY, *supra* note 5, at 81–83.

strongest point of your own argument has been the unreliability of a hostile witness, as demonstrated by his history.

Slightly different considerations may come into play when cross-examining an expert witness. In the Arran murder case, we can find a very good example of a so-called expert witness being readily discredited. Cosimo Latona had stated that he was a "guide" in the Arran mountains and that the place where the body was found was a dangerous one. This was to support the defense's theory that the dead man might have slipped accidentally. Graham Murray asked the following questions:

> MURRAY: "How long have you been in Arran?"
> LATONA: "About three years."
> MURRAY: "Are you a fisherman by trade?"
> LATONA: "Yes, a fisherman in the winter."
> MURRAY: "How many times have you guided people over the hills in Arran?"
> LATONA: "I did not guide any people until the body of Rose was found."
> MURRAY: "Had you ever been in Glen Sannox at all before Rose's body was found?"
> LATONA: "No."[27]

Today, such a witness is likely to be more than well qualified and to be fully in control of the evidence he presents.

The examples I have used so far suggest that advocacy should always be spoken. It would not, however, be correct to assume the answer to my question is clear. It is true that I have spent my career working with two traditions of predominantly oral advocacy: the Scottish tradition as well as the English tradition. Two points are, however, particularly noteworthy. One is that the Scottish tradition of oral advocacy is rather more recent than you might think. The other is that in England and Wales, much greater use has been made of written advocacy in a variety of different courts in recent years.

For part of the nineteenth century, written arguments, known as cases or minutes of debate, were extensively used in the Scottish Courts. For Court of Session actions, prior to 1825, parties supported their cases by extensive written memorials on both fact and law. It was open to parties at anytime in the progress of a case to introduce new issues of fact or law. A description of this practice appears in Lord Cockburn's journal for 26 May 1846:

> No modem can comprehend the lives of the well-employed "writing counsel" of the last generation, when every statement, every argument, every application, every motion was made in writing, and every party was always entitled to give in a written answer; eight out of every twelve hours of the lives of these men were spent over ink-stands. What tons of discussion—especially as no case in those days was ever done. Everything could be stated and re-stated 'til the client was fairly bankrupt or dead. There was always one excellent stock paper on each side, composed or revised by the best hand engaged. It was to this practice of good professional composition that the literature which has ever distinguished the law of Scotland was very much owing. Indeed, it has been thought that our old practice made better lawyers than can ever be made by oral discussion. When well done,

27. MUNKMAN, *supra* note 5, at 107.

> writing seems to have the advantage of inducing greater care. Men don't boggle at speaking nonsense which they would hesitate to put permanently down upon paper. But spoken words are shorter, and the judges cannot escape from hearing them.[28]

You might care to reflect on this quotation in the light of the words I quoted earlier from Francis Bacon.

The Judicature Act of 1825[29] changed the form of pleading, by requiring parties to distinguish statements of fact from pleas in law and to bind the parties to a particular statement of facts. The Act also sought to substitute, so far as possible, oral for written argument. Some written argument was, however, retained. It was possible to prepare "cases in writing" consisting of a copy of the record, and a separate argument in respect of each plea in law. Such "cases" could be required at a number of stages in an action:

(a) by the Lord Ordinary before deciding a question of relevancy before or after a proof or jury trial;[30]
(b) by the Lord Ordinary on reporting a case to the Inner House;[31] or
(c) by the Inner House itself.[32]

The effect of the changes from written to oral pleadings on Outer House and Inner House seems to have differed. Before I proceed to outline this, it might be helpful if I explain a little about the Outer and Inner House. The Court of Session is a Collegiate Court, where cases at first instance are heard by a single judge in the Outer House, so called because of its physical position. An appeal, described as "a reclaiming motion," went to the Inner House, who either "adhered to" or "departed from" the original judgment.

In the Outer House, although it appears that cases[33] were usually ordered in all matters of "intricacy or difficulty," the Lord Ordinary would nonetheless hear a full oral debate in addition. In the Inner House, by contrast, full "hearings in presence"[34] were apparently relatively rare, and discussion was limited to "a few minutes" based on the assumption that the judges had read the written arguments. Indeed, when a Parliamentary Select Committee reported on the Scottish Supreme Courts in 1840, it found that the judges of the Inner House sat in court for only approximately two hours each day, spending the remainder of the time (presumably) reading and writing.

As an alternative to ordering cases, the Inner House apparently, where points of difficulty were raised in argument, would sometimes appoint parties to prepare and lodge "minutes of debate,"[35] containing arguments on the point in dispute.

28. Lord Cockburn, Journal (1874).
29. 6 Geo 4 c. 120 (1825).
30. 6 Geo. 4 c. 1920 ¶ 10 (1825).
31. 6 Geo. 4 c. 120 ¶ 19 (1825).
32. 6 Geo. 4 c. 120 ¶ 21 (1825).
33. *See* R. Bell, A Dictionary of the Law of Scotland: Intended for the Use of the Public at Large, as Well as of the Profession (1838).
34. *See id.*
35. *See id.*

The use of written debate was not confined to the Court of Session. For a short period in the nineteenth century, when in a Sheriff Court (the lower court in Scotland) proof was concluded, the Sheriff could order minutes of debate or memorials on the proof or on the whole case before giving his decisions. This power, however, was subsequently removed.

During the course of the nineteenth century, various attacks were made on the use of written argument so that it fell largely into desuetude before formal repeal. It does seem very clear that the move from a system based on written pleadings in the eighteenth century to a system based on oral pleadings by the close of the nineteenth century was consciously modelled on procedure in the English courts.

In England and Wales, the most significant moves have been made toward the use of written advocacy in the field of civil appeals. This was largely in response to an ever-increasing workload, with the consequential problem of delay and growing backlogs. The current Master of the Rolls, Lord Donaldson, has since 1982 introduced a number of changes to the handling of appeals. These include the reading of appeal papers by judges in advance of a hearing, the filing of skeleton arguments, and the filing of a chronology of events setting out the basic facts of a case. This enables the advocate in a civil appeal to dispense with a recitation of facts and move straight to the ground of appeal.

The Commercial Court has been able to reduce delays in hearing cases, partly as a result of an additional judge and partly through a new and more flexible approach to listing procedures. In March 1990, the third edition of *The Practice and Procedure of the Commercial Court* was published.[36] The *Introduction to the Guide to Commercial Court Practice* states: "[I]t is the policy of the Court that in principle the trial or other hearing should take place at the earliest date that the parties can be ready."[37] The essence of this new approach is to ensure that the parties and the court are as fully informed as possible at the summons-for-directions stage about what is involved in a particular case with the aim that no dispute should be delayed in its resolution by reasons over which the court has control. This involves the early exchange of written information and the development of skeleton arguments. The overall result has been a significant reduction in the length of trials so that during the Whitsun and Trinity terms 1990 over fifty percent of cases lasted between one and two days and over eighty-six percent were completed in less than eight days.

In the English courts, both civil and criminal, first instance and appellate, the oral tradition has remained strong. Notwithstanding, much use has been made in the English courts of affidavit evidence. The Chancery Division has always used it extensively, and the great reduction in jury trials in recent years has made its use more frequent in the Queen's Bench Division. For example, in judicial review proceedings, the Divisional Court usually relies entirely on the affidavit evidence.

Although the oral tradition is still preferred in England, written advocacy has been more warmly received in recent years. My distinguished predecessor, Lord Hailsham, set in hand

36. A. Colman, The Practice and Procedure of the Commercial Court (3d ed. 1990).
37. *Id.* at 207.

a review of civil justice in response to the growing complexity and cost of the civil justice system in England and Wales. Among the recommendations of this review, which I will be introducing to the county courts in July, is the pretrial exchange of witness statements. The aim is to provide a sound basis for earlier, better informed settlements in appropriate cases, to improve pretrial preparation and shorten trials by helping to identify issues, and to reduce the need for lengthy oral evidence. This procedure was introduced into some parts of the High Court in 1986 and extended to the remainder in 1988.

I have, so far, looked at those systems of which I have direct personal experience, with the exception of the Scottish system in the early nineteenth century. It is, however, timely to look at the American system and in particular the system of civil appeals. Many aspects of the American system differ from that in England, Wales, and Scotland, despite the English heritage of the American legal system, including, for example, the use of law clerks and central staff attorneys.

As early as the mid-nineteenth century, time limits were imposed on oral argument in the Supreme Court, the first time limit being two-and-one-half hours per side. Since then, a number of steps have been taken to limit further all argument and to shorten the written briefs that are also provided. This has, I believe, led judges to rely primarily on the briefs with oral argument as a supplement. The brief follows a format specified in appellate rules and is limited in length, usually, I understand, to about fifty pages. It consists of five major sections: a statement of issues, a statement of the case, a statement of facts, argument, and conclusion. It is interesting to note that courts have felt it necessary to try and regulate the length of briefs submitted to them. The use of the word *brief* in this context implies a certain conciseness. I have evidence that this is not always the case, from a footnote to a 1980 Wisconsin district court case where the judge said:

> The story of the creation of the world is told in the book of Genesis in 400 words; the world's greatest moral code, the Ten Commandments, contains only 279 words; Lincoln's Immortal Gettysburg address is but 266 words in length; the Declaration of Independence required only 1321 words to establish for the world a new concept of freedom. Together the four contain a mere 2266 words. On this routine motion to amend a civil complaint, [Counsel] has filed a brief (not the primary one, just a reply brief) that contains approximately 41596 words spread over an agonizing 124 pages. In this case, the term reply "brief" is obviously a misnomer. Rather than impressive, the *brief is* oppressive. It points to the need for considering the adoption of a local rule limiting the number of pages Counsel may fill with written argument on pre-trial motions.[38]

I would not like to finish this necessarily brief summary of the use of written advocacy without referring in passing to the one instance I know of in which a written brief in the American style was used in England. This was the case of *Rondel v. Worsley*, in which Professor Michael Zander played a significant part. He acted for Rondel and, as a solicitor with no rights of audience in the higher courts, produced a written brief in the American

38. Marson v. Jones & Laughlin Steel Corp., 87 F.R.D. 151, 152 (E.D. Wis. 1980).

style. This was reluctantly accepted by the presiding judge but not regarded as a precedent for future cases.

Despite what I have said above about the use of written advocacy, oral advocacy remains a strong and essential part of the systems of criminal and civil justice in all the jurisdictions to which I have referred. Clearly this is more so in England, Wales, and Scotland than in the United States, but I do not think anyone would deny the potential significance of oral argument as a supplement to written briefs, as much as of incisive and powerful oral argument on its own. In the English and Scottish courts, both criminal and civil, first instance and appeal, the success or failure of a case depends largely on the strength of the advocacy presented. Indeed, in some continental systems, steps have been taken to reintroduce oral argument, in recognition of its utility in questioning the substance of a case and testing the arguments.

Well, Ladies and Gentlemen, I have set before you a summary of the facts. But is it possible to judge from this which of the two styles of advocacy is best? Best for what and against what criteria can we judge? I suspect a survey here might well come up with at least as many shades of opinion as I came across in my research for this lecture. Clearly, the experiences of our two jurisdictions are different, but there is no clear uniformity of opinion within either. Certainly, pressures of time and resources have made us all consider carefully how we manage the work of our courts, and I see little prospect of such pressure abating.

My own most recent experience as a judge lies in the House of Lords, the highest Appeal Court in our legal system. Again, there is no clear uniformity of opinion, but a number of my colleagues have come to the conclusion that our appellate oral advocacy, at least, is too lengthy and too diffuse. Some of the fault here may lie with the judges. It is sometimes difficult for a judge to resist the temptation to intervene during the course of the oral argument. There is also a tendency among some counsel to take an insufficiently disciplined approach and to take up a number of points of little apparent relevance to their arguments.

As a result of these concerns we are in the process of consulting those most closely involved on possible changes to procedure. These include replacing the appellant's and respondent's cases with a single Statement of Facts and Issues and setting down the appeal when the Statement is lodged. Perhaps most important, however, is the requirement that within seven days of the setting down of the appeal, each side will notify the judicial office of the time, in hours, that counsel consider necessary for each address that it is proposed should be made on behalf of the party. In normal circumstances, counsel will be expected to confine the length of the submissions to the time indicated in the estimates. Hopefully, this will have the desired effect, and my noble colleague Lord Templeman will not have cause to repeat his remarks, which could apply either to oral or written advocacy, in *Banque Keyser Ullman S.A. v. Skandiae (UK) Insurance Co.*[39] in August 1990. He said:

39. 3 W.L.R. 364 (1990).

> Before parting with this appeal I draw attention again to the length and complexity of the proceedings as they appear from the chronological account given earlier in this speech. As early as 1961 in an appeal which lasted 16 days Donovan L.J. recorded "That the questions in this case, one of fact, and four of the construction of the contract, have been resolved with the aid of only 55 authorities;" *Reardon Smith Line Ltd v. Ministry of Agriculture, Fisheries and Food* [1962] 1 Q.B. 42, 131. In *J H Rayner (Mincing Lane) Ltd v. Department of Trade and Industry* [1989] 3 W.L.R. 969, 986, I complained of an appeal to this House which occupied 26 days and for which copies of 200 authorities were available. I commented that the vast amount of written and oral material tended to obscure three fundamental principles decisive of the International Tin Council litigation. Proceedings in which all or some of the litigants indulge in over-elaboration cause difficulties to judges at all levels in the achievement of a just result. Such proceedings obstruct the hearing of other litigation. A litigant faced with expense and delay on the part of his opponent which threatened to rival the excesses of *Jarndyce v. Jarndyce* must perforce compromise or withdraw with a real grievance. In the present case the burdens placed on Steyn J. and the Court of Appeal were very great. The problems were complex but the resolution of these problems was not assisted by the length of the hearing or the complexity of the oral evidence and oral argument. The costs must be formidable. I have no doubt that every effort was made in the courts below to alleviate the ordeal but the history of these proceedings is disquieting. The present practice is to allow every litigant unlimited time and unlimited scope so that the litigant and his advisers are able to conduct their case in all respects in the way which seems best to them. The results not infrequently are torrents of words, written and oral, which are oppressive and which the judge must examine in an attempt to eliminate everything which is not relevant, helpful and persuasive. The remedy lies in the judge taking time to read in advance pleadings, documents certified by counsel to be necessary, proofs of witnesses certified by counsel to be necessary, and short skeleton arguments of counsel, and for the judge then, after a short discussion in open court, to limit the time and scope of oral evidence and the time and scope of oral argument. The appellate courts should be unwilling to entertain complaints concerning the results of this practice.[40]

As an advocate, I had the personal experience of appearing before a Court that discouraged lengthy oral argument: the European Court of Justice in Luxembourg. I know that the nineteenth John F. Sonnett lecture was given by the President of that Court, Ole Due, and you may therefore already be familiar with its practices and procedures. The usual practice is for the Court to invite the advocates appearing before it to indicate the length of time they will require to present their case. On one occasion when I appeared before the Court representing Her Majesty's Government, my opponent was asked how long he would take. His reply of one-and-one-half-hours caused the Court visible surprise. In the event, and no doubt discouraged by the Court's courteous but firm reaction to which I have referred, he easily accomplished his task in twenty minutes. Certainly, I am not aware that the generality of the advocates appearing before that Court find the time limits inadequate, particularly as the time limits are not fixed by any general rule but in an informal

40. *Id.* at 381.

discussion before the oral hearing begins. The limits thus agreed upon are for the advocates' speeches, and further time is often taken up by the judges' questions.

I do not think, however, that there would be a great deal of enthusiasm among my British colleagues for moving to your system in the appellate courts of restricting oral argument to fifteen to thirty minutes. The restriction can only work if judges devote a considerable amount of time to pre-reading material in advance of hearing a case; oral argument should undertake to emphasize and clarify the written argument appearing in the briefs theretofore filed.

Certainly, this is not universally welcomed in other jurisdictions where it has been introduced. Professor Ian Scott has told me that when he was doing some work for the Family Court of Australia, some of the judges told him that they resented having to pre-read vast amounts of material relating to listed cases when, in the event, the majority of them would settle. They also felt that, because they were dealing with a number of rather similar family disputes, pre-reading increased the danger that they would start to get the issues of one case confused with another.

Such reservations are, I am sure, not confined to the Australians. Indeed, during the preparation of this lecture, my attention was drawn to a book called Justice on Appeal by Carrington, Meador, and Rosenberg.[41] In a section on improving the efficiency of the American appellate courts, they regret the restriction of oral argument. I quote:

> Oral argument gives important service to the imperative of appellate justice. Specifically, it heightens the judges' sense of personal responsibility. It provides them with an opportunity to test their own thinking in a direct way with counsel available to correct error. Some judges assimilate ideas more readily by oral than by written transmission; and some ideas are more readily transmitted by oral means. Thus, the quality of decisions is likely to be enhanced.[42]

The authors do recognize that listening to oral argument can be time-consuming, but they do not regard such time as wasted. They go on to suggest that parties should perhaps be given the opportunity of waiving the right to oral argument in certain circumstances. This might save genuinely wasted time. Indeed, I think, it is important to recognize that time can be wasted in any form of advocacy. The substance of the case should be the indicator, and arbitrary time limits of any kind may not be wise.

The question I posed to myself at the beginning of this lecture was "The Advocate: Should He Speak or Write?" It will perhaps not surprise you if I say that my conclusion is that I, at least, cannot arrive at a universal answer to this question. I believe that the increase in the workload of all our courts is unlikely to diminish, and that against a background of finite resources, we must continually reexamine the way in which our systems operate with a view to securing greater efficiency and effectiveness, while maintaining or improving the quality of decision-making. Indeed, we can learn something from the observation of systems other than our own. I know that the regular Anglo-American

41. P. Carrington, D. Meador & M. Rosenberg, Justice on Appeal (West 1976).
42. *Id.* at 17.

exchanges have provided a useful source of ideas for some of the changes we have implemented. This may well accentuate the trend toward wider use of written material in England and Wales, but I am sure that it will not, and should not, lead to the exclusion of oral advocacy. I believe that each has an important role to play in any system. And, certainly for the systems with which I am most familiar, I would not like to see the introduction of fixed time limits for oral advocacy. Any limit should be adjusted to the circumstances of the particular case. Obviously, in a system that at first instance uses the jury trial system of judgment, oral testimony and argument must continue to have a firm place, but even when the first instance trial is before a judge or judges it may be difficult to decide in a conflict of testimony without oral evidence. The exact balance between oral and written advocacy will depend on many factors: the nature of the system, its historical development; its rules; the nature of the proceedings in question; and the training and experience of the advocate himself. On the last matter, if a system has advocates who specialize in appellate work, this may lead to a greater distinction between the methods of presentation at first instance work and on appeal. Although Chief Justice Warren Burger advocated specialization in appellate advocacy to the Royal Commission in England and Wales in the late 1970s, there has been no general distinction between first instance and appellate advocates in England and Wales. Remember, variety is the spice of life that gives it all its flavor. While proceedings in our courts are not dull, too-rigid proscription of styles of advocacy might cause them to become so. So, I answer my question by saying the advocate should both speak and write: the extent to which he does either should be determined in the light of the great variety of circumstances that can obtain in litigation, some of which I have mentioned.

Appellate Advocacy: Some Reflections from the Bench

Hon. Lawrence W. Pierce

Judge Lawrence W. Pierce delivered the twenty-first Sonnett lecture, *Appellate Advocacy: Some Reflections from the Bench*, on November 5, 1992.[1] Born in Philadelphia, Pennsylvania,[2] Judge Pierce earned a law degree from Fordham Law School in 1951 after graduating from St. Joseph's College (now St. Joseph's University) in 1948.[3] Prior to law school, Judge Pierce served in the Army from 1943 to 1946,[4] including an overseas deployment to Italy in World War II.[5] After law school, Judge Pierce's legal practice was wide-ranging, including posts with the Legal Aid Society, the Kings County District Attorney, and as the Deputy Commissioner of the New York Police Department.[6] In 1971, Judge Pierce was nominated by President Nixon and confirmed to a judicial seat in the Southern District of New York.[7] Ten years later, President Reagan appointed Judge Pierce to the Second Circuit Court of Appeals.[8] After a judicial career more than two decades long, Judge Pierce retired from the Second Circuit in 1995.[9]

In his Sonnett lecture, Judge Pierce gave astute guidance on appellate advocacy, providing valuable insight informed by his experience on the bench.[10] Tracing the historical development of appellate review from its Mediterranean roots to trials by combat and ordeal to modern day appellate practice, Judge Pierce contextualized and contrasted some of the issues of modern appellate process with more draconian historical practices.[11] Judge Pierce further remarked on efforts to streamline the ever-growing appellate docket

Introduction written by Michael D. Jenks, J.D., Class of 2015, Fordham University School of Law.

1. *See* Judge Lawrence W. Pierce, *Appellate Advocacy: Some Reflections from the Bench*, 61 Fordham L. Rev. 829, 829 (1993). This essay is adapted from the Twenty-First Annual John F. Sonnett Memorial Lecture delivered at Fordham University School of Law on November 5, 1992.

2. *See* Constantine N. Katsoris, Commemoration, *A Tribute to the Fordham Judiciary: A Century of Service*, 75 Fordham L. Rev. 2303, 2324 (2007).

3. *See* Lawrence Warren Pierce—Biographical Directory of Federal Judges, Fed. Judicial Ctr., http://www.fjc.gov/servlet/nGetInfo?jid=1887cid=999ctype=nainstate=na (last visited Mar. 10, 2014) [hereinafter Pierce Biography].

4. *See id.*

5. *See* John D. Feerick, *Dedication to the Honorable William Hughes Mulligan*, 7 Fordham Intell. Prop. Media & Ent. L.J. 1, 5 (1996).

6. *See* Pierce Biography, *supra* note 3.

7. *See id.*

8. *See id.*

9. *See id.*

10. *See generally* Pierce, *supra* note 1.

11. *See id.* at 829–33.

through, for example, reducing time for oral argument or issuing summary orders.[12] While acknowledging the necessity of addressing the demands of the resource-limited appellate process, Judge Pierce marked out a few key aspects that ought to command the attention of appellate practitioners: (1) preparing for the appeal process at the trial stage, (2) focusing the brief only on major issues, (3) giving attention to the particular style preferences of the judges hearing an appeal, and (4) focusing and emphasizing key points at oral argument.[13]

Judge Pierce reminded appellate attorneys that they should try to explain and simplify complex issues for the Court.[14] He cautioned against the "kitchen sink" approach, where lawyers make every conceivable point available to them, and encouraged them to focus on the one or two key points of the appeal.[15] Finally, he reminded the appellate attorney of the need to address court decisions that may appear adverse to her legal position.[16] By doing so, the attorney fulfills her ethical responsibility and also gives herself credibility and judicial respect.[17]

The insights Judge Pierce gave us in his Sonnett lecture are as valuable today as they were twenty years ago; the appellate advocate who heeds Judge Pierce's advice may assure herself that the appeal has been fully and effectively presented.[18]

1992 Sonnett Lecture

This annual lecture series is a fitting tribute to John F. Sonnett, who was highly respected public servant, a greatly admired senior partner at Cahill Gordon & Reindel, and one of Fordham's most distinguished alumni. As a federal appellate judge, I am especially pleased to discuss the topic of appellate advocacy, particularly in light of John Sonnett's renowned reputation as a master appellate advocate in both the public and private sectors.

In preparing these comments, I have drawn upon personal observations and experiences as both a circuit and a district judge. I will begin with a short discussion of some historical features of advocacy, followed by a brief overview of some modern-day considerations facing present day appellate advocates. I will discuss some strategic, practical, and ethical considerations relevant to my topic.

12. *See id.* at 833–34
13. *See id.* at 834–40.
14. *See id.* at 836–37.
15. *See id.* at 836.
16. *See id.* at 840–41.
17. *Id.*
18. Many of the points made by Judge Pierce continue to be made in recent texts and articles on appellate advocacy. *See, e.g.*, R. Aldisert, Opinion Writing (2d Ed. 2009); A. Scalia and B. Garner, Making Your Case: The Art of Persuading Judges (2008); and Richard A. Posner, *Judicial Opinions and Appellate Advocacy in Federal Courts—One Judge's View*, 51 Duq. L. Rev. 3 (2013).

HISTORICAL OVERVIEW OF APPELLATE ADVOCACY

Ancient Origins

A brief glimpse at a few historical features illustrates how much the processes of appellate advocacy have developed over time.

It has been suggested that appellate review first originated with the ancient civilizations of the Mediterranean Sea area.[1] For example, in ancient Athens, there existed a right to appeal decisions of the magistrate.[2] Some appeals were made to an assembly of as many as six thousand citizens—a majority of whom determined the outcome.[3] In a modern-day context, this would be akin to arguing an appeal before a capacity crowd at Radio City Music Hall.

Under our country's present court system, the United States Supreme Court is our highest level of appellate review. As far back as the ninth century, however, "appeals" were regularly made to an even higher authority. Although not formally considered "appeals" as we know them today, trial by ordeal and trial by battle were denominated as "appeals to the judgment of God."[4]

Trial by ordeal took several forms. For example, with the Ordeal of Iron, an accused might be required to carry a one-pound piece of red-hot iron in his hands for nine paces.[5] Thereafter, the hands of the accused would be bound. If after three days the wound had healed cleanly, the accused was determined to be innocent; if not, he was found guilty.[6] The outcome was thought of as God's judgment.[7]

Trial by combat worked on the same premise as trial by ordeal namely, that "'[t]he presumption of law [wa]s that God w[ould] give victory to him that hath right [on his side].'"[8] When an accused party chose to prove his case through trial by combat, he had the option of hiring a professional champion as a stand-in, as did his accuser.[9] Then, according

1. *See* Robert J. Martineau, Modern Appellate Practice: Federal and State Civil Appeals § 1.1, at 2 (1983).

2. *See* Robert J. Bonner, Lawyers and Litigants in Ancient Athens: The Genesis of the Legal Profession 35 (Benjamin Blom 1969) (1927).

3. *See id.* at 35–36; Douglas M. MacDowell, The Law in Classical Athens 30, 35–37 (1978). Although occasionally the whole body of heliasts, as they were known, convened, the usual course of action was to break the mass of people into sections known as "dicasteries," which were smaller panels consisting of 501 individuals for criminal cases and 201 individuals for civil cases. *See* Bonner, *supra* note 2, at 36.

4. A.T. Carter, A History of English Legal Institutions 200 (Fred B. Rothman & Co. 1986) (1902).

5. *See* Dick Hamilton, Lawyers and Lawbreakers 3 (Dorset Press 1991) (1979).

6. *See id.*

7. *See id.*

8. M.J. Russell, *Trial by Battle and the Writ of Right*, 1 J. Legal Hist. 111, 111 (1980) (quoting Co. Lit., fo. 294b. *Staunton v. Prior of Lenton* (1329), Dudg. *Orig.* 68, by Scrope J.).

9. *See* Julius J. Marke, *History in the Law Books*, N.Y. L.J., Sept. 15, 1992, at 4, 4.

to a strict code of procedure, both parties would battle from early morning until dusk.[10] If, "before the stars appeared," the accused or his stand-in had been vanquished, the accused was hanged on the spot.[11] If, on the other hand, the accused or his stand-in was successful in his defense, the accused was acquitted.[12] This manner of bizarre dispute resolution was not officially abolished in England until 1819.[13] Although we have obviously come a long, long way since those times, I am sure that many attorneys consider the arguing of an appeal today to be a very distinct ordeal, albeit of a clearly different order.

Under our present system, if an appellant files an appeal, it is the responsibility of the opposing party, the appellee, to defend the underlying decision. Historically, that was not always the case. Prior to 1272, under England's judicial system, the judge whose decision was being challenged had this responsibility.[14]

Looking back to the historical origins of our own federal appellate system, the Justices of the Supreme Court were at one time called upon to ride circuit.[15] Although the Justices served primarily as trial judges in this capacity, they did have appellate authority in certain cases.[16] The position of Supreme Court Justice in those days was by no means as dignified as it is today. Riding the circuit was rigorous work. Travel by road, by carriage, or by boat was slow, tedious, and oftentimes dangerous; accommodations could be bug-ridden and frequently dirty, and the food miserable.[17] No doubt, the trial and appellate attorneys involved also found it necessary to endure similar travails as they travelled to present their cases.

Modern Appellate Advocacy

While these historical features and the problems inherent in them no longer exist in our time, there are other aspects associated with our present-day system that merit reflection.

For example, the number of appeals has increased dramatically in recent decades. Just in the past forty years, the number of petitions for writs of certiorari to the United States Supreme Court has more than quintupled,[18] although the number of justices has remained unchanged. In the federal courts of appeals, the number of appeals filed has increased

10. *See id.*
11. *Id.*
12. *See id.*
13. *See* Robert Bartlett, Trial by Fire and Water: The Medieval Judicial Ordeal 13, 14–15 (1986); Marke, *supra* note 9, at 4; Russell, *supra* note 8, at 128.
14. *See* Martineau, *supra* note 1, at 3.
15. *See* Robert L. Stern, Appellate Practice in the United States 5 (2d ed. 1989).
16. *See id.*
17. *See* Jeffrey B. Morris, Federal Justice in the Second Circuit: A History of United States Courts in New York, Connecticut & Vermont 1787–1987, at 25–26 (1987).
18. *Compare The Supreme Court 1951 Term*, 66 Harv. L Rev. 89, 177 (1952) (1207 disposed, 146 remaining on docket) *with The Supreme Court 1991 Term*, 106 Harv. L. Rev. 19, 382 (1992) (5825 disposed; 945 remaining on the docket).

almost ten-fold in approximately the last three decades.[19] But, at least during that time, the number of judges in our courts of appeals has more than doubled.[20]

There are various theories as to the causes for this dramatic increase in appeals. One popular notion is that our society has become more litigious.[21] On the other hand, my colleague on the Second Circuit, Chief Judge Thomas Meskill, believes that the increase in the number of appeals flows directly from the initiatives of the United States government.[22] He has in mind governmental initiatives such as OSHA,[23] ERISA,[24] and Title VII.[25] He informs us that these and other federal acts have served to increase the number of cases litigated and, in turn, account in part for the increasing number of appeals filed in the federal courts.[26]

Whatever the causes, our courts of appeals, in an effort to deal with the ever-increasing number of appeals filed each year, have responded in a variety of ways. One approach to speeding along the proceedings has been to limit the time allotted for oral argument. The Second Circuit allows oral argument in almost every appeal, although severe time restrictions are usually imposed.[27] Other circuits also have turned to time limitations and impose still other restrictions on when oral argument will even be allowed.

One common approach to achieving timely dispositions of appeals is the use of summary orders.[28] Summary orders are an effective means of more promptly disposing of

19. In the federal courts of appeals, the number of appeals filed increased from 3900 in 1960 to 35,000 in 1987. *See* Robert L. Stern, *Remedies for Appellate Overloads. The Ultimate Solution*, 72 JUDICATURE 103, 103 (1988).

20. *See id.* (from 1960 to 1987, the number of circuit court judges "slightly more than doubled."); *see also* RICHARD A. POSNER, THE FEDERAL COURTS: CRISIS AND REFORM 357 (1985) (chart indicating that federal circuit judges numbered 63 in 1953, 66 in 1960, and 127 in 1983).

21. *Cf.* WALTER K. OLSON, THE LITIGATION EXPLOSION: WHAT HAPPENED WHEN AMERICA UNLEASHED THE LAWSUIT 1–2 (1991) (arguing that the United States is in the thralls of a litigation explosion that has been disastrous).

22. *See* Thomas J. Meskill, *Caseload Growth: Struggling to Keep Pace*, 57 BROOK. L. REV. 299, 300–01 (1991).

23. Occupational Safety and Health Act, 29 U.S.C. §§ 651–678 (1988 & Supp. II 1991).

24. Employee Retirement Income Security Act, 29 U.S.C. §§ 1001–1461 (1988 & Supp. II 1991).

25. Title VII of the Civil Rights Act of 1964, 42 U.S.C. §§ 2000e-2000e-17 (1988 & Supp. III 1992).

26. *See* Meskill, *supra* note 22, at 300–01.

27. The Second Circuit's Local Rules have been amended as follows:

> The judge scheduled to preside over the panel will set the time allowed for argument by each party after considering the appellant's brief and each party's request for argument time. Normally, ten or fifteen minutes will be allotted to each side. Parties on the same side of an appeal may be obliged to divide the time allotted to their side. Arguments in pro se appeals are normally five minutes per side. The clerk will notify counsel and pro se parties of all such time allotments.

2d Cir. R. 34(b) (effective Jan. 1, 1993).

28. Summary orders are succinctly written opinions with no precedential value. *See* Daniel Wise, *Circuit Court's Backlog Cut by 10 Percent; Appeals-Per-Panel Up; Week Added to Term*, N.Y. L.J., July 5, 1991, at 1, 3.

many of the cases on appeal. The Second Circuit, for example, used summary orders more often than any other device to dispose of appeals decided during the year ended June 30, 1991.[29] A summary order is most often accompanied by a succinctly written statement of the court's reasoning. It is almost invariably unanimous, and as the rule states, "Since these statements do not constitute formal opinions of the court and are unreported and not uniformly available to all parties, they [may] not be cited or otherwise used in unrelated cases before [the Second Circuit] or any other court."[30]

Another approach that could be utilized by our courts to deal with the increased volume of appeals is the filing of more per curiam, as opposed to full-blown, opinions. A per curiam opinion is usually a short opinion issued by the appellate panel as a whole, and thus, it does not bear the name of an individual judge as the writer. Per curiam opinions tend to be fairly succinct; oftentimes they deal primarily with a single, discrete issue. But, unlike summary orders, they *do* have precedential value.

Unlike summary orders and per curiam opinions, rulings from the bench, which at one time accounted for at least a small percentage of the court's dispositions, are rarely used today in the Second Circuit.

PROCESSES OF APPELLATE ADVOCACY IN THE AMERICAN LEGAL SYSTEM

Of the two methods of appellate advocacy—the written brief and the oral argument, some have criticized oral argument in recent years as being nothing more than an expensive habit that needs to be kicked.[31] This belief is strongly associated with Professor Robert Martineau, a highly respected academic, who disputes the view that oral argument plays an important role in the administration of justice in the appellate process. Professor Martineau maintains that if additional information is needed, there is no good reason why appellate judges cannot present written questions to counsel to gain the necessary insights.[32]

Not surprisingly, quite a few practitioners, scholars, and judges do not subscribe to this view. Indeed, the proponents of oral argument regard the opportunity to be heard as an essential element of the appellate process.[33] As Justice Brennan observed, "'I have had too many occasions when my judgment of a decision has turned on what happened in oral argument, not to be terribly concerned for myself were I to be denied oral argument.'"[34]

29. *See id.*

30. 2d Cir. R. 0. 23.

31. *See* Myron H. Bright, *The Power of the Spoken Word: In Defense of Oral Argument*, 72 Iowa L. Rev. 35, 35–36 (1986) (characterizing Professor Martineau's attack on oral argument).

32. *See* Robert J. Martineau, *The Value of Appellate Oral Argument: A Challenge to the Conventional Wisdom*, 72 Iowa L. Rev. 1, 32 (1986).

33. *See, e.g.*, Karl N. Llewellyn, The Common Law Tradition: Deciding Appeals 240 (1960); Frederick B. Weiner, *Oral Advocacy*, 62 Harv. L. Rev. 56, 58 (1948).

34. Commission on Revision of the Fed. Court Appellate Sys., *Structure and Internal Procedures: Recommendations for Change*, 67 F.R.D. 195, 254 (1975) (quoting Justice Brennan's comments at the 1972 Third Circuit Judicial Conference).

Proponents of oral argument point out that it serves as an important conduit for the exchange of information between judges and counsel. Judges are given the opportunity to discuss with counsel the issues they consider dispositive or particularly troublesome issues that may not have been briefed or at least not briefed fully. Counsel, in turn, are given the opportunity to gauge the judges' reactions to a particular line of argument and to modify their strategy, if that should be indicated. As Chief Justice Rehnquist has explained:

> You could write hundreds of pages of briefs, and, you are still never absolutely sure that the judge is focused on exactly what you want him [or her] to focus on in that brief. Right there at the time of oral argument you know that you do have an opportunity to engage or get into the judge's mental process.[35]

While the controversy over the merits of oral argument continues, and as argument time is increasingly whittled away, the significance of the brief becomes even more apparent. For example, in the Second Circuit, oral argument usually lasts not more than a half-hour. As a practical matter, in that period of time, counsel can actually address only a few points. The briefs, on the other hand, arrive in chambers approximately one month before oral argument is scheduled to be heard, and resort to them may occur for months after oral argument has ended. Therefore, it should be evident that the language used in a brief should be concise, cogent and convincing, such that the evidence supporting the facts "sing[s] out as clearly and simply as possible,"[36] and the legal discussion of the issues must be concentrated and persuasive.[37]

STRATEGIC, PRACTICAL, AND ETHICAL CONSIDERATIONS FOR SUCCESSFUL APPELLATE ADVOCACY

With these considerations in mind, I now turn to what I believe are some of the means that counsel might employ to make an appellate performance a more persuasive one.

Too often, attorneys forget that the potential for success on appeal *begins* at the pretrial preparation stage, *continues* during the trial phase (and perhaps post-trial phase), and generally *concludes* with the submission of one's brief and oral argument on appeal. If appellate and trial counsel are one and the same person, then it is essential to view what transpires at the trial through a prism of appellate considerations. If they are separate counsel, then it strikes me that, on occasion, it may be wise for appellate counsel to be associated with trial counsel both before and perhaps even during the trial to see to it that a proper record is made in the event that an appeal becomes necessary. That this course of action can have merit seems borne out by the fact that, more often than one would expect, cases are lost on appeal due to the failure of counsel at the trial level to make a proper record, or to raise

35. Bright, *supra* note 31, at 36–37 (quoting remarks of Chief Justice William H. Rehnquist at the *Jurists-in-Residence Program*, St. Louis University School of Law (Apr. 8, 1983)).
36. Irving R. Kaufman, *Appellate Advocacy in the Federal Courts*, 79 F.R.D. 165, 166 (1978).
37. *See id.* at 169.

arguments or objections, or to submit requests to charge for the judge's consideration in jury trials.

Developing a proper record can also be important in a case in which a pretrial dispositive motion has been made—e.g., a motion that seeks dismissal of a complaint for failure to state a cause of action or seeks a grant of summary judgment. Often, it is a wise course to have appellate counsel peruse such pretrial motion papers before they are submitted or before a response is filed.

On occasion, an attorney may find it difficult to make a satisfactory record at the trial level despite counsel's best efforts. Sometimes a busy trial judge will direct an attorney who is seeking to make a record, to "move along, counsellor." What then? Of the various steps that might be pursued by counsel at that point, in order to preserve an issue for appellate review, one option is to prepare a very short memorandum of law, for example by way of an offer of proof, and to hand it up to the judge that afternoon or the next morning, with a copy handed not just to the opponent, but also to the courtroom deputy for docketing and filing. Even if rejected, the trial transcript may reveal, especially if counsel makes it a point to insist upon it, that an attempt was made to make a record of the issue. This might well suffice to preserve the issue for appellate purposes.

Once at the appellate level, it is obvious that the briefs in even the most interesting case can become bogged down in a morass of technical issues and procedural points, such that the reader must struggle to "see the forest for the trees." This problem is particularly endemic to brief writing rather than to oral argument since time limitations imposed on oral argument can have the beneficial effect of winnowing out superfluous arguments.

Commonly, an appellate advocate will identify numerous issues that can be raised on appeal. When the issues are numerous, however, a wise course of action is to divide them into major and minor issues and then to elaborate only upon those that cry out to be addressed. Although good strategy may warrant developing one or two minor issues,[38] since they may represent just the needed additional tipping of the scales in one's favor, it is imperative that counsel avoid using an "everything but the kitchen sink" mentality in brief writing. While no one would dispute the importance of identifying relevant issues on appeal, few judges are apt to be impressed with a brief that asserts a half-dozen or more key points of error. In the words of the late Judge E. Barrett Prettyman, on the whole, "[t]rial judges make relatively . . . few errors."[39] When they do, such mistakes are frequently harmless in light of all the other evidence presented. Consequently, by asserting numerous grounds for reversal—some of which are not particularly strong—the court's attention may be needlessly diverted from the more compelling grounds, and the chance that the court will be convinced on any ground decreases significantly. As Judge Abner Mikva of the District of Columbia Circuit Court writes: "Asking attorneys to highlight the meat and

38. *See* E. Barrett Prettyman, *Some Observations Concerning Appellate Advocacy*, 39 Va. L. Rev. 285, 294 (1953).

39. *Id.* at 287.

potatoes of the case[] does not mean that the spices included in the entree[,] or the dessert that follows[,] should be taken off the menu. But it does suggest that serving eight different vegetables will detract from the main course."[40]

From a practical standpoint, a more concise, cogent brief presenting the strongest points and arguments usually makes the most sense. Appellate court rules may permit the filing of a primary brief of up to fifty pages and may allow an appellant to file a reply brief of up to twenty-five pages.[41] But consider that if one counts the number of appeals scheduled to be heard by a panel of judges on a particular day, and if one multiplies that by one brief for each party, plus a joint appendix, a reply brief, and an occasional sur-reply brief, in addition to the applicable cases and statutes, one can readily calculate the enormous amount of reading with which a judge and a judge's staff are faced to prepare for each sitting day. One may agree that it is better to have a shorter brief that will be read and studied in preparation for argument than a longer one that is skimmed and put aside for future study.

Not only is it important to select the issues to be presented on appeal with great care; one's phrasing of the selected issues is also tremendously important. Framing the issues often provides the opportunity to place emphasis or sharpen focus as to the questions presented. This calls for a thorough knowledge of the relevant law, as well as the adroitness to identify those portions of the record on appeal that are most likely to support your position. Counsel should accomplish this through the use of felicitous modes of expression.

It is important that one take care not to twist the record and issues out of shape. When judges see or hear mischaracterizations, they are left with the impression that the advocate is either unfamiliar with the case or is attempting to skirt issues on which counsel is vulnerable. To compound the problem, either the court or one's opponent will usually challenge or contradict mischaracterizations—and such challenges or even clarifications can diminish the persuasiveness of counsel's argument on appeal.

It should be evident that a clear discussion of the case is critical whether the case is criminal or civil, for each can present complicated fact patterns and still more complicated legal issues. If complex cases have been difficult for counsel to understand, they can be equally difficult for the judges and their staff to comprehend, at least initially. It is counsel's responsibility to reduce all segments of an appeal to understandable terms. I recall a patent attorney jesting that, before presenting a complicated patent case for trial or appeal, she would argue the case before her husband on the assumption that if he could understand it, anyone could, including the judges.

In my experience, in the course of writing an opinion, there tend to emerge both predictable and unpredictable hurdles that must be surmounted by the judge who is the opinion writer. A wise advocate may anticipate such hurdles and can often assist the court by suggesting ways of breaking through any such Gordian knots. For example, an appeal may be presented where the issue of whether there is jurisdiction is problematic, and yet, a care-

40. Abner J. Mikva, *Counsel Lack Selectivity in Appellate Advocacy*, LEGAL TIMES, Nov. 15, 1982, at 10.

41. *See* Fed. R. App. P. 28(g).

ful review of the merits may reveal that there simply was insufficient evidence to support the outcome in any event. In such a situation, an appellate advocate may find it advantageous to suggest to the court that, if feasible, the court assume jurisdiction *arguendo*, and then undertake to show the court that if the merits were to be reached, the outcome would quite clearly be in his or her favor. This is sometimes referred to as the "even if" approach.

What about using creative and expressive language in appellate arguments? One of the great tools lawyers utilize in preparation for an appeal is to study selected opinions of judges. In this regard, certain judges have very distinctive writing styles, the imitation of which might serve lawyers well in capturing the essence of an appeal. For example, the late Judge Irving Kaufman[42] believed that, in arguing appeals, appellants in particular should strive to tell an eloquent tale, in order to surmount what he called the appellate court's "natural disinclination" to reverse the district court's resolution of the controversy.[43] Frequently, it was Judge Kaufman's personal style to begin an opinion with strikingly expressive prose that in many ways placed the legal and factual issues in quite sharp focus.

For example, in one case, members of a religious organization sued the managers of the Nassau Coliseum, alleging First Amendment violations after persons were arrested there for distributing leaflets.[44] The attorney for the appellants summarized the issue tersely as follows: "The issue presented below was whether the plaintiffs have a First Amendment right to distribute non-commercial literature on property owned by the County. To resolve this issue it must be decided what type of forum that property represents."[45]

In an opinion upholding the district court's issuance of a preliminary injunction, Judge Kaufman chose to frame the issue this way:

> From the time of the founding of our nation, the distribution of written material has been an essential weapon in the defense of liberty. Throughout the years, the leaflet has retained its vitality as an effective and inexpensive means of disseminating religious and political thought. Today, when selective access to channels of mass communication limits the expression of diverse opinion, the handbill remains important to the promise of full and free discussion of public issues. For those of moderate means, but deep conviction, freedom to circulate fliers implicates fundamental liberties.[46]

Judge Kaufman was not alone in his expressive and expansive approach to opinion writing. For example, Judge Richard Cardamone[47] also has developed a distinctive writing

42. Prior to his death, Judge Kaufman served on the United States Court of Appeals for the Second Circuit, was the court's chief judge for many years, and was a distinguished Sonnett lecturer. For an article based on Judge Kaufman's Sonnett lecture, see Irving R. Kaufman, *Prison: The Judge's Dilemma*, 41 Fordham L. Rev. 495 (1973).

43. *See* Kaufman, *supra* note 36, at 167.

44. *See* Paulsen v. County of Nassau, 925 F.2d 65, 66–67 (2d Cir. 1991).

45. Brief for Appellant at 19, Paulsen v. County of Nassau, 925 F.2d 65 (2d Cir. 1991) (No. 90-7675).

46. *Paulsen*, 925 F.2d at 66–67.

47. Judge Cardamone serves on the United States Court of Appeals for the Second Circuit.

style. He tends to utilize analogies and aphorisms to focus the issues and facts sharply. For example, in a recent criminal case,[48] a defendant moved to suppress post-arrest statements on the ground that the authorities had violated *Miranda v. Arizona*[49] in obtaining such statements.[50] In an opinion upholding the district court's suppression order, Judge Cardamone used mythology to make his point. He wrote:

> After the defendant was given the prophylactic warnings and said he understood them and did not need a lawyer present when questioned, the arresting officer should have been satisfied that he was about to obtain a voluntary confession. But, like Semele who was not content with what she had, and used trickery to obtain more proof, the arresting officer in his eager pursuit of a confession also employed trickery to browbeat defendant into making a statement.[51]

By Judge Cardamone's reference to Semele, he used a character from classic mythology to make his point, for it was Semele who loved the god Zeus but was not content with his human guise and thus tricked him into revealing his god-like nature and wound up herself destroyed by his lightning.[52]

Even judges who have not adopted this expressive form or style of opinion writing may find themselves more sharply focused by an advocate's creative characterization of the issues on appeal. This especially may be the case at oral argument. It is precisely at this time that counsel should seek to give the appellate panel members a specific focus, setting forth as clearly as possible the heart and soul of the case.

Commonly, when an opinion is to be written regarding difficult or close issues, we send for, and listen to, the tapes of the arguments made on appeal. Occasionally, we listen to the arguments repeatedly. Some of our judges *always* listen to the tapes while engaged in the writing of an opinion.

Playing the tapes of the arguments can be the denouement of the writing process. By this point, the judge and the judge's law clerk have studied counsels' arguments in the briefs and have read the relevant cases and statutes. The reintroduction of the oral argument into the process, via the tapes, can be pivotal. One can listen for the nuances and for where counsel has placed emphasis. If counsel has been able to weave into his or her argument a Judge Kaufman—or Judge Cardamone-type expressive phrase, analogy, or aphorism of the key issue presented, it can have its greatest impact when the tapes are replayed. Creative expression can trigger important insights that assist the judge in carrying out his or her decision-making role.

Thus, although oral argument lasts a relatively short time, its importance should not be underestimated. Indeed, in the words of Judge Prettyman, it is a formidable task to

48. *See* United States v. Anderson, 929 F.2d 96 (2d Cir. 1991).

49. 384 U.S. 436 (1966).

50. *See Anderson*, 929 F.2d at 96.

51. *Id.* at 96–97 (footnote omitted).

52. *See id.* at 97 n.1 (citing C.M. Gagley, The Classic Myths 71–72 (rev. ed. 1939)).

"propel . . . other human minds into a certain channel to a certain result;"[53] yet oral argument can be particularly effective as a means of painting a picture for the judges. Those advocates who succeed in painting a clear and expressive picture may find that the judges more readily grasp and retain the position counsel is urging upon the court.

Most opinions filed in the Second Circuit are unanimous decisions. Appellate panel members, however, are not always of like minds in their views. Occasionally, a panel member will write a separate opinion from that of the majority. Such opinion either concurs with the majority's disposition of the case, but seeks to preserve a collateral, relevant argument for possible future development, or dissents to express disagreement with the majority.

To advance an argument on appeal that fails to convince the majority, but nevertheless is adopted in a minority opinion, may in itself be a significant achievement. For example, in seeking further appellate review, the advocate may be in a much stronger position in arguing the point in question if he or she can cite to a concurring or a dissenting opinion that agrees with the advocate's argument.

Moreover, if one is able to gain support for a position in a dissenting opinion, although the appellate court based its decision on the majority's contrary reasoning, an advocate may be in an improved posture in settlement negotiations. This is particularly true if the dissenting judge's views coincide with the views of other appellate courts or with perceived appellate court tendencies.

There are occasions when strategic considerations may prompt an appeal despite the expectation of an unfavorable outcome. A case may pose issues of first impression for the appellate court, and counsel may perceive that the facts of the particular case place the court at the cutting edge of an issue with broad implications.

Such an issue was presented in a recent appeal to the Second Circuit where the question was whether the statute of limitations in a securities case should be governed by the analogous state statute of limitations or whether the court should adopt a uniform federal statute of limitations, and, if so, for what length of time. The Second Circuit panel, in *Ceres Partners v. GEL Associates*,[54] adopted the uniform approach.[55] This was a cutting-edge issue on which the circuits were in conflict. Ultimately, this issue was resolved by the Supreme Court in a later case.[56]

In deciding whether to make a thrust into the appellate process when faced with novel or controversial issues and in plotting strategy, one must consider several factors, including: decisions in other circuits, dicta in prior cases, the overall reputation of the appellate court's tendencies, comments by lawmakers in the legislative history, discussions in treatises and law review articles, and reasoned speculation as to the current stance of the Supreme Court. These same considerations will also suggest the route to follow with respect to petitions for rehearing and suggestions for in banc review—although the odds for

53. Prettyman, *supra* note 38, at 285.
54. 918 F.2d 349 (2d Cir. 1990).
55. *Id.* at 364.
56. *See* Lampf, Pleva, Lipkind, Prupis & Petigrow v. Gilbertson, 111 S. Ct. 2773 (1991).

success on the en banc front are not great. Finally, in assessing whether to press an appeal on a cutting-edge issue, the advocate should gauge the likelihood of support from potential *amici curiae*.

One of the serious mistakes counsel can make while arguing an appeal is becoming defensive when questioned by a panel member who appears to be persuaded by the argument of his or her opponent. Often, the judge simply may anticipate being assigned the responsibility of writing the opinion and may be testing the strength of counsel's positions. Such questioning should be viewed as an excellent opportunity to deflate an opponent's arguments while advancing the strong points of one's own position. Indeed, some judges make it a practice to direct tough questions to the side that appears to have the better argument in an attempt to ensure that the envisioned outcome of the appeal is the correct outcome.

From a practical standpoint, an appellate advocate should make eye contact with each judge on the panel. It may be particularly desirable to make certain that this includes eye contact with female and minority panel members, since a male, majority-group attorney will sometimes incredibly make his presentation almost exclusively to a panel member of the same gender and race. While this invariably is inadvertent, it is a needless shortcoming.

Finally, while it is an attorney's duty to zealously represent his or her client, the attorney must be mindful to do so within the parameters of professional ethics guidelines.[57] There is an Ethical Consideration that states:

> Where a lawyer knows of legal authority in the controlling jurisdiction directly adverse to the position of his client, he should inform the tribunal of its existence unless his adversary has done so; but, having made such disclosure, he may challenge its soundness in whole or in part.[58]

While the Ethical Considerations are "aspirational" in nature,[59] a similar, mandatory Disciplinary Rule[60] sets forth a minimum level of conduct below which "no lawyer can fall without being subject to disciplinary action."[61]

While bringing an adverse ruling to the court's attention might seem like the last thing a zealous advocate would want to do, to fail to come forward with this information may be the equivalent of shooting oneself in the foot. Oftentimes, loss of credibility with the court can do more to undermine one's case than the adverse ruling—not to mention leaving the attorney vulnerable to sanctions. Indeed, appellate skills shine through most brightly when an advocate is able to distinguish or make a cogent argument as to why a seemingly adverse ruling is not apposite to the case at hand.

57. *See* Thomas R Newman & Steven J. Ahmuty, Jr., *Maintaining Credibility with the Court*, N.Y. L.J., Mar. 12, 1991, at 3, 3.

58. N.Y. Jud. Law app. EC 7–23 (McKinney 1992).

59. *See* N.Y. Jud. Law app. Preliminary Statement.

60. *See id.* DR 7–106B(l).

61. *See id.* Preliminary Statement.

The first time I encountered a clear-cut instance of such candor by an attorney was during my first year as a district judge. In the middle of the criminal trial, it became necessary for me to hold a sidebar conference. Both the defense attorney and the government attorney presented their arguments on the point being discussed. As I was about to rule on the matter, the defense attorney spoke up and told me that he wished me to know that a recent Second Circuit case had ruled adversely to his position. I no longer remember how I disposed of that issue, but now, more than twenty years later, whenever that attorney argues an appeal before me, I remember that occasion, and I respect his views as likely to be completely forthright.

CONCLUSION

In closing, it is important to keep in mind the words of the late Judge Kaufman: "Advocacy is not an end in itself, it is the means by which the judicial process attempts to arrive at truth and justice."[62] With that in mind, I hope others have found some interest in the overview that I have presented as I have seen it through my eyes.

62. Kaufman, *supra* note 36, at 172.

Law and Lawyers: The Road to Reform

Kenneth W. Starr

Kenneth Starr delivered the Sonnett lecture at Fordham University School of Law on November 3, 1994.[1] In his speech, entitled *Law and Lawyers: The Road to Reform*, he argued that the rise in punitive damage awards has, in part, contributed to the decline of civility in the practice of law.[2]

Starr is perhaps most well-known for his investigation of President William Clinton, which led to the latter's impeachment.[3] However, Starr has also enjoyed a long and distinguished career in the public, private, and academic sectors. Born on July 21, 1946 in Vernon, Texas, Mr. Starr was raised in San Antonio.[4] He attended college at George Washington University, received a master's degree from Brown University, and a law degree from Duke University Law School.[5]

Upon graduating from law school, Mr. Starr clerked for Fifth Circuit Judge David W. Dyer, and then for Supreme Court Chief Justice Warren E. Burger.[6] After completing his clerkships in 1977, Mr. Starr joined the law firm Gibson, Dunn & Crutcher at their Washington D.C. office.

In 1983, Mr. Starr was appointed to the D.C. Circuit Court of Appeals.[7] He served as a judge until he was named Solicitor General in 1989.[8] As Solicitor General, Mr. Starr argued over thirty-five cases before the Supreme Court.[9]

After serving as Solicitor General, Mr. Starr returned to private practice, joining the law firm Kirkland & Ellis and focusing on appellate practice, antitrust, federal courts,

Introduction written by Sophia Qasir, J.D., Class of 2014, Fordham University School of Law.

1. Kenneth W. Starr, *Law and Lawyers: The Road to Reform*, 63 Fordham L. Rev. 959 (1995). These remarks presented in this article were lightly edited and footnotes have been added, but they retain the form and style of the oral remarks.

2. *Id.* at 966.

3. *See* Communication from Kenneth Starr, Independent Counsel, Transmitting a Referral to the United States House of Representatives (Sept. 11, 1998), http://www.gpo.gov/fdsys/pkg/CDOC-105hdoc310/pdf/CDOC-105hdoc310.pdf.

4. *Bio of Ken Winston Starr, J.D.*, Baylor Media Commc'n (Feb. 15, 2010), http://www.baylor.edu/mediacommunications/news.php?action=story&story=69086.

5. *Id.*

6. *Baylor President and Chancellor Ken Starr*, Baylor Off. Pres. & Chancellor, http://www.baylor.edu/president/index.php?id=73711 (last visited Mar. 17, 2014).

7. *Id.*

8. *See* Press Release, Pepperdine University, Dean Ken Starr Honored with Portrait at the D.C. Circuit Court of Appeals, http://www.pepperdine.edu/pr/releases/2007/october/starrportrait.htm.

9. *Bio of Kenneth Winston Starr, J.D.*, *supra* note 4. In total, Mr. Starr has argued thirty-six cases before the Supreme Court. *Baylor President and Chancellor Ken Starr*, *supra* note 6.

federal jurisdiction, and constitutional law.[10] In 2004, Mr. Starr took an "of counsel" position at his firm and began teaching constitutional issues and civil procedure at Pepperdine Law School.[11] Notably, in 2006 Mr. Starr represented the petitioner school board[12] in *Morse v. Frederick*, in which a student was disciplined for holding a banner that read "Bong Hits for Jesus" at a school-sponsored function.[13] The Supreme Court granted certiorari and Mr. Starr successfully argued[14] the principle that a school board may restrict student speech when it can be reasonably viewed as promoting drug use.[15]

Mr. Starr remained at Pepperdine until 2010, when he was selected to be the Fourteenth President of Baylor University.[16] Mr. Starr also served on the faculty of Baylor Law School.[17]

In addition to these numerous accomplishments, Mr. Starr is a widely published author.[18] His writings include *First Among Equals: The Supreme Court in American Life* which traces the history of the Supreme Court since Chief Justice Earl Warren.[19]

In his Sonnett lecture, Mr. Starr discussed American society's distrust of political institutions and cultural suspicion of power.[20] This view, in Mr. Starr's opinion, extended to the judiciary and the legal profession as a whole.[21] Mr. Starr attributed this criticism to the increasingly aggressive techniques used by lawyers in pre-trial litigation, such as abusive discovery tactics.[22] Mr. Starr attributed the shift in lawyers' approach to litigation to the rising number of lawyers, increasing economic pressure,[23] and, in the case of tort law, the increasing award of punitive damages.[24]

Mr. Starr's remarks remain highly relevant in today's debate over tort reform[25] and the importance of civility and ethics in the legal profession. As the legal market continues to change, lawyers should bear in mind that they do not need to resort to "'in your face' stratagems"[26] to adequately represent their clients' interests.[27]

---

10. *Bio of Kenneth Winston Starr, J.D.*, *supra* note 4.

11. *Id.*

12. Brief for Petitioner, Morse v. Frederick, 551 U.S. 393 (2007) (No. 06–278).

13. Morse v. Frederick, 551 U.S. 393 (2007).

14. Transcript of Oral Argument, Morse v. Frederick, 551 U.S. 393 (2007) (No. 06–278), http://www.supremecourt.gov/oral_arguments/argument_transcripts/06–278.pdf.

15. *Morse*, 551 U.S. at 396.

16. *Baylor President and Chancellor Ken Starr*, *supra* note 6.

17. *Id.*

18. Mr. Starr is the author of over twenty-five publications. *Id.*

19. Kenneth W. Starr, First Among Equals: The Supreme Court in American Life (2002).

20. Starr, *supra* note 1, at 959–61.

21. *Id.* at 963.

22. *Id.* at 963–64.

23. *Id.* at 964.

24. *Id.* at 996.

25. *See, e.g.*, Jill W. Lens, *Procedural Due Process and Predictable Punitive Damage Awards*, 2012 B.Y.U. L. Rev. 1; Michael L. Rustad, *The Closing of Punitive Damages' Iron Cage*, 38 Loy. L.A. L. Rev. 1297 (2005).

26. Starr, *supra* note 1, at 964.

27. *See, e.g.*, Nicola A. Boothe-Perry, *No Laughing Matter: The Intersection of Legal Malpractice and Professionalism*, 21 Am. U. J. Gender Soc. Pol'y & L. 1 (2012); Donna C. Chin et al., *One Response to*

1994 Sonnett Lecture

My reflections this evening, which focus on our nation's justice system, reflect broader social concerns, going to the basic structure of American institutions and the precipitous decline in trust reposed in those institutions.

Let me not mince words. As a people, Americans have become highly distrustful and disrespectful of institutions, ranging from the basic social unit of the traditional nuclear family to churches and synagogues, schools and universities, and in this election season, of government itself. Courts—the justice system—are no exception to this powerful trend. In my view, the trend is broad-based and deep enough to be profoundly disturbing.

What explains this trend of distrust and disrespect? Part of the answer, I believe, lies in America's inherent, culturally rooted suspicion of power. We are, at bottom, an antipower society. We are a revolutionary society. Unlike the people of Canada, who peacefully separated from Britain,[1] we in the United States chose the path of violence.[2] We appealed to a higher authority. We appealed to Nature's God, to natural law, and ultimately, to the natural or inalienable rights, in Jefferson's words, of the individual to be free to make his or her own destiny.[3] That in large part was the American story that unfolded after the Revolution, especially the conquering of the frontier and expanding westward to the Pacific and beyond. We even hear this in our contemporary music, such as the country and western song (which I hear a lot in Little Rock) called "Independence Day."[4] The song has very little to do with the Fourth of July and much to do with individuality and autonomy.

That is another part of the answer of our cultural distrust of institutions. Culturally, we believe, above all, in the individual. The rights of the individual are of the highest order in our constellation of values. Thus, we as a people are inherently suspicious when government intrudes into the sphere of individuality and autonomy. This is an attribute that unites the ACLU in Greenwich Village and Sagebrush Rebellion leaders from the far West. Culturally, we favor not society, but the individual. We root for the little guy, the self-made woman, the self-made man. We talk about our freedom to define ourselves,

---

the Decline of Civility in the Legal Profession: Teaching Professionalism in Legal Research and Writing, 51 RUTGERS L. REV. 889 (1999); Raymond M. Ripple, *Learning Outside the Fire: The Need for Civility Instruction in Law School*, 15 NOTRE DAME J.L. ETHICS & PUB. POL'Y 359 (2001).

1. *See generally* ANNE-MARIE MAWHINEY, TOWARDS ABORIGINAL SELF-GOVERNMENT: RELATIONS BETWEEN STATUS INDIAN PEOPLES AND THE GOVERNMENT OF CANADA 1969–1984, at 23–26 (1994) (discussing the relationship between Canada and Britain); CARL WITTKE, A HISTORY OF CANADA (rev. ed. 1933) (explaining the influence of France and Britain on Canada's history).

2. *See* AMERICAN VIOLENCE: A DOCUMENTARY HISTORY 13–18 (Richard Hofstadter & Michael Wallace eds., 1970); CHARLES A. BEARD & MARY R. BEARD, A BASIC HISTORY OF THE UNITED STATES 102–19 (1944).

3. *See* Claude G. Bowers, *Jefferson and the American Way of Life*, *in* THE HERITAGE OF JEFFERSON 13, 13–15 (Claude G. Bowers et al. eds., 1944); DUMAS MALONE, JEFFERSON AND THE RIGHTS OF MAN 153 (1951); DAVID N. MAYER, THE CONSTITUTIONAL THOUGHTS OF THOMAS JEFFERSON 75–79 (1994).

4. Martina McBride, *Independence Day* (BMG).

to do what we want to do, and to be all that we can be, including marching to the beat of our own drummer. Cowboys, Lone Rangers, Henry David Thoreaus, Huckleberry Finns—these are our historic, traditional cultural icons. "Up the Organization," "Do Your Own Thing," "I Gotta Be Me"—these are our individualistic mottos and mantras.

The third reason for our growing distrust of institutions is scandal. Increasingly, we think our institutions lie to us and deceive us. Watergate was a cultural and political watershed in this respect. Since Watergate, we as a people are prepared to believe the worst. It was one thing for President Eisenhower to lie about the United States sending spy planes over the then Soviet Union, although it cannot be doubted that the shooting down of Gary Francis Powers's U-2 plane in 1958 sent shock waves of disbelief through the country.[5] We believed in our institutions, and we thought well of the President and believed what he had to say. "I like Ike" was an appropriate slogan for a country that sat together with their families and watched Fred McMurray in "My Three Sons" or "Leave it to Beaver." Adlai Stevenson was perfectly gracious and gallant in his unsuccessful quest for the Oval Office. Politics seemed not so nasty. That was when America was more tuned in to "Ozzie and Harriett," the "Donna Reed Show" and "I Love Lucy" than to Lenny Bruce and Reefer Madness. Kids in trouble meant an illegal six-pack, not an Uzi or a crack pipe. Quaint as it may seem, there was a time, not so long ago, when "60 Minutes" simply meant an hour in the day, not the reporting of yet another scandal befalling corporate, political or legal America.

These related themes—suspicion of power, the primacy of the individual and the culture of scandal—define our life together as a people in large measure in the 1990s (along with themes of inclusiveness, diversity and egalitarianism that are beyond the ambit of my remarks this evening).

My current role in Little Rock as independent counsel is illustrative of the confluence of these broad social trends. In the aftermath of Watergate, Senator Sam Ervin of North Carolina—who chaired the Senate select committee of the Watergate investigation and who became a folk hero in the mid-1970s—held hearings on whether an *independent* Department of Justice should be established.[6] This proposed independence of our nation's

5. *See* Quincy Wright, *Espionage and the Doctrine of Non-Intervention in Internal Affairs, in* Essays on Espionage and International Law 3, 17 (Roland J. Stranger ed., 1962); *see also* James Reston, *U.S. Concedes Flight Over Soviet, Defends Search for Intelligence; Russians Hold Downed Pilot a Spy*, N.Y. Times, May 8, 1960, at 1 (admitting that a plane equipped for intelligence purposes was flying over the Soviet Union). *See generally* Jef Verschueren, International News Reporting: Metapragmatic Metaphors and the U-2, at 33, 41–99 (1985) (analyzing the news coverage surrounding the downing of the U-2).

6. *See Removing Politics from the Administration of Justice: Hearings Before the Subcomm. on Separation of Powers of the Senate Comm. on the Judiciary*, 93d Cong., 2d Sess. (1974); *see also* William B. Gwyn, *The Indeterminacy of the Separation of Powers and the Federal Courts*, 57 Geo. Wash. L. Rev. 474, 484 (1989) (stating that Senator Sam Ervin proposed an "independent" Justice Department); Jeremy Rabkin, *At the President's Side: The Role of the White House Counsel in Constitutional Policy*, 56 Law & Contemp. Probs. 63, 78 (1993) (same).

law department was quite radical. The idea was that the Attorney General of the United States would be like the Chairman of the Federal Reserve Board, independent of the President of the United States. The idea, which was embodied in a piece of proposed legislation,[7] was rejected, but in its place—more modestly—came the Ethics in Government Act of 1978,[8] with its vision of independence. This is the moral vision of the "independent counsel," or what was once called the "special prosecutor." It means a prosecutor not appointed by the President or the Attorney General—the model of such memorable examples as Archibald Cox and Leon Jaworski—and who is appointed instead by the courts and who functions independently of the Executive Branch.

Why this independence from the executive branch? Why this independence from the President and any subordinate officer? The idea, again, is mistrust and suspicion of power. Just as no one should be the judge in his or her own case—the theory goes—we should not, as a matter of law, trust anyone appointed by the President or the Attorney General to investigate the President or other high ranking officers of the executive branch who are answerable to the President. We take a page from Lord Acton: "Power tends to corrupt, and absolute power corrupts absolutely."[9]

These trend lines are applicable to the courts as well. Judges, like others who wield power, can behave in ways that are viewed by the people as inappropriate or imperious. The great debate that swirls over *Roe v. Wade*,[10] the issue called right-to-die[11] and the unsettling world of Dr. Jack Kevorkian[12] is about morality, about competing visions of right and wrong, good and evil and differing moral visions about life—when life begins and who controls its termination.

But the debate is also about power and the appropriateness of courts making fundamental decisions about social policy in America. So here ideas and visions clash: Are judges and Justices of the Supreme Court simply protecting individual rights and liberties against majoritarian forces that would oppress or even enslave individuals? Or, on the other hand,

7. *See Removing Politics from the Administration of Justice: Hearings Before the Subcomm. on Separation of Powers of the Senate Comm. on the Judiciary*, 93d Cong., 2d Sess. (1974).

8. 5 U.S.C app. §§ 101–505 (Supp. V 1993).

9. J. Dalberg-Acton, *Acton-Creighton Correspondence*, *in* Essays on Freedom and Power 357, 364 (G. Himmelfarb ed., 1948).

10. 410 U.S. 113 (1973).

11. *See, e.g.*, Cruzan v. Director, Missouri Dep't of Health, 497 U.S. 261 (1990) (holding that clear and convincing evidence of an incompetent patient's wishes is required for the court to permit the termination of death-prolonging procedures); *In re* Quinlan, 355 A.2d 647, 663 (N.J. 1976) (stating that the Supreme Court has recognized the right of privacy, which presumably is broad enough to encompass a patient's desire to decline medical treatment); *see also* John A. Powell & Adam S. Cohen, *The Right to Die*, 10 Issues L. & Med. 169 (1994) (suggesting that our society continues to struggle with the debate over the right to die).

12. *See* Powell & Cohen, *supra* note 11, at 172; *see, e.g.*, Dan Colburn, *Debate on Assisted Suicide Gains Steam*, Wash. Post, May 10, 1994, at 8; Jacqueline Weaver, *Reflections on Life and How It Ends*, N.Y. Times, June 5, 1994, at 3.

are judges abusing their power? Are they usurpers, perhaps pursuing their moral vision of the good society, but in the process tearing at our democratic roots society and the right of the people, through elected representatives, to govern themselves?

Our suspicion of power readily includes judicial power. Courts, by their nature, tend to exalt the individual as against the organized forces of society. They protect individual liberty and dignity interests. This characteristic dovetails with one powerful current in our life as a society. We like the individual and individual rights, and so do courts. But, as to the third broad social current—scandal—the courts, themselves, sadly, have not been free from taint. Before the watershed of Watergate, Justice Abe Fortas resigned in disgrace,[13] and the specter of scandal engulfed Judge G. Harrold Carswell[14] and (in my opinion, unfairly so) Judge Clement Haynsworth.[15] Since that time, with astonishing regularity, sitting federal judges have been indicted, and at times convicted, of serious criminal offenses. More recent confirmation battles over various nominees to the nation's highest Court bear witness to scandal engulfing the Article III branch.[16] As I can personally attest, even appointments of independent counsel by a panel of judges, as provided by the Ethics in Government Act, have not been immune from controversy. Evil or improper motives have freely been attributed to judges with exemplary and lengthy records of distinguished service.

The scathing criticisms of our justice system, including the broadsides against the legal profession itself, can fully be understood only against the backdrop of this broader social and cultural context. But looming large in the criticism of courts and the law, and specifically in lawyers and in the legal profession, are features that are peculiar to the descent of our profession into the lower regions of public disrespect. In particular, our hard, cutting-edge individualism has resulted in a remarkably different litigation culture than the one John F. Sonnett[17] helped to nurture and preserve.

13. Bruce A. Murphy, Fortas: The Rise and Ruin of a Supreme Court Justice 55–77 (1988) (describing Fortas's career on the Supreme Court); The Supreme Court Justices 474 (Clare Cushman ed., 1993) (explaining that Fortas resigned from the Court after *Life Magazine* published a story about his involvement with an indicted stock manipulator).

14. *See Nomination of George Harrold Carswell to Be Associate Justice of the Supreme Court of the United States: Hearings Before the Senate Comm. on the Judiciary*, 91st Cong., 2d Sess. (1970).

15. *See Nomination of Clement F. Haynsworth, Jr. to Be Associate Justice of the Supreme Court of the United States: Hearings Before the Senate Comm. on the Judiciary*, 91st Cong., 1st Sess. (1970); *see also* John P. Frank, Clement Haynsworth, the Senate and the Supreme Court (1991) (discussing Haynsworth's nomination to the Supreme Court and suggesting that the defeat of his nomination was purely political).

16. *Nomination of Judge Clarence Thomas to Be Associate Justice of the Supreme Court of the United States: Hearings Before the Senate Comm. on the Judiciary*, 102d Cong., 1st Sess. 36 (1991).

17. John Sonnett, a 1936 graduate of Fordham School of Law, was known internationally as a preeminent trial and appellate lawyer. Prior to his death in 1969, Mr. Sonnett was a senior partner at the firm of Cahill Gordon & Reindel. Mr. Sonnett had also served as an Assistant Attorney General and Chief of the Antitrust Division of the United States Department of Justice. During

Several years ago, in downtown Los Angeles, the American Bar Foundation presented its fifty-year service award to a remarkable and distinguished practitioner from San Francisco, Moses Lasky. Mr. Lasky, in accepting the award marking his half-century of service to courts, clients and the legal profession, reminisced about his life in the law. Memories of great episodes in life, of relationships with great lawyers of integrity and wisdom, including lawyers of the other side, of teachers and mentors in the law came flooding through.

Then, the tone of the remarks shifted abruptly. Looking back over the span of five decades of law practice, Mr. Lasky suggested that sometime in the mid- to late 1970s, the practice of law changed. It stopped being fun. It became less civil, less genteel and considerably more commercialized.

It is by no means coincidental that the decline in professional satisfaction within the legal profession, captured by the pointed remarks of Moses Lasky, has been accompanied by growing expressions of disapproval by the American people of our profession and of the justice system more generally. Our explosive growth as a profession,[18] in terms of sheer numbers, has placed extraordinary burdens on our now endangered traditions of civility and professionalism. These baleful developments, along with bottom line economic pressures, is a story that is discouragingly familiar to bench and bar and need not be retold here.

In litigation, pretrial discovery is, and has been, the great battlefield. The age of gentility having been replaced by the culture of Jurassic Park,[19] albeit Jurassic Park in pin stripes, pitched battles are now waged, in an environment partaking of nonviolent but total war, by litigators and trial lawyers across the country. Zealous advocacy has been replaced by decidedly uncivil "in your face" stratagems designed to browbeat, to demean and to threaten.

How far we have come from the world envisioned by Judge Charles Clark of the Second Circuit, who served on the great court of Learned Hand and who was a primary architect of modem pretrial discovery.[20] That world was one of rationality, of informing parties to civil litigation of their respective strengths and weakness through pretrial discovery. Through such now familiar devices as written interrogatories, requests for production of documents and depositions of witnesses, including experts, parties would be able to come to grips with the realities of a case before the jury was in the box and society

World War II, Mr. Sonnett was special counsel to the Under Secretary of the Navy, and he conducted the final Navy investigations of the attack on Pearl Harbor.

18. In 1979, 57,676 people across the country took the bar examination. *See* The Lawyers Almanac 1981–82, at 284–85 (1981). In contrast, in 1992, 72,461 people across the county took the bar examination. *See* The Lawyers Almanac 1994, at 724 (1994).

19. Jurassic Park (Universal 1993).

20. Judge Clark was the Reporter to the original Federal Rule drafting committee. Jack B. Weinstein, *After 50 Years of the Federal Rules of Civil Procedure: Are the Barriers to Justice Being Raised?*, 137 U. Pa. L. Rev. 1901, 1903–04 (1989).

was put to the expense of a trial on the merits.[21] Discovery, then, was the great innovation to modernize, to streamline and to rationalize litigation and thereby to make the dispute resolution process less reliant on the courtroom cunning of skilled trial lawyers.

As years went on, discovery the solution, discovery the civil reformer's dream, became discovery the problem, discovery the nightmare.[22] From the shock of the activity of the defense counsel in the *Kodak* case,[23] to the swirling controversy over the conduct of the Seattle law firm of Bogle & Gates,[24] to the deposition techniques of Houston's legendary Joe Jamail,[25] a growing sense of disquiet and unease was spreading over lawyer behavior and law firm behavior. The ideal of Atticus Finch, the courageous lawyer carrying out an unpopular assignment with grace and dignity, was jettisoned and replaced by what judge after judge came to view as *lawyer as Rambo*, seen in courts across the country every day.

Two years ago, a very prominent and highly successful trial lawyer made a presentation for a group of litigators about how to conduct oneself in pretrial discovery.[26] In his Hobbesian world, litigation was simply a jungle. In his sinister world, the other side was not only not to be trusted, but just the opposite. The other side would deliberately deceive; they would improperly withhold or would fail to respond.

What to do? The lawyer advised his fellow lawyers as follows: "The answer is obvious: Be unreasonable. If you are unreasonable, the Judge will give you what you want."[27]

The trial lawyer went on to urge planning in advance, to anticipate that the other side would be obstreperous. Thus, he suggested: "You know what is coming when you are seeking discovery. Go ahead and prepare a draft motion to compel," he urged his listeners. "Try to develop evidence of slowness in response, bring this promptly to the judge's attention, and then try to get a default judgment entered against the other side."

This pattern is now a standard part of the modern litigator's playbook. It emphasizes attacks, presuming bad faith on the other side, immediate repairing to the trial judge with a laundry list of litigation sins by one's opponent and seeking the imposition of severe sanctions, including entry of default judgment.

21. *See generally* William A. Glaser, Pretrial Discovery and the Adversary System 9–12 (1968) (setting forth the aims of discovery, including to diminish the amount of trickery embedded in our legal system and to reduce the number of cases that go to trial).

22. *See* Theodore Y. Blumoff et al., Pretrial Discovery: The Development of Professional Judgment § 2.1, at 9–12 (1993).

23. *See* Berkey Photo, Inc. v. Eastman Kodak Co., 74 F.R.D. 613, 615 (S.D.N.Y. 1977).

24. *See* Washington State Physicians Ins. Exch. & Ass'n v. Fisons Corp., 858 P.2d 1054, 1074–79 (1993) (holding that trial court should have sanctioned the defendant or the defendant's attorneys for discovery abuse); Sharon Walsh, *State Court Sanctions Firm for Failure to Disclose*, Wash. Post, Nov. 29, 1993, § f (Financial), at 7.

25. *See* Paramount Communications Inc. v. QVC Network Inc., 637 A.2d 34,51–57 (Del. 1993) (discussing Jamail's misconduct with respect to discovery in an addendum to the opinion); Excerpts: *A Delaware Court Criticizes Deposition Behavior of Attorney*, Nat'l L.J., Feb. 21, 1994, at 22.

26. *See* James E. Butler, Jr. & Patrick A. Dawson, The Bench as Battleground: The Discovery Process is Broke and Only Judges Can Fix It (1992).

27. *Id.* at 4–5.

This brass-knuckles approach to litigation is now commonplace. In its most pathological form, it has come to have a name of its own-the *sanctions tort.*[28] Using sanctions prematurely, at times on the heels of wildly overbroad discovery requests, including requests for attorney client privileged material or attorney work product, which of course enjoy fundamental protection in our law,[29] the trial becomes one focused on the party's conduct and on the conduct of the party's counsel.

This is a new age of barbarism, and it is increasingly the order of the day. What drives this new age of barbarism is not unrelated to the themes articulated earlier—our aggressive individuality, or breaking bonds of professional community through an exaltation of the individual scrapping to get his or her way and achieve his or her goals, and, finally, the culture of scandal. It is the same value system in modern civil litigation as that undergirding negative advertising in politics. Do not debate the merits of issues; do not engage in the genuine clash of ideas. Manipulate, distort, and hopefully destroy. And in extreme situations, engage in character assassination. As in politics, the law and the legal profession have been demeaned and demoralized quite seriously in the eyes of the public.

This new age of litigation barbarism is most frightfully evident in the super-high stakes world of modern tort law. Tort litigation now means go-for-broke Rambo discovery tactics in this demoralized world now full blown upon us.

The engine driving the demonic machine is very simple to identify—dollars, very big dollars. It is the crassest, most greedy, avaricious dimension of the fearsome commercialization of the legal profession. Gunslinging competition is continually under way for the title, King of Torts, carrying with it not only fame and prestige but income levels that would impress even the partners of Goldman Sachs.[30] One trial lawyer now seeking federal elective office listed his earned income for the past twelve months as $12 million;[31] and this is a trial lawyer who has never had his trials on Court TV or featured in the *National Law Journal.* He is just a middle-class trial lawyer.

The astronomical, mind-boggling levels of income are traceable to one primary source—the modem-day phenomenon of punitive damages. Modern-day punitive damages are the modern-day lottery—not many winners, but a legion of wannabe winners who are competing vigorously in courtrooms across America. These are damages designed not to compensate an injured victim, but to punish and to deter antisocial conduct. As every first-year student learns, the purpose of damages in our civil law is to *compensate*, to make whole.

28. *See, e.g.*, Charles F. Herring Jr., *The Rise of the Sanctions Tort*, Tex. Law., Jan. 28, 1991, at 22 (describing the sanctions tort as a "whole new arena of outcome-determinative pretrial gamesmanship").

29. *See* Model Rules of Professional Conduct 1.6 (1983); Model Code of Professional Responsibility DR 4–101(B) (1980).

30. *See* Gary Taylor, *O'Quinn Shoots for 'Tort King' Crown*, Nat'l L. J., Oct. 17, 1994, at Al.

31. The attorney referred to is C. Fredrick Overby, a partner in the firm of Butler, Wooten, Overby & Chelley with offices in Atlanta and Columbus, Georgia.

Volume 2 of Blackstone's ancient commentaries[32] makes the point powerfully. The *criminal* nature of punitive damages, until recently, made scholarly commentators and defense attorneys uneasy. No lesser light than Prosser in his Law of Torts politely called punitive damages in the civil law "rather anomalous."[33] Indeed, our Yankee forebears in New Hampshire said over a century ago that it is difficult on principal to understand why, when the sufferer by a tort has been fully compensated for his suffering, he should recover anything more.[34] This from a New Hampshire Supreme Court opinion in 1873.

Punitive damage awards have become such a commonplace occurrence—albeit, so as not to overstate, not a daily occurrence—that we are no longer taken back by news of an award in the many millions, or even billions of dollars. It bears noting, however, that this is, all things considered, quite new, even though the concept of punitive damages is ancient in our law.[35] Indeed, statistics show that "hit-the-jackpot" levels of awards are quite novel.

A brief historical note: A recent study found that the largest punitive damages award in the nineteenth century—including verdicts set aside as excessive by reviewing courts—was a modest $4,500.[36] Translated into our cheapened coin of the realm, that is $58,000 in modern-day dollars.[37]

But if that seems like the unenlightened bad old days, as of 1955—when Adlai Stevenson was preparing a second time to square off against "I Like Ike"—the largest punitive damages award in the history of California was $75,000.[38] The movement toward large awards got under way in the 1960s and then took off on size in the 1970s and 1980s.

This, ironically, has come at a time of considerable regulatory activity and the growth of the modern administrative and regulatory state. That is, at a time when avenues of marketplace regulation at various levels of government, the need for common law instruments—through litigators on a case-by-case basis—would seem to have declined. There is, at least in theory, less of a gap than in the nineteenth century in terms of disincentives to engage in outrageous and wanton misconduct.

What flows from all of this? In my view, it is time to get at one of the root causes of that which is wrong with our life together as a profession. It is time to think the heretofore unthinkable and to reexamine the modern institution, by abolishing punitive damages. On reflection, it will be seen that this is not so unthinkable after all.

32. 2 William Blackstone, Commentaries 396.

33. W. Page Keeton et al., Prosser and Keeton on the Law of Torts § 2, at 9 (5th ed. 1984).

34. Fay v. Parker, 53 N.H. 342, 343 (1873).

35. *See* Gerald W. Boston, Punitive Damages in Tort Law § 1.2, at 2, §§ 1.7–1.10, at 11–16 (1993).

36. Brief of the American Institute of Architects et al. at 14, Pacific Mut. Life Ins. Co. v. Haslip, 499 U.S. 1 (1991) (No. 89-1279) (citing New Orleans, J. & G.N.RR. v. Hurst, 36 Miss. 660 (1859)).

37. *Id.*

38. *Id.* at 16.

Several states—Michigan,[39] New Hampshire,[40] Nebraska[41] and Washington[42]—do not have punitive damages. Yet, life seems to go on. And, despite their origins in ancient English case law, the law in England, upon close analysis, never evolved to the point, as in the United States, of accepting punitive damages that are expressly designed to do more than compensate.[43] And, as illustrated by *Rookes v. Barnard*,[44] a House of Lords decision from thirty years ago, punitive damages are generally prohibited at modern English common law.

Abolishing punitive damages would be an important, nontinkering step toward real reform in the law and in the profession. It would also be consistent with one of the bedrock concerns articulated at the outset of these remarks—the problem of power. Cutting across various philosophical and ideological lines, virtually every Justice on the Supreme Court in recent years—including Justice Brennan,[45] Justice Marshall,[46] Justice Blackmun[47] and, most recently, Justice Souter[48]—has expressed grave concern about runaway punitive damages awards.[49] That should go a long way toward establishing a moral consensus.

But the issues about competitiveness and other potential effects on our economic life will continue to spawn debate among economists. What should be clear, however, is that

39. *See* Fellows v. Superior Prods. Co., 506 N.W.2d 534, 536 (Mich. Ct. App. 1993) ("In Michigan, the courts of that State refuse to allow the recovery of punitive damages.") (citations omitted).

40. *See* Panas v. Harakis, 529 A.2d 976, 986 (N.H. 1987) ("This jurisdiction forbids the award of punitive damages.") (citing Fay v. Parker, 53 N.H. 342, 382, 397 (1873)).

41. *See* Braesch v. Union Ins., 464 N.W.2d 769, 777 (Neb. 1991) ("[P]unitive damages are not allowed in Nebraska.") (citing Abel v. Conover, 104 N.W.2d 684, 686 (1960)).

42. *See* Kennewick Educ. Ass'n v. Kennewick Sch. Dist. No. 17, 666 P.2d 928, 930 (Wash. Ct. App. 1983) ("It has long been established that recovery of punitive damages is contrary to the public policy of the State and will not be allowed unless expressly authorized by statute."); *see also* Spokane Truck & Dray Co. v. Hoefer, 25 P. 1072 (1891) (prohibiting punitive damages).

43. *See* Boston, *supra* note 35, §§ 1.3–1.6, at 2–10.

44. 1 All E.R. 367 (1964).

45. *See, e.g.*, Browning-Ferris Indus. v. Kelco Disposal, Inc., 492 U.S. 257, 281–82 (1989) (Brennan, J., concurring) (expressing concern that "punitive damages are imposed by juries guided by little more than an admonition to do what they think is best"). In *Browning-Ferris*, Justice Brennan suggested stricter scrutiny of punitive damages awards in cases where there is no statute to guide the jury's decision. *Id.* at 281.

46. *See, e.g.*, Rosenbloom v. Metromedia, Inc., 403 U.S. 29, 80–86 (1971) (Marshall, J., dissenting) (discussing the negative effect of punitive damage awards on freedom of the press).

47. *See, e.g.*, Pacific Mut. Life Ins. v. Haslip, 499 U.S. 1, 18 (1991). In *Haslip*, Justice Blackmun, writing for the majority, stated: "We note once again our concern about punitive damages that 'run wild.'" *Id.*

48. *See, e.g.*, TXO Prod. Corp. v. Alliance Resources Corp., 113 S. Ct. 2711, 2742 (1993) (O'Connor, J., dissenting). In *TXO*, Justice Souter joined in Justice O'Connor's dissent in which she expressed concerns with skyrocketing punitive damage awards. *Id.*

49. *See generally Haslip*, 499 U.S. at 9 ("This Court and individual Justices thereof on a number of occasions in recent years have expressed doubts about the constitutionality of certain punitive damage awards.").

we need to think rather creatively about how to abate the trend toward scorched earth, highly destructive and extremely high stakes litigation that is so demeaning and demoralizing to officers of the court. The old-fashioned virtues in law of honor, integrity, zealous advocacy, and respect for the other side and of the good faith of the other side is what John Sonnett stood for. It is these values that, in our own way, we should pursue in the memory of the great man whose contributions to this institution and to the courts of law we celebrate tonight.

Matters of Life and Death

Hon. Liam Hamilton

On March 28, 1996, Chief Justice of Ireland Liam Hamilton delivered the twenty-fourth Sonnett lecture.[1] This marked the third Sonnett lecture delivered by a Chief Justice of Ireland, following lectures by his predecessors, Chief Justice Cearbhall Ó Dálaigh and Chief Justice Thomas Finlay.

Born in Mitchelstown, County Cork in 1928, Chief Justice Hamilton had a lengthy public service career.[2] He worked as a civil servant and a High Court clerk before turning to the study of law.[3] He attended University College, Dublin and King's Inns, where he won the John Brooke Scholarship, awarded to the best final year student. He was called to the bar in 1956 and practiced law as a barrister for the next eighteen years.[4]

In 1974, he was appointed to the High Court and became its president in 1985.[5] During his time on the High Court, then-Judge Hamilton decided several important cases, including *Murphy v. Attorney General*[6] and *Kennedy v. Ireland*.[7] He also presided over a number of high-profile criminal trials as a judge of the Special Criminal Court.[8] From 1991 to 1994, he served as the sole member of a tribunal established to investigate allegations of illegal activity and fraud in the beef processing industry.[9] Judge Hamilton was elevated to Chief Justice in 1994, a position he held until he retired in 2000.[10]

For his Sonnett lecture entitled *Matters of Life and Death: Remarks*, Chief Justice Hamilton bravely chose to address two highly controversial topics: the right to life and the right to die.[11] More specifically, he set out to describe Irish constitutional law's response to such difficult issues as abortion and the right of an individual in a vegetative state to be removed from life support. In doing so, Chief Justice Hamilton tells the story

Introduction written by Nicholas Dowd, J.D., Class of 2015, Fordham University School of Law.

1. Liam Hamilton, *Matters of Life and Death: Remarks*, 65 Fordham L. Rev. 543 (1996).

2. *Former Chief Justice, Mr. Justice Liam Hamilton, Dies*, RTE News (Nov. 30, 2000), http://www.rte.ie/news/2000/1130/10468-hamilton/ (last visited Mar. 7, 2017).

3. *Id.*

4. *Former Chief Justices*, Supreme Court of Ireland, http://www.supremecourt.ie/supremecourt/sclibrary3.nsf/pagecurrent/B8E6388E466B6FB680257315005A41D3?opendocument&l=en (last visited Mar. 7, 2017).

5. *Id.*

6. [1982] IR 241 (H. Ct.) (holding joint taxation of married couples to be unconstitutional).

7. [1987] I.R. 587 (H. Ct.) (limiting State interference with private lives of individual citizens).

8. *Former Chief Justices*, *supra* note 4.

9. *Id.*

10. *Id.*

11. *See generally* Hamilton, *supra* note 1.

of a country grappling with its religious and cultural identity in the face of internationalism and evolving technology.

While the lecture is an outline of the struggle to find what Chief Justice Hamilton called "an Irish solution to an Irish problem," at the heart of that struggle are questions of obvious and lasting significance to the United States and the world.[12] Questions about the natural rights of individuals, the role of religion in the law, the meaning of "life," and even the question of who should be providing the answers to these questions continue to be divisive issues in society. Chief Justice Hamilton's poignant remarks on his country's search for an "Irish solution" thus provide valuable context and perspective as we continue to look for solutions of our own.

1996 Sonnett Lecture

I am extremely privileged and honored to have been invited to deliver the twenty-fourth Annual John F. Sonnett Memorial Lecture here at Fordham University School of Law.

My appreciation of such privilege and honor was accentuated when I read the list of previous lecturers who have delivered this lecture in memory of John F. Sonnett, a distinguished graduate of this university and this school of law, who devoted his life to the practice of law and to public service.

I am delighted to follow in their footsteps, particularly in the footsteps of my two predecessors as Chief Justice of Ireland, namely the late Cearbhall Ó Dálaigh and the recently retired Thomas Finlay.

I hope that you will find my address to you interesting because, in it, I propose to deal with two matters which are of common interest to our two countries, *viz.* the right to life and the right to die, but I intend to deal only with such rights under the Irish Constitution and the manner in which they have been dealt with by the Irish courts, producing an Irish solution to an Irish problem.

The authors of our 1937 Constitution, which came into effect on December 29, 1937,[1] in including a section on fundamental rights, could have had little idea of the revolutionary impact it would have on Irish society. The then-Taoiseach [Prime Minister] Mr. de Valera seems to have viewed the provisions as being mere "headlines for the Legislature"—standards for government to aim at, but not for courts to enforce.[2] Articles 40 through 44 gave express recognition to those rights most prized in Western liberal democracies—personal liberty, freedom of expression, equality before the law, ownership of property,

12. *Id.* at 543.

1. John M. Kelly, Fundamental Rights in the Irish Law and Constitution 8 (1961).
2. 68 DI Deb. cols. 216–17 (June 9, 1937).

and freedom of religious belief and practice.[3] The social policy of the Catholic Church also made itself felt, in the form of provisions recognizing the Family as "the natural primary and fundamental unit group of Society, and as a moral institution possessing inalienable and imprescriptible rights, antecedent and superior to all positive law."[4]

Article 42 recognizes the right of parents to educate their children, and pledges the State to support this "as guardian of the common good."[5]

Aside from such specific protections, the framers of the Constitution included some more general statements in Article 40, section three. They read as follows:

> 1. The State guarantees in its laws to respect, and, as far as practicable, by its laws to defend and vindicate the personal rights of the citizen.
> 2. The State shall, in particular, by its laws protect as best it may from unjust attack and, in the case of injustice done, vindicate the life, person, good name, and property rights of every citizen.[6]

The first generation of Irish judges had spent their working lives in a pure common law environment, where Parliament reigned supreme. Old habits die hard, and it is not surprising if a certain wariness and timidity colored judgments in the first few decades of the new constitutional era. But beginning in the 1960s, the two short sentences of Article 40, section 3 became the basis for a series of revelatory judgments which have changed Irish society, and indeed continue to do so.

Since these early years, a new race of right-conscious citizens has grown up; there has also been a new race of right-conscious young lawyers and gradually there has been a new breed of judges.

The first case to really break new ground was *Ryan v. Attorney General*[7] in 1963. Mrs. Ryan challenged the right of the State to fluoridate water supplied to her home without her consent.[8] She failed in her application, but Justice Kenny of the High Court held that a right of "bodily integrity" did exist, being one of an unenumerated list of rights protected by Article 40, section 3, subsection 1.[9] As to where those rights might be found, he said:

> In my opinion, the High Court has jurisdiction to consider whether an Act of the Oireachtas [Parliament] respects and, as far as practicable, defends and vindicates the personal rights of the citizen and to declare the legislation unconstitutional if it does not. I think that the personal rights which may be involved [sic] to invalidate legislation are not confined to those specified in Article 40 but include all those rights which result from the Christian and democratic nature of the State. It is, however, a jurisdiction to be

3. *See* Ir. Const. arts. 40–44.
4. *Id.* art. 41, § 1(1).
5. *Id.* art. 42, §§ 1, 5.
6. *Id.* art. 40, § 3(1)–(2).
7. 1965 I.R. 294 (Ir. S.C. 1964).
8. *See id.* at 296–97 (Kenny, J.).
9. *Id.* at 313.

> exercised with caution. None of the personal rights of the citizen are unlimited: their exercise may be regulated by the Oireachtas when the common good requires this. When dealing with controversial social, economic and medical matters on which it is notorious views change from generation to generation, the Oireachtas has to reconcile the exercise of personal rights with the claims of the common good and its decision on the reconciliation should prevail unless it was oppressive to all or some of the citizens or unless there is no reasonable proportion between the benefit which the legislation will confer on the citizens or a substantial body of them and the interference with the personal rights of the citizen. Moreover, the presumption that every Act of the Oireachtas is constitutional until the contrary is clearly established applies with particular force to this type of legislation.
>
> The next matter to be considered . . . is whether the general guarantee in Article 40, section 3, relates only to those personal rights which are specified in Article 40 or whether it extends to other unspecified personal rights of the citizen. If it extends to personal rights other than those specified in Article 40, the High Court and the Supreme Court have the difficult and responsible duty of ascertaining and declaring what are the personal rights of the citizen which are guaranteed by the Constitution.[10]

It is important to note that the personal rights which the courts are obliged to ascertain and declare are those *which are guaranteed by the Constitution* as arising from the Christian and democratic nature of the State.

Interestingly, Justice Kenny quoted a Papal Encyclical in support of the right to bodily integrity,[11] and his willingness to allow his reading of the Constitution to be informed by documents of a religious rather than a legal nature marked the beginning of a long and tortuous debate on the proper place of Christian moral teaching in Irish legal and political life. His identification of the State as Christian in nature was made baldly, Justice Kenny presumably feeling that it was too obvious to require proof. Since then, some judges have cited the Preamble to the Constitution in support of it. That begins: "In the Name of the Most Holy Trinity, from Whom is all authority and to Whom, as our final end, all actions both of men and States must be referred . . . [h]umbly acknowledging all our obligations to our Divine Lord, Jesus Christ, Who sustained our fathers through centuries of trial."[12]

The Supreme Court in *Ryan* reaffirmed the existence of unenumerated personal rights, though without reference to Justice Kenny's Christian/democratic theory.[13] However, within a decade came *McGee v. Attorney General*.[14] The Supreme Court, in striking down legislation penalizing the importation of contraceptives, found a constitutionally protected right of privacy within marriage.[15] Curiously, only one judge, Justice Griffin, referred to

10. *Id.* at 312–13.
11. *Id.* at 314.
12. Ir. Const. pmbl.
13. *See Ryan*, 1965 I.R. at 335–53 (Ó Dálaigh, C.J.).
14. 1974 I.R. 284 (Ir. S.C. 1973).
15. *See id.* at 312–14 (Walsh, J.).

the judgment of Justice Kenny in *Ryan*[16] Justice Walsh, generally recognized as the intellectual leader of the Court at that time, preferred to find the source of unnamed rights in the concept of *natural law.* To this end, he invoked the wording of the fundamental rights articles in the Constitution, saying:

> Articles 41, 42 and 43 emphatically reject the theory that there are no rights without laws, no rights contrary to the law and no rights anterior to the law. They indicate that justice is placed above the law and acknowledge that natural rights, or human rights, are not created by law but that the Constitution confirms their existence and gives them protection.
>
> . . .
>
> . . . The very structure and content of the Articles dealing with fundamental rights clearly indicate that justice is not subordinate to the law. In particular, the terms of s. 3 of Article 40 expressly subordinate the law to justice.[17]

While admitting that "[w]hat exactly natural law is and what precisely it imports is a question which has exercised the minds of theologians for many centuries and on which they are not yet fully agreed,"[18] the judge nonetheless felt that the Constitution imposed a duty on the Court to consider and decide upon what rights are protected by natural law, as and when parties to a case attempt to rely on such rights.[19]

He further stated:

> In this country it falls finally upon the judges to interpret the Constitution and in doing so to determine, where necessary, the rights which are superior or antecedent to positive law or which are imprescriptible or inalienable. In the performance of this difficult duty there are certain guidelines laid down in the Constitution for the judge. The very structure and content of the Articles dealing with fundamental rights clearly indicate that justice is not subordinate to the law. In particular, the terms of s. 3 of Article 40 expressly subordinate the law to justice. Both Aristotle and the Christian philosophers have regarded justice as the highest human virtue. The virtue of prudence was also esteemed by Aristotle as by the philosophers of the Christian world. But the great additional virtue introduced by Christianity was that of charity—not the charity which consists of giving to the deserving, for that is justice, but the charity which is also called mercy. According to the preamble, the people gave themselves the Constitution to promote the common good with due observance of prudence, justice and charity so that the dignity and freedom of the individual might be assured. The judges must, therefore, as best they can from their training and their experience interpret these rights in accordance with their ideal of prudence, justice and charity. It is but natural that from time to time the prevailing ideas of these virtues may be conditioned by the passage of time; no interpretation of the Constitution is intended to be final for all time. It is given in the light of prevailing ideas and concepts.[20]

16. *See id.* at 332–33 (Griffin, J.).
17. *Id.* at 310, 318 (Walsh, J.).
18. *Id.* at 318.
19. *See id.*
20. *Id.* at 318–19.

Explicit references to the Christian character of the State surfaced again in the case of *Norris v. Attorney General*,[21] which concerned a challenge to laws penalizing homosexual acts between males. Mr. Norris submitted that he had a constitutionally protected right of privacy—along the lines of the protection of marital privacy in *McGee* which was being infringed.[22] In denying the existence of such a right, a three-to-two majority of the Supreme Court (led by Chief Justice O'Higgins) was heavily influenced by the Christian ethos of the Constitution itself, and in particular the references to Jesus Christ and the Trinity in the Preamble. Chief Justice O'Higgins said:

> It cannot be doubted that the people, so asserting and acknowledging their obligations to our Divine Lord Jesus Christ, were proclaiming a deep religious conviction and faith and an intention to adopt a Constitution consistent with that conviction and faith and with Christian beliefs. Yet it is suggested that, in the very act of so doing, the people rendered inoperative laws which had existed for hundreds of years prohibiting unnatural sexual conduct which Christian teaching held to be gravely sinful. It would require very clear and express provisions in the Constitution itself to convince me that such took place.[23]

Both Justice McCarthy and Justice Henchy delivered trenchant dissenting judgments, yet neither felt able to deny or play down the importance of the Christian ethic in the identification of constitutional rights. The difference was one of emphasis: Both dissenting judges preferred to name charity, rather than justice, as the primary Christian virtue in a pluralist, democratic society.[24] Justice McCarthy commented on Justice Kenny's dictum in *McGee v. Attorney General*[25] as follows:

> In so far as the judgment of Kenny J., in referring to the Christian and democratic nature of the State, is a relevant identification of source . . . I would respectfully dissent from such a proposition if it were to mean that, apart from the democratic nature of the State, the source of personal rights, unenumerated in the Constitution, is to be related to Christian theology, the subject of many diverse views and practices, rather than Christianity itself, the example of Christ and the great doctrine of charity which He preached. Jesus Christ proclaimed two great commandments—love of God and love of neighbour; St. Paul, the Apostle to the Gentiles, declared that of the great virtues, faith, hope and charity, the greatest of these is charity.[26]

Norris was decided in 1983. That was also the year in which a referendum to amend the Constitution ignited the previously smoldering issue of abortion in Ireland. But to understand how this even came about, we must turn back the clock to January 1973 in America, and *Roe v. Wade*.[27] A majority of the United States Supreme Court, led by Justice Blackmun,

21. 1984 I.R. 36 (Ir. S.C. 1983).
22. *See id.* at 54–55 (O'Higgins, J.).
23. *Id.* at 64.
24. *See id.* at 75–78 (Henchy, J.); *id.* at 99–100 (McCarthy, J.).
25. 1974 I.R. 284 (Ir. S.C. 1973).
26. *Norris*, 1984 I.R. at 99 (McCarthy, J.).
27. 410 U.S. 113 (1973).

held that the right to privacy identified in *Griswold v. Connecticut*[28] extended to "a woman's decision whether or not to terminate her pregnancy."[29] Once the Irish Supreme Court had found a right to marital privacy in *McGee*, it was feared by some commentators that the Court might one day extend this right to cover abortions, in the same manner as *Roe v. Wade*. In truth, this seemed an unlikely prospect; abortion had been a statutory offence since 1861, and both popular and judicial opinion seemed to support this. Indeed, the majority in *McGee* went out of its way to point out that its decision had no bearing on the abortion issue, Justice Walsh commenting that "this case is not in any way concerned with instruments, preparations, drugs or appliances, etc., which take effect after conception"[30] and later: "Any action on the part of either the husband and wife or of the State to limit family sizes by endangering or destroying human life must necessarily not only be an offence against the common good but also against the guaranteed personal rights of the human life in question."[31] Justice Walsh repeated this observation in *G. v. An Bord Uchtdla*,[32] a 1978 case concerning adoption, and similar views were expressed by Justice McCarthy in the *Norris* case mentioned earlier.[33]

As President of the High Court, I gave judgment in the case of *Attorney General v. Open Door Counselling Limited and Dublin Wellwoman Centre Limited*,[34] subsequently appealed to the Supreme Court. In the course of the opinion I summarized the legislative history of abortion in Ireland:

> The right to life of the unborn has always been recognised by Irish law.
>
> It has been recognised at common law; by statute law; as one of the unenumerated personal rights which the State guaranteed by its laws to respect, and, as far as practicable, to defend and vindicate and is specifically acknowledged by the provisions of the Eighth Amendment to the Constitution. Abortion is an interference with and a destruction of the right to life of an unborn infant in the mother's womb and as such is an offence contrary to Irish law. Originally, it was an offence contrary to the common law. The common law misdemeanour of abortion applied, however, only after the child had quickened in the womb.
>
> The statute, (43 Geo. III, c. 58) of 1803 enacted that it should be a felony punishable by death to administer poison with intent to procure the miscarriage of a woman quick with child and a felony punishable with imprisonment or transportation for fourteen years to administer poison with a like intent to a woman who was not proved to be quick with child.
>
> As stated in the third edition of Smith and Hogan: Criminal Law p. 275, the distinction between quick and non-quick women gave rise to complications and this distinction

28. 381 U.S. 479 (1965).
29. *Roe*, 410 U.S. at 153.
30. McGee v. Attorney General, 1974 I.R. 284, 305 (Ir. S.C. 1973) (Walsh, J.).
31. *Id.* at 312.
32. 1980 I.R. 32, 69 (Ir. S.C. 1978) (Walsh, J.).
33. *See* Norris v. Attorney General, 1984 I.R. 36, 97–98 (Ir. S.C. 1983) (McCarthy, J.).
34. 1988 I.R. 593 (Ir. S.C. 1988). The relators in the case, the Society for the Protection of Unborn Children Ireland Limited, will be referred to hereinafter as "SPUC."

disappeared in the re-enactment of the law by the Offences Against the Person Act, 1839, which established substantially the law in its present form.

The current statute applicable is the Offences Against the Person Act, 1861. Section 58 of this Act provides that:

> Every Woman being with Child, who, with Intent to procure her own Miscarriage, shall unlawfully administer to herself any Poison or other noxious Thing, or shall unlawfully use any Instrument or other Means whatsoever with the like Intent, and whosoever, with Intent to procure the Miscarriage of any Woman, whether she be or be not with Child, shall unlawfully administer to her or cause to be taken by her any Poison or other noxious Thing, or shall unlawfully use any Instrument or other Means whatsoever with the like Intent, shall be guilty of Felony, and being convicted thereof, shall be liable, at the Discretion of the Court, to be kept in Penal Servitude for Life . . . or to be imprisoned for any Term not exceeding Two Years.

Section 59 of the said Act provides that:

> Whosoever shall unlawfully supply or procure any Poison or other noxious Thing, or any Instrument or Thing whatsoever, knowing that the same is intended to be unlawfully used or employed with Intent to procure the Miscarriage of any Woman, whether she be or be not with Child, shall be guilty of a Misdemeanour, and being convicted thereof shall be liable . . . to imprisonment for any term not exceeding two years.

The Health (Family Planning) Act, 1979, reaffirmed the acceptance by the Oireachtas of Sections 58 and 59 of the Offences Against the Person Act, 1861, as setting forth the law of abortion in this jurisdiction. Section 10 of the said Act provides that:

> Nothing in this Act shall be construed as authorising—
> (a) the procuring of abortion,
> (b) the doing of any other thing the doing of which is prohibited by Section 58 or 59 of the Offences Against the Person Act, 1861 (which sections prohibit the administering of drugs or the use of instruments to procure abortion or the supplying of drugs or instruments to procure abortion) or
> (c) the sale, importation into the State, manufacture, advertising or display of abortifacients.

Sections 58 and 59 of the Offences Against the Person Act, 1861, protected and protect the fetus in the womb and having regard to the omission of the words "Quick with child" which were contained in the statute of 1803 hereinbefore referred to, that protection dates from conception. Consequently, the right to life of the fetus, the unborn, is afforded statutory protection from the date of its conception.

Prior to the enactment of the Eighth Amendment to the Constitution the right to life of the unborn had been referred to and acknowledged by Walsh J. in the course of his judgment in *G. v. An Bord Uchtdla* [1980] I.R. 32 when he stated at p. 69 of the report:

> Not only has the child born out of lawful wedlock the natural right to have its welfare and health guarded no less well than that of a child born in lawful wedlock, but *a fortiori* it has

> the right to life itself and the right to be guarded against all threats directed to its existence whether before or after birth. The child's natural rights spring primarily from the natural right of every individual to life, to be reared and educated, to liberty, to work, to rest and recreation, to the practice of religion, and to follow his or her conscience. The right to life necessarily implies the right to be born, the right to preserve and defend (and to have preserved and defended) that life, and the right to maintain that life at a proper human standard in matters of food, clothing and habitation. It lies not in the power of the parent who has the primary, natural rights and duties in respect of the child to exercise them in such a way as intentionally or by neglect to endanger the health or life of the child or to terminate its existence. The child's natural right to life and all that flows from that right are independent of any right of the parent as such.

He then repeated what he had said in *McGee v. Attorney General* [1974] I.R. 284 at p. 312 of the report:

> any action on the part of either the husband and wife or of the State to limit family sizes by endangering or destroying human life must necessarily not only be an offence against the common good but also against the guaranteed personal rights of the human life in question.

> These passages clearly acknowledge:
>
> (1) the right to life of the unborn;
> (2) that that right springs primarily from the natural right of every individual to life;
> (3) the right includes the right to have that right preserved and defended and to be guarded against all threats to its existence before or after birth;
> (4) that it lies not in the power of a parent to terminate its existence, and
> (5) any action on the part of any person endangering human life must necessarily not only be an offence against the common good but also against the guaranteed personal rights of the human life in question.[35]

Nonetheless, support grew for an amendment to the Constitution explicitly recognizing the right to life of unborn children; the intention was to copper-fasten the existing situation, removing any possibility of a future court using *Roe v. Wade*–style reasoning to "frustrate" the democratic will of the people. Ideally, debate should have been confined to the merits of amending the Constitution in this fashion, but a series of emotionally charged campaigns on both sides quickly polarized positions and led many people to assume that a vote against the amendment was tantamount to overt support for the introduction of abortion. It is a pity that public discourse was diverted in this way; it is possible that the paucity of debate concerning the usefulness of the amendment, its actual wording, and whether it was likely to achieve its object, contributed in no small measure to the problems which were to come. In any event, no party, of any persuasion, foresaw the manner in which the Supreme Court would interpret those words in *Attorney General v. X*.[36]

35. *Id.* at 597–99 (Hamilton, P.).
36. 1992 1 I.R. 1 (Ir. S.C. 1992).

The Eighth Amendment to the Constitution was approved by a large majority of the people on September 7, 1983.[37] It reads: "The State acknowledges the right to life of the unborn and, with due regard to the equal right to life of the mother, guarantees in its laws to respect, and, as far as practicable, by its laws to defend and vindicate that right."[38]

The nature and extent of this right was first considered by the Supreme Court in the *Open Door* case, mentioned earlier. The defendants in this case:

> consider[ed] it essential to the service which they wish[ed] to provide that they should be at liberty to inform such women who wish to have an abortion outside the jurisdiction of the Court of the name, address, telephone number and method of communication with a specified clinic which they had examined and were satisfied was one which maintained a high standard.[39]

But it was declared by the Supreme Court:

> that the activities of the defendants, their servants or agents in assisting pregnant women within the jurisdiction to travel abroad to obtain abortions by referral to a clinic; by the making of their travel arrangements, *or by informing them of the identity and location of and method of communication with a specified clinic or clinics are unlawful, having regard to the provisions of Article 40, s. 3, sub-s. 3 of the Constitution.*[40]

Having so declared, this Court then ordered that:

> the defendants and each of them, their servants or agents be perpetually restrained from assisting pregnant women within the jurisdiction to travel abroad to obtain abortions by referral to a clinic, by the making for them of travel arrangements, *or by informing them of the identify and location of and the method of communication* with a specified clinic or clinics or otherwise.[41]

In the course of his judgment in that case, Chief Justice Finlay, having considered the admitted facts, stated that:

> I am satisfied beyond doubt that having regard to the admitted facts the defendants were assisting in the ultimate destruction of the life of the unborn by abortion in that they were helping the pregnant woman who had decided upon that option to get in touch with a clinic in Great Britain which would provide the service of abortion. It seems to me to be an inescapable conclusion that if a woman was anxious to obtain an abortion and if she was able by availing of the counselling services of one or other of the defendants to obtain the precise location, address and telephone number of, and method of communication

37. *See* John M. Kelly, The Irish Constitution 792 (Gerard Hogan & Gerry Whyte, 3d ed. 1994).

38. Ir. Const. art. 40, § 3(3) (enacted under the Eighth Amendment of the Constitution Act (1983)).

39. Attorney General v. Open Door Counselling Ltd., 1988 I.R. 593, 621 (Ir. S.C. 1988) (Finlay, C.J.).

40. *Id.* at 627 (emphasis added).

41. *Id.* (emphasis added).

with, a clinic in Great Britain which provided that service, put in plain language, that was knowingly helping her to attain her objective.[42]

The following year, SPUC brought a case against a students' union, seeking an order restraining them from publishing a booklet containing information about abortion services in the United Kingdom. In the particular circumstances, including SPUC's role in the *Open Door* case, and considering the nature and objects of the Society, the Supreme Court (four to one) was prepared to allow that SPUC did have legal standing to pursue its case.[43] SPUC sought injunctions against three more students' unions in *Society for the Protection of Unborn Children (Ireland) Limited v. Grogan*.[44] The High Court judge referred the case to the European Court of Justice "for a preliminary ruling on certain aspects of EC law."[45] Seven months later, the Court of Justice ruled that "it was not contrary to EC law for Ireland to prohibit the [students' unions] from distributing [abortion] information," where the clinics themselves are not involved in the said distribution.[46] However, the Court also held that lawful termination of pregnancy is "a service within the meaning of Article 60 of the Treaty of Rome"; therefore, the way was clear under EC law for foreign abortion clinics themselves "to disseminate information in Ireland about the services provided."[47] The ruling of the Court of Justice provoked an extraordinary political response, in the form of Protocol Number Seventeen to the Treaty on European Union, signed at Maastricht on February 7, 1992.[48] It purported to immunize the Eighth Amendment to the Constitution from any effects EC law might have on its application in Ireland.[49] However, the Protocol was soon overshadowed by events, specifically, the events which culminated in the case of *Attorney General v. X*.[50]

The "X." of the title was a fourteen-year-old schoolgirl.[51] Following an alleged rape, she found herself pregnant.[52] The girl and her parents concluded that the best course to pursue was to seek an abortion in England.[53] The parents informed the *gardaí* [police] of this course and also raised with them the possibility of having scientific tests carried out on the fetus in order to assist in identifying the father.[54] The police sought the opinion of the Director for Public Prosecutions ("DPP") on whether such evidence would be

42. *Id.* at 624.

43. Society for the Protection of Unborn Children (Ireland) Ltd. v. Coogan, 1989 I.R. 734, 741–42 (Ir. S.C. 1989) (Finlay, C.J.).

44. 1989 I.R. 753 (Ir. S.C. 1989).

45. *See* Kelly, *supra* note 37, at 794.

46. *Id.* at 795.

47. *Id.*

48. *See id.* at 795–96.

49. *Id.* at 795 (quoting the language of Protocol No. 17 to the Treaty on European Union).

50. 1992 1 I.R. 1 (Ir. S.C. 1992).

51. *Id.* at 41 (Finlay, C.).

52. *Id.*

53. *Id.*

54. *Id.*

admissible.[55] The DPP in turn informed the Attorney General, who applied for and obtained an interim injunction restraining the girl from having or arranging an abortion in Ireland, and preventing her from leaving the jurisdiction for nine months.[56] At this point the child and her parents were already in England; they cancelled the arrangements for the abortion and returned home to contest the injunction.[57]

Previous judicial pronouncements in relation to abortion had taken place in the dry atmosphere of theoretical argument; the contrast with this case cannot be overemphasized. Judges and lawyers alike are aware of the maxim "hard cases make bad law," and here was a case that pulled the heartstrings from every angle: A vulnerable, underage girl; sexually violated and impregnated against her will; behaving in obedience to the authorities at all times—even to the extent of returning home and cancelling the abortion appointment. Public sympathy was heightened by the oral evidence of a senior psychologist that she was in a disturbed emotional state, and might commit suicide. Public anger was aroused when it became known that it was her very willingness to help the *gardaf* that led to the Attorney General bringing proceedings—if the girl and her parents had said nothing, she would not have been stopped. And this time it was not merely the provision of information that was in contention: The State was seeking to restrict her *liberty to leave the country.*

This was the atmosphere in which the Court had to consider its judgment. The nation waited, and speculated, yet few foresaw the line that the Court took. The pro-life movement had sought by the Eighth Amendment to remove abortion from the judicial purview, but of course, once part of the Constitution, the Amendment itself fell to be interpreted solely and exclusively by the judiciary. In a judgment that convulsed the nation, four of the five Supreme Court judges held that, contrary perhaps to popular impression, the Eighth Amendment required that termination of pregnancy be allowed, albeit only where it was "established as a matter of probability" that there was "a real and substantial risk to the life" of the mother if such termination were not affected.[58] That was controversial enough, but to that, the Court added that "real and substantial risk" was not limited to physical conditions that endangered the mother's life, but could also encompass a psychological imbalance leading to possible suicide.[59]

By virtue of the enactment of the Eighth Amendment to the Constitution, Article 40, section 3, subsection 3 of the Constitution provides that "[t]he State acknowledges the right to life of the unborn and, with due regard to the equal right to life of the mother, guarantees in its laws to respect, and, as far as practicable, by its laws to defend and vindicate that right."[60] The right to life of the unborn therein referred to is not created by law or by the Constitution; the aforementioned Article merely confirms or acknowledges its existence and gives it protection.

55. *Id.*
56. *See id.* at 41–42.
57. *Id.* at 42.
58. *See id.* at 53–54.
59. *See id. at* 55.
60. Ir. Const. art. 40, § 3(3).

In the course of his judgment in this case, Chief Justice Finlay stated:

> I accept the submission made on behalf of the Attorney General, that the doctrine of the harmonious interpretation of the Constitution involves in this case a consideration of constitutional rights and obligations of the mother of the unborn child and the interrelation of those rights and obligations with the rights and obligations of other people and, of course, with the right to life of the unborn child as well.
>
> Such a harmonious interpretation of the Constitution carried out in accordance with concepts of prudence, justice and charity, as they have been explained in the judgment of Walsh J. in *McGee v. The Attorney General* [1974] I.R. 284 leads me to the conclusion that in vindicating and defending as far as practicable the right of the unborn to life but at the same time giving due regard to the right of the mother to life, the Court must, amongst the matters to be so regarded, concern itself with the position of the mother within a family group, with persons on whom she is dependent. with, in other instances, persons who are dependent upon her and her interaction with other citizens and members of society in the areas in which her activities occur. Having regard to that conclusion, I am satisfied that the test proposed on behalf of the Attorney General that the life of the unborn could only be terminated if it were established that an inevitable or immediate risk to the life of the mother existed, for the avoidance of which a termination of the pregnancy was necessary, insufficiently vindicates the mother's right to life.
>
> I, therefore, conclude that the proper test to be applied is that if it is established as a matter of probability that there is a real and substantial risk to the life, as distinct from the health, of the mother, which can only be avoided by the termination of her pregnancy, such termination is permissible, having regard to the true interpretation of Article 40, s. 3, sub-s. 3 of the Constitution.[61]

This was sufficient to dispose of what the Court considered to be "the substantive issue" in the case. In an *obiter* consideration of the right to travel, Chief Justice Finlay, Justice Egan, and Justice Hederman (who alone dissented on the substantive issue) were of opinion that the right to travel was not absolute, and could not *simpliciter* take precedence over the right to life: This meant that injunctions restraining travel abroad to procure abortions could be justified.[62] Justice O'Flaherty and Justice McCarthy, on the other hand, rejected such restrictions on travel. The former thought it would interfere to an unwarranted degree with the individual's freedom of movement and with family authority;[63] the latter felt that the court had no jurisdiction to curtail the right to travel on the basis of an intention, even if that intention were to commit a crime in another jurisdiction.[64]

Justice McCarthy was particularly incensed at what he perceived as a consistent failure to legislate in the area of abortion. He let his dissatisfaction be known in his judgment, saying:

61. *X.*, 1992 1 I.R. at 53–54 (Finlay, C.J.).
62. *See id.* at 57–58; *id.* at 62 (Hederman, J.); *id.* at 92–93 (Egan, J.).
63. *Id.* at 87–88 (O'Flaherty, J.).
64. *Id.* at 84–85 (McCarthy, J.).

In the context of the eight years that have passed since the Amendment was adopted . . . the failure by the legislature to enact the appropriate legislation is no longer just unfortunate; it is inexcusable. What are pregnant women to do? What are the parents of a pregnant girl under age to do? What are the medical profession to do? They have no guidelines save what may be gleaned from the judgments in this case. What additional considerations are there? Is the victim of rape, statutory or otherwise, or the victim of incest, finding herself pregnant, to be assessed in a manner different from others? The Amendment, born of public disquiet, historically divisive of our people, guaranteeing in its laws to respect and by its laws to defend the right to life of the unborn, remains bare of legislative direction.[65]

As a result of the cumulative effect of these decisions, the position was that:

(1) "if it is established as a matter of probability that there is a real and substantial risk to the life, as distinct from the health, of the mother, which can only be avoided by the termination of her pregnancy, such termination is permissible;"[66]

(2) the dissemination of information with regard to abortion services available outside the State was unlawful; and

(3) travel abroad for the purpose of obtaining an abortion was unlawful and could be restrained.

In an effort to deal with these issues, three proposed amendments to the Constitution were submitted to the people on November 25, 1992.[67] Two of these amendments were passed; these dealt with the freedom to travel and information relating to services lawfully available.[68] The one which was not passed was in the following terms:

It shall be unlawful to terminate the life of an unborn unless such termination is necessary to save the life, as distinct from the health, of the mother where there is an illness or disorder of the mother giving rise to a real and substantial risk to her life. not being a risk of self-destruction.[69]

The risk of self-destruction had been the ground upon which the Supreme Court in the X case had held the termination of pregnancy to be permissible.

Consequently, the rights as laid down by the Supreme Court in this case [*Attorney General v. X.*] prevail as no legislation dealing with the situation has been enacted by our Legislature.

The Legislature did, however, introduce legislation dealing with the regulation of information relating to services outside the State for the termination of pregnancies, and the provisions of this legislation were referred by the President to the Supreme Court for

65. *Id.* at 82.

66. *Id.* at 53–54 (Finlay, C.J.).

67. *See* Kelly, *supra* note 37, at 807.

68. *Id.*

69. Gerard Hogan, *Law, Liberty and the Abortion Controversy*, *in* LAW AND LIBERTY IN IRELAND 113, 113 (Anthony Whelan ed. 1993) (providing the text of proposed Twelfth Amendment of the Constitution Bill, defeated by the electorate on 25 November 1992).

a determination by it as to whether it or any provision thereof was invalid having regard to the provisions of the Constitution, and the Supreme Court held that it was not.[70]

By the time the Oireachtas had passed the bill regulating information on foreign abortion services, a new case[71] (and with it a new moral dilemma) was seizing the headlines. Once again, the courts were placed in a cauldron of emotion and passionate public debate, and asked to rule on the outer limits of the right to life, and the State's duty to preserve life. The facts were simple: A twenty-two-year-old woman had suffered three massive heart attacks during the course of a minor operation for which she had been given a general anesthetic.[72] From that time, she had been in a near-persistent vegetative state ("PVS"), kept alive by artificial nutrition and hydration.[73] In 1995, the woman was forty-five years old. She had remained in the same state, on life support, for twenty-three years. Her mother and brothers took the view that she should be allowed to die, by the removal of the artificial feeding mechanisms.[74] As the woman was a ward of court, however, it was necessary to apply to the High Court for a direction to this effect.[75] There, it was found as fact that, while the ward was not in a permanent vegetative state, "she was very nearly so and such cognitive capacity as she possessed was extremely minimal."[76] The High Court judge elaborated as follows:

> A fully PVS person cannot feel pain and has no capacity for pleasure or displeasure even though they may groan or grimace or cry, especially in response to painful stimuli, nor have they any realization whatever of their tragic situation. This is probably the ward's state but if such minimal cognition as she has includes an inkling of her catastrophic condition, then I am satisfied that that would be a terrible torment to her and her situation would be worse than if she were fully PVS. There is no prospect whatsoever of any improvement in the condition of the ward.[77]

On May 5, 1995, Justice Lynch granted the order sought by the ward's mother.[78] His decision was appealed by the Attorney General, the General Solicitor for Minors and Wards of Court who had been appointed her guardian *ad litem*, and the institution which had been caring for her.[79]

Leaving aside the question of court jurisdiction, the central issue that faced myself and the other judges of the Supreme Court was this: In speaking of the "right to life," what do

70. *See In re* Article 26 & *In re* Regulation of Information "Services Outside the State for Termination of Pregnancies" Bill 1995, 1995 2 I.RLM. 81 (Ir. S.C. 1995).

71. *In re* Ward of Court, 1995 2 I.L.RM. 401 (Ir. S.C. 1995).

72. *Id.* (Hamilton, C.J.).

73. *Id.* at 402.

74. *Id.*

75. *Id.*

76. *Id.*

77. *Id.* at 412–13 (citing High Court opinion of Justice Lynch).

78. *Id.* at 414 (Hamilton, C.J.).

79. *Id.* at 413–14.

we mean? What constitutes "life" in this context? It seemed clear to me then, as it does now, that:

> As the process of dying is part, and an ultimate inevitable consequence, of life, the right to life necessarily implies the right to have nature take its course and to die a natural death and, unless the individual concerned so wishes, not to have life artificially maintained by the provision of nourishment by abnormal artificial means, which have no curative effect and which are intended merely to prolong life.[80]

This right as so defined does not include the right to have life terminated or death accelerated and is confined to the natural process of dying. No person has the right to terminate or have terminated his or her life or to accelerate or have accelerated his or her death.

Euthanasia is not an acceptable concept in Irish constitutional jurisprudence. There is a difference between positive acts designed to end life, and the withdrawal of invasive medical treatment in order to allow nature to take its course. The right of a competent person to refuse medical treatment is not in doubt and it was the opinion of a majority of the Supreme Court that the ward had a similar right, excepting that the decision to refuse or not fell to the Court, exercising its discretion on her behalf, as she could not do so herself. It follows naturally that in so doing, the Court had paramount regard to the best interests of the ward herself. In this case, I and three other judges were of the opinion that her best interest lay in being allowed to die[81]—as the High Court judge had ordered.

Once again, this was a case which elicited considerable controversy. Identifying the proper legal and ethical boundaries of personal rights is never easy, particularly when matters of life and death are in issue. Nevertheless, such judgments must be made; lines have to be drawn. And although division may result, it is essential to the health of a pluralist society with a concern for human rights that such matters are raised, and brought to public attention. For perhaps the first time in Ireland, the *Ward of Court* case forced people into a conscious consideration of the new ethical problems being thrown up by our exponentially increasing technological ability. These problems will not go away, anymore than the technology which brought them into being will be "uninvented." As long ago as 1963, Martin Luther King warned western humanity: "The means by which we live have outdistanced the ends for which we live. Our scientific power has outrun our spiritual power."[82]

In considering these and other problems relating to life, the quality of life, and the role of the State in protecting it, the basic philosophical tools are already to hand: It is for the Court, and indeed for every citizen, to mould their understanding of fundamental human rights concepts in order to apply them to new situations. I have no doubt but that it is for the legislative organ of the State to decide the broader issues, including the redefinition of

80. *Id.* at 426.
81. *Id.* at 429–30; *id.* at 435 (O'Flaherty, J.); *id.* at 443 (Blayney, J.); *id.* at 465–66 (Denham, J.).
82. Martin Luther King, Strength to Love 74 (First Fortress Press 1981) (1963).

death. In the absence of such legislation, it is a matter for the courts to decide, when the issue is raised in proceedings before them: The issue cannot be avoided or ducked.

> I would echo the words of William Binchy, Professor of Law at Trinity College, Dublin, in which he challenges us not to bury our heads in the sand, but rather to face the moral and legal storms ahead, saying: I believe that in contemporary Ireland this is precisely the time when these questions should be examined afresh. We live in an exciting period when all the old orthodoxies have come under close scrutiny and debate. Without revitalisation and fresh endorsement, there would be a real danger that a society's value system might in time harden into a desiccated orthodoxy and come to be regarded merely as an external imposition of restrictive rules. The process of open debate and reconsideration creates an opportunity for new insights as well as a revitalised commitment to those values whose true worth may have become hidden from view.[83]

83. William Binchy, *Pluralism, Liberty and the Right to Life*, *in* Law and Liberty in Ireland 132, 132–33 (Anthony Whelan ed., 1993).

Lawyering for a New Age

Chief Judge Judith S. Kaye

Judge Judith Kaye delivered the twenty-fifth Sonnett lecture, entitled *Lawyering for a New Age*, on April 8, 1998.[1] The first woman to be appointed to the New York State Court of Appeals,[2] Judge Kaye served as Chief Judge for over twenty years, writing several prominent decisions and leading a variety of notable reforms to the New York state court system. Born in Monticello, New York, in 1938, Judge Kaye graduated from Barnard College in 1958 and was one of only ten women to graduate from New York University School of Law in 1962.[3] Judge Kaye spent several years at the law firm of Olwine, Connelly, Chase, O'Donnell & Weyher, where she was named the firm's first female partner in 1975.[4]

In 1983, then–New York governor Mario Cuomo nominated Judge Kaye to sit for New York's highest court, the New York State Court of Appeals.[5] As an Associate Judge, Kaye wrote several opinions in prominent criminal cases, including *People v. Smith*[6] and *Associated Press v. Bell*,[7] and established a reputation for upholding individual rights in cases like *Immuno AG v. J. Moor-Jankowski*[8] and via a concurring opinion in *People v. Scott*.[9]

In 1993, Judge Kaye was nominated and confirmed as Chief Judge of the New York State Court of Appeals, the first woman to ever hold the position.[10] As Chief Judge, she authored opinions in significant capital punishment cases such as *Hynes v. Tomei*[11] and *People v. Mateo*,[12] and further exhibited her commitment to individual rights in cases like *Kass v. Kass*.[13]

Introduction written by Michael B. Singer, J.D., Class of 2014, Fordham University School of Law.

1. Judith S. Kaye, *Lawyering for a New Age*, 67 Fordham L. Rev. 1 (1998). She acknowledges her counsel, Susan Knipps, for her superb assistance in preparing this article.

2. Steven C. Krane, *Judith Smith Kaye*, New York Unified Court System, http://www.nycourts.gov/history/legal-history-new-york/luminaries-court-appeals/kaye-judith.html.

3. *Id.*

4. *Id.*

5. *Id.*

6. 70 N.Y.2d 32, 468 N.E.2d 879, 470 N.Y.S.2d 706 (1984).

7. 70 N.Y.2d 32, 510 N.E.2d 313, 517 N.Y.S.2d 444 (1987).

8. 77 N.Y.2d 235, 567 N.E.2d 1270, 566 N.Y.S.2d 906 (1991).

9. 79 N.Y.2d 474, 593 N.E.2d 1328, 583 N.Y.S.2d 920 (1992).

10. Krane, *supra* note 2.

11. 92 N.Y.2d 613, 706 N.E.2d 1201, 684 N.Y.S.2d 177 (1998) (invalidating a death penalty statute).

12. 2 N.Y.3d 383, 811 N.E.2d 1053, 779 N.Y.S.2d 399 (2004) (reversing death penalty imposed on defendant due to circumstances in the case, while upholding jury verdict of murder in the first degree).

13. 91 N.Y.2d 554, 696 N.E.2d 174, 673 N.Y.S.2d 350 (1998).

Perhaps most notably, Judge Kaye wrote a vigorous dissent in *Hernandez v. Robles*,[14] in which a four-judge plurality rejected the right of same-sex couples to marry.[15] Judge Kaye, in a dissenting opinion that was far ahead of its time, argued that marriage is a fundamental right that should be available to same-sex couples, and that it is a court's duty to "safeguard individual liberties" and "protect constitutional rights."[16] In a prediction that has recently been validated, Judge Kaye concluded her opinion by writing, "I am confident that future generations will look back on today's decision as an unfortunate misstep."[17]

Judge Kaye was also an advocate for judicial reform, leading several important changes to the New York court system. Her tenure as Chief Judge saw the creation of the court's commercial division, the expansion of alternative forms of punishment focused on treatment and education, a revamped jury system, the restoration and renovation of courthouse facilities, and the founding of the New York State Judicial Institute.[18] Following a long and distinguished judicial career, Judge Kaye retired from the bench in 2008 and returned to private practice.[19]

Judge Kaye's Sonnett lecture, *Lawyering for a New Age*, focused on many of those reforms that she championed during her tenure as chief judge and further emphasized a renewed focus on "product" over "process" in legal representation.[20] One of the major initiatives Judge Kaye highlighted was the establishment and growth of drug treatment courts, an alternative form of adjudication focused on treatment rather than punishment.[21] In remarking on the early success of the initiative, Judge Kaye noted that hopes were high that the state would create 12 such courts.[22] As of September 25, 2013, New York State had 148.[23] Judge Kaye also discussed a need for jury reform,[24] as well as a shift in focus from lawyering as an adversarial system to one that instead produces the "right" results, whether that be from alternative dispute resolution methods (another major Judge Kaye reform),[25] a restructuring of case management and trial scheduling, or traditional forms of litigation.[26] This challenge to rethink the way the judicial system operates and the lawyer's role is one that continues to resonate within New York State, informing the education of young lawyers and the development of the legal profession.[27]

14. 7 N.Y. 3d 338, 855 N.E.2d 1, 794 N.Y.S. 2d 579 (N.Y. 2006).
15. *Id.* at 5 (plurality opinion).
16. *Id.* at 34 (Kaye, C.J., dissenting).
17. *Id.* Judge Kaye's prediction came true in United States v. Windsor, 570 U.S. 12 (2013).
18. Krane, *supra* note 2.
19. *Id.*
20. *See generally* Kaye, *supra* note 1.
21. *See id.* at 4–5.
22. *Id.* at 5.
23. *Drug Treatment Courts*, New York State Unified Court System, http://www.nycourts.gov/courts/problem_solving/drugcourts/index.shtml.
24. Kaye, *supra* note 1, at 6.
25. *Id.*
26. *See id.* at 7–11.
27. *See, e.g.*, Court Connected Alternative Dispute Resolution in New York State (2013); Unified Court Rules for New York State Trial Courts, Rule 202.70(G).

Judith Kaye died on January 7, 2016, at her home in Manhattan, from lung cancer. She had been diagnosed with the disease about five years before her death. She was seventy-seven years old.

1998 Sonnett Lecture

First and foremost, I thank you for the privilege of participating in this distinguished lecture series. The Sonnett lecture, for me, signals a provocative talk centering on lawyer professionalism, advocacy, and other issues touching on the great trust we have to deliver justice to the citizens of this state and nation. It is a formidable challenge to measure up to my predecessors at this podium.

While I have attended many of the Sonnett lectures, one in particular stands out for reasons only indirectly related to lawyer professionalism and the delivery of justice. It was the year my husband and I attended the lecture given by then-Chief Judge Sol Wachtler. By coincidence, that same evening we had tickets for a performance of Wagner's *Valkyrie* at the Metropolitan Opera, and we had neglected in advance to pass them on—or put more accurately, pass them off—to friends. While we were longtime, devoted opera-goers, even we had our limits. In fact, it was our practice to pass off *all* Wagner tickets. We just had neglected to do so that evening.

After Judge Wachtler's lecture, we found ourselves across the street from the Met, our tickets still in hand. So we wandered over to the opera house—just in time for Act Three, which proved to be one of the most moving, most dramatic, most spectacular acts in all of opera. We have been avid Wagnerians ever since. So we thank the Fordham Law School for that life-altering experience. The lecture was pretty good too.

That experience happens also to be highly relevant to my subject tonight—and not simply because of the proximity of the law school to the opera house. *Valkyrie* is the second of the four operas that make up Wagner's *Ring* cycle—and the *Ring* is above all a "Hymn to the Law."[1] The *Ring* glorifies the Rule of Law, in particular the importance of honoring contract obligations. This was amply demonstrated that fateful night when I saw Wotan banish his beloved daughter, Brunnhilde, from the Land of the Gods because she failed to keep a promise to him.

Scrupulous enforcement of the law is, of course, important, but I have often reflected on how things might have turned out had Wotan been a bit more attentive to other influences and just a little more open to change. After watching his precious Valhalla—the home of the gods, where all dead heroes were brought—go up in flames at the end of the *Ring*,

1. Charles Fletcher-Cooke, *Counsel's Opinion: The Ring and the Law*, 12 About the House 1 (1965), *reprinted in* Penetrating Wagner's Ring: An Anthology 135, 135 (John Louis DiGaetani ed., 1978).

I have speculated on what intermediate steps might have prevented that catastrophe. That, of course, brings me right to tonight's subject: change, and how we in the law must adjust to it.

Lawyering in a new age means, above all, lawyering in a time of innovation and flux. Tonight, I just want to sketch out some of the ways we in the courts are responding to emerging realities and talk as well about how these changes may affect the practicing bar.

Lawyers, of course, are completely comfortable with the notion that the substantive law must change and adapt to meet changing social conditions. But they are distinctly less comfortable with the idea that the structures of the justice system may also need to evolve to meet current demands. I suppose this should not be too surprising: my work uniform has not changed for centuries, and I do my job in a building smack out of ancient Athens. You do not need a degree in semiotics to conclude that ours is a profession that values formal stability and continuity.

But if we hope to be able to deliver swift and effective justice in the years ahead, the way we run our courts simply has to change, ionic columns notwithstanding. Just consider a few of the challenges facing our court system today.

First, there is the sheer volume of cases. Our relentlessly kinetic culture spins off myriad disputes—and increasingly these are brought to the courts for resolution. Last year, the New York State courts received close to four million new filings—more than ten times the number of cases that the federal district courts received nationwide.[2]

This press of filings compels us to expedite and innovate. Almost thirty years ago, Chief Justice Burger said that we could not afford to continue using cracker-barrel corner grocer methods to operate the courts in a supermarket age.[3] Today, even supermarket methods may be inadequate given the advent of online shopping. We must use every tool available to keep up with these enormous demands. We have finally gotten rid of all the rotary telephones in New York City courthouses—now it is on to interactive kiosks, wired benches, and video conferencing.

Huge numbers are only part of the story. The changed substance of today's cases is also a challenge. New technologies and new social mores create legal questions that no one even dreamed of when I went to law school. Over the past few years, the Court of Appeals has, for example, grappled with the issue of who should make decisions about prolonging or ending life for the terminally ill,[4] and more recently, the issue of determining the fate of frozen pre-embryos created by a couple now divorced.[5] We have recently considered

2. Data provided by the New York State Office of Court Administration and the Statistics Division of the Administrative Office of the United States Courts.

3. *See* Paul B. Wice, *Court Reform and Judicial Leadership: A Theoretical Discussion*, 17 JUST. SYS. J. 309, 309 (1995).

4. *See* Grace Plaza v. Elbaum, 82 N.Y.2d 10, 623 N.E.2d 513, 603 N.Y.S.2d 386 (1993); *In re* Westchester County Med. Ctr., 72 N.Y.2d 517, 531 N.E.2d 607, 534 N.Y.S.2d 886 (1988).

5. *See* Kass v. Kass, 91 N.Y.2d 554, 696 N.E.2d 174, 673 N.Y.S.2d 350 (1998).

whether faxes satisfy the Statute of Frauds,[6] whether wire funds that circle the globe twenty-four hours a day can be seized in New York,[7] and when claims accrue for that quintessentially postmodern trauma, computer keyboard-caused repetitive stress injury.[8]

Even when the legal issues are simple, the social realities underlying our cases can be extremely complex. As community institutions increasingly fail to influence individual behavior, and other branches of government gridlock and stall, more and more of society's most difficult problems are being outsourced to the courts. Drug addiction, homelessness, family violence—these are the issues that drive the dockets of our frontline urban trial courts. Adjudicating a parent neglectful due to drug abuse is easy. Crafting a disposition that will do something meaningful about it is not as easy.

As if the numbers and substance of today's cases were not enough, a final new challenge is the public's attitude toward the courts. Courts today face a public that, by and large, is cynical and distrustful of all government, including the judicial system. Courts can no longer just assume they enjoy the public's trust and respect. We have to achieve it in a new-fashioned way: we have to earn it.

All of these factors have led the New York State court system to undertake an ongoing program of court reform to make sure that we do what we do efficiently and, where appropriate, that we do it differently. Efficiency is a key value—but it is not the only value. When an ocean liner starts taking on water, you can devote a lot of your resources to efficient bailing operations. You might also, however, want to look around for where the leak is, or keep a closer watch for icebergs in the first place. Yes, we want to process cases faster—but we also want to process them better. A well-run court system does not just count its cases. It makes sure every case counts.

Slowly but surely, we are changing the way we deliver justice in this State. If I had to describe a methodology for our reforms, it would be this: we are looking at the substantive outcomes that our procedures actually achieve, and we are looking at our operations from the perspective of the public we are trying to serve. Let me give you an example of each approach in action.

I have mentioned drug abuse as an issue confounding the State courts, and its impact on our criminal justice system cannot be overemphasized. In recent years, drug offenses have consistently accounted for over forty percent of all felony indictments in New York State.[9] The effect goes far beyond these tens of thousands of cases. For many offenders, substance abuse fuels a pattern of criminal recidivism that causes them to cycle and recycle through the criminal justice system. They go into jail as substance abusers and thirty,

6. *See* Parma Tile Mosaic & Marble Co. v. Estate of Short, 87 N.Y.2d 524, 663 N.E.2d 633, 640 N.Y.S.2d 477 (1996).

7. *See In re* Liquidation of New York Agency & Other Assets of Bank of Credit and Commerce Int'l, S.A., 90 N.Y.2d 410, 683 N.E.2d 756, 660 N.Y.S.2d 850 (1997).

8. *See* Blanco v. AT&T, 90 N.Y.2d 757, 689 N.E.2d 506, 666 N.Y.S.2d 536 (1997).

9. Jason Scott, New York State Division of Criminal Justice Services, New York State Crime and Justice Trends 1992–1996 (1996).

sixty, or ninety days later they come out of jail as substance abusers, and not surprisingly are often soon re-arrested.

We can—and we do—work on processing these cases as efficiently as possible. But we also need to take a step back and ask, is there a better way to do this? Where is the leak here?

Once you start asking these kinds of questions, you start thinking about developing a court structure that will break, not merely interrupt, this destructive cycle of drugs-crime-jail, drugs-crime-jail. One model that we have been working on—like many jurisdictions around the country—is the drug treatment court.

Treatment courts look like ordinary criminal courts. When you first enter the Treatment Court in Brooklyn Supreme Court, for example, you will see a judge in a robe sitting at an elevated bench and counsel at their tables and so on. But if you look again, you will see that something fundamentally different is going on here—namely, a definite shift away from the traditional adversary model toward a team-based, problem-solving approach.

The basic idea behind these new tribunals is to use the coercive power of the court to get nonviolent offenders off drugs and out of the criminal justice system's revolving door. You do not see a lot of litigating in this court—in fact almost all of the defendants plead guilty. The focus in the treatment court is not on adjudicating past facts, it is on changing future behavior. The main tool is strict judicial supervision of the defendants' progress in drug treatment.[10]

That means the judges in these courts have a new role. No longer remote umpires of legal disputes, drug treatment court judges play an active role in the treatment process: monitoring compliance, rewarding progress, and sanctioning infractions.[11]

The lawyers also have new roles. The prosecution and defense are not sparring champions, they are members of a team with a common goal: getting the defendant off drugs.[12]

10. For a detailed description of the Drug Treatment Court operating in Brooklyn Supreme Court, see New York State Unified Court System, Brooklyn Treatment Court Report (1998); Jennifer Gonnerman, *Justice for Junkies*, VILLAGE VOICE (New York), June 3, 1997, at 50.

11. Judge Jo Ann Ferdinand, Presiding Judge of the Brooklyn Treatment Court, explained that: "The challenge of working in the Treatment Court is to figure out a role for the judge in the treatment process. It is very important that I be viewed as a judge—not a counselor, not a probation officer, not a friend. Defendants have to understand that if they fail to fulfill the treatment mandate, it will be a judge that responds. It is equally significant that their success is rewarded by a judge; it can be extraordinarily meaningful when a judge stands up and applauds." *Perspectives from the Bench*, TREATMENT: NEWS FROM THE BROOKLYN TREATMENT COURT (Fund for the City of New York), Winter 1998, at 2.

12. For a discussion of the teamwork approach in the Buffalo Drug Treatment Court, see JANE NADY SIGMON ET AL., AMERICAN PROSECUTORS RESEARCH INSTITUTE, ADJUDICATION PARTNERSHIPS: A GUIDE TO SUCCESSFUL COOPERATION 78–80 (1997). *See also* Sam Torres & Elizabeth Piper Deschenes, *Changing the Systenm and Making It Work: The Process of Implementing Drug Courts in Los Angeles County*, 19 JUST. SYS. I. 267,285 (1997) (finding that "[a]s intended, drug courts in Los Angeles County are operating in a non-adversarial manner with courtroom members, e.g., judge, district attorney, public defender, and treatment provider, functioning as a team").

When this goal is attained, everyone wins. Defendants win dismissal of their charges—not to mention improvement of their lives—and the public wins safer streets and reduced recidivism.

Indeed, the preliminary results are promising. Unlike many participants in voluntary treatment programs, defendants in our drug treatment courts overwhelmingly remain in treatment. While long-term impacts are still being studied, early figures show that recidivism rates in Treatment Courts are significantly lower than those in traditional courts.[13]

Having attended several drug court graduation ceremonies, I can tell you they are extremely moving events. Each graduate's personal achievement is recognized by applause and sometimes a few tears from family and court staff. "I didn't just get arrested," one recent graduate observed, "I got saved."

Looking at actual outcomes has led us to move away from a purely process-driven model of criminal adjudication to a problem-solving model. We now have eight such courts up and running across the State,[14] and hope soon to have twelve. We are piloting the same model in the Family Courts of New York and Suffolk Counties, where the courts' coercive power is not incarceration but removal of children from parents whose substance abuse causes neglect.[15]

At this point, drug courts may only be one small step for court operations, but they are a giant leap for our conception of how we can deliver effective justice.

Looking at court operations from the perspective of the public we serve can also cause small revolutions. My second example is a good illustration of this: jury reform. We all know the rhetoric about our jury system—the bulwark of our democracy, protector of our liberties—but when we looked at it from the citizen's perspective, we noticed that jury duty was about as cherished as a tax audit or a root canal. And rightly so. The system worked well for lawyers and judges—but for the jurors? We summoned the same people over and over again, made them wait in appalling assembly rooms, subjected them to unsupervised *voir dire* on the civil side and mandatory sequestration on the criminal side, never told them what was going on, never asked them what they thought about it, and paid them fifteen dollars a day for their time and trouble. This is how we treated the protectors of our liberty. This is how we dealt with one half million members of the public on whose trust and respect the "least dangerous branch" depends.

Obviously, when you start looking at the system from the public's perspective, a few things needed to change—like our entire summoning system, exemptions from service, jury facilities, and more than a few attitudes on the part of the bench and the bar. Change

13. *See* Drug Court Clearinghouse and Technical Assistance Project, Summary Assessment of the Drug Court Experience 2 (1997).

14. *See* Judith S. Kaye, *Changing Courts in Changing Times*, N.Y. L.J., Jan. 27, 1998, at S1 (describing New York's eight Drug Treatment Courts).

15. The Family Treatment Courts are discussed in my article *Changing Courts in Changing Tunes. The Need for a Fresh Look at How Courts Are Run*, 48 Hastings L.J. 851, 859–62 (1997), *available at* http://www.law.nyu.edu/sites/default/files/upload_documents/Changing%20Courts%20in%20Changing%20Times.pdf (last visited March 8, 2017).

of this magnitude—I am really talking about a cultural revolution—is not accomplished by just amending a few rules. It takes education and collaboration and years of effort. We have accomplished a lot in the four years that we have been at it.[16] But we have much, much more to do. Our goal is to build a system that lives up to the glorious rhetoric used to describe it.

Drug treatment courts and jury reform are two examples of what the New York State courts are doing to provide justice that is responsive to today's realities and public expectations. I could give you many others: domestic violence parts, the Commercial Division of the State Supreme Court, judicial case management initiatives, and our Midtown Community Court.

As lawyers in a new age, you can expect further court initiatives of this nature. You can, if you wish, wait until you bump into one to begin to think about the practice of law in an age of change and innovation. I want to encourage you, however, to take a more proactive approach. I want to challenge you to take a step back and think now about what models of lawyering make sense for this new era.

Changes in the courts themselves will not be the only thing affecting the practice of law in the future. With numbers of lawyers now nearing the one million mark,[17] the size and structure of the American bar has changed dramatically in recent years.[18] Some megafirms are growing;[19] other firms have imploded.[20] In-house departments are expanding.[21]

16. Major achievements to date include elimination of all statutory exemptions from jury service, reduction of average terms of service by more than fifty percent, improved juror facilities, increased juror compensation, elimination of mandatory sequestration in all but the most serious criminal trials, a "juror hotline," and juror exit questionnaires. *See* New York State Unified Court System, Jury Reform in New York State: A Second Progress Report on a Continuing Initiative (1998), *available at* http://ucs.ljx.com/jury2.htm (visited Aug. 3, 1998).

17. *See* Scott Carlson, *Attorneys Who Specialize in Patents, Corporate Deal-Making In Big Demand: Law Firms Nationwide Are Scrambling to Find Experienced Lawyers*, Milwaukee J. & Sentinel, Aug. 26, 1998, at 12 (reporting that the United States has an estimated 722,000 practicing lawyers, which is up ten percent from four years ago).

18. *See* Edward Frost & Margret Cronin Fisk, *The Profession After 15 Years*, NAT'L L.J., Aug. 3, 1993, at 1 (stating that the past fifteen years "have seen an astonishing evolution in the legal profession"); James Podgers, *Model Rules Get the Once-Over*, A.B.A.J., Dec. 1997, at 90, 90 (observing that "the landscape of legal practice has continued to change drastically" in the previous fifteen years).

19. *See* Frost & Fisk, *supra* note 18, at 1 (observing the "explosion in the size and scope of many big firms"); Martha Neil, *Biggest Firms Growing Fastest, Survey Shows*, CHICAGO DAILY L. BULL., Aug. 5, 1998, at 1 (stating that the "overall growth rate for large- and medium sized United States law firms doubled last year").

20. *See, e.g.*, *'94 Ends on Downbeat Note for Some in the Law*, N.Y. L.J., Jan. 3, 1995, at 1 (reporting that the "demise of major law firms continue[s] as such stalwarts as Shea & Gould, Lord Day & Lord, Barrett Smith and Bower & Gardener went out of business"); David Segal, *From Allies to Adversaries: The Fall of Nussbaum & Wald*, WASH. POST, Aug. 25, 1997, at F7 (discussing the aftermath of the implosion of Nussbaum & Wald).

21. *See* James S. Kakalik et al., *Discover, Management. Further Analysis of tile Civil Justice Reform Act Evaluation Data*, 39 B.C. L. REV. 613, 630–31 (1998) (reporting that "many large corporations have begun restructuring their relationships with legal service providers" and "have brought more

Competition is fierce as corporate clients zero in on the bottom line.[22] Government funds for legal services have been severely restricted.[23] All of this activity is taking place against a backdrop of increased public skepticism—warranted or not—about the value and integrity of our noble profession.

These changes, I believe, undercut that extreme model of lawyering—so ingrained in popular culture and the public's mind—that involves knee-jerk reliance on highly adversarial tactics to advance every client's cause. Put another way, Rambo litigators cannot all count on making it to Valhalla any more. This is not to say that there is still not a place for zealous advocacy—heart thumping, mind stretching, weekend ruining client representation. But a mindset that all disputes must be litigated and all litigation is war may prove to be about as useful as a 286 computer in the years ahead.

This is not because everyone is supposed to be nice in the new millennium. Rather, clients are now realizing that arms manufacturers and lawyers are probably the only ones who gain by policies of mutually assured destruction. It is very expensive to scorch the earth. As the increasingly competitive global economy grows, the market for this style of lawyering shrinks.[24]

Even if some clients still crave rampant adversarialism, courts are becoming less willing to tolerate it. Faced with enormous caseloads on the one hand and a public clamoring for swift justice on the other, more and more judges are becoming actively involved in case management issues—setting limits and time frames for discovery and motion practice. Differentiated case management—DCM, to the initiated—is one approach we are trying in the New York courts to keep cases on a sensible track for resolution in a timely manner.[25]

Furthermore, there is a final reason to think twice about the Rambo model: personal dissatisfaction within the legal profession. More and more we read reports of discontent and defection, lawyers from the newest to the most experienced are unhappy, unfulfilled, and looking to greener pastures outside the law.[26] For some, extreme adversarialism is one

---

of their legal work in-house in recent years"); Podgers, *supra* note 18, at 90 (observing the "proliferation of in-house counsel").

22. *See* Roger J. Dennis, Commentary, *The Epistemology of Corporate-Securities Lawyering: Beliefs, Biases and Organizational Behavior*, 63 Brook. L. Rev. 677, 682–83 (1997) (reporting a significant escalation of economic competition among lawyers).

23. *See generally* Gary Spencer, *Nets, State Bar Head Pinpoints Issues*, N.Y. L.J., June 24, 1998, at 1 (stating that government funding for legal services is under attack at the state capitol).

24. *See, e.g.*, *What Inhouse Attorneys Are Doing to Hold Down Costs*, Metropolitan Corp. Couns. (Mountainside, NJ), Dec. 1997, at 24 (discussing ADR as a means of cutting costs); *If You're Not Budgeting, You're Out: Corporate Clients Beef About Law Firm Billing*, Ill. Legal Times, Apr. 1996, at 1 (discussing strategies to contain litigation costs).

25. *See generally* Judith S. Kaye, *Changing Courts in Changing Time*, *supra* note 15, 48 Hastings L.J. at 853 (mentioning differentiated case management as a better way to process cases); Carl Tobias, *Nearing the End of Federal Civil Justice Reform in Montana*, 59 Mont. L. Rev. 95, 97 (1998) (noting that the Federal Judicial Center has recognized the benefits of differentiated case management).

26. *See, e.g.*, Mary Ann Glendon, A Nation Under Lawyers: How the Crisis in the Legal Profession Is Transforming American Society 85 (1994) (reporting that a recent poll of New

of the roots of their unhappiness.[27] That makes sense: how much joy can a steady diet of acrimony bring? Rethinking Rambo is therefore good for clients, good for courts, and ultimately, good for ourselves.

But what does that leave for New Age Lawyers to do? Plenty. Some of it may well be even more interesting than old age tasks like examining warehouses of documents. The forces of change are compelling lawyers, like courts, to look beyond process to the product. What is the substance of what is achieved? What value does it add? Success for New Age Lawyers cannot be measured by inches of papers filed. It is measured by the concrete difference the lawyering makes for the client.

John Feinblatt, Director of the Center for Court Innovation and New Age Lawyer extraordinaire, tells a story that illustrates this different outlook. As he tells it:

> When I was a twenty-eight-year-old lawyer fresh out of law school, I was assigned a case involving a man who was accused of brandishing a knife. Willie lived on the Bowery in New York City, was an alcoholic and was homeless. There was something else about Willie; he had some great legal issues, which as a newly minted lawyer I relished.
>
> Willie's case traveled through the courts for months as I challenged the legality of the search the police conducted and the admission of guilt he gave to the police. After motions, hearings and oral argument, I finally won the case. I say I won and not Willie because I was never quite sure Willie really needed me or that I had really helped him. I have often asked myself whether Willie needed a vigorous attorney or whether what he really needed was the help of an alcoholism counselor and the safety of a roof over his head.
>
> Some fifteen-plus years later, I have concluded that what Willie really needed was both.[28]

A focus on product, not just process, means a lawyer needs to think creatively about the best way to solve a client's problem. That may lead some New Age Lawyers to think about different court structures—like our drug treatment courts—that can better address the complex issues presented to them.

A focus on product, not just process, may lead other New Age Lawyers to consider alternative dispute resolution ("ADR") techniques to resolve their clients' problems. Increasingly, corporate clients are finding that ADR can make good business sense. Few cases end up being tried through to verdict.[29] ADR can help advance the "moment of truth" in the case—and save time, trouble, and money in the bargain. ADR does not

---

Jersey attorneys revealed that nearly one quarter were planning to leave the practice of law before retirement and that a Maryland Bar Association study showed that almost a third of the attorneys surveyed were not sure they wanted to keep practicing law).

27. *See, e.g.*, Sam Benson, *Why I Quit Practicing Law*, Newsweek, Nov. 4, 1991, at 10 (arguing that an adversarial system makes being ethical inherently difficult for lawyers).

28. John Feinblatt, *Making Communities Safe*, Speech at the Enterprise Institute (Oct. 28, 1995).

29. *See generally* Edwin J. Wesely, *Reflections on Court-Annexed ADR in the Eastern and Southern Districts of New York*, 37 Judges' J. 33, 33 (1998) (stating that ADR serves the interests of the courts by reducing their civil caseloads and backlog).

obviate the need for lawyers by any means. It is still essential that lawyers investigate facts, develop arguments, and present their case.[30] The difference is that with ADR, lawyers and clients work in partnership to solve a legal problem in a business-like manner.

In light of the growing interest in ADR for business cases, the New York State Supreme Court Commercial Division—hailed as a model for business courts around the country—includes a court-annexed ADR component, and the feedback we have been getting is good.[31]

ADR can also have a role beyond the business setting. In cases that have an element of interpersonal relations—matrimonial cases or neighbor disputes, for example—a less adversarial setting can allow the parties to work through emotional issues that may be driving the legal case. All the discovery in the world will not reveal that the client's main concern is that the husband not live in the former marital residence with his new girlfriend. Additionally, if the relationship is to be ongoing, such as a child custody dispute, uncovering and addressing the nonlegal conflicts may save everyone costly, painful future trips to the courthouse.

The New York State courts offer a number of programs in this area as well. Some programs are well-established—like our Community Dispute Resolution Centers that have been in operation since the early 1980s. Last year, these centers handled more than 23,000 matters, ranging from custody and visitation issues to Lemon Law arbitrations.[32] We have also recently begun piloting court-annexed ADR in matrimonial cases in selected counties, and we included a mediation program for landlord-tenant matters in our recent administrative overhaul of the New York City Housing Court.[33]

The new focus on creative problem solving may lead New Age Lawyers to seek out further alternatives to litigation. A number of examples of this approach were discussed at the symposium held here at Fordham last fall on Lawyering for Poor Communities in the twenty-first century. One particularly striking example, featured in the video "So Goes a Nation" that was shown at the conference, was the work of Brooklyn Legal Services

30. To help lawyers hone the necessary skills in this new area, the Association of the Bar of the City of New York recently offered a program on "Representing Clients in Mediation: There's More to It Than You Think." *See Corporate Counsel Organization Highlights*, METROPOLITAN CORP. COUNS. (Mountainside, NJ), Apr. 1998, at 39 (describing the program).

31. *See* Robert C. Meade, Jr., *Commercial Division ADR: A Survey of Participants*, N.Y. L.J., Oct. 17, 1997, at 1; *A Case Study in Successful Judicial Administration: Commercial Division, New York State Supreme Court*, N.Y. LITIGATOR, Aug. 1997, at 24. An online guide to the Commercial Division and its Alternative Dispute Mediation Program can be found at http://ucs.ljx.com/nycdlr/nycdhome.htm (visited Aug. 5, 1998).

32. New York State Unified Court System, Community Dispute Resolution Centers Program Annual Report 1–5 (1997). An online listing of the New York's Community Dispute Resolution Center Programs can be found at http://ucs.ljx.com/ cdrcp/index.html (visited Aug. 5, 1998).

33. *See* New York State Unified Court System, Housing Court Program: Breaking New Ground 11 (1997), *available at* http//ucs.ljx.com/hctprg.htm (visited Aug. 5, 1998).

Corporation A in developing a public health clinic for the Brownsville community.[34] To improve access to appropriate health care in that underserved neighborhood, the Legal Services attorney looked not to the courts but to intricacies of the state public finance system. The result: a seven-million-dollar bond offering to finance the transformation of an abandoned supermarket into a full-service family health care clinic. This is a new conception of the poverty lawyer—one who uses skills of a corporate transactional attorney to build community-based institutions for poor clients.

Finally, a new age focus on product, not just process, can also mean looking for ways to prevent disputes from arising in the first place. Rather than operating exclusively in a crisis management mode, lawyers can also function in a planning mode-designing policies and programs that reduce the chance of conflict. In a corporation, the lawyer might help set up mechanisms to deal with employee grievances before they morph into lawsuits. In a community, the lawyer might help develop student dispute resolution programs—like peer mediation—so that schoolyard spats do not escalate into armed conflicts.

Lawyering in the new age means lawyering in a time of challenge and a time of opportunity for improving the delivery of justice in society. That also means lawyering in a time of some risk—there is no such thing as a challenge or opportunity that is risk-free.

Do our several court innovations raise questions and issues that we need to be concerned with for the future? Of course they do. Our less adversarial problem solving courts cast both judges and attorneys in new roles—what impact will that have on ethical rules premised on an adversarial model? If a client's insistence on efficient resolution conflicts with a lawyer's notion of professional representation—sort of a managed care conflict, legal style—what then?

I raise these questions not to answer them, but to illustrate the kinds of issues that await us. What better setting than a law school to begin raising them? I have talked about what the courts have done, what lawyers can do. Let me not overlook the crucial role of law professors in preparing the next generation for these changing times and in helping us sort out which changes are helpful, which are unhelpful, and where to go next.

I began these remarks by discussing the relevance of an opera across the street more than a decade ago to my general topic of dealing with change. Being a great believer in meaningful coincidence, I naturally checked out the Met before coming into this auditorium today—and I was not disappointed.

I have spoken this evening about the risks of extreme adversarialism, the virtues of thinking "outside the box," and about new ways of resolving disputes. If you need further convincing on these points, I suggest you adjourn to the Opera House. Tonight's bill? *Romeo and Juliette.* If my words have not moved you, I guarantee that Shakespeare's story and Gounod's music will.

34. Videotape: So Goes a Nation: Lawyers and Communities (Sight Effects 1997). This video will be available to the public on CD-Rom as an attachment to 25 FORDHAM URB. L.J. (forthcoming Nov. 1998).

The Role of a Supreme Court in a Democracy

Hon. Aharon Barak

Aharon Barak delivered the Sonnett lecture on September 10, 2002. He was on Israel's Supreme Court for almost thirty years and served as Chief Judge of Israel's highest court for ten of those years. Prior to that, he was Israel's Attorney General and also served as Dean of the Hebrew University of Jerusalem Law School. As a professor, he lectured at Yale and Georgetown Law Schools.

Justice Barak was a most unlikely Sonnett speaker. He was born in Lithuania in 1936. Born Erik Brit, he was the subject of persecution in a ghetto and, at the end of World War II, hid in a wall to avoid death. His grandparents were killed during the Holocaust. After the war, his family was among the Jewish refugees who wandered across Europe and who eventually found their way to Israel. Once in Israel, Brit changed his name to Aharon Barak. Barak mastered Hebrew quickly, became a student leader, and went to law school.[1]

Justice Barak's Sonnett lecture was not published in the *Fordham Law Review*. He gave a similar lecture at Hastings Law School, which is reprinted herein with their permission. In both lectures, Justice Barak spoke on the subject of the role of a Supreme Court in a Democracy.[2] In his speech, he observed that he believes that, on occasion, judges do "legislate," should "legislate," and should acknowledge that this is occasionally part of the judicial process. He went on to discuss the considerations which a judge should bring to the process of legislating. He noted that on very rare occasions, a court should lead and not follow societal preferences or mores. He referred to these unique times as "Brown" moments.[3]

The role of the judiciary continues to be the subject of great debate.[4] The divisions among the current justices of the Supreme Court of the United States, as reflected in its

1. *See* Ari Shavit, My Promised Land: The Triumph and Tragedy of Israel (2013).

2. *See* Aharon Barak, *The Role of a Supreme Court in a Democracy*, 53 Hastings L.J. 1205 (2002). This article was delivered as the Matthew O. Tobriner Memorial Lecture on September 24, 2001 at the University of California, Hastings College of the Law, San Francisco, California. The annual Matthew O. Tobriner Memorial Lecture was established in honor of former California Supreme Court Justice and former Hastings faculty member Matthew O. Tobriner. Each year Hastings College of the Law sponsors a lecture by a distinguished legal scholar or prominent personality to build on the legacy of Justice Tobriner's outstanding accomplishments as a legal scholar and jurist. Parts of this lecture were previously published in *Israel Law Review* 33, no. 1 (1999). They are reprinted here with the permission of the *Israel Law Review*.

3. *See* Brown v. Board of Education, 347 U.S. 473 (1954) (declaring that "separate" was not "equal").

4. *See, e.g.*, Amy Coney Barrett, *Precedent and Jurisprudential Disagreement*, 91 Texas L. Rev. 1711 (2013); Cass R. Sunstein, *Unanimity and Disagreement on the Supreme Court*, 100 Cornell L. Rev. 769 (2015).

many 5-4 decisions, appear to revolve around the issues highlighted by Justice Barak. The topic will most likely be one that is debated forever. "Protecting liberty and equality and doing justice" were Judge Barak's "North Star."[5] We can probably all agree that this is a sentiment by which all judges should be guided.

2002 Sonnett Lecture

The role of the judiciary is to adjudicate disputes according to law. Adjudication involves three functions: fact determination (done mostly by the trial court), law application, and law determination. The third function—law determination—does not involve, in most cases, any creation. The law is known and determined. The court merely declares what the law is. The court is, in the words of Montesquieu, a "mouth that pronounces the words of the law."[1] However, there are hard cases. In such cases, the law is uncertain. There is more than one meaning to be given to the legal text. There is more than one solution to the legal problem. In such cases, law declaration also involves law creation. Prior to the judicial determination, the law (the constitution, the statute, the common law) spoke—even after all rules of interpretation were used—with a number of voices. After the judicial determination the law speaks with a single voice. The law was changed. A new meaning was created. The creation of a new norm—to be binding on all courts by the rule of precedent—is the main function of the supreme court in a democracy. Such creation involves discretion. The judge of a supreme court is not a mirror, passively reflecting the image of the law. He is an artist, creating the picture with his or her own hands. He is "legislating"—engaging in "judicial legislation." He does so in concrete cases, as an incidental and interstitial outcome of the adjudicative function.

Such "law creating" ("legislative") activity is not a reflection of judicial imperialism. It is an indication of the uncertainty inherent in the law itself. Law is not mathematics. Law is a normative system. So long as we cannot predict the future, so long as language does not enable generalizations that extend to all relevant situations, so long as we cannot overcome human limitation, we will have to live with uncertainty in law. Such uncertainty—and not any sense of judicial imperialism—is the source of judicial creativity. Such uncertainty derives from human limitations and the nature of society. Thus, there is no one legal answer to every legal problem. There are legal problems that have more than one answer. Indeed, we cannot and we do not want to have a legal system that has in advance all the legal answers to all the legal problems. Judicial creativity—judicial legislation—is natural to law itself. Law without discretion is a body without a spirit. Judicial

5. *See supra* note 2, at 1216.

1. Baron De Montesquieu, The Spirit of the Laws 191 (Thomas Nugent trans., D. Appleton & Co. 1900) (1748).

creativity is part of legal existence. Such creativity—"judicial lawmaking"—is the task of a supreme court.

Judges tend to hide their creative function. "We declare what the law is—we don't make it," is a common motto in many judgments from Blackstone's time onwards. Judges fear that public confidence in the judiciary will be affected if the public discovers the truth. "Personally," wrote Lord Radcliffe, "I think that judges will serve the public interest better if they keep quiet about their legislative function."[2] I disagree. The public has the right to know that we make law and how we do it; the public should not be deceived: "The right to know the architect of our obligations," wrote Professor Julius Stone, "may be as much a part of liberty, as the right to know our accuser and our judge."[3]

Judges tend to be apologetic about their creative role. They do so mainly because of their nonrepresentative character. But our nonrepresentative character—our nonpolitical accountability—is not a source of our weakness. It is the main source of our strength. Courts are not representative bodies, and it will be a tragedy if they become representative. Courts are reflective bodies; they reflect the basic values of their system. Thus, we should not be defensive in face of representational kinds of arguments. Democracy is not only representation. Democracy is also basic values, the center of which are human rights. When the majority takes away the right of the minority—this is not democracy. Democracy is a delicate balance between majority rule and individual rights. Furthermore, our creative power stems from the law itself. A constitution involves a delegation by the people to the judges of the power to interpret the constitution, and thus to create constitutional law; legislation is an authorization for judicial lawmaking in and around the statute. And the common law—our Lady of the Common Law—is the creation of judges for almost a thousand years. "I recognize without hesitation," wrote Justice Homes in 1917, "that judges do and must legislate."[4]

Thus, the main question is not whether "judges of the Supreme Court make law"; the main question is "how." How does a judge of a Supreme Court make law? How should we decide hard cases? A judge is not allowed to flip a coin, though it achieves full objectivity. How, thus, is judicial discretion in making law used?

In creating law, we should give expression to the basic values of our legal system. Those values are the key to constitutional and statutory interpretation. They are the force behind the common law.

Those values reflect ethical values of morality and justice; they include social values relating to public order, judicial independence, separation of powers, public peace, and security; they are based on concepts of reasonableness, tolerance, proportionality, good faith, and honesty. Those values include an aspiration to realize reasonable expectations

2. Lord Radcliffe, *The Lawyer and His Times*, *in* THE PATH OF THE LAW FROM 1967 9, 16 (Arthur E. Sutherland ed., 1968).

3. JULIUS STONE, SOCIAL DIMENSIONS OF LAW AND JUSTICE 678 (1966).

4. S. Pac. Co. v. Jensen, 244 U.S. 205, 221 (1917) (Holmes, J., dissenting).

and certainty in law. At the center of these fundamental values stand human rights—political, social and economic.

The judge learns about those basic values from the fundamental documents—such as the constitution—of his or her legal system. But those documents are not the only source. The judge learns about the basic values of his or her legal system from the aggregate national experience, from the nature of the political system as a democracy, and from understanding the basic concepts of the nation. The movement of his legal system through history, its social, political, and religious roots are the sources from which a judge learns about those basic values. And ultimately, he learns about those basic values "from reading life."

The values which direct the judge are the basic and fundamental values. They are not the outcomes of public opinion surveys; they are not populism carrying away the masses. They are not transient and revolving fashions. They are not blaring headlines. They reflect history, not hysteria. When a society is not faithful to its basic values, the judge is not to express the fleeting winds of the hour. He or she should express the deep values and the fundamental vision of society. When terror swept my country, and when bombs exploded in the street, the mood was "get the terrorists, interrogate them by any means, and find out where the bombs are." But, the Israeli Supreme Court said no. Dignity is a human right for everyone, including the terrorist. A state cannot use force against anyone—not even the terrorist that is planting a bomb in the supermarket. Those are our basic values as a democracy, and the Court, as an independent and nonrepresentative body, should express them. And I added:

> We are aware that this decision does make it easier to deal with that reality. This is the destiny of a democracy—it does not see all means as acceptable, and the ways of its enemies are not always open before it. A democracy must sometimes fight with one hand tied behind its back. Even so, a democracy has the upper hand. The rule of law and the liberty of an individual constitute important components in its understanding of security. At the end of the day, they strengthen its spirit and this strength allows it to overcome its difficulties.[5]

Of course, human rights are not the only values. The existence of the state, its security and public peace are also basic values. A charter of rights should not become a prescription for suicide. Human rights should not become tools for national destruction. Human rights need a community. Ensuring the political and social framework is a necessary condition for securing human rights themselves.

And here comes the main difficulty in judicial lawmaking. In the hard cases a judge is faced with a conflict between basic values. Dignity of the individual conflicts with state security; free speech conflicts with public order or privacy and reputation. Freedom of religion conflicts with freedom from religion. The dignity of the fetus conflicts with the dignity of the mother. We must solve those conflicts. But our legal system does not provide us with the necessary tools to reach a solution in every case. In many cases, we are

5. HCJ 5100/94, Pub. Comm. Against Torture in Israel v. Israel 53(4) PD 817, 845 (1999).

told that the solution to the conflict lies in a balance between the conflicting values. But neither our legal system nor philosophy provides us with an answer to the question what weight is to be assigned to each value and how should the judge balance the conflicting basic values. Balancing and weighing are, of course, metaphors. How do we decide which value is of greater importance in a particular case, and which supersedes other values?

Of course, the existence of discretion in those cases means that there are no fast rules as to how to weigh and balance in every case the conflicting basic values. But it does not follow that a judge can do whatever he or she wishes. There is no absolute discretion. Absolute discretion for judges, as well as any other public official, would be the beginning of the end of democracy. Furthermore, although there are no fast rules about weighing and balancing, it does not follow that every solution is as good as the other. There is good balancing and there is bad balancing. What makes good balancing? What makes a good solution?

Each individual judge has a different answer to that question. Every judge develops over the years his or her own philosophy of adjudication. It reflects personal history, life experience, and totality as an individual and as a judge. For many, this philosophy remains unexpressed and is based on intuition. For others, however, it is the result of an attempt to think through and articulate to oneself one's own approach to hard legal questions. It is the product of an attempt to identify the crucial considerations for the individual, and to order them appropriately. And, it is one's own attempt to shape one's judicial philosophy. Let me try to identify some of these considerations. In so doing, I make no claim to comprehensiveness. I make no claim to truth. I make, of course no claim that these considerations are binding on anyone in any legal system. My only claim is that I believe that if a judge in a democratic legal system would take them into account, he would be using his discretion in a better manner than if he ignored them.

My first point is this: the weighing and balancing of the conflicting values should be a rational process. Judicial discretion must manifest reason, not fiat. The method by which the judge weighs and balances is different from the method by which the legislature weighs and balances the same values. The legislative process is political. The judicial process is normative. The judicial weighing and balancing should, in Dworkin's term, "fit" within the normative scheme. No such requirement is imposed upon the political process. The judicial weighing and balancing should draw itself out of the existing normative structure. The weighing and balancing in one area of the law should be affected by the weighing and balancing in other areas of the law. Within the same legal system, a judge cannot decide, in one instance, that free speech is of great importance (for example, in a conflict between free speech and public order) and in another instance that free speech is of no importance (for example, in a conflict between free speech and the reputation of another). A judge is always faced with the need for harmony within the system. When a judge exercises judicial discretion, he does not perform a one-time act isolated from an existing normative order. Judicial discretion is used within the framework of a system and must fit into it. The legal system into which the judicial decision is introduced is not a frozen body. It is a living organism, and judicial discretion is one of the forces that fertilizes its cells. There must be harmony between the exercise of judicial discretion that develops the cells, on the one hand, and the development of the living organism, the legal system, on the other.

In general, organic growth of the legal system necessitates gradual development. The need to ensure the existence of the system demands evolution, not revolution. Usually, continuity, rather than a series of jumps, is involved. Of course, sometimes one cannot avoid sharp turns and dangerous leaps, but these occur in exceptional situations. Normally, the proper functioning of a legal system requires slow and gradual movement. Judicial discretion must fit into these frameworks. The judicial process is thus based on organic growth.

In most cases, a judge should reflect the deep public consensus, and not create it, but not in all cases. There comes a moment when the court should lead; where the court is the crusader of a new consensus. *Brown v. Board of Education* is a good example.[6] A supreme court cannot survive public confidence if it announces every week a new *Brown*. But, a supreme court will not survive public confidence if it misses the special moment to have a *Brown*.

The judge must determine the controversy before him. It is only natural for him to strive for a just solution to the parties before him, yet he cannot ignore the fact that his solution should fit into the existing normative fabric. Nor can he ignore the fact that his solution should be just for similar parties in the future. An ideal exercise of judicial discretion meets the triple test of integration with the past, justice in the present, and an appropriate norm for the future.

My second point is this: judicial discretion should be objective. The weighing and balancing of the conflicting values should be objective. Objectivity, of course, has many meanings. Here, I mean an intellectual process by which the judge reaches beyond himself to understand, from the perspective of his or her community, the social values that he is to weigh and balance. Objectivity stands in opposition to the subjective values of the judge. The judge's decision should reflect the deep values of his society, not his personal values.

Objectivity means giving expression to the general scale of values, not to the judge's own scale of values. It means that the judge frees himself, as far as he can, from all personal preferences. It means neutrality in the process of balancing. Objectivity means reflecting the deep consensus and the shared values of the society. It is only then that the judge would be able to look straight into the eyes of his nation and say: "I gave expression to your shared and profound values—not to my personal values." It is only then that he will be able to say to the legislator, whose statute he struck down as unconstitutional: "I gave expression, not to my personal values, but to the values of the constitution. The conflict is not between the court and the legislature; the conflict is between the legislature and the constitution."

This objectivity demands much from the judge and requires an element of mental accounting. He or she must be aware that his values may not be shared by everyone and that his personal views may be unique. He might attach great importance to issues that, within

6. 347 U.S. 483 (1954).

the legal system, are trivial and meaningless. The judge must be aware of his characteristics, and he must make every possible effort not to exercise his discretion on the basis of these subjective traits.

Judicial discretion should be consistent. Only thus will discretion fit into the legal system as a whole and become an integral part of it. A reasonable exercise of judicial discretion requires that in similar cases discretion be exercised in a similar manner. This is a fundamental requirement of justice. Of course, a judge might exercise his discretion in such a way as to cause a deviation from the existing law. Consistency does not require abstention from all change. Yet even here the judge should be consistent and neutral. He should apply the new rule in every similar case, and he should be prepared to deviate similarly when like circumstances arise. Herein lies one of the differences between the discretion of the judiciary and the discretion of the legislature. No legal obligation is imposed on the legislator to be consistent. He need not act neutrally. Not so the judge: his discretion should fit into the legal fabric. As a result, he must be consistent and neutral.

The judge is the product of his or her period. He lives at a given time and in a given society. The goal of objectivity is not to cut him off from his surroundings, but the opposite: to enable him to formulate properly the fundamental principles of his period. The goal of objectivity is not to "liberate" the judge from his past, his education, his experience, his faith and his values. On the contrary, its purpose is to stimulate him to make use of all of these in order to reflect as purely as possible the fundamental values of the nation. A person who is appointed as a judge need not change, but he must develop a sensitivity to the weight of his office and to the constraints it imposes. The judge must demonstrate both self-criticism and a lack of arrogance in a way that will enable him to avoid identifying himself with all he believes to be good and beautiful. He must demonstrate self-restraint that lets him separate his personal feelings from the inner feelings of the nation. He must demonstrate an intellectual modesty that permits him to say, "I erred, for I confused what I want with what I am entitled to." A judge who does not act accordingly and who imposes on the society all that is subjective in him will create tension between himself and his environment. As long as he or she persists in this, the tension between the judicial branch and the other branches will grow. The result of this tension may be hazardous for society, and above all, it may damage the status of the court and the public's confidence in it. Only through the use of objectivity and consistency will the judge have the trust of his legal community, a trust given to him as a neutral arbiter of conflicting values. And, without such trust, the judge cannot fulfill his function. The most important asset the judge possesses is the public's confidence in him. It is also among the most precious assets of the nation. This is the confidence that judging is done fairly, neutrally, while treating each side equally, and without any hint of personal stake in the outcome; confidence in the high moral standard of judging, and in the integrity of every individual judge. The judge has neither sword nor purse. All he has is the public's confidence in him. Public confidence is not a given. Its existence cannot be taken for granted. The public's confidence is a fluid matter. It must be nurtured. It is easier to damage it than to guard it. Years of effort may be lost forever because of one unfortunate decision. Therefore, in exercising his discretion, the judge should bear this need in mind. Every judge should act as though the public's confidence in the entire judicial system depended on the exercise of his balancing. Of course, there is not much one can do with just the public's confidence in adjudication. Yet, without it one cannot do anything. A judge should never reach a point, at which it can be said—as Justice Stevens said recently: "Although we may never know with complete certainty the identity of the winner of this year's Presidential election, the identity of the loser is perfectly clear. It is the nation's confidence in the judge as an impartial guardian of the rule of law."[7]

The need to ensure confidence does not mean the need to guarantee popularity, but rather, the need to preserve the public's sense that judicial discretion is being exercised objectively, through a neutral application of the laws and the fundamental values of the nation; that judicial discretion is exercised in order to maintain the articles of faith of the people and not the articles of faith of the judge; that the judge is not a party to the power struggles in the state, and that he is fighting not for his own power, but for the rule of law.

My third point is this: every judgment is a link in a chain. The world does not start with us, and hopefully will not end with us. Every judgment is one step in a long unending journey. We should always realize from where we come, and to where we are going. In solving hard cases, a judge should hold deep respect for tradition. Tradition means a sense of history. Tradition means an appreciation of precedent. Tradition means a fusion of the horizons of the past and the present; it means a dialogue between generations. Tradition creates continuity.

Judicial creativity, like the writing of a book in serial installments, is a continuous activity.[7] Judges who are no longer on the bench wrote the early chapter. Current judges write the continuation, but they do so by basing themselves on the past. *And* the chapters being written, as they are written, become part of the past, and new chapters, the fruits of new judge's labors, are written. Thus the judicial creation is achieved. It has no beginning and no end and is all continuity.

My fourth point is this: the judicial decision should fit into the general structure of the institutional-governmental systems. The judge who exercises discretion does so as part of the judicial branch. His or her judicial decision should match the fundamental concepts of the relations between his branch and the other branches of the state. These fundamental concepts stem from society's view of democracy and separation of powers. They are affected by society's view of the judicial function. Judicial lawmaking is not the only form of lawmaking or even the primary form. The other branches also create law. Judicial lawmaking should mesh with this overall lawmaking. The judge is not the only musician within the grand legal orchestra, and his playing must be in harmony with the rest of the music. Thus, for example, in the United States, separation of power leads to the nonjusticiability of the proceedings of Congress. In other countries, like Germany, Spain, and Israel, separation of powers—checks and balances—leads to the justiciability of those proceedings.

7. Bush v. Gore, 531 U.S. 98, 128–29 (2000) (Stevens, J., dissenting).

7. *See* Ronald Dworkin, *"Natural" Law Revisited*, 34 U. FLA. L. REV. 165 (1982).

My fifth point is this: in exercising discretion and in balancing conflicting values, a judge should be open-minded; he or she should be receptive to new ideas. He should realize that in a pluralistic society, there are many points of view and there is no single "right" solution. A judge should be aware of the complexity of the human being. Our approach should be holistic. When we construe one statute, we construe all statutes. During our life in law, we will face many conflicting theories: Naturalism, Positivism, Feminism, Law and Economics, Law and . . . and many others. There is some truth in all of them. They reflect different aspects of the human experience. We should learn from all of them. We should not become slaves to any one of them. Eclecticism—not purity—reflects the complexity of human nature and human relations.

A judge should lack any trace of arrogance. He should exercise humility. He should be aware of his personal strengths and weaknesses. He should know that he may fail. Though his decisions may be final, they are not infallible, and the judge may commit grave mistakes. He may misread the national way of life. He may not strike the proper balance between stability and change. Any theory of judging in a democracy should consider the possibility that mistakes can be made. And the judge should admit errors. The strength of our judgments lies in our ability to be self-critical and to admit our errors in the appropriate instances. Law hasn't started with us. It will not end with us. I myself make it a point to say openly in my judgment that I made a mistake in the past, and that correction by myself is needed. In one of my judgments I deviated from a previous judgment of mine. I wrote:

> This conclusion of mine contradicts the conclusion I reached in the previous judgment. In other words—I changed my mind. Indeed, since issuing the previous judgment, I have not stopped asking myself if my approach to the law is well-founded. I am not of the school that believes that the finality of a decision testifies to its correctness. We all make mistakes. Our professional integrity requires us to admit our mistake if we are convinced that we indeed erred. In our tough hours, when we question ourselves, the North Star that must guide us is the quest for truth that leads us to actualize the justice within the law. We must not become entrenched in our preconceived opinions. We must be ready to admit our mistakes.[8]

But what should a judge do when all this advice fails? How should he decide a hard case when rationality, objectivity, consistency, neutrality, continuity, tradition, and humility fail to lead to a single answer? There is no one answer to this question. Different judges have different answers. My answer is this: in that exceptional instance—and it is a very rare instance of the very hard case subjectivity is allowed to enter. The final decision will be shaped as Cardozo observed, by the judge's "experience with life; his understanding of the prevailing canons of justice and morality; his study of the social sciences; at times, in the end, by his intuitions, his guesses, even his ignorance or prejudice."[9] Of course, the judge should not cut corners in the decision-making process. He should not go straight to

8. CA 7048/97, Anonymous v. Minister of Def. 54(1) PD 721 (1997).
9. 53 Benjamin Cardozo, The Growth of the Law 86 (1924).

his subjective beliefs. There is a long objective road to travel. But, after all the objective means have been exhausted, he should be allowed to apply his subjective beliefs.

Those subjective beliefs differ, of course, from judge to judge, from one generation of judges to the next, from country to country. Every judge is part of his people. At times he lives in an ivory tower, but my tower is on the hills of Jerusalem, not on Mt. Olympus. As a judge, I am conscious of what is taking place in my country. It is my duty to study my country's problems, to read its literature, to listen to its music. A judge is a creation of his time. He moves with history. All of these conditions shape his judicial philosophy. And it is the judge's judicial philosophy that guides him in the hard cases. This philosophy may not contain the answer to all the difficult cases, yet it seems to me that without it, there is no proper solution at all.

I would like to point out the following two considerations that shape my judicial philosophy and my subjective beliefs when I use discretion in those very hard cases.

First, law is not an end in itself. It is a means for social order. The court has a social function. A supreme court does not merely solve disputes; it also creates law. It closes the gap between law and life. It preserves democracy both by protecting the political process and by guaranteeing human rights. It safeguards the rule of law. The judge is of course an objective arbiter. But he is an arbiter with a special function. We should realize that we are a social institution with a social function. It is our function, alongside the legislature, to preserve stability and change. "Law must be stable," said Professor Roscoe Pound, "and yet it cannot stand still."[10] Stability without change is stagnation; change without stability is anarchy. We must ensure stability through change. The law, like an eagle in the sky, is only stable when it moves. We should recognize that our function is to effect both stability and change, within the constitutional scheme, and through action that is sensitive to the other branches of government and to the idea of the separation of powers. But within these limitations, we should not view the closing of the gap between the law and the needs of the community as a function that is foreign to us.

Second, whenever all other objective considerations fail, the stage is set for reflection upon the most important value-justice. Of course, justice accompanies our judging throughout the adjudicative process. But at that final stage, when the objective considerations fail to produce one and only one answer, justice is foremost. At this point, law and justice unite. Law is justice, and justice is law. The justice does justice.

Let me end my lecture with a personal note.

When I was only three years old, World War II broke out. In 1941—when I was five years of age—my family and I were placed in a ghetto, in Kovnus, Lithuania. We were in hell. Out of 30,000 Jews in the Ghetto, only several hundred were saved. I am one of very few survivors. Almost all my family was killed. Most of the children of the Ghetto were shot in the streets. I was saved by miracles and the grace of a Lithuanian family. What is my lesson from this experience? It is not hatred; it is not hopelessness about the nature of the human being. Quite the opposite: my lesson is a belief in the human spirit; my lesson

10. Roscoe Pound, Interpretations of Legal History 1 (1923).

is the centrality of the human being; my lesson is equality among all of us; my lesson is that we are all made in the image of God. Protecting dignity and equality and doing justice is my North Star, which guides me in my difficult moments.

I see my role as judge as a mission. Judging is not merely a job. It is a way of life. An old Jewish Talmudic saying regarding judges is the following: "You would think that I am granting you power? It is slavery that I am imposing upon you."[11] But it is an odd sort of slavery, where the purpose is to serve liberty, dignity, and justice. Liberty to the spirit of the human being; dignity and equality to everyone; justice to the individual and to the community.

This is the promise which accompanies me to the courtroom daily. As I sit *at* trial, I stand *on* trial.

11. TB *Horayot* 10b.

The Secret Life of Judges

Hon. Dennis Jacobs

Judge Dennis Jacobs delivered the twenty-seventh Sonnett lecture, *The Secret Life of Judges*, on November 20, 2006.[1] When published, the lecture won a Green Bag Award for exemplary legal writing.[2]

Judge Jacobs served as Chief Judge for the United States Court of Appeals for the Second Circuit for nearly seven years, stepping down in August of 2013.[3] He is a native of New York City and graduated from Queens College in 1964.[4] Judge Jacobs went on to earn both his M.A. and J.D. from New York University.[5] He returned to Queens College as a lecturer before joining the law firm of Simpson, Thacher & Bartlett, where he became a partner in 1980.[6] During his time at Simpson Thacher, Judge Jacobs worked with the Bronx Legal Services to develop a program providing pro bono services to individual clients of the legal aid organization.[7] In 1992, President George H.W. Bush appointed Judge Jacobs to the Second Circuit, and in 2006 he took over as Chief Judge.[8]

As Chief Judge, Judge Jacobs authored a number of significant opinions, including *Windsor v. United States*,[9] in which the Second Circuit held that the Defense Against Marriage Act was unconstitutional, a decision upheld by the Supreme Court a year later.[10] Other notable decisions that Judge Jacobs authored include *United States v. Whitten*,[11] in which the court found that prosecutors may not use a defendant's demand for trial as

Introduction written by Austen Ishii, J.D., Class of 2015, Fordham University School of Law.

1. Dennis Jacobs, *The Secret Life of Judges*, 75 Fordham L. Rev. 2855 (2007).

2. *Exemplary Legal Writers 2007*, 11 Green Bag 2d 146 (2008).

3. Mark Hamblett, *In Handing Off Chief Judge Role, Jacobs Says: "I Kept Up My End,"* N.Y.L.J., Aug. 30, 2013, at 1.

4. *Judicial Profiles: Dennis Jacobs*, N.Y.L.J., http://judges.newyorklawjournal.com/profile/U.S._Second_Circuit_Court_of_Appeals/Dennis_Jacobs/Dennis_Jacobs-100076.xml (last visited Feb. 23, 2013).

5. *Id.*

6. *Id.*

7. Dennis Jacobs, Almanac of the Federal Judiciary.

8. Hamblett, *supra* note 3, at 1.

9. 699 F.3d 169 (2d Cir. 2012).

10. United States v. Windsor, 133 S. Ct. 2675 (2013).

11. 610 F.3d 168 (2d Cir. 2010).

evidence of his lack of remorse or refusal to accept responsibility,[12] and *Arar v. Ashcroft*, which held that there is no private right of action against government officials in the context of extraordinary rendition.[13]

Judge Jacobs was known not only for his legal opinions and "fiery dissents," but also for his administrative skills, which he used to reduce the backlog of cases plaguing the court, streamline the en banc system of review, and oversee the completion of renovations to the Thurgood Marshall U.S. Courthouse at 40 Foley Square.[14] Since stepping down as Chief Judge, Judge Jacobs has continued to serve on the Second Circuit, where his reasoned and efficient style has led lawyers arguing before him to comment that he is "an active questioner," "courteous but practical," and simply, "a wonderful judge."[15]

Judge Jacobs's Sonnett lecture, *The Secret Life of Judges*, focused on what he calls the "ambient bias" of judges to favor, empower, and enable the legal profession.[16] In his lecture, he described the judiciary's predisposition to "the lawyered solution," and the tendency of judges to craft legal doctrines without contemplating the economic consequences of the systems they put into place or considering whether nonlegalistic approaches might be better suited to the problems they face.[17]

Judge Jacobs warned of the insidious consequences of the secret bias: "the displacement of legislative and executive power, the subordination of other disciplines and professions, and the reduction of whole enterprises and industries to damages."[18] He ended his lecture with a call for judges to be more mindful of their bias in favor of the legal profession and "exercise the self-restraint and self-discipline" necessary to reduce the role of the judiciary while still elevating it "by considerations of honor, self-restraint, and respect for other influences."[19]

A year after Judge Jacobs's lecture, *New York Times* writer Adam Liptak wrote that the judge "put his views into practice" when Judge Jacobs penned a partial dissent in *Husain v. Springer*.[20] The case involved a lawsuit arising from a college newspaper that endorsed candidates for the school's student government.[21] Despite the fact that the suit involved only two dollars in damages, the majority found a violation of the First Amendment.[22] Judge Jacobs railed against what he saw as the court's rash decision to engage in extensive legal analysis over "a case about nothing," though he ultimately concurred in the majority's decision on the merits.[23] Like his lecture, Judge Jacobs's decisions continue to

12. *Id.* at 195.
13. 585 F.3d 559, 574 (2d Cir. 2009).
14. Hamblett, *supra* note 3, at 1.
15. Jacobs, *supra* note 1.
16. Jacobs, *supra* note 1, at 2856.
17. *Id.*
18. *Id.* at 2857.
19. *Id.* at 2863.
20. Adam Liptak, *With the Bench Cozied Up to the Bar, the Lawyers Can't Lose*, N.Y. TIMES, Aug. 27, 2007, at A10.
21. Husain v. Springer, 494 F.3d 108 (2d Cir. 2007).
22. *Id.* at 126.
23. *Id.* at 136 (Jacobs, J., concurring).

highlight the responsibility of judges to be mindful of the unseen undercurrents that influence their decisions.[24] The bias favoring lawyers in our legal system continues to this day to be a subject of ongoing debate.[25]

2006 Sonnett Lecture

Dean Treanor, distinguished faculty, students, alumni, colleagues, and fellow friends of Fordham University School of Law, I am honored more than I can say to be invited to deliver this distinguished lecture in the postcentennial year of this great law school—now, this venerable law school. I am going to express my gratitude by saying some things that matter to me, that are not often said, and that distill observations that have (increasingly) bemused me over the fourteen years that I have been a judge.

The title of my lecture gives little clue, I suspect, as to what I am going to say; but it is not a tease. I am going to talk about "The Secret Life of Judges," by which I mean a habit of mind that, among so many admirable features of the judicial mentality, amounts to a serious and secret bias. There is a social reluctance to talk about this kind of thing. It sounds sanctimonious. Then again, a neat thing about giving a lecture is that it disarms inhibitions about lecturing people. I get to be sanctimonious without worrying about it.

This lecture is about bias, the judge's inbred preference for outcomes controlled by proceduralism, the adversary system, hearings and experts, representation by lawyers, ramified complexity of doctrines and rules, multiple prongs, and all things that need and use lawyers, enrich them, and empower them vis-à-vis other sources of power and wisdom.

Let me make this bias concrete by example. If you arrived in an appellate court as counsel for a medical-malpractice plaintiff, and the three individuals on the bench were wearing white coats instead of black robes and had stethoscopes around their necks, I think your heart would sink. I could tell you that the three doctors deciding your case have taken an oath to be impartial as between patients and the medical profession and that they are conscientious, decent individuals who take seriously the obligation to be neutral. You would not be reassured: you would understand that there is (at least) an internalized bias that the doctors would not acknowledge because they would not notice it. A similar dread would come over the defendant's lawyer if the three judges each had a limb suspended in traction.

In our courts, judges are lawyers. They are all lawyers. Most of us have never been, nor want to be, anything else. We are proud of being lawyers. For many of us (like myself),

24. In fact, the case may have been about nothing (à la Seinfeld) other than legal fees for the lawyers. In *Husain v. Springer*, 193 F. Supp. 2d 664, 665 (E.D.N.Y. 2002), the prevailing party, having obtained two dollars in nominal damages, sought some $800,000 in legal fees as the "prevailing party" and was awarded over $200,000, which presumably was paid by New York taxpayers.

25. *See* Benjamin H. Barton, *The Lawyer's Monopoly—What Goes and What Stays*, 82 FORDHAM L. REV. 3067 (2014).

lawyering is our only talent (assuming we have any talent at all), and it is the source of as much esteem as we enjoy. Our calling says a lot about how our minds work, what we respect, and whom we trust.

I am not—I repeat, I am not—speaking about a bias based upon politics or agenda, economic class, ethnicity, or paraethnicity. When I refer to the secret life of judges, I am speaking of an inner turn of mind that favors, empowers, and enables our profession and our brothers and sisters at the bar. It is secret, because it is unobserved and therefore unrestrained—by the judges themselves or by the legal community that so closely surrounds and nurtures us. It is an ambient bias.

The result is the incremental preference for the lawyered solution, the fee-paid intervention or pro bono project, the lawyer-driven procedure, the appellate dispensation—and the confidence and faith that these things produce the best results. It is an insidious bias, because it is hard to make out, in the vast maze of judicial work and outcomes, the statutes, doctrines, and precedents that are woven together like an elaborate oriental rug in which the underlying image of the dragon emerges only after you stare for a while. I discern in this jumble a bias in favor of the bar and lawyers: what they do; how they do it; and how they prosper in goods and influence. This is the "figure in the carpet."[1]

This bias has several effects and ramifications. Judges all too frequently frame legal doctrines without considering the litigants' transaction costs. Considering how many of us conscientiously think hard about the economic consequences of the outcomes we adopt, it seems strange that our cases reflect an almost complete disregard and ignorance of the costs, uncertainties, and delays inflicted by the judicial process itself. I think that is because judges as lawyers cannot see as a problem the activity and busyness from which our brothers and sisters at the bar draw their livelihood, their career advancement, their distinction, and (often) their sense of purpose in life. All of this depends on the ceaseless turning of the legal machine.

Judges tend to assume that the adversary process assures a fair fight and a just outcome. And judges work hard to be fair as between the adversarial positions presented. But almost always, the adversaries on all sides are lawyers; so adversariness is no great engine for assuring fairness when it comes to the allocation of decision-making power between lawyers (adversaries all) and the institutions and populations outside our profession. The result is not that lawyers and the legal profession always win in court contests (even though they are on both sides); but, there is no doubt that they get to punch above their weight.

As I hope I have made clear, I am talking about altruistic litigation as well as hourly fee-paid work and work on contingency. For all the good that public interest lawyers do (and it is a great deal), some of it results in the short circuit of democratic decision-making and coerced policy choices. Thus, the threat of litigation often compels school boards to suppress all orthodoxies except those endorsed by the cadres of constitutional lawyers and constitutional law professors. A school-board member exercising fiduciary duties will bow

1. *See* Henry James, *The Figure in the Carpet*, *reprinted in* THE FIGURE IN THE CARPET AND OTHER Stories (Frank Kermode ed., Penguin Books 1986).

to anticipated demands rather than bear the cost of exercising or testing the board's own rights, if only because the cost of litigating a flag, a reference to God, a locker search, a dirty word, or something like that, can easily cost the school board the annual services of a music teacher or a teacher of remedial reading.

To my observation, judges are blind to this. I think that is because public interest litigation greatly enhances lawyer influence and—not at all incidentally—increases the influence and power of judges. Judges love these kinds of cases. Public interest cases afford a judge sway over public policy, enhance the judicial role, make the judge more conspicuous, and keep the law clerks happy.

Whether fee-paid or pro bono publico, when lawyers present big issues to the courts, the judges receive the big issues with grateful hands; the bar patrols against inroads on jurisdiction and independence and praises the expansion of legal authority; and together we smugly congratulate ourselves on expanding what we are pleased to call the rule of law.

Among the results are the displacement of legislative and executive power, the subordination of other disciplines and professions, and the reduction of whole enterprises and industries to damages. Examples come ready to hand, though, speaking as I do as a judge, I am constrained from citing specifics of controversies that may come before me. In generalities, let me observe:

> Judicial power over the legislature and the executive is dilated by constitutional litigation, much of which is lawyer-driven. Often, the plaintiff's standing is made to rest on largely notional, abstract harms (like annoyance or anxiety), and sometimes the existence of the plaintiff is a recruitment detail that is easily arranged.
>
> Through such constitutional litigation, judges get to direct the work of educators, police, child protection officers, and many other professionals who have training to discharge critical responsibilities that require their expertise and experience.
>
> Class actions and consent decrees allow judges to operate prisons and schools, to force appropriations, and to channel funds.
>
> In mass tort, judges hold in their hands the fate of vast enterprises and can cause their extinction, with capitalization forfeit to distribution between lawyers and plaintiffs and workers let go.

Judges who issue expansive rulings in these spheres enjoy wide esteem and reputation. There are judges whose fine reputations rest in part on the ability to handle and administer innumerable claims through litigation and settlement, pretty much without regard to whether the claims themselves are based on fraud, corrupt experts, perjury, and other things that would be deplored and persecuted by the legal profession if done within other commercial fields.[2]

2. This point has been made in the asbestos context. *See, e.g.*, Lester Brickman, *Ethical Issues in Asbestos Litigation*, 33 Hofstra L. Rev. 833, 911 (2005) ("[T]he pervasiveness of the absence of

The broadest judicial bias I see, and the one I will describe most vaguely, is the bias in favor of legal complexity. The volumes of the third edition of the Federal Reporter spread themselves like kudzu vine over the shelves of law libraries. I will offer no example, because I would be honor-bound to cite myself as a chief offender, but it is a problem when the complexity of the law causes laymen to view the legal process as either political or as essentially random. This phenomenon is made visible in the papers of pro se litigants, who rarely bother to read the trial court decisions that reject their claims, and proceed to appeal on the theory (perhaps not altogether misguided) that the sheer, ramified, sprawling patterns of law will (in the hands of the right judge) yield a substantial payment or a sweet revenge.

It is an observed fact that the complexity of doctrines and opinions (not to mention the discovery of new doctrines) evokes praise and respect from within the profession. But our highly ramified litigation system imposes vast costs on other fields of endeavor, on our democratic freedoms, and on the unrepresented and the nonlitigious.

The law reviews seem to have exhausted all topics dealing with bias in the law and the ethics and infractions of other professions. I asked one of my law clerks to check to see how many articles have dealt with the bias of judges toward the dominance and control of the legal profession, and my clerk came up dry.[3] That does not surprise me, because if judges have this unconscious bias, so (I think) do law professors, for the same reasons—and students, for the same (and other) reasons. Scholarly papers undertake to expose and demonstrate the institutional and cultural biases of the law in every direction but this one. It is not for me to say whether I am making the point of this lecture effectively; but at least I can say that the competition is thin.

Why do we not notice this bias that I am talking about? If you are with me so far, and you now agree (or started out believing) that judges have a bias in favor of legalism and the legal profession, you may wonder as I have, why it is not noticed. Actually, it is a very familiar phenomenon that we do not recognize our bias as such. One tends to assume that bias has a nasty face, and that decent people shrink away instinctively. But some forms of bias are culturally embedded and are exercised with popular or elite approval.

Bias is not a moral evil. Everyone feels tugs of loyalty; everyone should. The bias I am talking about is more finely characterized as a tropism, an instinctive turning to follow a source of vital energy. That is what the sunflower does. But it is one thing to turn to follow the sun, and it is another to follow the American Bar Association (ABA), the law schools, law clerks, and the sound of applause.

---

application of ethical rules to asbestos litigation and to a large extent, to asbestos bankruptcy proceedings as well, can only stand as an indictment of the courts, disciplinary authorities and indeed, the legal profession."); Lester Brickman, *On the Theory Class's Theories of Asbestos Litigation: The Disconnect Between Scholarship and Reality*, 31 PEPP. L. REV. 33, 37 (2003).

3. Subsequent to this lecture, Professor Benjamin Barton has posted a paper that discusses this bias. *See* Benjamin H. Barton, *Do Judges Systematically Favor the Interests of the Legal Profession?* (Apr. 3, 2007) (unpublished manuscript), *available at* http://papers.ssrn.com/sol3/papers.cfm?abstract_id=976478.

Judges are susceptible to the opinions of others in our profession. But the bias in favor of more law, more procedure, and more process is in great measure bred in the bone of a lawyer. A judge is trained in the law; virtually all of us have high self-approval and a high regard for our profession, its processes, its culture and values, and its judgments—the profession which (after all) did loft judges to the bench, where we presumably wanted to go.

The tropism in favor of what lawyers do, and our tendency to expand the spheres of activity in which lawyers act and control, comes clothed in virtue. It is seen by us mainly as respect for due process, as the open door of the courthouse, as a flowering of the rule of law—and so excesses are viewed with indulgence as a Tocquevillian quirk of the American character. But it is unbecoming for judges to dismiss this phenomenon. It matters that our conduct as judges is reinforced by the support and praise that we get from colleagues, lawyers, bar associations, and law schools. I think fair-minded people should recognize the dangers that arise when judges, as the final arbiters for allocating vast power, money, and influence, are all members of the same (self-regulating) profession—and often of the same professional groups and social environments. It is a matter of like calling unto like.

Judges adhere to tight ethical constraints that keep us honest in that way and to that degree; but (ironically) some of those same constraints tend to reinforce our professional bias by insulating us from the influences of politics and (non-law) commerce. Unless we make an effort, we can become disconnected from the values and perceptions of the larger public. The more we obey the constraints that isolate us within a circle of legal culture, the more we are left to be judged, evaluated, and flattered (or not) by the nourishing, attentive, knowledgeable circle of lawyers, law students, and professors—which (to make matters worse) includes often the most charming and scintillating people in the community.

The mystique of the judicial process, and its power and pretension in this country, is pretty much all based on the idea of neutrality. If that idea is deflated, by puncture or slow leak, it is bad for judges and for the larger community. Our work is subject to hostile critiques; and, if we do not acknowledge and restrain our bias, others will notice, and forces will marshal to rein us in.

These critiques are often classified as attacks on judicial independence, and resisted as interference, or dismissed as ignorant. Thus, a great theme of the legal profession is emphatic support for judicial independence. That is a good thing, and I enjoy my independence as much as the next judge; but judges should consider and appreciate that one effect (maybe a motive) of the bar's avid support of judicial independence is to make judges "independent" of many influences (good and bad) that compete with the dominant influence over judges that is exerted by fellow lawyers, bar associations, and law professors. This support of judicial power by the bar may be a pillar of law, but it can also operate as group loyalty, the protection of turf, or a reciprocal commitment to the ascendency of judges and lawyers.

This bias I am talking about keeps us from seeing obvious things. For example, bar associations nowadays are chiefly trade groups. It is naive to think that the legal profession is the only disinterested player in our economic life. And bar groups are highly political. The ABA has formally adopted and announced hundreds of positions on virtually every issue in political dispute: You can look them up. It lobbies for those views in legislatures; it promotes them in amicus briefs filed in the courts. Yet hundreds of federal judges are members; thousands in the state and local courts. The canons of judicial conduct[4] make space for that anomaly.

The canons broadly warn that "[a] judge should refrain from political activity."[5] But the same canon (7) has a proviso: "this should not prevent a judge from engaging in the activities described in Canon 4,"[6] which says that "[a] judge may serve as a member, officer, or director of an organization . . . devoted to the improvement of the law."[7] And the commentary positively "encourage[s]" a judge to "contribute to the improvement of the law" by various means, expressly including "through a bar association."[8] Hospitably, the commentary allows a judge to "receive as a gift travel expense reimbursement including the cost of transportation, lodging, and meals, for the judge and a relative incident to the judge's attendance at a bar-related function."[9]

The legal profession, like all other fields, should be able to tap the experience and wisdom of its leading members, judges among them. And there are times and places for that; at one time, the organized bar may have been such a forum. But now?

Judges who are members of the ABA are technically in an auxiliary for judges in which they presumably participate in the development of legal ideas. But allowing judges to join a trade association so that they can collaborate with the membership in developing the law seems to me to make matters much worse rather than better. In any event, the expedient of a judges' auxiliary would not be tolerated in any other ethical context. If there were a judges' auxiliary to the American Bankers Association or the Brotherhood of Pharmaceutical Manufacturers, I am sure they would love to have us, and would happily work with us on shaping legal improvements. What if there were a judges' auxiliary to the Tobacco Institute or the American Insurance Association that paid my way to their conventions (with my relative), where I could work with them shoulder to shoulder on beneficial improvements in the law? Why assume that the improvements favored by the ABA are less self-serving than the improvements favored by other professional and trade groups?

When the ABA considers improvements in the law, it usually comes down on the side of punitive damages, attorney's fees, the expansion of causes of action, and new areas of regulation that require maintenance by lawyers (such as speech at election time). I do not claim to be any better than the next one, but I would be uncomfortable being a guest of the ABA on well-oiled occasions when such improvements are discussed. All of this is made worse by the fact that the ABA often litigates as amicus curiae (and I will pass over without comment the ABA's evaluation of judicial nominees).

4. Code of Conduct for United States Judges (2000), *available at* http://www.uscourts.gov/guide/vol2/ch1.html.

5. *Id.* Canon 7.

6. *Id.* Canon 7C.

7. *Id.* Canon 4C.

8. *Id.* Canon 4 cmt.

9. *Id.* Canon 5C(4) cmt.

Of course, judges should be involved in the development of the law—case by case, chiefly. No doubt, judges also read some books, go to debates and forums, and attend seminars. But the idea that judges will develop the law under the sponsorship and aegis of a powerful interest group should provoke disquiet—and would, but for the fact that (with some notable exceptions) judges do not see this as an issue.

I sometimes think that the problem at bottom is a lack of respect by lawyers for other people. Judges live chiefly in a circle of lawyers. Our colleagues are lawyers; happily, our friends are lawyers (and I am hoping to keep some after this lecture); the only outside income a federal judge can earn (aside from royalties) is from teaching in law schools (with the idea, I suppose, that they furnish a nonpartisan environment); and the only political and trade organizations we can join are bar associations.

But outside that circle there are people who are just as fully absorbed by other pursuits that deserve consideration and respect. Judges need a heightened respect for how nonlawyers solve problems, reach compromises, broker risks, and govern themselves and their institutions. There are lawyers on the one hand; and just about everybody else is the competition in the framing of values and standards of behavior.

In that competition, judicial bias has eroded the independence and influence of doctors, medical administrators, insurance underwriters, engineers, manufacturers, the military, the police, wardens and corrections officers, the clergy, employers, and teachers and principals.

I think that judges ought to appreciate that they operate under an internalized conflict of interest when they deal with all of these categories of people, and others, and that (as someone observed) divided loyalties are rarely divided down the middle. There is a great danger that, by the subordination of other professions, callings, and centers of power (and of their judgment and discretion), we are losing indispensable influences.

Another consequence of biased vision is the assumption that if something is of great importance, it can be safely left to lawyers. That is fine when it comes to statutory interpretation and such, but lawyers lack humility in approaching great matters. As judges, we tend to assume that adversarial hearings and expert testimony will render the judge omnicompetent and fit to decide the great questions, and that a legal mind is the highest and most useful development of mental capacity.

The mind-set is that if something is of great importance—such as speech, thought, and expression; race, identity, and sexuality; life and death—it cannot be safely and properly left chiefly to anyone else. How else does one account for the fixation on issues such as capital punishment and the right to die, given that capital punishment cases are few (at least in these parts), and that death is coming for us as a certainty, regardless of whether we classify it as an entitlement? As we exercise power over all the basic, ultimate, and transcendent things, I think that judges should consider how we inevitably diminish the influence of doctors and juries, clergy and social workers, legislatures, and the ordinary citizen.

The legal mind is indispensable to lawyering, and for other purposes it is perfectly okay in its way. But it has its limitations. For example, every problem-solving profession—except ours—quickly adopts as preferred the solution that is simplest, cheapest, and most efficacious, or (as they say) elegant. Also, our legal mind is invasive: It has institutional advantages for subordinating other modalities of thought, and it presses those advantages. And it is triumphalist about its expansions of influence. The uninitiated, who lack the legal mind, are harnessed to our purposes as jurors or are put to the margins. What nonlegal professionals think can be dismissed as arbitrary and capricious, or (if needed to assist the legal process) can be classified as expert opinion, to be weighed by us and by our standards.

The legal mind can hold its own with the competition in terms of rigor; I have one, and I make no apology for it. But at least I have come to admit that, depending on the question, the legal mind may be insufficient or may be inferior to the moral imagination; the scientific method; the practical arts of healing, politics, and entrepreneurship; the promptings of loyalty, faith, and patriotism; and the experience and expertise found elsewhere and among others.

If you are not with me this far, you will have little interest in this last question: What can be done to correct this bias and to place the legal profession again on a footing of parity and fair competition with other professionals and activities that have a right to influence in our communities and our culture? In a nutshell, judges should lead the bar in exercising the self-restraint and self-discipline that is incumbent on a profession that has a virtual monopoly on legislative power and a monopoly by patent on the power of the judiciary, and that is largely self-regulating.

Other professions, by ethics or honor, exert the imagination and self-possession to avoid exercising all the power they have. Let me give an incendiary example.

When a military force occupies a conquered province, the military has vast power and may be tempted to run things in a way that best serves the dominance and comfort of the military profession. A military solution can be found for every challenge; such solutions fit the salient talents and skill-sets of military commanders. No doubt it is of the greatest convenience to the military and a great comfort to them to impose early curfews; to censor letters; to close the outspoken newspapers and the satirical magazines; to take over the radio, the police, and the prisons; to shoot looters; to draft strikers; to favor military justice; and to commandeer all the better hotels. I think there is a natural temptation for the military officers in charge to do all these things because these are measures that subordinate a lot of conduct that undermines military administration, and because no doubt lifelong professional military officers might believe that these measures are effective and fair and constitute the best design for the organization of the society under their thumbs. Others in the military might applaud the tidy administration that results.

We (in the profession of law) recoil from such measures in part because it is not our profession; it does not fit our salient talents and skill-sets; it puts to the margin what we do and the sphere in which we operate; and so we lack faith in it. It seems to us viscerally illegitimate.

But an enlightened military recognizes that imposition of all these measures on an ongoing or permanent basis improperly subordinates other spheres of life. The military types (I am not one) seem to control themselves through a concept of honor. Maybe judges should consider their example. I concede that a country could do worse than suffer rule by lawyers: I would prefer a tyranny of law to life under a military regime. But outside our professional sphere, the dominance of the legal profession and the judiciary is resented more than we appreciate.

As a matter of self-awareness and conscience, judges should accept that the legal mind is not the best policy instrument, and that lawyer-driven processes and lawyer-centered solutions can be unwise, insufficient, and unjust, even if our friends and colleagues in the legal profession lead us that way. For the judiciary, this would mean a reduced role, *but not a diminished one* if the judiciary is elevated by considerations of honor, self-restraint, and respect for other influences.

A Pillar of Democracy: Reflections on the Role and Work of the Constitutional Court of South Africa

Hon. Kate O'Regan

Justice Kate O'Regan is a former justice of the Constitutional Court of South Africa.[1] She was born in the United Kingdom and grew up in Cape Town, South Africa.[2] She obtained her B.A. and LL.B. from the University of Cape Town, an LL.M. from the University of Sydney, and a Ph.D. from the London School of Economics.[3] She spent four years as an attorney in Johannesburg, South Africa, specializing in labor and land rights law.[4] During this time, she was involved in the anti-apartheid movement and advocated for those adversely affected by apartheid land policy.[5] In 1994, after South Africa's historic transition to democracy, President Nelson Mandela appointed Justice O'Regan to the Constitutional Court of South Africa, where she served until 2009.[6] She served as chairperson for the Internal Justice Council of the United Nations, and currently serves on the boards of various NGOs in the field of human rights and constitutionalism.[7]

Justice O'Regan, in her 2012 John F. Sonnett Memorial Lecture at Fordham University School of Law, elaborated on the important role of the Constitutional Court of South Africa in shaping the developing constitutional order of that country.[8] She discussed the drafting of the South African Constitution, explained the composition of the Court, and described the role of the Court in *dealing* with differences in South African society, and adjudication of social and economic rights.[9] She emphasized the two distinct but

Introduction written by Alexandria Strauss, J.D., Class of 2015, Fordham University School of Law.

1. *See Justice Kate O'Regan: Personal Details*, Constitutional Court of South Africa, http://www.constitutionalcourt.org.za/site/judges/justicekateoregan/index1.html (last visited Mar. 11, 2014).

2. *See id.*

3. *See id.*

4. *See id.*

5. *See id.*

6. *See id.*; Bill Keller, *South Africa Keystone is Set: A Court Can Test Democracy*, N.Y. Times, Nov. 18, 1994, at A1.

7. *See Justice Kate O'Regan to Discuss South Africa's Constitutional Court at Sept. 13 Newman Lecture*, Yale Law School (Aug. 13, 2012), https://law.yale.edu/yls-today/news/justice-kate-oregan-discuss-south-africas-constitutional-court-sept-13-newman-lecture (last visited Mar. 24, 2017).

8. *See generally* Kate O'Regan, *A Pillar of Democracy: Reflections on the Role and Work of the Constitutional Court of South Africa*, 81 Fordham L. Rev. 1169 (2012).

9. *See generally id.*

interrelated roles of courts under the South African Constitution: protecting fundamental rights of citizens and fostering participatory government.[10]

Internationalism permeated Justice O'Regan's lecture, as she spoke of the importance of understanding constitutional interpretation in developing democracies in light of the contemporary revolutionary climate in the Middle East.[11] She began with a quotation inscribed on the New York State Supreme Court courthouse in Lower Manhattan and concluded with a quotation from former U.S. President Franklin D. Roosevelt.[12] In doing so, Justice O'Regan emphasized the role of foreign law and norms in interpreting South Africa's developing Constitution.[13]

Through her lecture, Justice O'Regan emphasized the critical role that constitutional interpretation has played in South Africa's pursuit of equality and morality.[14] Her work on the Constitutional Court of South Africa should serve as a model for the intersection between judicial interpretation and societal values for both South Africa and developing democracies across the world.[15]

2012 Sonnett Lecture

The true administration of justice is the firmest pillar of good government.[1]

In his memorable judgment in the matter in which the Constitutional Court declared the death penalty to be unconstitutional, *S v. Makwanyane*,[2] former Chief Justice Ismail Mahomed spoke of the new South African Constitution in the following terms:

> All Constitutions seek to articulate, with differing degrees of intensity and detail, the shared aspirations of a nation; the values which bind its people, and which discipline its government and its national institutions; the basic premises upon which judicial, legislative and executive power is to be wielded; the constitutional limits and the conditions upon which that power is to be exercised . . . and the moral and ethical direction which that nation has identified for its future. In some countries, the Constitution only formalises, in a legal instrument, a historical consensus of values and aspirations evolved incrementally from a stable and unbroken past to accommodate the needs of the future. The South African Constitution is different: it retains from the past only what is defensible and

10. *See id.* at 1186.
11. *See generally id.*
12. *See id.* at 1169, 1186.
13. *See id.*
14. *See generally id.*
15. *See generally id.*

1. This quote is inscribed on the facade of the New York Supreme Court courthouse at 60 Centre Street.
2. 1995 (3) SA 391 (CC).

> represents a decisive break from, and a ringing rejection of, that part of the past. . . . The contrast between the past which it repudiates and the future to which it seeks to commit the nation is stark and dramatic. . . . What the Constitution expressly aspires to do is to provide a transition from these grossly unacceptable features of the past to a conspicuously contrasting future founded on the recognition of human rights, democracy and peaceful co-existence and development opportunities for all South Africans, irrespective of colour, race, class, belief or sex.[3]

The powerful message of this passage is that the South African Constitution is a transformative document that recognizes that our society needs to change in fundamental ways and that articulates the values that are to guide the process of transformation. It is nearly eighteen years since constitutional democracy dawned in South Africa. Eighteen years in which constitutional democracy has been taking root and in which a strong form of judicial review has been undertaken by the courts. My purpose this evening is to describe to you the role of the courts, and particularly the Constitutional Court, in this new constitutional order.

To me, the real strength of understanding other societies and their constitutions (and indeed the South African Constitution permits courts when interpreting its Bill of Rights to look at foreign law)[4] is that it often liberates one from the habits and assumptions of one's own training and experience. It can facilitate the identification of strengths and weaknesses in one's own system and enable one to see more clearly the structural constraints that historical antecedents and present conditions impose. In so doing, it allows us to imagine different ways of being both democratic and respectful of human rights—the twin obligations of the modern state.

Before turning to the role of the Court, I am going briefly to describe how our Constitution was drafted. Then, I will discuss the genesis of the Court and how its members are appointed. And finally, I will describe the role of the Court under the Constitution by illustrating two aspects of our jurisprudence: how the Court deals with difference in our society and how it adjudicates social and economic rights—two of the most challenging areas of constitutional jurisprudence, in our democracy, as well as in many others.

THE PROCESS OF CONSTITUTIONAL CHANGE

How was the South African Constitution drafted?[5] The process that culminated in our Constitution commenced in the 1990s with the release from prison of the leaders of the liberation movements, the African National Congress, and the Pan-Africanist Congress. Four years of intense negotiations followed, which resulted initially in deadlock. The liberation movements wanted a constitution drafted by a democratically elected constituent

3. *Id.* at 487–88 ¶ 262 (internal quotation marks omitted).

4. S. Afr. Const., 1996 § 39(1)(c).

5. Some of this section of the speech draws on a speech I delivered at Trinity College Dublin in April 2000 and since published as *Cultivating a Constitution: Challenges Facing the Constitutional Court in South Africa*, 22 Dublin U. L.J. 1, 3–7 (2000).

assembly. The National Party government wanted a constitution drafted by negotiation prior to the first elections. Finally, it was agreed that a two-stage process to constitutional and political reform would be followed. A temporary or interim constitution was negotiated and enacted by the minority government. In terms of the interim constitution, elections would be held to elect a new Parliament.

The newly elected Parliament would have two roles: the first was as national legislature, and the second was as a Constitutional Assembly responsible for drafting a new constitution. The fears of the National Party were met, however, by an agreement that the new constitution would comply with certain constitutional principles agreed before 1994 and annexed as a schedule to the interim constitution. It was agreed that a new Constitutional Court would be established which would have the duty of determining whether the new constitution adopted by the Constitutional Assembly complied with the thirty-four constitutional principles set out in the interim Constitution. This compromise was the genesis of the Constitutional Court: it was to be established to decide if the new constitution was indeed constitutional!

The constitution-making process involved a high degree of public participation. Right from the start, key figures in the process identified the need to involve members of the public. Cyril Ramaphosa, speaking on January 24, shortly after the Assembly was convened, stated:

> It is therefore important that as we put our vision to the country, we should do so directly, knowing that people out there want to be part of the process and will be responding, because in the end the drafting of the constitution must not be the preserve of the 490 members of this Assembly. It must be a constitution which they feel they own, a constitution that they know and feel belongs to them. We must therefore draft a constitution that will be fully legitimate, a constitution that will represent the aspirations of our people.[6]

Ramaphosa was right. If, as Ismail Mahomed says, a constitution is not merely a legal document but is a charter that identifies the shared aspirations of a nation and its common values,[7] a process of public participation is essential.

Consulting the public in any society is never an easy task. In South Africa, a society (at the time) of more than 40 million people, many of whom live in poverty in rural areas, many of whom are not fully literate, and many of whom have only irregular access to print or electronic media, it is daunting indeed.[8] The approach adopted by the Constitutional Assembly was multifaceted. Advertisements were placed in the print and broadcast media calling for submissions to the Constitutional Assembly. In excess of 1.7 million submissions were received, the bulk of which were petitions on discrete issues. In addition, a series of public meetings were held throughout the Republic: attended by more than 20,000

6. Hassen Ebrahim, The Soul of a Nation: Constitution-Making in South Africa 239 (1998).

7. *Makwanyane* 1995 (3) SA at 487–88 ¶ 262.

8. *See* Ebrahim, *supra* note 6, at 241.

people and 717 organizations.[9] Of these meetings, Hassen Ebrahim, the executive Director of the Constitutional Assembly said:

> The public meetings held were extremely successful: discussions were lively, ideas original, and the exchange of views appreciated. These meetings also served to highlight the point that constitutions are about basic values affecting society and should be understood by even the least educated. It was a humbling experience to realize that constitutional debates and issues are not only the domain of the intellectual elite, but that they belong to everyone.[10]

In addition, there were television and radio programs broadcast to air the key issues under negotiation. By and large, these programs were structured as discussions between members of the Constitutional Assembly and members of civil society on issues under consideration in the Assembly such as the Bill of Rights, the separation of powers, the national anthem and flag, traditional leaders, and the death penalty.

A website was also created which contained a database of all the information produced by the Constitutional Assembly, including minutes, drafts, opinions, and submissions. It was early days for the Internet, especially in South Africa, but the site was very popular. The material on the site is currently being recaptured and indexed and it is hoped that it will soon be available on the Constitutional Court website (www.constitutionalcourt.org.za).

How successful was the process of public participation? That is difficult to evaluate. Its purpose was clearly twofold: a substantive one to allow members of the public to affect the actual provisions of the Constitution itself; and a process-based one, rooted in a conception of democracy that is participative rather than merely representative. No work has been done, as far as I am aware, on the extent to which the process of public participation affected the actual text of the Constitution, and I cannot helpfully speculate on it. Perhaps there is an interesting doctoral thesis to be written there.

And what of the process purpose of public participation? Independent market research at the time revealed that the campaign for public participation reached as many as sixty-five percent of South Africans.[11] The same research makes it clear that many members of the public were skeptical about the call for public participation.[12] Yet the sheer number of submissions received and the extent of participation in public meetings suggested that there was great interest and significant involvement in the process.

It is perhaps worth noting here that negotiated change has had to take place in many walks of South African life. Local government, for example, had been racially divided under apartheid, with each town having separate municipal councils based on race. In each municipal area, negotiations had to take place to arrange for the manner in which the separate councils would merge. Similarly, many public organizations, from school boards to

9. *Id.* at 244.
10. *Id.* at 245.
11. *Id.* at 243.
12. *See id.* at 239–50.

sporting codes, have had to renegotiate their ground rules of their organizations. These processes were often conflictual at first, but by and large, through compromise and negotiation, solutions to apparently intractable problems were reached.

Not surprisingly, then, inclusive processes that emphasize participation have become important values of our new constitutional democracy. They are widely accepted ground rules in many walks of South African life. And I think there can be no doubt that the public participation process around the Constitution contributed to this.

The importance of participation in law-making processes is also given expression in a wide variety of constitutional provisions. For example, the new Constitution requires both houses of Parliament to "facilitate public involvement" in their legislative and other processes.[13] The Constitutional Court has had to interpret these provisions on several occasions. Relying extensively on international law, the Court has held, by majority, that the provisions require Parliament to act reasonably to facilitate public involvement in law making. If Parliament unreasonably fails to facilitate public involvement, the consequence may be that the legislation enacted will be invalid, though any order of invalidity will ordinarily be suspended to enable Parliament to adopt a reasonable process to facilitate public involvement. The Court was clear that Parliament's view of what would constitute reasonable facilitation of public involvement would be respected by the courts.[14] As former Chief Justice Ngcobo said in his judgment:

> [T]he duty to facilitate public involvement must be construed in the context of our constitutional democracy, which embraces the principle of participation and consultation. Parliament and the provincial legislatures have broad discretion to determine how best to fulfil their constitutional obligation to facilitate public involvement in a given case, so long as they act reasonably. Undoubtedly, this obligation may be fulfilled in different ways and is open to innovation on the part of the legislatures. In the end, however, the duty to facilitate public involvement will often require Parliament and the provincial legislatures to provide citizens with a meaningful opportunity to be heard in the making of the laws that will govern them. Our Constitution demands no less.[15]

THE ROLE OF THE CONSTITUTIONAL COURT: FOSTERING A DEMOCRACY BASED ON PUBLIC REASON

The Constitutional Court is the final court of appeal in constitutional matters. Although somewhat resistant to precise definition, a constitutional matter is a matter that involves the interpretation or enforcement of a provision of the Constitution. Given the scope of the Bill of Rights in our Constitution, the range of constitutional matters is far broader than it would be were the Bill of Rights to be less expansive.

13. S. Afr. Const., 1996 §§ 59(1)(a), 72(1)(a).

14. *See* Doctors for Life Int'l v. Speaker of the Nat'l Assembly 2006 (6) SA 416 (CC) at 467 ¶ 124; *see also* Matatiele Municipality v. President of the Republic of S. Afr. (2) 2007 (6) SA 477 (CC) at 491–94 ¶¶ 50–55.

15. *Doctors for Life* 2006 (6) SA at 474 ¶ 145.

Right at the beginning, the Constitution declares that the "Constitution is the supreme law of the Republic," and "law or conduct inconsistent with it is invalid, and the obligations imposed by it must be fulfilled."[16] The corollary of this is that a court, "when deciding a constitutional matter within its power" *must* declare law or conduct that is inconsistent with the Constitution to be invalid to the extent of its inconsistency.[17] The Constitution then provides that the Court may make any "just and equitable" order.[18] Such an order may suspend the order of invalidity for any period and on any conditions in order to allow the competent authority, which may be Parliament, a provincial legislature, or an administrator, the opportunity to correct the defect. The court may also limit the retrospective effect of the order of invalidity.

The special role of the Constitutional Court is recognized by a rule that an order of constitutional invalidity in respect of an Act of Parliament, provincial legislation, or conduct of the President will have no force unless it is confirmed by the Constitutional Court.[19] Between five and ten cases are confirmed by the Court each year through this procedure.

The Appointment of Judges

The eleven judges of the Constitutional Court thus play an important and powerful role under our constitutional order. Not surprisingly, then, the procedure for appointment of judges under our Constitution also marks a distinct change from the past when judges were appointed by the member of Cabinet responsible for the administration of justice (the Minister of Justice). In 1994, for the first time, a Judicial Service Commission was established to participate in the process of the selection of judges.[20] Its first task was to assist in the appointment of judges to the Constitutional Court.

Under the terms of the 1996 Constitution, the Commission has twenty-three members[21]: the Chief Justice, who presides; the President of the Supreme Court of Appeal; the Minister of Justice; one Judge President (that is a judge who presides over one of the High Courts); four practicing lawyers; a professor of law; four presidential nominees; and ten members of Parliament (comprising four representatives from the National Council of Provinces [the upper house] and six representatives from the National Assembly—of these six, at least three must be members of the Opposition in Parliament).[22]

High Court judges and judges of the Supreme Court of Appeal (formerly the Appellate Division and the highest court of appeal in nonconstitutional matters) are appointed by the President on the advice of the Judicial Service Commission.[23] In practice, this has

16. S. Afr. Const., 1996 § 2.
17. *Id.* § 172(1)(a).
18. *Id.* § 172(1)(b).
19. *Id.* § 172(2)(a).
20. *Id.* § 178(1); *see* Judicial Service Commission Act 9 of 1994 (S. Afr.).
21. S. Afr. Const., 1996 § 178.
22. *Id.*
23. *See id.* § 174(6).

meant when vacancies arise, the Commission calls for nominations and then compiles a short list of candidates for interview. Interviews are held in public, though they are not televised. In the case of Constitutional Court judges, the transcripts of the interviews of the successful candidates for the Constitutional Court are available on the Court's website.

The Commission then sends to the President the names it recommends for appointment. As far as I am aware, the President has never rejected a name proposed by the Commission. The Constitution itself expressly requires that a key factor for the Commission to consider in appointing judges is "[t]he need for the judiciary to reflect broadly the racial and gender composition of South Africa."[24] In 1994, of 166 judges all but four were white men. Today the figure has changed significantly. The composition of the Constitutional Court bench in July 2011 was as follows: eight men (three white and five black) and two black women. The current Chief Justice is Mogoeng Mogoeng; and the Deputy Chief Justice is Dikgang Moseneke. Constitutional Court judges serve a maximum period of fifteen years.[25]

Why should we be concerned about the demographics of the bench? There is an extensive literature on why it is appropriate for a judiciary to be diverse,[26] but for me two reasons stand out. The first is that a diverse bench enhances the legitimacy of the judiciary in the eyes of the broader community. It is important in a diverse society that the bench is not seen to be the preserve of a particular group or elite, or this will damage the institution. Within this reason, however, lurks a danger that can be described as the siren of identity determinism. Your identity determines your judgments. If you are a black male judge, you will sympathize with a black male accused/complainant and your judgment will

24. *Id.* § 174(2).

25. *See* S. Afr. Const., First Amendment Act of 2001.

26. *See, e.g.*, Sean Cooney, *Gender and Judicial Selection: Should There Be More Women on the Courts?*, 19 Melb. U. L. Rev. 20 (1993); Rachel Davis & George Williams, *Reform of the Judicial Appointments Process: Gender and the Bench of the High Court of Australia*, 27 Melb. U. L. Rev. 819 (2003); Richard F. Devlin, *We Can't Go on Together with Suspicious Minds: Judicial Bias and Racialized Perspective in* R. v. R.D.S., 18 Dalhousie L.J. 408 (1995); Murray Gleeson, *Judicial Selection and Training: Two Sides of the One Coin*, 77 Australian L.J. 591 (2003); Regina Graycar, *The Gender of Judgments: Some Reflections on "Bias,"* 32 U. B.C. L. Rev. 1 (1998); Brenda Hale, *Equality and the Judiciary: Why Should We Want More Women Judges?*, 2001 Pub. L. 489; Claire L'Heureux-Dubé, *Making a Difference: The Pursuit of a Compassionate Justice*, 31 U. B.C. L. Rev. 1 (1997); Errol P. Mendes, *"Promoting Heterogeneity of the Judicial Mind": Minority and Gender Representation in the Canadian Judiciary*, *in* Ont. Law Reform Comm'n, Appointing Judges: Philosophy, Politics and Practice 91 (1991); Martha Minow, *Equalities*, 88 J. Phil. 663 (1991); Martha Minow, *Stripped Down Like a Runner or Enriched by Experience: Bias and Impartiality of Judges and Jurors*, 33 Wm. & Mary L. Rev. 1201 (1992); Jennifer Nedelsky, *Embodied Diversity and the Challenges to Law*, 42 McGill L.J. 91 (1997); Maryka Omatsu, *The Fiction of Judicial Impartiality*, 9 Can. J. Women & L. 1 (1997); Suzanna Sherry, *Civic Virtue and the Feminine Voice in Constitutional Adjudication*, 72 Va. L. Rev. 543 (1986); Patricia M. Wald, *Some Real-Life Observations About Judging*, 26 Ind. L. Rev. 173 (1992); Bertha Wilson, *Will Women Judges Really Make a Difference?*, 28 Osgoode Hall L.J. 507 (1990).

reflect this. The notion extends further: if you are a black male judge, you have an obligation to see the world in a particular way; and if you do not, you are to be criticized for that. Such reasoning must be rejected vigorously.

This is not to say that, as human beings, judges are not products of the societies within which they live; and that their race, gender, religion, schooling, and a variety of other factors have affected their beliefs and understanding of the world. But the task of judging in a democracy demands more of judges than that they merely give effect to a worldview inherited from their particular background. It demands a self-conscious appreciation of the impact of their background on their way of thinking and a conscientious attempt at all times to be impartial. In my view, the obligation of impartiality leads directly to the second important reason that our Constitution requires diversity on the bench.

In his direct and honest statement to the Truth and Reconciliation Commission, my former colleague Justice Ackermann remarked:

> Judges who believe that they are wholly free of prejudice delude themselves. It behoves us all to seek out rigorously, painful as that might be, our own particular prejudices, of whatever nature. We need to keep these constantly in mind and to endeavour actively and persistently to counteract them. Furthermore, we all need to understand the insidious influence of institutional culture and to appreciate the powerful effects of the class, social and political environments in which we live and work, and the potential that this has for making us insensitive to the context and views of others.[27]

So requiring diversity on a collegial court enables judges to interrogate their own prejudices or blind spots. The more alike judges are, the more likely that they will mistake prejudices for simple truths; the more different they are, the more likely that they will interrogate the correctness of their assumptions. If our backgrounds are the same, it is very comfortable and easy to reinforce the prejudices that such backgrounds foster. When we are different, prejudices masquerading as "common sense" or "the ways things are" are much more likely to be uncovered. If judges are, as the South African oath of office requires, to "administer justice to all persons alike without fear, favour or prejudice,"[28] we need to know where our prejudices lie. To me, therefore, this is the second reason for diversity on the bench: the fostering of judicial self-awareness is of great importance to me as a judge. It is a constant reminder not to delude myself that I am by nature impartial. Needless to say, it is a consideration that I like to draw to the attention of my colleagues from time to time as well!

The Work of the Court

The Constitutional Court has handed down 422 judgments in its first seventeen years of existence, a rate of just under twenty-five per year. This is not a prodigious judicial output

27. L.W.H. Ackermann, Submission to the Truth and Reconciliation Commission Re: The Role of the Judiciary, 115 S. Afr. L.J. 15, 54 (1998).
28. S. Afr. Const., 1996 sched. 2, item 6.

compared to other senior courts around the world. But that relatively low output needs to be assessed in the light of three considerations.

The first is that the Court has eleven members, and the general rule is that all eleven judges sit in every case. Although there is no doubt that the size of the Court is valuable in many respects, it probably slows down the process of decision-making and writing. Just, for example, to go round the table and permit every judge to air his or her views on a case will often take an hour.

Second, the Court receives far more applications for access to the Court than it actually enrolls for hearing. Each of these applications, which in the last four years that I was at the Court exceeded the number of cases heard on a ratio of between three and four to one (that is, an additional seventy-five to one hundred cases per annum to those that are actually enrolled for hearing) are considered by all the judges of the Court, unlike other senior appellate courts which often delegate this decision-making responsibility to a few judges. As our Constitution stipulates that a quorum of the Court is eight, no one can be turned away from the Court without at least eight judges having considered the matter.[29]

Finally, the issues that have come before the court in its first seventeen years have been some of the most difficult considered by courts anywhere. Some have attracted much public comment, such as the constitutionality of the death penalty, gay marriage, and some high profile criminal matters. Other issues have required the Court to grapple with issues relating to the interpretation and protection of social and economic rights—where there is no tried and tested path—and questions of constitutional structure and relationship that involve interpretation of the provisions of the Constitution other than the Bill of Rights.

How often does the Court declare an Act of Parliament to be inconsistent with the Constitution? According to my records, the Court has heard 147 such challenges and in ninety cases has upheld the challenge, an average of just under six times a year. Interestingly, the average has not declined markedly over the period. In the first five years, twenty-nine legislative provisions were declared to be invalid. In the following five years, twenty-nine legislative provisions were declared invalid, and in the seven years since, thirty-two provisions have been declared to be invalid.

It is important to realize that, in many cases, the declaration of invalidity is not controversial. Indeed, the rules of the Court provide that the relevant government minister responsible for the legislation must be given notice of the challenge and afforded an opportunity to oppose it. It is not infrequent that the Minister appears only to indicate that the government does not vigorously wish to argue that the legislation is constitutional, but only wishes to make submissions as to the appropriate order to be made by the Court to regulate the effect of the declaration of invalidity.

Sometimes, of course, the declaration of invalidity is controversial particularly with the public. The leading example of this is the death penalty case that I mentioned at the outset in which the legislative provision that provided for capital punishment was declared to be inconsistent with the Constitution and invalid. The Court directed all persons sentenced to

29. *Id.* § 167(2).

death would remain in custody until their sentences were substituted by lawful punishments.[30] Similarly controversial was the order in the case of *Minister of Home Affairs v. Fourie*[31] which declared section 30(1) of the Marriage Act 25 of 1961 to be inconsistent with the Constitution and invalid because it "does not permit same-sex couples to enjoy the status and the benefits coupled with responsibilities it accords to heterosexual couples."[32]

The model of judicial review adopted in the South African Constitution gives considerable powers to courts to determine the constitutionality of legislation, and once having done so, compels a court to declare legislation inconsistent with the Constitution invalid. Yet there are other provisions in the Constitution that make it plain that the Court must listen carefully to the reasons given by the legislature and executive for enacting legislation which limits rights entrenched in the Bill of Rights.

The model of rights adjudication is a two-stage model, perhaps most closely aligned with (though by no means identical to) the Canadian model.[33] This means that a court when considering a constitutional challenge to legislation asks two questions. The first is, does the legislation limit a right entrenched in the Bill of Rights—this exercise is by no means formal or automatic. The Court has adopted a careful approach to delineating the scope of rights, and a litigant bears the burden of establishing that his or her right is infringed by the legislation under attack. Should the Court decide that the legislation does limit a right, the next question that will arise is whether the limitation is "reasonable and justifiable in an open and democratic society based on human dignity, equality and freedom."[34] This affords the executive defending the constitutionality of legislation an opportunity both to lead evidence and present argument as to why the legislation is not unconstitutional.

How does the Court decide whether an infringement will nevertheless pass the test of justification? It considers whether the reason given by the government for limiting the right is sufficiently important to outweigh the impact it causes in limiting the right. This is essentially a proportionality analysis. The approach was summarized in an early decision of the Court as follows:

> In sum, therefore, the Court places the purpose, effect and importance of the infringing legislation on one side of the scales and the nature and effect of the infringement caused by the legislation on the other. The more substantial the inroad into fundamental rights, the more persuasive the grounds of justification must be.[35]

30. S v. Makwanyane 1995 (3) SA 391 (CC) at 453 ¶ 151.

31. 2006 (1) SA 524 (CC).

32. *Id.* at 585.

33. Section 1 of the Canadian Charter of Rights and Freedoms provides that the "rights and freedoms set out . . . [in this Charter are] subject only to such reasonable limits prescribed by law as can be demonstrably justified in a free and democratic society." Canadian Charter of Rights and Freedoms, Part I of the Constitution Act, 1982, *being* Schedule B to the Canada Act, 1982, c. 11, pt. 1, § 1 (U.K.).

34. S. Afr. Const., 1996 § 36(1).

35. S v. Bhulwana 1996 (1) SA 388 (CC) at 395 ¶ 18.

The process of limitations analysis therefore permits the Court to consider the reasons proffered by government for the legislation under attack. In so doing, it affords a government an opportunity to set out its reasons for the limitation to persuade the Court, and the broader society, of the legitimacy of both its purpose and method.

As we saw in relation to the legislature's obligation to public participation in the making of legislation, where the Court held that the legislature must openly and reasonably determine the extent of public participation it will facilitate in the making of any particular law, limitation analysis requires the government to disclose its reasons for enacting legislation which has infringed the Bill of Rights. The Court then assesses whether those reasons are sufficient given the nature of the limitation of rights concerned. In a real sense, the function of the Court here is twofold: most obviously, it serves as the guardian of fundamental rights; less obviously, but as importantly, it serves to create a forum for public debate about the reasons for the exercise of power. This role carries with it a conception of democracy that requires the exercise of public power to be accountable. Again and again, our Constitution confers power upon courts to enable citizens to hold public power accountable through requiring the disclosure of reasons for the exercise of power in a public and open forum.

"SOUTH AFRICA BELONGS TO ALL WHO LIVE IN IT, UNITED IN OUR DIVERSITY"

So proclaims the Preamble to our Constitution. What is the role of the courts and the Bill of Rights in realizing this goal? The challenge posed by the principle arises in a variety of different arenas: traditional leaders and customary law, religious and cultural practices, and the rights of noncitizens. The Court has had cases in all these areas. Tonight I only have time to discuss two. The first concerns customary law, and the second cultural and religious practices in schools.

As a matter of social practice, traditional leaders still play an important part in South African public life, particularly in the rural areas, and so does customary law. Our democratic Constitution recognizes traditional leadership and confirms that "[t]he institution, status and role of traditional leadership, according to customary law, are recognized, subject to the Constitution."[36] It also provides that "[t]he courts must apply customary law when that law is applicable, subject to the Constitution."[37]

The first important case where the Court has had to consider customary law was the case of Mrs. Bhe.[38] She came to court seeking relief on behalf of her seven- and ten-year-old daughters. The father of the children, Mr. Maboyisi Mgolombane died intestate in October 2002. He had been a carpenter and she a domestic worker and they lived together in an informal home in the giant township of Khayelitsha just outside Cape Town. Upon Mr. Mgolombane's death, his father was declared sole heir in the deceased estate according

36. S. Afr. Const., 1996 § 211(1).
37. *Id.* § 211(3).
38. Bhe v. Magistrate 2005 (1) SA 580 (CC).

to the customary principle of male primogeniture, Mr. Mgolombane having no surviving male children. The father intended to sell the family home in order to cover funeral expenses, which would have left Mrs. Bhe and the two young girls homeless. With the assistance of a local organization, Mrs. Bhe launched a constitutional challenge to the customary law rule of male primogeniture, which reached the Constitutional Court in 2004.

Speaking on behalf of the majority, Chief Justice Langa held that:

> The exclusion of women from inheritance on the grounds of gender is a clear violation of . . . the Constitution. It is a form of discrimination that entrenches past patterns of disadvantage among a vulnerable group, exacerbated by old notions of patriarchy and male domination incompatible with the guarantee of equality under this constitutional order.[39]

The Court thus declared that the rule of male primogeniture in customary law was inconsistent with the Constitution to the extent that it excludes women or extramarital children from inheriting property.

The message of the *Bhe* case, based on the express text of the Constitution, is that customary law is to be recognized as an important system of law in our society. Yet, like all laws in our legal system, it is subject to the Constitution and the Bill of Rights and, in this case, was held to be inconsistent with the right to be free from unfair discrimination. This is the first important principle of the Constitution's protection of diversity in our society: it embraces the pluralist character of our society but on express terms. The fundamental rights entrenched in the Constitution may not be impaired by any community or culture.

The second case that is illustrative of the approach to diversity in our constitutional framework is the case of Sunali Pillay.[40] Ms. Pillay was a fifteen-year-old student at a public school for girls in Durban. The school had a code of conduct which provided for a school uniform and which prohibited the wearing of jewelry at school, save for ear-studs (at the same level), watches, and medic-alert bracelets.

Ms. Pillay's family came originally from southern India and some of the women in her family had a tradition of wearing a nose stud, which is a widespread cultural and religious practice in Hindu communities in southern India. Contrary to the school rules, Ms. Pillay had her nose pierced and started wearing a tiny nose stud to school. The school objected but gave her three months' grace to allow the piercing to settle and then told her that she would have to remove the stud. When Ms. Pillay did not do so, the school asked her and her mother to explain on what basis they sought an exemption from the school's uniform code. Her mother explained that:

> It is a time-honoured family tradition. Sunali and I come from a South Indian family that has sought to maintain a cultural identity by respecting and implementing the traditions of the women before us. Usually, a young woman would get her nose pierced upon her physical maturity (the onset of her menstrual cycle) as an indication that she

39. *Id.* at 621–22 ¶ 91.

40. MEC for Educ. v. Pillay 2008 (1) SA 474 (CC), CCT 51/06 (Oct. 5, 2007). This is a yet unreported judgment of the Constitutional Court.

> is now eligible for marriage. While this physically oriented reasoning no longer applies, we do still use the tradition to honour our daughters as responsible young adults.[41]

After consulting experts on Hindu religion and culture, the school decided that this reasoning did not warrant an exemption to be made and proceeded with school disciplinary hearings against Ms. Pillay, who then approached the Equality Court. The matter wound its way through the court system to the Constitutional Court, which by a majority upheld Ms. Pillay's claim. In the end result, although the Court was divided on the precise order, the principle that underlay both judgments was the principle that, under our Constitution, diversity must not only be tolerated but fostered.

A SOUTH AFRICAN SPECIALITY: SOCIOECONOMIC RIGHTS

Time does not permit a full consideration of this aspect of the Court's jurisprudence, but I shall describe it briefly.

Rights that are protected are the right of access to adequate housing,[42] to a basic education,[43] the right of access to health care services, sufficient food and water, and social security.[44] Apart from education, the format of the rights is similar, so in the case of housing the right provides: "(1) Everyone has the right to have access to adequate housing. (2) The state must take reasonable legislative and other measures, within its available resources, to achieve the progressive realisation of this right."[45]

In including such rights within the Bill of Rights, South Africa went beyond the conventional terrain of a Bill of Rights in commonwealth countries. Most domestic rights instruments protect civil and political rights, such as the right to freedom of expression and association. Far fewer protect social and economic rights directly. However, a distinction between civil and political rights, on the one hand, and social and economic rights, on the other, was not followed when the Universal Declaration of Human Rights was adopted by the General Assembly of the United Nations in 1948.

Indeed, in a recent fascinating book,[46] Cass Sunstein has suggested that a key reason for the inclusion of both civil and political rights, as well as social and economic rights, was Franklin D. Roosevelt's insistence that the two were interrelated. FDR famously identified four essential human freedoms: freedom of speech, freedom to worship God in one's own way, freedom from want, and freedom from fear.[47] This led him to draft

41. *Id.* at 67 ¶ 131.
42. S. Afr. Const., 1996 § 26.
43. *Id.* § 29.
44. *Id.* § 27.
45. *Id.* § 26.
46. Cass R. Sunstein, The Second Bill of Rights: FDR's Unfinished Revolution and Why We Need it More than Ever (2004).
47. President Franklin D. Roosevelt, Address of the President of the United States to Congress (Jan. 6, 1941), *in* 87 Cong. Rec. 44, 46–47 (1941).

what he called "the second Bill of Rights," which contained social and economic rights.[48]

As a matter of normative desirability too, there is no difference between social and economic rights and civil and political rights. The desirability of ensuring that all citizens receive basic education, are properly housed, have access to food, clean water, and healthcare is not, I think, a controversial one. Indeed, social and economic rights are in some sense anterior to civil and political rights. The basic needs of human beings for shelter, nutrition, and clothing must be met before a lively interest in freedom of expression and association arises. It is for this reason that many international documents acknowledge the indivisibility and interdependence of social and economic rights, on the one hand, and civil and political rights on the other.

In the South African context, however, the inclusion and protection of social and economic rights in the Constitution had great significance. The real effect of centuries of colonialism, followed by decades of apartheid has been the impoverishment of black South Africans and the correlative enrichment of white South Africans. Our society is one of the most unequal in the world, and one in which the color of one's skin remains a strong predictor of socioeconomic status. Unless the basic needs of food, housing, and education are met, civil and political rights may seem mere luxuries. This might have carried the message that the Constitution contained a charter for whites and the wealthy while remaining oblivious to the needs of black South Africans who had been historically dispossessed and excluded.

The real challenge in entrenching social and economic rights is to determine the scope of their justiciability. There is a widespread view amongst politicians and lawyers that civil and political rights, on the one hand, and social and economic rights, on the other, are in some significant way conceptually different. Social and economic rights have been labeled "second generation" rights, while civil and political rights are considered "first generation." (I might point out that this categorization seems to me to be back-to-front—if food, water, and housing are indeed anterior as a matter of lived experience to civil and political rights, should they not be the first?)

The challenge is a complex one. Both civil and political rights, and social and economic rights may impose an obligation upon the government that is essentially negative in character. Do not limit my right to free speech. Do not evict me from my home. Enforcement of the negative obligations that rights impose is rarely controversial or difficult, whether the right concerned is the right of freedom of expression or the right of access to housing.

The justiciability of both, however, becomes more difficult when one has to consider whether the right not only imposes a negative obligation, but also a positive one. Does the state have a duty to make it possible for people to exercise their right of freedom of expression? Does the state have a duty to provide everyone with a house? Our intuitive anxiety about the justiciability of social and economic rights largely arises from our assumption that they primarily impose positive obligations upon government. And it is not different

48. *See* SUNSTEIN, *supra* note 46, at 61–95.

from the difficult questions that arise in the context of positive obligations that arise in respect of civil and political rights, whether it is the right to vote or the right to reasonable accommodation in disability law.

The South African Constitution helps to answer this question in relation to most of the social and economic rights by delineating quite carefully the extent of the positive obligation upon the state. So section 26(2) of the Constitution states: "The state must take reasonable legislative and other measures, within its available resources, to achieve the progressive realisation of the right."[49] I probably don't need to highlight the word "reasonable" in the section to you. It is indeed the key to the Court's approach to the justiciability of social and economic rights.

In the Nevirapine case,[50] in which the government proposed to establish only two sites per province for Nevirapine to be provided to HIV positive pregnant mothers, the question was whether that constituted a reasonable measure to achieve the right of access to health care.[51] Given that the manufacturers of the medication were furnishing it to the government for free, and given that it was clear that the government had the capacity to establish testing and counselling centers in excess of two per province, and given the World Health Organization's assessment of the value of Nevirapine in reducing mother to child transmission of HIV, the Court held that the government's plan was not reasonable.[52] The order the Court made was:

> It is declared that:
>
> (a) Sections 27(1) and (2) of the Constitution require the government to devise and implement within its available resources a comprehensive and co-ordinated programme to realise progressively the rights of pregnant women and their newborn children to have access to health services to combat mother-to-child transmission of HIV.
>
> (b) The programme to be realised progressively within available resources must include reasonable measures for counselling and testing pregnant women for HIV, counselling HIV-positive pregnant women on the options open to them to reduce the risk of mother-to-child transmission of HIV, and making appropriate treatment available to them. . . .[53]

The Court went on to declare that the current policy fell short of compliance with this declaratory order and the government was ordered, "without delay to: Remove the restrictions that prevent Nevirapine from being made available for the purpose of reducing the risk of mother-to-child transmission of HIV at public hospitals and clinics that are not research and training sites."[54] Finally, the Court ruled: "The orders made [above] do not preclude government from adapting its policy in a manner consistent with the Constitu-

49. S. Afr. Const., 1996 § 26(2).
50. Minister of Health v. Treatment Action Campaign (1) 2002 (5) SA 721 (CC).
51. *Id.* at 764–65 ¶ 135.
52. *Id.* at 754 ¶ 95.
53. *Id.* at 764–65 ¶ 135.
54. *Id.* at 765 ¶ 135.

tion if equally appropriate or better methods become available to it for the prevention of mother-to-child transmission of HIV."[55]

The approach of the Court to social and economic rights, as the text of the Constitution requires and consistent with its approach to its relationship with the legislature and executive in other areas, is to consider whether the measures established by government in any respect of a particular right, or aspect of it, are reasonable. In considering what will be reasonable, the Court said in an early case:

> Reasonableness must also be understood in the context of the Bill of Rights as a whole. The right of access to adequate housing is entrenched because we value human beings and want to ensure that they are afforded their basic human needs. A society must seek to ensure that the basic necessities of life are provided to all if it is to be a society based on human dignity, freedom and equality. To be reasonable, measures cannot leave out of account the degree and extent of the denial of the right they endeavour to realise. Those whose needs are most urgent and whose ability to enjoy all rights therefore is most in peril, must not be ignored by the measures aimed at achieving the realisation of the right.[56]

The protection of social and economic rights does not mean that every individual can come to court and demand a house. The Constitution requires only that government take reasonable steps progressively and within available resources to afford citizens access to housing. The court is thus serving as a public forum where government is called upon to explain its policies. This form of justiciability is as much about facilitating participative and responsive democracy, as it is about social and economic rights.

What is increasingly clear, however, is that the negative aspects of social and economic rights will provide real shields for citizens to protect them against the withdrawal of their access to health care, housing, and education. So, in one case, for example, the court held that the rules for the sale in execution of houses needed to be reconceived to ensure that a court, in ordering execution against immovable property, would take into account the right of access to housing and not make an order which would result in a person being rendered homeless, which would be disproportionate.[57] The Court reasoned that there would be circumstances in which it would be disproportionate or unjustifiable to permit execution against a home. Such was the case before the court, in which one of the applicants had purchased vegetables in an amount of approximately R190 (less than £13) and, as a result of the failure to pay that debt and an absence of any movable property to satisfy the judgment, was at risk of her home being sold in execution of the debt. The other applicant had borrowed R250 (less than £15) and faced the same result. The Court stated:

> [I]t is clear that there will be circumstances in which it will be unjustifiable to allow execution. . . . There will be many instances where execution will be unjustifiable because

55. *Id.*

56. Gov't of the Republic of S. Afr. v. Grootboom 2001 (1) SA 46 (CC) at 69 ¶ 44.

57. *See* Jaftha v. Schoeman, Van Rooyen v. Stoltz 2005 (2) SA 140 (CC) at 155–56 ¶¶ 31–34; *see also* Port Elizabeth Municipality v. Various Occupiers 2005 (1) SA 217 (CC) at 225–29 ¶¶ 14–23.

> the advantage that attaches to a creditor who seeks execution will be far outweighed by the immense prejudice and hardship caused to the debtor.[58]

It is perhaps surprising given our history that courts should have been given such an important role in our new constitutional democracy. But I hope that I have illustrated tonight, neither tendentiously, nor in a manner insensitive to my own judicial role, that the role of courts under the South African Constitution is twofold. The first is to protect the fundamental rights of South African citizens—not only civil and political rights, but also social and democratic rights. The second is to foster a process of public reason in our democracy by allowing citizens, through the process of litigation, to ask government for their reasons for the exercise of public power, which reasons are then scrutinized by the courts with careful attention to the need to protect the legitimate constitutional role of the legislature and executive. The important constitutional role entrusted to the courts should enhance the possibility of participatory and responsive government and also continue to facilitate the transformation of our broader society. I would like to end, perhaps surprisingly, with the words of FDR in his famous four freedoms speech to which I have already referred and which I think sums up the ongoing challenge of change in the South African Constitution: "Since the beginning of our . . . history," he said, "we have been engaged in change—in a perpetual peaceful revolution—a revolution which goes on steadily, quietly adjusting itself to changing conditions—without the concentration camp or the quicklime in the ditch."[59]

58. *Jaftha*, at 158–59 ¶ 43.
59. Roosevelt, *supra* note 47, at 47.